COMPUTERS IN SOCIETY
Privacy, Ethics, and the Internet

Edited by Joey F. George

Florida State University

PEARSON

Prentice
Hall

Upper Saddle River, New Jersey 07458

Library of Congress Cataloging-in-Publication Data

Computers in society : privacy, ethics, and the Internet / edited by
Joey F. George.
    p.   cm.
Includes bibliographical references.
ISBN 0-13-140660-4
    1. Computers and civilization.   2. Computers—Social aspects.   3.
Computers—Moral and ethical aspects.   I. George, Joey F.
QA76.9.C66C585   2003
303.48′33—dc21   2003045781

Executive Editor: David Alexander
Project Manager (Editorial): Kyle Hannon
Publisher and Vice President: Natalie E. Anderson
Editorial Assistant: Robyn Goldenberg
Media Project Manager: Joan Waxman
Senior Marketing Manager: Sharon K. Turkovich
Marketing Assistant: Danielle Torio
Managing Editor (Production): John Roberts
Production Editor: Renata Butera
Production Assistant: Joe DeProspero
Permissions Supervisor: Suzanne Grappi
Manufacturing Buyer: Michelle Klein
Cover Design: Kiwi Design
Cover Illustration/Photo: Terry Husebye/Getty Images, Inc.
Composition/Full-Service Project Management: BookMasters, Inc.
Printer/Binder: Courier/Westford

Credits and acknowledgments borrowed from other sources and reproduced, with permission, in this textbook appear on appropriate page within the text.

Pearson Education LTD.
Pearson Education Singapore, Pte. Ltd
Pearson Education, Canada, Ltd
Pearson Education–Japan
Pearson Education Australia PTY, Limited
Pearson Education North Asia Ltd
Pearson Educatión de Mexico, S.A. de C.V.
Pearson Education Malaysia, Pte. Ltd

10 9 8 7 6 5 4 3 2 1
ISBN 0-13-140660-4

To my teachers and to my students, and in memory of Rob Kling

Contents

v

Social Implications of Internet Use

The Internet, Government, and the Law

Digital Divides

Free Speech and the Internet

Introduction

It goes without saying that computers are becoming more and more pervasive in modern society. The changes computers bring about can be powerful and obvious or quite subtle. The microchips built into today's typical automobile have more computing power than a huge, mainframe computer of 30 years ago, but nobody thinks about the chips or the impacts they have on the car's performance or on the atmosphere when they are driving home from work. Yet the chips do have an impact: The car may not need a tune-up until it has traveled 100,000 miles, and potentially dangerous pollutants are reduced through a chip's increased control over the catalytic converter. Computer systems built and employed by organizations can have impacts just as powerful and as subtle, but few people think about them as they get cash from an ATM or pay their income taxes electronically or read an individualized version of the *Wall Street Journal* or some other national newspaper on their home computer each weekday. As one of the chief agents of change regarding the computerization of society, information systems (IS) professionals need to be aware of the implications their actions can have, at the individual, group, organizational, and societal levels. The choices IS professionals make in their work can have profound and unforeseen impacts on the people and organizations that come to rely on the systems IS professionals design and build, especially if the potential impacts are not even considered during the design and implementation process.

Plan of the Book

This book is divided into four sections: (1) Computers in Society, (2) Privacy, (3) Ethics, and (4) The Internet. The first section has five subsections: Views of Computing, The Information Society, Computers and Organizations, Computer-Based Monitoring, and Security and Reliability. The subsection on Views of Computing deals with the various ways that people think about computing and how it affects their lives. The second subsection is about the term "information society" and what that really means. The third subsection, on computers and organizations, is primarily about a phenomenon called "the productivity paradox." This subsection also includes an article commissioned specifically for this book by Steve Sawyer and Andrea Tapia on the social informatics view of computerization of work. The fourth subsection, on computer-based monitoring, includes articles about management monitoring of clerical work and professional work. Two of the three articles in this subsection were commissioned for this book: one by Joey George and Pam Carter and another by Terri Griffith. The final subsection in Part 1 is about computer security and reliability. The first of three articles in this subsection is about the exploits of one of the most famous of all American "hackers." The second article is an excerpt from an annual report on just how extensive computer security problems are in U.S. organizations. The final article by Judee Burgoon, Kent

Marett, and John Blair is about a research program investigating the successful detection of deception in computer-mediated communication.

Part 2 is about privacy. The focus is on privacy as it relates to computing in general and as it relates specifically to Internet use. The article by Mary Culnan was commissioned for this book. The next two articles deal with the relationship between trust and privacy for Internet commercial sites, and the results of a national survey in the United States on people's feelings about privacy and the Internet. The last two articles in this subsection come from *BusinessWeek*. They illustrate well the change in focus in privacy concerns from before and after the September 11, 2001, attacks on the United States.

Part 3 is about ethics. The first piece in this section is about the ethics of systems design. The second and third articles deal with the ethics of information systems professionals. The final article is a self-test on ethics, which allows you to determine whether the actions taken in the scenarios provided are ethical or not.

Part 4 of the book is about the Internet. Its 12 articles and five subsections are devoted to the social implications of the Internet. Topics include The Internet in the United States and the World; Social Implications of Internet Use; The Internet, Government, and the Law; Digital Divides; and Free Speech and the Internet. The first subsection has two articles, one on the Internet economy and the other on the global diffusion of the Internet. The second subsection looks at the so-called "Internet paradox," the idea that a communication medium created for social interaction may actually lead to socially isolated individuals. The third subsection includes articles on how U.S. law applies to cyberspace and on how to evaluate U.S. government Web sites. The latter article was commissioned for this book and is by Kim Thompson, Charles McClure, and Paul Jaeger. The subsection on digital divides covers both the racial and gender digital divides. Finally, the last subsection includes an article on why anonymity on the Internet may not be a good thing, the American Library Association's Library Bill of Rights, and a book chapter on free speech by one of the leading experts on cyberlaw, Lawrence Lessig.

▮▮▮ Support Materials

The text features a MyCompanion Web site (www.prenhall.com/george) where adopters can access a password-protected instructor's manual written by the text author.

Preface

The idea of creating this book originated years ago, when I organized and taught my first course on the social issues related to computing at the University of Arizona in 1991. To teach the class, I found and put together a set of articles from the popular and academic presses. This is common practice for a lot of faculty for a lot of courses, especially where frequent change in the topic requires constant updates in the assigned readings. However, I thought it would be nice to be able to put all those articles into a book—a single source for students taking my course and for students at other schools where their professors faced a similar problem. Publishers, however, are not wild about publishing books of readings, as I had found out in my efforts to publish such books for other doctoral seminars. Therefore, I never really pursued creating a book of readings about the social issues related to computers.

I was only able to teach the class once at Arizona, and it wasn't until the summer of 1998 that I was able to put together and teach another graduate level course on the social issues of computing. I created the course as part of the new masters program in MIS we were creating at Florida State University. I felt strongly that the masters program should have in it a course on social and organizational issues, so I was able to create the course and teach it. I have taught that course five times now, counting the academic year in which I am writing this preface and the one time I taught it at Louisiana State University. Each time I have taught the course, I have used a book of readings (not all publishers are wary of such books) and supplemented that with journal articles both in print and on the Web. With each passing year, the book of readings I was been relying on had become more and more out of date, and I was forced to increase the number of papers with which I had to supplement it. It became clear to me that I was soon going to have to teach the course without the readings book, just as I did back in 1991. However, I thought I would ask my editor at Prentice Hall, David Alexander, if there was any chance he would be interested in such a book. I had nothing to lose, so I was surprised when he showed some interest. Several months later, here we are, book in hand.

The book contains a total of 37 chapters. Thirty of these have been published before. Some are articles from the academic press, some come from the popular press, and some are book chapters. The remaining seven were written just for this book. In addition to the introductory chapter that I wrote, there are six chapters commissioned especially for this volume. I was able to convince some of the top people in the field to take the time to write chapters on their areas of expertise. You will not find these chapters anywhere else. Therefore, I want to wholeheartedly thank my friends and colleagues who contributed:

John "Pete" Blair, Michigan State University
Judee Burgoon, University of Arizona
Pamela Carter, University of Oklahoma

Mary Culnan, Bentley College
Terri Griffith, Santa Clara University
Paul Jaeger, Florida State University
Kent Marett, Florida State University
Charles McClure, Florida State University
Steve Sawyer, Pennsylvania State University
Andrea Tapia, Pennsylvania State University
Kim Thompson, Florida State University

I also had these commissioned chapters reviewed by other experts in the field. I want to thank them for taking the time to review the chapters and for the excellent suggestions they made that resulted in improved versions of all of the commissioned chapters. The reviewers were:

Diane Bailey, Stanford University
John Carlo Bertot, Florida State University
Lt. Col. David Biros, U.S. Air Force
Pamela Carter, University of Oklahoma
Lorrie Cranor, AT&T Labs

When I contacted David Alexander about the possibility of doing this book, I wrote the usual prospectus and table of contents. David and his staff then sent this out for review. I want to thank the people who reviewed the prospectus, especially because their comments helped convince David that he needed to publish this book. The reviewers were:

Robert Barger, Notre Dame University
Wolfgang Bein, University of Nevada–Las Vegas
Elizabeth Buchanan, University of Wisconsin–Milwaukee
Charles Crowley, University of New Mexico
Michael Maddox, George Mason University
Eric Santanen, Bucknell University
Jeffrey Stone, Pennsylvania State University

The book would never have happened, of course, without David Alexander, so I want to thank him for his initial interest and for making the book a reality. There also would not have been a book without the work of all the other people at Prentice Hall who made it possible, so I want to also thank Kyle Hannon, Maat Van Uitert, Suzanne Grappi, and Renata Butera for their many contributions. I also want to thank Jen Welsch of BookMasters, Inc.

Finally, I must thank my wife Karen and my two daughters Evan and Caitlin for allowing me to work on this project. Participating in a project like this always takes time away from other things, and I know that part of the time taken has been taken from my family. Thanks, guys, for letting me work on yet another book.

Joey F. George
Tallahassee, Florida
January 2003

PART

I

Computers in Society

⣿ Introduction

Not so long ago, an entire book on the social issues related to computing might have been limited to the topics covered in Part 1 of this book. The main reason is that, though it is a cliché, the Internet really has changed everything. The topics covered in Part 1 remain important to any consideration of the issues related to computing and society. The Internet has become a major force in our lives in a little more than 10 years, but computing has been around for over 50 years. Unlike the Internet's influence, the general influence of computing has grown and spread at a much more measured and gradual pace.

The growth in general computing and its influence is a lot like the story about the frog and a pot of boiling water. If you put a frog in a pot of hot water, it will jump out immediately. However, if you put a frog in a pot of tepid water, the frog will stay put, and as you gradually increase the water's temperature so that the water boils, the frog will stay in the water and eventually allow itself to be boiled to death. The reason is that a frog is not able to notice the very gradual increase in water temperature, so it does not react to the danger that it is in.

The increase and the diffusion of changes due to computing are like the water that slowly increases in temperature, and we are like the frog. Starting in the 1950s and spreading as the years have gone by, more and more aspects of our daily lives have come to be supported by computing. Of course, part of the reason for this is the continuing decline in the cost of computing relative to its power. Another part of the reason is the accompanying cost-performance improvements in related technologies such as memory.

Many of the impacts of computing on our lives are by design, such as more fuel-efficient cars, the ability to withdraw cash from our bank accounts no matter where we are in the world, efficient airline reservation systems, credit cards that are accepted all over the world, electronic data interchange for ships approaching ports, the hundreds of channels on satellite television, and so on. Clearly these applications of computing provide benefits for consumers and for the corporations that employ them. Yet these same applications have uses that their original designers may not have intended. For example, using information from ATM systems, credit card processors, and airline reservations systems, a government agency may be able to determine where a person has been and what they have purchased at a specific point in time. Information taken from a TV satellite may be used to make assumptions about an individual's consumer behavior or political views, and this information can then be sold to companies that will send the individual mail and spam e-mail in an effort to gain a sale or a political contribution.

The examples of unintended uses of computing in the previous paragraph focus on privacy, but other examples related to other social issues also can be drawn. Privacy has been associated with the growth of computing for decades; it is so important that it has its own section in this book. Before we get to privacy, however, we will examine other issues that have been associated with computing for decades and continue to be important. These issues are views of computing, the information society, computers and work organizations, computer-based monitoring, and security and reliability. First, though, is an introductory chapter that summarizes the findings to date on some of the earliest social issues associated with computing and that identifies other key issues that have recently emerged.

This introduction to Part 1, and the related introductions to the other sections, is organized as follows: After some initial remarks, brief comments on each article in the section will be presented. Comments will be followed by a list of Web sites related to the topics that are important to the section. A list of sources of additional readings is also provided.

▪▪▪ The Articles in Part 1

George, J. F. "Introduction to the Social Issues of Computing."

> This chapter provides an overview of social issues related to computing that were once considered vital and those that are now of central focus. Past issues include employment, deskilling, quality of work life, organizational structure, the existence of a technological elite, and privacy. Current issues include two "past" issues, the quality of work life although this time with a focus on white collar workers, and privacy, as well as the "new" issues of security, the degradation of social life, and digital divides.

Views of Computing

Shapiro, A. L. 1999. "Gaining Control." Chap. 3 in *The Control Revolution*. New York: Public Affairs.

> In "Gaining Control," a chapter from his book *The Control Revolution*, Shapiro talks about our attitudes towards computers and how they have evolved, including our attitudes towards the Internet and the relationship between the Internet and our sense of control.

Fisher, D. R., and L. M. Wright. 2001. "On utopias and dystopias: Toward an understanding of the discourse surrounding the internet." *Journal of Computer Mediated Communication* 6(2).

> Fisher and Wright summarize the positive, utopian views of the Internet, as well as the more pessimistic dystopian views. They also introduce a third, more modest view of the Internet, which they call the "technorealist perspective."

Anderson, D. P., and J. Kubiatowicz. 2002. "The worldwide computer." *Scientific American* 286(3): 28–35.

> Anderson and Kubiatowicz explore the possibilities of a future world where all of the millions of host machines on the Internet can work together to provide new Internet-wide applications through the development and use of an Internet-scale operating system.

The Information Society

Porat, M. U. 1978. "Global implications of the information society." *Journal of Communication* 28(1): 70–80.

> Porat's pioneering work on the information economy is summarized here in his 1978 article. Whereas an information society may be difficult to recognize, an information economy is fairly easy to identify.

Lyon, D. 1986. "From 'post-industrialism' to 'information society': A new social transformation?" *Sociology* 20(4): 577–588.

> Lyon argues that the much reported and anticipated transformation from an industrial society to an information society has not actually occurred.

Computers and Organizations

Brynjolfsson, E. 1993. "The productivity paradox of information technology." *Communications of the ACM* 36(12): 66–77.

> In this article, Brynjolfsson introduces the "productivity paradox," the observation that years of heavy investment in computing had not resulted in associated improvements in worker productivity. The productivity paradox was a topic of great concern in the early 1990s, before the emergence of the huge productivity gains that characterized the middle and end of the decade. At the time this article was written, the exact relationship between computing and productivity was still unclear.

Brynjolfsson, E., and L. M. Hitt. 1998. "Beyond the productivity paradox: Computers are the catalyst for bigger changes." *Communications of the ACM* 41(8): 49–55.

> Brynjolfsson and Hitt argue that computers are not necessarily automatically related to improvements in productivity. Instead, organizational factors are important to understanding how productivity can be improved through the use of computing, and the biggest gains seem to come when computing is combined with new business processes and strategies.

Dedrick, J., and K. L. Kraemer. 2000. "The Productivity Paradox: Is it Resolved? Is There a New One? What Does It All Mean for Managers?" Center for Research on Information Technology and Organizations, University of California at Irvine, Irvine, CA.

> Writing at the end of the 1990s, Dedrick and Kraemer conclude that the controversy over the productivity paradox has been put to rest. They raise the possibility of a new productivity paradox: Given the huge returns on investment from implementing computing, organizations are actually underinvesting in computing, not overinvesting.

Sawyer, S., and A. Tapia. "The Computerization of Work: A Social Informatics Perspective."

> Sawyer and Tapia investigate the forces that affect the computerization of work. They examine software development, systems implementation, and the knowledge-intensive work of real estate agents in order to understand the issues relevant to automating information work.

Computer-Based Monitoring

George, J. F. and Carter, P. "Computer-Based Performance Monitoring."

> For many years, computer-based performance monitoring generated a lot of controversy with regards to the monitoring of clerical workers. George and Carter write about studies of computer-monitored clerical workers in the early 1990s and discuss how monitored workers compare with nonmonitored workers in similar jobs.

Griffith, T. L. "Social and Technical Aspects of Electronic Monitoring: To Protect and to Serve."

> The monitoring of work by management is once again a popular topic, but the focus has shifted from clerical workers to white collar jobs. For these types of workers, much of the monitoring is of Internet use and e-mail. Griffith writes about how monitoring has traditionally been used to protect the organization but that it also has great potential for actually improving work for employees.

Simmers, C. A. 2002. "Aligning Internet usage with business priorities." *Communications of the ACM* 45(1): 71–74.

> Simmers writes about Internet usage policies for organizations and how they have been enforced through electronic monitoring.

Security and Reliability

Littman, J. 1996 "Pending Investigation." Chap. 3 in *The Fugitive Game*. Boston: Little, Brown & Co.

> "Pending Investigation" is a chapter from Littman's book *The Fugitive Game*, which is about serial hacker Kevin Mitnick. In addition to providing background on how Mitnick came to be a hacker, the chapter also illustrates an episode of "social engineering," which is essentially hacking without having to use a computer.

Excerpts from Power, R. 2002. "2002 CSI/FBI computer crime and security survey." *Computer Security Issues & Trends*, 8(2): 7–30.

> Every year since 1996, the Computer Security Institute, in conjunction with the Federal Bureau of Investigation, has conducted a survey of computer crime and security. This article is an edited version of the 2002 results.

Burgoon, J. K., K. L. Marett, and J. P. Blair. "Detecting Deception in Computer-Mediated Communication."

> Even with the most secure computer system, damage can still be done through the passing of deceptive information. Burgoon, Marett, and Blair write about their findings to date on the detection of deceptive information in computer-mediated communication. These initial findings come from a large multiyear study on deception and its detection.

Related Places to Go on the Web

One place to find information about social issues related to computing is the Web site for the Computer Professionals for Social Responsibility (www.cpsr.org/).

Some computing professional societies also have special interest groups devoted to computing and social issues. One example is the ACM Special Interest Group on Computers and Society (www.acm.org/sigcas/).

Commercial sites about computing and its effects on society are also available. An example is the Web site for *Wired* magazine (http:/www.wired.com/wired/current.html).

ADDITIONAL READING

Aiello, J. R., and C. M. Svec. 1993. "Computer monitoring of work performance: Extending the social facilitation framework to electronic presence." *Journal of Applied Social Psychology* 23(7): 537–548.

Attewell, P. 1987. "Big brother and the sweatshop: Computer surveillance in the automated office." *Sociological Theory* 5: 87–99.

Bell, D. 1973. *The Coming of the Post-Industrial Society.* New York: Basic Books.

Forster, E. M. 1947. "The Machine Stops." In *The Collected Tales of E. M. Forster.* New York: Alfred A. Knopf, 144–197.

Gates, W. H. 1996. *The Road Ahead.* New York: Penguin.

George, J. F. 1996. "Computer-based monitoring: Common perceptions and empirical results." *MIS Quarterly,* 20: 459–480.

Gibson, W. 1984. *Neuromancer.* New York: Ace Books.

Grant, R. 1990. *Silicon Supervisors: Computerized Monitoring in the Service Sector.* Washington, D.C.: ICIT Press.

Kling, R., and W. Scacchi. 1982. "The web of computing: Computer technology as social organization." *Advances in Computers* 21: 1–90.

Mowshowitz, A. 1976. *The Conquest of Will: Information Processing in Human Affairs.* Reading, MA: Addison-Wesley.

Mowshowitz, A. 1986. "Social dimensions of office automation." *Advances in Computers* 25: 335–404.

Nora, S., and A. Minc. 1981. *The Computerization of Society.* Cambridge, MA: MIT Press.

Orwell, G. 1949. *Nineteen Eighty-Four.* New York: Harcourt Brace Jovanovich.

Shimomura, T. 1996. *Takedown.* New York: Hyperion.

Turkle, S. 1995. *Life on the Screen: Identity in the Age of the Internet.* New York: Simon & Schuster.

U.S. Congress, Office of Technology Assessment. 1987. *The Electronic Supervisor: New Technology, New Tensions.* Washington, D.C.

Vonnegut, K. 1956. *Player Piano.* New York: Holt, Rinehart & Winston.

Weizenbaum, J. 1976. *Computer Power and Human Reason.* San Francisco: W.H. Freeman and Company.

Whisler, T. 1970. *The Impact of Computers on Organizations.* New York: Praeger Publishers.

Winner, L. 1977. *Autonomous Technology.* Cambridge, MA: MIT Press.

Introduction to the Social Issues of Computing

Joey F. George

Introduction

Every year it seems that the organization that accredits business schools in the United States changes its view of what should be taught in business school classes. This is reasonable and to be expected given that the business climate is dynamic, and students should be aware of the current state of the business world. In the early 1990s, the new emphasis was on international business and on social issues related to business, especially the teaching of ethics. (This was before the recent spate of business misconduct in the United States, which has resulted in another new push for the teaching of ethics.) I was asked by my department chair to compile a list of social issues being addressed in our classes in the MIS department. I will never forget one response I received from one of my colleagues. Although I have lost the actual message, it went something like this:

> Yes, it is important that we look at how computing has affected homelessness and poverty and hunger and world peace.

When I first read the message, I was stunned that someone could respond this way. The message was obviously sarcastic; my colleague was implying that computing, like so many seemingly neutral technological tools, obviously had no relationship at all to social issues. Yet across the many years that people have been studying computing, there have always been those who have concerned themselves with how computing might be affecting various aspects of society. My initial reaction was to respond to my colleague, lecturing him on all the various aspects of society where computing had been known to be effecting change. The list I provided was at that time well-known: employment effects, impacts on jobs and the quality of work life, changes in organizational structure, and so on. In fact, some of these topics had been studied for decades.

That my colleague was so unaware of the many ways that computing was having an impact on society surprised me. Yet his views were probably not too different from the views of millions of Americans at the time. Most people had just not taken the time to think about how computing was changing our lives. Some of us in academia were aware of the debates because we had read about them and had even written about them. In the early 1990s, computing was not as ubiquitous as it is today. Today, it is difficult to ignore computing, but even a dozen years ago, it was not that hard.

Before the personal computer arrived in the late 1970s (Apple and other companies) and early 1980s (the IBM PC especially), many Americans had never even seen a computer. The effects of computing on our lives and on our society were taking place behind the scenes through the use of computers by businesses and governmental organizations. That is why so many of the issues related to computing and society have an organizational and workplace focus. Even after the PC was introduced, it remained largely a business tool due to its relatively high cost and the lack of applications that most people would find to be useful in their homes. Some people bought these early personal computers for home, but most used them primarily for work purposes. It was not until the Internet was opened up to the average person, through its opening to commercial enterprise and the advent of the World Wide Web, that computing began to find a home in our homes. The spread of computing in the mid-1990s and on into the present has been at an amazing rate of speed.

Computing began to seep into our lives in other ways as well. Most home appliances, from dishwashers to microwaves, now include embedded processors. Our cars now include dozens of processors to control and monitor many aspects of performance. Videogames improved dramatically and then became portable. Portable game systems were soon followed by other handheld computers, such as MP3 players and personal digital assistants and mobile phones.

As computers have become distributed throughout so many different aspects of our lives, the social issues we have been concerned with have also changed. Many of the old debates about employment and so on have been settled. Some old issues such as privacy have become revived and have taken on new meanings and urgencies. New issues, such as the digital divide, which operates on so many levels, also have emerged.

The purpose of this introductory chapter is to acquaint you with social issues related to computing past and present. To that end, the next section covers the best known issues of the past: employment, job deskilling, quality of work life, organizational structure, the technological elite, and privacy. That section is then followed by one that explores current issues: quality of work life, privacy, security, the degradation of social life, and the digital divide. In neither case are these exhaustive lists, but they are illustrative of the social effects of computing past and present.

▮▮▮ Past Issues

Employment

Just as there was (and is) concern that machines would take over jobs in factories, many were also concerned that computers would take over jobs in offices. A 1960s era article in the *Harvard Business Review* was even titled "When the Computer Takes Over the Office" (Hoos 1960). The fear was that automating much of the work done by office workers would mean less for office workers to do, and hence fewer office workers. These fears were primarily for clerical workers, although some thought that managers' jobs were threatened as well (Leavitt and Whisler 1958). Fears of computer-induced unemployment were worse in Europe than in the United States (Attewell and Rule 1984).

It did not help that many computerization projects were (and still are) often justified on the basis of cost savings, most of which were to come from the need for fewer workers. However, most observers noted that, although some people may have lost their jobs due to office automation, the promised cost savings were rarely realized because in most cases, automation ended up resulting in more jobs and more people being hired. Interestingly enough, the massive layoffs predicted in the 1950s and 1960s did eventually occur—in the 1990s. It can be argued that this restructuring or downsizing of the white collar workforce was not a direct result of automation; rather, organizations were able to keep up with or even increase their workloads with fewer people by using computers to increase productivity. (See articles in this volume on the "productivity paradox" for more details).

Deskilling

Another concern about the impacts of computing in the work place dealt with the content of the job. It was widely believed (Zuboff 1982; Mowshowitz 1986) that the introduction of computing in the office would lead to jobs of lesser interest and challenge. The computer system would be designed to take over the more interesting parts of a job, leaving the worker to do little more than push buttons. This effect is called *deskilling*, as the skills needed to do the job originally have been removed and are now being done by the computer. Others argued that computing would actually improve jobs because computers would take over the tedious and repetitive aspects of work, leaving the really interesting and challenging part for the person to do (Bell 1976). Some called this *upskilling*. By and large, this issue has been settled. In a debate-stopping article, Attewell (1987) reported that there seemed to be about as much deskilling in automated jobs as upskilling, but that upskilling had the upper hand. Computing, then, seems to make work a little more interesting.

Quality of Work Life

As was the case for fears about computerization displacing workers, fears about how computers would affect the quality of work life grew out of similar concerns about machines in factories. During the Industrial Revolution, the quality of work life for many factory workers was horrendous. Think about how factory life was portrayed in Charles Dickens' writings, and the writings of other nineteenth-century authors, and you get a good idea of the popular notions of the quality of factory work life. Work was conducted at dizzying rates, there was not enough clean air and light, conditions were less than sanitary, and the work was physically dangerous. This type of work environment has been called a sweatshop, and the term is still applied today to many factory settings, especially in the textile trade. Some thought that work in the office would become like this after computerization (Garson 1988). The pace of work would be driven by the computer, people would feel great stress because of the fast pace, and they would suffer physically and emotionally because of it. Once improved surveillance techniques became available for office and particularly for clerical work, these techniques could be used to make sure that workers were keeping up with the computer-driven pace (Grant 1990). Most people who wrote about this computer-based performance monitoring believed that it was a universally bad practice. However, there is some evidence that monitoring is a malleable technology, and that managers have a lot of control over how it is used in the workplace (see the paper in this volume by George and Carter for more details). It may well be that how computerization affects the quality of work life has more to do with how the technology is implemented and with the context in which it is used than with the simple introduction of computerization alone.

Organizational Structure

The question of how computer technology would affect the structure of organizations has been a popular one at least since 1958, when Leavitt and Whisler brought it to the attention of the academic world with their now classic article, "Management in the 1980s." One of the key questions related to organizational structure was the extent to which computing affected where most decisions in an organization were made. There were basically four arguments: (1) computing was associated with centralization, (2) computing was associated with decentralization, (3) there was no necessary relationship between the two, or (4) the problem was best approached from a different perspective. Empirical support for centralization has come from many authors, including Mann and Williams (1958), Hoos (1960), Lee (1965), Reif (1968), and Whisler (1970). Meyer (1968), Klatzky (1970), and Pfeffer and Leblebici (1977) found some evidence that computing leads to decentralization.

Other scholars have concluded that there is in fact no relationship between computing and the decision-making location in the organization, that any changes in organizational structure that come about as a result of computing are the direct results of conscious managerial action. Finally, still others have suggested looking at the relationship between computing technology and organizational impacts from a different perspective. Davis et al. (1982) reasoned that the relationship between computing technology and organizations has changed because computing is now entrenched in organizations and that organizations are now altering computing rather than the other way around. Kraemer and Dutton (1979) maintained that this is how it has always been between computers and organizations, that those in power have always used the organization's resources to strengthen their positions and that computing is just another organizational resource.

In another debate-stopping article, George and King (1991) presented evidence from all sides of the debate, classifying much of the literature as either promoting a view of structure determined by technology or structure determined by managers. They concluded that the best explanation for changes in organizational structure that could be attributed to computing was a political model. Changes in structure associated with changes in computing were the result of concerted management action to preserve the current political status quo in the organization. To understand the relationship between computing and structure in an organization, it is necessary to also understand an organization's context, history, and power structure.

Technological Elite

When computing was first introduced into organizations, there were no computer science programs in universities and there were no vocational school courses on computer programming. Yet there was a real need for people who could design and build information systems and maintain them so they continued to operate. Given that computing was not well understood by most people in organizations, the few talented people who could design and build systems came to be seen as special. The special status given to early system developers and computer operators generated visions of a technological elite, a special priesthood of computing experts (Leavitt and Whisler 1958; Hoos 1960; Bell 1976). It was feared that these white-coated experts working behind glass walls would take on a special privileged role in the organization and that they would have undue influence in the organization's affairs. This view of how computing would affect organizations never quite came to pass.

Privacy Then

Interest in the relationship between computing and privacy has been cyclical (Burnhan 1983). In the 1960s, there was keen interest in privacy due to abuses in credit reporting in the United States. The result was the Fair Credit Reporting Act, passed in 1970. In the 1970s, there was again keen interest in privacy due to the Watergate scandal and the actions of the Nixon administration. The primary privacy law that exists in the United States, the Privacy Act of 1974, was passed during this period. During both of these periods of interest in privacy, the key issues related to the ability of people to inspect computer-based files about individuals that were held by organizations. Computer-based records of the day tended to be designed for and used for particular applications, making it difficult to compile data across files. People became concerned when the U.S. government or others considered ways to make it easier to compile data across files, as would be the case in the creation of massive centralized databases.

Another round of interest in privacy and computing occurred in 1990 and 1991, when the credit reporting firms were the primary source of consumer complaints to the Federal Trade Commission. Yet no new laws were passed at this time, because the credit reporting firms capitulated to some degree to government demands. After this controversy died down, there was little interest in privacy issues for several years until the advent of the Internet turned privacy once again into a mainstream concern. Internet privacy concerns will be covered in the next section. (There are five articles on privacy in this volume.)

▮▮▮ Current Issues

Quality of Work Life: White Collar Sweatshops

The impact of computing on the quality of work life continues to be an important example of how computing affects society. Whereas the focus of concern was previously on clerical workers, the focus has shifted recently to white collar workers: managers, professionals, and specialists. Only recently has computing begun to affect these workers and their jobs in direct ways (Fraser 2001). One key threat of computing to white collar jobs is surveillance. Many companies routinely monitor how professional workers use their e-mail and the Internet while at work. Another key threat is the ubiquity of computing. Most professionals have laptop computers, personal digital assistants, cell phones, and other computer-enabled and portable devices. The ready availability of these devices has made it possible for people to be able to work wherever they are, at whatever time of day or night. People can work from rooms, conference halls, and even from taxicabs. The concern is that ubiquitous computing has weakened the line between work and home, creating additional stress in white collar jobs and increasing the pace of work as well. These increases in stress and work pace are exacerbated by the apparent end of corporate loyalty to employees. For many white collar workers, the quality of work life is not as good as what their parents, in similar jobs, experienced.

Privacy and Surveillance Now

Surveillance used to be a concern only for clerical workers whose jobs were monitored by computer-based systems. Now it is a concern for white collar workers as well due to the common practice of monitoring e-mail and Internet use. Such monitoring practices are completely legal in the United States where managers are free to monitor the use of company-owned equipment and networks. However, surveillance concerns now extend beyond the workplace. This is due to the spread of Internet use. (See the articles in this volume by Simmers and Griffith on the monitoring of Internet use.)

In the United States, as of this writing, it is estimated that there are 166 million Internet users (NUA 2002; www.nua.net). This amounts to almost 60 percent of the population. Although this high level of Internet penetration is typical of industrialized Western countries, the estimate for the number of Internet users worldwide is 580 million, or about 10 percent of the world's population. These numbers continue to increase every year.

When a person goes online to use the Internet, that individual immediately begins to create a trail that shows where they have gone, what pages they have looked at, and how much time was spent on each page. Let's say that you go online to do some shopping. As you move from site to site on the Internet, you leave a record of every page you visited and how long you were there. Someone looking at that data could determine what you were interested in by focusing on the things you spent the most time looking at. The next time you visited a site, you might get a customized page just for you, based on what you looked at. Retailers such as Amazon.com do this routinely. The same thing would not happen to you in a typical retail mall. When you visit a shopping mall, no record is made of what you looked at and for how long as you make your way through the various departments of various stores. You have a level of anonymity in the mall that you do not enjoy on the Internet. This lack of anonymity on the Internet worries a lot of people. This is a social issue related to computing that was unimaginable even 10 years ago.

Security

Security is another issue that used to be restricted to corporations and government agencies that owned and ran large computing operations. The security threats to such organizations remain and have in fact increased dramatically as criminals who would attack their systems have gotten better and bolder. Security also has become an issue for other computer users, especially over the last couple of years.

After people started buying personal computers for their homes, security was an issue only to the extent that someone was likely to come into their houses and walk away with their computers. Even after more and more people began to use the Internet, security was not a problem as most people used dial-up connections and did not use their computers as Internet hosts. However, as high-speed direct connections spread, so, too, do direct threats to personal computers in people's homes. Constant direct connections increase the opportunity for others to locate and attack home computers.

The Internet has also worsened the threat of attack by becoming a key meeting place and exchange market for hackers and crackers and others who would break into other people's systems. Hacking tools are readily available on the Internet, and hackers and crackers can easily exchange information in chat rooms and using other Web-based communication tools. Most people are aware of the dramatic increase in the number and type of computer viruses, worms, and Trojan horses that have been spread through the Internet and e-mail in the past few years. Security has suddenly become an issue that typical users must confront on an almost daily basis. (This volume contains three articles related to security.)

Degradation of Social Life

Just as many social observers feared that television would lead to changes in social life, many now fear that the Internet will also change social life, and not necessarily for the better. As with television, time spent online is time that cannot be spent interacting with friends and family, playing sports or cards, or engaging in conversation. In fact, as the Internet is primarily a communications tool, personal contact with people close by may be given up for contact with new friends online. Chat rooms may be substituted for conversations around the dining room table. Internet hearts may be substituted for card games with the family. Interactive video games played online with people all around the world may be substituted for a pickup game of basketball at the neighborhood park. Some fear that, as people move further and further into the virtual world, they become less and less able to function in the real world, weakening the social networks that allow communities to function. (See the papers in the section on the social implications of Internet use for more detail.)

Digital Divides

The digital divide refers to differences in the availability of computing, especially in terms of Internet access, between two different groups. Most people think of the digital divide applying to different ethnic groups, such as the differences between white Americans and African-Americans. Although such use of the term is certainly valid, there are actually many types of digital divides. There are the divides between young and old, between rich and poor, between urban and rural, between the developed world and the developing world, and so on. (It is interesting to note that the digital divide between men and women, although quite wide in the early days of the Web—way back in the early 1990s—has essentially closed today.) The U.S. government has dealt with the digital divides in the United States by applying the idea of universal access, borrowed from policy regarding the telephone, to the Internet (U.S. NTIA 1993). The result has been the establishment of the e-rate, a tax paid on telecommunication use, which has provided for expanded Internet access in public schools and public libraries.

If Internet access is crucial to social interaction and societal development, the existence of digital divides raises interesting and painful questions about society. What happens if certain segments of the population are shut out and left behind? What is the best way to close the gaps? (See the three articles in this volume on digital divides for more information.)

▪ ▪ ▪ Conclusion

As mentioned earlier in this chapter, these lists of computing effects are only suggestive, not exhaustive. Computing and the Internet have touched so many different aspects of our lives that a truly comprehensive book on the many social issues related to computing would be a huge endeavor to compile, and probably a huge endeavor to carry around because such a book would be quite large. Instead of being comprehensive, this book is intended to introduce the relationships between society and computing to those who have not thought about such issues very much. My hope is that those who are interested in what they read here will follow the reference lists in each article, as well as the lists of additional readings and related Web sites in the part introductions, to find out more about issues in which they are interested. Given the ubiquity of computing in modern society, issues that tie together computing and society can no longer be ignored or automatically dismissed out of hand.

REFERENCES

Attewell, P., and J. Rule. 1984. "Computing and organizations: What we know and what we don't know." *Communications of the ACM* 27(12): 1184–1192.

Attewell, P. 1987. "The deskilling controversy." *Work and Occupations* 14(3): 323–346.

Bell, D. 1973. *The Coming of the Post-Industrial Society*. New York: Basic Books.

Burnham, D. 1983. *The Rise of the Computer State*. New York: Random House.

Davis, J., V. Dhar, W. King, and J. Teng. 1982. "The impact of the organization on the computer." Working paper,

Graduate School of Business, University of Pittsburgh, Pittsburgh, PA.

Fraser, J. A. 2001. *White-Collar Sweatshop*. New York: W.W. Norton & Co.

Garson, B. 1988. *The Electronic Sweatshop*. New York: Simon and Schuster.

George, J. F. and J. L. King. 1991. "Examining the computing and centralization debate." *Communications of the ACM* 34(7): 62–72.

Grant, R. 1990. *Silicon Supervisors: Computerized Monitoring in the Service Sector*. Washington, D.C.: ICIT Press.

Hoos, I. 1960. "When the computer takes over the office." *Harvard Business Review* 38(4): 102–112.

Klatzky, S. R. 1970. "Automation, size, and the locus of decision making: The Cascade effect." *Journal of Business* 43(2): 141–151.

Kraemer, K., and W. Dutton. 1979. "The interests served by technological reform." *Administration and Society* 11(1): 80–106.

Leavitt, H., and T. Whisler. 1958. "Management in the 1980s." *Harvard Business Review* 41–48.

Lee, H. C. 1965. The Impact of EDP Upon the Patterns of Business Organization and Administration. Albany, NY: State University of New York, Albany.

Mann, F. C., and L. K. Williams. 1958. "Organizational impact of white collar automation." *Annual Proceedings of Industrial Relations Research Associates*, pp. 59–68.

Meyer, M. W. 1968. "Automation and bureaucratic structure." *American Journal of Sociology* 74: 256–264.

Mowshowitz, A. 1986. "Social dimensions of office automation." *Advances in Computers* 25: 335–404.

NUA Internet Surveys. www.nua.com. Accessed October 2, 2002.

Pfeffer, J., and H. Leblebici. 1977. "Information technology and organization structure." *Pacific Sociological Review* 20(2): 241–261.

Reif, W. E. 1968. "Computer technology and management organization." Bureau of Business and Economic Research, College of Business Administration, University of Iowa, Iowa City, IA.

U.S. National Telecommunications and Information Administration. 1993. *The National Information Infrastructure: The Administration's Agenda for Action*, Version 1.0.

Whisler, T. 1970. *The Impact of Computers on Organizations*. New York: Praeger Publishers.

Zuboff, S. 1982. "New worlds of computer-mediated work." *Harvard Business Review* 142–152.

Gaining Control

ANDREW L. SHAPIRO

On the first page of his bestseller *The Road Ahead*, Bill Gates writes that he was initially drawn to computers as a child because "here was an enormous, expensive, grown-up machine and we, the kids, could control it." Though the young Gates and his friends were too young to drive or do other adult things, in the realm of computers they could be kings. "We could give this big machine orders and it would always obey," he recalls. "To this day it thrills me to know that if I can get the program right it will always work perfectly, every time, just the way I told it to."[1]

Gates is not alone in feeling that computers put him in charge. In Steven Levy's *Hackers*, a young computer wizard points out that "the computer. . . was just some dumb beast following orders, doing what you told it to in exactly the order you determined. You could control it. You could be God."[2]

Statements like these seem to celebrate the ability to control the machine itself, to domesticate it like some wild beast. Yet claims of control increasingly go further. Sherry Turkle, a psychologist and MIT professor, says that computer hobbyists often report that their machines provide them with a sense of mastery and order that is absent from other parts of their lives.[3] As one frequent user puts it, "I can't control the rest of the world but I can control my computer. . . ."[4]

There is something peculiar about this juxtaposition. What does "controlling" a machine, even a powerful computer, have to do with "controlling" one's life? How can playing computer games, for example, possibly compensate for powerlessness in work or politics?[5] One form of authority is limited to the operation of a box of silicon and wires; the other has to do with wielding influence in the real world. On a crude level, perhaps assertive behavior in one sphere of life can offset helplessness in other spheres.[6] But there is something deeper here: a relationship between the use of computers and the desire to increase one's relative control of the external world. To understand this connection, and particularly its relation to the Net, we need to step back briefly to consider how our attitudes toward computers have evolved.

▌▌▌ Taming the Machine

Before PCs became commonplace in the 1980s, most people thought of computers (if they thought of them at all) as mammoth objects with inscrutable vacuum tubes, blinking lights, and whirling magnetic tapes. This fearsome vision of computers—straight from sci-fi movies and TV shows—was abetted by the fact that these machines were scarcely seen in everyday life. They were, for the most part, operated by highly trained scientists in the exclusive enclaves of the academy, government, and large corporations. But with the remarkable improvement of the microprocessor, computers became increasingly small, affordable, and available. They entered our workplaces, schools, libraries, and homes.

Still, in their early years, PCs continued to provoke confusion and suspicion among the general public. Those who used computers regularly were stereotyped as geeks, misanthropes, even malevolent misfits. This view was born mostly out of ignorance. But it also reflected the fact that, reasonably or not, most people saw computers as mind-numbingly complex, boring, and perhaps even belittling. Recognizing this, the smartest entrepreneurs set out to build computers that would empower individuals rather than intimidate them.

The creative minds at Apple Computer understood the challenge better than anyone. In 1984, Apple released the Macintosh, the first commercial PC with a graphical user interface and a mouse. Instead of having to plow through dark fields of cathode-green text, remembering obscure commands, one could simply point and click through a soothing façade of simple, aesthetically pleasing icons: a desktop, menus, folders and files, dialog boxes, a trash can. Where earlier computer designs had seemed alienating, cold, and confusing, the Macintosh was humanizing, warm, and likable.

"User-friendly" was the term that evolved to describe this new computer interface, yet there was more to it than just amiability and simplicity. Apple consciously sold customers on the idea that the Macintosh was a computer for a new type of user—for "the rest of us," as the company put it. Nowhere was this strategy more evident than in their brilliant television advertisement introducing the Macintosh. It ran only once, in January 1984 during the Super Bowl, but caused such a stir that many who didn't see it undoubtedly heard about it. In the ad, a young woman liberates a horde of downtrodden info-age serfs from the gray, sterile tyranny of Big Brother—in this case, not the intrusive state of Orwell's *1984*, but Apple's powerful and lumbering rival, IBM.

Where IBM's PC was the computer of the establishment, Macintosh would be the tool of the creative, the young, the cutting-edge. The Mac appealed to those who felt threatened—not just by the complexity of computers, but by the prospect of becoming a cog in some routinized authoritarian scheme. Later, when Microsoft copied the Mac approach with its Windows operating system, the genius of the graphical interface would become universally appreciated. But it was Apple that first realized what we needed in order to become comfortable with computers. We needed more control.

In part, this meant being liberated from the drudgery of a text-only interface with the PC. As Steven Johnson explains, the graphical interface gave us the benefit of "direct manipulation," the ability to "get your hands dirty, move things around, make things happen."[7] Freed from having to learn arcane written commands, users could concentrate on what they wanted their computers to do *for* them rather than what their computer demanded *of* them.

Word-processing programs gave us new authority over the written word. Unconstrained by the permanence of ink and page, we could free-associate, type aimlessly, then cut, paste, and rearrange. We could spellcheck, highlight, and change the look of our documents a hundred times. Spreadsheets and personal finance programs gave us the ability to manipulate and keep track of numbers in new ways. Graphics programs allowed even the least artistically inclined to appear talented. And an endless surfeit of games indulged the imagination. In all these cases, software designers were writing code with the specific goal of enabling the individual. Every new release came with more options, more opportunity for customization.

The Macintosh and the now-ubiquitous Windows operating systems have extended this ethic to the point of allowing each user to personalize even the basic elements of the interface. On a Mac, for example, a user can name her hard drive, change the background colors on the screen, rearrange the desktop, and customize menus and commands. Personal computers have truly become personal. Apple emphasized this point with its "What's on your Powerbook?" ad campaign, which showed unlikely pairs of individuals and lists of the sundry items—addresses, screenplays, math equations—they stored on their portable Powerbook computers.[8] It's not just a box, Apple was telling us, it's an extension of you.

Even for those of us who use computers on a daily basis, these individual-oriented features may go largely unnoticed, if not unused. But they represent a broader philosophy of computing and technology generally—one that encourages each of us to feel as if the machine works, as Bill Gates put it, "just they way I told it to." Personal satisfaction has become perhaps the central value in our use of computers. And why not? This new emphasis on gratification and comfort has allowed us to transform what were sources of confusion into sources of power.

Now, with the reach and flexibility of the Internet, we can extend that power outward: from the tidy, inward focus of managing our files and applications to an increasingly externalized control—a remote control—of our interactions with the information and inhabitants of the whole world.

Just as you grew accustomed to choosing fonts and customizing your desktop, you'll now choose online communities and customize your news. You saved time by not having to rewrite a cover letter; now you'll post an evolving resume online and—if you're fortunate to have the right skills and experience—find work easily. That finance program helped you balance your checkbook. Tomorrow you'll save money online by having a software agent find the lowest price for a product you want. (Indeed, software agents, or bots, will likely carry out all sorts of tasks for you.)

The same way that PCs enabled us to take command of aspects of our personal lives, the Net will give each of us more of an opportunity to take command of our interactions with the world at large.

Reflect again, then, on the relationship between controlling a computer and controlling one's life. The Net means that the two could become increasingly intertwined. Sitting in front of a computer screen in your bedroom or office, it may be hard to see how a click here and there can really affect anything beyond the box, let alone your four walls. But connect that box to an outside line and things start to happen. As you gain access to newly personalized information, your perception of the world changes. Publish online and caucus with fellow travelers, and you can change other people's views. Sign a digital petition and influence the political process. Buy stocks—or groceries—online and affect the economy. Telecommute from home and redefine work, while reducing auto traffic and air pollution. These are the types of individual actions that are helping to produce a revolution in control.

▪▪▪ The Disappearance of Cyberspace

With all this potential for personal control, it's noteworthy that cyberspace has so far mostly been described as "out of control." Average users often find it confusing and disorderly. Critics describe a chaotic medium overrun by porn, hate speech, and mindless flame wars. But oddly enough, this exaggerated sense of clutter and disarray actually proves just how much the Internet is defined by the potential for individual control.

I recognized this when I was telling a friend of mine about the premise of this book. He looked skeptical. "Personal control?" he said. "When I go online, I feel totally lost. There's nothing to guide you or tell you what to do."

Exactly. No one is in control—except you. And if you're fairly new to the Net, then it may well feel frenzied and unmanageable. You're not powerless because someone else is pulling the strings, though. You're just beginning to realize that the strings are there for you to pull yourself.

In time, as we become more familiar with online interaction and navigation, and as new software tools are developed, the Net will become more domesticated. Design will likely be simpler, information will be easier to find, and the whole experience will become more predictable and routine. Norms and rules will develop. Soon enough, naysayers will realize that cyberspace is no more dangerous or perplexing than physical space. Indeed, it will become increasingly difficult to distinguish the two, as cyberspace will simply become a way of looking at the world.

Many of the digital vanguard seem to think otherwise. They have urged us to see cyberspace as if it were elsewhere, a place with its own law and sovereignty. In 1996, for example, cyber-activist John Perry Barlow wrote a Declaration of the Independence of Cyberspace, which minced no words about the illegitimacy of governments exercising jurisdiction over the "space" in which people interact online:

> Governments of the Industrial World, you weary giants of flesh and steel, I come from Cyberspace, the new home of Mind. On behalf of the future, I ask you of the past to leave us alone. You are not welcome among us. You have no sovereignty where we gather. . .
>
> I declare the global social space we are building to be naturally independent of the tyrannies you seek to impose on us. You have no moral right to rule us nor do you possess any methods of enforcement we have true reason to fear.
>
> Governments derive their just powers from the consent of the governed. You have neither solicited nor received ours. We did not invite you. You do not know us, nor do you know our world. Cyberspace does not lie within your borders. . . [9]

Barlow, a former Grateful Dead lyricist and self-described "cognitive dissident," would probably be the first to admit that his pronouncements are equal parts theater and theory. But he is not the only visionary who has described cyberspace as a place where communities exist, altercations occur, and cultural practices congeal.[10]

Some legal scholars even have asserted that cyberspace should have its own law and legal institutions, and have questioned whether state-based governments should have jurisdiction over online activity. We should, they say, see cyberspace "as a district 'place' for purposes of legal analysis by recognizing a legally significant border between Cyberspace and the 'real world.'"[11]

This cannot be right. Though the sentiments are well-intentioned and understandable—some Internet users may feel they are somewhere else when they interact online, and there are real legal difficulties that arise because of transnational communications—it would be a mistake, conceptually and practically, to erect a barrier between online and offline activity. Cyberspace is not somewhere "out there," a world apart from flesh and blood, asphalt and trees. Our actions online have (need it even be said?) a real impact on the lives of other human beings. When a fraudulent securities offering on the Net causes novice investors to be bilked of their hard-earned money, for example, that's a "real world" injury.

In short, cyberspace is too important to be thought of as elsewhere. Rather, we should think of it as being right here. In fact, it is so close to us, so increasingly significant and indispensable, that it will eventually recede from the fore and even disappear. Disappear, that is, in the same sense that the wallpaper pattern in your bathroom eventually becomes so familiar that it fades away and escapes notice.

▮▮▮ A Lens on Life

Fascination with cyberspace's exotic unfamiliarity is to be expected, for this is how we treat every new technology at its inception. As online interaction becomes less foreign and more a part of everyday existence, though, it makes sense to think of cyberspace not as a place or even a metaphorical space, but as a lens on life. The Net is an interface with which we can do almost anything: learn, work, socialize, transact, participate in politics. It allows us to control other things—the information we are exposed to, the people we socialize with, the resources of the physical world.

Thinking of the Net in terms of control even makes etymological sense. The word "cyberspace," made popular by science-fiction writer William Gibson in the mid-eighties, derives from *cybernetics*, which is the science of "control and communications theory."[12] Cybernetics, in turn, was coined half a century ago by a group of scientists led by Norbert Wiener, and was based on the ancient Greek word *kubernetes*, which meant "steersman" (as in the steering of a ship) or "governor." Cyberspace, then, can be thought of as an interface of personal control—a way that we steer reality or govern life.

Governing life? By tapping a computer keyboard? Yes, it may sound a bit far out. Most folks are just trying to get connected to America Online or hoping to figure out how to get rid of all the junk email that is clogging their email boxes. Yet this somewhat bewildered preoccupation with the Net's mechanics will pass as the technology becomes increasingly familiar.

In the early days of the telephone, people shouted into the receiver and conversation was stilted, yet now phone interaction is as natural for most of us as face-to-face contact. In the first years of radio, families gathered resolutely around the console at fixed hours each week to listen to programs. Today, the radio is a constant companion: It wakes us up, keeps us company in the car, and envelops us in the supermarket and at the office. (Indeed, few people listen to the radio any longer while *not* engaged in some other activity—driving, working, cleaning house.)

An even better comparison might be the adoption of alphabetic writing or spoken language. We don't think about letters as we write or grammar as we speak (unless we're learning a new language). Alphabets and language are our most taken-for-granted communication tools. They are so familiar that they just disappear. Similarly, just as the original Macintosh operating system worked because it was a fairly unobtrusive interface between the user and the resources of the personal computer—and a good interface wants nothing more than to be invisible[13]—the Net will increasingly be our inconspicuous interface with the world, another taken-for-granted way of understanding and filtering reality.[14]

More important than the ordering of the Net itself, then, is the way that it will let us reorder our lives. In other words, as the mystery of Internet communication fades, we will concentrate less on the computer and the network, and more on what the technologies allow us to do. *Allow*, though, is the operative word. Just because technology enables a revolution in control does not mean that it's a sure thing. To start with, we have to make it happen.

REFERENCES

1. Bill Gates, *The Road Ahead*, rev. ed. (New York: Penguin, 1996), 1–2.
2. Quoted in Steven Levy, *Hackers: Heroes of the Computer Revolution* (Garden City, N.Y.: Anchor Press/Doubleday, 1984), 284.
3. "Many hobbyists used the kind of control they felt able to achieve with their home computers to relieve a sense that they had lost control at work and in political life." Sherry Turkle, *Life on the Screen: Identity in the Age of the Internet* (New York: Simon and Schuster, 1995), 32.
4. Quoted in Molly O'Neill, "The Lure and Addiction of Life On Line," *New York Times*, March 9, 1995, C1, C6.
5. Turkle cites the case of a middle-aged lawyer who is passionate about playing games on his computer because, he says, "with these games I'm in complete control. It's a nice contrast with the rest of my life." Turkle, *Life on the Screen*, 67.
6. Renshon, *Psychological Needs*, 49–50.
7. Steven Johnson, *Interface Culture: How New Technology Transforms the Way We Create and Communicate* (San Francisco: HarperEdge, 1997), 21.
8. The ad can be found in the June 1995 issue of *Wired*.
9. John Perry Barlow, Declaration of the Independence Cyberspace, February 9, 1996 (at www.eff.org/pub/Publications/John *Perry*Barlow/barlow_0296.declaration).
10. See, for example, Howard Rheingold, *The Virtual Community: Homesteading on the Electronic Frontier* (Reading, Mass.: Addison-Wesley, 1993).
11. David R. Johnson and David Post, "Law and Borders: The Rise of Law in Cyberspace," *Stanford Law Review* 48 (1996): 1367, 1378.
12. "We have decided to call the entire field of control and communications theory . . . by the name Cybernetics." Norbert Wiener wrote in 1948. Norbert Wiener, *Cybernetics: Or Control and Communication in the Animal and the Machine* (Cambridge, Mass.: MIT Press, 1961), 11. Wiener himself may have been unaware that 150 years earlier a French physicist also used the term cybernetics to refer to a branch of political science which he described as the science of governance. See Kevin Kelly, *Out of Control: The Rise of Neo-Biological Civilization* (Reading, Mass.: Addison-Wesley, 1994), 120.

   The term cyberspace was first used by William Gibson, in his science-fiction story "Burning Chrome," *Omni*, July 1982, 72. It was made popular in his novel *Neuromancer* (New York: Ace Books, 1984).
13. See Donald A. Norman, *The Invisible Computer: Why Good Products Can Fail, the Personal Computer Is So Complex, and Information Appliances Are the Solution* (Cambridge, Mass.: MIT Press, 1998).
14. To a degree, television has played this role over the last few decades, influencing our personal and social life, our understanding of issues, and our political system. In fact, a small precursor to the control made possible by the Net can be seen in the changes wrought by the television remote control. That little clicker meant that rather than watching TV passively, we could shuttle between programs, mute the volume, and avoid commercials (often to the consternation of broadcasters and advertisers). It's a shift that is being recapitulated on a much more dynamic scale in our use of the Net. Like the TV remote, the networked computer gives us more power, only now the experience we can control is not just television, but almost the full scale of our human interactions.

On Utopias and Dystopias: Toward an Understanding of the Discourse Surrounding the Internet

DANA R. FISHER
LARRY MICHAEL WRIGHT

Introduction

On 26 July 2000, the San Francisco District Court ruled that Napster, the Internet-based music sharing software, was, in the words of Judge Marilyn Hall Patel, "essentially a program to facilitate the downloading and uploading of music . . . pirating be damned is the sense one gets" (Grimaldi 2000, p. A01). Although a final decision regarding the future of Napster is pending, this case has evoked responses from all sides of the issue, claiming that Napster has "changed the world" (Greenfeld 2000, p. 62). Whether the software has made the world better or worse depends on whom you ask. One side of the issue is voiced in the words of David Boies, lead attorney for Napster, who says that "that is a new technology that threatens . . . control."[1] On the other side, the technology has been called a part of the revolution by mainstream sources such as *Time Magazine* (Cohen 2000).

Such extreme responses are not unique to the online music-sharing software. Similar polarized discussions have focused on many different aspects of the Internet since it became accessible to mass society in the early 1990s. Given the different responses to the Internet's effects, it is important to consider the discourse surrounding

"On Utopias and Dystopias: Toward an Understanding of the Discourse Surrounding the Internet," D. R. Fisher and L. M. Wright, *Journal of Computer Mediated Communication*, Vol. 6, No. 2, 2001. Copyright © 2001.
[1]www.thestandard.com/article/display/0,1151,16593,00.html.

this medium of communication as it will likely affect how the technology is utilized by society in the future. Much of this discourse can be described along the lines of utopian and dystopian visions of the Internet (see, for example, Wellman 1997). The medium is heralded for its democratic potential. One such example is provided by Tsagarousianou (1998, p. 3), who claims that the technology will offer "a new arena for communication, a new public sphere that can replace the old one now crippled by commodification and fragmentation." At the same time, others argue that it will only make it easier for people to remove themselves from public life and the sense of civic engagement that goes with it (see, for example, Wilhelm 2000). The question of whether the Internet will remain largely free of regulation or whether it will be commodified is an important one. Of even larger importance, however, is understanding this extremely bifurcated discourse surrounding the development and diffusion of the Internet and all of its many applications such as Napster.

This paper explains the varying responses to the Internet as depicted by the academic and popular literature on the topic. We argue that the utopian/dystopian dichotomy found in the discourse surrounding the Internet is consistent with what Ogburn (1964) describes as a cultural lag. This lag suggests that the effects of technology may not be visible to social actors until some time after its introduction. As a result of this lag between the introduction of a technology and its cultural adaptation, both utopian and dystopian accounts of technologies such as the Internet are more likely to reflect authors' own preferences and values rather than an account of the technology's impact on the material and social conditions of society.

The paper is separated into three sections. First, we present Ogburn's notion of the cultural lag and describe its strengths and weaknesses. Next, we provide a review of the literature on the Internet, focusing our attention on the literature that discusses potential utopian and dystopian effects on society. Finally, we explain what the notion of the cultural lag brings to our understanding of the academic literature to date. By looking back to this earlier theory of technological diffusion, we hope that we will have a better understanding of the exceptionally polarized discussion surrounding the technology, how it fits historically within the context of other communication technologies, as well as how we can use these debates to develop a more critical view of the technology's potential effects on society.

▪▪▪ Cultural Lag

One possible way to begin to understand the extreme interpretations of Napster and other applications of the Internet is to turn to William Ogburn's work on the cultural lag. Although the notion of the cultural lag provides a framework to discuss technology and society, it is not without critics (Fischer 1992; Meyrowitz 1985; Mumford 1962; Segal 1994; Toffler 1970). As such, we will briefly discuss the model's limitations before describing its utility.

Perhaps the most potent criticism of the theory is that it is technologically deterministic (see, for example, Mumford 1962). Although Ogburn does entertain the possibility that the effects of culture and technology are reciprocal, he proceeds as though technology is an autonomous independent variable affecting the dependent variable of culture. In Ogburn's own words, "in nearly all cases [of cultural lag] the independent variable proved to be a scientific discovery or mechanical invention" (1964, p. 90).

In addition to the strongly deterministic theme in his work, the cultural lag also suffers from a teleological bias. Specifically, the notion of the cultural lag suggests that the identification of a problem is carried out by a single, unified culture. The presence of such a telos in Ogburn's work may have contributed to the assumption concerning consensus that we see in academic circles today: Scholars tend to be much more likely to argue over defining the problem to be studied than they are to decide how to alleviate the problem. Because of this shift in scholarship, theories such as that of the cultural lag have been overlooked. Although an important point to note, analyzing the relationship between the cultural lag and the theoretical scholarship that followed is beyond the scope of this study. It is important to recognize, however, the weaknesses in the theory that have contributed to its recent unpopularity. Even with these weaknesses, this theory of technological diffusion and adoption is very useful in understanding the extreme responses to applications such as Napster as well as other technologies of the Internet.

As a social theorist in the 1960s, Ogburn's project was to understand technology's adoption and the visions of its future. In *On Cultural and Social Change*, Ogburn writes about the theory of the cultural lag to explain the temporal difference in social causation (1964, p. 88). In other words, this theory explains the time lag between a technology's invention, its distribution to society, and the social adjustment that follows (Westrum 1991, p. 53). While the lag exists, unrealistic interpretations of the technology abound. In Ogburn's theory, some technologies are quickly followed by social institutional change and others are not.

In the author's own words, cultural lags exist because "technology moves forward and the social institution lags behind in varying degrees" (1964, p. 133). They occur "when one of two parts of culture which are correlated changes before or in greater degree than the other part does, thereby causing less adjustment between the two parts than existed previously" (Ogburn 1964, p. 86). Ogburn not only believed that the cultural lag could best be seen with technology, he felt that technology was responsible for most social change. "In our times in the Western world, technology and science are the great prime movers of social change. That this is so is an almost universal observation" (1964, p. 91).

The theory of cultural lag specifies that societies as a whole do not universally change in response to introductions of new technology. Ogburn points out that there are four stages to a cultural lag: technological, industrial, governmental, and social philosophical (1964, p. 134). With the introduction of a new technology, different sectors of society accept and adopt it at different speeds. The theory states that industry is the first sector to adjust to and acquire the technology.

After the industrial sector responds to the new technology, government structures adjust. One of the main ways that the state deals with new technology is by regulating it. Ogburn states that "technology cracks the whip, but because these extra liaison bodies do not develop rapidly and properly in the effort to make the lethargic governmental structure work, the institutions of society slip out of gear, and humanity suffers because of it" (1964, p. 143). Without governmental structures dealing with and regulating technology, the fourth stage of the cultural lag, that of social philosophies, cannot adjust. It is not clear that this lag inevitably causes suffering to humanity, however it does, in the words of Carey, cause the "satanic and angelic images that have surrounded, justified, and denigrated" technology without realistically assessing its actual capabilities and limitations (1988, p. 2). It is within this fourth stage of the cultural lag that scholarship understands technology. While the lag exists, academic discussions regarding the topic tend to be skewed.

Although conceptually simple, cultural lags are difficult to distinguish. Ogburn addresses why identification is so difficult. "In the long perspective of history, though, lags are not visible because they have been caught up. They are visible phenomena largely at the present time" (1964, p. 95). In contrast to mainstream historical theories that claim that the only way to see social and political phenomena is through hindsight,

Ogburn's theory of cultural lag states that hindsight hinders identification of historic lags; once the lag has disappeared, the period of the cultural lag is forgotten.

Given the temporal qualities of the cultural lag, it is much easier to conceive of and distinguish lags in newer technologies than in older ones. Although it is no longer possible to see the actual cultural lags surrounding the diffusion of the earlier forms of communications technology, the four stages of cultural lag can be frequently identified. Examples of cultural lags in earlier communication technologies are provided by the telephone and the television. Both of these technologies were identified as tools for democracy, as well as artifacts that would bring about the loss of privacy, the homogenization of society, indecent communication, and even revolution (see, for example, de Sola Pool 1983; Fischer 1992; Greenberger 1964; Grossman 1995; Jones 1997; Marvin 1988; Meyrowitz 1985). In both cases, business was the first to embrace these technologies and take advantage of their capabilities. Television, for example, "was construed—as both a commodified communications apparatus . . . and a market" (Breslow 1997, p. 237; see also Moran 1994).

More important to this paper, however, is the fact that both of these technologies have been perceived as being "variously imagined as harmless and harmful" in their social effects (Moran 1994, p. 38). On the positive side, for example, television was viewed as a utopian technology that would cause "equalization of many different types of people" (Meyrowitz 1985, p. 155). Because access to the television and its programming does not necessarily follow the traditional social stratification of society, it was seen as a democratizing force that "would bring culture, education, and information to the masses" (Grossman 1995, p. 167). On the negative side, however, television has been accused of homogenizing American culture and its "regional spheres" (Meyrowitz 1985, p. 145).

The Internet has been said to be as powerful, if not more powerful than these older technologies. A 1999 *Time Magazine* article, in fact, claimed that the Internet is a "technological wonder, every bit as revolutionary as the light bulb or the telephone. [It] is going to shape our lives in the century ahead" (Okrent 1999, p. 38). As such, the cultural lag and the extreme interpretations of the technology that follow may be more extreme as well.

Thirty-plus years after the notion of the cultural lag was first proposed, technology plays an even greater role in social change; and the Internet, as one of the newer and more diffused technologies, is having effects on societies around the world. Not only does technologically driven social change extend beyond the Western world, but it has also become the *product* of social change as well as the driving force behind it (see, for example, Haraway 1997; Wellman et al. 1996). The Internet illustrates this point clearly: It not only drives society to change its behaviors but it responds to society as well. In fact, as the Internet's capabilities grow and its effects extend to more and more of the world's population, predicting how the technology will develop and how it will change society is a difficult task. Not only is it close to impossible to forecast the effects of the Internet on society, but also the medium itself continues to change at a remarkable rate. In the words of Leiner et al. (1997), "One should not conclude that the Internet has now finished changing." Napster provides an ideal case of the continuing changes on the Internet. This new technology, developed by a college dropout, is reported as having been downloaded by over 32 million people in one year.[2]

Like the earlier technologies of the telephone and television, both utopian and dystopian visions of the Internet have been put forth. Computer and networking technology "is producing a sweeping set of transformations in every corner of social life"

---

[2]www.napster.com/

(Winner 1986, p. 99). The Internet has been heralded as the most powerful democratizing force in communications (Association for Progressive Communications 1997). Not only does it have the capabilities to give a voice to the powerless, but it is also said to be able to give the powerless access to the world (Fisher 1998). In addition to its democratizing forces, the Internet has been celebrated as a potential tool for American politics. Scholars such as Tsagarousianou claims that it is the locale of "a new public sphere" (1998, p. 3; see also, Buchstein 1997; Dean 1997; Mukerji and Simon 1998; Rheingold 1993; Schneider 1996; Ward 1997).

At this point in the diffusion of the Internet, it is important to identify what Carey (1988, p. 2) would call the "satanic and angelic images" within the discourse surrounding this new technology in order to fit these visions realistically into the technology's actual capabilities and limitations. Unique to the Internet is its ability to work like a number of different communications technologies. Because there are different resources on the Internet that use different modalities of communication, Ogburn's cultural lag is even more visible than it was in the older communications technologies. In the section that follows, we focus on the extreme interpretations of the Internet that inundate the literature on the technology during this period of the cultural lag.

▮▮▮ Utopian and Dystopian Visions of the Internet

As we have already argued, one of the effects of a cultural lag are extreme and unrealistic interpretations of the technology within the discourse surrounding it. This antinomy pits the political utility of emerging information technology with the potential for that same technology to further fragment society and increase anomie among its members. In the section that follows, we describe this dichotomy in terms of utopian and dystopian positions.

Perhaps the most salient aspect of the utopian position is the implied notion that there are technological solutions to social problems (see, for example, Budge 1996; Cox 1999; Ward 1997). These solutions are often described in terms of technology's effects on communitarian and populist forms of democratic participation. The communitarian argument suggests that the Internet will facilitate civic engagement by increasing the ease of communication among citizens by transcending geographic and social boundaries. The argument suggests that the bonds produced by this interaction will in turn encourage the formation of new deliberative spaces and new forms of collective action. The populist model, in contrast, emphasizes technology's role in altering the interaction between citizens and government. Ward (1997) points out that the mechanisms of change are typically described in terms of online referenda and initiatives.

The utopian position is largely premised on the notion that the communication medium is paramount in determining effects (McLuhan 1964). This approach usually touts the democratic potential of computer-mediated communication by referencing the actual design of the network. Through this network that provides communicative interaction, democratic participation and a sense of community are facilitated (Rheingold 1993). Stated simply, utopians posit that cyberspace will make it easier for people to communicate both politically and otherwise. The utopian position tends to follow through with one of Habermas's main interests (1992, 1989), arguing that the communicative action, which emerges as a result of this interaction, can limit the subversion of deliberative democracy at the hands of market-driven imperatives.

In contrast to the utopian perspective that focuses on the effects of the Internet on society, the dystopian position has its roots in understanding the phenomenon of the experience (see, for example, Barber 1998; Slouka 1995; Stoll 1995). Rather than viewing the Internet merely as a tool, the dystopian position emphasizes the potential of the medium to affect communication in such a way that it may negatively alter the practices and spaces of communication that had previously nurtured democracy. One such interpretation can be seen in the work of Timothy Luke, who says that as a result of the Internet, "Power shifts focus, speed overcomes space, orders become disordered, time moves standards, community loses centers, [and] values change denomination as the settings of industrialized human agency are completely shaken" (1998, p. 125).

The dystopian argument claims that democracy crumbles as the social fabric of society becomes fragmented and people become more isolated from one another. Within many of the dystopian arguments, the influence of Arendt's arguments concerning totalitarian regimes are visible (Holub 1991). In particular, the effect of society's reliance on communications technology will be the same results as Arendt found in her work on the "iron band of terror" (1973). The dystopian position also argues that a similar fragmentation will result if face-to-face interactions are supplanted by mediated ones (Barber 1998).

In addition to the loss of strong bonds among members of a society, many critics agree that the Internet will limit connections between central and peripheral actors in society (see, for example, Castells 1998; Luke 1998; Soros 1998). Participants at the center of an information-based communicative structure and those on the periphery of that structure will be less connected than ever before. In addition, the Internet is expected to disturb political life through what Derrida calls "accelerated rhythms" (1994). Rather than facilitating political engagement among citizens, this accelerated rhythm is described by dystopians as impending thoughtful deliberation.

Beyond these dominant themes of utopian and dystopian visions of the Internet, it should be noted that a third theme, which can be described as technorealism, is also represented in the literature (see, for example, Bimber 1998; Calhoun 1998; Monberg 1998). This position tends to be held by journalists and technology professionals as well as academics and usually takes a more modest approach to claims concerning the Internet's potential impact (Wilhelm 2000). It usually presents a more tempered view of the Internet's effects on society in comparison to the utopian and dystopian positions. Calhoun (1998, p. 381), for example, argues that ultimately the effects of the Internet "matter much more as a supplement to face-to-face community organization and movement activity than as a substitute for it." Technorealistic ideas are diverse, but they seem to be premised on the idea that is best expressed by Monberg (1998), who says that whatever questions we are asking about the Internet today, the only thing we can know for certain is that we are asking the wrong questions. This notion that the medium is too new for scholars to determine effects is consistent with Ogburn's idea of a cultural lag.

In addition to the academic predictions of the Internet's impact on society, there have been a number of popular pronouncements concerning the technology. Utopian and dystopian visions of technology are probably most clearly manifest in artifacts of mass culture such as novels, art, and the media. Ever since Gibson's *Neuromancer* was released in 1984, his work has embodied a dystopian vision of what the world is becoming with the advent of the Internet. His characters create the technology but are eventually trapped/controlled by it. Stephenson's *Snow Crash* (1992), in contrast, presents a mixed utopian/dystopian cyberworld in which people can possess superpowers through their Internet alter egos. In the end, the young and the hip save the day from the potential evil that has threatened to destroy the Internet as they know it. Like the novel, corporate advertising has also promoted utopian visions of the technology. In an MCI/Worldcom advertisement, for instance, different voices state "there is no race, there is no gender . . . I can be whoever I want to be."

Dystopian interpretations of the Internet are no less prevalent today. Both privacy and content on the Internet have been a subject of great social concern and represent two of the most dominant debates about the potential negative effects of this communication technology. Stories about cyber-lurkers and personal information being obtained through the Internet prevail. Questions about content on the Internet confront Internet users from all sectors of society. At a recent conference, for example, an academic argued that with all of the indecent information and cyber-smut on the Internet, it was an open question whether it was appropriate to use the Internet for publication or distribution of scholarly work. Similarly, the popular media have recognized the dystopian aspects of the Internet. "All the trash, flotsam and spillage of our society gets its moment there, where the tiniest obsession has its spot on the shelf, right next to Bach and charity and sunsets" (Okrent 1999, pp. 39–40).

⬛ ⬛ ⬛ Discussion and Conclusion

As the technology diffuses across American society and more people log on to the Internet, dystopian and utopian claims about the technology's capabilities grow. In 1996 for example, the U.S. Congress attempted to limit free speech on the Internet through the Communications Decency Act. Although the Supreme Court overturned the act on the grounds of the First Amendment, criticism of the *indecent* speech in many different areas of the Internet are still widespread and come from organizations as diverse as the Anti-Defamation League and Roman Catholics (see, for example, Harmon 1997). At the same time, people around the world are celebrating the democratizing capabilities of this new technology (see, for example, Fisher 1998; Haraway 1997; Sclove 1995). The actual structure of the pending regulations have strong implications for the diffusion of the technology both throughout the United States and beyond it to other countries in the developed and developing world.

Ogburn's notion of a cultural lag points to the future while focusing on the present. In doing so, the idea also aids us in understanding the extreme responses to the technology and helps us to be more critical of the academic literature on the subject. James Carey (1988) states that new communications technologies repeat old patterns of diffusion. "We are dealing with an old story rather than a new one. Although the computer and satellite have reduced time to a picosecond, an instantaneous present, and the globe to a point where everyone is in the same place, this is simply the latest chapter in an old tale. The habits of mind and structures of thought that seem characteristic of our age, particularly the talk of communications revolution and exalted hopes and equally exaggerated fears of the media, are repetitions so predictable as to suggest undeviating corridors of thought" (1988, p. 2).

The case of Napster provides a timely example of the latest chapter in this old tale. Although actors from all sides of the issue argue over the utopian and dystopian effects this technology will have on business and society, in time society will adjust to the cultural lag and interpretations will become more realistic. As was the case with the telephone, television, or even the fax machine, while society became used to the capabilities of the technology, claims about their effects on society became less extreme.

Whether one views the Internet and all of its technological trappings as a panacea for problems facing democracy or not, the truth about the Internet's capabilities, like most truth, lies somewhere in between these utopian and dystopian interpretations. In order to understand realistically this technology that is changing society, we must recognize the extreme readings of its effects as what they are: products of a cultural lag between the diffusion of the Internet across society and society's adoption of the technology.

REFERENCES

Arendt, H. 1973. *The Origins of Totalitarianism*. San Diego: Harvest.

Association for Progressive Communications. 1997. *Global Networking for Change*. London: Association for Progressive Communications Women's Networking Support Program.

Barber, B. 1998. *A Passion for Democracy: American Essays*. Princeton, NJ: Princeton University Press.

Breslow, H. 1997. "Civil society, political economy, and the Internet." In S. G. Jones (Ed.), *Virtual Culture: Identity and Communication in Cybersociety*. London: Sage Publications.

Buchstein, H. 1997. "Bytes that bite: The Internet and deliberative democracy." *Constellations* 4: 248–263.

Calhoun, C. 1991. "The infrastructure of modernity." In Haferkamp and Smelser (Eds.), *Social Change and Modernity*. Berkeley: University of California Press.

Carey, J. W. 1988. *Communication as Culture: Essays on Media and Society*. Boston: Unwin Hyman.

Castells, M. 1989. *The Information City*. Cambridge: Basil Blackwell Ltd.

Cohen, A. 2000. "A crisis of content." *Time*. 2 October, 68–72.

De Sola Pool, I. 1983. *Forecasting the Telephone: A Retrospective Technology Assessment of the Telephone*. New Jersey: ABLEX Publishing.

Dean, J. 1997. "Virtually citizens." *Constellations*, 4: 264–281.

Derrida, J. 1994. *Specters of Marx*, translated by Paggy Kamuf. New York: Routledge.

Fischer, C. S. 1992. *America Calling: A Social History of the Telephone to 1940*. Berkeley: University of California Press.

Fisher, D. R. 1998. "Rumoring theory and the Internet: A framework for analyzing the grassroots." *Social Science Computer Review* 16(2): 158–168.

Gibson, W. 1984. *Neuromancer*. London: Gollancz.

Greenberger, M. 1964. The computers of tomorrow. *Atlantic Monthly*, 213(5): 63–67. www.theatlantic.com/unbound/flashbks/computer/greenbf.htm.

Greenfeld, K. T. 2000. "Meet the Napster." *Time*. 2 October, 60–68.

Grimaldi, J. 2000. "Napster ordered to shut down: Piracy of music judge says." *The Washington Post*, 27 July, A01.

Grossman, L. K. 1995. *The Electronic Republic: Reshaping Democracy in the Information Age*. New York: Viking Publishing.

Habermas, J. 1992. "Further reflections on the public sphere." In C. Calhoun (Ed.), *Habermas in the Public Sphere* (pp. 421–461). Cambridge, MA: MIT Press.

Habermas, J. 1989. *The Structural Transformation of the Public Sphere*. Cambridge, MA: MIT Press.

Haraway, D. J. 1997. *Modest_witness@Second_millennium. Femaleman©_Meets_Oncomouse™*. New York: Routledge.

Jones, S. G. (Ed.) 1997. *Virtual Culture: Identity and Communication in Cybersociety*. London: Sage Publications.

Leiner, B. M., V. G. Cerf, D. D. Clark, R. E. Kahn, L. Kleinrock, D. C. Lynch, J. Postel, L. G. Roberts, and S. Wolff. 1997. "A brief history of the Internet." http://www.isoc.org/internet-history/.

McLuhan, M. 1964. *Understanding Media: The Extensions of Man*. New York: McGraw-Hill.

Marvin, C. 1988. *When Old Technologies Were New: Thinking About Communication in the Late Nineteenth Century*. New York: Oxford University Press.

Meyrowitz, J. 1985. *No Sense of Place: The Impact of Electronic Media on Social Behavior*. New York: Oxford University Press.

Monberg, J. 1998. "Making the public count: A comparative case study of emergent information technology-based publics." *Communication Theory* 4: 426–454.

Mukerji C., and B. Simon. 1998. "Out of the limelight: Discredited communities on the Internet." *Sociological Inquiry* 68: 258–273.

Mumford, L. 1939. *Technics and Civilization*. San Diego: Harcourt Brace & Company.

Ogburn, W. F. 1964. *On Cultural and Social Change: Selected Papers*. Chicago: University of Chicago Press.

Okrent, D. 1999. "Raising kids online: What can parents do?" *Time Magazine* 10 May, 38–43.

Rheingold, H. 1993. *The Virtual Community: Homesteading on the Electronic Frontier*. New York: Harper Perennial.

Schneider, S. M. 1996. "Creating a democratic public sphere: A case study of abortion conversation on the Internet." *Social Science Computer Review* 14: 373–393.

Segal, H. P. 1994. *Future Imperfect: The Mixed Blessings of Technology in America*. Amherst: University of Massachusetts Press.

Solve, R. 1995. *Democracy and Technology*. New York: Guilford Press.

Stephenson, N. 1992. *Snow Crash*. New York: Bantam Books.

Toffler, A. 1970. *Future Shock*. New York: Bantam Books.

Tsagarousianou, R. 1998. "Electronic democracy and the public sphere: Opportunities and challenges." In R. Tsagarousianou, D. Tambini, and C. Bryan (Eds.), *Cyberdemocracy: Technology, Cities and Civic Networks*, London: Routledge.

Tsagarousianou, R., D. Tambini, and C. Bryan, 1998. *Cyberdemocracy: Technology, Cities and Civic Networks*. London: Routledge.

Ward, I. 1997. "How democratic can we get? The Internet, the public sphere, and public discourse," *JAC: A Journal of Composition Theory* 17: 365–379.

Wellman, B. 1997. "The road to utopia and dystopia on the information superhighway." *Contemporary Sociology* 26: 4.

Wellman, B., J. Salaff, D. Dimitrova, L Garton, M. Gulia, and C. Haythornthwaite. 1996. "Computer networks as social networks: Collaborative work, telework, and virtual community." *Annual Review of Sociology* 22: 213–238.

Westrum, R. 1991. *Technologies and Society*. Belmont, CA: Wadsworth Publishing.

Wilhelm, A. 2000. *Democracy in the Digital Age*. New York: Routledge.

The Worldwide Computer

An Operating System Spanning the Internet Would Bring the Power of Millions of the World's Internet-Connected PCs to Everyone's Fingertips

DAVID P. ANDERSON
JOHN KUBIATOWICZ

When Mary gets home from work and goes to her PC to check e-mail, the PC isn't just sitting there. It's working for a biotech company, matching gene sequences to a library of protein molecules. Its DSL connection is busy downloading a block of radio telescope data to be analyzed later. Its disk contains, in addition to Mary's own files, encrypted fragments of thousands of other files. Occasionally one of these fragments is read and transmitted; it's part of a movie that someone is watching in Helsinki. Then Mary moves the mouse, and this activity abruptly stops. Now the PC and its network connection are all hers.

This sharing of resources doesn't stop at her desktop computer. The laptop computer in her satchel is turned off, but its disk is filled with bits and pieces of other people's files, as part of a distributed backup system. Mary's critical files are backed up in the same way, saved on dozens of disks around the world.

Later, Mary watches an independent film on her Internet-connected digital television, using a pay-per-view system. The movie is assembled on the fly from fragments on several hundred computers belonging to people like her.

Mary's computers are moonlighting for other people. But they're not giving anything away for free. As her PC works, pennies trickle into her virtual bank account. The payments come from the biotech company, the movie system and the backup service. Instead of buying expensive "server farms," these companies are renting time and space, not just on Mary's two computers but on millions of others as well. It's a win-win situation. The companies save money on hardware, which enables, for instance, the movie-viewing service to offer obscure movies. Mary earns a little cash, her files are backed up, and she gets to watch an indie film. All this could happen with an Internet-scale operating system (ISOS) to provide the necessary "glue" to link the processing and storage capabilities of millions of independent computers.

Internet-Scale Applications

Although Mary's world is fictional—and an Internet-scale operating system does not yet exist—developers have already produced a number of Internet-scale, or peer-to-peer, applications that attempt to tap the vast array of underutilized machines available through the Internet. These applications accomplish goals that would be difficult, unaffordable, or impossible to attain using dedicated computers. Further, today's systems are just the beginning: We can easily conceive of archival services that could be relied on for hundreds of years and intelligent search engines for tomorrow's Semantic Web [see "The Semantic Web," by Tim Berners-Lee, James Hendler and Ora Lassila; *Scientific American*, May 2001]. Unfortunately, the creation of Internet-scale applications remains an imposing challenge. Developers must build each new application from the ground up, with much effort spent on technical matters, such as maintaining a database of users, that have little to do with the application itself. If Internet-scale applications are to become mainstream, these infrastructure issues must be dealt with once and for all.

We can gain inspiration for eliminating this duplicate effort from operating systems such as Unix and Microsoft Windows. An operating system provides a virtual computing environment in which programs operate as if they were in sole possession of the computer. It shields programmers from the painful details of memory and disk allocation, communication protocols, scheduling of myriad processes, and interfaces to devices for data input and output. An operating system greatly simplifies the development of new computer programs. Similarly, an Internet-scale operating system would simplify the development of new distributed applications.

An ISOS consists of a thin layer of software (an ISOS agent) that runs on each "host" computer (such as Mary's) and a central coordinating system that runs on one or more ISOS server complexes. This veneer of software would provide only the core functions of allocating and scheduling resources for each task, handling communication among host computers and determining the reimbursement required for each machine. This type of operating system, called a microkernel, relegates higher-level functions to programs that make use of the operating system but are not a part of it. For instance, Mary would not use the ISOS directly to save her files as pieces distributed across the Internet. She might run a backup application that used ISOS functions to do that for her. The ISOS would use principles borrowed from economics to apportion computing resources to different users efficiently and fairly and to compensate the owners of the resources.

Two broad types of applications might benefit from an ISOS. The first is distributed data processing, such an physical simulations, radio signal analysis, genetic analysis, computer graphics rendering, and financial modeling. The second is distributed online services, such as file storage systems, databases, hosting of Web sites, streaming media (such as online video), and advanced Web search engines.

▪▪▪ What's Mine Is Yours

Computing today operates predominantly as a private resource; organizations and individuals own the systems that they use. An ISOS would facilitate a new paradigm in which it would be routine to make use of resources all across the Internet. The resource pool—hosts able to compute or store data and networks able to transfer data between hosts—would still be individually owned, but they could work for anyone. Hosts would include desktops, laptops, server computers, network-attached storage devices, and maybe handheld devices.

The Internet resource pool differs from private resource pools in several important ways. More than 150 million hosts are connected to the Internet, and the number is growing exponentially. Consequently, an ISOS could provide a virtual computer with potentially 150 million times the processing speed and storage capacity of a typical single computer. Even when this virtual computer is divided up among many users, and after one allows for the overhead of running the network, the result is a bigger, faster, and cheaper computer than the users could own privately. Continual upgrading of the resource pool's hardware causes the total speed and capacity of this über-computer to increase even faster than the number of connected hosts. Also, the pool is self-maintaining: When a computer breaks down, its owner eventually fixes or replaces it.

Extraordinary parallel data transmission is possible with the Internet resource pool. Consider Mary's movie, being uploaded in fragments from perhaps 200 hosts. Each host may be a PC connected to the Internet by an antiquated 56K modem—far too slow to show a high-quality video—but combined they could deliver 10 megabits a second, better than a cable modem. Data stored in a distributed system are available from any location (with appropriate security safeguards) and can survive disasters that knock out sections of the resource pool. Great security is also possible, with systems that could not be compromised without breaking into, say, 10,000 computers.

In this way, the Internet-resource paradigm can increase the bounds of what is possible (such as higher speeds or larger data sets) for some applications, whereas for others it can lower the cost. For certain applications it may do neither—it's a paradigm, not a panacea. And designing an ISOS also presents a number of obstacles.

Some characteristics of the resource pool create difficulties that an ISOS must deal with. The resource pool is heterogeneous: Hosts have different processor types and operating systems. They have varying amounts of memory and disk space and a wide range of Internet connection speeds. Some hosts are behind firewalls or other similar layers of software that prohibit or hinder incoming connections. Many hosts in the pool are available only sporadically; desktop PCs are turned off at night, and laptops and systems using modems are frequently not connected. Hosts disappear unpredictably—sometimes permanently—and new hosts appear.

The ISOS must also take care not to antagonize the owners of hosts. It must have a minimal impact on the non-ISOS uses of the hosts, and it must respect limitations that owners may impose, such as allowing a host to be used only at night or only for specific types of applications. Yet the ISOS cannot trust every host to play by the rules in return for its own good behavior. Owners can inspect and modify the activities of their hosts. Curious and malicious users may attempt to disrupt, cheat or spoof the system. All these problems have a major influence on the design of an ISOS.

▪▪▪ Who Gets What?

An Internet-scale operating system must address two fundamental issues—how to allocate resources and how to compensate resource suppliers. A model based on economic principles in which suppliers lease resources to consumers can deal with both issues at once. In the 1980s researchers at Xerox PARC proposed and analyzed economic approaches to apportioning computer resources. More recently, Mojo Nation developed a file-sharing system in which users are paid in a virtual currency ("mojo") for use of their resources and they in turn must pay mojo to use the system. Such economic models encourage owners to allow their resources to be used by other organizations, and theory shows that they lead to optimal allocation of resources.

Even with 150 million hosts at its disposal, the ISOS will be dealing in "scarce" resources, because some tasks will request and be capable of using essentially unlimited resources. As it constantly decides where to run data-processing jobs and how to allocate storage space, the ISOS must try to perform tasks as cheaply as possible. It must also be fair, not allowing one task to run efficiently at the expense of another. Making these criteria precise—and devising scheduling algorithms to achieve them, even approximately—are areas of active research. The economic system for a shared network must define the basic units of a resource, such as the use of a megabyte of disk space for a day, and assign values that take into account properties such as the rate, or bandwidth, at which the storage can be accessed and how frequently it is available to the network. The system must also define how resources are bought and sold (whether they are paid for in advance, for instance) and how prices are determined (by auction or by a price-setting middleman).

Within this framework, the ISOS must accurately and securely keep track of resource usage. The ISOS would have an internal bank with accounts for suppliers and consumers that it must credit or debit according to resource usage. Participants can convert between ISOS currency and real money. The ISOS must also ensure that any guarantees of resource availability can be met: Mary doesn't want her movie to grind to a halt partway through. The economic system lets resource suppliers control how their resources are used. For example, a PC owner might specify that her computer's processor can't be used between 9 A.M. and 5 P.M. unless a very high price is paid.

Money, of course, encourages fraud, and ISOS participants have many ways to try to defraud one another. For instance, resource sellers, by modifying or fooling the ISOS agent program running on their computer, may return fictitious results without doing any computation. Researchers have explored statistical methods for detecting malicious or malfunctioning hosts. A recent idea for preventing unearned computation credit is to ensure that each work unit has a number of intermediate results that the server can quickly check and that can be obtained only by performing the entire computation. Other approaches are needed to prevent fraud in data storage and service provision.

The cost of ISOS resources to end users will converge to a fraction of the cost of owning the hardware. Ideally, this fraction will be large enough to encourage owners to participate and small enough to make many Internet-scale applications economically feasible. A typical PC owner might see the system as a barter economy in which he gets free services, such as file backup and Web hosting, in exchange for the use of his otherwise idle processor time and disk space.

▪▪▪ A Basic Architecture

We advocate two basic principles in our ISOS design: a minimal core operating system and control by central servers. A computer operating system that provides only core functions is called a microkernel. Higher-level functions are built on top of it as user programs, allowing them to be debugged and replaced more easily. This approach was pioneered in academic research systems and has influenced some commercial systems, such as Windows NT. Most well-known operating systems, however, are not microkernels.

The core facilities of an ISOS include resource allocation (long-term assignment of hosts' processing power and storage), scheduling (putting jobs into queues, both across the system and within individual hosts), accounting of resource usage, and the basic mechanisms for distributing and executing application programs. The ISOS should not duplicate features of local operating systems running on hosts.

The system should be coordinated by servers operated by the ISOS provider, which could be a government-funded organization or a consortium of companies that are major resource sellers and buyers. (One can imagine competing ISOS providers, but we will keep things simple and assume a unique provider.) Centralization runs against the egalitarian approach popular in some peer-to-peer systems, but central servers are needed to ensure privacy of sensitive data, such as accounting data and other information about the resource hosts. Centralization might seem to require a control system that will become excessively large and unwieldy as the number of ISOS-connected hosts increases, and it appears to introduce a bottleneck that will choke the system anytime it is unavailable. These fears are unfounded: A reasonable number of servers can easily store information about every Internet-connected host and communicate with them regularly. Napster, for example, handled almost 60 million clients using a central server. Redundancy can be built into the server complex, and most ISOS online services can continue operating even with the servers temporarily unavailable.

The ISOS server complex would maintain databases of resource descriptions, usage policies and task descriptions. The resource descriptions include, for example, the host's operating system, processor type and speed, total and free disk space, memory space, performance statistics of its network connections, and statistical descriptions of when it is powered on and connected to the network. Usage policies spell out the rules an owner has dictated for using her resources. Task descriptions include the resources assigned to an online service and the queued jobs of a data-processing task.

To make their computers available to the network, resource sellers contact the server complex (for instance, through a Web site) to download and install an ISOS agent program, to link resources to their ISOS account, and so on. The ISOS agent manages the host's resource usage. Periodically it obtains from the ISOS server complex a list of tasks to perform.

Resource buyers send the servers task requests and application agent programs (to be run on hosts). An online service provider can ask the ISOS for a set of hosts on which to run, specifying its resource requirements (for example, a distributed backup service could use sporadically connected resource hosts—Mary's laptop—which would cost less than constantly connected hosts). The ISOS supplies the service with addresses and descriptions of the granted hosts and allows the application agent program to communicate directly between hosts on which it is running. The service can request new hosts when some become unavailable. The ISOS does not dictate how clients make use of an online service, how the service responds or how clients are charged by the service (unlike the ISOS-controlled payments flowing from resource users to host owners).

▪▪▪ An Application Toolkit

In principle, the basic facilities of the ISOS—resource allocation, scheduling and communication—are sufficient to construct a wide variety of applications. Most applications, however, will have important subcomponents in common. It is useful, therefore, to have a software toolkit to further assist programmers in building new applications.

Code for these facilities will be incorporated into applications on resource hosts. Examples of these facilities include:

Location independent routing. Applications running with the ISOS can spread copies of information and instances of computation among millions of resource hosts. They have to be able to access them again. To facilitate this, applications name objects under their purview with Globally Unique Identifiers (GUIDs). These names enable "location independent routing," which is the ability to send queries to objects without knowing their location. A simplistic approach to location independent routing could involve a database of GUIDs on a single machine, but that system is not amenable to handling queries from millions of hosts. Instead the ISOS toolkit distributes the database of GUIDs among resource hosts. This kind of distributed system is being explored in research projects such as the OceanStore persistent data storage project at the University of California at Berkeley.

Persistent data storage. Information stored by the ISOS must be able to survive a variety of mishaps. The persistent data facility aids in this task with mechanisms for encoding, reconstructing and repairing data. For maximum survivability, data are encoded with an "m-of-n" code. An m-of-n code is similar in principle to a hologram, from which a small piece suffices for reconstructing the whole image. The encoding spreads information over n fragments (on n resource hosts), any m of which are sufficient to reconstruct the data. For instance, the facility might encode a document into 64 fragments, any 16 of which suffice to reconstruct it. Continuous repair is also important. As fragments fail, the repair facility would regenerate them. If properly constructed, a persistent data facility could preserve information for hundreds of years.

Secure update. New problems arise when applications need to update stored information. For example, all copies of the information must be updated, and the object's GUID must point to its latest copy. An access control mechanism must prevent unauthorized persons from updating information. The secure update facility relies on Byzantine agreement protocols, in which a set of resource hosts come to a correct decision, even if a third of them are trying to lead the process astray.

Other facilities. The toolkit also assists by providing additional facilities, such as format conversion (to handle the heterogeneous nature of hosts) and synchronization libraries (to aid in cooperation among hosts).

An ISOS suffers from a familiar catch-22 that slows the adoption of many new technologies: Until a wide user base exists, only a limited set of applications will be feasible on the ISOS. Conversely, as long as the applications are few, the user base will remain small. But if a critical mass can be achieved by convincing enough developers and users of the intrinsic usefulness of an ISOS, the system should grow rapidly.

The Internet remains an immense untapped resource. The revolutionary rise in popularity of the World Wide Web has not changed that—it has made the resource pool all the larger. An Internet-scale operating system would free programmers to create applications that could run on this World Wide Computer without worrying about the underlying hardware. Who knows what will result? Mary and her computers will be doing things we haven't even imagined.

Further Information

The Ecology of Computation. B. A. Huberman. North-Holland, 1988.

The Grid: Blueprint for a New Computing Infrastructure. Edited by Ian Foster and Carl Kesselman. Morgan Kaufmann Publishers, 1998.

Peer-to-Peer: Harnessing the Power of Disruptive Technologies. Edited by Andy Oram. O'Reilly & Associates, 2001.

Related Links

Many research projects are working toward an Internet-scale operating system, including:

Chord: www.pdos.lcs.mit.edu/chord/
Cosm: www.mithral.com/projects/cosm/
Eurogrid: www.eurogrid.org/
Farsite: http://research.microsoft.com/sn/farsite/

Grid Physics Network (Griphyn): www.griphyn.org/
OceanStore: http://oceanstore.cs.berkeley.edu/
Particle Physics Data Grid: www.ppdg.net/
Pastry: www.research.microsoft.com/~antr/pastry/
Tapestry: www.cs.berkeley.edu/~ravenben/tapestry/

Global Implications of the Information Society

MARC URI PORAT

"As with life itself, the prognosis for an information society is mixed, the remedy inconclusive."

The U.S. is now an information-based economy. By 1967, 25 percent of GNP originated in the production, processing, and distribution of information goods and services. In addition, over 21 percent of GNP originated in the production of information services by the private and public bureaucracies for purely internal uses. By 1970, close to half of the U.S. workforce was classified as "information workers," holding a job where the production, processing, or distribution of symbols is the main activity. This group of workers earned over 53 percent of all labor income.[1]

In this article, I shall discuss some of the many international implications flowing from this transformation of the U.S. economy: How do exports of information goods and services fit into foreign policy? What is "cultural exportation," and how is it viewed internationally? What about human rights issues and the use of information technologies? How important is the export of technological and scientific information?

The group of industries which produce, process, or transmit knowledge, communication and information goods or services are termed the "primary information sector."

On the service side, these industries include the electronic and print media, advertising, education, telecommunications services, components of finance and insurance, libraries, consulting, and research and development firms. On the goods side are

"Global Implications of the Information Society" by Marc Uri Porat, *Journal of Communications*, Vol. 28, No. 1, 1978, pp. 78–80. Copyright © 1978. Reprinted by permission of Oxford University Press.
[1]A complete exposition of the definitions, sources, methods, and findings is available in (6). Marc Uri Porat is a Fellow of the Aspen Institute's Program on Communication and Society. The author wishes to express appreciation for helpful suggestions from Glen O. Robinson (Aspen Institute), Frederick T. C. Yu (Columbia University), Morris Crawfore (Department of State), Francesca Jessup (Amnesty International), and Elizabeth Vermilye (Department of Commerce).

This article is based on a paper commissioned for the United States Information Agency entitled "The U.S. as an Information Society: International Implications," July 1, 1977.

included computer, communication, and electronic equipment manufacturers, office and business machines, measuring and control instruments, and printing and printing presses. A detailed measurement effort (covering over 70 industries and over 6,000 products measured at the seven-digit Standard Industrial Classification level) yielded the result that in 1967, 25.1 percent of valued added (GNP) originated in the primary information sector. One quarter of GNP is bound up with the information activity — goods and services for sale.

In addition, we know intuitively that noninformation firms (e.g., auto, steel, and petroleum) and governments produce and consume information of a wholly "internal" type. Every institution consumes some mixture of research and development, design, management, accounting, legal services, clerical and marketing information "services." Firms and governments hire "information labor" (e.g., managers and secretaries) and invest in "information capital" (e.g., computing, communications, and office machines.) These are essentially *information inputs* to noninformation activities. The information services produced in a nonmarket context, i.e., not specifically exchanged in an established market, are labeled the "secondary information sector." A detailed estimate reveals that these activities, often associated with private and public bureaucratic *information overhead*, generated (in 1967) some 21.1 percent of value added (GNP).

Together, the primary and secondary information sectors accounted, in a formal National Income and Product Accounts sense, for 46 percent of GNP in 1967. We assume that the figure is somewhat higher in 1977, although it has not yet been measured.

> *An economy can also be characterized by the distribution*
> *of its workforce across various activities.*

The conventional classification of labor is a tripartite sectoring scheme — agriculture, industry, and services. But if we create a fourth sector — information — and include all the workers who hold an informational job,[2] a most interesting picture emerges.

Figure 1 shows the four sector aggregation of the U.S. labor force. In Stage I (1860–1906), the single largest group was agricultural workers. During this stage, the United States is characterized as an agricultural society.

In Stage II (1906–1954), we see that the industrial workforce is predominant, reaching a peak of around 40 percent in 1946. During this stage, the United States is characterized as an industrial society. In the 1950s, the industrial workforce began to decline, and is presently about 25 percent of U.S. labor.

In Stage III (1954–present), information workers comprise the largest group. From a low of five percent of the workforce in 1860, the information sector of U.S. labor has grown to about 47 percent of the workforce. In 1967, this group earned over 53 percent of all employee compensation, as shown in Table 1.

> *On the strength of the GNP and labor data, the*
> *United States can now be called an "information society."*

There are many phrases for the same phenomenon. Fritz Machlup (4) called it a "knowledge economy."[3] To Brzezinski, it is a "technetronic age, to Dahrendorff, it is

---

[2]Including teachers, selected managers, selected clerical workers, selected professionals (e.g., accountants, lawyers), and people who work with information machines (e.g., computer and telephone operators). The criterion for including an occupation in the information sector is as follows. The information-handling aspect of the job overshadows the noninformation aspects; conversely, the noninformation aspects are clearly ancillary to the informational.

[3]The quote is attributed to Kenneth E. Boulding, who has also written extensively on the knowledge industries (see 2). The emergence of a large and uncharted service sector was the theme of V. R. Fuchs in *The Service Economy* (3), but he did not, however, carry through Machlup's idea of a "knowledge industry."

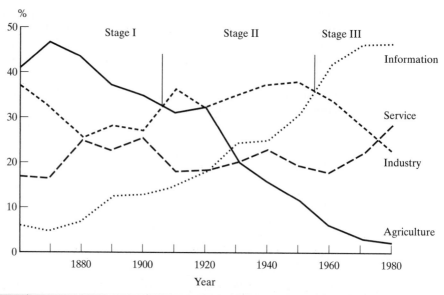

▪▪▪▪▪▪▪▪▪▪▪▪▪ **FIGURE 1** Four Sector Aggregation of the U.S. Workforce by Percent, 1860–1980 (using median estimates of information workers)

"post-capitalist," to Etzioni, it is "post-modern." Daniel Bell first coined the term "post-industrial," and succinctly describes the essence of the transformation as follows:

> In *pre-industrial societies*—still the condition of most of the world today—the labor force is engaged overwhelmingly in the extractive industries: mining, fishing, forestry, agriculture. Life is primarily a game against nature.... *Industrial societies* are goods-producing societies. Life is a game against fabricated nature. The world has become technical and rationalized.... A *post-industrial society* is based on services. Hence, it is a game between persons. What counts is not raw muscle power, or energy, but information (1, emphasis added).

The essential difference between an industrial and an information society is that the locus of economic activity and technological change has shifted away from manufacturing "objects" towards handling information and symbols. The plow and farming techniques heralded the agricultural economy; the steam engine and manufacturing techniques transformed first Europe and then the United States into an industrial economy; the computer and telecommunications are now propelling the United States into the information economy. This economic realignment, which eventually ripples outside the U.S. borders and onto the shores of our trading partners, has further implications for the nature of the international economy.

> *But is information intrinsically a valuable*
> *commodity, or is it a "leech"*
> *on the productive sectors of the economy?*

No one doubts that information can be a lucrative source of both profits and employment. The primary information sector, which *sells* information goods and services, accounted in 1967 for 25 percent of GNP. The secondary (or overhead) sector employs one out of five workers, and accounted for 21 percent of GNP. But unless the information is *productive*, it is not supportable in the long run.

TABLE 1 Typology of Information Workers and 1967 Compensation[a]

Markets for Information	*Employee Compensation ($ millions)*
Knowledge producers	*46,964*
Scientific and technical workers	18,777
Private information service	28,187
Knowledge distributors	*26,265*
Educators	23,680
Public information disseminators	1,264
Communication workers	3,321
Information in Markets	
Market search and coordination specialists	*93,370*
Information gatherers	6,132
Search and coordination specialists	28,252
Planning and control workers	58,986
Information processors	*61,340*
Nonelectronic based	34,317
Electronic based	27,023
Information Infrastructure	
Information machine workers	*13,167*
Nonelectronic machine operators	4,219
Electronic machine operators	3,660
Telecommunication workers	5,288
Total Information	243,106
Total employee compensation	454,255[b]
Information as % of total	53.52%

[a]Employee compensation includes wages and salaries and supplements
[b]Excluding military workers
Source: Computed using BLS Occupation by industry matrix, Census of Population average wages.

Consider, for the moment, information as a *resource*, analogous to natural, labor, and capital resources. A firm needs information goods and services (such as computers and managers) to produce its output. A rational firm buys a computer or hires a manager only if it can extract a surplus from the "investment"—the return is greater than the outlay and as large as any alternative investment opportunity.

Information thus enters as a productive input and increases domestic output. In the case of invention, the application of new information mobilizes idle resources, opens new markets, and improves the efficiency of existing processes. Information *creates* wealth in this context.

But the production of information also consumes capital and labor resources, which are "taken" from other sectors of the economy, hence pushing up the price of labor and capital to other sectors of the economy. Assessing the productivity of information workers and bureaucratic process is very hard indeed, leading to a popular (although unproven) assumption that information can be a wasteful activity. In this context, information detracts from domestic input.

Whether information contributes to domestic production through new inventions and increased efficiency—or detracts from it as an unproductive resource "sink"—can only be settled by research which has not yet been done. However, projections of the U.S. labor force reveal that the growth of the information work force has slowed dramatically. According to the Bureau of Labor Statistics, between 1970 and 1980 the information sector will grow at a net rate of 0.04 percent—not much faster than the overall U.S. labor force. It seems that our bureaucracies are glutted and can absorb no more information workers.

The prospects for new growth for the information economy can come from only two sources of demand: domestic and foreign. Domestically, the primary information sector will expand if new entrepreneurial ventures are undertaken: breakthroughs in business and home applications such as "information utilities" and teleconferencing, or new technologies such as microprocessors, fiber optics, and mass storage manufacturing.

Foreign markets are the other obvious sources of demand for U. S. information goods and services. Internal pressures to export information goods and services have already resulted in aggressive marketing by U.S. multinationals—both in the developed countries (including the Soviet Bloc) and the less developed nations. The secondary information sector is now exported as a "hidden cost," as part of the price of a noninformation good, and explicitly in the form of scientific and technological knowledge.

*An industrial society sheds its chrysalis
and becomes an information society when
every aspect of its economy becomes
dependent on information machines.*

The foreign appetite for U.S. information machines is exceeded only by demand for U.S. guns and butter. The export of computers in 1975 exceeded $2.2 billion. Over $1.1 billion worth of telecommunications systems were bought from U.S. manufacturers. In terms of balance of payments, these information technologies generated a huge $2.4 billion surplus for the United States in 1975. The only trade problem on the horizon is the alleged "flooding" of consumer electronics markets by Japanese exporters. (In 1975, the United States imported $2,067 million of radios, TVs, high fidelity equipment and calculators, and exported $652 million.) But in the arena of computers, peripherals, microwaves, switching equipment, terminal equipment, satellite ground stations, and computer software, U.S. firms are dominant.

The less developed nations, who are grappling with industrial technology, are in the odd position of "leapfrogging" over an entire stage of economic evolution. A country like Brazil is simultaneously developing an industrial *and* information infrastructure. It makes no sense to import modern industrial technology without its concomitants—computer process control, computerized management techniques, and rapid communication between all sectors (business, government, households). Thus as the managerial trappings of modern industry are informational, the demand for U.S. information goods will continue to be strong.

Where computers and communications are used for economic modernization (i.e., in support of industrialization), the United States is clearly committed to encouraging such development. The quality of life is at stake, and dovetails with a fixture of U.S. foreign aid policy—raising the developing nation's standard of living.

But modernization or development are not "neutral" words. As they are often equated with Westernization, in a development context, information technology becomes a *political fact* as well as an economic resource. The establishment of U.S. administrative procedures, accounting and financial practices, and managerial control is not an apolitical development. There is nothing inherently political about computers, except that the dearth of native scientific and technical talent often means that U.S. advisors become a part of the technology transfer. And *that* is a political decision.

This point is dramatized by the case of computer exports. The same computer can be used in the service of "modernization" to design a water irrigation project, manage a national innoculation program, or coordinate interindustry balanced growth. It can also handle logistical support for an army, assist in the design of nuclear weapons, serve as a pinpoint missile guidance control system, or digest foreign intelligence data. A computer is both a tool of economic development and a strategic weapon. It is a plow at one moment, a gun at the next, and this basic duality of purpose cannot easily be severed.

The uses of information systems—both telecommunications and computers—also pose foreign policy problems in the arena of human rights. No one takes issue with a country's basic need to communicate internally and with its neighbors. No modern economy (much less a Western-oriented industrial economy) can survive without efficient domestic telecommunications systems. With that presumption, huge exports of advanced systems have recently been approved, mostly to Third and Fourth World nations such as Iran, Saudi Arabia, and Indonesia. But what about the use of telecommunication systems in domestic surveillance—massive eavesdropping and wiretapping—and systematic violation of (what the U.S. defines as) basic human and civil liberties. It is now a fairly simple matter to monitor telephone conversations using highly automated equipment. Telephone pairs of dissidents and political "undesirables" are simply programmed into a computer, and conversations are routinely tapped and recorded.

Computers, a requisite of economic improvement and development, can also be used to maintain extensive personal dossiers on political dissidents. The National Council of Churches recently revealed that an IBM computer system (370/145) might be deployed for just that purpose by DINA, Chile's infamous secret police. DINA has been implicated in numerous violations of human rights, including a regime of sudden "disappearances" of dissidents, extended incarceration without formal charge, and outright torture.[4]

Hence the sale of U.S. information systems can be a highly political decision: Does the United States have the right to dictate to its clients how they may or may not use an imported system? How does a nation guarantee in advance that an information system will be used to promote economic development rather than abuse human rights?

Information services exports are potentially as troublesome as the export of information goods.

Information services are divisible into three basic types: (1) financial, insurance, accounting and *data base* information; (2) *cultural exports*, such as film, television, radio, books, newspapers and magazines; and (3) *knowledge exports*, represented by patent royalties, and management and consulting fees. All generate their share of political problems.

U.S. and European firms produce mountains of financial data that flow freely across international borders. This linking of commerce is as natural as the flow of goods in a mercantile or industrial age. The new resource of value is information: invoices, bills of lading, freight movement, personal travel, financial instruments, private bank accounts, personnel records. The European data market alone is projected to exceed $5 billion by 1980.

---

[4]An overview discussion of the issue, including the viewpoints of the National Council of Churches, Amnesty International, the United Nations, IBM, CDC, and Burroughs, appears in (5). See also the March and May 1977 issues of *Computer Decisions*.

But some new and troubling policy problems have arisen in connection with the *protection of privacy*. The laws protecting personal information differ considerably between countries, and have not yet been harmonized. Only two nations, Sweden and W. Germany, have passed stringent privacy laws. The EEC and OECD are jointly concerned that a country with weak privacy laws can be used as a "data-haven," wherein an unethical firm subverts its own country's strict privacy laws by setting up a subsidiary in a less stringent foreign host. In fact, the United States has been identified as a particularly attractive haven. Foreign firms wishing to fly a U.S. "flag of convenience" can enjoy two advantages: (1) the United States does not have comprehensive privacy legislation to cover personal data bases, and (2) the U.S. can offer the necessary technical support—computer hardware and software and advance telecommunications— that may not be available in some other haven such as Turkey.

As a remedy, a convention or a treaty on "transborder data flows" is now under consideration by the OECD. Some U.S. firms maintain that the true purpose of such a treaty is a European attempt to suppress competition from the U.S. firms in the lucrative data markets. This view is rebuffed by European countries, who claim that their true concerns are for protection of privacy.

> *Another growing source of income from abroad is
> the sale of U.S. media products like television
> programming, feature films, books, and magazines.*

Third World nations in particular, often without a developed national media industry, simultaneously seek and resent U.S. cultural products. It is always cheaper to import U.S. entertainment than to produce television and film domestically. A Minister of Culture or Education, facing both a tight budget and the impossible requirement of filling up at least eight hours a day of television programming, has every incentive to import rather than produce domestically.

But the claim is heard that such items are "cultural propaganda," that they are a force of "cultural imperialism," that the portrayal of U.S. lifestyle in television programs transmits ideological fare along with entertainment. The proponents of the "cultural imperialism" argument point to the overwhelmingly dominant position of the U.S. media in the world media market. The defense states that nations can unilaterally restrict such imports by simply refusing to buy. Here the argument takes a new twist: New direct broadcasting technologies by communication satellites may obviate a nation's right to reject U.S. cultural exports. The subject has been repeatedly debated in UNESCO-sponsored conferences. However, it is difficult to assume that many private households could build and conceal illegal rooftop dish antennas to receive satellite transmissions. Thus, the question is wholly political, not technical.

> *As outputs of the secondary information sector,
> knowledge exports are embodied in patent royalties,
> management and consulting fees, and process licensing fees.*

Knowledge is being sold—"know-how," "show-how," organizational experience, scientific and technical information, and managerial information. As in the television programming case, a Minister of Science and Industry has little incentive to invest in a domestic "knowledge industry." A research and development lab or a management consulting company is just the tip of a very large iceberg of industrial production experience. Dealing with the global market, in either the role of an importer or exporter, requires sophisticated knowledge. Buying this knowledge is always cheaper than trying to produce it domestically.

In fact, the United States has established a foreign aid program specifically in the area of scientific and technical information. Much of the relevant information can be acquired for very little cost; organizations such as the World Bank and the IMF proffer a dose of information along with a low interest loan; many U.S. firms are in the business of "selling" information as a consulting or management contract; and lastly, when a multinational sets up a manufacturing subsidiary as a joint venture with another country, patent royalties and management fees for the use of U.S. technology and U.S. management know-how are often part of the deal.

The concept of "technological colonialism" arises from this last feature. We often see an influx of U.S.-trained technicians, managers, and scientists—a highly visible presence that has often been the target of political criticism. The critics argue that when a country buys technical or scientific knowledge (in the form of patent royalties and management fees), it concurrently imports a form of economic organization that mirrors the West. It is almost unavoidable. Management organizational hierarchy, economic concepts about productive efficiency, the price system, financing techniques, marketing techniques, demand management—these are the correlates of Western technology.

The export of film and television programs in 1973 amounted to $324 million. By contrast, the knowledge exports (patents, management fees) were $3,034 million—nearly ten times the amount of film rentals and royalties (see 6, Vol. 8, p. 9; 7). A technological system of production, once installed, is a most enduring cultural artifact.

> *One of the more assuring propositions*
> *about future economic growth is that an*
> *information economy is not as constrained*
> *by natural resources as an industrial economy.*

The emergence of an information society means that knowledge production and distribution will continue to play critical roles in future economic growth. Firms and individuals that understand the value of information, know how to access and use information, and can discriminate between knowledge and noise, will always be more "successful" than those who cannot.

An information society is geared to the production and distribution of information—its workforce is well-educated, literate, versed in symbol manipulation, comfortable with the use of information machines (such as telephones, computers, photocopiers). An information society can be a vibrant source of new knowledge, invention and progress, whose benefits extend beyond our shores.

An information society is also a technocratic or a bureaucratic society. The creative premium has shifted from physical craftsmanship and pride to specialization and organizational gamesmanship. The manager-scientist-professional is the new knight, absorbing the old powers of the capitalist, the landlord, the general and the priest.

Information is the most curious of all resources. It is infinitely renewable—the act of consumption does not destroy the information, and it can be used repeatedly and simultaneously by many people. Information does not even depreciate with use. On the contrary, the more one uses certain types of information (knowledge, the law), the more valuable they become. Information goods and services do not require huge inputs of natural resources or energy, and generate only modest waste or environmental pollution.

Although this view is appealing on the surface, note that 21 percent of GNP is bound up with bureaucratic information production in non-information firms. In a resource-connected recession, the manufacturing, energy, food, and transportation industries are hard hit. Preliminary evidence indicated that the information bureaucracy is the first economic luxury to hit the street (6, vol. 1, chapter 10). Although the primary information sector is fairly insensitive to resource issues, the secondary information sector is not.

*The guideposts along the way are domestic
and international information policies.*

We can, with guidance, have a bright future as an information society. The capital and human infrastructure is in place, and can be mobilized with great force. But many domestic issues regarding the domestic flows of social and economic issues need to be resolved—contradictions between the Privacy Act and the Freedom of Information Act; First Amendment issues and the bounds of commercial speech; the federal paperwork burden; the Copyright Act—these are all elements of information policy.

Domestic policy will also focus on the structure of the information industries—issues of competition vs. regulation in the telephone industry; the boundary between communications and computing; the future of electronic funds transfer systems and electronic mail—these also are elements of information policy. And finally, attention will necessarily focus on the international implications—the exports of information goods and services, cultural exports, and technological and scientific information transfer. We cannot be definitive about the information society because that era is still evolving about us. As with life itself, the prognosis for an information society is mixed, the remedy inconclusive.

REFERENCES

1. Bell, Daniel. *The Coming of Post-Industrial Society*. New York: Basic Books, 1973, pp. 126–127.
2. Boulding, K. E., "The Economics of Knowledge and the Knowledge of Economics." In D. M. Lamberton (Ed.) *Economics of Information and Knowledge*. Middlesex, England: Penguin Books, 1971.
3. Fuchs, V. R. *The Service Economy*. New York: National Bureau of Economic Research.
4. Machlup, Fritz. *The Production and Distribution of Knowledge in the United States*. Princeton, N.J.: Princeton University Press, 1962.
5. Nadel, Laurie, and Hesh Wiever. "Would You Sell a Computer to Hitler?" *Computer Decisions*, February 1988.
6. Porat, Marc Uri. *The Information Economy: Definition and Measurement* (nine volumes). U.S. Government Printing Office, Washington, D.C., July 1977.
7. Teplin, M. "U.S. International Transactions in Royalties and Fees: Their Relationship to the Transfer to Technology." *Survey of Current Business* 53(12): December 1975.

From "Post-Industrialism" to "Information Society": A New Social Transformation

DAVID LYON

The rapid introduction and widespread diffusion of information technology (IT) within the advanced societies raises numerous questions of great interest for sociology. Among them is the broad question of whether we are at the threshold of a new kind of society. Naturally enough, this issue features prominently in futurist television shows, popular paperbacks, and the press. But the kinds of claims made—such as that we are constructing a "wired society" (Martin 1978) or experiencing a "third wave" (Toffler 1980), dependent on the "wealth of information" (Stonier 1983)—warrant more systematic social analysis.

Among the concepts put forward to encapsulate what is going on, the "information society" is clearly a leading candidate. Given the newness of the technologies, and the relatively recent realization of their potential to affect all areas of life, it would be surprising if sociological debate were already crystallizing around a single concept. But the growing number of references to the "information society" (or to related categories, such as "information workers") makes it a suitable focus for discussion of research on the social dimensions of the new technology, and the specific question of whether we should revise one of our basic means of characterising "society" today.

The emergence of this concept within serious social analysis is explicable. Firstly, the social (not to mention economic and political) significance of information technology is rapidly being established as a phenomenon worthy of social investigation (sometimes on dubious grounds, as we shall see). Secondly, whereas "post-industrialism," the only previous potential usurper of "industrial society" concepts, was *negatively* and thus rather vaguely defined, "information society" promises concrete clues as to the dominant features of the burgeoning social formation. Thirdly, just as Daniel Bell more

From "Post-Industrialism to Information Society" by David Lyon, *Sociology*, Vol. 20, No. 4, pp. 577–78.

than any other single contributor placed "post-industrialism" on the sociological agenda, so he has also put his weight behind the "information society" concept.

Some discussions of "information society" evoke a sense of *déjà vu*, not to mention impatience, in the light of extensive critiques which have already been made of "post-industrialism" (Kleinberg 1973, Kumar 1978). On the other hand, the "social forecast" of "post-industrial society" was issued by Bell and others well before the technological breakthroughs associated with the silicon chip. While it may appear premature to hail the consequences of this as a "Micro Revolution" (Large 1984), the increases in speed, flexibility and efficiency in information handling, along with the decreases in component costs, do have far-reaching actual and potential social ramifications. Trying to gauge the extent and meaning of such ramifications, whether or not they amount to "information society," is a valid sociological enterprise.

In what follows, I examine the current debate over the "information society" concept. Firstly, I uncover the roots of this concept in the literatures of post-industrialism, of futurism, and of what might be called the "social consequences of new technology." Secondly, I survey attempts to clarify or criticise the idea of "information society," with particular reference to the social role of "information" and of "information activities." I also comment on the failure to include analysis of power relations (local and global) in some versions of the "information society" thesis. Thirdly, I suggest where the most fruitful lines of inquiry seem to lie. While this need not necessarily entail abandonment of the "information society" concept, I propose a number of crucial qualifications. In particular, the spectres of economic and technological determinism must be laid, and renewed emphasis given to the social *shaping* as well as social *consequences* of new technology.[1]

▪▪▪ The Roots of the Information Society Idea

The roots of the information society idea are intertwined in a fairly complex manner. It is hard to disentangle the diverse strands of attempted social prediction, government policy, futuristic speculation and empirical social analysis. For instance, a Canadian government report, *Planning now for the information society* (Science Council of Canada 1982), is clearly geared towards identifying a national technological strategy in microelectronics. But it depends on social scientific concepts such as the "information economy," indulges briefly in quoted "predictions" (for instance that by the year 2000 "smart" highways for semiautomated driving will enter early development), and refers to empirical studies of the impact of microelectronics on, among other things, women's work.

One strand that is readily identifiable, however, is the idea of post-industrialism, especially the version associated with Daniel Bell. Several writers refer hopefully to the "information society" future (for instance, Nora and Minc 1981), but frequently fall back on the language of post-industrialism. In essence, this is the view that, as "agrarian" was replaced by "industrial" society as the dominant economic emphasis shifted from the land to manufacture, so "post-industrial" society emerges as a result of the economic tilt towards the provision of services. The increased part played by science in the productive process, the rise to prominence of professional, scientific and technical groups, plus the introduction of what we now call "information technology," all bear witness to a new "axial principle" at the core of the socioeconomic system. This "axial principle," the "energising principle that is the logic for all the others," is the centrality of "theoretical knowledge" (Bell 1974: 14).

Bell argues that the information society is developing in the context of post-industrial society. He forecasts the emergence of a new social framework based on telecommunications which "may be decisive for the way economic and social exchanges are conducted, the way knowledge is created and retrieved, and the character of work and occupations in which men (sic) are engaged." The computer plays a central role in this "revolution" (1980: 500).

Bell also sketches other significant features of information society. Information and telecommunications, as they shorten labour time and diminish the production worker, actually replace labour as the source of "added value" in the national product. Knowledge and information supplant labour and capital as the "central variables" of society. He comments on the "pricing" of information, and the way in which the "possession" of information increasingly confers power on its owner. Bell acknowledges but sidesteps the ambiguities involved in identifying a "service sector" by proposing that economic sectors be divided into "extractive, fabrication, and information activities." This way, he claims, one may monitor the penetration of information activities into more traditional areas of agriculture, manufacturing and services.

Bell underlines what he sees as the expansion of these areas in the wake of information technology. He foresees major social changes resulting from the establishment of new telecommunications infrastructures. These in turn will intensify concern about population distribution, national planning, centralization, privacy, and so on. The "fateful question", when all is said and done, is whether the promise will be realised that "instrumental technology" will open "the way to alternative modes of achieving individuality and variety within a vastly increased output of goods" (1980: 545).

Of course, Bell's is not the only version of the post-industrialism thesis. Alain Touraine's European alternative, for instance, takes account of the same socioeconomic trends as those isolated by Bell, but views the post-industrial society as a somewhat less harmonious product of them. Arguing that our image of class has been too deeply bound up with the "era of capitalist industrialization," Touraine challenges the bland post-industrial assumption that class struggle is a thing of the past, and invites us to consider the "fundamental importance of class situations, conflicts and movements in the programmed society" (1974:28). He identifies the major new cleavage between on the one hand the technocrats, and on the other a more disparate grouping whose livelihood and lifestyle is governed by their practice. The principal opposition between the two great classes or groups of classes hinges not so much on property-ownership but "comes about because the dominant classes dispose of knowledge and control *information*" (1974:61).

During the 1970s a number of theories appeared, purporting both to document the emergence of "new classes" — "the knowledge class" (Gouldner 1979) or the "professional-managerial class" (Ehrenreich 1979) — and to bid "farewell to the working class" (Gorz 1980). Novel class alignments, it appeared, were bound up with changing technologies and shifts in educational qualification and skill. As we shall see, however, the effort to identify new lines of class cleavage has sometimes deflected attention from those which still operate within societies adopting IT, namely, property relations.

▪▪▪ Social Forecasters and Social Planners

The roots of the "information society" idea are not only found in sociology. Futurists (such as Toffler 1980, Naisbitt 1984) and "social impact of technology" commentators also contribute. They tend to share the belief that technology "shapes" social relationships.

One of the many cheerful "social forecasts" comes from Tom Stonier. "Living in a post-industrial world" he avers, "means that not only are we more affluent, more resourceful and less likely to go to war, but also more likely to democratise" (1983:202). Increasing prosperity is a common "information society" theme.

By "more resourceful" Stonier means that IT will enable us to conquer the environmental and ecological problems associated with industrialism. Again he touches on a common theme. James Martin also stresses the "non-polluting, non-destructive" quality of IT itself as a major point in its favour (Martin 1978:4). New communications technologies hold out the next promise—the demise of war ("as slavery disappeared in the industrial era" Stonier 1983:202). And lastly, IT ushers in the world of "computer democracy". More information availability, plus push-button referenda, open the door for the first time to genuinely responsive participatory government. This, along with the burden of administration being thoroughly automated, is the contented futurist's world of "information society."

A short step away from the futurist's vision is the forecaster's proposal. Japan was first to produce such a proposal, in the shape of *The plan for information society: A national goal toward the year 2000* (1972). Lacking natural energy resources, the Japanese were acutely aware of the fragility of their economy in the face of recession. Yoneji Masuda's work (translated into English as *The information society as postindustrial society*, 1981) has been central to the process of establishing the "national plan." The idea of "computopia" is given concrete shape by Masuda, who links together the futurist dream ("the goal. . . . is a society that brings about a general flourishing state of human intellectual creativity, instead of affluent material consumption," 1981:3) with actual "new towns" in Japan and "information society infrastructures" elsewhere.

Japan's Tama New Town, with its built-in network of coaxial cables, Canada's *Telidon* (videotex) programme, and Sweden's *Terese* project, which monitors regional development using new telecommunications, are cited as relevant examples of such "infrastructures." They are significant because Masuda sees information society as "a new type of human society." For him, "*production of information values and not material values will be the driving force.*" At the same time, past experience within industrial society may be used as a "*historical analogical model for future society*" (1981:29).

Masuda's assumption that the history of industrial society may be used as an analogy for what will happen in information society brings us back to the core of the sociological question. Is it legitimate to claim that the steam engine was to industrial society what the computer is to information society, so that, one, the new technology shapes the resulting social and political formation, and two, a qualitatively different kind of society emerges?

Within the same sociological question lies the problem of exactly what the social consequences—and the social determinants—of the diffusion of information technology are. Even if one remains sceptical about the capacity of the computer to transform the world in quite the way envisaged by a Stonier or a Masuda, it is clear that IT is a major phenomenon with a broad potential social impact.

Some predictions about IT's effects exude confidence, especially those whose plausibility rests on identifying a big proportion of the workforce as "information processors." Barron and Curnow, for example, put the proportion at around 40 percent (1979). Against this, Trevor Jones is more cautious (1980). He insists that a sector-by-sector analysis is required before any overall survey can be attempted. Productivity varies between sectors, as does the pace of change and new technology take-up rates. Close analysis also reveals job-loss, deskilling, and increased workplace surveillance associated with new technology, which suggests continuities rather than discontinuities with "industrial society."

Clearly, other factors than "technology" enter the picture. Government policy for example has an impact on the way IT is developed. In Britain, the Alvey programme for developing IT is heavily weighted in favour of commercial rather than university research, which affects both the traditional role of the latter, and the kinds of "product" of research.

This brings us to the sociological critique of the "information society" concept. The further one moves from grand national IT plans and from futuristic forecasts of the conditions prevailing within the computerised society, and the nearer one gets to actual social analysis in which technology is not perceived as a quasi-autonomous force acting upon society, the more questionable the information society concept appears.

The Critique of "Information Society"

The "information society" concept has inherited several symptoms of the troubles which beset "post-industrialism." The post-industrialists failed to justify the significance given to trends such as the growth of theoretical knowledge and "services." Their idea of a leisure society, based on automated manufacture, and a vast array of services, with a cultural system embodying self-expression, political participation, and an emphasis on the quality of life, does not seem to have materialised, at least not for the majority of the populations of the advanced societies.

Much of the exaggeration and sociological sleight of hand involved in post-industrialism has been adequately exposed (most economically in Kumar, 1978). For instance, the *quantity* of research and development (R&D) in a given economy tells us nothing about the social *role* of scientific and technical knowledge, the price put on it, or the power of those who manipulate it. The fact that R&D is often financed for political rather than social reasons, and developed for military rather than economic purposes, gives the lie to any idea that universities may have become crucibles of power in the new world. (Add to this the current squeeze on university funding, plus the politicization of science and technology policy, and the notion of "powerful" universities becomes even more of a chimera.) The so-called "new class" is probably less strong than some post-industrialists imagined, either as an enlightened elite or as an exploitative class (see further, Badham 1984).

Kumar, whose work draws together diverse strands of the critique of post-industrialism, concludes that a qualitatively different social world has not appeared. When one has distinguished between "white collar" and "service" work, shown that some "professionalization" in fact involves "relabelling" (the plumber becomes a "heating engineer"), and deflated the idea that more PhDs means a bigger stock of social knowledge, the claims about a "new social transformation" begin to wear somewhat thin. The agenda of questions for post-industrial society, says Kumar, is remarkably reminiscent of the agenda of *industrial* society. In his words,

> Beneath the post-industrial gloss, old scarred problems rear their heads: alienation and control in the workplaces of the service economy; scrutiny and supervision of the operations of private and public bureaucracies, especially as they come to be meshed in with technical and scientific expertise. Framing all these is the problem of the dominant constraining and shaping force of contemporary industrial societies: competitive struggles for profit and power between private corporations and nation states, in an environment in which such rivalries have a tendency to become expansionist and global. (1978:231)

Kumar points out that the early sociologists foresaw in *industrialism* exactly those trends which are now touted as signs of post-industrialism, such as Weber's observation of the increasing application of calculative rationality to the productive order. Something not dissimilar applies to "information society" as well.

Having said that, today's "information society" theorists lay great store by the notion that "information work" is becoming increasingly significant within the economy, especially as IT is more widely diffused. It is not just that theoretical knowledge is more important for production, but that so-called "information operatives" are increasingly visible within all kinds of occupations. The big question, of course, is who these information operatives are, and what contribution their work makes to patterns of social relationship.

Studies of the occupational structure made by Marc Porat (1977) are frequently taken as the basis for bold predictions. Taking the U.S. national accounts as his basis, Porat calculated (in 1967) that almost 50 percent of the workforce was engaged in the "information sector," and received just over 50 percent of total employee remuneration. But Porat fails to explain what is meant by "information", so that while rent collectors and judges *are* in the "information" sector, doctors are an "ambiguous occupation," straddling the "service" and "information" sectors. He simply defines "information" as "data that have been organized and communicated", and decides who is and is not an "information worker" on the basis of whether the worker derives an income from handling such information. No reference is made to the purpose, function, or context of "information work," and thus any clues about informative *power* are missing.

"Information work" is a category deserving careful analysis, without which we cannot know who makes decisions, and on what basis, or with what effect. Newman and Newman (1985) argue that a theory of information is a vital prerequisite to that. They propose the (economist's) formula that information is "that which destroys uncertainty." Information's importance to the economy lies in its contribution to economic adaptation through decisions made by firms, unions, governments, regulatory bodies, and consumers. And it must be seen in relation to organizational processes which shape labour markets and work situations. On this showing, "information work" has to do with specific decision-taking (as in top management), while "knowledge work" (as with the R&D scientist) has to do with the broader framework within which "information" questions are asked.

Beyond this, the "information society" thesis stands or falls on the question of which sectors of the economy are actually expanding, and which contracting. Politically, this is a crucially sensitive area. Government puts all its eggs into the IT basket on the assumption that IT will contribute to the creation of wealth and employment in the long run. It is to this question we now turn.

▪▪▪ Information: A New Socioeconomic Factor?

In *The new service economy* (1983), Jonathan Gershuny and Ian Miles attempt to break out of the sectoral paradigm which has guided popular economic thinking since the 1960s. They doubt whether much sense may be made of today's social-economic realities by appealing to the traditional "march through the sectors" of development, from primary through secondary and into tertiary production. Both post-industrial and information society theories are dubious because they are built on this "march" idea. They obscure, for instance, the extent to which the tertiary services sector grew *because of* growth in manufacturing, and thus the extent to which services would not simply soak up surplus displaced from manufacturing.

Gershuny and Miles offer both an alternative reading of sectoral shifts, which details many nuances *within* the too-frequently homogenised services sector, and indicate the growing significance of information technology within the service subsectors. Thus they acknowledge that "information" (-processing, -storing, and -transmitting) is a factor which must increasingly be taken into account in contemporary social-economic analysis. But they rightly stress that "information" cannot validly be viewed as a "separate" sector. *All* sectors are becoming more "information intensive."

The "march through the sectors" appears more and more "simplistic and naïve" as one follows Miles and Gershuny's (1986) arguments further. By distinguishing on the one hand between marketed and nonmarketed services, and on the other between intermediate producer and intermediate consumer services (the latter often refer to services finally controlled by the consumer, involving entertainment or DIY) they illustrate that far more than mere "consumer demand" is operating. Political and management decisions are also crucially important.

The work of Gershuny and Miles helps collapse the "information society" idea into a question of *alternative* possibilities rather than the "evolution" of the next "stage of development." But I do have a caveat which I think is more than a cavil. It centres on the use of the term "*wave.*" They say that "informatics are clearly central" to "a future growth wave" (1986:26).

A recent revival of interest in the "Kondratiev wave" has stimulated analytical debate, especially among those searching for a way out of economic recession (see, for example, Freeman 1984, but also Marxist versions such as Wallerstein 1980). The difficulty, as Tom Kitwood (1984) points out, is that a metaphor may be raised to the status of theory, at the expense of careful analysis both of actions of the *dramatis personae*, and of major social processes such as militarism and government policy. Given Miles and Gershuny's critique of technological determinism, and their awareness of the problems surrounding the new "informatics" infrastructure, their use of the "wave" metaphor seems a little surprising.

Nevertheless, the main message derived from Gershuny and Miles about the "information society" stands: The "march through the sectors" idea is of little help in determining what role "information" has today. Information activities take place throughout the economy, for varying reasons, and with differing impacts on processes such as employment.

At the same time, informatics has risen very rapidly over the past decade as a source of "added value" and a means of wealth creation. Is this another reason for revising our concepts? Are we moving "beyond" industrial capitalism?

▪▪▪ Information Society: Beyond Industrial Capitalism?

It is hard to justify the claim that "information society" takes us beyond industrial capitalism. On the one hand, information *is* being treated as though it were a commodity, to be priced within the marketplace. Vast transnational corporations such as IBM are involved in the commercial exploitation of information-related hardware, software, and services. On the other hand, the kinds of issues which have absorbed social analysis of industrial capitalism are reappearing in the information-intensive context—alienation and exploitation of the labour force, management and state monitoring and surveillance, and ethnic, gender and class cleavages.

In the USA, Herbert Schiller's critique of the "information society's" transcendence of capitalism is probably best known (1981). In his words,

> The new communications technologies that have been discovered, the
> mode of their invention, the processes by which they have been installed, the

factors which determine their utilization, the products that have been forth-coming, and the beneficiaries of the new systems and means of information transfer, are phenomena understandable best in terms of long-established and familiar market-based criteria. (1981:xii)

As in Britain, big corporations are given public assistance at the R&D stage, then the enterprises have to "pay their own way" in the market. Needless to say, those who *cannot* pay (either for new cable television "entertainment" or for new educational, commercial, personal, or medical services) will rapidly become aware of what is termed "information inequality." It would indeed seem that property relations retain their importance *within* the "information economy."

But it is not only within nations that information inequality seems to be grow-ing. The so-called "information explosion" is a global phenomenon, in which the less developed countries are at a distinct disadvantage. The transfer of technology and skills happens slowly, if at all, so that indigenous growth is unlikely. But the transna-tional corporations not only continue to locate their plant in the most economically viable settings within the so-called Third World, they also maintain a commanding position because of their superior technological capabilities (see Rada 1982, Littler and Salaman 1984).

Britain also has its "information society" critics. Frank Webster and Kevin Robins, for instance, see the activities of the transnationals which monopolise IT and shape innovation as expressions of the "needs of capital." They argue that the British Conservative government's "free market/strong state" policy shows extensive collu-sion between it and big business. IT will actually "facilitate the institution of the rule of capital across ever wider spheres of social existence." This is felt, they say, both in the workplace (through the discipline of the labour process), the public sphere (as a tool of administrative and political processes), and the private sphere (through the further pri-vatisation of leisure) (1981:266–7, and forthcoming).

The rapid growth of IT raises the question of what exactly is happening to capital-ism, which is of particular interest to Marxists (see Mandel 1978). Harry Braverman's controversial work on "deskilling" is also about the restructuring of capital, hence "labour *and monopoly capital*" (1974). The quest for profit within capitalism, and its impact on relations between labour and capital, is crucial here. In its "monopoly" phase, capitalism has developed at least two kinds of response to the crisis which has been with us since the 1960s. One has to do with labour intensification, technological innovation, and the rationalization of work, the other with the international movement of capital via multinational corporations.

Debate over Braverman's work (for instance, Wood 1982) has served to highlight the question of whether or not capitalism is being "transcended" in "information soci-ety." The extent to which Braverman is correct to claim that deskilling and labour con-trol are part of a capitalist ploy to extract surplus value (an alternative view is sketched in Rosenbrock 1984) cannot be determined here. But it is clear that resistance to deskilling and to management control and pacing of tasks is at the core of a number of socialist and union strategies to cope with new technology, as well as more academic attempts to explain its social impact (Gill 1985).[2]

One other area of concern is IT and women's employment. The two main aspects of this are, firstly, the lack of opportunities for technical education and training for women, and secondly, that women continue to bear the brunt of deskilling, low pay, and unemployment as word processors, automation and IT-enabled homeworking are extended (see, e.g., Cockburn 1983). Are these concerns qualitatively different from those which have exercised the minds of students of industrial capitalism, especially since the last war? It would seem that only one thing has changed. The debate is now focused around the diffusion of information technology.

▮▮▮ Information Society as a Problematic

Given the massive alterations in the way of life and in patterns of social, economic and political relationships which actually and potentially accompany the diffusion of information technology, focusing sociological attention on these is clearly a priority. The danger (in view of who pays for research) is that the scope of such studies will be restricted to the social *consequences* of new technology, and on "adaptation to change." It is a danger because the technology is then taken as given, rather than as the outcome of economic, political, and technical choices (although the socially-constraining effects of those choices should also be analysed).[3]

So what concepts should we use in attempting to analyse these changes? My own suggestion is that, rather than discarding the "information society" concept, we should grant it the status of a "problematic." A "problematic" is a "rudimentary organization of a field of phenomena which yields problems for investigation" (Abrams 1982:xv). What would its features be?

Firstly, it must be very clear what "information society" does *not* involve. The technological determinism lying not far beneath the surface of some accounts is rejected. Likewise the idea that a new "technocracy," in which power resides with a knowledgeable or "information-rich" class, is vulnerable to critique from both within and outside of Marxism. Also, any view which ignores the palpable fact that no social-economic development takes place today in isolation from the *world* economic system must be subjected to severe criticism.

Secondly, alternative explanations must be offered. Technological determinism may be countered with analyses of the *social shaping* of new technology, the diverse contributions of governments, labour unions, corporations, universities, and consumers (see MacKenzie and Wajcman 1985). Predictions about the growing power of intellectuals or, rather, the technically knowledgeable, are thrown in doubt by the continuing salience of property relations to the analysis of IT. The same economic activities are also inherently *international* in scope.

Negatively and positively, then, such criteria alert us to significant features of the "information society" problematic. Two final comments are in place. Firstly, social analysis must grapple with the social implications of the *fusion* of technologies represented by the phrase "information technology" (as begun, for instance in Bannon 1982, Bjorn-Andersen 1982, and Forester 1985). This involves eroding the conventional division of labour between "communication studies" on the one hand, and "computing/ automation studies" on the other. For instance, issues raised by the decline of public service broadcasting are no longer relevant only to "communications and media studies." The burgeoning of communication between computers, and the emergence of the commercial database brings "public service" questions to the heartland of computing (journals such as *Media, Culture and Society* are relevant here).[4]

Secondly, as social analysis exposes *alternative* options in the adoption of new technology which are in fact available to government, industry, and the public, discussion of strategies for *shaping* new technology will become more relevant. Such analysis can serve to indicate the conditions under which ethical considerations and social hopes might be released. The yawning credibility gap between futurist dreams and the hard realities of government, transnational, and military involvement in IT demands a sense of urgency about research within the "information society" problematic. It also indicates a vital role for serious social analysis within the policy-making process.

NOTES

1. Comments from Jay Blumler, Howard Davis, Anthony Giddens, and anonymous referees helped my revision of this article.
2. See also the new journal, *New Technology, Work and Employment*, issued to supplement *The Journal of Industrial Relations*.
3. Relevant literature is monitored in *New Technology: social and economic impacts*, a periodical edited by Lesley Grayson, and published by Technical Communications, 100 High Avenue, Letchworth, SG6 3RR, UK.
4. For instance, the journal *Media Culture and Society* has now committed itself to debating the "information society" concept. See the editorial by Nicholas Garnham and Richard Collins in volume 7, number 1, January 1985.

REFERENCES

Badham, R. 1984. "The sociology of industrial and postindustrial society," *Current Sociology*, 32:1.

Bannon, L. (*et al.* eds.) 1982. *Information Technology: impact on the way of life*. Dublin: Tycoply.

Barron, I. and Curnow, R. 1979. *The Future with Microelectronics*. Milton Keynes: Open University Press.

Bell, D. 1974. *The Coming of Postindustrial Society: a venture in social forecasting*. Harmondsworth: Peregrine.

Bell, D. 1980. "The social framework of the information society," in Forester 1985, q.v.

Bjorn-Andersen, N. (*et al.* eds.) 1982. *Information Society: for richer, for poorer*. Oxford: North-Holland.

Braverman, H. 1974. *Labour and Monopoly Capital*. New York: Monthly Review Press.

Cockburn, C. 1983. *Brothers: male dominance and technological change*. London: Pluto.

Ferguson, M. (ed.) 1986. *New Communications Technologies and the Public Interest*. London: Sage.

Forester, T. (ed.) 1985. *The Information Technology Revolution*. Oxford: Basil Bnackwell.

Forester, T. (ed.) 1980. *The Microelectronics Revolution*. Oxford: Basil Blackwell.

Freeman, C. 1984. "Keynes or Kondratiev: How can we get back to full employment?" in Pauline Marstrand (ed.) 1984, q.v.

Gershuny, J. and Miles, I. 1983. *The New Service Economy*. London: Frances Pinter.

Gill, C. 1985. *New Technology, Unemployment and Work*. Cambridge: Polity Press.

Gorz, A. 1980. *Farewell to the Working Class*. London: Pluto.

Gouldner, A. 1979. *The Rise of the Intellectuals and the Future of the New Class*. London: Macmillan.

Jones, T. (ed.) 1980. *Microelectronics and Society*. Milton Keynes: Open University Press.

Kitwood, T. 1984. "A farewell wave to the theory of long waves." *Education, Culture and Society (Universities Quarterly)* 38:2, 158–78.

Kleinberg, B. 1973. *American Society in the Post-Industrial Age*, Columbus: Merrill.

Kumar, K. 1978. *Prophecy and Progress: the sociology of industrial and postindustrial society*, Harmondsworth: Allen Lane.

Large, P. 1984. *The Micro Revolution*, London: Fontana.

Litter, C. and Salaman, G. (eds.) 1985. *The Social Shaping of Technology*. Milton Keynes: Open University Press.

Mandel, E. 1978. *Late Capitalism*. London: Verso.

Mandel, E. 1980. *Long Waves in Capitalist Development*. Cambridge: Cambridge University Press.

Marstrand, P. (ed.) 1984. *New Technology and the Future of Work and Skills*. London: Frances Pinter.

Masuda, Y. 1981. *The Information Society as Postindustrial Society*. Bethesda, MD: World Futures Society.

Martin, J. 1978. *The Wired Society*. Harmondsworth: Penguin.

Miles, I., and Gershuny, J. 1986. "The social economics of information technology" in Ferguson 1986, q.v.

Naisbitt, J. 1984. *Megatrends*. New York: Warner Books.

Newman, J. and Newman, R. 1985. "Information work: the new divorce?" *British Journal of Sociology* 24: 497–515.

Nora, S., and Minc, A. 1980. *The Computerisation of Society*. Cambridge, MA: MIT Press (ET of *L'informatisation de la société*, Paris: La Documentation Française).

Rada, J. 1982. "A third world perspective," in Gunter Friedrichs and Adam Schaff, *Microelectronics and Society: for better or worse*. London: Pergamon.

Reinecke, I. 1984. *Electronic Illusions*. Harmondsworth: Penguin.

Rosenbrock, H. H. 1984. "Designing automated systems: need skill be lost?" in Pauline Marstrand (ed.) 1984.

Shiller, H. 1981. *Who Knows: information in the age of the Fortune 500*. Norwood, NJ: Ablex.

Science Council of Canada 1982. *Planning Now for an Information Society: tomorrow is too late*. Ottawa: Science Council of Canada.

Stonier, T. 1983. *The Wealth of Information*. London: Thames Hudson.

Toffler, A. 1980. *The Third Wave*. London: Pan.

Touraine, A 1974. *The Postindustrial Society*. London: Wildwood House.

Wallerstein, E. 1980. *The Capitalist World Economy.* Cambridge: Cambridge University Press.

Webster, F. and Robins, K. 1981. "Information technology: futurism, corporations and the state," *Socialist Register*, 247–269.

Webster, F. and Robins, K. (forthcoming) *Information Technology: a Luddite analysis.* Norwood, NJ: Ablex.

Wood, S. (ed.) 1982. *The Degradation of Work? Skill, deskilling, and the labour process.* London: Hutchinson.

The Productivity Paradox of Information Technology

ERIK BRYNJOLFSSON

The relationship between information technology (IT) and productivity is widely discussed but little understood. Delivered computing power in the U.S. economy has increased by more than two orders of magnitude since 1970 (Figure 1) yet productivity, especially in the service sector, seems to have stagnated (Figure 2). Given the enormous promise of IT to usher in "the biggest technological revolution men have known" [29], disillusionment and even frustration with the technology is increasingly evident in statements like "No, computers do not boost productivity, at least not most of the time" [13].

The increased interest in the "productivity paradox," as it has become known, has engendered a significant amount of research, but thus far, this has only deepened the mystery. The Nobel Laureate economist Robert Solow has cleverly characterized the results: "we see computers everywhere except in the productivity statistics." Although similar conclusions are repeated by an alarming number of researchers in this area, we must be careful not to overinterpret these findings; a shortfall of evidence is not necessarily evidence of a shortfall. Furthermore, recent work [7] suggests that the return to IT spending may in fact be much higher than previously estimated.

This article summarizes what we know and do not know, distinguishes the central issues from diversions, and clarifies the questions that can be profitably explored in future research. After reviewing and assessing the research to date, it appears that the shortfall of IT productivity is as much due to deficiencies in our measurement and methodological tool kit as to mismanagement by developers and users of IT. The research considered in this article reflects the results of a computerized literature search of 30 of the leading journals in both information systems (IS) and economics (see sidebar for a comprehensive list of literature searched), as well as discussions with leading researchers in the field. In what follows, the key findings and essential research references are highlighted and discussed.

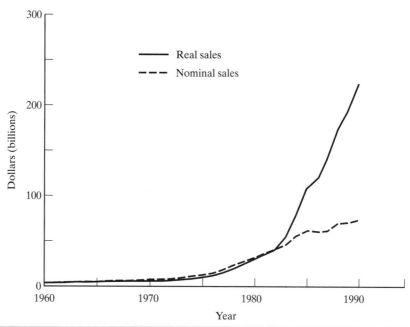

▪ ▪ ▪ ▪ ▪ ▪ ▪ ▪ ▪ ▪ ▪   **FIGURE 1** Real Purchases of Computers Continue to Rise

Based on data from Bureau of Labor Statistics, Productivity and Testing (1990 data is prepublication.)

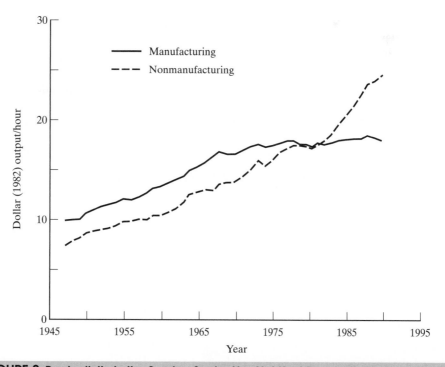

▪ ▪ ▪ ▪ ▪ ▪ ▪ ▪ ▪ ▪ ▪   **FIGURE 2** Productivity in the Service Sector Has Not Kept Pace with That in Manufacturing

Source: Commerce Department Census of Shipments, Inventories and Orders using BEA deflators (data for 1991 are estimates.)

▪▪▪ Dimensions of the Paradox

Productivity is the fundamental economic measure of a technology's contribution. With this in mind, CEOs and line managers have increasingly begun to question their huge investments in computers and related technologies. While major success stories exist, so do equally impressive failures (see [18]). The lack of good quantitative measures for the output and value created by IT has made the MIS manager's job of justifying investments particularly difficult. Academics have had similar problems assessing the contributions of this critical new technology, and this has been generally interpreted as a negative signal of its value.

The disappointment in IT has been chronicled in articles disclosing broad negative correlations with economywide productivity and information worker productivity. Econometric estimates have also indicated low IT capital productivity in a variety of manufacturing and service industries. The principal empirical research studies of IT and productivity are listed in Table 1.

Economywide Productivity and the Information Worker

The Issue

One of the core issues for economists in the past decade has been the productivity slowdown that began in the early 1970s. Even after accounting for factors such as changing oil prices, most researchers find there is an unexplained residual drop in productivity as compared with the first half of the postwar period. The sharp drop in productivity roughly coincided with the rapid increase in the use of IT (Figure 1). Although recent productivity growth has rebounded somewhat, especially in manufacturing, the overall negative correlation between economywide productivity and the advent of computers is the basis for many of the arguments that IT has not helped U.S. productivity or even that IT investments have been counterproductive.

This link is made more directly in research by Roach [27] focusing specifically on information workers, regardless of industry. While in the past, office work was not very capital-intensive, recently the level of IT capital per ("white-collar") information worker has begun approaching that of production capital per ("blue-collar") production worker. Concurrently, the ranks of information workers have ballooned and the

TABLE 1 Principal Empirical Studies of IT and Productivity		
Economywide or Cross-Sector	*Manufacturing*	*Services*
Osterman [23]	Loveman [19]	Cron and Sobol [10]
Baily and	Weill [32]	Strassman [30]
Chakrabarti [2]	Morrison and	Franke [14]
Roach [26]	Berndt [21]	Harris and Katz [16]
Brooke [6]	Barua et al. [4]	Alpar and Kim [1]
	Siegel and	Parsons et al. [25]
	Griliches [28]	Noyelle [22]
	Brynjolfsson and	Roach [27]
	Hitt [7]	Brynjolfsson and Hitt [7]

▪▪▪▪▪▪▪▪

ranks of production workers have shrunk. Roach cites statistics indicating that output per production worker grew by 16.9% between the mid-1970s and 1986, while output per information worker decreased by 6.6%. He concludes: "We have in essence isolated America's productivity shortfall and shown it to be concentrated in that portion of the economy that is the largest employer of white-collar workers and the most heavily endowed with high-tech capital." Roach's analysis provides quantitative support for widespread reports of low office productivity.[1]

Comment

On closer examination, the alarming correlation between higher IT spending and lower productivity at the level of the entire U.S. economy is not compelling because so many other factors affect productivity. Until recently, computers were not a major share of the economy. Consider the following order-of-magnitude estimates. IT capital stock is currently equal to about 10% of GNP. If, hypothetically, the return on IT investment were 20%, then current GNP would be directly increased about 2% (10% × 20%) because of the existence of the current stock of IT. The 2% increase must be spread over about 30 years, since that is how long it took to reach the current level of IT stock. This works out to an average contribution to aggregate GNP growth of 0.06% in each year. Although this amounts to billions of dollars, it is very difficult to isolate in our five-trillion-dollar economy because so many other factors affect GNP. Indeed, if the marginal product of IT capital were anywhere from −20% to +40%, it would still not have affected aggregate GNP growth by more than about 0.1% per year.[2]

This is not to say that computers may not have had significant effects in specific areas, such as transaction processing, or on other characteristics of the economy, such as employment shares, organizational structure, or product variety. Rather it suggests that very large changes in capital stock are needed to measurably affect total output under conventional assumptions about typical rates of return. The growth in IT stock, however, continues to be significant. At current growth rates, changes at the level of aggregate GNP should be apparent in the near future if computers increase productivity.

As for the apparent stagnation in white-collar productivity, one should keep in mind that relative productivity cannot be directly inferred from the number of information workers per unit output. For instance, if a new delivery schedule optimizer allows a firm to substitute a clerk for two truckers, the increase in the number of white-collar workers is evidence of an increase, not a decrease, in their relative productivity and in the firm's productivity as well. Osterman [23] suggests this is why clerical employment increased in the 1970s after the introduction of computers and Berndt and Morrison [5] confirm that IT capital is, on average, a complement for white-collar labor, even as it leads to fewer blue-collar workers. Unfortunately, more direct measures of office worker productivity are exceedingly difficult. Because of the lack of hard evidence, Panko [24] has gone so far as to call the idea of stagnant office worker productivity a myth, although he cites no evidence to the contrary.

---

[1]For instance, Lester Thurow has noted that "the American factory works, the American office doesn't," citing examples from the auto industry indicating that Japanese managers are able to get more output from blue-collar workers (even in American plants) with up to 40% fewer managers.

[2]In dollar terms, each white-collar worker is endowed with about $10,000 in IT capital, which at a 20% return on investment (ROI), would increase his or her total output by about $2,000 per year as compared with precomputer levels of output. Compare to the $100,000 or so in salary and overhead that it costs to employ this worker and the expectations for a technological "silver bullet" seem rather ambitious.

A more direct case for weakness in the contribution of IT comes from the explicit evaluation of IT capital productivity, typically by estimating the coefficients of a production function. This has been done in both manufacturing and service industries, as reviewed in the following subsections.

The Productivity of IT Capital in Manufacturing

The Issues

There have been at least six studies of IT productivity in the manufacturing sector, summarized in Table 2. A study by Loveman [19] provided some of the first econometric evidence of a potential problem when he examined data from 60 business units. As is common in the productivity literature, he used ordinary least-squares regression to estimate the parameters of a production function. Loveman estimated that the contribution of IT capital to output was approximately zero over the five-year period studied in almost every subsample he examined. His findings were fairly robust to a number of variations on his basic formulation and underscore the paradox: While firms were demonstrating a voracious appetite for a rapidly improving technology, measured productivity gains were insignificant.

Barua et al. [4] traced the causal chain back a step by looking at the effect of IT on intermediate variables such as capacity utilization, inventory turnover, quality, relative price and new product introduction. Using the same data set, they found that IT was positively related to three of these five intermediate measures of performance, although the magnitude of the effect was generally too small to measurably affect return on assets or market share.

Using a different data set, Weill [32] was also able to disaggregate IT by use, and found that significant productivity could be attributed to transactional types of IT (e.g., data processing), but was unable to identify gains associated with strategic systems (e.g., sales support) or informational investments (e.g., email infrastructure).

Morrison and Berndt have written a paper using a broader data set from the U.S. Bureau of Economic Analysis (BEA) that encompasses the whole U.S. manufacturing sector [21]. They examined a series of highly parameterized models of production in their paper, found evidence that every dollar spent on IT delivered on average only about $0.80 of value on the margin, indicating a general overinvestment in IT.

TABLE 2 Studies of IT in Manufacturing

Study	Data Source	Findings
Loveman [19]	PIMS/MPIT	IT investments added nothing to output
Weill [32]	Interviews and Surveys	Contextual variables affect IT performance
Morrison and Berndt [21]	BEA	IT marginal benefit is just 80 cents per dollar invested
Barua et al. [4]	PIMS/MPIT	IT improved intermediate outputs, if not necessarily final output
Siegel and Griliches [28]	Multiple gov't. sources	IT = using industries tend to be more productive; government data is unreliable
Brynjolfsson and Hitt [7]	IDG; Compustat; BEA	The return on investments in IT capital is over 50% per year in manufacturing

List of Literature Searched

Literature searched included *Communications of the ACM, Database, Datamation, Decision Sciences, Harvard Business Review, IEEE Spectrum, IEEE Transactions on Engineering Management, IEEE Transactions on Software Engineering, Information & Management, Interfaces, Journal of Systems Management, Management Science, MIS Quarterly, Operations Research, Sloan Management Review, American Economic Review, Bell (Rand) Journal of Economics, Brookings Papers on Economics and Accounting, Econometrica, Economic Development Review, Economica, Economics Journal, Economist (Netherlands), Information Economics & Policy, International Economics Review,* and the *Journal of Business Finance.*

Articles were selected if they indicated an emphasis on computers, information systems, information technology, DSS, ES, or high technology combined with an emphasis on productivity. A longer version of this article, including a more comprehensive bibliography of articles in this area, is available from the author.

Defining the Paradox: Some Key Terms

Information technology can be defined in various ways. Among the most common is the category "Office, Computing and Accounting Machinery" of the U.S. Bureau of Economic Analysis (BEA), which consists primarily of computers. Some researchers use definitions that also include communications equipment, instruments, photocopiers and related equipment, and software and related services.

Output is defined as the number of units produced times their unit value, proxied by their "real" price. Establishing the real price of a good or service requires the calculation of individual price "deflators" that eliminate the effects of inflation without ignoring quality changes.

Labor productivity is calculated as the level of output divided by a given level of labor input.

Multifactor productivity (sometimes more ambitiously called "total factor productivity") is calculated as the level of output for a given level of several inputs, typically labor, capital and materials. In principle, multifactor productivity is a better guide to the efficiency of a firm or industry because it adjusts for shifts among inputs, such as an increase in capital intensity, but lack of data can make this consideration moot.

Finally, Siegel and Griliches [28] used industry and establishment data from a variety of sources to examine several possible biases in conventional productivity estimates. Among their findings was a positive simple correlation between an industry's level of investment in computers and its multifactor productivity growth in the 1980s. They did not examine more structural approaches, in part because of troubling concerns they raised regarding the reliability of the data and government measurement techniques.

Most recently, a study of 380 large firms between 1987 and 1991 (over 1,000 observations in all) was completed by Brynjolfsson and Hitt [7]. Using essentially the same methodology as used by Loveman and by Berndt and Morrison, they found the return on investment for IT capital was over 50% per year and the return to spending on IS labor was also very high.

Comment

All authors make a point of emphasizing the limitations of their respective data sets. The MPIT data, used by both [4] and [19], can be particularly unreliable.

The BEA data may be somewhat more dependable, but one of the principal conclusions of Siegel and Griliches [28] was that "after auditing the industry numbers, we found that a nonnegligible number of sectors were not consistently defined over time."

The importance of data quality is underscored by the fact that different estimates of the contribution of IT were obtained when different data sets were used. Indeed, Brynjolfsson and Hitt [7] attribute the statistical significance of their findings not only the more recent time period of their data, but also to larger size of their data set, which enable them to estimate returns for all factors with greater precision.

However, the generally reasonable estimates derived for the other, non-IT factors of production in all of the studies indicate that there may indeed be something worrisome, or at least special, about IT.

The Productivity of IT Capital in Services

The Issues

It has been widely reported that most of the productivity slowdown is concentrated in the service sector [27]. Before about 1970, service productivity growth was comparable to that in manufacturing, but since then the trends have diverged significantly. Meanwhile services have dramatically increased as a share of total employment and to a lesser extent, as a share of total output. Because services use over 80% of IT, this has been taken as indirect evidence of poor IT productivity. The studies that have tried to assess IT productivity in the service sector are summarized in Table 3.

One of the first studies of the impact of IT was performed by Cron and Sobol [10], who looked at a sample of wholesalers. They found that on average, IT's impact was not significant, but that it seemed to be associated with both very high and very low performers. This finding has engendered the hypothesis that IT tends to reinforce existing

TABLE 3 Studies of IT in Services

Study	Data Source	Findings
Cron and Sobol [IO]	138 medical supply wholesalers	Bimodal distribution among high IT investors: either very good or very bad
Strassman [30]	Computerworld survey of 38 companies	No correlation between various IT ratios and performance measures
Roach [27]	Principally BLS, BEA	Vast increase in IT capital per information worker while measured output decreased
Harris and Katz [16]	LOMA insurance data for 40	Weak positive relationship between IT and various performance ratios
Noyelle [22]	U.S. and French industry	Severe measurement problems in services
Alpar and Kim [1]	Federal Reserve Data	Performance estimates sensitive to methodology
Parsons et al. [25]	Internal operating data from 2 large banks	IT coefficient in translog production function small and often negative
Brynjolfsson and Hitt [7]	IDG; Compustat; BEA	The return on IT investments is over 60% per year in services

management approaches, helping well-organized firms succeed but only further confusing managers who have not properly structured production in the first place.

Strassmann also reports disappointing evidence in several studies. In particular, he found that there was no correlation between IT and return on investment in a sample of 38 service sector firms: some top performers invest heavily in IT, while some do not. In many of his studies, he used the same MPIT data set discussed previously and had similar results. He concludes that "there is no relation between spending for computers, profits and productivity" [30].

Roach's widely cited research on white-collar productivity, discussed previously, focused principally on the dismal performance of IT in the service sector [27]. Roach argues that IT is an effectively used substitute for labor in most manufacturing industries, but has paradoxically been associated with bloating white-collar employment in services, especially finance. He attributes this to relatively keener competitive pressures in manufacturing and foresees a period of belt-tightening and restructuring in services as they also become subject to international competition.

There have been several studies of the impact of IT on the performance of various types of financial services firms. A recent study by Parsons, Gottlieb and Denny [25] estimated a production function for banking services in Canada and found that overall, the impact of IT on multifactor productivity was quite low between 1974 and 1987. They speculate that IT has positioned the industry for greater growth in the future. Similar conclusions are reached by Franke [14], who found that IT was associated with a sharp drop in capital productivity and stagnation in labor productivity, but remained optimistic about the future potential of IT, citing the long time lags associated with previous "technological transformations" such as the conversion to steam power.

Harris and Katz [16] looked at data on the insurance industry from the Life Office Management Association Information Processing Database. They found a positive relationship between IT expense ratios and various performance ratios, although at times the relationship was quite weak. Alpar and Kim [1] note that the methodology used to assess IT impacts can also significantly affect the results. They applied two approaches to the same data set. One approach was based on key ratios and the other used a cost function derived from microeconomic theory. They concluded that key ratios could be particularly misleading.

Using a standard production function approach, Brynjolfsson and Hitt [7] found that for the service firms in their sample, return on investment averaged over 60% per year.

Comment

Measurement problems are even more acute in services than in manufacturing. In part, this arises because many service transactions are idiosyncratic, and therefore not subject to statistical aggregation. Unfortunately, even when abundant data exist, classifications sometimes seem arbitrary. For instance, in accordance with a fairly standard approach, Parsons et al. [25] treated *time* deposits as inputs into the banking production function and *demand* deposits as outputs. The logic for such decisions is often difficult to fathom, and subtle changes in deposit patterns or classification standards can have disproportionate effects.

The importance of variables other than IT also becomes particularly apparent in some of the service sector studies. Cron and Sobol's finding of a bimodal distribution suggests that some variable was left out of the equation [10]. Furthermore, researchers and consultants have increasingly emphasized the theme of reengineering work when introducing major IT investments [15]. A frequently cited example is the success of the Batterymarch services firm. Batterymarch used IT to radically restructure the investment management process, rather than simply overlaying IT on existing processes. In sum, while a number of the dimensions of the "IT productivity paradox" have been overstated, the question remains as to whether IT is having the positive impact expected. In particular, better measures of information worker productivity are needed, as are explanations for why IT capital has not clearly improved firm-level productivity in manufacturing and services. We now examine four basic approaches taken to answer these questions.

▪▪▪ Four Explanations for the Paradox

Although it is too early to conclude that the productivity contribution of IT has been subpar, a paradox remains in the difficulty of unequivocally documenting any contribution, even after so much effort. The various explanations that have been proposed can be grouped into four categories:

1. *Mismeasurement* of outputs and inputs
2. *Lags* due to learning and adjustment
3. *Redistribution* and dissipation of profits
4. *Mismanagement* of information and technology

The first two explanations point to shortcomings in research, not practice, as the root of the productivity paradox. It is possible that the benefits of IT investment are quite large, but that a proper index of its true impact has yet to be analyzed. *Traditional* measures of the relationship between inputs and outputs fail to account for *nontraditional* sources of value. Second, if significant lags between cost and benefit may exist, then short-term results look poor but ultimately the payoff will be proportionately larger. This would be the case if extensive learning by both individuals and organizations were needed to fully exploit IT, as it is for most radically new technologies.

A more pessimistic view is embodied in the other two explanations. They propose that there really are no major benefits, now or in the future, and seek to explain why managers would systematically continue to invest in IT. The redistribution argument suggests that those investing in the technology benefit privately but at the expense of others, so no net benefits show up at the aggregate level. The final type of explanation examined is that we have systematically mismanaged IT: There is something in its nature that leads firms or industries to invest in it when they should not, to misallocate it, or to use it to create slack instead of productivity. Each of these four sets of hypotheses is assessed in the following subsections.

Measurement Errors

The Issues

The easiest explanation for the low measured productivity of IT is simply that output is not being measured correctly. Denison [12] makes a wide-ranging case that productivity and output statistics can be very unreliable. Most economists would agree with the evidence presented by [3] and [22] that the problems are particularly bad in service industries, which happen to own the majority of IT capital. It is important to note that measurement errors need not necessarily bias IT productivity if they exist in comparable magnitudes both before and after IT investments. However, the types of benefits managers attribute to IT—increased quality, variety, customer service, speed and responsiveness—are precisely the aspects of output measurement that are poorly accounted for in productivity statistics, as well as in most firms' accounting numbers [7]. This can lead to systematic underestimates of IT productivity.

Plotting the Paradox: Some Key Trends

The price of computing has dropped by half every 2 to 3 years (Figure 3a and Figure 3b). If progress in the rest of the economy had matched progress in the computer sector, a Cadillac would cost $4.98, while 10 minutes' worth of labor would buy a year's worth of groceries.[1]

There have been increasing levels of business investment in IT equipment. These investments now account for over 10% of new investment in capital equipment by U.S. firms (Figure 4). Information processing continues to be the principal task undertaken by the U.S. work force. Over half the labor force is employed in information-handling activities.

Overall productivity growth has slowed significantly since the early 1970s and measured productivity growth has fallen especially sharply in the service sector, which consumes over 80% of IT (Figure 2). White-collar productivity statistics have been essentially stagnant for 20 years (Figure 5).

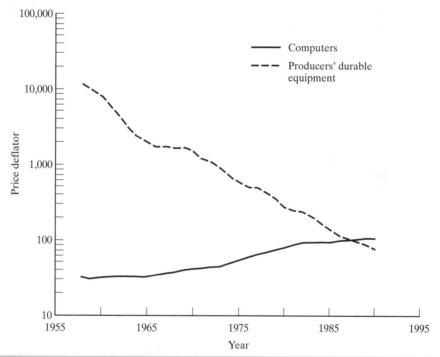

▮▮▮▮▮▮▮▮▮▮▮ **FIGURE 3A** The Cost of Computing Has Declined Substantially Relative to Other Capital Purchases

Based on data from U.S. Department of Commerce, Survey of Current Business (1990 data is prepublication.)

---

[1]"This comparison was inspired by the slightly exaggerated claim in Forbes, (1980), that "If the auto industry had none what the computer industry has done, . . . If Rolls-Royce would cost $2.50 and get 2 million miles to the gallon."

(continued)

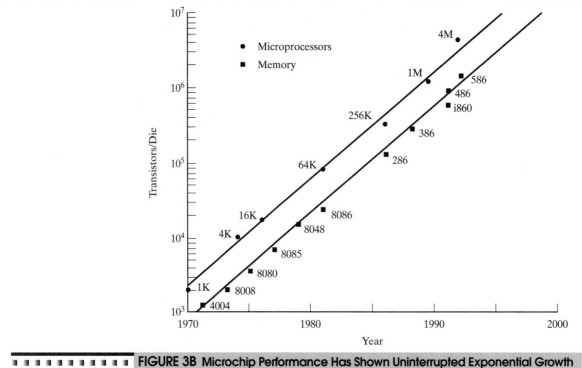

FIGURE 3B Microchip Performance Has Shown Uninterrupted Exponential Growth

Data provided by Intel.

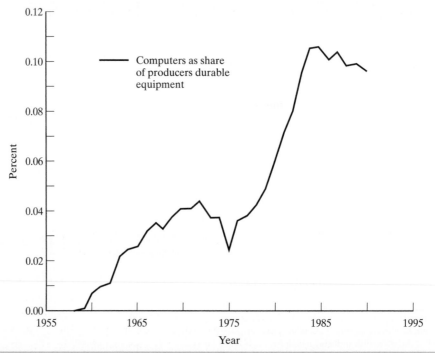

FIGURE 4 Computer Hardware Comprises About 10% of Investment in Producers' Durable Equipment

Based on data from BEA, National Income and Wealth Division (1990 data is prepublication.)

(continued)

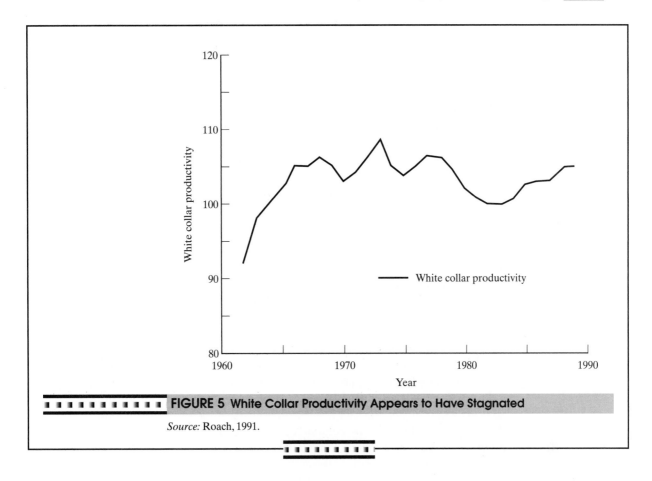

FIGURE 5 White Collar Productivity Appears to Have Stagnated

Source: Roach, 1991.

The measurement problems are particularly acute for IT use in the service sector and among white-collar workers. Since the null hypothesis that no improvement occurred wins by default when no *measured* improvement is found, it probably is not coincidental that service-sector and information-worker productivity is considered more of a problem than manufacturing and blue-collar productivity, where measures are better.

Output Mismeasurement   When comparing two output levels, it is important to deflate the prices so they are in comparable "real" dollars. Accurate price adjustment should remove not only the effects of inflation but also adjust for any quality changes. Much of the measurement problem arises from the difficulty of developing accurate, quality-adjusted price deflators. Additional problems arise when new products or features are introduced. This is not only because they have no predecessors for direct comparison, but also because variety itself has value, and that can be nearly impossible to measure.

The positive impact of IT on variety and the negative impact of variety on measured productivity has been econometrically and theoretically supported by Brooke [6]. He argues that lower costs of information processing have enabled companies to handle more products and more variations of existing products. The increased scope has been purchased at the cost of reduced economies of scale, however, and has therefore resulted in higher unit costs of output. For example, if a clothing manufacturer chooses to produce more colors and sizes of shirts, which may have value to consumers, existing productivity measures rarely account for such value and will typically show higher "productivity" in a firm that produces a single color and size. Higher prices in industries with increasing product diversity is likely to be attributed to inflation, despite the real increase in value provided to consumers.

In services, the problem of unmeasured improvements can be even worse than in manufacturing. For instance, the convenience afforded by 24-hour automatic teller machines (ATMs) is a clear example of an unmeasured quality improvement. How much value has this contributed to banking customers? Government statistics implicitly assume it is all captured in the number of transactions, or worse, that output is a constant multiple of labor input! In a case study of the finance, insurance and real estate sector, where computer usage and the numbers of information workers are particularly high, Baily and Gordon [3] identified a number of practices by the Bureau of Economic Analysis (BEA) which tend to understate productivity growth. Their revisions add 2.3% per year to productivity between 1973 and 1987 in this sector.

Input Mismeasurement   If the quality of work life is improved by computer usage (less repetitive retyping, tedious tabulation and messy mimeos), then theory suggests that proportionately lower wages can be paid. Thus the slow growth in clerical wages may be compensated for by unmeasured improvements in work life that are not accounted for in government statistics.

A related measurement issue is how to measure IT stock itself. For any given amount of output, if the level of IT stock used is overestimated, then its unit productivity will appear to be less than it really is. Denison [12] argues the government overstates the decline in the computer price deflator. If this is true, the "real" quantity of computers purchased recently is not as great as statistics show, while the "real" quantity purchased 20 years ago is higher. The net result is that much of the productivity improvement the government attributes to the computer-*producing* industry, should be allocated to computer-*using* industries. Effectively, computer users have been "overcharged" for their recent computer investments in the government productivity calculations.

To the extent that complementary inputs, such as software or training, are required to make investments in IT worthwhile, labor input may also be overestimated. Although spending on software and training yields benefits for several years, it is generally expensed in the same year that computers are purchased, artificially raising the short-term costs associated with computerization. In an era of annually rising investments, the subsequent benefits would be masked by the subsequent expensing of the next, larger round of complementary inputs. On the other hand, IT purchases may also create long-term liabilities in software and hardware maintenance that are not fully accounted for, leading to an underestimate of the impact of IT on costs.

Comments

The closer one examines the data behind the studies of IT performance, the more it looks like mismeasurement is at the core of the "productivity paradox." Rapid innovation has made IT-intensive industries particularly susceptible to the problems associated with measuring quality changes and valuing new products. The way productivity statistics are currently kept can lead to bizarre anomalies: To the extent that ATMs lead to fewer checks being written, they can actually lower productivity statistics. Increased variety, improved timeliness of delivery and personalized customer service are additional benefits that are poorly represented in productivity statistics. These are all qualities that are particularly likely to be enhanced by IT. Because information is intangible, increases in the implicit information content of products and services are likely to be underreported compared to increases in materials content.

Nonetheless, some analysts remain skeptical that measurement problems can explain much of the slowdown. They point out that by many measures, service quality has gone down, not up. Furthermore, they question the value of variety when it takes the form of six dozen brands of breakfast cereal.

Lags

The Issues

A second explanation for the paradox is that the benefits from IT can take several years to show results on the "bottom line." The idea that new technologies may not have an immediate impact is a common one in business. For instance, a survey of executives suggested that many expected it to take at much as five years for IT investments to pay off. This accords with a recent econometric study by Brynjolfsson et al. [8] which found lags of two-to-three years before the strongest organizational impacts of IT were felt. In general, while the benefits from investment in infrastructure can be large, they are indirect and often not immediate.

The existence of lags has some basis in theory. Because of its unusual complexity and novelty, firms and individual users of IT may require some experience before becoming proficient. According to models of learning-by-using, the optimal investment strategy sets short-term marginal costs greater than short-term marginal benefits. This allows the firm to "ride" the learning curve and reap benefits analogous to economies of scale. If only short-term costs and benefits are measured, then it might appear that the investment was inefficient.

Comment

If managers are rationally accounting for lags, this explanation for low IT productivity growth is particularly optimistic. In the future, not only should we reap the then-current benefits of the technology, but also enough additional benefits to make up for the extra costs we are currently incurring.

Redistribution

The Issues

A third possible explanation is that IT may be beneficial to individual firms, but unproductive from the standpoint of the industry as a whole or the economy as a whole: IT rearranges the shares of the pie without making it any bigger.

There are several arguments for why redistribution may be more of a factor with IT investments than for other investments. For instance, IT may be used disproportionately for market research and marketing, activities which can be very beneficial to the firm while adding nothing to total output [2]. Furthermore, economists have recognized for some time that, compared to other goods, information is particularly vulnerable to rent dissipation, in which one firm's gain comes entirely at the expense of others, instead of by creating new wealth. Advance knowledge of demand, supply, weather, or other conditions that affect asset prices can be very profitable privately even without increasing total output. This will lead to excessive incentives for information gathering.

Comment

Unlike the other possible explanations, the redistribution hypothesis would not explain any shortfall in IT productivity at the firm level: Firms with inadequate IT budgets would lose market share and profits to high IT spenders. In this way, an analogy could be made to models of the costs and benefits of advertising. The recent popularity of "strategic information systems" designed to take profits from competitors rather than to lower costs may be illustrative of this thinking. On the other hand, the original impetus for much of the spending on electronic data processing (EDP) was administrative cost reduction. This is still the principal justification used in many firms.

Mismanagement

The Issues

A fourth possibility is that, on the whole, IT really is *not* productive at the firm level. The investments are made nevertheless because the decision makers are not acting in the interests of the firm. Instead, they are increasing their slack, building inefficient systems, or simply using outdated criteria for decision making.

Many of the difficulties researchers have in quantifying the benefits of IT would also affect managers. As a result, they may have difficulty in bringing the benefits to the bottom line if output targets, work organization and incentives are not appropriately adjusted. The result is that IT might increase organizational slack instead of output or profits. This is consistent with arguments by Roach [27] that manufacturing has made better use of IT than has the service sector because manufacturing faces greater international competition, and thus tolerates less slack.

Sometimes the benefits do not even appear in the most direct measures of IT effectiveness. This stems not only from the intrinsic difficulty of system design and software engineering, but also because the rapidly evolving technology leaves little time for time-tested principles to diffuse before being supplanted.

A related argument derives from evolutionary models of organizations. The difficulties in measuring the benefits of information and IT discussed previously may also lead to the use of heuristics, rather than strict cost/benefit accounting to set levels of IT investments.[3] Our current institutions, heuristics and management principles evolved largely in a world with little IT. The radical changes enabled by IT may make these institutions outdated. For instance, a valuable heuristic in 1960 might have been "get all readily available information before making a decision." The same heuristic today could lead to information overload and chaos [31]. Indeed, the rapid speedup enabled by IT can create unanticipated bottlenecks at each human in the information processing chain. More money spent on IT will not help until these bottlenecks are addressed. Successful IT implementation process must not simply overlay new technology on old processes.

At a broader level, several researchers suggest that our currently low productivity levels are symptomatic of an economy in transition, in this case to the "information era" [11, 14]. For instance, David [11] makes an analogy to the electrification of factories at the turn of the century. Major productivity gains did not occur for 20 years, when new factories were designed and built to take advantage of electricity's flexibility which enabled machines to be located based on work-flow efficiency, instead of proximity to waterwheels, steam engines and power-transmitting shafts and rods.

Comments

While the idea of firms consistently making inefficient investments in IT is anathema to the neoclassical view of the firm as a profit maximizer, it can be explained formally by models such as agency theory and evolutionary economics, which treat the firm as a more complex entity. The fact that firms continue to invest large sums in the technology suggests that the individuals within the firm that make investment decisions

---

[3]Indeed, a recent review of the techniques used by major companies to justify IT investments revealed surprisingly little formal analysis. See [9] for an assessment of the IT justification process.

Why Haven't Computers Measurably Improved Productivity?

1. *Measurement Error*: Outputs (and inputs) of information-using industries are not being properly measured by conventional approaches.
2. *Lags*: Time lags in the payoffs to IT make analysis of current costs vs. current benefits misleading.
3. *Redistribution*: It is especially likely that IT is used in redistributive activities among firms,

making it privately beneficial without adding to total output.
4. *Mismanagement*: The lack of explicit measures of the value of information makes it particularly vulnerable to misallocation and overconsumption by managers.

---

are getting some benefit or at least believe they are getting some benefit from IT. In general, however, we do not yet have comprehensive models of the internal organization of the firm and researchers, at least in economics, are mostly silent on the sorts of inefficiency discussed in this section.

▬▬ Conclusion

Research on IT and productivity has been disappointing, not only because it has only exacerbated apprehension about the ultimate value of billions of dollars of IT investment, but also because it has raised frustrating concerns with the measures and methods commonly used for productivity assessment. Only by understanding the causes of the "productivity paradox" can we learn how to identify and remove the obstacles to higher productivity growth.

The section "Dimensions of the Paradox" presented a review of the principal empirical literature that engendered the term "productivity paradox" regarding poor IT performance. While a number of dimensions of the paradox are disturbing and provoking, we still do not have a definitive answer to the question of whether the productivity impact of IT has actually been unusually low. The section "Four Explanations for the Paradox" focused on identifying explanations for a slightly redefined "paradox": Why has it been so difficult to unambiguously document productivity gains from IT thus far? The four principal hypotheses are summarized in the sidebar "Why Haven't Computers Measurably Improved Productivity?" It is common to focus only on the mismanagement explanation, but a closer examination of the principal studies and the underlying data underscores the possibility that measurement difficulties may account for the lion's share of the gap between our expectations for the technology and its apparent performance. Indeed, the study with the largest and most detailed data set [7] found no productivity shortfall.

Where Do We Go From Here?

Even with substantive improvements in our research on IT and productivity, researchers must not overlook that fact that our tools are still "blunt." Managers do not always recognize this and tend to give a great deal of emphasis to studies of IT and productivity. Because they are written for an academic audience, the studies themselves are usually careful to spell out the limitations of the data and methods, but sometimes only the surprising conclusions are reported by the media. Because significant investment decisions are based on these conditions, researchers must be doubly careful to communicate the limitations as well.

While the focus of this article has been on the productivity literature, in business-oriented publications a recurrent theme is the idea that IT will not so much help us produce more of the same things as allow us to do entirely new things in new ways [15, 20]. For instance, [6] makes a connection to greater variety but lower productivity as traditionally measured. The business transformation literature highlights how difficult and perhaps inappropriate it would be to try to translate the benefits of IT usage into quantifiable productivity measures of output. Intangibles such as better responsiveness to customers and increased coordination with suppliers do not always increase the amount or even intrinsic quality of output, but they do help make sure it arrives at the right time, at the right place, with the right attributes for each customer. Just as managers look beyond "productivity" for some of the benefits of IT, so must researchers be prepared to look beyond conventional productivity measurement techniques.

If the value of IT has not yet been widely documented—the one certainty is that the measurement problem is becoming more severe. Developed nations are devoting increasing shares of their economies to service- and information-intensive activities for which output measures are poor. The comparison of the emerging "information age" to the industrial revolution has prompted a new approach to management accounting [17]. A review of the IT productivity research indicates an analogous opportunity to rethink the way productivity and output are measured.

Acknowledgments

This research was sponsored by the MIT Center for Coordination Science, the MIT International Financial Services Research Center, and the MIT Industrial Performance Center. Special thanks to Michael Dertouzos and Tom Malone for inviting me to pursue this topic for a study at the MIT Laboratory for Computer Science. I would like to thank Ernie Berndt, Geoffrey Brooke, Chris Kemerer, Richard Lester, Jack Rockart and seminar participants in Cambridge, New York, and London for valuable comments. Marshall van Alstyne provided excellent research assistance.

References

1. Alpar, P. and Kim, M. A comparison of approaches to the measurement of IT value. In *Proceedings of the Twenty-Second Hawaiian International Conference on System Science* (Honolulu, Hawaii 1990).

2. Baily, M. and Chakrabarti, A. Electronics and white-collar productivity. In *Innovation and the Productivity Crisis*, Brookings, Washington, DC; 1988.

3. Baily, M.N. and Gordon, R.J. The productivity slowdown, measurement issues, and the explosion of computer power. *In Brookings Papers on Economic Activity.* W.C. Brainard, and G.L. Perry. The Brookings Institution, Washington, D.C., 1988.

4. Barua, A., Kriebel, C. and Mukhopadhyay, T. Information technology and business value: An analytic and empirical investigation. Working Paper, University of Texas, Austin, Tex. May 1991.

5. Berndt, E.R. and Morrison, C.J. High-tech capital, economic and labor composition in U.S. manufacturing industries: An exploratory analysis. National Bureau of Economic Research Manuscript, Apr. 24, 1991.

6. Brooke, G. Information technology and productivity: An economic analysis of the effects of product differentiation. Ph.D. dissertation, University of Minnesota, 1991.

7. Brynjolfsson, E. and Hitt, L. Is information systems spending productive? New evidence and new results. *International Conference on Information Systems* (Orlando, Fl., 1993).

8. Brynjolfsson, E., Malone, T., Gurbaxani, V. and Kambil, A. Does information technology lead to smaller firms? *Manag. Sci.* To be published.

9. Clemons, E.K. Evaluation of strategic investments in information technology. *Commun. ACM 34*, I (1991), 22–36.

10. Cron, W.L. and Sobol, M.G. The relationship between computerization and performance: A strategy for maximizing the economic benefits of computerization. *J. Inf. Manag. 6* (1983), 171–181.

11. David, P.A. *Computer and Dynamo: The Modern Productivity Paradox in a Not-Too-Distant Mirror.* Center for Economic Policy Research, Stanford, Calif. (1989).

12. Denison, E.F. *Estimates of Productivity Change by Industry: An Evaluation and an Alternative.* The Brookings Institution, Washington, DC, 1989.

13. *Economist.* Working harder, doing less. (1990), 17.

14. Franke, R.H. Technological revolution and productivity decline: Computer introduction in the financial industry. *Tech. Forecast. Soc. Change 31* (1987).

15. Hammer, M. Reengineering work: Don't automate, obliterate. *Harvard Bus. Rev.* (July–Aug. 1990), 104–112.

16. Harris, S.E. and Katz, J.L. Predicting organizational performance using information technology managerial control ratios. In *Proceedings of the Twenty-Second Hawaiian International Conference on System Science* (Honolulu, Hawaii, 1989).

17. Kaplan, R. Management accounting for advanced technological environments. *Sci. 245* (Sept. 1989), 819–823.

18. Kemerer, C.F. and Sosa, G.L. Systems development risks in strategic information systems. *Info. Softw. Tech. 33*, 3 (Apr. 1991), 212–213.

19. Loveman, G.W. An assessment of the productivity impact on information technologies. MIT Management in the 1990s working paper #88-054, July, 1988.

20. Malone, T. and Rockart, J. Computers, networks and the corporation. *Sci. Am.* 265, 3 (1991), 128–136.

21. Morrison, C.J. and Berndt, E.R. Assessing the productivity of information technology equipment in the U.S. manufacturing industries. National Bureau of Economic Research Working Paper #3582, Jan. 1990.

22. Noyelle, T., Ed. *Skills, Wages, and Productivity in the Service Sector.* Westview Press, Boulder, Col. 1990.

23. Osterman, P. The impact of computers on the employment of clerks and managers. *Industrial and Labor Relations Review 39* (1986), 175–186.

24. Panko, R.R. Is office productivity stagnant? *MIS Q.* (June 1991), 190–203.

25. Parsons, D.J., Gottlieb, C.C. and Denny, M. Productivity and computers in Canadian banking. University of Toronto, Dept. of Economics working paper #9012, June, 1990.

26. Roach, S.S. America's white-collar productivity dilemma. *Manuf. Eng.* (Aug. 1989), 104.

27. Roach, S.S. Services under siege—The restructuring imperative. *Harvard Bus. Rev.* (Sept.–Oct. 1991), 82–92.

28. Siegel, D. and Griliches, Z. Purchased services, outsourcing, computers and productivity in manufacturing. National Bureau of Economic Research WP#3678, Apr., 1991.

29. Snow, C.P. Government science and public policy. *Science 151* (1966), 650–653.

30. Strassmann, P.A. *The Business Value of Computers.* Information Economics Press, New Canaan, Conn., 1990.

31. Thurow, L. Economic paradigms and slow American productivity growth. *Eastern Eco. J. 13* (1987), 335–343.

32. Weill, P. *Do Computers Pay Off?* ICIT Press, Washington, D.C., 1990.

Beyond the Productivity Paradox

Computers Are the Catalyst for Bigger Changes

ERIK BRYNJOLFSSON
LORIN M. HITT

Why Should We Care About Productivity?

An important question that has been debated for almost a decade is whether computers contribute to productivity growth. Productivity isn't everything. However, as noted by the economist Paul Krugman, in the long run it is almost everything. Productivity growth determines our living standards and the wealth of nations. This is because the amount a nation can consume is ultimately closely tied to what it produces. By the same token, the success of a business generally depends on its ability to deliver more real value for consumers without using more labor, capital, or other inputs.

Productivity is a simple concept. It is the amount of output produced per unit of input. While it is easy to define, it is notoriously difficult to measure, especially in the modern economy. In particular, there are two aspects of productivity that have increasingly defied precise measurement: output and input. Properly measured, output should include not just the number of widgets coming out of a factory, or the lines of code produced by a programming team, but rather the value created for consumers. Fifty years ago, tons of steel or bushels of corn were a reasonable proxy for the value of output. In today's economy, value depends increasingly on product quality, timeliness, customization, convenience, variety, and other intangibles.

Similarly, a proper measure of inputs includes not only labor hours, but also the quantity and quality of capital equipment used, materials and other resources consumed, worker training and education, and even the amount of "organizational capital" required, such as supplier relationships cultivated and investments in new business processes. The irony is that while we have more raw data today on all sorts of inputs and outputs than ever before, productivity in the information economy has proven harder to measure than it ever was in the industrial economy.

Where does productivity growth come from? By definition it doesn't come from working harder—that may increase output, but it also increases labor input. Similarly, using more capital or other resources does not necessarily increase productivity. Productivity growth comes from working smarter. This usually means adopting new production technologies and techniques.

The greatest increase in productivity has historically been associated with a particular class of technologies: "general purpose technologies." The steam engine was an important general purpose technology. It could be used in a variety of new applications, from driving spinning looms in a newly mechanized factory to powering locomotives in a new transportation system. Electricity was another key technology that set off a chain of innovation in the 1890s.

What general purpose technology might hold a similar promise in the 1990s? The obvious answer is information technology. Driven by Moore's law—the doubling of the number of transistors per chip every 18–24 months—computer technology has advanced at an exponential rate for several decades (see Figure 1). Ultimately, however, these trends in basic computer power only provide greater inputs into production. The question remains: Are computers increasing output? Are computers pulling their weight?

On the one hand, amazing success stories abound: the billions of dollars already being transacted by firms like Dell and Cisco via the Internet are only the latest example. On the other hand, there is no shortage of stories about cost overruns, abandoned systems investments and other IT failures. Some authors have even described the idea that computers have substantial business benefits as "the big lie of the information age" [12]. Anecdotes can be found to bolster either side of the debate.

A better way to determine if computers are living up to their promise is by studying broader data sets that contain hundreds or even thousands of observations. The idea is that unusually "lucky" or "unlucky" experiences with computers will tend to average out and we will be left with a clearer picture of the underlying relationship. We have reviewed several such studies, many of which were originally presented at the Workshop on Information Systems and Economics (WISE), across a wide range of technologies, industries and applications. We find that a consensus is beginning to emerge: Computers *are* pulling their weight [1–3, 8, 10].

In addition, a second, even more important finding is clearly evident in the data. While the average returns to IT investment are solidly positive, there is huge variation across organizations; some have spent vast sums on IT with little benefit, while others have spent similar amounts with tremendous success. Today, the critical question facing IT managers is not "Does IT pay off?" but "How can we best use computers?"

Fortunately, the same methodologies used in investigating the first question can be directed toward the second question, and a number of provocative results are emerging. Most importantly, the greatest benefits of computers appear to be realized when computer investment is coupled with other complementary investments; new strategies, new business processes and new organizations all appear to be important in realizing the maximum benefit of IT. This change is rarely easy since many organizations will require a painful and time consuming period of reengineering, restructuring and organizational redesign in order to best utilize their IT investments. However, once these investments in change are made, these companies will be positioned to reap the benefits of continued technological progress in the computer industry, while others may be left further and further behind.

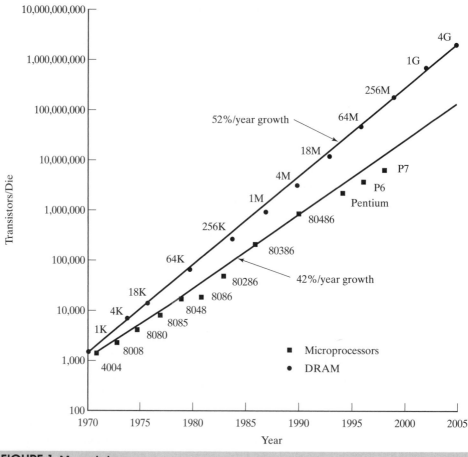

▮▮▮▮▮▮▮▮▮▮▮ **FIGURE 1** Moore's Law

The number of transistors that can be placed on a semiconductor die doubles approximately every 18 months.

▬▬▬ The Productivity Paradox

Attention was first drawn to the "productivity paradox" by a simple but provocative study, "America's Technology Dilemma: A Profile of the Information Economy" by Morgan Stanley's chief economist Steven Roach published in Morgan Stanley's April 22, 1987 economics newsletter series. He attempted to explain why the measured productivity growth rate in the U.S. economy has slowed substantially since 1973. Roach observed that the amount of computing power per white-collar worker in the service industry was growing dramatically over the 1970s and 1980s, yet the measured productivity of this sector was flat. His conclusion was that the tremendous increase in computerization has had little effect on economic performance, particularly for those sectors of the economy with large numbers of "information workers."

Other studies also showed little evidence of a link between computer investment and productivity using data on computer investment in manufacturing industries or in a sample of business units of large firms. A few studies found positive effects on intermediate factors such as cost efficiency or market share, but it was still difficult to tie these benefits to the bottom line. Furthermore, despite the tremendous advances in computer power, the aggregate statistics suggest that productivity has grown more slowly since 1973 than it did between 1950 and 1973. By the late 1980s, the conventional wisdom was that computers were not contributing significantly to productivity. As succinctly stated by Robert Solow in the *New York Times Book Review* (July 12, 1987) "we see the computer age everywhere except in the productivity statistics."

However, while these results generally found little evidence of a relationship between IT and productivity, there was also little evidence that computers were unproductive. In particular, many people pointed to the inadequacies of productivity measurement. One problem is that until recently overall computer investment was relatively small compared to overall capital investment and labor expenditure. Economist Zvi Griliches in his presidential address to the 1996 annual meeting of the American Economic Association likened the search for IT value to looking for a needle in a haystack. However, even as the magnitude of IT investment grows larger, he notes that there are still systematic biases in conventional productivity measurement that prevent an accurate assessment.

Most productivity metrics are oriented around counting things: number of employees, pounds of nails, or number of checks processed. As long as computers allow firms to produce more of the same product at lower costs, these metrics work reasonably well. But there is strong evidence that managers are not simply making IT investments to cut costs. When managers are asked, "Why do you invest in IT?" surveys suggest that customer service and quality consistently rank above cost savings as the prime motivation for making investments [3].

The quirks of productivity measurement are easily seen in banking. ATMs reduce the number of checks banks process so, by some measures, banking output and productivity decrease. The increases in convenience ATMs have created go uncounted in conventional productivity metrics, while their costs are counted. At an aggregate level, banking labor productivity is measured, like all sectors, as the ratio of an output metric to number of employees. But since the aggregate level of the true "output" of banks is difficult to measure, most conventional analyses have shown that labor productivity has essentially been flat. Not surprisingly, when you can easily count the costs of computer investment but have a difficulty assessing the benefits, particularly those that take time to be realized, IT can look like a bad investment.

An "Information Payoff?"

In the early 1990s data became available that allowed a reexamination of some of the previous results on IT productivity. This data, for the first time, enabled researchers to look at the IT investment behavior and productivity of large numbers of firms rather than focusing on higher level aggregates such as manufacturing industries or the whole economy. This microlevel approach had a number of advantages. While there is only one U.S. economy and only a few dozen manufacturing industries, this data allowed analyses to be conducted on hundreds of firms over several years. The increase in sample size enabled much more precise estimates of IT contributions, improving the chance of identifying the needle in the haystack.

Firm-level data also enables the measurement of at least some of the intangible value that was being created by computers even if this value could not be directly observed. If consumers are willing to pay more for increases in quality or convenience, then a firm's revenue will reflect some of this increase in intangible value. However, these differences will not appear at the industry level; high-quality firms force low-quality firms to lower their prices to remain competitive. Therefore, overall industry revenues will not necessarily increase as firms computerize. While some of the value from IT investments made by firms and passed on to consumers through competition will not be observed—at least some of this intangible value can be captured in productivity measurements.

Initial firm-level studies of IT and productivity found that a dollar of IT capital is associated with a substantial increase in revenue each year [1, 2, 11]. Other analyses have replicated these basic findings using different sets of econometric assumptions, different characterizations of IT (mainframes, PCs, IS staff or some combination), and different subsets of the economy (manufacturing vs. services) [3, 8]. Across all these studies there is a consistent finding that IT has a positive and significant impact on firm output, contradicting claims of a "productivity paradox."

In fact, in these studies the returns to IT appear to be quite high. This raises the possibility that computers are not only pulling their weight but contributing substantially more. However, at least part of this high rate of return is required to compensate for rapidly falling prices of computer equipment. In addition, these returns may represent more than just the returns to the technology. Technology is only one component of an IT investment; there are usually large expenditures on training, process redesign and other organizational changes accompanying a systems investment. This doesn't change the conclusion that computers contribute to increased output, although it does make exact rate of return calculations more difficult.

▪▪▪ Beyond the Averages

While computers on average appear to be productive, this fact alone is not enough for an IS manager to make good investments. In fact, the difficulty of establishing the overall value of IT may indicate that the value that IT brings to a firm varies enormously from company to company. When we plot the relationship between IT and productivity in Figure 2, two features stand out. First, when a line is fitted through these points, it slopes upward, which suggests that firms with more computers are compensated by increased output. However, more strikingly, there is an enormous amount of variation around this line; some firms have high IT investments and are highly productive, others have similar investments but poor performance. What explains the difference?

One way to start thinking about the sources of variation is to divide the benefits of IT into two parts: those that are unique to a particular firm, and those that appear due to variation in spending across firms. These two dimensions can be distinguished by a statistical technique known as a firm effects model. Applying this technique, we found that the measured benefits of IT were reduced by almost half when firm effects were included [1]. One interpretation of this result is that about half of IT value is due to unique characteristics of firms, while the remaining part is shared generally by all firms. What goes on inside the "black box" of the firm has a substantial influence on the productivity of IT investments.

To obtain a better characterization of the organizational factors that affect IT value, we can look at the relationship of IT investment to productivity over different time periods. If organizational changes can be made instantaneously with IT investments, then it should not matter whether we look at one-year changes in the firm or five-year changes. However, if there is some lag or adjustment time required to match organizational factors and IT investments, we would expect to see more benefits over longer time periods. The statistical results were striking (Figure 3). While short-term benefits were about what would be expected if they had "normal" returns, long-term benefits were substantially larger: from 2 to 8 times as much as short-term benefits [3].

Our interpretation is that the organizational factors that unlock the value of IT are costly and time consuming. This could explain why the effects rise (these changes take substantial time and are put in place incrementally) and why IT appears unusually productive in the longer term: The long-term benefits are not just the returns from IT but

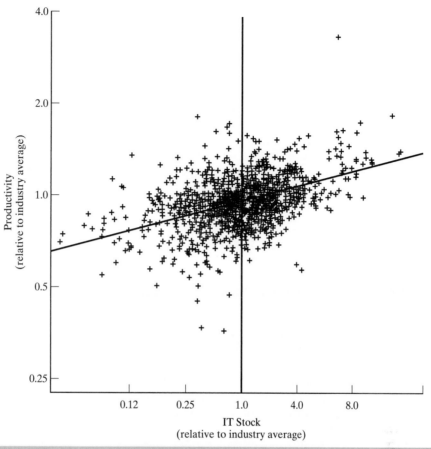

▮▮▮▮▮▮▮▮▮▮▮ **FIGURE 2** Variation in Productivity and IT Investment Across Firms

The vertical axis (labeled "Productivity") is multifactor productivity, defined as output divided by a weighted sum of inputs (in constant 1990 dollars). The horizontal axis (labeled "IT Stock") represents the total IT inputs in a firm. Both productivity and IT input are centered at the industry average. The points are approximately 1,300 individual observations representing an individual firm in a particular year.

returns from a system of technology and organizational changes; for every dollar of IT there are several dollars of organizational investments that, when combined, generate the large rise in measured firm productivity and value.

The Arrival of the "New Organization"

Tom Malone [11], Peter Drucker, and others recognized that general changes in the economy as well as the increased diffusion of IT into the workplace would facilitate and necessitate a dramatic restructuring of organizations. For example, Drucker's article, "The Coming of the New Organization" [9], predicted that technology-rich firms will increasingly shift toward flatter, less hierarchical organizations in which highly skilled workers take on increasing levels of decision-making responsibility. Similar ideas underlie other management trends such as business process redesign, the emergence of "high-performance work systems" and the shift from "mass production"-style manufacturing to flexible "modern manufacturing." In essence, these all represent organizational changes that exploit low-cost communications and information processing capabilities created by IT.

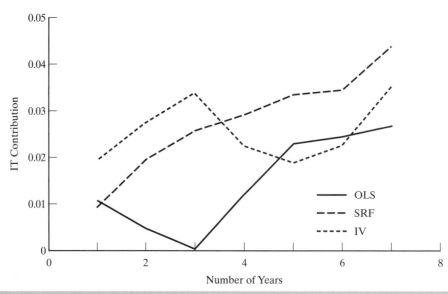

▪ ▪ ▪ ▪ ▪ ▪ ▪ ▪ ▪ ▪ ▪ ▪ **FIGURE 3** Productivity of IT Investments over Time

The vertical axis represents estimates of the productivity growth contribution of IT capital. The numbers are estimated output elasticities of IT capital, which represent the percentage change in output for a small percentage change in the quantity of IT. The value would be approximately 0.01 if IT has a "normal" rate of return. These estimates were computed by linear regression and the different lines represent different statistical techniques. "OLS" refers to ordinary least squares. "SRF" (semi-reduced form) is similar to OLS except that labor expense was not included in the list of inputs to reduce biases on the IT estimates from reverse causality between output and labor expense. "IV" represents instrumental variables regression which is an alternative way of addressing reverse causality. Further discussion of this analysis appears in [3].

Do these types of practices actually make a difference? The initial answer appears to be yes. Recently completed studies suggest that organizations that utilized decentralized decision making and have employees with greater levels of skill and education appear to invest more in information technology [10]. Irrespective of how IT is measured, there is a consistent positive relationship between the use of these technologies and a set of work practices that include the use of self-directed work teams, greater levels of individual decision authority, particularly over method and pace of work, increased investments in training and screening for education, and incentive systems that reward and encourage high team performance. Part of this relationship is due to the fact that organizations that employ large numbers of educated workers, particularly professionals, or employ technology- and skill-intensive production processes are likely to use more IT and adopt decentralized structures. However, the relationship between IT and the new organization of work goes beyond that which would be predicted by the composition of the work force and is present both within and between industries.

A cynical explanation of these results is that firms adopting the new work practices are wasteful users of IT; they spend too much or are too quick to adopt various management fads including IT investment and the new work practices. In fact, the opposite appears to be true. In addition to spending more on IT, these firms also appear to receive slightly higher returns on their IT investments. When we look at combinations of IT and work practices in the 2 × 2 matrix shown in Figure 4 we see that firms that couple IT investments with decentralized work practices are about 5% more productive than firms that do neither. However, firms can actually be *worse off* if they invest in computers without the new work systems.

IT / Decentralization	Low	High
High	0161 (.0191) N = 47	.0455 (.0177) N = 69
Low	0 (n/a) N = 69	-.0366 (.0197) N = 47

▪ ▪ ▪ ▪ ▪ ▪ ▪ ▪ ▪ ▪

FIGURE 4 Productivity Effects of IT and Decentralization

Each quadrant contains the average productivity, the standard error of the productivity estimate (in parenthesis) and the number of firms from our sample in each group. Productivity is defined as multifactor productivity: output divided by input costs (in constant 1990 dollars). The productivity numbers are relative to the "low-low" quadrant (which is set to zero as a reference point). More firms line up on the diagonal (high-high, low-low) than on the off-diagonals indicating that IT and decentralization are correlated. Reproduced from [4].

In addition to getting more total benefits from IT, these organizations also appear to be adopting IT at a faster rate. In 1994 this amounted to only about a 50% difference in overall IT investment intensity, however, this gap is growing by 10% per year. Over the next decade, these decentralized and empowered organizations may begin to pull away from their industrial age counterparts in performance as they are better able to exploit increasingly inexpensive information technology. These results suggest that it is becoming increasingly important to organize in ways that leverage the value of IT. While these types of results may not hold across all possible settings, the general trend is clear. So why do so many organizations still retain the old structure?

A plausible reason is that these types of organizational changes are time consuming, risky, and costly. Redesigning management infrastructure, replacing staff, changing fundamental firm practices such as incentive pay and promotion systems and undertaking a redesign of core business processes are not easy. In many cases this may involve abandoning business practices that may have been successful for decades in favor of work systems with which the organization has little experience, or adopting an abrupt, radical, and discontinuous change in organizational structure. The large number of documented difficulties and failures of change of this magnitude suggests that making these types of changes is indeed costly.

The experience of one firm we visited is instructive. It spent millions of dollars to implement a new computerized manufacturing process. Top management was wise enough to understand that fundamental changes in work practices would also be required. For instance, to exploit the new, more flexible equipment, they proposed a sharp reduction in work-in-process inventories and more frequent product change-overs in production lines. Despite the best of intentions, there were initially no significant gains in either productivity or flexibility [5].

The reason was that workers maintained the old ways of doing things, not in a conscious effort to sabotage the new manufacturing system, but simply because they had too many ingrained habits. For example, one worker explained, "The key to productivity is to avoid change-overs and keep the machines running at all times." This was a

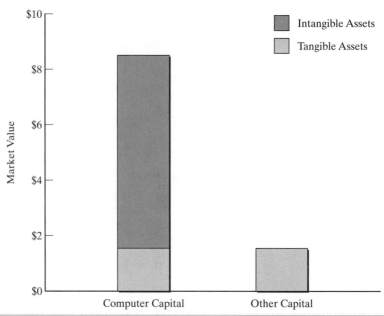

FIGURE 5 Relative Market Value of Computer Capital

Estimates of the market value of computers relative to the market value of other assets from [5]. This analysis suggests that a one-dollar change in IT capital is associated with a change of about $10 in market value for the average firm in our sample. For this to be an equilibrium, there must be about $9 of unmeasured intangible associated with each dollar of measured IT capital.

very useful rule of thumb with the old, inflexible equipment, but it nullified the benefits of the new machines. Effectively, the huge investment in flexibility machinery was being used mainly to make the new machines work just like the old machines! Interestingly, management's attempts to empower line workers with more decision-making responsibility were not much more successful. Several workers confessed that they had no interest in having more decision-making responsibilities—when chatting with their colleagues at work, they preferred to discuss sports rather than statistical process control.

Eventually, the firm was successful in managing this change, and they ultimately surpassed their production goals. The unmistakable lesson was that purchasing computerized equipment was the smallest part of the overall cost of creating a new manufacturing system. The biggest costs were in changing the organization.

One way to think about these changes is to treat the organizational costs as an investment in a new asset. Firms make investments over time in developing a new process, rebuilding their staff or designing a new organizational structure, and the benefits from these investments are realized over a long time period. Our earlier results suggest that these types of organizational assets need to be matched to information technology assets in order to be maximally valuable.

To get an idea of the potential magnitude of these assets, one can look at how the stock market values different types of assets owned by the firm (see Figure 5). For large corporations, a dollar of most types of capital is valued by the stock market at about a dollar. However, for these same corporations a dollar of computer hardware appears to be associated with about $10 of market value [6]. While it could be true that IT is extraordinarily productive, it seems more reasonable to argue that this extra $9 represents the value of hidden complementary organizational assets. For instance, with each dollar a firm spends on enterprise resource planning software like SAP's R/3 system, it typically spends $3–4 on consultants who implement the new system. Even bigger costs are incurred in employee retraining and time spent redesigning business processes. However, in the end, the firm has a new system with lasting value—they own a new asset. These types of assets don't show up on a firm's balance sheet but accompany and complement IT investments.

▪▪▪ What We Now Know About Computers and Productivity

Research on computers and productivity is entering a new phase. While the first wave of studies sought to document the relationship between investments in computers and increases in productivity, new research is focusing on how to make more computerization effective. Computerization does not automatically increase productivity, but it is an essential component of a broader system of organizational changes which does increase productivity. As the impact of computers becomes greater and more pervasive, it is increasingly important to consider these organizational changes as an integral part of the computerization process.

This is not the first time that a major general purpose technology like computers required an expensive and time-consuming period of restructuring. Significant productivity improvement from electric motors did not emerge until almost 40 years after their introduction into factories [7]. The first use involved swapping gargantuan motors for large steam engines with no redesign of work processes. The big productivity gains came when engineers realized that the factory layout no longer had to be dictated by the placement of power transmitting shafts and rods. They reengineered the factory so that machines were distributed throughout the factory, each driven by a separate, small electric motor. This made it possible to arrange the machines in accordance with the logic of work flow instead of in proximity to the central power unit.

It has also taken some time for businesses to realize the transformative potential of information technology to revolutionize work. However, the statistical evidence suggests that revolution is occurring much more quickly this time.

REFERENCES

1. Brynjolfsson, E. and Hitt, L. Computers as a factor of production: The role of differences among firms. *Economics of Innovation and New Technology 3*, 3–4 (May 1995), 183–199.
2. Brynjolfsson, E. and Hitt, L. Paradox lost? Firm-level evidence on the returns to information systems. *Manag. Sci. 42*, 4 (Apr. 1996).
3. Brynjolfsson, E. and Hitt, L. Computing productivity: Are computers pulling their weight? MIT and Wharton working paper, November, 1997; www.ccs.mit.edu/erik/.
4. Brynjolfsson, E. and Hitt, L. Information technology and organizational design: Firm-level evidence. MIT, Stanford, and Wharton working paper, January 1998; www.ccs.mit.edu/erik/.
5. Brynjolfsson, E., Van Alstyne, M., and Renshaw, A. The matrix of change. *Sloan Management Review 38*, 2 (Winter 1997), 37–54; www.ccs.mit.edu/mo.
6. Brynjolfsson, E. and Yang, S. Intangible benefits and costs of computer investments: Evidence from the financial market. In *Proceedings of the International Conference on Information Systems* (Atlanta, GA., Dec. 1997).
7. David, P.A. The dynamo and the computer: A historical perspective on the modern productivity paradox. *American Economic Review Papers and Proceedings 1*, 2 (1990), 355–361.
8. Dewan, S. and Min, C. The substitution of IT for other factors of production: A firm-level analysis. *Manag. Sci. 43*, 12 (Dec. 1997), 1660–1675.
9. Drucker, P.F. The coming of the new organization. *Harvard Business Rev. 66*, 1 (Jan.–Feb. 1988), 45–53.
10. Lichtenberg, F.R. The output contributions of computer equipment and personnel: A firm-level analysis. *Economics of Innovation and New Technology 3*, 3–4 (May 1995), 201–217.
11. Malone, T. Is empowerment just a fad? *Sloan Management Review 38*, 2 (Winter 1997).
12. Schrage, M. The real problem with computers. *Harvard Business Rev. 75*, 5 (Nov.–Dec. 1997), 178–183.

The Productivity Paradox: Is It Resolved? Is There a New One? What Does It All Mean for Managers?[1]

KENNETH KRAEMER
JASON DEDRICK
Prepared for the CRITO Consortium Industry Advisory Board Panel: The End of the Productivity Paradox?

▪▪▪ The Productivity Paradox: Are We Really Irrational?

Has the productivity paradox been put to rest, and has a new paradox emerged in its place? These questions continue to vex the economics community, including its most powerful member, Federal Reserve chairman Alan Greenspan, and to concern the IT industry, IT users, and management researchers.

The whole issue arose over a decade ago, when Nobel Prize winning economist, Robert Solow, famously remarked, "You can see the computer age everywhere but in the productivity statistics." This offhand comment became the Quip that Launched a Thousand Production Functions, as researchers were driven to solve the apparent contradiction to economic theory. For if Solow was right, it meant that businesses were investing billions of dollars on technology with no apparent payoff. Such a massive, widespread phenomenon would certainly call into question the fundamental economic principle that investors and managers are not systematically irrational.

The Productivity Paradox: Is It Resolved? Is There a New One? What Does It All Mean for Managers? by J. Dedrick and K.L. Kraemer, CRITO, February 2001. Copyright © 2001 Kenneth Kraemer and Jason Dedrick. Reprinted by permission of the authors.
[1]This research has been supported by grants from the CISE/IIS/CSS Division of the U.S. National Science Foundation and the NSF Industry/University Cooperative Research Center (CISE/EEC) to the Center for Research on Information Technology and Organizations (CRITO) at the University of California, Irvine. Industry sponsors include: ATL Products/Quantum, the Boeing Company, Canon Information Systems, IBM, Nortel Networks, Conexant, Microsoft, Seagate Technology, Sun Microsystems, Whirlpool Corporation.

Interestingly, Solow's quip was based entirely on circumstantial evidence, i.e., the fact that U.S. companies had invested over a trillion dollars in IT the previous decade, but U.S. productivity growth remained well below the rates seen in the earlier post-war period. However, it stimulated other economists such as Martin Baily, Stephen Roach, Gary Loveman, and Robert Gordon to conduct more rigorous analyses and they found that the impacts of IT on productivity were not obvious. So the productivity paradox became a thorn in the side of economic theory, a concern for businesses trying to improve profits, and an issue for government policymakers trying to spur productivity and economic growth. If true, it also threatened the IT industry, whose products might be seen as having little economic value in spite of the rapid technological progress that marked the industry.

▪ ▪ ▪   Resolving the Paradox

The first reaction to the productivity paradox was to try to explain why it might exist. These explanations were summarized by Eric Brynjolfsson (1993) into four categories: (1) measurement errors of IT capital due to rapid price and quality changes, and failure of economic statistics to measure qualitative improvements in the output of service industries; (2) time lags, an argument made by Paul David (1990), which said that IT would not have a measurable impact on productivity until it reached a critical mass of diffusion and experience; (3) management practices, which had not yet evolved to take advantage of the potential of the technology; and (4) redistribution, i.e., IT might help individual firms relative to competitors, but not increase productivity in the whole economy.

A second reaction was to develop more sophisticated models to tease out the relationship between IT and productivity. Studies in the early 1990s by Brynjolfsson and Loren Hitt (1993), and by Frank Lichtenberg (1993), found evidence that refuted the productivity paradox at the firm level, showing that IT investment was indeed strongly correlated with higher levels of output. At the country level, a study by Kraemer and Dedrick (1994) of Asia-Pacific countries showed a significant relationship between IT spending and GDP growth. These studies were followed by additional studies at the firm and country level, as summarized in Table 1.

The studies at the firm level confirmed that IT investment was correlated with better performance, at least for the relatively large companies that were included in most studies. They also show that firms with decentralized organizations performed much better than those with centralized organizations. At the country level, most studies came to the interesting conclusion that wealthier industrialized countries showed a positive and significant relationship between IT and productivity, but that there was no evidence of such a relationship for developing countries. Dewan and Kraemer (1998) hypothesized that this gap was due to the low levels of IT investment relative to GDP in developing countries, and to the lack of necessary infrastructure and experience to support effective use of IT (harking back to David's time lag argument).

The final element of the productivity paradox seemed to be put to rest when the U.S. economy experienced a surge of productivity growth in the late 1990s, nearly returning to the levels of the 1950s and 1960s, and supporting a rate of non-inflationary economic growth that had been considered impossible a few years earlier. The timing of this upswing, coming about 40 years after the introduction of business computers and 20 years after the invention of the PC, supported David's argument for a relatively long time lag between the introduction of a technology and its impact on productivity.

Optimists declared the emergence of a New Economy, in which IT-led productivity (and other factors such as globalization) would lead to a long period of inflation-free prosperity. By the end of 2000, however, the collapse of the technology-led NASDAQ

TABLE 1 Summary of IT Payoffs Studies

Study and Date	Sample	Findings
CRITO studies		
Kraemer and Dedrick, 1994	12 Asia-Pacific countries, 1984–1990	IT investment positively correlated with GDP and productivity growth.
Dewan and Kraemer, 1998 and 2000	36 countries	IT capital positively correlated with labor productivity in developed countries. IT capital shows no significant correlation with productivity in developing countries.
Kraemer and Dedrick, 2001	43 countries	Growth in IT investment correlated with productivity growth. Level of IT investment (% of GDP) not correlated with productivity growth.
Melville, 2001	31 industries, 1965–1991	IT returns are positive for U.S. as a whole. Benefit of IT increases with time. Higher IT returns accrue to high growth industries.
Plice, 2001	Six industry sectors for 38 countries	IT capital shows 5–8 times higher ROI than non-IT capital for developed countries.
Gurbaxani, Melville and Kraemer, 1998	1694 firms, 1987–1994	Degree to which employees are networked is positively correlated with firm output.
Gilchrist, Gurbaxani and Town, 2001	Panel of *Fortune* 1000 U.S. firms, 1987–1993	IT productivity is greater in producer firms than in user firms.
Tallon, Kraemer, Gurbaxani, 2000	150 firms, 1998–1999	Greater alignment of IT with business strategy results in greater IT payoffs.
Ramirez, 2001	200+ U.S. firms, 1998	Firm use of employee involvement, TQM and re-engineering enhances IT returns.
Other studies		
Lichtenberg, 1995	U.S. firms 1988–1991	One IS employee can be substituted for six non-IS employees without affecting output.
Hitt & Brynjolfsson, 1997; Brynjolfsson & Hitt, 1997	600+ large U.S. firms, 1987–1994	Firms that adopt IT and decentralized organizations are 5% more productive than those that adopt only one of these.
Brynjolfsson and Yang, 1998	*Fortune* 1000 U.S. firms, 1987–1994	The market value of $1 of IT capital is the same as $10 of other capital stock.
Pohjola, forthcoming	39 countries, 1980–1995	IT investment shows 80% gross returns for OECD countries. No significant returns for developing countries.
Oliner and Sichel, 2000	U.S. 1991–1995 and 1996–1999	IT capital accounts for about 2/3 of the acceleration in productivity growth after 1995.

▪▪▪▪▪▪▪▪▪▪

market and a slowing of the U.S. economy brought out pessimists who said that the New Economy was little more than a brief bubble.

The productivity resurgence of the late 1990s raised two new questions: (1) How much of the resurgence could be attributed to IT use? and (2) Are the gains sustainable, or are they a short-term phenomenon? These questions led to new studies that attempt to measure the relative importance of IT in the productivity gains of the late '90s, and to forecast the staying power of those gains. Most of these studies came to optimistic conclusions on both issues, as economists such as Dale Jorgenson and Tim Bresnahan, and even previous skeptics such as Martin Baily and Daniel Sichel, came to the conclusion that the gains from IT were real and probably sustainable even through an economic downturn.

The only major dissenter is Robert Gordon, who argues that much of the late '90s gains were cyclical, and that virtually all of the productivity gains in the U.S. economy were concentrated in the durable goods sector, particularly the computer and telecommunications equipment industries. Perhaps most important is the opinion of Greenspan (and Fed economists such as Sichel), who apparently has become convinced that IT-led productivity is real and that the economy can sustain higher non-inflationary growth rates than previously thought.

A New Paradox?

Returning to the various studies on IT and productivity, a new paradox appears to have emerged. It is simultaneously one which vexes IT industry executives and challenges the principles of economics as much as the initial productivity paradox. IT industry executives wonder why business executives do not invest much more in IT than they already do, given that IT returns are so large and acknowledged by noted economists and distinguished policymakers alike. Overall, IT investment represents about four percent of GDP, has shown a 12% annual increase on average over the last twenty years, and shows no evidence of decline as business executives continue to report that they plan increased investments.

Reinforcing views of the IT industry, and presenting a challenge to economics, is the claim by Brynjolfsson and others (including a new CRITO study by Plice, 2001), that IT investments not only show high returns, but much higher returns than non-IT investments. These studies argue that there is actually a massive *underinvestment* in IT at both the firm and country level. This suggests that managers and investors may still be acting irrationally, in this case by spending too little on IT and thus foregoing highly profitable investments (or leaving $100 bills laying on the floor, to use one author's expression). If true, economic theory is again in trouble, and boards of directors should be sacking management teams en masse for failing to take advantage of such opportunities.

However, we would argue that claims of massive underinvestment in IT should be viewed cautiously. First, the production function models used in most analyses are only models, which are useful but simplified views of the real world. Also, these models show correlation but not causality. Causality could run in either direction (e.g., successful companies or rich countries invest more in IT because they have the resources to do so), or there may be a third factor that is driving both IT spending and productivity growth (e.g., increasing education levels in the work force, or a shift of the economy to more information intensive activities due to financial deregulation). Thus there should be some hesitance to translate the elasticities in a production function into varying rates of return on investment.

Even if one is willing to take that leap, other factors come into play. First of all, the high rates of depreciation for IT investments mean that *net* returns on investment are much lower than gross returns, and taking into account the large standard deviations in the results of many studies, it is possible that the net returns to IT investments are in line with non-IT investments. Second, the risks involved with IT investments may be larger than non-IT investments, due to rapid technology changes, frequent time and cost overruns, and occasional outright failures of IT projects. These risks are keenly felt by managers whose jobs may be at stake in the case of a well-publicized failure.

If, in spite of all of these factors, firms are still underinvesting in IT, it might be due to the very difficulty of forecasting and measuring the returns on such investments. Few firms that we have interviewed have put in place the means to monitor the returns on specific projects or investments. An Economist Intelligence Unit (1999) survey indicated that only about 50% of business executives use some kind of ROI evaluation for IT projects. Even fewer evaluate projects after implementation. In the absence of measures of

IT returns, IT spending is often treated as a budget item rather than an investment, and capped at some percentage of total revenues. Another factor could be the shortage of IT professionals, which might make it impossible to carry out all of the projects with potentially positive returns. Labor market rigidities and lag times in educational choices can leave skills shortages in place for years (or even decades in some countries).

Finally, it is possible for firms to be investing at an optimal level in IT but still to have underinvestment at the national level. This is because the social returns on investment might be greater than the private returns, as is the case with education and R&D. Brynjolfsson (1995) argues precisely this when he says that IT creates a consumer surplus. If this is the case, there may be an argument for governments to promote IT use through measures such as training programs, accelerated depreciation rates, tax policies that treat software spending as an investment (as the U.S. now does), and liberalization of telecommunications markets to lower the cost of Internet access.

▪ ▪ ▪ What Are the Implications for Managers?

How should executives and managers view the results of these studies as they make their own decisions about IT investments and related management decisions? We recommend the following considerations:

• The original productivity paradox has been resolved. On average IT spending does pay off, and there is no need to fear that technology investments are a systematic waste of scarce resources. Rather, managers should be concerned with whether their own IT investments are paying off, and what they can do to maximize the returns on those investments.

• As for the new paradox, in spite of the optimistic findings about the high returns on IT investments, managers cannot simply give $1 to their favorite IT vendors and expect to get $2 in return. First, the results are an average and not a guarantee of any company's likely return. Second, as many of the studies point out, the most important variables are organizational structure and management practices. In fact, a study by Brynjolfsson and Hitt (1998) found that companies who invest heavily in IT within centralized organizations perform worst of all. Our own studies found that management practices such as IT alignment with business strategy, employee involvement, total quality management and re-engineering, enhance IT returns (Tallon, Kraemer, and Gurbaxani, 2000; Ramirez, 2001). At the case study level, we can compare Dell Computer, which has been very successful investing in IT to refine and extend its well-designed direct business model, to Compaq, which invested heavily in an SAP implementation to improve the performance of its complex indirect business model, with poor results.[2]

• So the biggest concern for managers should be restructuring their organizations and implementing effective management practices. In such an environment, IT investments are likely to be most productive. Figure 1 is a stylized graph which illustrates the relationship between IT investment and productivity, and two ways in which a firm might increase productivity. The trend line shows the average relationship for a large number of firms, as seen in some of the firm level studies in Table 1. But suppose a firm is at point A, meaning it is spending a relatively low share of revenues on IT, and is also below the trend line, meaning it is getting a below average return on its IT investment (probably due to poor management practices). If that firm increases its IT investment without changing its management practices, it is likely to move parallel to the trend line to point C, an expensive way to make modest gains in productivity. On the other

---

[2]For Dell, see Kraemer et al., 2000. For Compaq, see Dedrick and Kraemer, 1999.

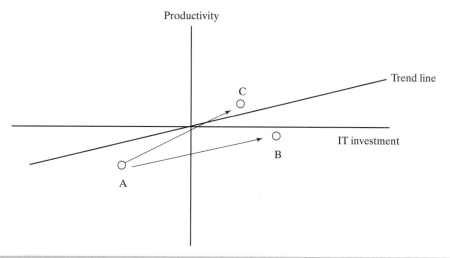

FIGURE 1 Two Paths for Improving Productivity with IT

hand, if it increases IT spending (even to a lesser extent), while making corresponding changes in its structure and processes, it could move to point B—a greater gain at a lower cost. As several interviewees put it, "The key is getting the business processes right. Then the IT might be simple or complex, and the investment small or large, but the payoff will be there in any case because of the joint investment."

- Research points to several managerial practices that are shown to complement IT investments and improve firm performance. Based on our surveys and case studies, and the work of others, we would identify the following lessons for managers:

    - Aligning IT investments with business strategy is critical to success. This has been stated often in the management and IS literature, yet large numbers of firms still suffer from poor alignment of IT and business objectives. A key to achieving alignment is greater interaction between business executives and IT executives—involving IS executives in business planning on the one hand and involving business executives more in IS planning and investment decision making on the other hand (Tallon, 2000).

    - Decentralized organizations are more successful overall, and show better returns on IT investments. The model associated with many successful high-tech companies is the "virtual company," which is decentralized internally and has strong links to external suppliers, customers and business partners. This model allows for flexibility and responsiveness in dynamic markets, and allows firms to focus their attention on core, strategic functions, while leveraging the capabilities of business partners for other activities. IT and e-commerce play a vital role in coordinating the internal and external relationships in such a model.

    - Decentralized IT organizations, coordinated by a strong CIO, appear to be effective in many cases. Two well-known case studies of successful IT use are Dell Computer and Cisco Systems. Each has a strong CIO who is responsible for setting architectural and infrastructure standards, and designating certain application standards across the company. But IT projects are largely staffed and funded within functional departments, which have leeway in determining their own spending priorities and choosing applications relevant to their own operations. Compaq, which formerly was highly centralized, has since moved more responsibility and staffing to individual business units, partly in response to complaints about the centralized, top-down approach taken to the SAP implementation.

- IT is most effective when implemented in conjunction with complementary practices such as total quality management and process redesign. This is the finding of survey research and is reinforced by case studies. For instance, Apple Computer attempted to introduce SAP into a dysfunctional business environment in the mid-1990s, and ended up abandoning the effort. In 1997, Apple jettisoned several product lines and reorganized into a simpler structure, then began implementing SAP with much better results (both in terms of the implementation itself, and performance measures such as inventory turnover).

- Benchmark against other companies to understand where you are in terms of IT investment and performance measures. Most companies have no idea how they rank in relation to their peers and competitors in variables such as IT spending levels, structure of IT costs (e.g., hardware, software, outside services), or perceptions of IT effectiveness on the part of IT managers and other executives. Participating in benchmark studies such as those conducted by CRITO and various research firms can provide baseline data for measuring the effectiveness of IT.

- Develop internal methods to measure returns on IT projects, and to learn from successes and failures in order to reduce risk and improve performance in the future. Such metrics need to be developed by teams that include IT managers and managers of functional units so that they measure outcomes that are most important to business strategies (one aspect of alignment). Measuring the impacts of IT on broad performance variables such as revenue per employee or return on assets is very difficult, so there is a need to develop process-oriented variables that can be translated into dollars and cents impacts. For instance, inventory turnover improvements can be directly attributed to IT investments and related process changes. It should then be possible to translate such an improvement into a measure of cost savings if the cost of carrying inventory can be estimated.

  As projects are completed, it is valuable to gather feedback from IT staff and others involved as to what problems were faced, how they were solved, and what impact the new systems had on specific operations. This information can be documented and made available through knowledge management systems for others in the company to use. There should also be mechanisms in place for people to interact with others outside their usual work groups and share practical information and experience. Such development of institutional knowledge can enhance IT performance and also help better align the IT function with overall business strategy.

▪▪▪ What Are the Implications for the IT Industry?

- Celebrate. The IT industry's products and services do improve customers' productivity, and the resolution of the productivity paradox should encourage IT users to continue to invest. Quietly counter the naysayers (who seem to attract media attention) by seeing that positive results get attention.

- Promote education and learning about the organizational and management practices that enhance the returns from IT investments and decrease the likelihood of failed investments. Realizing returns from IT investments is not a simple matter. It requires appropriate infrastructure, human capabilities and organizational learning. Employing what is known about successful management practices will help to ensure smart investments.

• Tone down the marketing rhetoric that creates unrealistic expectations about IT returns. The IT industry is notorious for hyping every minor innovation as "revolutionary" and for making extravagant claims about the capabilities of its products. Such rhetoric confuses customers and IT professionals alike. More importantly, it sets customers up for disappointment if a product turns out to be simply useful, and leads to skepticism on the part of users. IT companies would do well to heed the admonition "under promise and over deliver."

• Be a model of success for your customers. Show them how you use your own technology to improve your performance. Most economists do not agree with Robert Gordon that nearly all of the productivity gains of the past few years can be attributed to the IT industry itself, but there is no doubt that the IT industry has shown exceptional productivity gains and is a heavy user of IT itself. Companies such as Dell, Oracle, and Cisco promote themselves as models of how to use IT and the Internet effectively. This not only helps sell products, but it puts the whole company on alert that others are watching, so the company must be a model of effective IT use.

BIBLIOGRAPHY

Baily, Martin N. (1986). "What has happened to productivity growth?" *Science*, 234(4775): 443–451.

Bresnahan, Timothy, Erik Brynjolfsson, and Lorin Hitt (2001). "Information technology, work organizational and the demand for skilled labor: Firm-level evidence." *Quarterly Journal of Economics*, in press.

Brynjolfsson, Erik (1993). "The productivity paradox of information technology." *Communications of the ACM*, 36(12): 66–77.

Brynjolfsson, Erik (1995). "The contribution of information technology to consumer welfare." Working paper, MIT Sloan School of Management.

Brynjolfsson, Erik, and Lorin Hitt (1996). "Paradox lost? Firm-level evidence on the returns to information systems spending." *Management Science* 42: 541–558.

Brynjolfsson, Erik, and Lorin M. Hitt (1998). "Beyond the productivity paradox: Computers are the catalyst for bigger changes." *Communications of the ACM* 41(8) August.

Brynjolfsson, Erik, and Lorin M. Hitt (2000). "Computing productivity: Are computers pulling their weight?" Working paper, MIT Sloan School of Management.

David, Paul A. (1990). The Dynamo and the Computer: An Historical Perspective on the Productivity Paradox." *American Economic Review, Papers and Proceedings*. 80: 315–348.

Dedrick, Jason, and Kenneth L. Kraemer (1999). "Information technology in a company in transition: Compaq Computer." Center for Research on Information Technology and Organizations.

Dewan, Sanjeev, and Kenneth L. Kraemer (1998). "International dimensions of the productivity paradox." *Communications of the ACM* 41(8): 56–62.

Dewan, Sanjeev, and Kenneth L. Kraemer (2000). "Information technology and productivity: Evidence from country level data." *Management Science*, 46(4):548–562.

Economist Intelligence Unit (1999). *Assessing the Strategic Value of Information Technology*. New York: EIU.

Gilchrist, Simon, Vijay Gurbaxani, and Robert Town (2001). "Productivity and the PC revolution." Working paper, Center for Research on Information Technology and Organizations.

Gordon, Robert J. (forthcoming). "Does the 'New Economy' measure up to the great inventions of the past?" *Journal of Economic Perspectives*.

Gurbaxani, V., N. Melville, and K. Kraemer (1998). "Disaggregating the Return on Investment to IT Capital," Proceedings of the International Conference on Information Systems, Helsinki, Finland.

Jorgenson, Dale W., and Kevin J. Stiroh (2000). "Raising the speed limit: U.S. economic growth in the information age." May 1. Available from kwhelan@frb.org.

Kraemer, Kenneth L., and Jason Dedrick (1994). "Payoffs from investment in information technology: Lessons from the Asia-Pacific region." *World Development*, 22(12): 1921–1931.

Kraemer, Kenneth L., and Jason Dedrick (2001). "Information technology and productivity: Results and policy implications of cross-country studies." In Pohjola, Matti (ed.) *Information Technology, Productivity and Economic Growth: Implications for Economic Development*. Oxford University Press.

Kraemer, Kenneth L., Jason Dedrick, and Sandra Yamashiro (2000). "Refining and extending the direct model with information technology: Dell Computer Corp." *The Information Society,* 16(1): 5–21.

Lichtenberg, Frank R. (1995). "The output contributions of computer equipment and personnel: A firm level analysis." *Economic Innovations and New Technology* 3: 201–217.

OECD (2000). "The role of information and communications technology in growth performance." In *A New Economy? The Changing Role of Innovation and Information Technology in Growth.* Organisation for Economic Cooperation and Development.

Oliner, Stephen D., and Daniel E. Sichel (2000). "The resurgence of growth in the late 1990s: Is information technology the story?" Washington, DC: Federal Reserve Board.

Melville, Nigel (2001). "Impact of IT investment: An industry analysis." Working paper, Center for Research on Information Technology and Organizations.

Plice, Robert (2001). "A contribution to the empirics of IT returns." Working paper, Center for Research on Information Technology and Organizations.

Pohjola, Matti (2001). "Information technology and economic growth: A cross-country analysis." In Pohjola, Matti (ed.) *Information Technology, Productivity and Economic Growth: Implications for Economic Development.* Oxford University Press.

Roach, Steven, "America's technology dilemma: A profile of the information economy." New York: Morgan Stanley.

Sichel, Daniel E. (1999). "Computers and aggregate economic growth: An update." *Business Economics,* April: 18–24.

Tallon, Paul, Kenneth L. Kraemer, and Vijay Gurbaxani (2000). "Executives' perceptions of the business value of information technology: A process-oriented approach," *Journal of Management Information Systems,* 16(4): 145–173.

Tallon, Paul (2000). "A process-oriented assessment of the alignment of information systems and business strategy: Implications for IT business value." PhD dissertation, University of California, Irvine.

The Computerization of Work: A Social Informatics Perspective*

STEVE SAWYER
ANDREA TAPIA

In this chapter we focus on the computerization of work. We do so because work continues to be a powerful lens for understanding both organizations and society. What we do for work helps to shape, and is also shaped by, the nature and structure of civil society, local community, the organization of industry and government, family relations, and personal identity. That is, and paraphrasing Karl Marx, the means of production (working) help to structure society. To support and enable work we have developed a range of social institutions, corporate organizations, and a wide (and ever-growing) range of computer-based systems. These computer systems include applications such as word processing and office suites, groupware, integrated software development environments, mobile infrastructures, and enterprise systems, to name a few. As we develop in this chapter, the increasing level of computerization (by which we mean the pervasiveness and importance of computer-based systems) in work may be helpful but is often problematic.

Why is it that office workers will use electronic mail extensively but show little interest in systems that control and regulate work flow? Why do organizational leaders face resistance when trying to implement automated production controls? Why are many potentially productivity-enhancing systems used at lower than expected levels once implemented? We write this chapter with the intent that our findings can provide insights into these and similar questions. The findings we report here regarding the computerization of work can be used to guide information systems and work-process designers, organizational decision makers, and scholars in their research.

To help understand current, and guide future, computerization of work efforts, we make two points. First, we make the case that a social informatics perspective provides an excellent conceptual frame from which to view the computerization of work. A social

93

informatics perspective focuses on the social and organizational consequences of using computers. Such a perspective is problem oriented and contextually relevant, viewing work as it occurs. This approach typically highlights unexpected and unintended effects. Second, within this frame we highlight the added insights possible due to taking a functional view of computing. A functional view of computing is one focused on understanding how computers are used. This is often done by studying specific groups of people in specific settings, here represented by reporting on three specific types of work.

To best make our points we organize this chapter into four sections. In the first section we discuss the concepts of work and computerization and provide evidence on the increasing level of computerization in work. In the second section we build on these concepts and more fully develop the social informatics perspective as a framework for understanding the computerization of work. And, in doing this, we also develop our functional conceptualization of computer use. In section three we explain our selection of, and summarize results from, studies of three different forms of work: packaged (vendor) software developers, organizational technologists, and residential real estate agents. In section four we present and discuss three broad findings that our work highlights: (1) functional insights of computerization, (2) the omnipresence of articulation work (the work done to ensure the computer does what is needed or expected), and (3) ongoing power shifts, due in part to computerization in the workplace.

■■■ Work and Computerization

The numbers of people using computers at work continue to grow, as the numbers in Table 1 help make clear. The increasing degree of convergence among computing and communicating systems, evidenced by the merging of cable and computing networks, the rise of mobile networks, and the increasing ability to transmit larger files due to greater bandwidth, underlie this growth in computer use at work. Moreover, the range of computing devices being used is expanding so that the concept of computer time (the time spent in front of a computer terminal) is ever more appropriately seen as "screen time" (the time spent in front of some form of computing device whether it is with a workstation, mobile phone, personal digital assistant, medical diagnostic system, etc.). For example, doctors use computers in the conduct of diagnosis, to scan medical literature, to track patient records, to communicate with others by phone, and perhaps even to play downloaded music on MP3 players while in the operating room. Car mechanics do the same, though they play their music in a different form of "operating room."

These two examples make clear what the 1999 National Research Council (NRC) report on the *Changing Nature of Work* says in detail: The computerization of work can be described in a number of ways. Here we use a three-part division of work and computerization: as directly involved with using computers, as indirectly involved with using computers, and as not using computers (see Table 1). Direct users of computers

TABLE 1 The Computerization of Work in the United States*				
Type	*2000*	*1990*	*1980*	*1970*
Direct: IT sector	4.1	3.5	2.5	1.2
Direct: Users	10.3	8.2	4.1	1.4
Indirect users	69.1	57.7	12.4	7.3
Total number	110.9	102.7	95.8	80.1

*Numbers in millions and approximate.
Sources: NRC, 1999; OECD, 2001; Kling, 1990.

can further be seen as comprising two forms of computerization. One form of direct users of computers in work are those workers who design, develop, install, operate, train, and support computers, computer-based applications, and other forms of information technology (IT). This work is often called the "IT sector." (note 1)

A second form of direct users of computers consists of those workers who use computers in their everyday work. Examples of this form of work computerization include: small business owners running their own accounting and customer tracking software, use of sophisticated diagnostic systems by mechanics in vehicle repair, and real estate agents' extensive use of linked mobile communications and Web-based systems (such as the multiple listing service, or MLS). These workers may be direct users of computer-based systems, but only to support primarily noncomputing elements of their work. The number of less "sophisticated" direct users is also large and increasing. For example, point-of-sale (POS) systems in retail stores are a form of what might be called tertiary computerization. The person (which is increasingly becoming the customer) who is scanning items through the POS terminal is engaged in computerized work, albeit primarily doing data collection. This segment of the population, increasingly seen as the engine of the economy, represents many professional and technical workers such as doctors, engineers, and scientists (Barley 1996; Barley and Kunda 2001; Kling 1990).

Beyond these two forms of directly computerized workers are indirect users of computers at work. Indirect users include many service workers whose work schedules, task allocation, and work monitoring are computerized (via automated scheduling and work tracking systems). For example, many hourly workers are required to clock in and out of their jobs, and this tracking is increasingly done via software, and the records are digitized. Indirect users have traditionally been an underreported and understudied area of computerization, primarily because most studies of computerization focus on high-status primary and secondary users (Clement 1994). However, recent changes to workforce contexts (at least in the use) due to legal and policy changes (such as changes to welfare policies, pressure on immigration polices such as H1-B visa quotas, and globalization pressures) are likely to spur increased attention to this form of work and the effects on it from computerization. Estimates of the number of people who are indirect users of computers at work are obviously difficult to make. The issue, however, is that even nonusers (and we imply that larger numbers of these nonusers) are being affected by computerization of work processes, of which their non-computer-using work is part.

Computing-based work is also expanding. U.S. Bureau of Labor Statistics (2002) data indicate that occupations that rely on using computers are projected to be the fastest growing types of work, with employment expected to have double-digit percentage increases between 2000 and 2010. Working with computers is often lucrative, especially for direct users of computers. Simply, future job opportunities will be excellent for most workers who use computers. Professional and administrative workers enjoy the best future work prospects. This is due in part to a continuing demand for higher (and broader) level skills needed to keep up with changes in computer-based technologies.

This high-level evidence makes clear that the computerization of work is extensive, expanding, and highly valued. And, as Zuboff (1988) made clear, the uses of computing are changing the structural properties of work; mediating workers from the work via sensors used to collect (and make digital) data; the ability to transmit, store, and manipulate data; and the increased expectation that this digitization and decision support is part of all work. Increased automation is the engine behind the steady and extensive productivity improvements in manufacturing, the means to deliver services and products in financial and other knowledge-based industries, and a growing form of automating service work. While simplistic, the computerization of work has been an important basis for the growth of the postindustrial, knowledge-based economy that Porat and others have foretold (e.g., Porat 1977; Bell 1976). More detailed analyses make clear that the computerization of work is a complex, large-scale phenomena (Benner 2002).

Work

Work's pervasiveness helps to mask the conceptual difficulties of explaining what it means. In this chapter we characterize work as the set of roles that a worker enacts and the tasks they are charged to do. This characterization raises the roles of agency and governance, suggesting that an individual's work must be understood relative to what others are doing. McGrath and colleagues note that this perspective implies that a person's social needs and ego status are also tied to the production elements of work (McGrath 1990; McGrath and Hollingshead 1994). In doing this, they make clear that work is more than agency and governance, it is also identity and socialization (Hackman and Oldham 1980; Hackman 1977).

In this chapter we focus on a specific type of working where the worker's knowledge needs (skill, experience, and education) is a much greater component of their effort than is manual labor (heads-in, not hands-on focus). We do so because this so-called knowledge-intensive work is increasingly the focus of computerization efforts. Knowledge work is also characterized by the increased level of interdependence (among tasks, resources and people) and the temporal nature of these interdependencies. Further, knowledge-intensive work is often characterized by abstractions such as what is embodied in production processes that guide worker's tasks and actions. This process abstraction further elevates the issues of work governance because it requires both worker and supervisor to use abstractions. That is, it is difficult to "see" a partially complete software program, so it often described via abstractions such as modules, features, and lines of code.

The issues with control of knowledge, importance of interdependencies, and the required abstractions about work processes means that governance is a contested space in knowledge-intensive work. This is because knowledge disparities often lead to power disparities (White 1981). More generally, the governance of work has always been a contested space (as the rise of industrial engineering, industrial relations, professional management, and federal mediation forums indicate). So, knowledge-intensive work is also a forum for the negotiation (and perhaps transfer) of social power among different types of workers (Zuboff 1988; Kling and Iacono 1984, 2001; Clement 1994; Barley and Kunda 2001).

Computerization of Work

Computerization of work efforts are extensive and ongoing, as we noted earlier, but the effects of computerization are less clear. Often, computerization efforts are conceived as directly affecting work, primarily as a means to either replace labor or increase throughput and quality. Scholars have noted that this simple view of computerizing work is problematic (Attewell 1996, 1998; Roach 1998; Landauer 1996; Kling 1996; Kling and Dunlop 1995).

Computerization of work efforts are typically undertaken for one or more of the following reasons: The first is to use computer-based systems to enable the conduct of current tasks. This is often done by substituting use of computer-based systems for manual processes. The second is to link, and often speed-up, the conduct of work tasks and processes. This is often done through using rules, decision aids, and other representations to assist workers in their tasks. The third is to use it as a means (or platform) to leverage future operations (Ciborra 1996). This platform argument is often phrased as a means for investing in future capabilities. Beyond these high-level goals there is also the continued effort to upgrade, connect, and even repair current systems. This effort may also support other work goals, but often is done to continue allowing for current operations (such as upgrading office suite software to maintain compatibility with other applications).

▄▄▄ A Social Informatics Perspective

Social informatics is the large, diverse, and growing body of research and study that examines social and organizational aspects of computerization, such as the roles of computers in social and organizational change and the ways that the uses of computers are influenced by social and organizational structures and actions (Kling 1999; Sawyer and Eschenfelder 2002; Kling, Sawyer, and Rosenbaum 2003). Social informatics is not a theory or a method. Social informatics provides a set of empirically grounded orienting principles that makes explicit particular elements of the socio-technical perspective regarding developing, deploying, and using computers.

Three broad findings that arise from the empirical basis of social informatics research help focus our attention on work and computerization. The first finding is that computers are embedded in, and also help to shape, the context of their use. For example, Ward, Wamsley, Schroeder, and Robins (2000) investigate the assumption that computerization promotes autonomy, organizational change, and greater responsiveness. Their analysis of computing implementations and uses at the U.S. Federal Emergency Management Administration (FEMA) helps to show how existing control structures within the agency shape budgeting for computers. The resulting systems reinforce existing power structures in the organization. They explain that the Reagan-Bush administration's emphasis on national security led to the allocation of most FEMA computing resources to civilian defense-related projects and the location of the agency information resources management office to be in the civilian defense division. This allocation process left other parts of the agency, including the disaster planning division, suffering for lack of computing resources and unable to deal effectively with major U.S. natural disasters such as Hurricane Hugo, Hurricane Andrew, or the Loma Prieta earthquake. They conclude that government investment in computing does not automatically produce greater responsiveness, as the larger social context shapes the programs in which the computer systems are procured, implemented, and used.

The second common finding drawn from social informatics research is the often paradoxical and unintended effects of computerization. These effects typically vary by both level of analysis and the ways in which computers are used. For example, Adams and Sasse (1999) studied the work practices and environments that contribute to improper use of passwords. Their findings challenge the idea that organizations can achieve greater system security through use of strict security regulations such as periodic forced password changes, multiple unique passwords for different systems, and requirements for non-dictionary-word-based passwords. They suggest that more strenuous security measures may in fact decrease overall security. In explaining their thesis, they describe both contextual and cognitive factors leading to password misuse. For instance, they explain how certain types of work tasks encourage group sharing of passwords, for example, if a workgroup is sharing access to a particular set of files. In these instances, the security mechanisms interfered with the group-based nature of their work. That is, required use of individual passwords interfered with the work done by the employees. The study suggests that security applications developers and departments need to improve their understanding of work practices in order to develop applications and processes that comport with work practices.

In a second example of the paradoxical and unintended consequences of computerization, Walsham (1998) reports how the use of groupware, ostensibly designed to improve communication, may actually harm group interactions. Participating pharmaceutical sales representatives reported that the software did help to achieve one of the intended goals: Use lessened the need for face-to-face communications as certain interactions could be done electronically. Through analysis of the social context surrounding the system, Walsham also reports that reduction in face-to-face time harmed overall group communication by removing opportunities for social networking and relationship building.

The third common finding drawn from social informatics research is that computers and computer-based systems are not neutral artifacts: There is agency in their design and, due to their configurational nature, there is agency in their use. For example, Kraut, Dumais, and Koch (1989) highlight the ways in which computerization of phone operators was designed to reduce the number of human operators, limit the work autonomy of the remaining operators, increase managerial control, and increase throughput (of answered calls). Clement and Halonen (1998) show how computerization efforts can advantage one group over another. They examine how user groups and information systems specialists in a large utility company differed in their conceptualizations of a "good" system and good systems development practice. According to Clement and Halonen, for the users, a good system was customized for different offices such that use required minimum knowledge of office-specific codes. Good development practice required code customization for each office, resulting in the existence of multiple unique versions of the software and a great deal of ad hoc programming. From the information systems perspective, good systems development practice required standardization, version control, and minimal code changes. This approach led to the creation of a less user-friendly system that required more end-user expertise. Clement and Halonen's study also showcases the ways in which different conceptualizations of a good system, and good systems development practices, benefit one group more than another. User groups favored the ad hoc, customized development practices because they resulted in a more flexible, customizable, user-friendly system. The information systems group preferred a more structured, systematized approach to development because it resulted in a more easily manageable software product.

Conceptualizing Computerization

Conceptualizing the connections among doing work and using computers requires a more detailed depiction of computing than is often developed in direct effects models (Kling and Lamb 2000). Direct effects models of computing (and even models of mediating effects) characterize computers as endogenous to their setting of use (MacKenzie 1992). That is, the computer is seen as an external force, perhaps as an agent of change, and the features of this tool are easily understood (both in terms of use and outcomes). This tool view suggests that a computer-based system need not be connected to the scenes of its use (Orlikowski and Iacono 2001). This further suggests a form of stable meaning for a computer: Tools do not change over time, unless these changes are designed into new forms of the tool (such as additional features in new releases of software). The implied stability of meaning inherent in a tool view tends to minimize the changing nature of tool use due to the context of its use.

Alternatively, computers can be seen as they are used: embedded into particular and specific social milieu (Mackenzie 1992; Orlikowski and Iacono 2001; Jackson, Poole, and Kuhn 2002). This social constructivist view suggests that the meaning, value, and ascribed outcomes of computer use are developed in relation to how they function in particular situations and not to the set of features that they designed to support (Jackson, Poole, and Kuhn 2002). This functional perspective suggests that computers are part of a web of meaning that includes the current understanding of both the computer's and people's roles, the rules and norms of use, and the larger work context and incentive structures in which all of these are developed (Taylor 1982, 1986; Kling and Scacchi 1982). This functional view of computerization leads observers and scholars to making explicit the connections (interdependencies) among computer-based systems and the elements of work described previously. (note 2)

A functional conceptualization leads to viewing computing as supporting (1) communication and coordination, (2) access to information, (3) production support, (4) controlling and monitoring, and/or (5) entertainment. That is, computer-based systems can enable people to communicate and coordinate more (and often more easily) with one another (and even with other things like sensors). Computers can function to provide for greater (and perhaps easier) access to data (where access can mean search, retrieval, storage, and manipulation of data). Computers can function to enhance production efforts, such as the use of business rules, automated processing, information processing, and other forms of information processing and computation. People can also use computers to assist them in controlling and monitoring (from mundane things such as password protection to the use of sophisticated sensor networks to monitor people's movements). And, though not often considered in work settings, computers can be used for entertainment and enjoyment. This can range from making pleasing interfaces to the sharing of music and playing online and individual gaming on or via computers. Clearly, combinations of these functions are pos sible (if not certain). That is, the control, production, coordination, and access functions are all enabled by the interdependent systems and common data structures inherent in enterprise systems (e.g., Markus, Axline, Petrie, and Tanis 2000; Markus and Tanis 2000).

▮▮▮ Three Studies of Work

We use the three findings of social informatics as a means to frame the analysis of our empirical studies of work and computerization. As a basis for discussing these findings, we first review the empirical work from studies of packaged software developers, organizational technologists, and residential real estate agents. The conceptual rationale for focusing on these occupations is two-part, as we outline below and summarize in Table 2. First, each represents a distinct form of knowledge work. Second, each group of workers were (and are) using forms of computerization that were (and are) considered important to the ways in which their work will be done. (note 3)

Packaged Software Developers

Our first source of evidence on computerization of work comes from 10 years studying packaged software developers (see Sawyer and Guinan 1998; Sawyer and Carmel 1998; Sawyer 2001a, 2001b, 2000). We focused on software developers because their work requires a high level of abstraction and knowledge about the domain of development, development methods and tools, and group and team processes. We specifically focused our studies of work on developers who made products to sell to the open market (as opposed to internal or sole-source customers), which we call packaged software developers. Examples of packaged software are Peoplesoft, DB2, Word, and Autocad. The rewriting of IRS tax code software is not done by packaged software workers.

Because software is often lauded as the United State's (and perhaps the world's) largest source of innovation (even after the failure of many "dot-com" companies at the end of the twentieth century), we sought to better understand the roles of computerization in packaged software development. We focused on two computerization efforts relative to packaged software developers. The first computerization effort was the push in the early 1990s to use a range of computer-aided software engineering (CASE) tools (Guinan, Cooprider, and Sawyer 1997). (note 4) The second computerization effort, and partially a response to issues with CASE use, was the emphasis on supporting developer coordination needs using e-mail and common access to work

TABLE 2 Forms of Knowledge Work and Computerization

Type of Work	*Knowledge Aspects*	*Computerization Aspects*
Packaged software developers	Design abstractions Design methods and tools Group and team processes	Computer-aided Software Engineering (CASE) tool suites Collaborative computing spaces
Organizational technologists	Work process abstractions Requirements elicitation Project and change management Group and team processes	Enterprise Integration (EI) software Work flow and database components Client/server and distributed computing
Residential real estate agents	Work process abstractions Professional norms and rules Home and community data Professional networks	Multiple listing service (MLS) and Web tools to search the MLS Integrated mobile and land-line telephony and personal digital assistants

products and the use of collaborative rooms to support development (e.g., Sawyer, Farber, and Spillers 1997).

Packaged software developers work for organizations whose primary function is to make software for sale to others via markets (as opposed to internal customers or direct contractual arrangements). With the potential for huge rewards, packaged software development work reflects many attributes of the entrepreneurial legend: individualistic orientation, long work hours, determination, and a willingness to take on risk. Packaged software development organizations are designed around highly individualistic work practices. Rugged individuals—software cowboys—are respected, even revered, in most packaged software organizations. The individualistic, rule-abhorring developer is not as attractive to most traditional (internal-to-an organization) software development departments who typically seek process-oriented workers.

Packaged software firms function in an environment of intense time-to-market pressure relative to IS development efforts. This is due, in part, to packaged software being such a high-profile industry today under continual scrutiny by investors, stockholders, Wall Street analysts, and hundreds of technology media sources. Success is typically measured by profits and revenues, market share, and good product reviews in trade journal and trade shows (such as COMDEX). Most traditional development efforts are measured by user satisfaction, user acceptance, quality, and cost. Developers in packaged software firms are in "line" positions, whereas the in-house software developers are in "staff" positions. In packaged software shops, developers are the primary producers of revenue for the company. Thus, developer needs are central to production.

To support developer individualism and product innovation needs in packaged software development the product itself is the focal point and the process, with its engineering orientation, is both secondary and less mature. For example most packaged software firms rely on software development guidelines or templates, not strict development methods. Software product teams tend to be small, loosely controlled in terms of work, though product design is often carefully controlled by two or three "core" team members. Teams tend to be product loyal over time and exhibit high cohesion among members.

Organizational Technologists

Our second source of evidence on the computerization of work is drawn from 6 years studying organizational information technologists (see Eschenfelder, Heckman, and Sawyer 1998; Sawyer and Southwick 2002; Sawyer 2001b). By organizational technologists, we mean the information systems staff of an organization. This includes the programmers, network administrators, database specialists, systems analysts, trainers, end-user support staff, technical management, and consultants and contractors used to support the organization's computing infrastructures, systems, and applications. These people work inside larger organizations to support the development, implementation, operations, and support users of the organization's computing infrastructures.

We studied organizational technologists because, in the late 1990s, their work began shifting from developing, maintaining, and operating internally constructed systems to that of enabling the acquisition, implementation, and operations of vendor-developed enterprise resource planning (ERP) systems (Markus and Tannis 2000). The computerization of work efforts included both the changes to the technologists' work (and their work focus) and the ways that these systems change the work of those who were to use these integrated production and control systems.

The changes to organizational technologists' work increased their need to understand work processes at an abstract level and to focus less on technical operations and more on user requirements and the ways in which the ERP systems would enable user needs. This change increased the need for organizational technologists to lead and manage project (and organizational) change and to work with vendors, consultants, and the line workers. The technical change to organizational technologists' work has been just as dramatic. They have had to learn how to work with new technologies such as distributed and client/server computing (instead of mainframes), software packages (instead of software languages), and integrated applications based on work flow and database connectivity (instead of stand-alone modules).

The basis of ERP is an integrated set of application modules connected to a common database. These modules provide partial automation support for business processes (such as ordering, finance, payroll-HR, product process flow, etc.). The common database allows for improved worker and managerial control, amplifies the focus on (production) processes, and improves access to data. Improved coordination and communication are not the intent of ERP. However, the process orientation and level of effort needed to implement such large systems demand extensive collaboration and communication (Sawyer and Southwick 2002).

In the organizations that we studied, the central information technology group promoted extensive user involvement, often leading to the forming of dozens, if not hundreds, of user/technologist committees to assist in implementing the new distributed computing systems. Most of these committees were led by line, not technology, people. A second aspect of the decentralization of the technologists was the creation of a distributed technical staff program. Distributed technical staff serve as network managers, troubleshooters, trainers, and local computer "gurus" (Eschenfelder, Heckman, and Sawyer 1998).

ERP system implementations are typically conceived as a multiproject effort. The order and priority of these projects is defined by negotiating among key stakeholders such as senior line managers, technology vendors, executive leaders, and internal technologists. The criteria that helped to structure these negotiations included user/functional needs, availability of needed software, political gain, and resources. Selecting a vendor-provided software (the ERP) forced the organizational technologists to shift their focus from mainframe to client/server computing and comprehend the new, interdependent, enterprisewide modules and data architectures.

Organizational technologists' work has been affected in at least two ways: (1) how workers view the tasks they do and (2) how they interact with others. Workers' tasks, for example, are more interdependent, have higher levels of visibility, greater variety, less autonomy in selection (i.e., often they must respond to what others have done), and demand a broader variety of skills to complete. This is a difficult adjustment for many because they had become familiar with the relative simplicity (and monochronicity) of supporting a stable (mainframe) technology.

Technologists are also responsible for more tasks. Because the tasks demand new ways of sequencing and are more interconnected, workers are having to participate in more task sharing, where many people contribute to completing one task. Thus, the worker's day is often more fragmented (polychronic) as they constantly connect with others to complete these shared tasks.

Residential Real Estate Agents

Our third source of evidence about the computerization of work is drawn from 4 years studying residential real estate agents (Crowston, Sawyer, and Wigand 2001; Sawyer, Crowston, Wigand, and Allbritton 2003). We focused on this form of work for several reasons. The work of residential real estate agents is information intensive, based on a distributed and emergent work process, has unique contractual structures such as agency relationship among agents, brokers, local agencies and national franchises, and is undergoing rapid computerization.

The rapid computerization is reflected in changes to the technologies of access, coordination, and production. For example, relative to production, in the late 1990s much of the information contained in their databases of houses (known as the multiple listing service, or MLS) was made available on the Web. This effort also centralized access to the MLS data as MLS franchises are local, but common access is done through a Web portal using sophisticated query and tracking tools to search and monitor the MLS. At the same time, rapid improvements in mobile phone technologies allowed agents to integrate land-line phones (and voice mail) with their mobile phones to link these to electronic lists of buyers and sellers, and to manage all of this with little technical support (or specific technical know-how).

Residential real estate agents' work is transaction based and is bounded by a set of legal and regulatory codes. It is focused on moving information around and relies on the agent's ability to keep track of an abstract and very contingent process that requires extensive coordination of a range of people. Agents serve as intermediaries between buyers and sellers of houses, providing both information and process knowledge (the sale of a house is culminated in its "closing," though the actual steps in the closing process are contingent on a range of factors).

The role of real estate agents is to bring together the seller and buyer of a property and to advise both of these principals, independently, regarding their responsibilities in the transaction. In the United States two agents are typically involved in a transaction. The listing (or seller's) agent assists a seller in marketing a property by helping to determine an asking price, guiding the seller to make the property attractive, advertising it, and screening potential buyers. When offers to buy the property are received, the seller's agent advises the seller in the negotiations and details of the transaction. The second (typically known as the buyer's) agent helps a buyer find suitable properties among those offered for sale and narrow the selection to a specific property. The buyer's agent advises the buyer on the purchase. Thus, the typical house sale/purchase has the buyer and seller negotiating with the intermediation of the buyer's agent and the seller's agent.

In most cases, the seller pays both agents, and this is part of the closing settlement. When listing a property, the seller contracts to pay the seller's agent a commission, usually a percentage of the sales price, when the transaction closes. These commissions are typically in the range of 5 to 7 percent of the value of the property. (note 5) In all states of the United States, agents are affiliated with a real estate firm that employs, or is headed by, a broker. Real estate firms range in size from a single agent-broker to dozens of agents along with clerical and managerial staff. Some agencies are franchises of national chains (e.g., Better Homes and Gardens or RE/Max); others are local. Agents enter into listing contracts on behalf of the broker, get a variety of services from the firm and, in return, give the firm a share of their commissions. These relationships are contractual, as agents are independent contractors rather than employees of the agency. A highly productive agent has the bargaining power to negotiate for additional services or a more favorable division of the commission. In other words, the organizational structure of the real estate industry is primarily contractual, agents essentially act as "companies of one." Independent agent-brokers provide their own resources.

▮▮▮ Findings, Discussion, and Implications

The focus in this section is on the commonalities regarding the ways in which context, uses of Information and Communication Technologies (ICT), and the effects of these uses can be seen across levels of analysis. In doing this, we acknowledge that these findings are not orthogonal, rather, they can be interdependent, leading to possibly reinforcing or contradictory observations in specific settings.

From our work we observe that:

1. *A functional view of computerization provides insight into how changes to work might be better understood*. The values of, and responses to, computerization of work are similar if compared by function.

2. *Articulation is an omnipresent part of the computerization of work*. Articulation appears to be a constant, and perhaps growing, component of computerized work. This contradicts the simple view that articulation is a transient effect of learning to use and make use of a new computer-based system.

3. We note that computerization, and particularly the increased emphasis on identifying and semiautomating work processes, leads to extended conflicts regarding *power shifts among different occupations that must work together*.

Functional Insights on Computerization

A functional explanation of work's computerization provides additional insight into the effects of using computer-based systems. In Table 3 we summarize these insights. In all three forms of work reported on here, the functional uses of the control elements of the various types of computer-based systems are limited. Moreover, control elements of computer-based systems are typically underappreciated and often actively resisted. Packaged software developers did not like the constraints of version control, the organizational technologists did not like project-control software, and real estate agents valued software that allowed them to monitor people visiting their properties or interacting with their Web sites. Agents did not like franchise-level monitoring of their sales and listings.

In all three work settings, production elements of the computer-based systems were often co-opted in use. That is, their uses in practice were different from the intended (or designed-in) uses. Software developers made very selective uses of which production elements they used, though their work is enacted through programming environments and software-based development tools. Organizational technologists relied on a range of diagnostic, diagramming, and documentation tools. Simple digital forms were the primary production technologies used by real estate agents.

TABLE 3 Summary of the Functional Perspective on Computing

Function of Computing	*Findings*
Control	Limited use, often resisted. This contrasts with managerial perspective on the value of computing for control.
Production	Co-opted in use, not used as expected by designers or managers. Shaped by local use.
Coordination	Extensively used and valued. Often features of systems are co-opted for coordination functions.
Access	Extensively used, tied to both production and coordination.
Entertainment	Not explored in this study.

All three groups of workers used computer-based systems to access data. Reports, code libraries, and data (of all sorts) were often sought, used, and even stored. Software developers relied on the code repository of the CASE tool and created shared spaces for their work in the collaborative work space. The ERP is predicated on simplified data access and powerful query and reporting tools. The MLS and the search tools provided even greater access for both real estate agents and customers (albeit at different levels of access).

Coordination elements were used by all workers and were often seen as primary functional value of the system being used. All three sets of workers used e-mail often, leaving the e-mail application running continuously. Packaged software developers also coordinated via notes in code and on documents, using these as notes and as tracking documents. Organizational technologists made extensive use of Web pages (for meeting minutes and updates), listservs, and the telephone. Real estate agents were the most extensive coordinators; cell phones, faxes, and e-mail were considered indispensable. This is possibly because much of their work is about coordination and communication.

Omnipresent Articulation

The second common finding is the additional effort needed to use any computer-based system. Too often this extra work is conceived as merely a transient phenomena tied to implementation—a training and learning cost. Clearly implementation is a period of added articulation. However, our evidence is that any computer-based system adds work. That is, even if a computerization effort alters or removes some work, it adds other work. The added articulation work we observed includes:

• Effort needed to develop work-arounds and extra time needed for coordination (meetings, calls, and tracking of status) to oversee processes and data, work out problems, and plan (e.g., Suchman 1996, 2000).

• Increased cognitive loads placed on workers. This is often due to clumsy computerization. That is, as work pressures increased (perhaps due to temporal pacing), computerized systems often demanded more attention from their users or failed to work when needed (e.g., Woods and Patterson 2001).

Examples of the added efforts to develop work-arounds are evident in the organizational technologists' work. They struggled, on a daily basis, to adjust the functionality of the ERP to meet the needs of line workers, altering work practices, changing configurations, rewriting reports, and even developing PC-based databases and spreadsheets to supplement the missing features of the ERP. Software developers were also constantly working around the limitations of their programming environments. Given the need to work together, they even knocked down walls and reconfigured their computers so they could more easily work from a common screen (Sawyer, Farber, and Spillers 1997). A substantial portion of a real estate agent's job is coordination and articulation as they work to close a house. Their reliance on cell phones and mobile devices is reflected in their frustration when the phone does not work. As an aside, when computerization is conceived as a means to increase work productivity, articulation work is even more disappointing as it is often not expected or budgeted. Thus, the extra work is being done even as the expectations are that work should be easier.

Power Shifting

The third common finding is that the computerization of work tends to lead to shifts of power. These power shifts often center on work structuring (or restructuring), changes to the locus of decision rights, rights of access, and/or the use of resources. These all play parts in the increased focus on governance of computer-system-dependent processes. In essence, these new semiautomated processes are a new form of organizing. For example, the bulk of computerization efforts in software development were to automate elements of the software development process. Organizational technologists participated in an increased automation of the processes of implementation even as that effort was designed to increase the level of automation in the organization's work processes. Real estate agents were increasingly using computer-based systems to automate elements of their processes of finding clients (both buyers and sellers) and selling houses.

Examples of power shifts shaped the work changes from all three of our domains. Software developers strove to collaborate, even as they resisted managerial monitoring. Organizational technologists tried to retain oversight of the technical infrastructure and the project order, even as users and vendors gained more power. Real estate agents worked to differentiate their services and minimize the likelihood that they would be disintermediated (Sawyer, Crowston, Wigand, and Allbritton 2003).

From a computerization perspective, we further note that in these efforts, control and production functions were either underused or used differently than originally intended (or designed). This was especially the case if these functions were focused on controlling the worker. However, coordination and access functions were valued, used (!), and often appropriated for use by workers in ways not expected or intended (Eschenfelder and Sawyer 1998; Orlikowski 1993).

Another form of power shifting is the use of computer-based systems to do things unimagined at first (Sproull and Kiesler 1991). This is in contrast to first-order (simple automation) and second-order (new ways of working) effects. For example, the development of team rooms by software developers and the shifting of house searches to buyers (via searching the online MLS) suggest that computerization of work efforts can have unintended and unforeseen positive effects. This is likely due to the pressures of articulation forcing workers into having to confront, domesticate, and resolve the computerization efforts effects on their work. That is, long-term computerization efforts are socially shaped, and the systems are configurable (Quintas 1994; Fleck 1994).

▪▪▪ Conclusion

In this chapter we have focused on the computerization of work. In doing this, we have shown that the computerization of work is intimately linked to the larger social context in which these efforts take place. We have also shown that a social informatics perspective provides a useful lens to help explore this cross-level relationship. Further, we developed a functional characterization of computerization and drew from our own empirical work to show how this characterization provides increased intellectual precision about computerization of work efforts. Finally, we have identified three common findings about the computerization of work. As we summarize in the last few paragraphs, these findings can serve as tentative propositions for researchers in this area, as a set of design parameters for computing systems developers, and as a set of guidelines for those involved in leading, managing, and supporting work.

For researchers in this area, the findings developed from our overview of computerization of work studies lead to three suggestions for future research. First, that the contextualist and sociotechnical orientation provided by social informatics is an important conceptual lens to guide future research efforts. Second, the functional characterizations of computing provides added insight into the possible roles of, and likely responses to, computer-based systems. Third, the three common findings are worthy propositions for future empirical testing.

For designers, there are at least two pieces of guidance that can be derived from the findings reported in this chapter. First, systems design must be rooted in a deep understanding of the work that the system is designed to enable or support. Second, characterizing computing as a set of functions suggests that designers work to relate how particular features of their system map to user functions, and, as a part of that, to amplify the systems coordination and access functions, while minimizing the control and production aspects. For systems designed to enable control and production, this further suggests that linking these functions with coordination and access functionality may lead to a higher level of acceptance and use. Although the findings from the work summarized in this chapter do not speak directly to entertainment functionality, we speculate that this is an increasingly important (or at least opportunistic) element to explore in future systems designs.

For those involved in leading, managing, and supporting work, the findings from this study provide two insights. First, and analogous to the advice we provide to designers, it is critical to understand the contextualized and often abstracted patterns of process that underlie knowledge-intensive work. Second, it is important to understand that the value propositions, acceptance, and uses of new computing systems can be better understood as differing by function. This understanding can guide implementation plans and future work design. For example, computerization of work efforts that allow for increased coordination, access (and possibly entertainment), functionality are likely to be more readily received than are those that focus on control and production. If control and production are the important functions being pursued in computerization of work efforts, they may be more acceptable to the workers if these goals are intimately tied to coordination and access (and possibly entertainment) functionality.

Returning to how we began this chapter, the attention and interest in computerization of work continues to be offset by the remarkably large number of these efforts that substantially underperform in practice. The way forward is not tied to developments of new and currently unknown new computing technologies as much as it is intimately tied to both a better understanding of the complex and contextual nature of work and to a better way to think of, describe, and design the computerized artifacts that might support work.

ENDNOTES

1. In reporting these numbers, we echo the concerns about estimating workforce numbers. See the NRC monograph and Kling (1990) for extended discussions on the problems with estimating workforce numbers.

2. This explicit relationship reflects the socio-technical nature of work. That is, the complex interdependencies among the technical elements of work (such as the uses of computers) and the roles, norms, actions, and values of the people doing the work are difficult

to treat independently. Socio-technical approaches to understanding work were first developed in the Tavistock tradition (Mumford 2000). Various forms of socio-technical theorizing such as social construction of technology (SCOT), social-shaping of technology (SST), and network models (such as Hughes' reverse salients and Latour's actor network theory) have been developed to guide the analysis of socio-technical relations (Mackenzie and Wacjman 1999).

3. Two pragmatic reasons further guided selecting these three forms of work and computerization. First, the contexts and the uses of computers were interesting to us. Given the extended field work that work studies entail and the multiyear nature of the work, our enthusiasm for doing this research hinged, in part, on our personal interests. Second, gaining access (both physical and legal) to sites and people in those sites led us away from some forms of work (such as biotechnology) simply because there were no biotechnology firms nearby.

4. These are also known as integrated programming environments (IPE) and integrated development environments (IDE).

5. Although exact figures are not kept, using 6 percent as a base commission, in 1998 total commissions exceeded $38 billion. In 1999 this grew to be greater than $41 billion. Current exact sales price and sales volume data are available online from the National Association of Realtors at http://nar.realtor.com/research/home.htm.

REFERENCES

Adams, A., and Sasse, M. A. (1999). "Users are not the enemy." *Communications of the ACM, 42* (12), 40–46.

Attewell, P. (1996). "Information technology and the productivity challenge." In *Computerization and Controversy*, Rob Kling (ed.). San Diego, CA: Academic Press.

Attewell, P. (1998). Research on Information Technology Impacts. Available online at www.nap.edu/readingroom/books/esi/appb.html#attewell.

Barley, S. (1996) "Technicians in the workplace: Ethnographic evidence for bringing work into organization studies." *Administrative Science Quarterly, 41,* 404–441.

Barley, S., and Kunda, G. (2001). "Bringing work back in." *Organization Science 12* (1), 76–95.

Bell, D. (1976). *The Coming of Post-Industrial Society: A Venture in Social Forecasting*. New York: Basic Books.

Benner, C. (2002). *Work in the New Economy*. Malden, MA: Blackwell.

Bureau of Labor Statistics. (2002). "*Labor Force Statistics from the Current Population Survey.*" U.S. Department of Labor. Available online at http://data.bls.gov/cgi-bin/surveymost. Accessed December 12, 2002.

Carmel, E., and Sawyer, S. (1998). "Packaged software development teams: What makes them different?" *Information Technology & People 11* (1), 7–19.

Ciborra, C. (1996). "The platform organization: Recombining strategies, structures, and surprises." *Organization Science 7* (2), 103–118.

Clement, A. (1994). "Computing at work: Empowering action by 'low-level users.'" *Communications of the ACM 37* (1), 52–63.

Clement, A., and Halonen, C. (1998). "Collaboration and conflict in the development of a computerized dispatch facility." *Journal of the American Society for Information Science, 49*, 1090–1100.

Crowston, K., Sawyer, S., and Wigand, R. (2001). "The interplay between structure and technology: Investigating the roles of information technologies in the residential real estate industry." *Information Technology &People* 14 (2), 163–183.

Eschenfelder, K.R. (2003). "The importance of articulation work to agency content management: Balancing publication and control." Proceedings of the 36th Annual Hawaii International Conference on Systems Sciences, IEEE Computer Society Press.

Eschenfelder, K., Heckman, R., and Sawyer, S. (1998). "The distribution of computing: The knowledge markets of distributed technical support specialists." *Information Technology and People 11* (2), 84–103.

Fleck, J. (1994). "Learning by trying: The implementation of configurational technology." *Research Policy 23*, 637–651.

Guinan, P., Cooprider, J., and Sawyer, S. (1997). "The effective use of automated application development tools." *IBM Systems Journal 36* (1), 124–139.

Hackman, J. (1977). "Work Design." In *Improving Life at Work*, R. Hackman and J. Suttle (eds.), Santa Monica, CA: Goodyear, 96–162.

Hackman, J., and Oldham, J. (1980). *Work Redesign*. Boston: Addison-Wesley.

Jackson, M., Poole, M. S., and Kuhn, T. (2002). "The social construction of technology in studies of the workplace." In *The Handbook of New Media*, L. Lievrouw and S. Livingstone (eds.), London: Sage, 236–253.

Kling, R. (1999). "What is social informatics, and why does it matter?" *D-Lib Magazine, 5* (1). Available at www.dlib.org:80/dlib/january99/kling/01kling.html. Accessed February 12, 2001.

Kling, R. (1996). *Computerization and Controversy: Value Conflicts and Social Choices*, 2nd ed. San Diego, CA: Academic Press

Kling, R. (1990). "More information, better jobs? Occupational stratification and labor-market segmentation in the United States' information labor force." *The Information Society 7* (2), 77–107.

Kling, R., and Dunlop, C. (1995). "Controversies about computerization and the character of white collar worklife." *The Information Society 9* (2), 1–29.

Kling, R., and Iacono, S. (2001). "Computerization movements: The rise of the Internet and distant forms of work." In J. Yates and J. Van Maanen (eds.), *Information Technology and Organizational Transformation: History, Rhetoric, and Practice.* Thousand Oaks, CA: Sage Publications, 93–136.

Kling, R., and Iacono, S. (1984). "The control of information systems developments after implementation." *Communications of the ACM 27* (12), 1218–1226.

Kling, R., and Lamb, R. (2000). "IT and organizational change in digital economies: A socio-technical approach." In B. Kahin and E. Brynjolfsson (ed.), *Understanding the Digital Economy—Data, Tools and Research:* Cambridge, MA: MIT Press.

Kling, R., Rosenbaum, H., and Sawyer, S. (2003). *Information Technologies in Human Contexts: Learning from Organizational and Social Informatics.* Medford, NJ: Information Today.

Kling, R., and Scacchi, W. (1982). "The web of computing: Computer technology as social organization." *Advances in Computers 21,* 1–90.

Kraut, R., Dumais, S., and Koch, S. (1989) "Computerization, productivity, and the quality of work-life." *Communications of the ACM 32* (2), 220–228.

Landauer, T. (1996). *The Trouble with Computers: Usefulness, Usability, and Productivity.* Cambridge, MA: MIT Press.

Latour, B. (1987). *Science in Action: How to Follow Scientists and Engineers Through Society.* Cambridge, MA: Harvard University Press.

Mackenzie, D. (1992). "Economic and sociological explanation of technical change." In R. Coombs, P. Saviotti, and V. Walsh (eds.), *Technological Change and Company Strategy.* London: Academic Press, 26–48.

MacKenzie, D., and Wajcman, J. (1999). *The Social Shaping of Technology.* Philadelphia: Open University Press.

Markus, M., Axline, S., Petrie, D., and Tanis, C. (2000). "Learning from adopters' experiences with ERP: Problems encountered and success achieved." *Journal of Information Technology 15* (4), 245–266.

Markus, M., and Tanis, C. (2000). "The enterprise experience: From adoption to success." In *Framing the Domains of IT Research: Glimpsing the Future Through the Past,* R. Zmud (ed.), Cincinnati, OH: Pinnaflex Educational Resources, 173–207.

McGrath, J. (1990). "Time matters in groups." In J. Galeghar, R. Kraut, and C. Egido (eds), *Intellectual Teamwork, Social and Technological Foundations of Cooperative Work.* Hillsdale, NJ: Lawrence Earlbaum Associates, 23–61.

McGrath, J., and Hollingshead, A. (1994). *Groups Interacting with Technology.* Thousand Oaks, CA: Sage.

Mumford, E. (2000). "Socio-technical design: An unfulfilled promise or a future opportunity?" In R. Baskerville, et al. (eds.), *Organizational and Social Perspectives on Information Technology.* New York: Kluwer.

National Research Council. (1999). *The Changing Nature of Work.* Washington, D.C.: National Academy Press.

OECD. (2001). *Organization of Economic Cooperation and Development, Science, Technology and Industry Scorecard, 2001: Towards a Knowledge-Based Economy.* Organization of Economic Cooperation and Development, Report 92-2001-02-1-2987.

Orlikowski, W. (1993). "Learning from Notes: Organizational Issues in Groupware Implementation." *The Information Society 9* (3), 237–250.

Orlikowski, W., and Barley, S. (2001). "Technology and institutions: What can research on information technology and research on organizations learn from each other?" *MIS Quarterly 25* (2), 145–165.

Orlikowski, W., and Iacono, S. (2001). "Desperately seeking the 'IT' in IT research—A call to theorizing the IT artifact." *Information Systems Research 12* (2), 121–124.

Porat, M. (1977). The Information Economy: Definition and Measurement United States Office of Technology Special Publication 77–12(1), Washington, D.C.: Department of Commerce, Office of Telecommunications.

Quintas, P. (1994). "Programmed innovation: Trajectories of change in software development." *Information Technology & People 7* (1), 25–47.

Roach, S. (1998). "No productivity boom for workers." *Issues in Science and Technology 14* (2), 49–56.

Sawyer, S., Crowston, K., Wigand, R., and Allbritton, M. (2003). "The social embeddedness of transactions: Evidence from the residential real estate industry." *The Information Society 18* (1), 1–21.

Sawyer, S. (2001a). "Effects of conflict on packaged software development team performance." *Information Systems Journal 11* (2), 155–178.

Sawyer, S. (2001b). "Information systems development: A market-oriented perspective." *Communications of the ACM 44* (11), 97–102.

Sawyer, S. (2000). "Packaged software: Implications of the differences from custom approaches to software development." *European Journal of Information Systems 9* (1), 47–58.

Sawyer, S., and Eschenfelder, K. (2002). "Social informatics: Perspectives, examples, and trends." B. Cronin (ed.), In *Annual Review of Information Science and Technology.* Medford, NJ: Information Today Inc./ASISI, 427–465.

Sawyer, S., Farber, J., and Spillers, R. (1997). "Supporting the social processes of software development teams." *Information Technology & People 10* (1), 46–62.

Sawyer, S., and Guinan, P. (1998). "Software development: Processes and performance." *IBM Systems Journal 37* (4), 552–569.

Sawyer, S., and Southwick, R. (2002). "Temporal issues in ICT-enabled organizational change: Scenes from an ERP implementation." *The Information Society 17* (4), 263–280.

Sproull, L., and Kiesler, S. (1991). *Connections: New Ways of Working in the Networked Organization.* Cambridge, MA: MIT Press.

Suchman, L. (2000). Human/Machine Reconsidered. Working paper, Department of Sociology, Lancaster University. Available online at www.comp.lancs.ac.uk/sociology/soc0401s.html. Accessed December 5, 2002.

Suchman, L. (1996). "Supporting articulation work." In R. Kling (ed), *Computerization and Controversy,* 2nd ed. San Diego: Academic Press.

Walsham, G. (1998). "IT and changing professional identity: Micro-studies and macro-theory." *Journal of the American Society for Information Science 49* (12), 1081–1089.

Ward, R., Wamsley, G., Schroeder, A., and Robins, D. B. (2000). "Network organization development in the public sector: A case study of the Federal Emergency Management Administration (FEMA)." *Journal of the American Society for Information Science 51* (7) 1018–1032.

White, W. (1981) "Where do markets come from?" *American Journal of Sociology 87* (3), 517–547.

Woods, D., and Patterson, E. (2001). "How unexpected events produce an escalation of cognitive and coordinative demands." In P. Hancock and P. Desmond (eds.), *Stress, Workload, and Fatigue* Mahwah, NJ: Lawrence Earlbaum, 290–302.

Zuboff, S. (1988). *In the Age of the Smart Machine.* New York: Basic Books.

Computer-Based Performance Monitoring

JOEY F. GEORGE
PAMELA E. CARTER

⚎ Introduction

Due to technological advances and decreasing technology costs during the 1980s, organizational managers began utilizing information technologies in a widespread fashion to increase the productivity and efficiency of their enterprises. One such information technology, computer performance monitoring, was used by an increasing number of organizations during the mid to late 1980s. Computer monitoring is the practice of collecting, storing, analyzing, and reporting information regarding employee activities or performance directly through their use of computerized systems (Nebeker and Tatum 1993; U.S. Office of Technology Assessment 1987). Today, many organizations monitor employees through computerized systems. Estimates vary on the extent of computer monitoring in the workplace, but the trend seems to be growing. The now defunct Office of Technology Assessment reported in 1987 that approximately 25 to 35 percent, or 4 to 6 million, U.S. clerical employees and 1 to 2 million professional, technical, and managerial employees were subject to computer monitoring in the workplace. Fourteen years later, the American Management Association (2001) reported that 82 percent of member organizations surveyed reported using electronic monitoring and surveillance. Organizational managers, when justifying the use of computer monitoring, point to benefits such as improved performance measurement objectivity, accuracy, and consistency; improved feedback to employees; and increased overall productivity.

However, there are also strong critics of computer monitoring (cf. Clement 1984; Marx 1985; 9to5 1990; Nussbaum 1992; Smith, Carayon, Sanders, Kim, and LeGrande 1992). Negative impacts related to employee quality of work life issues, such as higher levels of negative health and stress effects, dehumanizing and unsatisfying work environments, and privacy invasion, are often attributed to computer monitoring. Unfortunately, given the prevalence of computer monitoring in organizations, there is comparably little academic research published on the effects of computer monitoring (see Ambrose and Adler 2000, for a review). Additionally, there have been few published field studies of computer performance monitoring, and there have been no published field studies that compare the quality of work life of computer-monitored and non-computer-monitored clerical employees.

In this chapter, we begin by defining computer-based monitoring, followed by a discussion of how monitoring has traditionally been portrayed in the popular press. The next section presents some detailed information about monitoring and how it is actually implemented as a business practice in a set of five organizations. Monitored workers in these sites are then compared to nonmonitored workers in similar jobs. The chapter ends with some concluding thoughts.

▪▪▪ What Is Computer-Based Monitoring?

Computer-based monitoring is the use of computerized systems to automatically collect information about how an employee is performing his or her job. Although theoretically anyone who uses a computer at work can be subject to such monitoring, there is a specific range of jobs to which monitoring practices have historically been applied. These jobs include airline reservation agents, telephone operators, data entry clerks, telemarketing clerks, and insurance claims clerks. They also include some stock brokers and computer programmers.

Computer-based monitoring is not a single practice. In fact, there are at least three different forms of computer-based monitoring. Lund (1991) distinguishes between two different categories of monitoring: computerized work performance monitoring systems (CWPMS) and what he calls "service observation." CWPMSs typically take two different forms. Most clerical workers whose work is monitored usually use both a computer system and a telephone system to perform their daily work tasks. Either the computer system or the telephone system can function as a CWPMS. In the first instance, the worker may use the computer system to take customer orders, and the CWPMS component is used to record such information as the number of orders taken or the sales amount of each order. In the second instance, the telephone system used to talk with customers can also be used to collect information on the number of calls taken, the average length of the calls, the time available to take calls, and so on. Service observation refers to having someone, usually a supervisor or a trainer, listen to and/or record phone conversations between employees and customers.

As Lund (1991) points out, it is important to distinguish between organizations where performance information is used as the basis for pay increases and promotions and those where the information is used to discipline employees who are not working at established levels. Just as monitoring consists of several different distinct practices, organizations that use monitoring have the ability to use the information they gather in many different ways.

▪▪▪ How Is Computer-Based Monitoring Portrayed?

Most popular accounts of monitoring come from what Rebecca Grant calls the advocacy literature (Grant 1990), that is, books and articles written by people who advocate the restricted use or outright abolition of computer-based monitoring practices. Most of the evidence provided in the advocacy literature comes from anecdotes or interviews with a handful of select people.

Most of the advocacy literature reports on monitoring are based on conversations with one or two people or on studies conducted in one or few organizations, with one or few informants. Findings from these limited samples are then ascribed to all employees who are monitored and all organizations that employ monitoring. The advocacy literature rarely reports that monitoring may affect people differentially. Instead, articles typically report that whatever monitoring does to people, it does to all of them in the same way. Similarly, the advocacy literature rarely reports that monitoring practices can have any positive value or that some employees may actually like being monitored by a computer. Nor are any distinctions made between monitoring practices within or between organizations. Rather, computer-based monitoring is portrayed as a uniform practice, always with the same (negative) effects, wherever it is used.

The general conclusion from the advocacy literature on employee attitudes toward computer-based monitoring is that workers uniformly dislike these practices, as reflected in the following quote from a clerical worker as stated in a 9to5 report: "We're tired. The stress level in there—I mean there's nto [sic] a week in there where somebody doesn't cry . . . You sit there, I have done it myself, and just key-enter and cry, you know, and this is every week" (1985, p. 35). Taking a more center-of-the-road perspective, Marx and Sherizen (1989) write that "Workers may feel violated and powerless in the face of the new monitoring technologies" (p. 402).

The advocacy literature routinely reports direct causal relationships between computer-based monitoring and increased stress and incidents of stress-related illnesses. One of the most celebrated cases is that of Harriet Ternipsede, an airline reservations agent who suffered a nervous breakdown because she was monitored at work (Piller 1993; Ternipsede 1993). The 9to5 (1985) report also associated health problems, such as headaches, nausea, exhaustion, and other stress-related symptoms, with monitoring.

What Is Computer-Based Monitoring Really Like?

To determine what computer-based monitoring was really like in organizations, the first author conducted a study of monitoring in Arizona, beginning in the summer of 1991 and ending in the spring of 1993. Since the late 1980s, several organizations that relied on computer-based monitoring for employee evaluation had relocated to Arizona. These organizations included retail catalog operations, insurance claims processing centers, airline reservations offices, and telecommunications facilities, among others. Five organizations agreed to take part in the study: the customer service department of a utility, two catalog operations, one airline reservations office, and one facility that employed communications workers. Two sites were local organizations and three were part of large U.S.-based service organizations. The data reported here come from 61 employees of Company A, 8 from Company B, 62 from Company C, 64 from Company D, and 77 from Company E, for a total of 272 respondents (Table 1).

In each of the five organizations, the respondents were subject to computer monitoring systems that recorded performance data though their computer and telephone systems. In all organizations, this performance data was used for evaluation and the determination of bonuses or annual pay raises. However, the average number of calls monitored per employee and the manner in which they were monitored (e.g., real time versus delayed) differed by organization. (See George 1996, for greater detail regarding each site.) In the sections that follow, we will focus on three different dimensions of computer-based monitoring and how they varied across the organizations studied. These dimensions are: (1) variation in work environments and monitoring practices, (2) variation in how performance information is used for evaluation, and (3) variation in employee perceptions of their work and of monitoring.

TABLE 1 Differences in Monitoring Practices Across Sites

Factor	Company A	Company B	Company C	Company D	Company E
Type of company	Catalog	Utility	Communications	Catalog	Reservations
Number of stations	560	10	312	76	676
Number of employees on the phones	800–1,000, 1,600 max	10	900	107	1,000
Center is	1 of 10	1 of 1	1 of 8	1 of 1	1 of 8
Starting pay (per hour)	$4.73 to $6.23	$7.94	$5.50 to $6.66	$5.00	$5.77
Evaluation results in	Bonus twice per year	Annual pay raise	Annual pay raise (plus awards)	Annual pay raise	Annual pay raise
Average number of calls per hour per employee (actual performance unless quota specified)	Approx. 15 (avg. of 4 minutes per call)	Winter: 10 per hour; Summer: 19 per hour	Approx. 500 per day (approx. 63 per hour)	Quota of 9 calls per hour	Approx. 16 to 31 per hour (2 to 4 minutes per call)
Part-time/ Full-time	Part-time only	Full-time only	90% full; 10% part	85% part; 15% full	95% full; 5% part
Hours open	15 per day	9 per day	24 hours	13.5 per day	18 per day
Training	Formal (40 hours)	Informal (2 weeks)	Formal (12 days)	Formal (2 weeks)	Formal (7 weeks)
Number of calls monitored per employee	At least 3 every 6 months (taped)	5 to 6 every 6 months	About 35 per month	3 to 4 forms per month; many calls per form	40 per quarter (13 to 14 per month)
Posting of statistics	By Employee	Not done but available	By team	By employee	By team and employee

▪▪▪ Variation in Work Environments and Monitoring Practices

Table 1 provides a summary of work and monitoring practices in the five Arizona organizations studied. The first four variables listed illustrate differences in work environments: Companies A, C, and E are rather large, with Company D being more moderately sized, and Company B's operations being very small. Yet, despite the differences in size, each operation has at least four levels of hierarchy: (1) a center or department manager, (2) an intermediate level of management, (3) supervisors, and (4) people answering the phones. In each workplace, employees who answer the phones work in cubicles, each of which is equipped with a personal computer or terminal. There is also a phone jack for the phone headset each person uses. Cubicles are typically open and arranged in clusters of four or five, and in the large sites, dozens of such clusters are located in a single large room. The extent to which cubicles can be personalized varies across sites, as do regulations that cover work performed there. In Company C, employees may not bring food into the cubicle and can only drink water from a special container. In Company A, reading materials are prohibited. In Company D, there are few regulations, as cubicles are highly personalized and the first author observed several pulp novels stacked in cubicles.

The number of workstations at each site is of course reflected by the number of employees on the phones. The larger the site, the more likely it is to be one of several such centers which together make up a larger organizational unit, as is the case for Companies A, C, and E. Where this is true, the actual computer system software used by the phone personnel runs at a remote site. In one of the smaller research sites in the study, the system being used was a turnkey system (Company B). In the remaining site (Company D), the system was developed in-house. Both of these systems were on site.

All sites collect performance information through a phone-based CWPMS and through service observations. They also collect information through their primary computer systems. In all five sites, performance information is used for determining awards. In only one site, Company A, the information determines if the employee qualifies for a bonus awarded twice per year. The amount of the bonus is determined by the performance of the entire center. There are no pay increases at Company A. As can be seen in Table 1, Company A had the lowest starting rate of pay; Company B had the highest. Companies A, C, and E run contests to increase performance. Company C also gives out awards for excellent service levels.

Company A hires people for part-time jobs only, and they average 20 to 25 hours per week on a prearranged schedule. Company B hires people on a full-time basis only. Companies C, D, and E favor full-time employment, but all three companies do have some part-time employees. With the exception of Company B, all sites run multiple shifts. The hours of operation are determined by the nature of the work being done. Company C, staffed by telecommunications workers, is the only site open 24 hours per day. The number of phone calls each worker is asked to handle is also partly determined by the nature of the work, but even here there are variations. The operators at Company C handle much shorter calls, so they handle more of them, about one per minute. Companies A and D are both in the catalog business, but workers at Company A take 60 percent more calls per hour. Although there are daily, weekly, monthly, and seasonal variations in the amount of work in all five sites, management at Company B were the only ones to identify the number of calls per hour per employee as a dichotomy, where the summer workload is about double that for the winter. This is probably due to the fact that Companies A, C, D, and E all make adjustments in their staffing depending on the anticipated workload, whereas Company B employs the same number of people in the summer and the winter, despite the much heavier summer workload.

The monitoring practices and personnel used for service observation vary greatly across sites. In Company A, at least three calls are listened to and recorded over a 6-month basis. Personnel in the training department record the calls and also observe the computer screens used for the order. These calls are rated by a supervisor and played back to the employee at the biannual evaluation meeting. Company B rarely records calls and the supervisor or his or her manager listens to five or six calls per month. No formal checklist is used to judge the quality of the phone call; instead, it is done subjectively. In Company C, about 35 calls are monitored each month (these are typically short), and they are evaluated on a monitoring form. Calls are not recorded. In Company D, three to four evaluation forms are filled out for each employee by trainers who listen to the calls. Each form represents several calls. Calls are recorded, but only for two reasons: When an employee is having problems that need to be documented or to record an especially well-done call and provide positive feedback. In Company E, call observation occurs about 40 times per quarter for each salesperson. This works out to about 13 or 14 per month. Calls are evaluated on a standard form, which has room for 10 call ratings. The form has two parts, one to evaluate the call itself (greeting, using the caller's name, friendliness, listening) and one to evaluate sales techniques used in the call. Sometimes, for training purposes, a group of people in a meeting room will listen to a live call and evaluate it as it occurs.

The degree of public access to computer-based monitoring information (i.e., whether it is posted and in what form) also varies. Company B does not post the information, but it is readily available in reports generated by the system. These reports are printed in the main work area, and information is listed by employee extension number. Employees know everyone else's number and constantly compare their statistics to those for others. In Companies A and D, the information is posted in the main work area by individual. Company C posts some information by individual, using the operator number as the identifier, and other information by team. The team-based information is the first thing you see as you enter the facility on the way to the main work area. At Company E, employees can access their performance statistics and compare them to those of other workers from their computers.

▮▮▮ Variation in the Evaluation Process

Despite the extensive amount of information collected on each employee, these organizations do not use all of it in the formal evaluation of their employees. Each organization selects a different subset of data that management considers important in making evaluations (Table 2). In Company A, the single most important factor considered is attendance. If the attendance and tardiness measure is below expected levels, the other measures listed in Table 2 will not even be considered. Even if these other measures are exemplary, if performance on attendance and tardiness are below par, the employee will not receive a bonus for that period. Customer service and the evaluation of the monitored phone calls are considered to be the next most important criteria and are considered to be equal in importance. Interestingly enough, Company A collects quite a few quantitative statistics through its phone system, but these statistics are not used in the formal employee evaluation. If there are problems in these areas, however, the problems are discussed with the employee.

In Company B, all employees that work for the utility are evaluated using the same form. Particular criteria for evaluation of telephone customer service clerks are written out in detail in a separate document. Each of the seven broad categories on the general evaluation form is broken down into a list of job-specific criteria. "Quality of work" is one of the seven evaluation criteria on the general form. For telephone clerks, quality is determined from information collected through listening to calls (e.g., "courtesy," "listening

TABLE 2 Criteria Used for Evaluation

Company A	Company B	Company C	Company D	Company E
Attendance and tardiness	Quality	Accuracy	Job knowledge	Revenue
Monitored calls	Customer and employee relations	Courtesy	Quality/accuracy	Customer service
Customer service	Adaptability to change	Attendance	Quantity	Selling tickets by mail
Team effectiveness	Initiative	Percent stationed	Follows instruction	
Measured but not used:	Quantity	Average work time	Cooperation	
• Talk time	Accepts responsibility	Business conduct	Dependable/attendance	
• Handling time	Economy of work performance	Safety in work habits		
• No. calls				
• Break time				

skills"), through the computer (e.g., "checks all screens available"), and through the phone system (e.g., "leaves work station during work hours only for customer service business"). Part of the evaluation of customer/employee relations is also determined through information collected through listening to calls. Information collected through the phone system ("available at 8:01 A.M.," "reports to work on time and complies with break policies," "meets 430 minutes availability on the phones") is used to help determine initiative. Information from both the phone ("total calls divided by number of employees") and computer systems ("performs online direct input on customer accounts," "checks the history file on all inquiries") are used to determine the quantity measure.

The list of evaluation criteria under Company C also come from the company's official evaluation form. Accuracy and courtesy are the most important factors, as the center must attain certain levels for both attributes. Both are determined from monitoring phone calls. The evaluation of attendance is based on time-card data. Percent stationed—the ratio of the amount of time operators are logged on to their station taking calls to the amount of time they should be logged on—is collected through the computer system. Average work time, the time spent on calls, is also tracked through the computer. Business conduct is a more subjective measure, based on how the operator conducts himself or herself in the center and how he or she handles such issues as adherence to rules and attitude.

In Company D, the same form used for evaluation of all employees is also used for phone clerks. The items listed in Table 2 reflect the criteria listed on this form. Elements of the quantity evaluation are collected through the computer and phone systems. The measures from the computer include: number of orders taken, number of sales of Federal Express deliveries, number of items sold that the customer did not originally call to buy, number of credit applications taken. Statistics collected using the phones include: time available to take calls, time plugged in but not available, time idle, and the number of calls lost (i.e., people who hung up before their calls were answered). Quality and accuracy are determined with information collected through monitoring phone calls.

Finally, in Company E, the criteria for performance evaluation had changed just prior to the beginning of the research project. Attendance, which used to account for 20 percent of performance, was no longer counted in the formal evaluation. The calling statistics gathered through the call management system were no longer used either. Instead, revenue generated was worth 60 percent, customer service (through call observation) counted 30 percent, and selling tickets-by-mail counted for the remaining 10 percent.

▪▪▪ Variation in Employee Perceptions

Although we cannot attribute differences in employee attitudes toward their jobs solely to the monitoring practices in each workplace, these practices, and their role in performance evaluation, do have an effect on how workers feel about their jobs. Table 3 lists the levels of satisfaction workers at each site reported with regard to three separate areas: (1) satisfaction with the computer-based monitoring aspects of their jobs, (2) satisfaction with the phone-based monitoring aspects of their jobs, and (3) their overall job satisfaction.

In general, respondents in all four sites seem to be satisfied with performance measurement done through the computer (Table 3, Question 1). Company B had the lowest proportion of respondents who indicated they were somewhat satisfied with the practice, at 43 percent, and Company C had the highest, at 75 percent. In Company A, almost 40 percent of the respondents said they were very satisfied with the practice.

TABLE 3 Responses by Site to Satisfaction Questions*

	(1) Satisfaction with Computer Monitoring	(2) Satisfaction with Phone Monitoring	(3) Overall Job Satisfaction
Company A			
Not too	9%	10%	5%
Somewhat	52	52	41
Very	39	31	54
Company B			
Not too	14	63	0
Somewhat	43	25	63
Very	29	13	37
Company C			
Not too	7	24	13
Somewhat	75	51	55
Very	15	18	30
Company D			
Not too	14	27	22
Somewhat	55	42	38
Very	29	19	37
Company E			
Not too	15	22	10
Somewhat	51	42	48
Very	29	21	38

****Key to table**: All three questions used a four-point scale, with 1 for "Not at All Satisfied," 2 for "Not Too Satisfied," 3 for "Somewhat Satisfied," and 4 for "Very Satisfied."*

Regarding their satisfaction with phone conversations monitored by supervisors, Company B has the lowest proportion of workers somewhat satisfied with the practice. Only 25 percent of respondents in Company B reported being somewhat satisfied with the practice, compared to 40 to 50 percent of respondents in the other three sites. Company B also had the largest proportion of respondents who said they were not too satisfied with the practice: 63 percent. The differences seem clearly related to monitoring practice: Company B was the only participating organization where service observation was totally subjective, with no official forms, rating systems, or explicit criteria used to evaluate the quality of worker interactions with customers.

Finally, in terms of overall satisfaction with their jobs (Table 3, Question 3), the largest proportion of respondents indicating they were very satisfied were at Company A (54 percent!). There were few differences in overall job satisfaction at companies B, D, and E (37 to 38 percent reported being very satisfied). Companies B and C had the largest proportions of respondents who reported being somewhat satisfied with their jobs (63 percent and 55 percent, respectively). It is important to remember that each of these five organizations used very similar procedures to collect data about workers both through their computers and through listening to their phone conversations with customers, yet there are clear variations in how satisfied workers were with monitoring practices and with their jobs. It seems clear that the mere presence of computer-based monitoring is not the sole factor affecting how these workers felt about their jobs. Monitoring practices varied across organizations, and worker reactions varied as well.

▦ How Do Monitored Employees Compare To Nonmonitored Employees?

All of the organizations studied in Arizona monitored all of their employees, thus it was not possible to compare monitored to nonmonitored employees in these sites. Still, we were interested in how workers who were monitored compared on measures of work life quality to similar workers who were not monitored. Even though the workers studied in Arizona varied in terms of how they reacted to monitoring, the writers in the advocacy literature would still be correct about monitoring, to some extent, if non-monitored workers had more favorable perceptions of their quality of work life than did monitored workers in similar jobs. To compare monitored and nonmonitored workers, we used data about nonmonitored workers, which had been collected by the first author and others in about the same time period (1990).

The sample of nonmonitored workers consisted of both clerical and professional employees. Usable data were available for 72 clerical workers. These clerical employees worked at 10 different organizations and held order entry, accounting, and word processing positions. Seven organizations were located in California and three in Arizona. All organizations were private sector, for-profit organizations and ranged in size from over 2,500 employees to fewer than 250 employees. All respondents worked in a heavily computerized work environment, and none were subject to computer-based monitoring.

We found at least two distinct differences between computer-monitored and non-computer-monitored clerical employees, regardless of their organizational context, when referencing specific dimensions of their quality of work life (see Carter and George 2000 for more detail on how these comparisons were made). Computer-monitored clerical employees perceived their work as more *routine* than non-computer-monitored clerical employees. Perhaps computer-monitored clerical employees are better informed as to what "performance" is expected given that their performance on the job is monitored. Knowing what behaviors are expected may increase the likelihood that those particular behaviors are more routinely carried out.

Computer-monitored clerical employees also experienced lower levels of *work effort* than non-computer-monitored clerical employees. Again, knowing what behaviors are expected and rewarded, computer-monitored clerical employees may be more likely to stick to the minimum effort needed to perform satisfactorily. Considered together, the routineness and work effort results suggest that monitored clerical employees may employ "work to rule" behaviors. Prior findings that computer monitoring has a negative effect on work quality also support this assertion. A "work to rule" aspect of computer performance monitoring has not been specifically investigated but warrants further research.

However, we did not find significant differences between monitored and nonmonitored clerical employees regarding their perceived *working conditions* or *extent of supervision*. Instead, for working conditions, what differences we did find were between clerical employees working in different organizations. These differences may be due to differences in the supervisory behaviors employed along with other social influences within each organization. The organizations with the best and worst working conditions and with the highest and lowest levels of supervision all employed computer-based monitoring. This suggests that the mere presence of computer monitoring does not significantly affect clerical employees' reactions to their working conditions or to their perceived extent of supervision. Therefore, other factors within an organization appear to be important influences.

A closer analysis of the extent of supervision variable did reveal a significant difference with regard to employees' perceptions of their supervision that occurred specifically through computing equipment. Computer-monitored clerical employees had significantly higher perceptions of being closely monitored through their computing equipment. However, the range of perceptions from employees of monitored organizations (mean range of 3.41 to 6.17 on a seven-point scale), with two monitored organizations being significantly different from all other monitored organizations, again suggests that there may be other factors influencing the effects of computer performance monitoring.

Interestingly, the means of the two non-computer-monitored organization groups regarding their perceptions of supervision through computing equipment were 2.04 and 2.37 with standard deviations of 1.47 and 1.37, respectively. Although significantly different from the computer-monitored groups, these numbers suggest that some clerical employees not subject to computer monitoring may believe, or at least entertain the thought, that they are computer monitored given that their responses overlap with the responses from monitored employees. Perhaps these beliefs are influenced by mass media reports, communications with peers who are subject to computer monitoring, or suspicions of supervisory behaviors. Indeed, some employers do electronically monitor their employees without their knowledge (American Management Association 2001). In any case, this raises the question of whether "computer monitoring" effects are limited to employees who are actually monitored by their employers through computing equipment.

There was no significant difference between the computer-monitored group and the non-computer-monitored group perceptions of the extent of their general supervision. Computer-monitored and non-computer-monitored clerical employees appear to perceive their extent of general supervision similarly. However, there was a great deal of difference among the monitored organization group perceptions, with four out of six monitored pairs being significantly different from each other. It seems likely, from these results, that social and or supervisory behavior factors play a role at least as significant as, if not greater than, the computer monitoring factor itself. Again, this undermines the sole dependence on the presence of monitoring practices for understanding all dimensions of computer performance monitoring in the work place.

⋕⋕⋕ Conclusions

Millions of employees are monitored through electronic devices every day in many different types of jobs. At the same time, many employees, particularly in the United States, react negatively to being monitored electronically. Our lack of understanding and knowledge regarding the key factors involved in this phenomenon is somewhat unsettling. It does not appear as if computer monitoring or other types of electronic surveillance are going to disappear anytime soon. In fact, their usage is increasing. In addition, monitoring practices are being extended more and more to white-collar workers, whose e-mail and Internet use at work are being increasingly monitored.

The Arizona study reported on here indicates that computer-based monitoring is not a simple, monolithic workplace practice. Although all five of the organizations studied collected similar data about their employees, using very similar means, they each had their own unique way of using some or all of that data for performance evaluation. At the extreme (Companies A and E), none of the usual data associated in the advocacy press with computer-based monitoring was used at all in the performance evaluation process. And, as might be expected from a realization of the variety of approaches used in organizations that monitor clerical employees, there was also a variety of responses to monitoring and its use. Satisfaction with monitoring and with the job itself varied from location to location.

Computer monitoring in the workplace has been a volatile issue for a number of years. Although most organizational managers recognize the benefits that may be gained from computer monitoring (e.g., increased productivity and improved performance measurement), many organizations have either scaled down or phased out their electronic surveillance activities because of negative employee reactions (Journal of Commerce 1997). The question for managers, then, is whether computer performance monitoring itself has so great a negative effect on employees' quality of work life that other factors, which might produce more positive effects, cannot outweigh or eliminate negative computer monitoring effects.

The results of the comparison of monitored and nonmonitored clerical workers suggest that: (1) computer performance monitoring itself may not have negative effects on all dimensions of an employee's quality of work life, and (2) other factors are important influences on employees' quality of work life. Negative effects on employees' quality of work life resulting from the presence of computer performance monitoring may be lessened or mitigated through other factors, such as supervisory behaviors and communications or other communications from mass media, coworkers, peers, or the technology itself. Purposeful management of these factors and their impact on employees may allow managers to reap the benefits of computer performance monitoring while minimizing negative effects for employees. However, as is the case with most social science research, additional research is needed to build upon the results presented here and to further our knowledge of the effects of computer monitoring on employees' quality of work life. This is especially the case today in view of the increased spread of monitoring to white collar employees.

REFERENCES

Ambrose, M.L. and Adler, G.S. (2000). Designing, implementing, and utilizing computerized performance monitoring: Enhancing organizational justice. *Personnel and Human Resources Management*, **18**, 187–219.

American Management Association. (2001). 2001 AMA survey: Workplace monitoring & surveillance. Available at www.amanet.org/research/archives.htm. Accessed August 22, 2002.

Carter, P., and George, J.F. (2000). Computer Performance Monitoring and Employee Quality of Work Life. Florida State University working paper.

Clement, A. (1984). Electronic management: The new technology of workplace surveillance. *Canadian Information Processing Society, Session 84*, Calgary, Alberta, 259–266.

George, J.F. (1996). Computer-based monitoring: Common perceptions and empirical results. *MIS Quarterly*, **20**, 459–480.

Grant, R. (1990). *Silicon Supervisors: Computerized Monitoring in the Service Sector*. ICIT Press, Washington, D.C.

Journal of Commerce. (1997). The Rising Rate of Snooping. August 7.

Lund, J. (1991). Computerized work performance monitoring and production standards: A review of labor law issues. *Labor Law Journal*, **42** 195–203.

Marx, G.T. (1985) I'll be watching you. *Dissent*, **32**, 27–34.

Marx, G.T., and Sherizen, S. (1989). Monitoring on the job, in T. Forester (ed.), *Computers in the Human Context*. The MIT Press, Cambridge, MA, 397–406.

Nebeker, D.M, and Tatum, B.C. (1993). The effects of computer monitoring, standards, and rewards on work performance, job satisfaction, and stress. *Journal of Applied Social Psychology*, **23**, 508–536.

9to5, National Association of Working Women. (1985). *Hidden Victims: Clerical Workers, Automation, and the Changing Economy*, Cleveland, OH.

9to5, Working Woman Fund. (1990). *Stories of Mistrust and Manipulation: The Electronic Monitoring of the American Workforce*, Cleveland, OH.

Nussbaum, K. (1992). Workers under surveillance. *Computerworld*, **26**, January 6, 21.

Piller, C. (1993). Bosses with X-ray eyes. *Macworld*, July, 118+.

Smith, M.J., Carayon, P., Sanders, K.J., Lim, S-Y., and LeGrande, D. (1992). Employee stress and health complaints in jobs with and without electronic performance monitoring. *Applied Ergonomics*, **23**, 17–27.

Ternipsede, H. (1993). Is electronic workplace monitoring stressful to workers? *Congressional Quarterly Researcher*, **3**, 1025.

U.S. Congress, Office of Technology Assessment. (1987). *The Electronic Supervisor: New Technology, New Tensions*.

Social and Technical Aspects of Electronic Monitoring: *To Protect and to Serve**

TERRI L. GRIFFITH

The *2001 American Management Association survey on electronic monitoring and surveillance found the following rationales for monitoring:*

- Legal liability
- Security concerns
- Productivity measurement
- Legal compliance
- Performance review

Although productivity measurement and performance review could be considered as starting points for employee development, most of the literature on electronic monitoring discusses strong concerns related to more negative outcomes, such as employee privacy and stress. It seems that current organizational use of electronic monitoring (defined here as the practice of collecting information on employee behavior through computers, telephones, or other electronic systems) is more about protection, and less about service.

Protection and service do not have to result from separate systems. Protection in the discussion to follow is largely focused on employee supervision, employee evaluation, and the like. This same information can be used for service; that is, to improve employee welfare through performance tracking with an eye to tracking for bonuses, tracking of work processes for the purpose of identifying improvement areas, and so on. In general, the two approaches of protection and service can also be thought of as enforcement versus learning.

This chapter is written to two audiences: First, to managers in situations where electronic monitoring is a tool for managing performance or maintaining security; and second, to employees looking to better understand the rationale for this monitoring and how to apply monitoring for their own benefit. My goal is to provide a general overview of electronic monitoring and to suggest that there is much more to be gained from considering service versus protection.

The key to *understanding* electronic monitoring is to realize that it is the perception of the monitoring that has influence in the organization, and that this perception is a *combination* of the technology's capabilities and how employees understand its use. The key to *using* electronic monitoring is to only focus on protection/enforcement where necessary (e.g., to protect the organization against legal action), while directing much greater attention to the possibilities electronic monitoring affords through service/process improvement. Perhaps a mix of roughly 5 percent protection to 95 percent service would be a reasonable approach. Unfortunately, anecdotal evidence suggests that current use is reversed—95 percent protection to 5 percent service. Yes, electronic monitoring is for organizational protection, but it should also serve in developing employee practice.

In the following sections, I will describe the current form and prevalence of electronic monitoring in work organizations, provide a short background on the legal and policy issues surrounding monitoring, and consider the joint optimization of technical and managerial tools for monitoring. The last sections of the chapter push for integrating monitoring into the way we work. This approach requires that monitoring be seen as a tool for employees—as well as managers.

▪▪▪ What Does Monitoring Look Like?

One survey of 435 members of the American Management Association (2001) examined monitoring varying from video surveillance to keystrokes and Internet connections. They found that use of monitoring ranged from a high of 61.6 percent of organizations monitoring Internet connections to a low of 7.6 percent of organizations performing storage and review of voice mail messages. Table 1 provides a summary of their results.

Although the American Management Association survey provides an interesting baseline, it is also important to take a more fine-grained approach to the form and use of electronic monitoring in organizations. The following is a discussion of a variety of

TABLE 1 Activities Commonly Monitored in Organizations Responding to 2001 AMA Survey	
Activity	*Percent Reporting (%)*
Monitoring Internet connections	61.6
Storage & review of e-mail messages	46.9
Storage & review of computer files	36.3
Video recording of employee job performance	11.7
Recording & review of telephone conversations	8.5
Storage & review of voice mail messages	7.6
Total, active monitoring of communication and performance	73.6
Telephone use (time spent, numbers called)	41.6
Video surveillance for security purposes	33.3
Computer use (time logged on, keystroke counts, etc.)	20.5
Total, all forms of electronic monitoring and/or surveillance	77.7

▪▪▪▪▪▪▪▪▪

Adapted from the American Management Association's (2001) summary of their most recent data collection.

dimensions that are critical to consider. The overall approach is one of understanding the possibilities to make good management decisions.

As can be seen in Table 1, not all monitoring is alike. Some monitoring is focused on the process of the work being performed (e.g., statistical process control of manufacturing processes). Other monitoring provides real-time surveillance of employee actions on the job (e.g., listening to phone-based customer service representatives). The perspective argued for here is that no one particular form of monitoring is evil, an invasion of privacy, or a cure-all for performance ills. Instead, the performance and social outcomes of electronic monitoring are the results of what is monitored and how that information is understood and used.

Monitoring varies on these (and certainly in the future, other) dimensions:

- What is monitored

  Individuals versus groups of employees
  E-mail (who is contacted, content of message)
  Voice mail
  Internet use (locations visited, files downloaded, etc.)
  Telephone use
  Work process (keystroke tracking, time on task, software used, work performed, etc.)
  Broad Internet use (search for postings on job/resume boards, search for employee postings on public discussion boards, etc.)

- Who receives the information

  Only the employee
  Only the manager
  Manager and employee
  The work group
  Public

- Timing of the monitoring

  Real time ("eavesdropping," systems that signal certain types of use, etc.)
  Summaries (daily, weekly, etc.)
  Archiving for later search

- Purpose of monitoring

  Legal (avoiding sexual harassment legal action, Securities and Exchange Commission rules, etc.)
  Work improvement (identification of common errors, study of work process to find opportunities for greater efficiency, etc.)
  Company policy enforcement (no use of e-mail for personal communication, etc.)
  Knowledge management (finding organizational experts on particular topics, e.g., Knowledgemail, Tacit 2002)

- Employee involvement

  Access to results
  Notification of monitoring policies and procedures
  Employee involvement in interpretation of results

Outcomes of monitoring have been found to depend on different components of these factors. For example, studies have found that video monitoring is perceived to be more fair if employees are given advance notice of the monitoring (Hovorka-Mead, Ross, Whipple, and Renchin 2002); task performance can be *lowered* if employees are not given control over monitoring (Douthitt and Aiello 2001); employee performance varies based on whether monitoring is human or electronic in nature (Griffith 1993a);

although health problems and stress are positively related to the number of tasks monitored but negatively related to employee's ability to discuss the monitoring (Hawk 1994). One study of five organizations (customer service for a utility, two catalog operations, one airline reservations office, one communications firm) found that although the companies collected similar sets of performance data, they all used the data in different ways, resulting in different findings regarding employee satisfaction, work-related illnesses, and perceptions of supervision (George 1996).

The key to understanding and effectively using electronic monitoring is to understand that the outcomes are the result of both social and technical aspects of its use. The next section raises some of the social issues around legal and policy considerations.

▪▪▪ Legal and Policy Issues

This section is not intended to be a summary of the current laws. This choice was made for two reasons: One, these laws are constantly in flux given changes in statutes and case law; second, the legal issues are especially complex given the global nature of many of the affected jobs and their status regarding the laws of different countries. One summary of U.S. laws are available online at www.gcwf.com/gcc/graycary-c/practice-a/privacy/ecompriv.doc_cut.htm (Gray Cary Ware and Freidenrich LLP, 2002). For international issues you are urged to do an Internet search focused on your particular topic (www.findlaw.com is a good starting point).

Broadly speaking, electronic communications made on company-owned technologies (e.g., computers, networks, telephones) are not private. One of the best known cases involved Epson International. In *Flanagan et al. vs. Epson America, Inc.* [Case No. BC007036, Los Angeles County Superior Court (1991)]:

> . . . employees alleged that they were told that their e-mail was private and confidential, and that no one informed them that it could be intercepted or read. They claimed that the employer stressed the privacy and security of the system, and issued secret passwords to prevent unauthorized access.
>
> However, the employer systematically intercepted, copied, and read employee e-mail. The trial court ruled that the California Penal Code provision protecting confidential communications was not intended to apply to e-mail, and also rejected the plaintiffs' Federal Wire Tapping Act claims because the equipment used for interception of the messages was provided by the employer. (Brobeck Phleger & Harrison LLP 1999)

Most legal and human resource experts suggest that having a stated policy on both communications use (e.g., whether personal use of any type is allowed, types of Internet sites that are barred from access), and the employer's approach to monitoring and enforcing such policies, are a first step to effectively managing Internet and telecommunications issues in the firm. Examples of such policies can be found at www.email-policy.com/Sample-email-policies.htm (Email-policy.com 2002). Please note that this citation is provided for informational purposes only and should be used only in consultation with appropriate legal counsel.

Limited empirical work has been done on the value of particular policies and practices. The most effective approach is to gather information both from those involved in decisions regarding monitoring and those being monitoring (George and Griffith 2002), yet such studies seem to be lacking in the literature. Robert Mitchell and Tameka

Jones (2002) do provide data from the decision makers. In their study of 37 small businesses in Arkansas they found that 100 percent at least stated that employees could be disciplined for inappropriate use of technology, though only 38 percent had formal policies in place. Table 2 provides summaries the content of those formal policies.

Although formal policy statements are not absolute protection from invasion of privacy claims, discrimination, or harassment suits, they may diminish the risk of exposure to the employer (Brobeck Phleger and Harrison LLP 1999).

The above policies are one example of how social features of monitoring (e.g., dissemination of formal policies regarding Internet use) may help influence behavior. However, a full-blown effort to both increase organizational efficiency and effectiveness while minimizing legal risk requires a more holistic approach—a joint optimization of the social and technical components of monitoring.

TABLE 2 Contents of Computer-Based Monitoring Policies (Mitchell & Jones, 2002)

Policy Content	Organizations with Formal Policies (%)
States that employees can be disciplined for inappropriate use of technology	100
Prohibits accessing inappropriate Web sites (e.g., sexually explicit photographs)	85
Limits use of organization equipment/systems to business use	79
Prohibits downloading, viewing, communicating, and storing defamatory, criminal, or confidential information (e.g., trade secrets, hate mail)	79
Prohibits illegally downloading/transferring software/files (e.g., copyright protected music)	79
Prohibits transferring documents that could be the basis for sexual harassment or discrimination suits (e.g., jokes)	79
Prohibits unauthorized release of confidential or proprietary information	79
Identifies circumstances under which computer use is monitored	64
Identifies circumstances under which e-mail is monitored	57
Restricts employee use of encryption software to that approved by the organization	57
Identifies appropriate e-mail etiquette, such as language and subject matter	57
Identifies privacy expectation	50
States that passwords are not a guarantee of privacy	50
Identifies circumstances under which Internet use is monitored	50
States that employees can be held liable for civil and criminal penalties for illegal use of technology	42
Defines employee expectations relating to system use and limitations	36
Requires that all transmission include employer's header and reflect the employer (i.e., prohibits use of anonymous remailers)	36
Identifies an agreement for employees to efficiently use computer-based resources	29
Includes a disclaimer that the organization is not liable for material viewed or downloaded by employees	21

Adapted from Mitchell and Jones (2002).

▪▪▪ Joint Optimization of Social and Technical Components of Monitoring

Joint optimization is an idea drawn from the study of socio-technical systems (e.g., Trist and Bamforth 1951). Basically, social and technical components of the organization have to be managed in concert. The social components include the employees, managers, trainers, and others, as well as their perceptions and understandings of the work, rules, and policies. The technical components include the capabilities of the technology (e.g., what can and cannot be monitored, the speed at which the information can be consolidated, etc.). Joint optimization means that all the social and technical components are considered at the same time as an approach to monitoring in the organization is developed.

To fully understand this joint optimization also requires that we understand the strong role that perception plays. Technology capabilities may be one thing on a specification sheet and quite another when actually implemented in the organization. Similarly, the monitoring policy may legally mean one thing, but understood and acted upon in the organization completely differently. (For a detailed discussion of how such systems come to be understood, please see Griffith 1999.) The more implementation and training are considered and supported, the more likely it is that employees and managers will understand the organization's monitoring in the same way.

Implementation and training need to acknowledge the full organizational system (e.g., people, technology, policies/procedures, context, and organizational structure). The implementation approach for introducing monitoring must understand that one cannot change just one thing in an organization, such as introducing monitoring, without also taking into account how people will learn about the monitoring, be reinforced regarding monitoring's use, how policies and procedures may need to be adjusted, and so on. Organizational changes are not introduced into vacuums or static environments, and the implementation process must take this into account. Once the full force and method of the implementation are assessed, training can be developed to support the implementation process.

Training about monitoring should cover both the technical and social components of the process. Why is monitoring needed? How will it be conducted? What organizational policies/procedures will be changed or introduced? What improvements could be made in the approach being implemented? Each of these questions will help to design training that brings manager and employee understanding in-line with one another and with the needs of the organization and its people.

The direction that this joint optimization takes can be managed top down, bottom up, or as a negotiation. The negotiated approach is more likely to result in successful and clearly understood implementations of monitoring (Griffith, Tansik, and Benson 2002), but even a top-down approach can be effective if the full range of dimensions mentioned earlier are taken into consideration.

▪▪▪ How to Use Monitoring Effectively[1]

Some organizations believe that electronic monitoring in organizations should be restricted (for a list of such organizations, see The National Workrights Institute 2002). However, monitoring can be an effective tool for increasing organizational effective-

---

[1]The following suggestions are based on foundation of management research. Although these particular suggestions have not been formally validated by organizational research, each builds from a breadth of sources. Interested readers are urged to search the Internet or journal archives using the terms "electronic monitoring" and "computer monitoring," coupled with their particular focus of interest.

ness and efficiency if implemented and used in appropriate ways. The following section presents particular examples of effective monitoring methods.

Five rationales for monitoring in organizations were proposed at the beginning of this chapter: legal liability, security concerns, productivity measurement, legal compliance, and performance review. In this section, the list will be narrowed to two: protection and service.

However, before touching on the form that monitoring of these types can take, we must consider the first step that must be common to both forms: policy notification — publicizing appropriate Internet and e-mail use, how monitoring is used, and what action can follow based on the information gained. Without clear implementation and training, the outcomes of monitoring cannot be predicted.

Protection

Monitoring for the enforcement of legal, industry, or policy infractions should be designed as any organizational security system. The rules should be made clear through the aforementioned policy notification and then those rules should be applied without bias. Depending on the risk profile (meaning cases where immediate termination is not required), the organization may want to adopt a policy of sending a Web transgression report card. Cabletron is described as using a monthly e-mail "to embarrass" employees (Deo 2000). However, such feedback does not need to be embarrassing, but rather a clear indicator of appropriate and inappropriate behavior. Feedback provides the organization with the opportunity to make clear the rules and outcomes related to Internet use, using the technical capabilities of monitoring to effectively manage the perceptions (social aspects) of Internet use.

Service

Electronic monitoring has great potential for service and work improvement. Effective management has generally focused on the ability of managers to make process suggestions, and electronic monitoring increases the detail of the information on which these suggestions are based. Although most early electronic monitoring focused on jobs with relatively standard tasks (customer service representatives, airline reservation staff, word processing employees, etc.), current tools can assess a variety of data from all levels of the organization. The following are just brief examples of either extant or possible forms of monitoring that can provide service to the employee, as well as work improvement. The success of each would clearly be dependent on the related training, implementation, incentive programs, and feedback from management or other knowledgeable parties.

Knowledge Management   Tacit's Knowledgemail product uses a confidential search of "noun phrases" in outgoing e-mail to identify particular expertise within the organization. This is electronic monitoring, combined with privacy controls and personal choice (you can opt out of the system), for the purpose of organizational knowledge management.

Time Management   Self-monitoring could provide employees with feedback regarding how they are spending their time. Personally, I would like a tool that notifies me when I have spent more than 5 minutes looking for just the "right" graphic to include in a presentation. The notification would let me make a cost-benefit judgment regarding the use of my time.

Knowledge Management and Training   Hughes Aircraft had a system known as CVITS (Computer Video Integrated Technology System). This information tool was connected to powerful microscopes that were used in the inspection of microchips (for a more complete description, see Griffith 1993b). Two types of monitoring were used. Real-time video monitoring of the microscope images was used to allow supervisors to follow the work process without entering the clean room. Archival monitoring was used as digital images were saved of any chip defects; the description of the defect was also recorded. The power came in the ability to document the forms of the errors and provide feedback to production. Additional benefit was gained as the inspectors could quickly view a "classic" example of a particular error type with what they were seeing in the current chip. They could also call for expertise from their supervisor through the video connection. Training was also to be improved as errors could easily be tracked to identify problem areas, either with individual skills or where improvement in error descriptions needed to be made.

Peer-to-Peer Review Customer service representatives are sometimes managed as teams. In this situation, they may be able to rotate responsibilities for doing "performance checks." Peers listen into customer calls and then highlight particularly effective or ineffective approaches. In the most powerful system, time would be taken to have these feedback sessions with the full group.

Enterprise Incentive Management (EIM) As stated by Robb (2002), "EIM analyzes, tracks, and pays bonuses, commissions and other types of variable compensation" (p. 73). As an enterprise system, EIM takes the power of Enterprise Resource Management and applies it for improved incentive compensation. Employees can quickly track transaction information that before would have been combined from a variety of systems, a cumbersome process that would reduce the motivational power of the incentive program by making the behavior/outcome relationship more opaque.

Location Systems Global Positioning Systems (GPSs) are becoming so small that they can be attached to everything from trucks, to children, to clothing (e.g., Petersen 2002). Hospitals are using them to track the location of nurses and other employees. Although some nurses find this to be an invasion of privacy, one expert suggests that the monitoring be assessed as would any other health-care tool—based on whether or not it serves the patient (Salladay 2001). Some hospitals have linked the location system to the paging system, allowing for faster (and quieter) pages. Salladay (2001) notes that discussing these issues with the staff is key; hospitals need to avoid losing even one valued employee who might feel insulted by the system.

Training Support Tools such as VisVIP (National Institute of Standards and Technology 2002) allow Web navigation to be tracked. Stephen Eick (2001) suggests that tracking the patterns of user navigation can help Web designers to create more usable sites. Such tracking could be used for changing the social, as well as the technical, side of the system. Web use is becoming a larger part of many jobs, yet most of us have never received formal training in Web navigation. We start up a search engine and wander from there. Consider the power of tracking Web navigation and then providing structures for more efficient use. Live trainers, perhaps modern forms of reference librarians, could look at user "trails" and suggest alternatives for future use. Perhaps Google (www.google.com) or some other algorithmically based search engine could provide artificial intelligence training suggestions. Again, the idea is to look at the opportunities for *both* social and technical improvements. It would seem that current use of Web tracking software is focused on the technology and not the people.

The above examples largely focused on the "to serve" portion of the chapter's title. Service is broadly meant to improve the welfare of the employee by improving the work process. This is in contrast to "protection," which is more focused on enforcing extant policies and procedures. Service is about learning. Protection is about the status quo. There are ample examples of electronic monitoring system's focus on protection. The bias here is an attempt to even the focus.

▮▮▮ The Future

Employees and management must work together to find the best use of monitoring systems. In many cases, the information gathered from the monitoring is more valuable to the employee than to management. Detailed feedback can be critical for performance improvement, and it may not be necessary to always involve management in the process. Instead, expertise for interpreting the data may come from peers, the employees themselves, and, especially as we continue to develop both the social and technical sides of monitoring, artificial intelligence systems. Tools could be developed to help us better learn to do our jobs. Our own information could guide this learning and feedback could be immediate.

These positive outcomes are less likely if we do not look to see who really needs the information. We are just beginning to develop information policies and are even further behind on testing their benefits. One point is clear, we do not want legal fears to cause us to overlook organizational benefits. Just as tools for monitoring, sorting, and gaining knowledge benefit from e-mail are being developed, so, too, are tools for making e-mail disappear.

Omniva (www.omniva.com) provides such a tool. E-mail or other documents are created with "policies." These attached policies determine when the document will "disappear" (Omniva 2002). The policies can also control whether e-mail or documents can be forwarded or sent outside the organization's network. Although such systems have benefits to organizations hoping to control their documents, they may also be killing a knowledge management opportunity, causing vast amounts of rework (e.g., presentations must be created from scratch, rather than built from prior files) or spawning further legal issues. Several Wall Street banks are being investigated for not preserving all business communications—including e-mail—they have sent (both internally and externally) over the last 3 years (McGeehan 2002). Certainly implementing such policies should be done with the help of both legal and knowledge management consultation.

▮▮▮ Summary

To protect and to serve. This subheading was chosen for its connection to law enforcement. In 1955, Officer Joseph S. Dorobeck submitted this winning entry to the Los Angeles Police Department's motto contest (Anonymous 1963). Just as there is a system of checks and balances in law enforcement, there needs to be a system of checks and balances in how we apply technology. Electronic monitoring can clearly protect organizations and employees. However, much more attention needs to be paid to how electronic monitoring can also serve by providing learning, development, and other benefits.

This discussion proposed a variety of opportunities for service: knowledge management, training support, peer-to-peer review, time management, and enterprise incentive management. These are just a sampling of the possibilities for turning the focus of electronic monitoring to that of service, rather than simply the heavy hand of protection.

REFERENCES

American Management Association. (2001). *2001 AMA Survey: Workplace Monitoring & Surveillance: Policies and Practices*. Available at www.amanet.org/research/pdfs/emsfu_short.pdf. Accessed on October 20, 2002.

Anonymous. (1963). *To Protect and to Serve*. Available at www.lapdonline.org/general_information/ dept_mission_statement/department_motto.htm. Accessed on October 24, 2002.

Brobeck Phleger and Harrison LLP. (1999). *Labor & Employment Update: Sex, Lies and E-Mail Systems*. Brobeck, Phleger & Harrison LLP. Available at www. library.lp.findlaw.com/articles/file/firms/bph/bph000074/ title/subject/topic/computers%20%20technology %20law_internet/filename/computerstecnologylaw_1_79. Accessed on October 20, 2002.

Deo, D. (2000). Workers Online Being Watched: More Fired over Misuse of Equipment. *Chicago Sun-Times*, August 4, p. 19.

Douthitt, E. A., and Aiello, J. R. (2001). The Role of Participation and Control in the Effects of Computer Monitoring on Fairness Perceptions, Task Satisfaction, and Performance. *Journal of Applied Psychology 86* (5), 867–874.

Eick, S. G. (2001). Visualizing Online Activity. *Communications of the ACM 44* (8), 45–50.

Email-policy.com. (2002). *Sample email policies*. Available at www.email-policy.com/Sample-email-policies.htm. Accessed October 20, 2002.

George, J. (1996). Computer-Based Monitoring: Common Perceptions and Empirical Results. *MIS Quarterly 20* (4), 459–480.

George, J. F., and Griffith, T. L. (2002). *The Great Unknown: How Computer-Based Monitoring Affects White-Collar Workers*. Unpublished manuscript.

Gray Cary Ware & Freidenrich LLP. (2002). *Electronic Communication*. Available at www.gcwf.com/firm/ groups/privacy/electronic_comm.html. Accessed October 20, 2002.

Griffith, T. L. (1993a). Monitoring and Performance: A Comparison of Computer and Supervisor Monitoring. *Journal of Applied Social Psychology 23* (7), 549–572.

Griffith, T. L. (1993b). Teaching Big Brother to be a Team Player: Computer Monitoring and Quality. *Academy of Management Executive, 7*, 73–80.

Griffith, T. L. (1999). Technology Features as Triggers for Sensemaking. *Academy of Management Review 24* (3), 472–488.

Griffith, T. L., Tansik, D. A., and Benson, L., III. (2002). Negotiating Technology Implementation: An Empirical Investigation of a Website Introduction. *Group Decision and Negotiation 11*, 1–22.

Hawk, S. R. (1994). The Effects of Computerized Performance Monitoring: An Ethical Perspective. *Journal of Business Ethics 31* (12), 949–957.

Hovorka-Mead, U. D., Ross, W. H. J., Whipple, T., and Renchin, M. B. (2002). Watching the Detectives: Seasonal Student Employee Reactions to Electronic Monitoring with and Without Advance Notification. *Personnel Psychology 55* (2), 329–362.

McGeehan, P. (2002). Wall St. Banks May be Fined for Discarding E-Mail Traffic. *New York Times on the Web*. www.nytimes.com

Mitchell, R. B., and Jones, R. (2002). Policies Controlling Use of Computer-Based Resources in Small Businesses. *Journal of Computer Information Systems*, Summer, 77–83.

National Institute of Standards and Technology. (2002). *VisVIP*. Available at www.zing.ncsl.nist.gov/WebTools/ VisVIP/overview.html. Accessed October 24, 2002.

Omniva. (2002). *Policy Manager Enterprise Edition*. Available at www.disappearing.com/products/ policy_manager/. Accessed October 20, 2002.

Petersen, A. (2002). Tiny New Gizmos Help People Find Misplaced Keys, Glasses. *Wall Street Journal*, October 15, p. D1.

Robb, D. (2002). Automation Gives Variable Compensation a Boost. *HR Magazine,* August, 73–77.

Salladay, S. A. (2001). Snooping on Nurses. *Nursing 31* (4), 22.

Tacit. (2002). *Knowledgemail*. Available at www.tacit.com/ products/knowledgemail/. Accessed October 20, 2002.

The National Workrights Institute. (2002). *Electronic Monitoring in the Workplace*. Available at www.workrights.org/ issue_electronic/em_legislative_brief.html. Accessed October 20, 2002.

Trist, E. L., and Bamforth, K. W. (1951). Some Social and Psychological Consequences of the Long-Wall Method of Coal-Getting. *Human Relations* (4), 3–38.

Aligning Internet Usage with Business Priorities

Regulating Internet Activities So That Targeted Outcomes Remain Within Acceptable Limits

CLAIRE A. SIMMERS

It is becoming increasingly clear the Internet is now a critical component of the 21st century business landscape. Using the Internet can create many desirable organizational outcomes—lowering the cost of communication, meeting customer needs, supply chain management, and improving business practices and integration [3]. However, using the Internet can also generate undesirable outcomes—loss of intellectual property, sexual harassment lawsuits, productivity losses due to excessive Web surfing, security threats, and network bandwidth overload. Hence, employers have an obligation to proactively manage the Internet-connected workplace, maintaining a middle ground between "no access" and "unrestricted access" to benefit both the organization and the employees. This aligning process—Internet policy management (IPM) [2]—is the regulation of Internet activities so that targeted outcomes remain within acceptable limits. The essential components of IPM are:

- An explicit and clearly communicated Internet usage policy (IUP);
- Tools for monitoring and recording Internet and email usage;
- End-user training; and
- Application of discipline measures.

Many people assert that Internet monitoring should be avoided because it fosters a "Big Brother" environment and is an invasion of privacy. Others take the position that the best way to manage the Internet is to have either no usage or severely limited usage. However, either too much or too little Internet management can be dysfunctional for an organization. For instance, optimal outcomes will be achieved when businesses restrict usage by policy and check the policy by monitoring/filtering software. At one end of the spectrum, if there is no access or if access is severely limited, organizational outcomes may suffer. Blocking is problematic because it is difficult to keep updated and easier to get around. At the other end of the spectrum, vague, not monitored/enforced, or no policies expose the organization to a number of legal, financial, and operational risks such as losses of confidential information, network congestion, threats to network integrity, diversion of employee attention, and increased legal liability. [4]

An IUP defines appropriate behavior when using company Internet resources and outlines the ramifications for violations. An effective IUP can even allow for personal surfing and email. Policy templates can be found by searching for "Internet policies" with any search engine [6] and at Elron Software [2]. Once a draft IUP is written, an organization's management and legal staff should review it and widely publicize it through seminars, performance reviews, and informal discussion sessions. It should be given to all new employees.

An IUP isn't sufficient to reduce excessive surfing, viewing sexually explicit material, confidential data leaks, viruses, or viewing violent content. Many companies do little more than ask their employees for compliance to a formal usage policy; for a growing number of businesses, this just isn't enough. There's increasing sentiment among executives that a more hands-on approach to Internet management is needed. In a recent Dataquest survey of 200 U.S. business executives, 82% said Internet usage should be monitored at their companies, but only 34% said they have already instituted such a program. Web monitoring is expected to jump from 34% in 1999 to 66% by the end of 2001 [1].

Employers must be honest about monitoring, announcing when the monitoring will happen, and why and how it will be done. Monitoring should not be put in place to catch people but to reinforce the business usage of the Internet and the responsibilities that employees have to use this resource properly. The technical aspects of monitoring are not a major hindrance in IPM. There are many monitoring and blocking solutions available. For example, many routers allow ports to be disabled, denying specific Internet traffic. Blocking servers are popular alternatives, with many of these products combined with firewalls and proxy servers. There are several NT-based proxy alternatives; proxy servers can be configured to permit specific traffic to pass through to the network [6]. However, for more optimal alignment of usage with business priorities, a full service provider of Internet management solutions such as SurfWatch Software, a Los Gatos, California-based division of Spyglass Inc. and Elron Software Inc., a Burlington, Massachussetts-based division of Elron Electronic Industries, should be considered [5].

The monitoring function of the IPM should be more than the technology [2]. It should include:

- Periodic (weekly, monthly, bimonthly) generation of Internet usage reports to allow feedback on policy compliance;
- Discussion of these reports at appropriate levels of the organization;
- Actions taken against those who violate policy, per action steps established in the IUP;
- Addition of Web sites identified in usage reports as inappropriate to the filtering feature of the monitoring tool; and
- Periodic review and update of the IUP.

We explore how eight organizations manage usage by policy and enforce the policy by monitoring/filtering software, thus enhancing alignment of individual Internet usage with organizational priorities.

▪▪▪ The Case Studies

Each of the eight organizations thoughtfully determined their policy in accordance with their overall mission, carefully communicated this policy, and then installed a monitoring solution. Elron Software collected the data for an ongoing research project involving the study of the adoption and implementation of IPM. IS professionals responsible for establishing and maintaining an Internet protection and security presence at their organizations were interviewed [2]. The cases are a cross section of organizational types, including two public companies, three nonprofits, one school, and two private firms.

20th Century Fox

20th Century Fox, the largest of the organizations studied, is principally engaged in broadcasting and distribution of feature films and television programs. Although securing the Internet and email was a primary concern, the protection of company data, network, and servers was a high priority. 20th Century Fox wanted to have a powerful reporting tool without high administrative overhead or hardware cost. Jeff Uslan, the manager of information protection, said, ". . . we really needed a way to break down specific Internet usage traffic by employees . . . to enforce our IUP." Uslan found Web-based monitoring software with full text analysis was the most efficient way to track user access. What was employee reaction to the monitoring of their Internet usage? "Being adults and being reasonable people, our employees understand we have to provide a 'safe haven,'" said Uslan. Content filtering and monitoring software at 20th Century Fox makes it workable to tap the power of the Internet by providing unlimited Internet access to all employees.

Bard Manufacturing

Bard Manufacturing specializes in air conditioners and heat pumps. All employees have Internet access. The Internet has proven to be a tremendous resource for the company's overall business. Ray Crooks, the IS professional, was already considering an investment in more network bandwidth to compensate for increased Internet traffic, and there was also concern over other negative consequences such as Web surfing abuse by employees and liability for potential sexual harassment. Internet monitoring could not be a labor-intensive effort at Bard, so after a free, 30-day trial of Web Inspector—an Internet monitoring tool from Elron Software—Crooks was able to document several problems: visits to pornographic Web sites, incorrect network configuration, and access to personal email accounts. Crooks adopted the monitoring software and sent a company-wide email message explaining the new policies. With this monitoring, Bard was able to proactively manage Internet usage, avoiding major abuse and lost productivity.

JFK Medical Center

At JFK Medical Center, one of the largest hospitals in New Jersey, thousands of employees ranging from doctors and nurses to executives and staff members have Internet access. "There is a ton of valuable information our employees can access via the Internet that is critical to the efficiency and effectiveness of this institution," said Bill Thorpe, a system analyst. "However, there is a lot of garbage out there. Our concern is focused primarily on protecting JFK from legal liabilities. Saving our bandwidth and improving employee productivity are also important goals." With thousands of employees at JFK, Thorpe does not have the time or the manpower to manually monitor where people are going on the Internet. Thorpe reviewed several different filtering products and chose one that was content and context sensitive, reducing the number of false positives, and had extensive reporting capabilities, providing cost analysis and cost-per-minutes data. Thorpe worked with the human resources department to develop an IUP, configuring the monitoring software to enforce this policy. Employees know they have the freedom to use the Internet as a business tool, but usage will be monitored and comprehensive reports generated, allowing specific issues to be addressed.

Lake Charles Memorial Hospital

The nonprofit Lake Charles Memorial Hospital is one of the largest facilities serving Southwest Louisiana and Southeast Texas with about 1,000 employees across the hospital's six locations. "I knew we needed an email policy and a way to enforce it, otherwise we could be held liable if an employee was exposed to inappropriate Internet content," said Ron Westmoreland, the system administrator. "We wanted a solution that was accurate, flexible, and scalable." After finalizing the hospital's policy for email usage, it was communicated to current employees and is part of the orientation process for new-hires. "We explained the reasons why email shouldn't be abused and employees were informed that we now had the ability to monitor email content in order to enforce the policy," said Westmoreland. The policy also states that occasional personal use of the hospital's email system is acceptable. Employee response to the monitoring has been positive as Lake Charles allows employees some freedom to explore the Internet.

New Mexico Mortgage Finance Authority

The New Mexico Mortgage Finance Authority (MFA) is a housing agency for the state. "On every level of this organization we need to be organized and in control," says Doug Flint, the systems administrator. The MFA has an integrated system linking all of its systems together and all employees have Internet and intranet access. MFA did not want labor-intensive policing of the Internet, and wanted to ensure a productive and healthy environment. "We did suspect a couple of people were abusing Internet usage, but really we decided to start monitoring Internet access out of common sense—the smart thing to do," said Flint. Monitoring was a learning process at MFA. According to Flint: "At first we made the rules too strict, but over time we came to understand what kind of protection we needed and were able to find a policy that worked for us."

Irvington High School

Irvington High School, with a student body of 1,600 students, is located about 40 miles southeast of San Francisco. Bill Stanley, the technology coordinator said, "In a school setting, Internet access is fraught with many hazards." By "hazards," Stanley refers to surfing abuse by students and faculty. "We want to encourage students to perform online research and gain a larger worldview, but teenagers often have a tendency to move outside the educational constraints," he said. Stanley decided a tool to filter and monitor Internet usage was needed to allow user-customization of keywords for blocking, but more importantly emphasized monitoring and reporting. It is impossible to block all the current and potential content-offensive sites, but with the development of an IUP and monitoring software, the school is able to use the Internet to enrich the curriculum.

Bricker and Eckler

Bricker and Eckler is one of Ohio's leading law firms. "We have lots of attorneys that work from home," said Eric Schmidt, chief information officer. "We want them to each have efficient access to all of our resources. We told every employee they are being monitored because I really think it is important to let them know up front." Utilizing an authentication program provided by the company firewall and a high-speed Internet connection, the attorneys are able to securely conduct client research and transmit confidential data over the Internet. Prior to rolling out the Internet resource throughout the firm, however, Schmidt and the firm's managing partner developed and clearly communicated a policy for Internet usage.

Davis and Kuelthau, S.C.

Davis and Kuelthau, a full-service law firm with five offices throughout Wisconsin, is dedicated to "educating its clients about the law to ensure they have the tools necessary to identify legal problems and minimize the risk of legal consequences." According to Brian Drier, the firm's IS manager, "Organizations look to us as experts in advising how to protect themselves from these kinds of Internet problems, so we lead by example and take the same precautions within our own company. Our position is that the Internet is a fantastic resource," said Drier. "We wanted to open up this resource to all employees for personal and professional use, but we knew it needed to be managed properly. Our biggest concerns were legal liabilities and productivity." By using monitoring software, Davis and Kuelthau was able to preserve investment in critical Internet resources and make intelligent planning and forecasting decisions with flexibility and customizability.

▪▪▪ Conclusion

While these eight organizations have many differences, there is a common goal — to use the communication and productivity enhancing power of the Internet while minimizing risks and costs and maximizing employee freedom and privacy. To accomplish this, they chose to adopt IPM, integrating policies and monitoring. Filtering and monitoring software is increasing in popularity; the International Data Corporation, a leading market research firm, estimates 3.9 million businesses will implement Web-filtering software by 2003, and 80% of large companies will purchase Web-filtering software in the next 12–24 months [2]. The organizations in this discussion found flexibility and customizability, low maintenance, a high degree of accuracy, multiple features, ease of use, and integration with current technologies in monitoring software. They deployed the latest Internet technologies to streamline business processes, trim costs, and offer customers and suppliers the ease of electronic communication while protecting organizational information and resources, and respecting employee rights. In short, the eight organizations leveraged the power of the Internet while responsibly and proactively managing its use. To companies that are hesitant about providing Internet access, IPM offers a way to reduce the risks, and as these cases demonstrate, it is not only large companies that can benefit from IPM.

REFERENCES

1. D'Antoni, H. Web surfers beware: Someone's watching. *Info. Week 772* (Feb. 7, 2000), 167–168.
2. Elron Software, Inc. (Mar. 2001); www.elronsw.com.
3. Mandel, M.J. and Hof, R.D. Rethinking the Internet. *Bus. Week* (Mar. 26, 2001), 117–141.
4. Ohlhorst, F.J. Filtering software blocks headaches, litigation. *Computer Reseller News 926* (Jan. 1, 2001), 53–54.
5. Roberts, B. Filtering software blocks employees' Web abuses. *HRMagazine 44*, 9 (Sept. 1999), 114–120.
6. Wonnacort, L. Policing the Internet: If your users can't surf responsibly, you may have to monitor them. *Info World 21*, 13 (Mar. 29, 1999), 13–14.

Pending Investigation

Jonathan Littman

"Hi, Lew," Kevin greets his friend in his hangdog voice. It's January of 1992. He's talking on the phone from his dad's apartment in Calabasas, and he's got that awful pang in his gut. Kevin Mitnick trusts his instincts. He decides he better check to see if the line is being tapped.

Mitnick phones the remote Pac Bell central office in Calabasas, on Las Virgenes Street.

"You have one of our boxes there," he informs the technician.

Mitnick's launching another social engineering attack.

Mitnick listens to the tech walk down the frame and then return.

"Yeah, here it is."

"And the monitor number on that box was?"

Kevin Mitnick knows exactly what questions to ask. He knows that when Pac Bell wants to wiretap somebody they first create a new phone line, what they call a "monitor number" in the local central office. On the steel and wire frame where the phone lines run, Pac Bell connects the monitor line to the target line through a special interface box. Next, Pac Bell security personnel in Oakland phone the monitor line and enter the touchtone security code 1-2-3-4 to activate the wiretap.

And Kevin Mitnick knows some other things Pac Bell would prefer he didn't. The taps are referred to as pen registers, or Dial Number Recorders, DNRs. All the phone numbers dialed from each tapped line print out at the Pac Bell security office in Oakland. And Mitnick is one of a handful of hackers who know the taps also transmit voice, and can also be used to eavesdrop on conversations.

Mitnick's got the monitor number. One more phone call and he figures he'll get the number of the actual wiretap.

His car radio's playing a familiar ad as he cruises with his cell phone. "This is Tom Bodette for Motel Six, and we'll leave the light on for you."

Mitnick dials Pac Bell security in San Francisco.

"Hi, this is Tom Bodette," Mitnick drawls.

Shit. I can't believe I used that name!

"We've got a box here with your name and number. I'm going to have to disconnect it," Bodette continues.

The security investigator is being helpful. And why not? She's one of the half dozen phone company professionals in California that makes sure citizens are being properly wiretapped. Intercepts. That's what Pac Bell calls them. It sounds less threatening than a wiretap.

"Do you need to do it now?" the security woman asks.

"Yeah. You ready?" primes Bodette.

"Go ahead."

"OK. Hold on a minute. I'll be right back."

This is the fun part. Mitnick cups his hand over the phone for a couple of minutes and works himself into character.

"I, HUFF, HUFF, disconnected it. HUFF, HUFF. Can you give me some help connecting it back to the frame?"

The Pac Bell security woman rattles off the LEN, the line equipment number, of the wires the box has to be tied back into.

"I don't have Cosmos handy," Bodette casually offers, mentioning the Pac Bell computer database. "What's the phone number?"

Kevin Mitnick is so smooth that the security professional doesn't even pause.

"It's 55—"

Hook, line, and sinker.

Kevin is half right. There is a wiretap out of the local Calabasas central office, but it's on the phone of Teltec Investigations, a nearby Calabasas private detective firm. By coincidence, Mitnick's father, Alan, knows a private detective who works at the firm, a guy named Mark Kasdan. Mitnick senior invites him over, Kevin fills the detective in on what he's learned, and then Kasdan brings Kevin down to the firm's offices for a little show-and-tell.

The detectives don't believe Mitnick at first, the things he says he knows, the things he claims he can do. But as Mitnick starts to prove his encyclopedic knowledge of phones and computers, they take him seriously. The detectives confide why they think their phones are being tapped. Teltec was investigated for allegedly using stolen codes to run TRW credit reports on individuals, and the three-year statute of limitations on the case is about to expire. Perhaps, they tell Mitnick, the recent wiretap is a sign of renewed law enforcement interest.

The on-ramp light turns green, and Mitnick guns it onto the crowded 101 freeway at Sherman Oaks. His probation officer has given him permission to take the long drive to Vegas, where his mother and grandmother live, for his brother's funeral.

The death of his half brother has hit Mitnick hard. The facts are sketchy. On the evening of January 7, 1992, Adam Mitnick was found dead in Echo Park, a neighborhood notorious for gangs and drugs. They had been close. It was Adam who arrived at the gate at Lompoc when Mitnick's prison term was up. They were talking about renting an apartment together. Adam had started his own business selling miniblinds and had enrolled in college. That's what gnawed at Kevin. His brother had sworn he'd quit heroin.

To the Los Angeles police department the death of Adam Mitnick was just one of the hundreds of overdoses each year that clog its files. But Kevin Mitnick had to investigate, and before long he learned that Adam was found in the passenger seat of his own BMW, slumped against the dash.

So who had driven his half brother to Echo Park to die? Mitnick learned Adam had visited his uncle that same night, the same uncle who was addicted to heroin.

Suddenly, Kevin Mitnick didn't want to know any more about how his brother ended up dead at just twenty-one. It reminded him too much of his family.

Mitnick's parents divorced when he was three, and he lived in a series of unmemorable apartments in the San Fernando Valley. Although Kevin saw his father rarely, he liked him and looked up to him. The Mitnick men were salesmen, smooth tongued, sharp and successful. Mitnick said his dad worked for Capitol Records, and then sold home improvement contracts. *Los Angeles Magazine* would list him as one of the most successful businesses in the San Fernando Valley, but court records told another story. Alan Mitnick filed for bankruptcy in the mid 1980s, and Los Angeles criminal filings included charges for forgery, grand theft, and battery.

Crime was no stranger to the Mitnick family. Mitnick's aunt, Chickie Leventhal, ran Chickie's Bail Bonds in Los Angeles. Mitnick's uncle worked in construction, but Southern California court files were full of civil actions filed against him. By the late 1980s his uncle's life began to unwind. There were charges for possession of controlled substances and drug paraphernalia. In 1989, he was charged with grand theft and sentenced to a year in county jail and three years probation. Incredibly he served part of his term in the same Jewish halfway house with his nephew, after Kevin's DEC conviction. But Mitnick's uncle wasn't rehabilitated. The following year he fled probation. He had at least three aliases: Jay Tenny Brooks, Richard Stewart, and William Contos. And years later he would be charged and convicted of manslaughter. During a robbery he shot and killed a man.

Kevin was often left to fend for himself. His father was more interested in Adam. His mother, Shelly Jaffe, was busy just trying to make ends meet, waitressing at a couple of Jewish delicatessens on Ventura Boulevard. Mitnick appeared eager to work, toiling as a delivery boy and kitchen helper at one of the delis, and helping out in the office of a local synagogue. When Kevin was ten or twelve, he'd push carts back into the slots at the local Safeway for Blue Chip stamps. He was proud of his Jewish faith and displayed his framed Bar Mitzvah certificate on his dresser.

But like everything else in the Mitnick household, even Kevin's faith was a bit off-kilter. Mitnick's stepfather was an active member of the radical Jewish Defense League. When Mitnick was eight or ten his stepfather would take him out into the desert near Los Angeles and let him watch while they fired automatic weapons at posters of Hitler.

Kevin was a loner, uninterested in sports and too shy for girls. At thirteen he learned how to punch out his own bus transfers, and after school he'd ride out toward San Bernardino and the desert, or down the coast to Long Beach. His grandmother was proud of Kevin for memorizing the routes and schedules. No one in the family would think to scold him for tricking the transit district out of bus fare. Kevin's little game was an ingenious system of babysitting himself, of creating a travel opportunity for a boy whose mother rarely had the time to take him anywhere.

One afternoon on the bus, Kevin met a fat boy. They'd ride together to Beverly Hills, eat junk food, and gawk at the homes of the movie stars. Soon Kevin too was fat and ate almost constantly. Bob Arkow, a bus driver, struck up a conversation with the kid on his empty bus one day. He'd noticed his T-shirt emblazoned with "CBers Do It on the Air." Mitnick told him he was into citizens band radio, and the driver asked if he'd heard about ham radio. That's all it took to get him started. Mitnick went to the ham radio outlet, picked up some books, and in no time earned his own ham radio license.

As a ham radio operator Mitnick had his own call sign, and could radio other ham operators around the world. The parallels to hacking were great. Mitnick didn't have to pay for his radio messages. His call sign was his identity, or "handle," and he was part of a worldwide community of radio enthusiasts. Though cellular phones were years off into the future, he was already mastering their basic principle—radio.

To Arkow, Mitnick was just another thirteen-year-old boy with a new toy, making on-air personal attacks on other ham radio operators. Soon, he was able to manipulate the phone system to harass people too. He began rummaging through phone company dumpsters for discarded manuals and reading Bell technical journals at the library. Just as Mitnick rode L.A.'s buses free, he could travel the long distance lines wherever and however he pleased.

Lewis De Payne discovered Mitnick one day while listening to one of his ham radio fights. They became fast friends, though De Payne was several years older than the fifteen-year-old. De Payne admired the young enthusiast's obsessive streak. Mitnick could be whoever he wanted over the radio or on the phone. He'd call a Pac Bell switching center and impersonate an angry supervisor, and if one person wouldn't give him what he needed, he'd just dial someone else.

His mother couldn't afford to buy him a personal computer so Mitnick roamed like a techno gypsy from one Radio Shack to another, slipping in a communications program disk and using the store's modem to dial any computer he wished. His teachers at Monroe High School described him as clever, until he began using its computers to hack into the files of other schools. He dropped out and was later expelled from a community college for similar pranks.

Those who crossed Mitnick did so at their own risk. He attached a hospital's $30,000 in long distance charges to the home phone bill of a ham radio enthusiast he hated. His goal was power. Mitnick had little interest in making money with his phone and burgeoning computer skills. For kicks, he tracked Susan Thunder, a prostitute who had fallen hard for De Payne, finding out where she lived and turned tricks, shutting off her phone service, forwarding her calls, and broadcasting her sex talk on ham radio. In 1981, after Mitnick and De Payne talked their way into a late-night unauthorized visit of a Pac Bell computer operations center, Thunder planned her revenge. The computers of a San Francisco leasing company nearly ground to a halt, and the operators arrived one morning to find the floor littered with printouts carrying threats and the names of Roscoe and Mitnick. It wasn't long before an investigator from the district attorney's office chased young Mitnick on the 405 freeway and handcuffed him at gunpoint. The charges were burglary, grand theft, and conspiring to commit computer fraud. Thunder testified for the prosecution and the juvenile court ordered a diagnostic psychological study of Mitnick and sentenced him to a year's probation.

By 1984, Mitnick had a job and a black Nissan with the conspicuous vanity plate "X-HACKER." But the D.A.'s office was already back on his tail, investigating allegations Mitnick was harassing people on MIT's computers and hacking into phone company computers. Mitnick's new office job was a convenient place to make his pretext calls to Pac Bell and run TRW credit checks for kicks. But the day before the D.A. served its search warrant, a man identifying himself as a Los Angeles Police Department detective called into the warrant section of the LAPD to confirm a probation violation warrant on Mitnick.

It was Mitnick, presumably, checking to see if he was wanted, and when he got the bad news, he went underground, not to resurface until the summer of 1985, after his arrest warrant expired. He enrolled at a Los Angeles technical school, the Computer Learning Center, and impressed his instructors. In 1987, he surprised everyone by dating a pretty, petite woman named Bonnie Vitello. They were soon married.

Love brought out another side of Mitnick. The impulsive hacker lost weight, danced at nightclubs, and shared romantic trips up the California coast. But Mitnick hadn't gone cold turkey. To start with, Bonnie Vitello happened to work for GTE, a phone company. Like an addict, Mitnick would periodically escape into cheap motels with a computer and modem for hacking binges, and sure enough, in 1987, he was busted again, this time for hacking into the computers of a small Santa Cruz UNIX software maker. The charge was reduced to a misdemeanor when he agreed to explain how he did it, and Mitnick was given three years probation.

He was on the verge of being hired by Security Pacific Bank, but calls from an enemy ham radio operator and an LAPD detective scuttled the job offer. Mitnick tried to get into security, and even filed a fictitious business name, Security Software Services, in Sherman Oaks in April of 1988. But by that summer, Kevin Mitnick had a new plan. He wanted to learn more about Digital Equipment Corporation's latest VMS operating system for its powerful minicomputers. He didn't just want the operating system, however, he wanted the source code, the genetic blueprint, to discover more about its vulnerabilities. With the source code, Mitnick could understand more about the complex program. He could also plant the seeds of his own future games. At the least, he'd know better where to attack. And if he was truly bent on creating mayhem, he could try to send the software back to Digital's distribution centers, implanted with his own Trojan horse programs, secret back doors to enable him to manipulate the system at will.

But once again Mitnick was caught red-handed. Lacking his own powerful computer, he'd been forced to stash his loot at the University of Southern California's computers, and, not surprisingly, the university's system administrators had noticed his bulging files. There was no evidence Kevin Mitnick planned to sell the software, modify it, or even redistribute it. But what Mitnick looked upon as simple copying, the government viewed as theft.

Kevin Mitnick was a serial hacker, and he'd given no one any reason to believe he intended to quit.

2002 CSI/FBI Computer Crime and Security Survey

RICHARD POWER

The "Computer Crime and Security Survey" is conducted by CSI with the participation of the San Francisco Federal Bureau of Investigation's (FBI) Computer Intrusion Squad. The aim of this effort is to raise the level of security awareness, as well as help determine the scope of computer crime in the United States.

Now in its seventh year, the annual release of the survey results is a major international news story, covered widely in the mainstream print and broadcast media. Furthermore, throughout the year, the survey results are referenced in numerous presentations, articles and papers on the nature and scope of computer crime.

Based on responses from 503 computer security practitioners in U.S. corporations, government agencies, financial institutions, medical institutions and universities, the findings of the "2002 Computer Crime and Security Survey" confirm that the threat from computer crime and other information security breaches continues unabated and that the financial toll is mounting.

Here are the results of the seventh annual survey, together with some insights from subject matter experts, as well as a few of my own comments. If the survey continues beyond the seven-year cycle it has now completed, it will be designed differently and reflect new priorities.

But it has certainly met its objectives to raise the level of security awareness throughout the world, help determine the scope of computer crime, foster cooperation between federal law enforcement and the private sector and promote sound information security practices within organizations.

▪▪▪ Who We Asked

Most respondents work for large corporations. The heaviest concentrations of respondents are in the high-tech (19%) and financial services (19%) sectors. Manufacturing is the next largest industry segment (11% of respondents).

Federal (8%), state (8%) and local (3%) government agencies, taken together, comprise 19% of respondents.

Organizations in other vital areas of the national infrastructure also responded—for example, medical institutions (8%), telecommunications (5%) and utilities (3%).

The responses come from organizations with large payrolls—for example, 24% reported 10,000 or more employees and 12% reported from 5,001 to 9,999 employees.

Thirty-seven percent of respondents in the commercial sector reported a gross income over $1 billion, 8% reported gross income of from $501 million to $1 billion, and 16% reported gross income of from $100 million to $500 million.

▪▪▪ What They Used

For the fifth year in a row, we asked what kind of security technologies respondents were using. And, as we have discussed in previous years, the results were compelling.

For example, although 89% of respondents have firewalls and 60% use IDS, 40% report system penetration from the outside; and although 90% of respondents use anti-virus software, 85% of them were hit by viruses, worms, etc.

▪▪▪ The Trends Continue

Highlights of the "2002 Computer Crime and Security Survey" include the following:

- Ninety percent of respondents (primarily large corporations and government agencies) detected computer security breaches within the last twelve months.
- Eighty percent acknowledged financial losses due to computer breaches.
- Forty-four percent (223 respondents) were willing and/or able to quantify their financial losses. These 223 respondents reported $455,848,000 in financial losses.
- As in previous years, the most serious financial losses occurred through theft of proprietary information (26 respondents reported $170,827,000) and financial fraud (25 respondents reported $115,753,000).
- For the fifth year in a row, more respondents (74%) cited their Internet connection as a frequent point of attack than cited their internal systems as a frequent point of attack (33%).
- Thirty-four percent reported the intrusions to law enforcement. (In 1996, only 16% acknowledged reporting intrusions to law enforcement.)

Respondents detected a wide range of attacks and abuses:

- Forty percent detected system penetration from the outside.
- Forty percent detected denial of service attacks.
- Seventy-eight percent detected employee abuse of Internet access privileges (for example, downloading pornography or pirated software, or inappropriate use of e-mail systems).
- Eighty-five percent detected computer viruses.

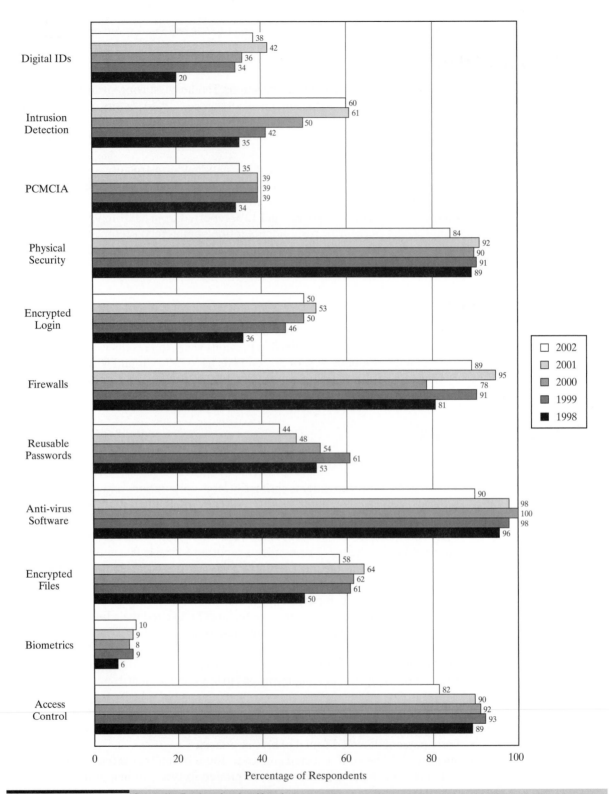

Security Technologies Used

Percentage of Respondents

Source: Computer Security Institute, CSI 2002 Computer Crime and Security Survey.
2002: 500 Respondents/99%   *1999: 501 Respondents/96%*
2001: 530 Respondents/99%   *1998: 512 Respondents/98%*
2000: 629 Respondents/97%

■ ■ ■ WWW Crime Has Become Commonplace

For the fourth year in a row, we asked our respondents some questions about their WWW sites.

Here are the results:

- Ninety-eight percent of respondents have WWW sites.
- Fifty-two percent conduct electronic commerce on their sites.
- Thirty-eight percent suffered unauthorized access or misuse on their Web sites within the last twelve months. Twenty-one percent said that they didn't know if there had been unauthorized access or misuse.
- Twenty-five percent of those acknowledging attacks reported from two to five incidents. Thirty-nine percent reported ten or more incidents.
- Seventy percent of those attacked reported vandalism.
- Fifty-five percent reported denial of service.
- Twelve percent reported theft of transaction information.
- Six percent reported financial fraud.

WWW crimes range from cyber vandalism (e.g. Web site defacement) at the low end to theft of proprietary information and financial fraud at the high end.

Despite a brief decline in the weeks after 9/11, Web site defacements, the most prevalent form of cyber vandalism, increased globally during 2001, according to Mi2g (www.mi2g.com).

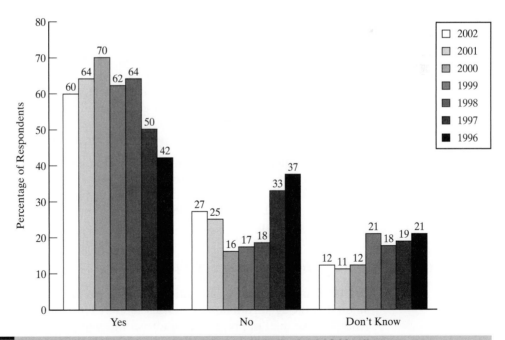

■ ■ ■ ■ ■ ■ ■ ■ ■ ■ ■ **Unauthorized Use of Computer Systems Within the Last 12 Months**

Source: Computer Security Institute, CSI/FBI 2002 Computer Crime and Security Survey.

2002: 481 Respondents/96%   *1998: 515 Respondents/99%*
2001: 532 Respondents/99.6%   *1997: 391 Respondents/86%*
2000: 585 Respondents/91%   *1996: 410 Respondents/96%*
1999: 512 Respondents/98%

▪▪▪ Hemorrhaging from Theft of Proprietary Info?

In 1997, when we first asked questions about "types of attack" and "financial losses," 20% of respondents acknowledged detecting theft of proprietary information. In 2002, the percent of respondents acknowledging theft of proprietary information was the same. The high was in 2001, when 25% reported theft of proprietary information; the low was in 1998 when only 18% reported it.

But while the percent of respondents acknowledging theft of proprietary information has remained relatively steady, the total financial losses due to this type of activity among respondents willing and/or able to quantify their losses, as well as the average loss derived from the aggregate totals, has soared.

In 1997, 21 respondents quantified their losses. The highest reported loss was $10M, the average loss was $954,666, the total losses reported were $20,048,000. In 2002, 26 respondents quantified their losses. The highest reported loss was $50M, the average loss was $6,571,000, total losses reported were $170,827,000.

Why the significant increase in quantified financial losses due to theft of proprietary information when the percent of respondents reporting that type of activity has remained fairly constant?

Naomi Fine of Pro-Tec Data (www.pro-tecdata.com), a leading authority on economic espionage and information protection, explains.

The obvious answer is that those seeking information are more effective, perhaps because of more sophisticated technologies and techniques, at taking more valuable information. But the steady rise can also be attributed to two additional factors that have been rising exponentially over the same years as the study:

1. increased recognition that information has value.
2. increase in perceived value of information.

In other words, while organizations like the Society for Competitive Intelligence Professionals help gatherers hone information collection skills, and the Internet makes it easier for information thieves to gather information used to bait and lure targets, the targets feel the pain of the loss more now because of an increased awareness that information translates into market differentiation, competitive positioning and even top line "revenues."

Another interesting trend in the data over the seven year life span of the survey is that the percent of respondents reporting U.S. domestic corporate competitors as a likely source of attack has gone either sideways or down: 51% in '97, 48% in '98, 53% in '99, 44% in '00, 49% in '01, 38% in '02. Perhaps the EEA, signed into law by President Clinton in 1996, really has had an impact.

▪▪▪ Hemorrhaging from Financial Fraud?

Like theft of proprietary information, financial fraud accounts for a disproportionate amount of the aggregate financial losses cited by those willing and/or able to quantity. And also like theft of proprietary information, while the losses attributed to financial fraud have increased significantly, the percent of those respondents acknowledging detection of financial fraud has remained fairly constant.

In 1997, when we first asked questions about "types of attack" and "financial losses," 12% of respondents acknowledged detecting financial fraud. In 2002, the percent of respondents acknowledging financial fraud was the same. The high was 14% in 1998 and 1999, when 14% reported financial fraud; the low was in 2000 when only 11% reported it.

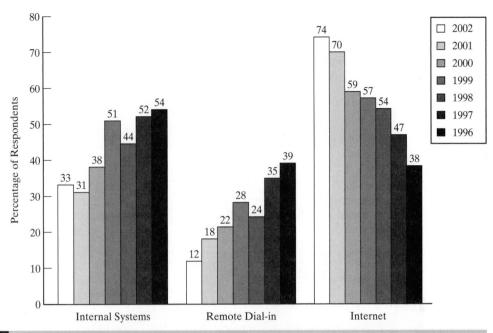

Internet Connection Is Increasingly Cited as a Frequent Point of Attack

Source: Computer Security Institute, CSI/FBI 2002 Computer Crime and Security Survey.

2002: 481 Respondents/96% *1999: 324 Respondents/62%* *1997: 391 Respondents/69%*
2001: 384 Respondents/72% *1998: 279 Respondents/54%* *1996: 174 Respondents/40%*
2000: 443 Respondents/68%

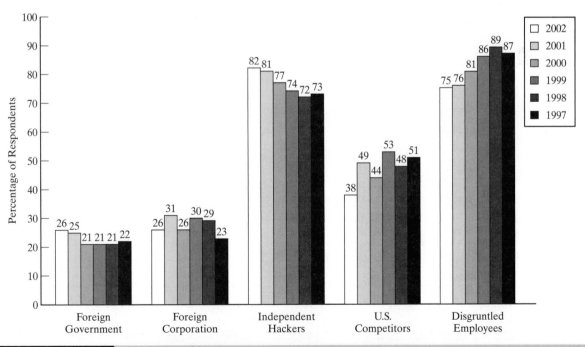

Likely Sources of Attack

Source: Computer Security Institute, CSI/FBI 2002 Computer Crime and Security Survey.

2002: 414 Respondents/82% *2000: 583 Respondents/90%* *1998: 428 Respondents/54%*
2001: 484 Respondents/91% *1999: 460 Respondents/88%* *1997: 503 Respondents/89%*

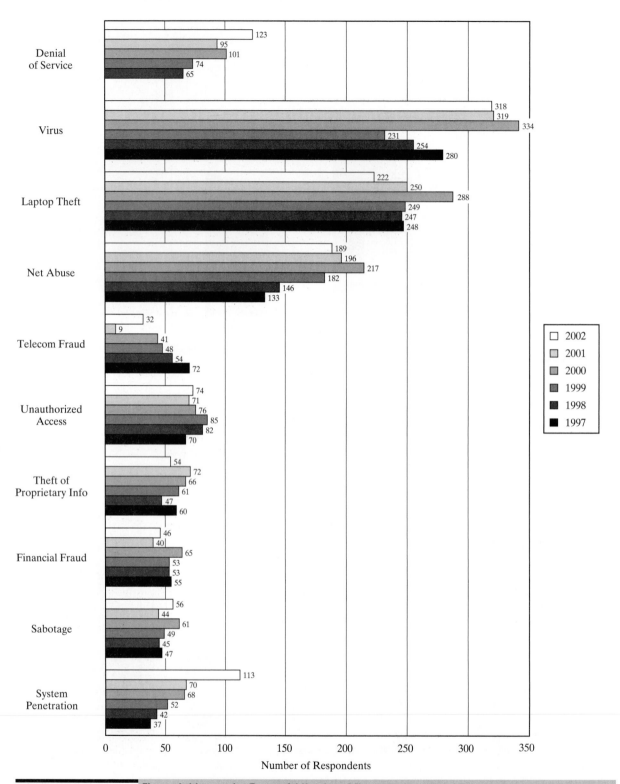

Financial Losses by Type of Attack or Misuse

Source: Computer Security Institute, CSI/FBI 2002 Computer Crime and Security Survey.

2002: 404 Respondents/80%   *1999: 376 Respondents/73%*

2001: 344 Respondents/64%   *1998: 512 Respondents/98%*

2000: 477 Respondents/74%   *1997: 422 Respondents/75%*

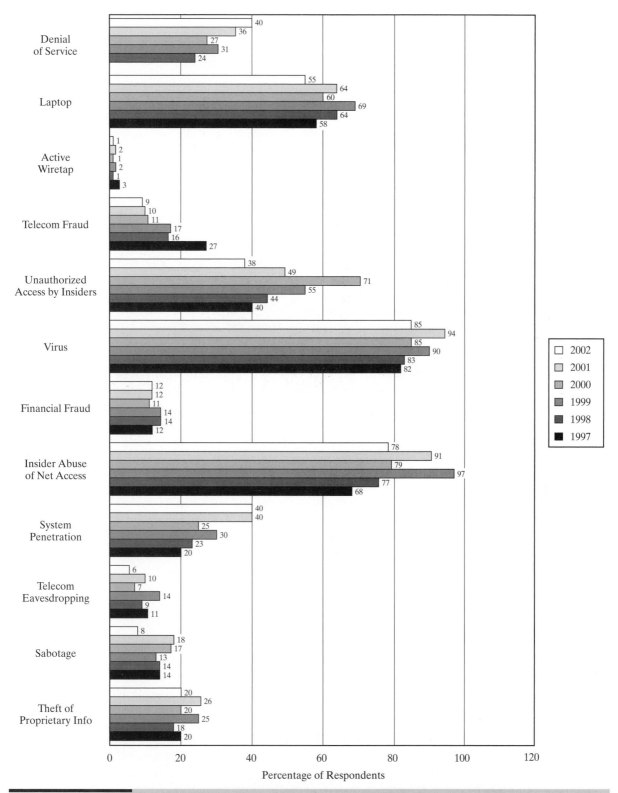

Denial of Service
- 40 (2002)
- 36 (2001)
- 27 (2000)
- 31 (1999)
- 24 (1998)

Laptop
- 55 (2002)
- 64 (2001)
- 60 (2000)
- 69 (1999)
- 64 (1998)
- 58 (1997)

Active Wiretap
- 1 (2002)
- 2 (2001)
- 1 (2000)
- 2 (1999)
- 1 (1998)
- 3 (1997)

Telecom Fraud
- 9 (2002)
- 10 (2001)
- 11 (2000)
- 17 (1999)
- 16 (1998)
- 27 (1997)

Unauthorized Access by Insiders
- 38 (2002)
- 49 (2001)
- 71 (2000)
- 55 (1999)
- 44 (1998)
- 40 (1997)

Virus
- 85 (2002)
- 94 (2001)
- 85 (2000)
- 90 (1999)
- 83 (1998)
- 82 (1997)

Financial Fraud
- 12 (2002)
- 12 (2001)
- 11 (2000)
- 14 (1999)
- 14 (1998)
- 12 (1997)

Insider Abuse of Net Access
- 78 (2002)
- 91 (2001)
- 79 (2000)
- 97 (1999)
- 77 (1998)
- 68 (1997)

System Penetration
- 40 (2002)
- 40 (2001)
- 25 (2000)
- 30 (1999)
- 23 (1998)
- 20 (1997)

Telecom Eavesdropping
- 6 (2002)
- 10 (2001)
- 7 (2000)
- 14 (1999)
- 9 (1998)
- 11 (1997)

Sabotage
- 8 (2002)
- 18 (2001)
- 17 (2000)
- 13 (1999)
- 14 (1998)
- 14 (1997)

Theft of Proprietary Info
- 20 (2002)
- 26 (2001)
- 20 (2000)
- 25 (1999)
- 18 (1998)
- 20 (1997)

Legend:
- □ 2002
- 2001
- 2000
- 1999
- 1998
- ■ 1997

Percentage of Respondents

Types of Attack or Misuse Detected in the Last 12 Months (by percent)

Source: Computer Security Institute, CSI/FBI 2002 Computer Crime and Security Survey.

2002: 455 Respondents/90%	*2000: 583 Respondents/90%*	*1998: 428 Respondents/83%*
2001: 484 Respondents/91%	*1999: 460 Respondents/88%*	*1997: 503 Respondents/89%*

▪▪▪ Other Serious Problems: Viruses, Worms, etc.

Theft of proprietary information and financial fraud account for perhaps two-thirds of the financial losses reported by respondents. Yet only 20% report incidents of theft of proprietary information, and only 12% report incidents of financial fraud.

Furthermore, throughout the seven-year life of the survey, these ratios have held fairly steady.

So what does the rest of the story tell us? What types of attacks or breaches are the most common? And what kind of financial losses do they incur?

It will probably be no surprise to you that malicious code attacks (i.e., viruses, worms, etc.) have proven year in and year out to be the most common incidents reported in the survey.

In 1997, 82% of respondents reported virus and worm contaminations. In 2001, the year in which the survey results reflected those hit by "I Love You," the percent of respondents reporting viruses, etc. peaked at 94%.

In 1997, financial losses due to viruses, etc. were reported by 165 respondents for an aggregate total of $12,498,150 with an average of loss of $75,746 per organization.

In 2001, financial losses due to viruses, etc. were reported by 186 respondents for an aggregate total of $45,288,150 with an average loss of $243,845 per organization.

In 2002, although the percent of respondents reporting virus and worm outbreaks dropped from 94% the previous year to 85%, the total financial losses reported by the 188 respondents who were willing/and or able to quantify actually increased from $45,288,600 to $49,979,000 with an increase in the average loss from $243,845 per organization in 2001 to $283,000 per organization in 2002.

While the 2001 results reflect the impact of "I Love You," the 2002 results would reflect those respondents hit by CodeRed, Nimda and Sircam.

Computer Economics (www.computereconomics.com) estimates that the worldwide economic impact of Code Red was $2.62 billion, the worldwide economic impact of SirCam was $1.15 billion and the world economic impact of Nimda was $635 million. Computer Economics further estimates the worldwide economic impact of "I Love You" in 2000 at $8.75 billion and that of Melissa and Explorer in 1999 at $1.10 billion and $1.02 billion respectively.

▪▪▪ Other Serious Problems: Net Abuse, etc.

Of course, not all cyber crime involves trade secret theft, financial fraud or sabotage. Greed and revenge are not the only motives. Some cyber crimes are crimes of passion. And, indeed, some security breaches are not even criminal in nature, but can nevertheless be costly due to lost productivity, civil liability damages, etc.

The number of respondents reporting employee abuse of network and Internet privileges (for example, downloading pornography or inappropriate use of e-mail systems) dropped from 91% in 2001 to 78% in 2002, and yet, financial losses attributed to this type of abuse, etc. soared from $35,001,650 with an average loss per organization of $357,160 in 2001 to $50,099,000 with an average of $536,000 in 2002. How and why?

Organizations are more sensitive to the costs of the problem. They are watching their workforce more closely. They are more in control of what is going on. They are getting tougher. They are making examples of people. The Internet filtering and monitoring technology they have invested in is paying off.

High-profile crackdowns on Net abuse at Dow Chemical Co., the *New York Times*, Computer Associates International, First Union Corp., Edward Jones, Livermore

National Lab and numerous U.S. government agencies have whetted the appetite of other organizations.

Organizations are taking the problem seriously.

According to the American Management Association, seventy-three percent of U.S. businesses monitored their employees' Internet use last year.

Organizations are cracking down harder than ever.

Websense, an Internet filtering provider, reports that nearly two-thirds of U.S. companies disciplined workers for misusing Internet privileges while working, and a third of them—ranging in size from 6 to over 150,000 employees—have terminated workers that use the Internet to loaf.

Organizations are spending lots of money on it.

International Data Corp. forecasts that the Internet filtering technology market will grow by close to 50% per year, reaching $636 million (707.8 million euros) world-wide by 2004.

And the well-funded crackdown is world-wide.

The Privacy Foundation estimates that the number of employees under such surveillance is at 27 million, just over one-quarter of the global online workforce, i.e., those employees who have Internet and/or e-mail access at work, and use it regularly.

The problem isn't simply insiders accessing pornographic sexual content.

For example, the Informa Media Group projects that e-gambling revenue will rise to $14.5 billion worldwide by 2006. Informa believes that by that time, the U.S. will claim 24% of e-gambling revenue, and Europe will claim 53%. The Society for Human Resource Management reports that 30 percent of employees dive into NCAA office

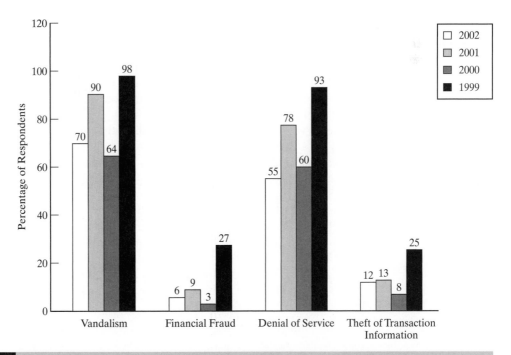

WWW Site Incidents: What Type of Unauthorized Access or Misuse?

Source: Computer Security Institute, CSI/FBI 2002 Computer Crime and Security Survey.

2002: 166 Respondents/33% *2000: 93 Respondents/14%*

2001: 78 Respondents/14% *1999: 44 Respondents/8%*

gambling pools. According to PC Data Online, approximately 14 million people visited sports Web sites during last year's NCAA college basketball tournament, aka "March Madness." Websense estimates organizations could suffer $504 million in lost productivity due to employees checking scores and viewing game Webcasts during work hours.

For corporations and government agencies, net abuse is a problem that effects the bottom line.

▦ To Report or Not to Report

The aim of the annual CSI/FBI Computer Crime and Security Survey is not only to gather data on the dark side of cyberspace, but to foster greater cooperation between law enforcement and the private sector so that there is a viable deterrent to cyber crime.

For the first three years, only 17% of those who suffered serious attacks reported them to law enforcement.

In 1999 survey, 32% answered that they had reported such incidents to law enforcement. A positive step forward.

In 2000, the percent of respondents who reported intrusions to law enforcement dropped to 25%.

In 2001, the percent of those who reported intrusions to law enforcement rose again to 36%.

In 2002, the percent of those who reported intrusions to law enforcement held relatively steady at 34%.

The trend is still upward.

▦ The Truth Is Out There

The CSI/FBI Computer Crime and Security Survey is a non-scientific, informal but narrowly focused poll of information security practitioners. Its aim is to heighten security awareness, promote information protection, and encourage cooperation between law enforcement and private sector.

The survey is at best a series of snapshots that give some sense of the "facts on the ground" at a particular time. The findings are in large part corroborated by data from other reputable studies, as well as by real-world incidents documented in open source publications. I also suggest that the findings of the CSI/FBI survey are strengthened by having six straight years of data to draw on.

The CSI/FBI survey results should be taken, in my opinion, as raw intelligence (something that some companies are trying to charge you a lot of money for). They should not be used as the basis for actuarial tables or sentencing guidelines. They should not be used as a basis to extrapolate some pie in the sky numbers on intrusions or financial losses for the whole economy or the whole of the Internet. They should be used as an intelligence resource for your own thinking about the emerging trends in cyber crime. Nothing more, nothing less.

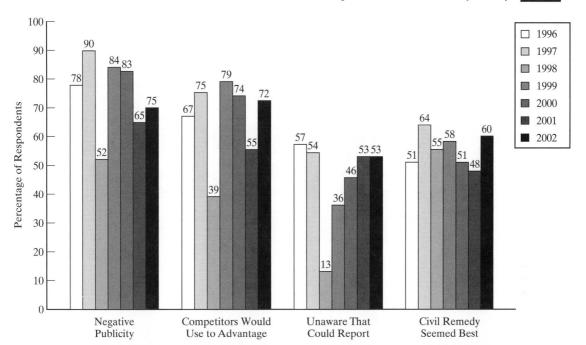

The Reasons Organizations Did Not Report Intrusions to Law Enforcement

Source: Computer Security Institute, CSI/FBI 2002 Computer Crime and Security Survey.

2002: 143 Respondents/28%   *1998: 96 Respondents/19%*
2001: 151 Respondents/28%   *1997: 142 Respondents/25%*
2000: 209 Respondents/32%   *1996: 64 Respondents/15%*
1999: 107 Respondents/20%

Detecting Deception in Computer-Mediated Communication*

JUDEE K. BURGOON
KENT MARETT
J. P. BLAIR

Detecting Mediated Deception

In every field, organization, and walk of life that makes use of effective decision making, reliable and timely information is of the utmost importance. Information technology is widely considered a key enabler of informed decision making. Not only do these relatively new tools and systems allow for great speed, volume, and flexibility in information transmission and communication with others, they also allow for the ready access of information archives. Up to this point, however, the risk associated with gathering biased and erroneous information has not been neutralized by technology. The sad fact is that information technology offers prime opportunities for inaccurate and purposely deceptive information to be passed along to decision makers, and currently it is mainly up to the human users of technology to detect any deception.

The Nature of Deception and Mediated Communication

This chapter focuses on deceptive information and its impact on people who use computer-based modes of communication, also referred to as computer-mediated communication. By the term *deception* we refer to the fabricated information knowingly transmitted by one person with the intent of creating a false conclusion in others. Deception can come in many forms, from simple "white lies" and exaggerations to misdirection, concealments, and complex fabrications. Obviously, lies also can range in the lev-

Detecting Deception in Computer-Mediated Communication by Judee K. Burgoon, Kent Marett, and John P. Blair. Copyright © 2002 Kent Marett. Reprinted by permission of the author.
*Portions of this research were supported by funding from the U.S. Air Force Office of Scientific Research under the U.S. Department of Defense University Research Initiative (Grant #F49620-01-1-0394, Judee Burgoon, Principal Investigator) and the U.S. Army Research Institute (Contract #DASW01-98-K-009, Judee Burgoon, Principal Investigator). The views, opinions, and/or findings in this report are those of the authors and should not be construed as an official Department of Defense position, policy, or decision.

els of maliciousness. Magicians use misdirection to divert an audience's attention away from the sleight of hand enabling an entertaining visual trick. The history of warfare is loaded with examples of propaganda and disinformation to divert an enemy's attention, with much more life-threatening consequences. All of these forms of diverging from "the truth, the whole truth, and nothing but the truth" fall under the umbrella of deception.

Computer-mediated communication (CMC), though commonly associated with text-based communication such as e-mail, actually includes any form of electronic communication that relies on computers for message transmission. Examples include use of Microsoft's NetMeeting tool, which can be used for text messaging, audio-conferencing, or videoconferencing; AOL's Instant Messenger; videoconferencing technologies such as PictureTel; and group decision support tools such as GroupSystems. Even cell phone communication falls under this general category of electronically mediated communication. Our interest in this chapter is in the use of these technologies for decision making and similar task-related communication.

Vulnerabilities in Electronic Communication

A brief moment's reflection should bring to mind numerous ways in which deception can affect decision making. After all, deception may be found in all phases of data gathering, information fusion, and determination of alternatives. The use of information technology to aid in these decision-making phases is commonplace and includes the use of data warehousing, expert systems, and computer-based communication media, among other systems. Should omitted, exaggerated, ambiguous, and fabricated information become fused with valid information, the resulting decision that relies on it will suffer. Computer systems are thus prime candidates for perpetuating deceptive information (Zmud 1990). Unreliable information preserved in IT artifacts provides one example. The latent effects of deceptive information contained within a database, for instance, may not be realized for some time after it has been recorded and stored. Further, the difficulties derived from deceptive information can become magnified, considering the ease with which technology such as e-mail, teleconferencing, and wireless communication can spread information quickly. Because many people place undue trust on information delivered by computers and have limited ability to observe the information's creation, the difficulty of detecting deception is exacerbated. Opportunities for deceivers to plan, rehearse, and edit their messages prior to transmission may place recipients at a further disadvantage.

The Challenge of Detecting Mediated Deception

One goal of research on deceptive communication is to develop methods that will improve the chances of humans in detecting deceptive information. Extensive prior research has shown that the average person is unsatisfactory at recognizing deception. Most studies place human accuracy at little better than 50 percent, with accurate detection of truth far more accurate than the detection of deceit (Park and Levine 2001). This is considered the result of several factors: the common bias of humans to regard incoming communication as truthful; the lack of a uniform set of reliable indicators of deceit; and the potential of heightened suspicion to backfire and lead to false alarms. To study whether the same poor rates of accuracy occur when communication is electronically mediated, we have begun a program of research to determine how deceit is perpetrated and detected when communication is electronically mediated. The ultimate goal of this program is the design and development of technologies that can assist humans in detecting deceit. There is no guarantee that the same verbal, nonverbal, and paralinguistic indicators of deception found in face-to-face encounters generalize to other media, especially computer-based media, hence the need for the new research program.

Our Research Goals

Clearly, research must be undertaken to establish some understanding of deceptive communication via information technology. The following sections describe our initial attempts at gaining a foothold with electronic modalities. Two objectives have served as the initial goals for this research effort. First, we wish to identify reliable cues of deception under computer-mediated and electronic communication modalities. Indicators to deception found in traditional oral, face-to-face conditions, such as changes in gestures, smiling, or posture, are not relevant in text-based or audio-based computer-mediated communication. A practical use of such a list could be to incorporate the cues into the training of information-gathering personnel and decision makers who use computer-based communication. Simply put, when using the "new media" and attempting to successfully detect deception, a new profile of cues is in order.

The second main goal of our research is the development of software that can automate detection or aid in augmenting the human user's ability to detect deception. We intend to develop a set of tools for computer-assisted and computer-automated analysis of potentially dubious messages and information. This goal is related to the goal of establishing a set of reliable electronic cues, because the cues would be the basis of the computerized analysis. Automated software that can parse and analyze an incoming message based on the cues to deception hold much practical importance. Information technology has certainly improved human performance by reducing the time it takes to accomplish many other time-and labor-intensive tasks, and we believe the task of filtering electronic messages for deceptive indicators falls in the same category. It is hoped that eventually, an automated deception detection system will be able to aid computer users by manually annotating suspicious communications. It is worth noting that completely replacing human detectors with automated tools is unrealistic and infeasible. Detection software cannot replace the human capacity to recognize, integrate, and interpret subtle and highly variable behavioral anomalies. However, computer-based tools working in conjunction with human detection strategies and skills should lead to a stronger link in the information processing chain.

The following sections report on several experiments as our first steps in progressing toward achieving the two goals. First, we report a study investigating mediated interpersonal deception over multiple modalities. Next, we describe two "mock theft" experiments that involved computer-based interviewing and software analysis of the transcripts. This will be followed by an account of an experiment examining deceptive communication over group support software. Finally, we present the results of a pilot study in textual resume faking. Although still early in the research process, these experiments, beyond yielding encouraging results, offer insight into the kinds of experiments that can be undertaken to gain greater knowledge about computer-mediated deceit and the requirements for creating computer-assisted tools.

▪▪▪ Experiments in Mediated Interpersonal Deception

Surviving in the Desert

Our first foray into deception under computer-mediated conditions explored how use of electronic communication alters users' perceptions of one another's truthfulness and trustworthiness. Funded by a contract from the U.S. Army Research Institute's Research and Advanced Concepts Office, the project did not look at deceptive indicators per se but rather at how perceptions of another's deceptive communication during face-to-face decision making differ from text, audio, and audiovisual forms of mediated communication. Face-to-face (FtF) communication served as our benchmark against which to compare computer-mediated communication (CMC) to see if mediating the communication process really did make a difference.

The task we used was a variation on a familiar group ranking task. In this case, we gave our participants a scenario in which they were in a jeep that had crashed in the Kuwaiti desert and their task was to decide what was most and least important to salvage. Specifically, they had to rank-order 12 objects such as a mirror, compass, tarp, jackets, water, pistol, and a book on edible plants in the desert in terms of importance of salvaging them from their combustible jeep. The beauty of this task is that it is one for which NASA experts had already established rankings based on their own knowledge and expertise, which meant we could compare our rankings with an objectively "best" set of rankings.

Here is how the experiment unfolded. Business and communication students reported to a research laboratory to participate in an experiment on new forms of communication. They were paired with another student and assigned to one of four communication conditions: FtF, text, NetMeeting audioconferencing, or NetMeeting videoconferencing. Those in the FtF condition worked with their partner in the same room, facing one another and with computers available off to each side. Those in the mediated conditions were placed in separate rooms at computer stations and did not see their partner prior to the experiment. They began by each reading the following scenario on their computer:

> You are on a reconnaissance mission in the Kuwaiti desert when your jeep crashes, killing several members of your group. The rest of you are uninjured. The nearest outpost is 45 miles east. When you don't report back for the evening, others will know you are missing and know generally, but not specifically, where you are. The terrain is dry and rugged. A nearby shallow water hole is contaminated by worms, animal leavings, and dead mice. The temperature will reach 108 degrees, and you are dressed in lightweight summer clothes with hats and sunglasses. The remaining survivors are able to salvage the following items. Rank these items according to how important they are to your survival, with 1 for the most important to 12 for the least important.

Before completing their rankings, participants read a handout we had created to look like material from an encyclopedia entry entitled "Imperative Information: Surviving in the Desert." We thought that if they had more information to exchange, their discussions would last longer and have greater validity. Unbeknownst to their partners, in half of the teams we asked one person to deceive his or her partner by advocating a position contrary to what the experts recommend. Specifically, we told them to advocate leaving the jeep in search of help as the best plausible solution, despite the experts' advice to stay put. We also asked them to mislead the other participant into believing that clothing, shelter, and communication are less important for survival than they really are. To make their task as clear as possible, we listed three issues on which they were to provide faulty and misleading information:

- Leaving the jeep, with proper equipment to find your way (e.g., the compass, map), is a must for survival.
- Communication devices (e.g., the rearview mirror, the flashlight) are unlikely to be useful in the desert.
- Shed all unnecessary clothing (e.g., rain-gear) to make walking easier.

In the other half of the teams, we omitted any such instructions. This meant that half of our teams had deception present and half did not. Thus, deception was one independent variable. The other independent variable was the modality in which teams interacted.

Those in the FtF condition turned their swivel chairs to face one another for their discussion. Those in the text condition completed their discussion in Microsoft NetMeeting's chat window, those in the audio condition had the full duplex audio enabled, and those in the video conferencing condition not only could use voice communication via the computer but could also see each other and themselves in small windows displayed on their computer screens. (Those in the latter two conditions could not use the chat windows.)

After reading the encyclopedic information and, where applicable, the deception instructions, participants completed their individual rankings of the 12 salvageable items and then discussed their rankings with their partner, the goal being to arrive at a consensually agreed-upon set of final rankings. Following the discussion, participants once again worked independently, completed their final rankings, and completed ratings of each other's communication, credibility, and truthfulness.

What did we find? First, deception made a big difference in how "naïve" participants judged their deceptive or truthful partner in terms of their communication and credibility. As with so many previous studies conducted exclusively under FtF conditions and with different tasks, deceivers were seen as less involved than truth-tellers. Partners also judged deceivers as less receptive, less composed, less dominant (i.e., more subdued and submissive than assertive), less persuasive, less similar to themselves, and less understanding than did partners of truth-tellers. In the same vein, deception affected judgments of credibility and attraction. Deceivers were judged as less truthful, trustworthy, competent, and sociable, and attractive as task partners.

Second, modality had some impact on perceived communication and credibility. Communicators were judged as the most receptive, receivers felt the greatest sense of connection with them, and receivers felt the most understood under the audio modality. As for credibility, they felt their partner was the most dependable and helpful in the FtF condition, followed closely by the audio condition. They also thought their partner's behavior was the most usual and expected under the FtF condition.

As might be expected, those interacting with deceivers made poorer quality decisions than those interacting with truthful partners. Decision quality was lowest under the audio modality, but this was due to those interacting with deceivers doing least well under audio. Given that partners were seen as the most persuasive and attractive as task partners in the audio condition, we speculate that deceivers were able to use that modality to be especially persuasive and prevent their partners from moving toward the high-quality decision advocated by experts. This differs from what we had found with an earlier study involving social conversation in which participants were most sensitive to deception in the audio condition and least so in the text condition. In fact, in that study, participants in the text condition actually thought deceivers were more truthful and trustworthy than truth-tellers. The one common thread through these studies is that modality influences communication, trust, other aspects of credibility, and ultimately, performance. Teasing out which modalities produce which communication patterns and elicit the most trust remains a task for further analysis and experimentation.

These findings from our first ventures into mediated deception produced two very important conclusions. First, under the right conditions, users of mediated forms of communication are able to pick up on deception when it is present. Their ratings of both their partners' communication and their partners' credibility reveal that they were attuned to differences in their partners' manner of communicating, and these differences had a negative impact on their willingness to trust the partner. These findings mirrored what we had found in FtF experiments, suggesting that it was not the task alone or deceivers' difficulty in pulling it off successfully that led to their poorer performances and credibility. The findings were encouraging, as they signaled that there should be indicators of deceit in mediated messages as well as nonmediated ones. Our task would be to uncover just which features of language, the voice, and visual nonverbal cues were responsible for these impressions and which could be incorporated into computer tools to assist users in detecting deception. At the same time, we recognized that the positions we had asked our deceivers to advocate—leaving the jeep, discarding communication devices, and discarding protective clothing—might have prompted skepticism and undermined deceivers' credibility from the start. With more subtle and practiced forms of deception, we would expect detection to become more challenging.

The second important conclusion was that detection of deceit may vary according to modality. We could not assume all modalities would function the same way or lead to the same degree of accuracy in detecting deception. This meant that we could not just focus our efforts on text communication, for example, nor could we assume that what was true of text messages would necessarily be applicable to voice message or other modalities. The challenge before us was a significant one but also a very exciting one, to figure out just how deception detection changes from one form of CMC to the next. The next investigations were designed to delve more specifically into the verbal and nonverbal behaviors indicative of deceit and the ways in which CMC altered users' manner of communicating.

Mock Theft Experiments

Traditionally, deceptive displays have been thought to arise from one of four causes: emotion, arousal, cognitive difficulty, and image or behavioral control (Vrij et al. 2000; Zuckerman, DePaulo, and Rosenthal 1981). First, three common types of emotions are associated with deception. These emotions include guilt, fear, and excitement. The amount of emotion that a person will experience during deception depends on numerous individual differences and situational factors. According to the emotional approach, feelings of guilt and fear will increase the amount of arousal that deceivers experience and this arousal will be exhibited in the suspect's behavior. Furthermore, the act of deception itself is thought to activate physiological arousal, with deceivers experiencing more nervousness and anxiety than truth-tellers. Such nervousness is thought to "leak out," in other words, to show up inadvertently in outward behavior. There is some debate about how emotionally arousing deception is and the effects of any such arousal on verbal and nonverbal displays. For example, many scholars note that much deceit takes the form of low-stakes, garden-variety white lies, evasions, and the like. Such deceit is unlikely to evoke much fear, guilt, or anxiety. Too, people seem to be quite adept at lying, which should reduce the degree of physical activation and emotion that deception triggers. Moreover, proponents of Interpersonal Deception Theory (IDT) (Buller and Burgoon 1996) argue that even if deception does elevate arousal, moderate levels of arousal should actually cause senders to be more believable. This is because senders who are aroused are likely to pay more attention to their communication attempt and therefore to craft more believable messages. If this is correct, senders who are experiencing moderate levels of arousal should be judged as more truthful than those who are not aroused. On the flip side, other scholars (e.g., Ekman 1992) believe that all arousal will produce some cue leakage and that this leakage will be interpreted as deception by receivers. If this is correct, then senders who are experiencing any level of arousal should be judged as more deceptive than those who are not aroused.

The basic premise of the cognitive difficulty approach states that lying is more mentally complex and taxing than telling the truth. Therefore, lying takes more cognitive effort than telling the truth. This is because the liar must make his or her story consistent and plausible with the facts as well as consistent with his or her previous statements, whereas the truth-teller need simply recall the information from memory. This additional effort is believed to be detectable in behavioral cues, and therefore receivers should be able identify those who are experiencing greater cognitive "load."

If this is correct, then deception should have reliable behavioral indicators associated with this greater cognitive effort.

The image or behavioral control approach states that deceivers are aware that they may give themselves away through their behavior and so attempt to exert control over their behavior so as to maintain a credible image. Therefore, deceivers, in an attempt to appear truthful, will attempt to suppress these behaviors. The control of these behaviors is believed to be difficult and may result in over-control such as adopting more rigid posture and reductions in involvement. If this approach is correct, deceivers should attempt to control their behaviors more so than truthful subjects and in ways that are indicative of too much restraint.

To explore the above predictions, we conducted a pilot study. The general purpose of the design was to test our experimental procedures, questionnaires, and coding procedures and to gain an initial picture of how well we could identify linguistic and content features that differ under text as compared to FtF communication. Sixty students were recruited from a multisectioned communication class by offering them credit for participation and the chance to win money if they were successful at their task. Half of those students were assigned the role of interviewer and half the role of interviewee. Of those who became interviewees, 16 were randomly assigned to be "thieves," that is, those who would be deceiving about a theft, and 14 became "innocents," that is, those who would be telling the truth.

Interviewees in the deceptive condition were assigned to "steal" a wallet that was left in a classroom. In the truthful condition, interviewees were told that a "theft" would occur in class on an assigned day. All of the interviewees and interviewers then appeared for interviews according to a preassigned schedule. We attempted to motivate serious engagement in the task by offering interviewers $10 if they could successfully detect whether their interviewee was innocent or guilty and successfully detect whether they were deceiving or telling the truth on a series of the interview questions. In turn, we offered interviewees $10 if they convinced both the naïve (i.e., student) interviewer and a trained interviewer that they were innocent and that their answers to several questions were truthful. An additional incentive was a $50 prize to be awarded to the most successful interviewer/interviewee.

All interviewees completed a written statement before they were interviewed. This gave them the opportunity to reflect on the events of the day in question and also to rehearse their story. Interviewees were then interviewed by a naïve interviewer under one of the two modalities—face to face (FtF) or text chat—followed by a FtF interview conducted by one of two trained male interviewers. These interviews followed a standardized Behavioral Analysis Interview format that is taught to criminal investigators all over the country (see Inbau, Reid, Buckley, and Jayne 2001, for additional details on this type of interview). Following the interview, interviewers rated interviewees on their credibility, judged their truthfulness on selected interview questions, and made their assessment of whether the interviewee was telling the truth about stealing the wallet. Interviewees completed a questionnaire that asked them to report their actual level of truthfulness on several of the questions and to report their level of positive or negative arousal, perceived cognitive difficulty, attempted control, and perceived success.

This pilot study yielded some very interesting results, far more than we had anticipated for a beginning effort. Many of the general beliefs about the effect of deception on arousal, cognitive load, control, and motivation were not supported. Specifically, deceptive subjects did not experience more arousal or cognitive load than truthful subjects. However, deceptive subjects did report more control and motivation than truthful subjects. Only motivation was significantly positively correlated with the judgments of the interviewers. This correlation provided support to the IDT view of motivation that more motivated subjects will be more successful at being judged as truthful. We also conducted some linguistic analyses. Although none of these analyses met traditional standards of statistical significance, they do suggest that there may be some differences in the language used by truthful and deceptive subjects. Specifically, "innocents" (truthful participants) tended to use more words, more complex language, and more avoidance language than did deceptive subjects. Speculatively, when deceivers have time to plan out their deceits and even rehearse them—as they did in this case by doing a written statement first—they may actually produce messages that aim to be persuasive and therefore require more, not less, verbiage and complex vocabulary, but they may also attempt to mask their true intentions by using language that detaches them from direct responsibility for what they are saying.

This pilot experiment also helped us to hone our methods and measures for the main experiment, in which we intended to expand modalities to include an audio condition. The effects of motivation on deceptive displays are in dispute. Traditionally, it has been believed that motivation facilitates performance, especially overlearned performances. It has also become commonly accepted that too much arousal can be detrimental, causing what we all know as "choking under pressure." Within the realm of deception, these principles should lead to the prediction that increasing arousal aids deceivers in crafting more convincing messages unless the arousal is extreme. However, scholars have begun to take issue with these general premises. DePaulo's motivation impairment effect (DePaulo and Kirkendol 1992) suggests that deceptive suspects who are more motivated will experience a decrement in their ability to produce effective nonverbal performances due to involuntary leakage of telltale deception cues, but they will experience enhancement of their ability to craft effective verbal displays. The result should be that compared to receivers who have access to verbal cues (as would happen in text messages), receivers who have access to nonverbal cues (as would happen with audio or FtF communication) will judge motivated deceivers as more deceptive than unmotivated ones. However, IDT suggests that motivation can facilitate some nonverbal as well as verbal performances while hindering others, depending on which behaviors are being examined. This is because IDT contends that many verbal and nonverbal behaviors are strategically produced by senders, rather than being involuntary indicators, and that such behaviors will show careful and effective behavioral management. If this is correct, motivated deceivers should be judged as more truthful than less motivated deceivers, and this should be true of truth-tellers as well.

Our main experiment, then, examined the three factors of motivation, deception, and modality. There were a number of dependent measures included in this investigation, and all of the interviews are being transcribed and coded behaviorally. Because the investigation is still in progress, we report here only the preliminary results on arousal, cognitive difficulty, behavioral control, and credibility.

Briefly, here is how the methods changed from the pilot study: We were concerned about the impact that mediated communication would have on the four factors just discussed. To explore the impact of mediation on the four factors, three interviewing modalities were used: face-to-face, audio, and text/chat. Participants were randomly assigned to conditions. The basic scenario was similar to the first study. Deceptive participants were asked to "steal" a wallet from a classroom on an assigned day. Truthful participants were told that a wallet would be stolen on a specific day.

In the FtF condition, the interviewer sat in the room with the interviewee and conducted the interview. In the audio condition, the interviewer sat in a room that was separate from the interviewee, and the interviews were conducted using two-way radios. In the text/chat condition, the interviewer and interviewee sat in different rooms, and the interview was conducted using a chat program.

Some preliminary findings of this study are presented here. In general, experimentally induced motivation, communication modalities, and guilt had a major impact on the participants' reported anxiety, cognitive load, attempted control, self-reported motivation, and partner-rated credibility. Specifically, guilty subjects reported more anxiety, more cognitive load, and more motivation than innocent participants. For deceivers, motivation remained high regardless of whether we offered extra incentives to perform well or not; among truth-tellers, motivation was much lower without some external "boost." High-motivation deceivers also thought the task was more cognitively taxing than did high-motivation truth-tellers. Yet this greater difficulty did not translate into impaired credibility. Deceivers were as credible as truth-tellers under high motivation, whereas deceivers were far less credible under low motivation.

As for modality effects, participants also reported more anxiety in the FtF and audio conditions than they reported in the text condition. Interestingly, participants reported significantly more cognitive effort in the audio condition than in the FtF or text conditions. This was contrary to our expectations and might be due to the participants' lack of familiarity with using two-way radios. There was a near-significant difference in the amount of attempted control that the participants reported in the different modalities. The subjects reported more attempted control in the FtF and audio conditions than in the text condition. As we acquire more data, this difference may become significant. Subjects also reported the most motivation in the FtF condition, with less motivation reported in the audio condition and the least amount of motivation reported in the text condition.

The implications for detecting deceit under CMC lie especially in the modality effects. Generally, the participants reported less anxiety, cognitive load, attempted control, and motivation in the text conditions than in the FtF and audio conditions. Because the four factors are believed to be the causes of deceptive verbal and nonverbal displays, it is likely that deception will be more difficult to detect in text-based communication than in FtF communication, but it may be easier to detect when CMC is audio based. Current research is exploring this possibility in more detail.

Deception in Group Systems

Deception detection is not just a one-on-one affair. Deception may also occur in groups. Accordingly, another experiment delving into various communication media was designed to determine the differences between lying to one individual and lying to a group of people, specifically to determine if it is more difficult to successfully deceive multiple people at the same time. Considering that previous studies in deception have found that the average person detects 50 percent of lies or less (Miller and Stiff 1993), this experiment centered on the relationship between receivers. Receivers in groups may be better able to detect lies based on a larger aggregate of knowledge among the group, as well as by maintaining a different perspective on the discussion while in the role of observer. Receivers can also interact among themselves, and may possibly verify any suspicions that arise when receiving a deceptive message. By expressing their doubts with others who may have perceived the same deception, this adds a complicating factor with which a deceiver must contend.

Groups of three college students were asked to attend a meeting in which they would brainstorm ideas for increasing tourism to the local community. Before each meeting began, one of the group members arrived early and was asked to argue for a predetermined method of boosting tourism, unbeknownst to the other two group members. This member was asked to make up facts and invent stories in order to sway the other members' opinions toward this method, in effect to deceive them. Deceivers were informed that they stood to win a cash prize should they persuade the others to vote the assigned method as one of the top two choices brainstormed during the meeting. These instructions came complete with a request to refrain from telling the other group members about their deceptive task. Each person was given the opportunity to decline this unexpected role, but all of the potential deceivers readily agreed to deceive their group partners.

The deceiver was not the only group member to receive special instructions. Three-fourths of the receivers were warned (via written instructions) that one of their partners could use the meeting to serve their own interests, and that any false information accepted by the group would "reflect poorly on all the group members." These forewarned receivers were promised a cash reward for each untruthful comment they contested. Again, the instructions were accompanied by a request to avoid mentioning any of this to the other group members. By attempting to arouse the suspicion in half of the receivers, this meant that the other half of the receivers were naïve to any possible deception.

Because information technology allows multiple people to communicate simultaneously using alternative means, group meetings were either conducted using verbal communication or over computer-mediated media using a computer-aided group support system (GSS). The use of a text-based medium should effectively prevent most nonverbal indicators of deceit from reaching a receiver. Although the group meetings were conducted around a traditional boardroom table, half the groups spoke with each other directly, while the other half used the GSS. In all, 18 group meetings with a deceptive group member were completed, with five groups in both the FTF/one suspicious receiver and the GSS/one suspicious receiver cells, and four groups in the FTF/two suspicious receivers and the GSS/two suspicious receiver cells.

Results showed that regardless of which modality was used, receivers did not detect many of the lies. In fact, in this experiment they performed even more abysmally than in previous studies, detecting only 11 percent of the deceptive statements overall. Both the naïve and suspicious group members performed poorly. This result demonstrates that receivers are susceptible to deception, even when working in tandem and even when forewarned. Another unexpected finding was that the deceivers using the computer-based media tended to lie more than those in the verbal condition. The deceivers in the GSS groups submitted an average of 1.89 lies per meeting, compared to the 1.11 lies contributed by the face-to-face deceivers.

While the detection performance of group members left much to be desired, post hoc analysis showed that lies were more detectable after the fact. The two transcripts from the study containing the most deceptive statements were prepared and distributed to 17 disinterested, third-party volunteers. The volunteers were told only to find the lies in the transcripts. The volunteers produced successful deception detection rates much closer to those traditionally found in the deception literature, including an average of 44 percent of the deceptive statements in one transcript and 59 percent in the other, for an overall average of 51 percent successful detection. This rate is similar to accuracy rates in other studies, but this analysis further illustrates the naturally poor detection ability in average people. Even when presented with transcripts rampant with deception, the volunteers were only slightly better than chance at detecting deception.

One interesting side note of this study regards the behavior of the individuals assigned the role of deceiver. Although the findings just presented were derived from a total of 18 groups, there were 31 other groups of subjects that participated. These groups were omitted from the data analysis for the simple reason that the subject receiving the instructions to deceive did not do so. This was a surprising observation in itself, that these participants showed a strong disinclination toward lying to their fellow group members. When reviewing the discussion transcript with these "nondeceivers" afterwards, the majority either felt that they had been persuasive enough without lying or that they were "not good at coming up with things out of thin air." Others questioned whether the reward itself was real, which was unexpected. Interestingly, this "nondeceptive" behavior occurred in both the FtF and CMC meetings. Whether this is due to the task, the addition of a second receiver, or the mere physical presence of the other members and GSS facilitator has yet to be resolved.

Resume "Enhancement"

The last study we will report here involved the use of resume deception, otherwise known as applicant faking. In recent years, there have been several high-profile cases of coaches and officials in the athletic world who have been relieved of their duties for falsifying information on their resumes. This is apparently an everyday occurrence, as some human resource studies have shown that from one-third up to 40 percent of all job applicants exaggerate resume information to some degree, no matter what field or what level the position may be (Challenger 1997). Apparently, many of these exaggerations are never caught. One possibility for the inaccurate detection in the resume review process is that much of the exaggerated information is extremely difficult to contest, and the necessary background checks to do so are time-consuming and costly. Other than an interviewer asking probing questions and uncovering deception, applicant faking should be simple to get away with.

In the experiment described here, our objective was to determine the ease with which deceptive information is encoded and the strategies used for doing so in preparation for subsequent studies that would focus on detection of such information. Study participants reserved individual times to come in for a "resume review" and were asked to bring copies of their resume. Upon arrival, they were given the consent form to peruse and sign, while the researcher briefly examined the resume. The students were assured that their resume looked fine, and then were told that the MIS department was considering a scholarship to be offered to the top student in the future. They were asked to fill out an application for the award to help us set the standard requirements for potential applicants. In doing so, they were told to make themselves appear as competitive as possible, as if they wanted to be the strong favorite to win. Twenty-five students participated.

After finishing the application, the true nature of the study was revealed to the student. The student then went through the application and pointed out any deceptive changes that had been made. Not surprisingly, it took very little prompting for the subjects to understand how to make their resume appear more competitive. All but two of the students admitted to altering resume information in one way or another. The most commonly exaggerated application blanks were the student's overall grade point average and positions held in MIS organizations, both altered by 48 percent of the subjects. Other commonly altered blanks included positions held in MIS-related firms (44 percent); letter grades in individual classes; GPA in the major; knowledge, skills, and abilities (KSA's); and the duration of MIS organization membership (36 percent each). It is worth noting that several subjects claimed that they would be a little hesitant lying about certain things that could be easily verified, such as their GPA and individual class grades, and they would be more creative given more time to reflect and strategize.

Other interesting revelations came to light during discussion with the subjects. Most of the subjects had not compared their resumes with or had even viewed their classmates' resumes, so their faking had not been informed by others. Many of the subjects were familiar with the practice of resume enhancement, and some went so far as to explain the deceptions performed by friends and acquaintances. In fact, when relating the percentage of overall applicants who enhance their resumes in the actual job market, some subjects believed that the number was too low.

There are a couple of key differences in this experiment than from most deception studies. First of all, the target of deceptive resume information is not always known. Applicants may know the identity of the organization they are communicating with, but probably do not know the specific department manager or human resource professional who will be screening each resume. Therefore, personal information in these cases cannot be tailored for a specific receiver, making anything other than a generic deceptive strategy infeasible. Another difference is that in the written application medium, an applicant will not have the opportunity to defend or expound upon a piece of deceptive information. Until some form of interview is initiated, the communication between applicant and screener is inherently static. The application or resume must stand alone in terms of transferring information from one party to the other.

Subsequent experiments will have "screeners" interviewing the deceitful applicants. For now, this study serves to show that wherever there are opportunities for individuals to engage in self-serving behavior, there is the distinct possibility that any information they provide may be inaccurate. This means that information in databases, in online employment applications or credit applications, and the like may contain exaggerated and self-enhancing information.

Additionally, the strategies utilized by the study participants, such as exaggerating least easily verified information, are probably indicative of those used in any one-to-many communication situation. Detecting such deceits may prove to be especially challenging if the exaggerations are slight enough to still seem plausible and not send up any red flags. In light of the robustness of human truth biases, such information may easily escape careful scrutiny when it appears in databases or text-based CMC, where other nonverbal indicators of deceit are missing.

▮▮▮ Conclusions and Implications

Clearly, much work remains to be done to gain a better understanding of deception in CMC before reliable and valid tools for its detection can be built. Human communication is extraordinarily complex. Creating software that accounts for that complexity is consequently quite challenging. The experiments described here have formed a foothold in this area toward the twin objectives of identifying reliable indicators of deception in electronic media and developing automated detection software. Because the second goal is dependent on the achievement of the first goal, the first phase of the research has naturally focused on determining what indicators are reliable and effective at discriminating truth from deception. Because there is no single profile of behaviors that applies universally to all communication contexts, and because good science requires replication before drawing firm conclusions, the research program will necessarily be devoted for some time to assessing what indicators are applicable to what circumstances, or, put differently, what features of communication contexts, tasks, and modalities influence the ways in which truthful and deceptive communications are expressed.

Our initial experiments have already yielded important conclusions in that regard. As seen in the desert survival experiment, the modality used for communication affects both performance and how receivers respond to partners. Each modality appears to have unique properties that in and of themselves affect perceived communication, credibility, and ability to detect deceit. In many cases, trust is highest in FtF communication. The use of electronic media may withhold many of the cues that FtF communicators have available, leading computer users to have a higher level of skepticism. Whether use of CMC modalities leads to receivers judging communicated messages more carefully or simply responding to them mindlessly with a blanket reduction in truth bias remains to be seen. And even the reduction in truth bias was not uniform. There were many instances where trust was highest in the text, audio, or AV condition. This often depended on whether the communicator was being truthful or deceptive, a finding that indicates receivers can discriminate between truth and deception in CMC modalities. But their detection abilities still remain far below what is desirable. In any event, computer users picked up on some noticeable differences when they were being deceived, and either consciously or subconsciously picked up on the related indicators. Other studies, such as the follow-up mock theft experiment and one experiment in progress featuring resume interviews over different modalities, will hone in on prospective reliable indicators. Besides nonverbal indicators, the mock theft experiments have also exposed some behavioral and attitudinal differences between deceivers using mediated communication and deceivers using oral, FtF communication. Specifically, those using audio and text-based messaging were less anxious, less motivated/aroused, and exerted less control over their communicative performance, with audio users suffering higher cognitive demand. Linguistically, the guilty parties may have used more complex language and fewer words overall to explain themselves, although this is a very speculative conclusion given that there were no statistically significant differences. Perhaps these findings will better inform an understanding of deceiver behavior when using computer-mediated communication.

The use of communicative technology by virtual work teams and other groups should not be ignored, and we have begun investigating the detection of deception among multiple persons. Initially, it appears that receivers are no better at detecting deception in a group than when alone, and the results presented here suggest that they may be worse. More study is needed to verify this. Other group software needs to be investigated as well. Work has begun using group support systems, but e-mail, chat, teleconferencing, use of databases, and other differences in synchronicity and parallel communication may produce differences in deceptive behavior. Again, one of the main purposes for this research is to potentially automate deception detection, and it is for computer-based media like these that we hope to incorporate the automation once each has been specifically investigated.

Although more work will be required to validate a list of deceptive indicators available in computer-mediated environments, the results so far have been encouraging. More and more communication, both in the workplace and in private, is being conducted using information technology, and signs point only to increasing usage. Logic tells us that deceptive information will be a significant part of this process, so the need for understanding ways to detect it will be more vital than before. The work described here serves as a springboard from which future needed research on deception in computer-mediated environments can be launched.

REFERENCES

Buller, D., and Burgoon, J. (1996). Interpersonal deception theory. *Communication Theory, 6*, 203–242.

Challenger, J. (1997). Job hunters resorting to questionable ethics. *HRMagazine*, February, p. 27.

DePaulo, B., and Kirkendol, S. (1989). The motivation impairment effect in the communication of deception. In J. Yuille (Ed.), *Credibility Assessment* (pp. 51–70). Duerne, Belgium: Klewer.

Ekman, P. (1992). *Telling Lies: Clues to Deceit in the Marketplace, Politics, and Marriage* (Vol. 2). New York: WW Norton and Company.

Miller, G., and Stiff, J. (1993). *Deceptive Communication*. Newbury Park, CA: Sage Publications.

Park, H., and Levine, T. (2001). A probability model of accuracy in deception detection experiments. *Communication Monographs, 68*, 201–210.

Vrij, A., Edward, K., Roberts, K., and Bull, R. (2000). Detecting deceit via analysis of verbal and nonverbal behavior. *Journal of Nonverbal Behavior, 24*(4), 239–263.

Zmud, R. (1990). Opportunities for strategic information manipulation through new information technology. In J. Fulk & C. Steinfeld (Eds.), *Organizations and Communication Technology* (pp. 95–116). Newbury Park, CA: Sage Publications.

Zuckerman, M., DePaulo, B., and Rosenthal, R. (1981). Verbal and nonverbal communication of deception. In L. Berkowitz (Ed.), *Advances in Experimental Social Psychology* (Vol. 14, pp. 1–59). New York: Academic Press.

PART II

Privacy

Introduction

Privacy is and always has been a central issue in the relationship between computing and society. Concerns over privacy come from concerns about record keeping, the ownership of records, and who has the ability to see and change records. Keeping records is nothing new—records have been kept since people have been able to write, and even before then in oral form. However, until very recently, finding and accessing a single record, such as how much someone owes on their home mortgage, was difficult. Such information was on paper and probably not stored in a place that the public was able to access. Accessing additional records from different sources about the same person was even more difficult. Sifting through the resulting information to form a dossier about that person was probably not even worth the effort except in exceptional circumstances. In fact, personal records kept in an individual's home came to be protected in the U.S. Constitution in the protection against unreasonable search and seizure in the Fourth Amendment.

With the advent of computing, however, all of that has changed. With data kept in many places and in compatible formats, much of which is available over the Internet, gaining access to or creating a dossier is about as easy as gaining access to a particular piece of data. Computers make it a lot easier to compile data from many different sources and to essentially use each datum like a piece of a jigsaw puzzle to put together a meaningful picture of a person. Computers also make it easy to use inference to fill in the missing pieces to complete the whole. If you do not want to do the hard work yourself, plenty of vendors on the Web will be glad to sell you a dossier on the individual of your choice.

It was not always easy to use computers to find and integrate data. In the early days of automation, different computers could not talk with each other and converting data from one machine to be read by another was a monumental task. Data files were created for specific applications, and the same piece of data could be coded in different forms and formats. Creating a personal dossier with computer data was too expensive except for the most important purposes. Today, however, with cheap, powerful computing, relatively easy data conversion, and the massive public storage system that is the Internet, creating personal dossiers is cheap and relatively simple.

People in different countries have different views about the privacy of computerized data. For example, the European Union and the United States have very different approaches and hence very different laws. The European Union restricts the collection and dissemination of data by businesses; the United States has very few laws that deal with business. These differing approaches and laws emerge from different attitudes about the role of government and commerce and from different recent histories.

In the United States, the interests in privacy are cyclical. Spurts of interest have emerged at one or two specific points in each of the past decades since computerization began to grow. These periods of interest generally result in very specific new laws. Particular concerns have been with the credit reporting industry in the 1960s and again in the early 1990s. Direct marketers have also been a target of privacy advocates, but these marketers remain largely unregulated. In the United States, people have traditionally trusted commercial interests more than they have trusted the government. One exception to this general rule is the Watergate period in the early and mid-1970s, the time in which America's only comprehensive privacy legislation, the Privacy Act of 1974, was passed. Current times are also exceptions to the rule, as most Americans now are concerned with how merchants are using their personal data on the Internet, whereas few are concerned about new federal government programs to collect and integrate massive amounts of personal data in the name of homeland security (e.g., the newly created Information Awareness Office).

Still, privacy has become a central and ongoing concern among Americans for most of the last half-dozen years, breaking the pattern of only sporadic, cyclical interest. The Internet is clearly the impetus for this sustained interest, and the events of September 11, 2001, have provided an impetus of their own. This is an important time for privacy in the United States. It will be fascinating to watch how things develop over the next decade.

▪▪▪ The Articles in Part II

Culnan, M. "Consumer Privacy, Technology, and Policy."

> Mary Culnan is widely recognized as one of the experts on privacy in the management information systems community. In this commissioned chapter, Culnan presents a comprehensive overview of the important issues surrounding consumer privacy. In addition to explaining why consumer privacy is an important issue, she discusses fair information practices and different ways to implement them. She ends with comments on consumer privacy in a post-September 11 world.

Hoffman, D. L., T. P. Novak, and M. Peralta. 1999. "Building consumer trust online." *Communications of the ACM* 42(4):80–85.

> Hoffman, Novak, and Peralta report on how concerns over privacy, especially over the use of personal information, prevents many potential consumers from making purchases over the Web. After careful analysis of a large dataset of Web users, they recommend short-term and longer-term steps Web merchants can take to build consumer trust.

Excerpts from Fox, S., et al. 2000. "Trust and privacy online: Why Americans want to rewrite the rules." The Pew Internet and American Life Project, Washington, D.C., pp. 5–17.

In May 2000, the Pew Internet & American Life Project surveyed over 2,000 Americans, over 1,000 of whom were Internet users, to discover their attitudes toward privacy and the Internet. This excerpt from their report provides an overview of their basic findings, from the conditions under which Web users will share their personal information, to the conditions under which they will provide false information on Web sites, to their anxieties about the Web and what happens to the information users provide online.

Green, H., M. France, M. Stepanek H., and A. Borros. 2000. It's Time for Rules in Wonderland." *Business Week*. March 20, 83–88, 92, 94, 96.

In March of 2000, one of the key privacy concerns related to the Internet was the collection and sale of personal information collected online from Web users. Given the possible dampening effects of such concerns on Web business, *Business Week* set out a four-point plan that would allow privacy and e-commerce to peacefully coexist.

France, M., H. Green, J. Kerstetter, J. Black, A. Salkever, and D. Carney. 2001. "Privacy in an Age of Terror." *Business Week*. November 5, 83–88.

By November of 2001, concerns about privacy had shifted dramatically due to the terrorist attacks in the United States on September 11, 2001. Instead of concerns over personal data used or sold by Web merchants, the threat now came from the U.S. government and its increased surveillance power and practices that followed from the September 11 attacks. This article examines these threats to privacy.

▪▪▪ Related Places to Go on the Web

Many different organizations that focus on privacy issues maintain extensive Web sites. These organizations provide in-depth, timely information on privacy issues, and they do so from many different perspectives. The list here is by no means comprehensive, but it provides a place to start.

> American Civil Liberties Union (www.aclu.org)
> ACM Public Policy pages on privacy (www.acm.org/usacm/privacy/)
> Cato Institute (www.cato.org)
> Center for Democracy and Technology (www.cdt.org)
> Electronic Frontier Foundation (www.eff.org)
> Electronic Privacy Information Center (www.epic.org)
> Privacy Rights Clearinghouse (www.privacyrights.org)

ADDITIONAL READING

Bennett, C. J., and R. Grant. 1999. *Visions of Privacy: Policy Choices for the Digital Age.* Toronto: University of Toronto Press.

Byford, K. S. 1998. "Privacy in cyberspace: Constructing a model of privacy for the electronic communications environment." *Rutgers Computer & Technology Law Journal* 24:1–74.

Culnan, M. J. 1993. "How did they get my name? An exploratory investigation of consumer attitudes toward secondary information use." *MIS Quarterly* 17:341–364.

Culnan, M. J., and R. J. Bies. 2003. "Consumer privacy: Balancing economic and justice considerations." *Journal of Social Issues* 59(2), 323–342.

Culnan M. J., and P. M. Regan. 1995. "Privacy issues and the creation of campaign mailing lists." *The Information Society* 2:85–100.

Etzioni, A. 2000. *The Limits of Privacy.* New York: Basic Books.

Garfinkel, S. 2000. *Database Nation.* Sebastopol, CA: O'Reillly & Associates.

Laudon, K. C. 1986. *The Dossier Society: Value Choices in the Design of National Information Systems.* New York: Columbia University Press.

Lyon, D. 1994. *The Electronic Eye: The Rise of Surveillance Society.* Minneapolis: University of Minnesota Press.

Rule J., D. McAdam, L. Steams, and D. Uglow. 1980. *The Politics of Privacy.* New York: New American Library.

Smith, H. J. 1994. *Managing Privacy: Information Technology and Corporate America.* Chapel Hill, NC: University of North Carolina Press.

Smith, H. J., S. J. Milberg, and S. J. Burke. 1996. "Information privacy: Measuring individuals' concerns about organizational practices." *MIS Quarterly* 20(2):167–195.

Westin, A. F. 1967. *Privacy and Freedom.* New York: Atheneum.

Whitaker, R. 1999. *The End of Privacy.* New York: The New Press.

Consumer Privacy, Technology, and Policy

MARY J. CULNAN

Introduction

In the competitive global marketplace, privacy is an important issue because of a fundamental tension between business and consumer interests. Specifically, organizations need to collect and use personal information to remain competitive while consumers find some methods of collection and use of their personal information to be unfair and an invasion of their privacy. As a result, privacy is at the center of an ongoing public debate about who controls how our personal information is used.

The focus of this chapter is information privacy rather than physical privacy. Information privacy is the ability of individuals to control the terms under which their personal information is acquired and used (Westin 1967). Personal information is information identifiable to a specific individual. Examples of personal information include a name or account number. This definition of privacy reflects an implicit understanding that privacy is not absolute; instead, the individual's privacy interests are balanced with the information needs of society at large in our roles as consumers, citizens, and employees.

Information privacy has three "faces": marketing, lookups, and security. "Marketing" refers to the ways that organizations reuse the personal information they collect from and about their customers in the normal course of doing business. Generally, the interest here is not in any particular person but in being able to target groups of individuals based on their behavior or demographics in order to deliver personalized offers. For example, a grocery store may wish to make a special offer to its best customers. It is interested in identifying these people based on their purchases, but it is not particularly interested in the specific people who are members of the group. With marketing, privacy concerns typically arise when information collected for one purpose, such as completing a transaction, is used for other unrelated purposes such as sharing a customer list with another organization, without the person's knowledge or permission.

"Lookups" differs from marketing in that for lookups, personal information is used to identify a specific individual by name. Lookups are often used to make decisions that involve risk, such as extending credit or making a job offer, or in a legal procedure. In these instances, it is important to match the correct individual with their personal information. Identity theft, where someone obtains enough personal information about an individual to establish credit fraudulently in the person's name, is one of the main privacy concerns associated with lookups.

"Security" refers to the privacy breaches that result from unauthorized access to personal information. These breaches often occur because an organization has failed to protect personal information during either transmission or storage. Security breaches may also result in identity theft or credit card fraud. Although some equate privacy with security, there are some important differences. Privacy is about use and permission whereas security is about protecting information. You can have security without privacy, but you cannot have privacy without security. Whereas both security and lookups apply across the three roles of consumer, citizen, and employee, marketing applies primarily to our role as consumers.

The focus of this chapter is consumer privacy, particularly the use of personal information by organizations for marketing to their current and prospective customers. However, many of the issues discussed are also relevant to citizen and employee privacy. The chapter continues with a general discussion of consumer privacy concerns and the role new technology plays in raising privacy concerns. Next, we discuss alternatives for implementing a set of principles, fair information practices that can address privacy concerns that are shaped by the fairness of organizational information practices. Third, we present an overview of global privacy issues and organizational considerations related to managing consumer privacy concerns. Finally, the chapter concludes by raising some issues about consumer privacy in the post-September 11 world.

▰▰▰ Why Is Consumer Privacy an Issue?

In a world where organizations can no longer personally know their customers, advances in technology, combined with a need to serve customers as individuals, have fueled the collection of personal information. It is possible for firms to efficiently gather, store, use, and exchange vast amounts of consumer information that are needed in a business environment characterized by largely anonymous, impersonal relationships. Data mining is used to perform sophisticated analysis on massive databases of transaction data that provide the basis for designing marketing programs for individual customers. Instantaneous access to a consumer credit report containing their bill-paying history means credit can be extended on the spot. Online access to a customer's history by a customer service representative enables standardized, impersonal encounters with anyone who answers the 800-number to assume the appearance of a personal relationship. These uses of information benefit consumers through greater convenience, access to personalized offers, and other benefits such as loyalty programs and benefit organizations by creating customer loyalty and reducing costs. Yet these same advances in technology that can create benefits for both consumers and organizations are simultaneously raising privacy concerns because of the potential for surveillance.

There are typically two drivers of information privacy concerns: incompatible use of personal information and new technology. Privacy concerns arise when organizations use information they collected for one purpose in ways that are unrelated to why the information was collected without the individual's knowledge or consent. When personal information is used in ways that are legal but that consumers do not expect, they may perceive these uses to be unfair. This is more likely to be the case if the personal information is sensitive, as is the case for medical or financial information. For example, customers who picked up prescriptions at an Eckerd pharmacy signed a form acknowledging receipt for the prescription. In small print, the form also authorized Eckerd to use the data the customer had provided in order to have their prescription filled for an incompatible use—marketing. Eckerd would automatically send customers who had signed the form information about new drugs, and possibly about alternatives to the drugs they had been prescribed. Although many consumers may not object to receiving offers generated from other types of purchases, they did object to having sensitive medial information they believed to be confidential used for marketing. The settlement reached with the Florida Attorney General required Eckerd to change its practices and to endow a $1-million chair in ethics at a Florida university (Dorschner 2002).

Second, new technologies expand the scope of personal information collection, resulting in new privacy concerns. For example, Internet cookies initially raised serious privacy concerns because of their potential to record people's surfing patterns, when people in fact thought they were surfing anonymously. Today, a new tracking technology has the potential to raise similar concerns in the off-line world. Radio frequency identification (RFID) tags consist of a small chip that, once imbedded in a product, broadcasts tracking information. While initially designed to improve supply chain efficiency, the potential exists to match products with consumers. Prada, the upscale retailer, is testing the technology in its New York store, and Gillette has announced it will test RFID's to track its products from manufacturing to store shelves. See the Web site for MIT's Auto-ID Center for more information (www.autoidcenter.org).

▪▪▪ Beyond the Consumer Transaction: Privacy and the Second Exchange

In marketing, consumer transactions have traditionally been conceptualized in terms of a single utilitarian exchange where value in the form of goods or services is given in return for money or other goods (Bagozzi 1975). Culnan and Milberg (1998) call this exchange "the first exchange." However, consumer transactions increasingly include a "second exchange" where the consumer makes a nonmonetary exchange of their personal information for value such as higher quality service and personalized offers or discounts. It is the second exchange that provides the ongoing flow of customer information needed to support marketing relationships and to run the business. For organizations, the challenge is to create a willingness in consumers to participate in the second exchange and to disclose their personal information by making the second exchange fair.

The second exchange is not new. In earlier times, data from the second exchange were maintained in ledgers or in the proprietor's head. Technology, however, has transformed the information from the second exchange into a competitive asset by connecting the point-of-sale to one or more databases. Table 1 illustrates how technology has increased the scope of the second exchange from an anonymous cash transaction where no information was provided to wireless technologies where the transaction, the consumer, their transaction data, and their location are known. As a result, organizations can compile detailed profiles about their operations and their customers. This allows organizations to more accurately match their product or service offerings with their customers and to develop loyalty programs or other benefits for their customers (Winer

TABLE 1 Technology and the Second Exchange		
Context	*How Information Is Collected*	*What Information Is Collected*
Face-to-face (customer not identified)	Cash register without scanner	None
Face-to-face (customer not identified)	POS scanner	+ Inventory
Face-to-face or direct marketing	Customer order or loyalty program	+ Customer (name, purchase history)
Online	Cookies or clickstream data	+ Browsing behavior
Wireless	Device transmits information	+ Location

2001). However, for organizations to capitalize on the competitive advantages of the second exchange, customers have to be willing to disclose their personal information.

▪▪▪ Promoting Consumer Disclosure of Personal Information

Laufer and Wolfe (1977) hypothesized that individuals should be willing to disclose personal information in exchange for some economic or social benefit subject to an assessment that their personal information will subsequently be used fairly and that they will not suffer negative consequences in the future. In other words, individuals will exchange personal information as long as they perceive adequate benefits will be received in return—that is, benefits which exceed the perceived risks of information disclosure. Consumers then behave as if they are performing a "cost-benefit" analysis on a case by case basis in assessing the outcomes they receive as the result of providing personal information to organizations.

Creating a willingness in consumers to disclose personal information, then, requires that organizations develop an explicit strategy to manage the second exchange. Consumers should continue to disclose personal information as long as they perceive that they receive benefits that exceed the current or future risks of disclosure. Implied here is an expectation that organizations not only need to offer benefits that consumers find attractive, but they also need to be open and honest about their information practices so that consumers both perceive disclosure to be a low risk proposition and can also make an informed choice about whether or not to disclose.

As trust reflects a willingness to assume the risks of disclosure, developing information practices that address the perceived risk of disclosure should result in positive experiences with the organization over time, increasing the consumer's perceptions that the organization can be trusted (Mayer, Davis, and Schoorman 1995). Trust creates switching costs that raise the costs or effort associated with changing firms, increasing the likelihood that the consumer will continue in the relationship with the firm. To sustain trust, the organization's information practices as perceived by the consumer must be consistent with the policies it disclosed.

For firms and consumers to realize these benefits, however, consumers must be willing to disclose their personal information and, thereby, surrender a measure of their privacy. We now turn our attention a set of principles, fair information practices, which can address consumer privacy concerns by making the second exchange fair.

▪▪▪ Fair Information Practices

Fair information practices are procedures that provide individuals with control over the disclosure and subsequent use of their personal information and govern the interpersonal treatment that they receive (Organization for Economic Cooperation and Development [OECD] 1980). Fair information practices balance the competing organizational and individual interests around the use of the individual's personal information and serve as the basis for privacy laws in the United States and elsewhere. Although the OECD's 1980 Guidelines reflect global norms for the ethical use of personal information, the actual coverage and implementation of fair information practices in the United States and elsewhere varies, reflecting cultural and legal differences (Milberg, Burke, Smith, and Kallman 1995).

Currently, the most widely accepted U.S. definition of fair information practices reflects a subset of the OECD Guidelines and is based on four elements: notice, choice, access, and security (Federal Trade Commission [FTC]:2000). *Notice* means that when individuals provide personal information, they have the right to know what, if any, information is being collected and how it will be used. *Choice* means that individuals should have the right to object when personal information is collected for one purpose and will be used for other unrelated purposes or shared with third parties, unless this sharing is required by law. *Access* means that individuals should have the right to see their information and correct errors. *Security* means that organizations should be good stewards of personal information by ensuring data integrity and that data are secure from unauthorized access during both transmission and storage. Finally, a reliable mechanism should exist to impose sanctions for noncompliance with these principles (FTC 2000).

Fair information practices, therefore, mediate privacy concerns raised by disclosure and subsequent use of personal information by empowering the individual, *even if people do not choose to invoke the procedures.* They also provide an assurance that the organization will adhere to a set of principles that most people find acceptable. Fair information practices, then, if followed, signal to the consumer that the firm can be trusted with the information they disclose via the second exchange. From the organization's perspective, fair information practices allow the organization to capitalize on the opportunities provided by information technology and to freely use the information it collects as long as its practices are consistent with what it has disclosed in its privacy notice. Observing fair information practices, then, is good for business (Culnan and Bies 2003).

▪▪▪ Implementing Fair Information Practices: Three Different Approaches

Although there is consensus in principle that the aforementioned elements of fair information practices should be used to protect consumer privacy, there is no consensus about how they should be implemented. Two issues are relevant here. First, what is the appropriate mix of law, self-regulation, and technological solutions in protecting privacy? In most of the developed world (e.g., Europe), fair information practices are implemented primarily through omnibus laws. In the United States, however, for consumer privacy, fair information practices are implemented though a combination of laws, self-regulation, and technological solutions (Schwartz and Reidenberg 1996).

Second, how should the basic elements of fair information practices, that is, notice, choice, access, and security, be operationalized across the three implementation methods? What constitutes effective notice and how and when should it be delivered to consumers? Can the same disclosure meet both the consumer information and legal compliance requirements of notice? What constitutes incompatible use of personal information collected for a particular purpose (meaning choice needs to be offered), and should choice take the form of "opt in" (where information *may not* be reused or shared unless the consumer *consents*) or "opt out" (where the information *may* be reused or shared unless the consumer *objects*)? Clearly, sharing personal information with third parties requires choice, but what about sharing information among affiliated companies with the same corporate parents for offerings that are unrelated to the original transaction? What kinds of information should be included under access? Should consumers have access to all information that the organization has acquired or inferred about them or only the information related to their transactions with the firm? What constitutes appropriate security for a small business versus a large corporation and how specific should this disclosure be to promote consumer trust without providing a roadmap to hackers? These questions characterize the current policy debates about consumer privacy. We now turn our attention to the three different approaches to implementing fair information practices: government regulation, industry self-regulation, and technology.

Government Regulation

The U.S. government has typically adopted a reactive approach to enacting consumer privacy legislation. For example, Congress typically steps in only when a clear problem has been identified, often by the media, and then focuses on developing a narrowly targeted (sectoral in contrast to an omnibus) solution (see Schwartz and Reidenberg 1996). In some instances, this has resulted in sectoral legislation for specific types of records, as in the case of credit reports and video rental records, or for classes of sensitive information, such as medical information, financial information, and information collected from young children. Table 2 lists some of the major U.S. consumer privacy laws. See Rotenberg (2002) for the text of these and other privacy laws. For personal

TABLE 2 Major U.S. Consumer Privacy Laws

Law	Year Enacted	Type of Information Regulated
Fair Credit Reporting Act (FCRA)	1970	Credit reports
Cable TV Privacy Act	1984	Cable subscriber records
Video Privacy Protection Act	1988	Video rental and sales records
Telephone Consumer Protection Act (TCPA)	1991	Telemarketers
Driver's Privacy Protection Act	1994	Private sector access to drivers license and motor vehicle registration data
Telecommunications Act of 1996	1996	Telephone toll records
Children's Online Privacy Protection Act (COPPA)	1999	Personal information collected online from children under 13 years of age
Gramm-Leach-Bliley Act (GLBA)	1999	Financial information
Health Insurance Portability & Accountability Act Rules (HIPAA)	2002	Medical records

information collected and used by the federal government, the Privacy Act of 1974 provides comprehensive protection. However, no such comprehensive legislation exists for information collected and used by the private sector, particularly information collected online; therefore, organizations also need to self-regulate in order to address consumer privacy concerns.

Self-Regulation

Self-regulation is not the same as a pure market solution where consumers with privacy concerns should favor firms with strong privacy policies and avoid those firms that do not protect privacy. With self-regulation, industry develops rules and enforcement procedures that substitute for government regulation (Swire 1997). For self-regulation to effectively address privacy concerns, organizations need to voluntarily adopt and implement privacy policies that are based at a minimum on the four elements of fair information practices described previously. Effective compliance procedures and enforcement mechanisms need to be implemented so that consumers will have the confidence that an organization plays by the rules, and that there are negative sanctions if they do not. In other words, firms need to say what they do and do what they say.

Merely disclosing that an organization observes fair information practices even when combined with strong internal controls may not adequately address consumer concerns about trust, particularly if the individual lacks first-hand experience with the company. In such cases, trust may be fostered if there is an assurance to the consumer by a trusted third party that an organization's practices conform to the policies it disclosed. Web site privacy seals are one example of a mechanism that was created to provide third party assurances to consumers based on a voluntary contractual relationship between the organization and the seal provider. See TRUSTe at www.truste.org and BBBOnline at www.bbbonline.org for examples. Both programs also are based primarily on the organization completing a self-assessment that is then reviewed by the seal program. The American Institute of Certified Public Accountants (AICPA) has developed a similar program through its Web Trust program (see www.aicpa.org). The Web Trust program differs from the other two seal programs in that this seal is awarded based on the results of regular external audits rather than a self-assessment.

Currently, there is little evidence that self-regulation has been fully implemented and is effective. In 2000, the FTC surveyed the privacy disclosures posted by 335 consumer-oriented dot-com Web sites. They found that although 88 percent posted some type of privacy disclosure, only 41 percent had disclosures implementing the first two elements of fair information practices, notice about the site's information practices and choice about having personal information shared with third parties; and only 20 percent implemented, at least in part, all four elements of notice, choice, access, and security (FTC 2000). A follow-up survey conducted in 2001 found similar results suggesting that self-regulation for online privacy has reached its upper limits (Milne and Culnan 2002).

Technology Solutions for Individuals

There are also two emerging types of technology-based solutions for privacy. One type provides consumers with greater control over the disclosure of their personal information, the other helps organizations keep their privacy promises. The Platform for Privacy Preferences (P3P) is one example of the former. P3P is a standard sponsored by the World Wide Web consortium (W3C). Web sites encode their privacy policies in a machine-readable version using XML, allowing Web browsers and other P3P user agents to find them automatically. In some implementations, users can encode their preferences in the user agent. The user agent will compare the P3P policy with the user's preferences and display any differences (Cranor 2002). See www.w3c.org/P3P for more information.

As of January 2003, Ernst & Young reported that 18 percent of the top 500 Web sites and 28 percent of the top 100 Web sites had adopted P3P. See www.ey.com/privacy for the P3P Dashboard Report, which tracks P3P adoption by industry. On the user side, currently three user agents have implemented P3P. Microsoft's Internet Explorer and Netscape Navigator allow individuals to manage the use of cookies as well as provide notice about the Web site's privacy policy. The AT&T Privacy Bird is a user agent that notifies the user whether or not the Web site's practices conflict with the user's preferences. See http://privacybird.com for more information. Other technology tools for individuals include the ability to visit Web sites anonymously, to manage cookies, or to manage one's online identity (Lester 2001).

Enterprise Technology Solutions

Two new types of enterprise tools help organizations keep the privacy promises that they make to individuals. The first type of tool analyzes Web sites for potential problems such as the absence of links to the privacy policy or the use of cookies or forms to collect personal information (e.g., Watchfire's WebCPO and IDcide's Privacy Wall). The second type of tool incorporates rules for data use into the firm's database at the level of the individual data element to automatically prohibit use of personal information in ways that conflict with the preferences a consumer has registered with the organization (e.g., IBM's Tivoli Privacy Manager or ZeroKnowledge's Enterprise Solutions).

Tools of this type can reduce the need for human oversight. For decentralized organizations with very large Web sites or large customer databases and whose practices vary for different groups of customers, it may be impossible to perform effective manual oversight. This may place the organization at risk for a deceptive trade enforcement action by the Federal Trade Commission if the organization's practices are found to vary from the promises made in the privacy policy. Technology tools may help to minimize this risk. See www.ftc.gov for examples of FTC enforcement actions.

Looking to the Future

In the future, a mix of self-regulation, technology, and law plus a vigilant media will be required to successfully protect consumer privacy and to address the range of consumer preferences related to their personal information. Self-regulation is unlikely to work 100 percent of the time, as there will always be bad actors or organizations who have not implemented the substance of fair information practices, creating a need for baseline privacy legislation. However, the penalties imposed by law are rarely enough to restrain organizations where there is no commitment to comply. At the same time, innovative uses of information technology will inevitably outstrip existing laws and social norms, necessitating a national, even global, conversation about what constitutes fair use of personal information. Therefore, the voice of activists and the media will continue to play an important role in mobilizing public outrage over unfair practices while at the same time helping to lead the broader social conversation on the fair use of personal information in the global economy. We now turn our attention to privacy as a global issue.

▮▮▮ Global Privacy Issues

Significant cross-cultural differences exist regarding privacy. As a result, privacy has emerged as an important issue for global organizations. The European Data protection Directive was enacted in 1995 to ensure that privacy concerns did not impede free flows of personal information among members of the European Community (EC). The Directive defines omnibus requirements for the collection and use of personal information for government and the private sector and requires each country to have a government agency responsible for privacy. Member countries are required to enact legislation to implement the provisions of the Directive. See Rotenberg (2002) for the text of the Directive.

The Directive also has important implications for countries, such as the U.S., which are not members of the EC. Article 25 of the Directive prohibits the transfer of personal of information to a third country, such as the United States, unless the third country ensures an adequate level of privacy protection. Article 26 specifies a limited number of exceptions to Article 25. Given the absence of both omnibus privacy legislation governing the private sector and a federal privacy office, the United States was deemed not to have an adequate level of protection. This meant that U.S. companies could be prohibited from transferring personal information about their European customers or employees to the United States.

The U.S. response to the Directive was the Safe Harbor, which was negotiated by trade negotiators from the Commerce Department and the European Community. The agreement was finalized in July 2000. The Safe Harbor principles require participating organizations to self-certify that they will observe fair information practices as defined by the Safe Harbor principles and a set of Frequently Asked Questions (FAQs). Enforcement is provided by the U.S. government agency with responsibility for regulating that industry. Organizations that choose to participate in the Safe Harbor are deemed to be adequate (see www.export.gov/safeharbor). What is interesting about the Safe Harbor is that participating organizations may provide stronger privacy rights to Europeans than they do to their U.S. customers.

Organizations that need to transfer data from Europe but do not want to join the Safe Harbor have several options. These include processing all personal information in Europe, obtaining the individual's unambiguous consent to the transfer, or maintaining that the transfer is necessary to fulfill the contract with the individual. Finally, the data exporter and the data importer (including European and U.S. subsidiaries of the same organization) may sign a contract that conforms to the terms specified by the European Community in 2001.

▮▮▮ Implementing Privacy: Organizational Considerations

U.S. business for the most part has adopted a reactive approach to managing consumer privacy concerns. For example, a 1990 Harris-Equifax survey found that no more than 25 percent of firms in privacy-intensive industries wanted to be a leader in developing new privacy policies. Smith (1994) investigated how seven different organizations in four industries (retail banking, insurance, credit card issuers, credit bureaus) responded to growing public concerns about consumer privacy, which had generated negative publicity for the organizations. He observed a three-phase cycle of response: drift, external threat, and reaction. Rather than address privacy issues proactively, these firms delegated responsibility for privacy to lower-level managers. New policies were developed only in reaction to an external threat or crisis.

In the *drift* phase, top management essentially abdicates responsibility for managing privacy to lower and midlevel managers to craft their own practices, if any. If any privacy matter is raised, each manager handles it on an ad hoc basis. In the second phase, organizations perceive a *threat* to their legitimacy, resulting from their practices of gathering or using personal information about their customers (e.g., credit card holders, retail bank customers). This threat often took the form of negative publicity in the press or media or legislative scrutiny. In the final phase, now that privacy has become a strategic issue, top management engages in a forceful *reaction*. Typically, efforts are made to codify existing practices and create new formal procedural safeguards to protect privacy.

There are two potential explanations for the reactive posture of business. First, there is no obvious competitive dynamic in the marketplace to suggest that firms can benefit financially from acting proactively, meaning that there is no assurance that the benefits of taking a proactive approach to privacy, such as potentially increasing market share, will outweigh the costs. Second, Osterhus (1997) argues that there are also two types of risks that act as disincentives to adopting prosocial policies. First, if a firm is discovered to have practices that do not match its privacy claims, this can lead to negative media coverage, decreased sales, and possibly a deceptive trade action by the FTC. Therefore, many firms approach consumer privacy issues as problems to be resolved or constraints to be managed rather than market opportunities to be leveraged into strategic advantages. When business has responded to the threat of legislation, it is either to avoid unwanted regulation or to help shape legislation when legislation was unavoidable.

Previously, firms had few market incentives to implement privacy initiatives. Despite their concerns, consumers continued to participate in marketing programs. Today, the "trust gap" described previously that has emerged in the online arena threatens this participation as consumers engage in privacy-protective behavior such as declining to do business with companies they do not trust (Harris Interactive 2002). This trust gap reflects a way in which consumer privacy concerns potentially threaten business interests, suggesting it is in the self-interest of business to address these concerns in a meaningful way. Further, we have begun to see new business opportunities in the privacy space in terms of products, services, and jobs (Lester 2001).

As the previous discussion illustrates, privacy has traditionally been a hard sell to business. This chapter takes a different view. Rather than being at odds with each other, the competitive need to use personal information should be able to peacefully coexist with consumer privacy interests. Because fair information practices build trust and trust is the lynchpin in building long-term customer relationships, protecting privacy represents an opportunity rather than a threat (Cavoukian and Hamilton 2000). Organizations, then, need a strategy to capitalize on this opportunity.

▮▮▮ Developing a Culture of Privacy

In consumer-facing organizations, most business processes involve personal information. Further, as we have seen, technology continues to create new opportunities to collect personal information. As a result, privacy is an organizational issue that is likely to become more, not less, important over time. Therefore, organizations need to develop a strategy for managing the second exchange, the personal information they collect, in the same way that they have formalized processes for managing the first exchange, the firm's product and service offering. Managing privacy effectively means that the organization needs to do more than write a privacy policy. It needs to treat privacy as a core business issue and create and maintain a culture of privacy. Creating and maintaining a culture of privacy involves four ongoing steps: champion, assess, evaluate, and implement.

First, developing a culture of privacy requires a champion from top management to signal the importance of privacy to the organization. Roles, responsibilities, and ownership for privacy need to be identified. The organization may decide to name a chief privacy officer. See Cavoukian and Hamilton (2002) for a more information about this newest member of the top management team. A privacy policy committee representing the relevant functions across the organization such as marketing, information systems, legal, consumer affairs, and operations should be appointed.

In the second step, the organization needs to conduct a privacy audit to assess current uses of personal information by the firm and its business partners. Best practices and legal requirements for privacy and security should be identified. Then the organization should develop its privacy policy.

In the third step, the organization needs to create education and awareness programs for its employees and develop and implement a communication strategy for its customers that "says what you do" with personal information. Third-party service agreements and contracts should be revised to reflect the privacy policy. The organization may also need to align some of its own information practices with the privacy policy based on the results of the privacy audit. Finally, privacy needs to be made part of the business case for new uses of customer information. Additional issues to be addressed during implementation include whether the organization should apply for a privacy seal, join the Safe Harbor, or implement P3P on its Web site.

Fourth, the organization needs to conduct periodic assessments to ensure that its practices comply with its policy and that you "do as you say." At this point it may be appropriate to consider using some of the enterprise privacy technologies discussed earlier to assist with these assessments. Employees need to be retrained. The external environment needs to be monitored for new issues related to technology, regulation, and public opinion. The privacy policy committee should meet regularly to address any new or ongoing issues.

▪▪▪ Consumer Privacy in the Post-September 11 World

Finally, the larger question is what are the long-term effects on our democratic society of an economy fueled by consumer data? The Gartner Group estimates that by 2004, 30 times more personal information will be routinely collected than is the case today and that the next hot-button privacy issue will be that extensive data collection or monitoring will be required for customer service (Hallawell 2001). Before the Internet, these data flowed largly from transactions initiated by the consumer, such as using a credit card or an ATM, joining a loyalty program, or entering a sweepstakes. Today, the Internet automatically provides data about our transactions as well as surfing habits to Web site owners as well as advertisers. Wireless systems and other forms of mobile technology yield not only data about what we do, but also where we are. In the future, it is predicted that even our home appliances and many products will be wired. What are the consequences to individuals and to society at large of this collective loss of privacy?

In the 1970s, some of the earliest concerns about privacy in the United States resulted from a government proposal to create a centralized database of personal information collected by the federal government. In the wake of these privacy concerns, plans for the database were scrapped and omnibus legislation, the Privacy Act of 1974, was enacted. The Privacy Act implemented fair information practices for personal information collected by the U.S. government.

Actions by the U.S. government since September 11 are once again raising concerns about the privacy of citizens. Here the concern is not a centralized database of government information, but the blurring of the boundaries between information about us in our separate roles as citizens, consumers, and employees or students. Consider, for example, Total Information Awareness (TIA), a Department of Defense research program to acquire massive amounts of data on all American consumers including bank records, tax filings, credit-card purchases, medical data, and phone and e-mail records. These records would then be mined for evidence of suspicious activity (Black 2002). Critics of TIA argue that such a program would undermine the privacy of all Americans with no clear security payoff, and in February 2003, Congress voted to suspend funding for TIA (Clymer 2003). Two public interest organizations, the Electronic Privacy Information Center (www.epic.org) and the Center for Democracy and Technology (www.cdt.org), provide good coverage of these issues.

Consumer data stored on corporate servers do not enjoy the same legal privacy protections that are afforded to information stored on home computers by the Fourth Amendment to the Constitution. Just as in the consumer arena where people are willing to disclose personal information if the benefits exceed the risks, most people are willing to trade some privacy for increased security, but we should ensure that any loss of privacy in fact results in a genuine increase in security. In the post-September 11 world, the rules for government access to our consumer data in the name of national security also merit a serious ongoing national conversation to ensure the appropriate balance between the privacy of our consumer data and our national security.

REFERENCES

Bagozzi, R. P. 1975. "Marketing as exchange." *Journal of Marketing 39: 32–39.*

Black, J. 2002. "Snooping in all the wrong places." *Business Week Online,* www.business/week.com, December 18.

Cavoukian, A. and T. J. Hamilton. 2002. *Privacy Payoff: How Successful Businesses Build Customer Trust.* New York: McGraw Hill.

Clymer, A. 2003. "Conferees in congress bar using a pentagon project on Americans." *New York Times,* February 12, p. A1.

Cranor, L. F. 2002. *Web Privacy with P3P.* Sebastapol, CA: O'Reilly.

Culnan, M. J., and R. J. Bies. 2003. "Consumer privacy: Balancing economic and justice considerations." *Journal of Social Issues 59 (2) 323–342.*

Culnan, M. J., and S. J. Milberg. 1998. *The Second Exchange: Managing Customer Information in Marketing Relationships.* Unpublished manuscript, Georgetown University.

Dorschner, J. 2002. "Eckerd to pay for ethics chair at Florida A&M to settle complaints over marketing efforts." *Miami Herald,* July 11. www.herald.com.

Federal Trade Commission 2002. *Privacy Online: Fair Information Practices in the Electronic Marketplace.* Washington, D.C.: Federal Trade Commission.

Hallawell, A. 2001. *Mr. President, It's Time for New Privacy Protection Methods.* Stamford, CT: Gartner Group.

Harris Interactive. 2002. *Privacy on and off the Internet: What Consumers Want.* Hackensack, NJ: Privacy and American Business.

Laufer, R. S., and M. Wolfe. 1977. (Privacy as a concept and a social issue: A multidimensional developmental theory.) *Journal of Social Issues 33: 22–42.*

Lester, T. 2001. "The reinvention of privacy." *Atlantic Monthly,* March, pp. 27–39.

Mayer, R. C., J. H. Davis, and F. D. Schoorman. 1995. "An integrative model of organizational trust." *Academy of Management Review* 20: 709–734.

Milberg, S. J., S. J. Burke, H. J. Smith, and E. A. Kallman. 1995. "Values, personal information privacy, and regulatory approaches." *Communications of the ACM* 38: 65–74.

Milne, B. R., and M. J. 2002. "Using the content of online privacy notices to inform public policy: A longitudinal analysis of the 1998–2001 U.S. Web Surveys." *The Information Society 18:* 345–359.

Organization for Economic Cooperation and Development. 1980. *Guidelines on the Protection of Privacy and Transborder Flows of Personal Data.* Washington, D.C.: Organization for Economic Cooperation and Development.

Osterhus, T. L. 1997. "Pro-social consumer influence strategies: When and how do they work?" *Journal of Marketing 61:* 16–29.

Rotenberg, M. 2002. *Privacy Law Sourcebook 2002: United States Law, International Law, and Recent Developments.* Washington, D.C.: Electronic Privacy Information Center.

Schwartz, P. M., and J. R. Reidenberg. 1996. *Data Privacy Law.* Charlottesville, VA: Michie.

Smith, H. J. (1994). *Managing Privacy: Information Technology and Corporate America.* Chapel Hill, NC: University of North Carolina Press.

Swire, P. P. 1997. "Markets, Self-Regulation, and Government Enforcement in the Protection of Personal Information." In U.S. Department of Commerce (ed.), *Privacy and Self-Regulation in the Information Age,* pp. 3–19. Washington, D.C.: National Telecommunications and Information Administration.

Westin, A. F. 1967. *Privacy and Freedom.* New York: Atheneum.

Winer, R. S. 2001. "A framework for customer relationship management." *California Management Review* 43: 89–105.

Building Consumer Trust Online

How Merchants Can Win Back Lost Consumer Trust in the Interests of E-Commerce Sales

DONNA L. HOFFMAN
THOMAS P. NOVAK
MARCOS PERALTA

Moving some Web consumers along to the purchase click is proving to be difficult, despite the impressive recent growth in online shopping. Consumer online shopping revenues and related corporate profits are still meager, though the industry is optimistic, thanks to bullish forecasts of cyberconsumer activity for the new millennium. In 1996, Internet shopping revenues for U.S. users, excluding cars and real estate, were estimated by Jupiter Communications, an e-commerce consulting firm in New York, at approximately $707 million but are expected to reach nearly $37.5 billion by 2002 [1]. Meanwhile, the business-to-business side is taking off with more than $8 billion in revenues for 1997 and $327 billion predicted by 2002 just in the U.S., according to Forrester Research, an information consulting firm in Cambridge, Mass. [4]. On the consumer side, a variety of barriers are invoked to explain the continuing difficulties.

There are, to be sure, numerous barriers. Such factors as the lack of standard technologies for secure payment, and the lack of profitable business models play important roles in the relative dearth of commercial activity by businesses and consumers on the Internet compared to what analysts expect in the near future. Granted, the commercial development of the Web is still in its infancy, so few expect these barriers to commercial development to persist. Still, commercial development of the Web faces a far more formidable barrier—consumers' fear of divulging their personal data—to its ultimate commercialization.

The reason more people have yet to shop online or even provide information to Web providers in exchange for access to information, is the fundamental lack of faith between most businesses and consumers on the Web today. In essence, consumers simply do not trust most Web providers enough to engage in "relationship exchanges" involving money and personal information with them.

Our research reveals that this lack of trust arises from the fact that cyber-consumers feel they lack control over the access that Web merchants have to their personal information during the online navigation process. These concerns over privacy span the dimensions of environmental control and secondary use of information control [6].

Environmental control, or the consumer's ability to control the actions of a Web vendor, directly affects consumer perception of the security of online shopping. In the physical world, a consumer may be concerned about giving out credit card information over the telephone to an unknown voice within a mail-order company. On the Web, consumers may fear typing in credit card information to any commercial Web provider. Similarly, a commercial Web provider may fear the efforts of a hacker intent on stealing credit card numbers.

Control over secondary use of information reflects consumers' perceived ability to control the use of their personal information for other purposes subsequent to the transaction during which the information is collected [2]. On the Web, this lack of trust is manifested in consumers' concern that Web providers will sell their personal information to third parties without their knowledge or permission.

Unlike traditional retail environments in the physical world, where consumers feel they have only limited choices, such perceptions concerning information privacy on the Internet have a striking negative influence on consumer willingness to engage in relationship exchanges online.

▬ ▬ ▬ Consumer Privacy Perceptions

We investigated key consumer perceptions of privacy by analyzing consumer responses to two biannual surveys: the spring 1997 *Nielsen Media Research/ CommerceNet Internet Demographics Study* [10] and the 1997 Georgia Tech Graphics, Visualization, and Usability Center's *GVU 7th WWW User Survey* [11].

The Nielsen study is representative of the U.S. as a whole, so the sample we examined (1,555 Web users) projects to the approximately 45 million Web users ages 16 and over in the U.S. at the time of the survey. The GVU survey is based on a self-selected sample of respondents to a Web-based form and tends to represent more experienced Web users from around the world. It is not representative or projectable to the larger Web user population, but the large sample size we analyzed (14,014 Web users) provides important insights into many Web users' attitudes toward privacy.

Analyzing the GVU data, we found that consumer expectations of privacy depend on the medium. In traditional media, it is well known that consumer attitudes toward privacy invasion range from tolerance to resigned disgust. But in electronic media, consumers are making it clear their need for control and protection is intense. A whopping 87% of Web users think they should have complete control over the demographic information Web sites capture, and over 71% feel there should be new laws to protect their privacy online.

While almost 20% of Web users in the survey (international in scope, though most respondents were from the U.S.) say magazines have a right to sell their demographic data to other firms for direct marketing purposes, only 12% say Web sites and third-party agencies have the same right. Similarly, almost 21% of Web users like receiving direct mail solicitations, but only 6% of Web users want to receive junk email.

The behavior of today's commercial Web providers is responsible for these attitudes. Many cybermarketers lack faith in consumers, thinking that if they ask consumers to opt in, most will opt out. Some cybermarketers treat online consumers poorly, in ways that bring to mind the practices of unscrupulous direct marketers in the physical world. Our analysis revealed that the primary barriers to consumers' providing demographic data to Web sites are related to trust and the nature of the exchange relationship. Nearly 63% of consumers who decline to provide personal information to Web sites report it is because they do not trust those who are collecting the data. Moreover, 65% report that providing such information is not worth the risk of revealing it, and 69% of Web users who do not provide data to Web sites say it is because the sites provide no information on how the data will be used.

The strength of these responses is hardly surprising, considering that 86% of commercial Web sites provide no information of any kind on how any demographic data collected will be used, or even whether data is being collected [9]. Consumers respond accordingly, either by withholding their personal data or by providing false data. Almost 95% of Web users have declined to provide personal information to Web sites at one time or another when asked, and 40% who have provided demographic data have gone to the trouble of fabricating it.

Despite this consumer resistance, our research suggests that consumers do realize that personal data is important to Web marketers and, perhaps surprisingly, report being interested in providing such information. Would it shock many marketers to know that almost all Web users (92%) would, in principle, give demographic data to Web sites? And that most consumers (over 62%) also understand that Web sites need information about their visitors to market their sites to advertisers.

But commercial Web sites are their own worst enemies. Contrary to the conventional wisdom, the enabling conditions for giving up information are not product discounts, access to the site, or value-added services. Indeed, 67%–75% of all Web users are decidedly uninterested in selling their personal data to Web sites for financial incentives or access privileges. In other words, consumers do not view their personal data in the context of an economic exchange of information, as many commercial Web providers believe.

Instead, Web consumers report wanting another type of exchange—characterized by an explicit social contract executed in the context of a cooperative relationship built on trust. The enabling condition for providing personal data is clear: Over 72% of Web users said they would give Web sites their demographic information if the sites would only provide a statement regarding how the information collected would be used.

But while consumers clamor for full disclosure and informed consent, the few Web sites that do tell their visitors they are tracking them and recording their data follow the traditional opt-out model. The default position of even the best opt-out policy is that unless the Web site is otherwise informed, it is free to use consumers' data in any (presumably legal) way it sees fit. Opt-out information privacy policies thus place the entire information-protection burden on the consumer while offering none of the control and setting up an environment of ipso facto mistrust between Web provider and consumer.

Although questionable security is a major deterrent to online shopping, concerns regarding the secondary use of information loom large, discouraging consumers from engaging in online relationship exchanges. Control over secondary use of information is likely to be a sticking point. Over 80% of Web consumers simply do not want Web sites to resell their personal information to other businesses.

▪▪▪ Consumer Attitudes and Cyber Behavior

The Internet threatens consumer information privacy in new and extreme ways. Unlike the case with consumer behavior in the physical world (When was the last time a consumer refused to shop for groceries over privacy invasion fears?), this threat has pushed many consumers to opt out of various forms of commercial participation in the Internet, including providing personal information to Web sites for marketing purposes.

The security issues raised by environmental control are shared by commercial Web providers and consumers. In contrast, the secondary use of information is a source of conflict between commercial Web providers and consumers. Although this conflict also exists in the physical world, the issue takes on greater urgency online, owing to the special characteristics of the Internet.

Data mining and data warehousing opportunities are being exploited as never before due to the capabilities of the Internet, high-speed networks, and terabyte data storage. In contrast, consumer information in the physical world is stored in a much wider variety of databases and data formats and is much more difficult to combine, analyze, and access.

Online shopping potentially allows commercial Web providers to collect much more detailed consumer behavior information than they can from most physical shopping trips. Commercial Web providers can collect not only the same information available in most physical transactions—identity, credit history, employment status, legal status—but also such additional information as electronic address, specific history of goods and services searched for and requested, other Internet sites visited, and contents of the consumer's data storage device.

Finally, with the notable exception of single-source data, such as supermarket scanner data, most secondary uses of information in the physical world have been limited to aggregate data involving generalizations across groups of consumers or inferences and assumptions about behavior based on broad indicators, such as geography and demographics.

Secondary use of information captured online can more easily follow individual-level behavior. Highly touted by many Internet marketers is the idea that data specifically linked to a single identifiable person can be used to customize a product or service to a potential customer, in the interest of maximizing the likelihood of consumer acceptance of the offer. Despite the growing consumer awareness of the potential of such customization, the practice generally proceeds without explicit consumer permission or knowledge.

It should come as no surprise that most consumers therefore avoid engaging in relationship exchanges online. In 1997, although more than 45 million individuals age 16 and over had used the Web in the U.S. at least once, only 4.5 million, or 10%, had ever purchased a product or service on the Web [8]. It is also worth noting, for the sake of perspective, that almost 123 million people, or nearly 62% of the U.S. population in 1997, had no access to the Internet and had never used it, and another 32 million Americans had access but had yet to use the Internet even once.

Figure 1 shows that Web consumers' top online-shopping concerns are related to control over information privacy and to trust, as opposed to the operating risks of remote shopping, and that these concerns influence their stated likelihood of buying something. In light of increasing security concerns, the likelihood of buying online decreases.

The same is true for secondary use of information control and trust, except that these concerns are most pronounced for both those Web users most likely and those least likely to shop online.

Figure 2 shows the relationship between the degree of online experience (closely correlated with and described by us here as "skill") and the reasons for not shopping

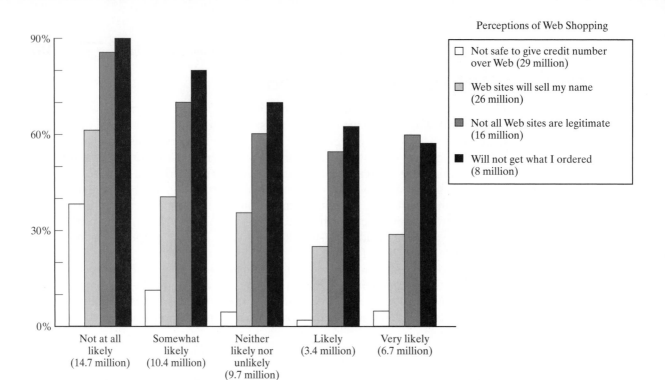

FIGURE 1 How Consumer Attitudes Influence Intent to Buy on the Web

Note: Analyses based on data from the 1997 CommerceNet/Nielsen Internet Demographic Survey (base: 45 million U.S. Web users).

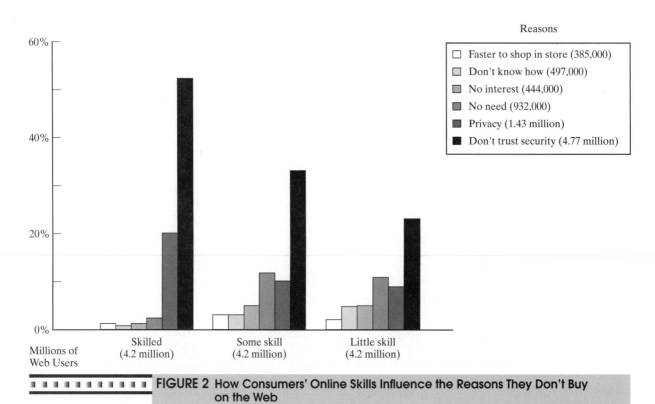

FIGURE 2 How Consumers' Online Skills Influence the Reasons They Don't Buy on the Web

Note: Analyses based on data from the 1997 CommerceNet/Nielsen Internet Demographic Survey (base: 12.6 million nonbuyers not at all likely to buy in the future who gave reason(s) for nonbuying, 31% of all nonbuyers; nonbuyers are 90% of all Web users).

online. We considered only Web users who have never shopped online and never plan to. Overall, the most important reasons nonbuyers uninterested in online shopping give for not shopping online are not functional but are related to issues of control over their personal information.

It is dramatically apparent that negative perceptions regarding security and privacy *increase* along with levels of online proficiency. The reverse is true for the functional reasons Web users do not shop online, including no perceived need, no interest, no knowledge of how to shop online, and the belief that it is faster to shop in stores made of bricks and mortar. In essence, the more experience one acquires online, the less important are the functional barriers to online shopping and the more important are concerns of control over personal information.

▪▪▪ Commercial Development of the Web (Short- vs. Long-Term)

Each stage of the online purchasing process involves dissimilar and conflicting interests for consumers and commercial Web providers [3]. During the search stage, for example, the Web provider wants to glean consumer information—the better to build a database of customer navigation and eventual purchase profiles. And the consumer wants to minimize the amount of personal information disclosed while maximizing the amount of information obtained about the product.

In the near term, this conflict of interest cannot be easily resolved, but we can address it by giving consumers the opportunity to be anonymous or pseudonymous when engaging in information exchanges and online transactions. Traceable anonymity gives Web providers no clues about consumers' identities but leaves this information in the hands of a third party. Traceable pseudonymity attaches a nom de plume, or pseudo-identity, that can be traced back to the consumer by someone, not necessarily the Web provider [5]. These functions can be ensured through the use of pseudonymous and third parties acting as mediators. At the same time, consumer anonymity or pseudonymity has to allow Web providers to receive the minimum information necessary—but only the minimum—to complete the exchange; for example, authentication, certification, confirmation, payment, and nonrepudiation in the case of an online transaction.

This short-term solution is appealing because it is likely to stimulate consumers' commercial online transactions by preserving their information privacy. It has the added attraction of opening the door to a long-term solution.

Ultimately, the most effective way for commercial Web providers to develop profitable exchange relationships with online customers is to earn their trust. The way to achieve trust is simple, though it departs radically from traditional business practice and will be difficult for many companies to implement. Trust is best achieved by allowing the balance of power to shift toward a more cooperative interaction between an online business and its customers [7].

Recognizing consumers' rights to data ownership on the Internet is an important first step in this rebalancing process. At a minimum, it means market-driven industry acceptance and enforcement of opt-out policies regarding information exchange. Eventually, the industry should accede to consumer demand and move toward opt-in, informed-consent policies in computer-mediated environments. However, it is likely that U.S. federal regulatory effort will be required.

A more consumer-oriented information privacy model will lead to commercially valuable relationship exchanges with important benefits for consumers and companies doing business on the Internet [12]. Consumers will be in control of their personal information—a notion consistent with customization of customer needs in online environments. Companies will be rewarded with consumer trust, willingness to disclose personal information, and increased loyalty. Moreover, as with open standards in computing and networking technology, cooperative models promote the healthy development of the electronic marketplace.

REFERENCES

1. Achs, N. *1998 Online Shopping Report: Strategies for Driving Consumer Transactions.* Jupiter Communications, Digital Commerce Group, New York, 1997 (www.jup.com).
2. Culman, M. Consumer awareness of name removal procedures: Implications for direct marketing. *J. Dir. Mark. 9,* 2 (Spring 1995), 10–19.
3. Driscoll, M., Roberts, C., Lyons, E., Jain, G., and Nuckols, J. *Secure Online Payment Systems.* Owen Electronic Commerce Student Working Paper, 1997 (mba.vanderbilt.edu/student/mba98/Jeffrey.nuckols/secure_online_payment/secure_payments_frames.html).
4. Erwin, B., Modahl, M. and Johnson, J. Sizing inter-company commerce: Business trade and technology strategies. *The Forrester Report 1,* (July 1997) (www.forrester.com).
5. Froomkin, M. Flood control on the information ocean: Living with anonymity, digital cash, and distributed databases. *Univ, Pittsburgh J. Law and Commer, 395,* 15 (1996) (www.law.miami.edu/froomkin/articles/ocean.htm).
6. Goodwin, C. Privacy: Recognition of a consumer right. *J. Public Policy Mark, 10,* 1 (spring 1991), 106–119.
7. Hoffman, D., and Novak, T. A new marketing paradigm for electronic commerce. *Inf. Soc.: An Int. J. 13,* 1 (1997), 43–54.
8. Hoffman, D., and Novak, T. *Privacy and electronic commerce.* Handout prepared for Electronic Frontier Foundation/Silicon Valley Industry Briefing with Ira Magaziner on Global Electronic Commerce and Personal Privacy Protection (Aug. 5, 1997).
9. Landesberg, M., Levin, T., Cuttin, C., and Lev, O. *Privacy Online: A Report to Congress.* Federal Trade Commission, June 1998 (www.ftc.gov.).
10. *Nielsen. Media Research. Nielsen Media Research/CommerceNet Internet Demographics Study,* Spring 1997 (www.nielsenmedia.com/commercenet/).
11. Pitkow, J., and Kehoe, C. *7th WWW User Survey.* Georgia Tech Research Corp., June 1997 (www.gvu.gatech.edu/user_surveys/).
12. Wang, H. Lee, M., and Wang, C. Consumer privacy concerns about Internet marketing. *Commun. ACM 41,* 3 (Mar. 1998), 63–70.

Trust and Privacy Online: Why Americans Want to Rewrite the Rules

SUSANNAH FOX

▪▪▪ Section One: Americans Want a Privacy Guarantee

Privacy has emerged as a central policy concern about the Internet as more Americans go online every day—and recent weeks have brought a ceaseless number of new allegations about privacy violations by Internet companies. In the past three months, a series of events have heightened sensitivities.

In June, the federal Office of National Drug Control Policy (the so-called "drug czar's" office) was found to be using Internet tools called cookies to track Web surfers' drug-related information requests. After a storm of criticism that this might allow the drug czar's office to clandestinely record citizens' online activities, the federal Office of Management and Budget banned the use of cookies on federal government Web sites.

In July, the Federal Trade Commission forced a bankrupt toysmart.com to abandon its plans to sell off customer data to the highest bidder. The firm had promised site users that it would not divulge information gleaned from tracking users' activities on the site, but a court-appointed overseer believed the customer list was a valuable asset that could be sold to help pay off the firm's creditors. That same month, Senator John McCain (R-Ariz.) introduced legislation that would require commercial Web sites to notify consumers about what kinds of personal information they collect and how they use it. Microsoft announced new third-party cookie controls for Internet Explorer, actively warning consumers and allowing them to reject cookies, which could be used to track their activities all across the Web. Fifty Dow Chemical Company employees were fired after a search of their email revealed pornography or violent images. The Clinton Administration and the Federal Trade Commission set privacy standards so favorable for online advertisers that shares in Doublelick rose 13 percent in one day. The FBI came under fire from Congress and civil liberties groups for developing

191

Very Concerned About Privacy	
Women, minorities, those with less online experience, and older Americans are the MOST concerned about keeping their personal information private	
All Americans	60%
Not online	64%
Internet users	54%
Women	62%
Men	57%
African-American	72%
Hispanic	62%
White	57%
Less than 6 mos. online experience	62%
More than 3 years online experience	50%
Ages 51–64	67%
Ages 18–29	46%
Source: Pew Internet & American Life Project May–June 2000 Poll.	

"Carnivore," a wiretapping device that silently intercepts all traffic to and from a suspect's email account.

Early this month, Toysrus.com was accused of feeding shoppers' personal information to a data-analysis firm without revealing the relationship to consumers. In response to complaints, Toysrus.com added information to their privacy policy about how customer data is treated, but denies that the information is sold to outside vendors. One week after the customer lawsuit was filed, Amazon.com and Toysrus.com announced a strategic alliance and restated their commitment to consumer privacy online. And this past week, Pharmatrak Inc., a Boston technology firm, acknowledged tracking consumers' activities on health-related sites without informing the public.

Not surprisingly, a great many online Americans are fretful about the things that could happen online and the way in which data about them might be gathered and used. An overwhelming majority of Internet users (86%) are concerned about businesses or people they don't know getting personal information about themselves or their families. Some 54% say they are "very concerned."

Americans Want the "Opt-in" Option

These wired Americans are anxious to take charge of their online lives and resoundingly prefer a different privacy protection scheme from the one promoted by major Internet industry and government leaders. Seven in ten Internet users (71%) say that people who use Web sites should have the most say over how Internet companies track users' activities.

Indeed, Internet users reject the notion that the government and Internet companies are the best stewards of their personal privacy. Two-thirds say Internet companies should not be allowed to track users' activities and 81% contend there should be rules governing how that tracking is done. Asked who would do the best job setting those rules, 50%

of online Americans said Internet users themselves would be best, 24% said the federal government would be best, and just 18% said Internet companies would be best.

And they are clear what that policy should be. Some 86% of Internet users favor an "opt-in" privacy policy and say that Internet companies should ask people for permission to use their personal information. This is the kind of system that has been adopted by the European Union. By contrast, the self-regulation plan recently embraced by the Clinton Administration, the Federal Trade Commission, and a consortium of Internet advertisers is an "opt-out" scheme that would compel consumers to take steps to protect their privacy.

Many Will Share Information—If They Can Choose When and Where

When Internet users are given the choice between sharing their personal information or not being able to use a Web site, 54% have provided their real email address, name, or other personal information. Of those who have never done this, 23% (or 10% of all Internet users) say they are *willing* to provide that information in order to use a site. This two-thirds majority (64%) demonstrates that many Internet users are willing to enter into an exchange with Internet companies. That said, a solid majority of Internet users still do not think companies should track their behavior online without asking users' permission.

The Making of Cookies

The strong urge of online Americans to protect their privacy and put the onus on companies to get permission before exploiting data or passing it along to others is a pipe dream considering the current privacy arrangement on most Internet sites. Cookies are bits of encrypted information deposited on a computer's hard drive after the computer has accessed a particular Web site. The Web site stores these bits of information so when the same site is accessed again by that same computer, the Web site can recognize the computer and provide the same layout, shopping cart, search information, or even user's name with the exact personalization each time the site is visited. (No reliable figures exist about how many Web sites install cookies.) Some cookies track the activities of a user at a particular Web site. Others can track the user from Web site to Web site.

Netscape created cookies in 1994 as a special browser feature to make life easier for people browsing the Web. The concept is similar to that of a computer's preferences file. It keeps track of how the user wants a site to look or function. Once the preferences are set, the user does not have to input routine information upon each visit. Its creators thought it would be especially useful in enabling "shopping cart" services on Web sites. The idea was to allow consumers to click from page to page choosing items to buy, while a virtual clerk kept track of the items until the consumer was ready to check out. Cookies also allowed a site owner to observe which displays attracted the consumer's attention and which needed some sprucing up. Netscape did not initially inform consumers about the clandestine activity on their hard drives and probably did not foresee the firestorm that would follow.

Chris Sherman has written for About.com that some believe the term cookie "comes from the story Hansel and Gretel, who marked their trail through a forest by regularly dropping crumbs along their path. Of course Hansel and Gretel used bright stones, not cookies to mark their trail; nonetheless, the legend persists."

After the media reported on the technology in January 1996, Netscape added a tool to disable cookies for the next version of their Web browsing software. But it was

Online Tracking		
Young people are more likely to say online tracking is helpful, because the company can provide information that matches their interests.		
	Helpful	*Harmful*
All Internet users	27%	54%
Ages 18–29	36%	47%
Ages 30–49	25%	54%
Ages 50–64	23%	56%
Source: Pew Internet & American Life Project May–June 2000 Poll.		

not very easy to do the disabling. Web site users had cookies implanted on their machines unless they took affirmative steps to reject cookies—a classic "opt-out" scheme. A user had to dig two menu screens down in his browser to find the place to opt out of cookies. There seemed to be no anticipation at the time that the use of cookies would create a problem. In 1996, Alex Edelstein, Netscape's product manager for Navigator 2.0, declared that cookie technology was an insignificant issue and would "blow over."

For a while, the use of cookies exploded and there were few complaints from consumers. Cookies themselves are not inherently bad or necessarily invasive to one's privacy. And they are instrumental in activating some of the Web's most appealing features. Web publications like iVillage.com use cookies to identify the preferences of regular readers and then direct appealing, tailored content to them. Merchants like Amazon.com use cookies to speed ordering and to suggest products to return customers. Soon enough, Web advertisers saw the possibility that cookies could help Web sites monitor users' activities and help discern consumer tastes. With that kind of information Web sites could deliver customized information to users.

Third-party advertising networks like Doubleclick sprang up to oversee banner ads on Web sites. These networks designed cookie files that track a user's activities all across the Web and trigger advertisements according to each user's apparent interests and needs. It is Web sites' ability through cookies to glean user's tastes and lifestyle that has led to the current debate about the appropriate ways to do tracking and maintain the privacy Americans want. In the most comprehensive and extreme cases, a Web company could build a profile of an Internet user that combines information about her purchases, her taste in music, the investment information she seeks, the health issues that concern her most, and the kind of news stories that seize her interest.

Unarmed in the Privacy Wars

The rise of third-party ad networks has raised the issue of cookies to prominence in legal and policy-making circles. But fewer than half of Internet users are aware of cookies. Eight in ten Internet users (79%) think it's common for Internet companies to track Web activities, yet only 43% of Internet users know that creating cookies is the way this is done. Of those who can identify cookies, just 24% set their browsers to refuse cookies. That means just 10% of all Internet users have set their browsers to reject cookies.

To a considerable degree, members of the two groups most likely to be targeted by Internet companies—those who click on ads online and those who buy things online—

are unaware that their computers' hard drives are implanted with cookies. The Pew Internet project survey found that 69% of Internet users have clicked on a Web advertisement and about 46% have bought products online. Yet only about half of each of those groups know what a cookie is. Of those shoppers and ad-clickers who are aware of cookies, just a fifth choose to block the tracking devices and surf more anonymously (23% of ad-clickers and 20% of online buyers). That means almost 90% of Internet users who shop online are being tracked by cookies and many are unaware that is happening.

There are other notable differences between groups when it comes to cookie awareness. Men are more likely than women to say they know what a cookie is (51% of online men; 34% of online women). Internet veterans are much more likely than Internet novices to say they know what a cookie is. Sixty percent of users who have been online for three or more years know what a cookie is, compared to just 23% of new users.

The Verdict on Tracking

A majority of Internet users (54%) are certain that online tracking is harmful because it invades their privacy. Advocates of cookies make the case that consumers will eventually come to appreciate cookies because they allow sites to provide information that is important and relevant to an individual Web user. In the case of advertising and marketing, cookie advocates argue that there's a great deal of waste that everyone hates in mass marketing through the mails (junk mail) and the media. These advocates argue that the ideal world created by cookies and tracking is one where the clutter of information and advertisements is cut to a minimum and only useful material is put in users' and consumers' hands. There is a distance to go, though, before that argument persuades Internet users. Only 27% say that tracking is helpful because it allows Web sites to tailor information for users.

Richard Purcell, director of the Corporate Privacy Group at Microsoft, says that new cookie controls for Internet Explorer will be part of a set of "empowerment tools" for consumers that will soon be available in the upgraded browser. Users will be alerted when a site tries to place a third-party cookie—that is, one that could help track their activities all across the Web. "We don't want to tell businesses how to act, beyond being truthful, but instead we want to let consumers be a force to be reckoned with," says Purcell. Purcell believes that consumer education is the key to allaying Internet users' fears—not behavior modification on the part of the industry.

Hard-Core Privacy Protectionists

While online Americans say they are concerned about breaches of privacy and that control is important to them, about half of all Internet users are trusting valuable personal information to Web companies that require it. Fifty-four percent of Internet users have provided their real email address, real name, or other personal information in order to use a Web site.

Of the 45% of Internet users who have not provided real personal information to a site, 61% are hard-core privacy defenders and say they are not willing to provide that information in order to use a site. This hard-core group is more likely to believe that tracking is harmful, that online activities are not private, and that there is reason to be concerned about businesses getting their personal information. Women and men are equally likely to be in this hard-core group, as are new and veteran Internet users. Young people (18–29 years old) are more likely to say they are not willing to provide personal information, as are users who go online only from home.

▪▪▪ Section Two: Guerrilla Tactics

There is a small group of Internet users resorting to "guerilla tactics" to defend their privacy online. About a quarter of Internet users have provided a fake name or personal information in order to avoid giving a Web site real information about themselves. A fifth of online Americans have used a secondary email address to avoid giving a Web site real information. Just one in ten Internet users have sent an encrypted email and only one in twenty have used software that hides their computer identity from Web sites.

Men are more likely to engage in these guerrilla tactics than women. Twenty-eight percent of men have provided fake personal information to a Web site, compared to 19% of women. Twelve percent of men have used encryption to scramble their email, compared to 6% of women. Seven percent of men have used identity-masking software, compared to 4% of women.

Young people and those with more online experience are also more likely to resort to lying in order to protect their personal information. Thirty-five percent of 18–29 year olds have provided fake personal information, compared to 22% of 30–49 year olds and 17% of 50–64 year olds. Only 18% of the newest users (online for six months or less) have provided fake personal information, compared to 31% of those with three or more years of online experience.

The use of online deception tactics such as fake names highlights the compartmentalization that is the basic tool of people who want to control their privacy. Judith Donath, an MIT professor who studies identity and online behavior, says that until Web sites design spaces that are clearly public or clearly private, users will have trouble choosing what information to share and what to hide. She adds that such fundamental decisions about what to share "shouldn't be about reading the fine print" of a Web site's privacy policy, but instead should be as obvious as the difference between staying in the privacy of your own home versus walking down the street. When a user is in "public" Internet space such as an online store, she suggests, the user would be correct in assuming that her movements were watched. When the user was in "private" space, he would have a right to expect that nothing about his activities there would be monitored, gathered into a profile, or sold to anyone or any firm unless he authorized it. Just as people act one way in their dens and another way at a party, Internet users want to make sure that the Internet world recognizes nuances about when "public" and viewable events are occurring as opposed to "private" and sensitive communications.

Internet users are pretty savvy about at least one safeguard: passwords. Sixty-eight percent of Internet users use different passwords when they register at various Web

Privacy Warriors	
Percentage of Internet Users Who Have:	
Provided a fake name or personal information to a Web site	24%
Used a secondary email address to avoid giving real information to a Web site	20%
Sent an encrypted email that has been scrambled to keep other people from reading it	9%
Used software that hides your computer identity from Websites you visit	5%
Source: Pew Internet & American Life Project May–June 2000 Poll.	

sites. Men are more likely than women to use different passwords (72% of men, compared to 64% of women).

▪▪▪ Section Three: A Punishing Mood

Internet users may not know all the tricks when it comes to protecting their privacy online, but they know problems when they see them. And if their trust is betrayed, they want vengeance.

If an Internet company violated their own privacy policy and used personal information in ways that it said it wouldn't, 94% of Internet users said the company should be punished. When given four choices of punishment, 11% of Internet users say the company's owners should be put in jail, 27% say the company's owners should be fined, 26% say the site should be shut down, and 30% say the site should be placed on a list of fraudulent Web sites.

If an Internet company cheated its customers or committed a fraud online, again, 94% of Internet users said the company should be punished. When presented with the same four options, 26% of Internet users say the company's owners should be put in jail, 22% say the company's owners should be fined, 33% say the site should be shut down, and 13% say that placing the site on a "fraudulent site" list is the right punishment.

Men are somewhat more passionate to punish dot-com executives. Fourteen percent of online men say a privacy-violating company's owners should be put in jail, compared to 7% of online women. Thirty percent of online men think a fraudulent company's owners should be put in jail, compared to 22% of online women.

More experienced Internet users are also less forgiving. Thirteen percent of veteran Internet users (three or more years of experience) would put the privacy-violating executives in jail, compared to 7% of the newest users (less than six months of experience). Thirty percent of veteran users say jail is the right place for owners of a fraudulent company, compared to 23% of the newest users.

Jason Catlett, founder of Junkbusters Corp. and a privacy advocate, argues the case for punishment this way: "Many Americans know that violation of copyright is a crime, and many believe that violation of their privacy should be a crime too. Why is distributing a corporation's software without its permission called 'piracy,' while distributing a person's information without permission is called 'sharing'?"

The Federal Trade Commission currently lacks the authority to enforce privacy standards on commercial Web sites, unless the content is directed at children. In May this year, the FTC released a report on privacy online that noted "only 20% of the busiest sites" implement the four widely-accepted fair information practices: (1) notice, displaying a clear and conspicuous privacy policy; (2) choice, allowing consumers to control the dissemination of information they provide to a site, (3) access, opening up the consumer's personal information file for inspection, and (4) security, protecting the information collected from consumers. The commission maintained that industry self-regulation had fallen short. Even as it agreed to a self-regulation scheme with Internet advertisers, the FTC called on Congress to expand the agency's enforcement power "to ensure adequate protection of consumer privacy online."

▪▪▪ Section Four: Fear Versus Trust

This survey's attempt to assess the level of trust online found three strong and sometimes conflicting patterns. In their attitudes, Internet users express considerable fears about a number of problems they might face online. They report, though, that the actual incidence of online problems is not very substantial. Finally, despite those fears, they behave in surprisingly trusting ways in many sensitive online areas. However, those fears cannot be discounted because they do seem to inhibit some groups, especially Internet novices and parents, from participating in some kinds of Internet activities.

Many Anxieties

A strong sense of distrust shades many Internet users' view of the online world and the uneasiness has grown in the past two years. Eighty-six percent of Internet users say they are concerned about businesses or people they don't know getting personal information about them or their families. Seven in ten Internet users are concerned about hackers getting their credit card number and six in ten are concerned about someone learning personal information about them because of things they've done online. More than half of Internet users worry about receiving bad medical information online or downloading a virus to their computer. Nearly half of Internet users worry about seeing false news or financial reports online. Forty-six percent are not confident that their online activities are private. Only 10% of Internet users are "very confident" that the things they do online are private and will not be used by others without their permission.

Older users are more concerned than younger users about the integrity of the information they see on the Internet. Fifty-nine percent of Internet users 50–64 years old are concerned about people spreading false rumors online to affect stock prices, compared to 37% of 18–29 year old users and 49% of 30–49 year old users. Fifty-five percent of Internet users 30–49 years old are concerned about seeing false or inaccurate news reports online, compared to 40% of 18–29 year old users and 50% of 50–64 year old users.

Credit Card Concerns: Not Much Different from the Offline World

It is important to understand that while Americans are concerned about their privacy online, there is no evidence in this survey that the Internet is a more menacing threat to privacy than activities in the offline world. In the case of credit card information, Americans' online concerns are no greater than the concerns they have offline. Of all those Americans who had used their credit card to buy something over the phone, 56% said they worried about someone else getting their credit card number. Of all those with Internet access who used their credit card to buy something online, 54% said they worried about someone else getting their credit card number. And the proportion of those using credit cards online has leaped in the last five years. Only 8% of Internet

Uptick in Online Worries		
Percentage of Internet Users Who Worry. . .	1998	2000
. . . their email will be read by someone besides the person they sent it to	20%	27%
. . . someone might know what Web sites they've visited	21%	31%
. . . they'll get a computer virus when they download information	42%	54%

Source: Pew Internet & American Life Project May–June 2000 Poll and The Pew Research Center for the People and the Press 1998.

users had used their credit card to make a purchase online in 1995, compared to 48% of Internet users who had done this by June 2000.

This survey found that 19% of Internet users (and 15% of all Americans) have been victims of credit-card fraud or identity theft. A vast majority of those who had been victimized (80%) said the theft occurred offline. Only 8% reported that the thief got the information because the consumer had provided it online. That means that fewer than 3% of Internet users have had their credit card information swiped online.

Viruses and Unwanted Email

The most frequent online problems are tied to email, but that has not seemed to affect the Internet's most popular activity. Almost everyone who goes online (98%) knows what a computer virus is and one in four Internet users (25%) has had a computer infected by a virus. According to CERT, the Internet security emergency response team at Carnegie Mellon University, the number of "security incidents" reported held steady at about 2,400 per year in the mid-1990s. But such incidents grew to 3,700 in 1998, nearly 10,000 in 1999, and 8,836 through the first two quarters of 2000. An infected email message is the most likely suspect for Internet users who have had a virus—46% cite that suspicion.

Users who go online from both home and work are the most fearful of computer viruses, possibly because they are more likely to have downloaded a virus and would miss the Internet the most if their access were taken away. Seventy-five percent of home-and-work users say they are worried, compared to just 51% of work-only users (who are often protected by impenetrable firewalls) and 52% of home-only users. Thirty-one percent of home-and-work users have had a computer infected with a virus, compared to 30% of work-only users and 18% of home-only users. Nevertheless, email users are very fond of this form of communication; and the people most victimized by viruses are the most likely to express affection for email. In a March 2000 Pew Internet Project poll, 83% of home-and-work users said they would miss the Internet if they could no longer go online, compared to 54% of work-only users and 71% of home-only users.

Viruses are not the only stink bombs lurking in Americans' email in-boxes. Twenty-eight percent of Internet users have received an offensive email from someone they have never heard of. Men and women are equally likely to have received an offensive email, as are Internet users across all age, education, and income groups. Veteran users—Americans who have been online for more than three years—are the most likely to have received an offensive email from a stranger. Thirty-six percent of veteran users said that has happened to them, compared to just 14% of users with less than six months of experience online.

In a March 2000 Pew Internet Project poll, 37% of email users reported that they get a lot of spam or unwanted email messages. For those who feel inundated by unwanted email, 70% say the offending messages are sales solicitations, 17% say the emails are from other people they don't care to hear from as much, and 7% say the unwanted emails come from list-serves, or online discussion groups.

Email continues to be the most popular online activity – 92% of Internet users have ever sent an email and 48% do this on a typical day.

Work Surveillance and Discipline

The incentive to monitor Internet users' behavior is not simply confined to those who want to sell them products and services. There are legal encouragements to monitor online actions. Business executives can be sued if they do not maintain a safe and harassment-free work environment. That gives these executives encouragement to watch what happens on their computer systems. Moreover, the Internet is bursting with opportunities for workers to use their computers for fun or profit that is not related to their jobs. That can prompt executives to make sure workers are productively engaged when they are on the clock.

The Pew Internet Project survey shows how aggressively firms are already acting on those incentives. Eleven percent of all Americans and 17% of Internet users know someone who was fired or disciplined because of an email they sent or a Web site they went to at work. The survey suggests this kind of thing is happening most frequently at the level of those with the highest paying, most sophisticated jobs. Americans with higher levels of education and income are more likely to know someone in that situation. Fifteen percent of Americans with a college degree know someone who was fired or disciplined because of online activities, compared to 3% of Americans with have not finished high school. Nineteen percent of Americans with a household income exceeding $75,000 per year know someone in that situation, compared to 8% of those whose household income falls below $30,000 per year.

Yet many Internet users continue to conduct personal business during working hours. According to the Pew Internet Project's four-month tracking poll, 10% of Internet users who only go online from work are surfing the Web "just for fun" or to pass the time on a typical day. In addition, on that typical day, 8% of work-only Internet users are looking for information online about a hobby or interest; 3% are looking for a new job; 4% are looking for information about books, movies, music or other leisure activities; and 5% are checking sports scores on that day.

Making Friends and Meeting Strangers

Twenty-six percent of Internet users have responded to an email from a stranger and 25% of Internet users have made friends with someone online. Men are much more likely to respond to an email from someone they've never met or talked to than women. Some 31% have done that compared to 20% of women. Young people are also more likely to have responded to unexpected emails than older Internet users—31% of 18–29 year olds have responded to a stranger's email. After age thirty, an Internet user's likelihood to respond drops significantly, with 25% of users between 30–49 years old and 22% of 50–64 year olds responding to a stranger's email.

The incidence of making friends online has held steady for years. Pew Research Center polls show that 23% of Internet users reported that they had made a friend online in 1995 and a similar percentage reported that in 1998. As with responding to emails from a stranger, men are more likely to make friends online with 29% claiming an online friend, compared to 21% of women. Twenty-eight percent of those with a high school education or less have made friends online, compared to 18% of those with a college degree.

And although most Internet users are wary of other people, only 4% have ever felt personally threatened when they were online.

Dating and Support-Group Sites

Despite their privacy concerns, Americans are finding ways to reach out to each other online. Large majorities of those who email family and friends say email is useful for these communications (88% and 90%, respectively). Half of those who email friends

(51%) say the electronic communication has brought them closer, while among those who email family 40% say it has brought them closer to their families.

Nine percent of Internet users have gone to a dating site and 36% have gone to a support group site or one that provides information about a specific medical condition or personal situation. Interestingly, men are twice as likely as women to visit a dating site (12% of men have done this, compared to 6% of women). Women are almost twice as likely as men to visit a support-group site (44% of women have done this, compared to 29% of men).

Online Calendars or Address Books

Internet users are also taking advantage of online services that aim to simplify their lives, despite their concerns about security risks. Twenty-two percent of Internet users have entrusted their personal calendar or address book to a Web site service. Internet users who upload intimate life details such as anniversaries and doctor's appointments may well be nervous that the Web calendar company will protect their privacy. Nor surprisingly, many of the sites are part of the TRUSTe privacy program and post very tough-sounding policies. For example, the Daily Drill site states, "Your calendar and all its information is absolutely private and will never ever be shown to anyone else. Period."

Women and African-American users are more likely to use these types of sites, despite the fact that these groups are among the most frequent to say they are concerned about their online privacy.

▪▪▪ Section Five: Why Privacy Concerns Could Limit the Net's Potential

Concerns about privacy are notably higher among some groups, especially Internet novices (those who first got online within the past six months), parents, older Americans, and women. In some instances, these fears are associated with lower participation in some online activities, especially commercial and social activities. There is no way to know yet whether these groups will eventually become more comfortable and less fearful in the online world or whether their wariness will permanently limit their use of the Internet until their concerns about protecting personal information are met.

Internet Newcomers and Veterans

Fifteen percent of Internet users just got online in the last six months. These users are more likely to be highly concerned about privacy and Web site security than more experienced Internet users. Sixty-two percent of Internet users with less than six months of experience are "very concerned" about businesses and people they don't know getting personal information about them or their family. In comparison, 50% of Internet users with three or more years of experience feel that way.

These pronounced privacy concerns among newer Internet users are driven in part by their fears about the technology, rather than first-hand experience with fraud or other online invasions. For example, new users are no more likely than experienced users to have been victims of any kind of credit card fraud. Some 19% of these newcomers have had their credit card number stolen, compared to 23% of Internet

Cookie Awareness	
Internet Experience:	Know What a "Cookie" is
<6 mos.	23%
6–12 mos.	25%
2–3 yrs.	42%
3+ yrs.	60%

Source: Pew Internet & American Life Project May – June 2000 Poll.

veterans who have suffered the same problem. And very few in each group have been victims of credit card theft online.

New users are less likely than Internet veterans to know what a "cookie" is. Among those who know what a cookie is, veteran users are the most likely to set their browser to accept them—72% of users with three or more years of experience allow Web sites to track their activities using cookies, compared to 55% of users with two or three years of experience. The percentage of new users who block cookies is too small to accurately evaluate.

New users are much less likely than veteran users to lie to protect their personal information. Only 18% of the newest users (online for six months or less) have provided fake personal information to a Web site, compared to 31% of those with three or more years of online experience.

The more time someone has been online, the more likely they are to be confident about Web site security. For example, an equal proportion (23%) of the most experienced Internet users (3+ years of experience) and relatively new users (6–12 months of experience) have had their credit card or other personal information used without permission. But only 46% of the most experienced Internet users say they worry about online credit-card theft, compared to 70% of less-experienced users.

This lack of confidence is reflected in the fact that Internet newcomers are also less likely to purchase products or services online. Twenty-seven percent of users who got access within the last six months have bought something online such as books, music, toys, or clothing, compared to 60% of users who have been online for three or more years. Only 18% of the newest users have purchased an airline ticket or made a hotel reservation online, compared to 36% of the most experienced Internet users.

New users are more wary and less friendly online than veteran users. Just 18% of Internet users with less than six months of experience have responded to an email from someone they don't know, compared to 34% of those with three or more years of experience. Eighteen percent of new users have made a friend online, compared to 28% of veteran users.

The Parents' Story

Forty-two percent of Internet users are parents and they bring a unique perspective to the privacy debate. Eighty-four percent of parents think Internet companies should have to ask for permission to use any personal information that they collect, compared to 76% of non-parents. Parents with Internet access whose children also go online are much more nervous about computer viruses, perhaps out of concern that their children will unwittingly infect the family machine. Sixty-two percent of these "wired family" parents worry about downloading a virus to their computer, compared to 50% of non-parents and 54% of all Internet users.

Now What Have You Downloaded?	
Do you ever worry that you'll get a computer virus when you download information?	
Internet users	54%
Online parents whose children go online	62%
Online non-parents	50%

Source: Pew Internet & American Life Project May–June 2000 Poll.

Parents who are online are less friendly and more wary of other people than non-parents online. Only 20% of parents have responded to an email from someone they didn't know, compared to 30% of non-parents. Parents are also less likely to make friends online—20% of parents said they had, compared to 28% of non-parents.

It's Time for Rules in Wonderland

Here's Business Week's *Four-Point Plan to Solve the Internet Privacy Mess*

HEATHER GREEN
MIKE FRANCE
MARCIA STEPANEK
AMY BORRUS

If Lewis Carroll had written about Alice's adventures today, she would find herself passing through the looking glass and into cyberspace. She would meet up with dodos, duchesses, and eggheads, some of whom would spout the rough equivalent of "Twas brillig, and the slithy toves. . . ." The journey also would be full of rude surprises. As in Carroll's books, she would eventually discover who she really was. But many others she had never met would learn about her, too. Indeed, with every click of the mouse, a bit more of her privacy would vanish down the rabbit hole.

These days, a lot of people are stumbling on similar unpleasant surprises. Thanks to a string of privacy gaffes involving DoubleClick (DCLK), RealNetworks (RNWK), Amazon.com (AMZN), and other major Web sites, consumers are learning that e-commerce companies have an intense interest in their private information. For about 9 cents, some medical data sites will sell you your neighbor's history of urinary tract infections. Your speeding tickets, bounced checks, and delayed child-support payments are an open book. In the background, advertising services are building profiles of where people browse, what they buy, how they think, and who they are. Hundreds of sites already are stockpiling this type of information—some to use in targeted advertising, others to sell or trade with other sites.

Gold Rush   It will get worse. The tricks being played today are child's play compared with what's coming. Web sites that want to know you better will soon be able to track your movements on Web phones, palm devices, and video games, and parse the data with more subtle software. Online services can be layered with mounds of data about each person. Interactive TVs, for instance, have the potential to correlate the Web sites you visit at work with the ads you see at home in the evening.

Web surfers don't need extra proof that this gold rush for personal data is alarming. In a new Business Week/Harris Poll, 92% of Net users expressed discomfort about Web sites sharing personal information with other sites. The public outcry has grown so loud that in February, search engine Alta Vista Co. promised to ask explicit permission before sharing visitors' personal information with other companies. On Mar. 2, DoubleClick bowed to public pressure on a similar point: The company, which serves up ads on many Web sites, has created anonymous digital snapshots, or "profiles," of millions of cybersurfers, based on where they browse and what they do online. DoubleClick had planned to link profiles with much more specific information, including names and addresses culled from real-world databases that cover 90% of American households. The company dropped that controversial plan, and within days, smaller rival 24/7 Media Inc. abandoned a similar strategy.

Anonymous tracking and profiling by DoubleClick and 24/7 can be very subtle. But sometimes privacy violations hit you in the face. We have all heard the examples of sociopaths who stalk their victims online. We have seen the statistics on "identity theft," in which criminals suck enough personal data off the Net to impersonate other people. Perhaps these are extreme examples. Even without them, many cybersurfers are starting to feel that they have spent quite enough time at this particular Mad Tea Party. They are ready for privacy rules that set some plain and simple boundaries. In the March Business Week/Harris Poll, 57% of respondents said government should pass laws on how personal information is collected. "What's going on today is exponentially more threatening to those who want to protect privacy," says Eliot Spitzer, New York's state attorney general who has proposed privacy legislation. People can't make informed decisions on the Net because they lack the necessary information. "What we're confronting is a market failure," says Spitzer.

Responding to a growing chorus of privacy-related complaints, some states have drafted legislation ranging from curtailing the sale of personal information to the creation of a privacy ombudsman. But this piecemeal, state-by-state approach is a muddle. Scattershot laws will only create more confusion. Over time, they will choke budding e-business in complex litigation and red tape.

Business Week believes there is a better way. Instead of a conflicting patchwork of state rules, the federal government should adopt clear privacy standards in the spirit of the Fair Information Practices—a philosophical framework for privacy protection that has been adopted worldwide over the past 25 years. The broad principles are essential:

- Companies conducting business online should be required by law to disclose clearly how they collect and use information.
- Consumers must be given control of how their data are used.
- Web surfers should also have the ability to inspect that data and to correct any errors they discover.
- And when companies break the rules, the government must have the power to impose penalties. "All of these bits you are sending out are your digital DNA," says Tara Lemmey, president of the Electronic Frontier Foundation. "You should have control of that."

Regulation flies in the face of the approach industry has been championing. For the past four years, Net companies have insisted that they can police themselves on privacy. "Industry initiatives and market forces are already doing a good job," says Daniel J. Jaye, co-founder of Engage Technologies Inc., which dishes up ads on the Web.

In other words, the market will punish companies that fall afoul of consumers. Bringing in the government, execs say, will pile bureaucratic layers on top of the Net. This could undercut the very promise of efficiency that many online businesses are counting on. The Internet, they say, is supposed to draw companies closer to their customers, allowing them to anticipate their desires. With profile data, they can target their ads, slash wasteful and random marketing costs, design products faster, and build higher profit margins. Profiling provides the underpinnings of a new way of doing business upon which the Net Economy is built.

Laws that require businesses to seek users' permission before they collect or use data about Web-surfing habits could kill this goose, they say. And why do that, industry execs ask, when they are making such fine strides in protecting consumer privacy? As a positive sign, Net businesses trumpet a May, 1999, Federal Trade Commission survey in which 66% of companies queried had privacy policies.

Self-Regulatory Sham We are not persuaded by these arguments. Few Web sites give consumers real choices over the data that get collected online. There is no proof that if given a choice—especially bolstered with financial incentives proffered by Web merchants—consumers won't willingly hand over some personal data. As for privacy policies, the same FTC survey showed that while more than 90% of companies polled collected personal information, fewer than 10% actually followed all of the established Fair Information Practices.

In short, self-regulation is a sham. The policies that companies have posted under pressure from the government are as vague and confusing as anything Lewis Carroll could have dreamed up. One simple example: When people register at Yahoo! Inc. (YHOO) for one of its services, such as My Yahoo, they are asked to provide their birth date and e-mail address—ostensibly as a safeguard if they forget their user name and need prompting. But Yahoo also uses that information for a service called the Birthday Club, sending product offers from three to five merchants to users via e-mail on their birthday.

Don't look for transparency here. Most sites don't limit how they or their partners use consumer information. And Web sites can transfer information to partners without telling their own customers. Many sites also change their practices at will and without warning.

Because privacy breaches are so corrosive to consumer trust, some Web execs actually welcome broad national standards. IBM (IBM) and Walt Disney Co. (DIS) have decided not to advertise on Web sites that don't have privacy policies. Privacy codes must be clearer, says Chris Larsen, CEO and founder of E-Loan Inc. (EELN), an online loan service that has its privacy policies audited. "I think the industry has squandered the opportunity to take care of this on its own." IBM Chairman Louis Gerstner doesn't go that far. But he has warned Net executives that they must get serious. "I am troubled, very troubled, by leaders who have failed to recognize our responsibility in the transformation of the new economy," he says.

We hope other Web execs are listening closely. The policies we propose are in the best interests of Web businesses. If more consumers can be assured that their personal information is safe, more of them will flock to the Net—and click, not exit. There are other explicit benefits for the industry. Privacy standards create a level playing field, so companies don't fall into an arms war, each trying to collect the most data—at any cost.

"Business will benefit from the right level of government involvement," says Nick Grouf, founder of PeoplePC, which offers cheap PCs and Net connections. "Standards are good, but they need some teeth, and this is where government becomes a good partner."

Federal Standard   In the long term, the privacy protection that Business Week espouses will make life simpler for businesses on the Net. More than 20 states already are moving to enact some kind of guarantees. A minimum federal standard of online privacy would decrease the cost and complexity for companies. It also would increase trust. If businesses really want to be close to their customers, trust is paramount. This approach also will shrink the gap that has arisen between the U.S. and Europe, where privacy already is recognized as a right. The Europeans have stood firm, putting American companies in the peculiar position of extending greater privacy protection in Germany or France than at home.

It's time to iron out the inconsistencies. Here are our prescriptions for protecting personal privacy without jeopardizing the promise of e-commerce . . .

▮▮▮ Our Four-Point Plan

E-privacy and E-commerce can coexist. Here's how to safeguard both.

1—Display Your Practices

Privacy policies seem like very simple things. Companies put up a notice online about how they gather and use information, and it's win-win from there. Consumers get the lay of the land, and Net companies pass on to consumers the responsibility for their online privacy.

If only it were that simple. These little postings have actually been the focus of rancorous debates for years. The tricky thing is that once policies are up there for all to see, companies are legally obligated to uphold them. That's one reason sites have dragged their feet in putting them up. Or should we say down? The statements are usually buried at the bottom of the page, and seem to be drafted by life-forms on a distant planet.

It's time that policies be written for mere mortals. Not many sites do a great job of explaining how information is tracked, used, and disclosed to partners. Consider the privacy policy of search engine Ask Jeeves (ASKJ). The company first says it always asks permission before providing information to partners. Yet on a registration form, the choice given to consumers is that information is shared unless you say otherwise. To confuse matters further, the policy later states that: "Ask Jeeves sometimes co-sponsors [sweepstakes and contests] with other companies, in which case the user's individual contact and demographic information is likely to be shared with participating sponsors. [The] information will not be released . . . without the user's consent." So which is it: Is your information automatically shared unless you go the extra step to object? Or is it kept private unless you pipe up and give the green light? When asked directly, Ask Jeeves says it depends. Depends on what? It's fine for companies to have different options, but too vague possibilities baffle consumers, rendering privacy notices useless.

One solution might be simple icons that help to navigate the policies. Like the "Information" sign that is recognized around the world, these symbols could be standardized: a large "p" signifying "privacy policy" could be placed on the top right-hand side of the page, on a registration form, in an electronic shopping cart, or anywhere that information is collected on a site. Often it's not clear, upon registration, whether you need to locate an "opt-out" button and click on it to stop the site from sharing your information with others, or whether the site intends to ask your permission each time it wants to pass information to another site. Icons could help clarify this.

Second Opinion   Simple road signs on the Info Highway may seem trivial, but understanding the full measure of privacy policies is no joke. They resemble contracts. Indeed, they are generally the only privacy-related feature on sites than can actually trip a lawsuit. In January, New York District Attorney Spitzer used privacy policy violations by Chase Manhattan Bank (CMB) and Sony Music Entertainment Inc.'s Info Beat to curtail their sharing of data. "We have an obligation to define reasonable boundaries," he says. "We have to articulate what privacy rules should be and then how to enforce them."

It isn't enough to have just any old policy, though. The statements need to follow the Fair Information Practices, clearly laying out how each site addresses choice, access, and security. Policies should outline how a person's information is shared and how to limit its use. Contact numbers or e-mail addresses should be available. And the date on when the policy was last changed should be clearly stated. Web execs make a good argument when they say that it's hard to know how they will use data in the future. But they should alert consumers when the policy changes. Amazon.com (AMZN), for example, says it doesn't sell or trade information now, but adds: "We may choose to do so in the future." The only notice the company says it will give is a change in its policy online.

The sharing of information is a white-hot button in the privacy debates. And for good reason. A Georgetown University survey of the privacy policies on health-care sites showed how common this is. Of 21 sites sampled, six offered assessments on health conditions that were actually run by other companies. Some companies shared names, ages, and e-mail addresses, which makes it hard for users to know who has their personal data or which privacy policy to rely on.

In the best of all worlds, companies should bind partners with whom they share data to their privacy policies. At the very least, they should inform consumers that they plan to transfer personal information to a partner. That way, consumers can check out the partner's privacy policy and make an informed decision about whether they want to participate.

Defining Terms   It's all too vague on Yahoo's Web site. That's partly because the No. 1 site on the Net has what's known as a "universal registration," where people sign up once and are entitled to a host of different services—from e-mail to auctions to private personal calendars. But the universal registration information also ties in with other services offered through partners, such as the reservation service Travelocity provides. While details about data-sharing practices are explained on Yahoo (YHOO), they are buried many clicks deep in so-called terms of service agreements, which aren't marked as privacy policies.

Some companies, such as PeoplePC and eBay, have very clear policies that give descriptions of how information could be passed to partners and naming some partners as examples. They also try to provide some level of surety. For instance, eBay Inc. says that before it provides personal information to partners, it lets users see the data it has collected. That's a step forward, but still limiting. To prevent eBay from sharing your data, you must choose not to use the service. And for those who give the O.K.? Once the information is transferred in these co-branded services, eBay says it has no control over how partners use the data.

It's crucial that these partnerships, data-gathering techniques, and customer options are spelled out, especially for Net newbies. Companies must be clear about how they define "personally identifiable information," because that description can change from site to site. Just as vital, they need to spell out the technology used to track and profile consumers. RealNetworks, which overhauled its privacy policies this fall after being accused of compiling information about the musical tastes of users, has a straightforward approach. It breaks out every tracking technique it uses and explains them simply and effectively. In contrast, CBS SportsLine explains that it uses IP addresses to identify users and their shopping carts but doesn't bother to explain what an IP address is. For the record: This is a trackable number assigned to your PC every time you connect to the Web.

Clearly, privacy policies are backbreakers to write. But it seems the hardest part about them for any company is coming up with a privacy philosophy that they will stick to. Once this hurdle is crossed, however, the positive impact might resonate into the brick-and-mortar world as well. Privacy policies governing credit reports, drug prescriptions, and more could follow the new model for the Internet.

2—Give People a Choice

Right now, there's only one way you can be sure that the sensitive details of your life won't spill out over the Internet: Don't log on in the first place.

Short of doing that, consumers who surf the Web do so at their own peril. There are practically no laws to stop sites from ferreting out as much personal information about you as they can get their hands on—and then turning around and selling it to the highest bidder. If an AIDS patient visits a health site to investigate the side effects of the drug AZT, that site is free to market the information to drug companies, insurers, or anyone else.

Things don't have to be this open. What is needed is a way to give consumers more control over what is collected about them and more say over how it can be used. Proposed new federal and state laws would require Web sites to allow consumers to "opt out" of a company's data-collecting and resale operations. How? The new laws would force sites to display a box, which, for example, could be checked off by AIDS patients if they didn't want health-care sites to track the screens they read, store their credit card numbers, or resell any of that information.

Opting Options   Of course, many Web sites already let visitors opt out. But most of those opt-out boxes are buried. Some of the proposed new privacy laws, such as a Senate bill being sponsored by Ron Wyden (D-Ore.) and Conrad Burns (R-Mont.), would require every Web site to offer a clearly written, prominently displayed opt-out box. Under such bills, consumers who arrive at the home page of Yahoo, Amazon, or eToys (ETYS), would be able to find the opt-out box right under their nose, perhaps on the upper righthand corner of their screen.

But even such prominently placed boxes might not be protection enough. Studies indicate that people who may otherwise be worried about online privacy are not going to stop their surfing long enough to read a few sentences of dense boilerplate, and then click on a box. That's why some politicians and privacy advocates are pushing even tougher protections. Rather than put the burden on consumers to opt out, they want to put the burden on companies to get Web surfers to opt in. Before a site could start collecting and selling most data, it would have to get people to check a box giving it permission to do so. A controversial Senate bill to do this has been proposed by Robert Torricelli (D-N.J.).

Industry reaction to giving consumers more choice ranges from genuine enthusiasm to hyperventilating hostility. Among critics, opt-out legislation is generally regarded as the lesser evil. But because information technology is evolving rapidly and the Internet soon will be widely available on tiny cell phones and other devices, some online executives worry that a bulky, federally required opt-out notice might not fit. "Having laws get down to pixel counts and screen layouts won't work," says Max Metral, chief technology officer for PeoplePC.

Nonetheless, most Web executives can live with opt-out. But they are terrified of opt-in. Execs worry that many people simply won't be willing to make the extra effort that opting in requires. As proof, some cite the Children's Online Privacy Protection Act, a 1998 law that limits the collection of information about kids under 13. Among other things, COPPA requires parents to opt in, by written letter or fax to the site, before their children can use online chat rooms and message boards. Just ask Julie Richer, president of San Francisco-based cyberkids.com, a site that targets 7- to 12-year-olds. Richer says COPPA has caused message board and chat room traffic to plummet by more than 40%.

But the objections to the opt-in rule go beyond the issue of reduced traffic. Advertising revenues might also suffer under Torricelli's opt-in proposal. There would be less free information available, making it harder for companies to put together the kinds of demographic profiles that allow them to target customers more precisely. Says DoubleClick (DCLK) President Kevin Ryan: "The Torricelli legislation would have a very negative impact on the Internet."

There's no doubt that opt-in would hike the cost of doing business online. But it's not as bad as its detractors claim. For one thing, companies would be able to lure people to opt-in by offering Web surfers cash and other incentives. It also would earn the goodwill of privacy-conscious Web surfers. One convert is Gregory Miller, chief Internet strategist for MedicaLogic, a Hillsboro (Ore.) site offering online health information, and a member of the Federal Trade Commission's new advisory committee for online access and security. His company supports opt-in on the theory that customers will be attracted to a site that takes privacy concerns seriously. "If you ask someone for permission to market to them, you build a loyal customer," says Miller. "It's our job to convince the consumer that it's a good idea to opt in by being truthful and showing what the benefit is." One way MedicaLogic would do this: It could persuade diabetes sufferers to surrender their personal information by offering timely updates on advances in treatment. "There are so many users out there, and the Net is growing so rapidly, that you can still get a reasonable return on your investment. People can be persuaded to opt in," says Miller.

Ideally, the best way to protect privacy on the Net is to combine the best elements of both opt-out and opt-in—as the European Union does. Opt-in methods are relatively extreme, so they should be used only for the most sensitive information—your chronic heart problems, for example, or the details of your financial holdings and your sexual preferences. And rules should be strict. No pre-checking of the opt-in box allowed. Instead, companies should be forced to describe what type of information they will be collecting and what they will be doing with it. Finally, opt-in also should be required before a company can resell any information about a Web surfer to a third party or share it with an ad network, since this offers few benefits to the surfer.

Apart from these extreme situations, the rule should be opt-out. Yes, it will be a pain in the neck to offer consumers this much control over how their information is used. But the bigger hurt could come from doing nothing and watching Web surfers opt out of the Internet.

3—Show Me the Data

Americans gained a precious thing from the Fair Credit Reporting Act of 1970: the right to inspect their credit records and find out why the bank turned them down on a car loan or a mortgage. No such privileges exist when it comes to online profiles, and it won't be easy to invent them. But some experts say the same kinds of tools Web sites use to track visitors could be used to provide at least a partial window into the data banks that store online profiles.

First, the downsides of doing that: The information a Web site collects is often strewn among multiple databases. Companies may not have the resources to query each one every time a surfer gets curious. What's more, the profile of your browsing habits may be based on cookie files—the bits of identifying code that Web sites deposit on your hard drive so they can monitor your comings and goings. If that's the case, those profiles may be linked only to the computer you browse from, not to your identity in the outside world. Do you really want to request access to that profile? The site would have to authenticate you. And in the process, it would acquire even more information about you than it started with. "It's clear that many systems on the Web were designed without much thought to privacy," says David M. Kristol, a member of the technical staff at Lucent Technologies Inc.'s Bell Labs. "These systems may be quite difficult to retrofit."

Hard, but not impossible. Some of these challenges seem tailor-made for smart software solutions. "If there's data in a database, it's there so that you can access it," says Lorrie Cranor, an AT&T Labs researcher who chairs a privacy working group at the World Wide Web Consortium.

Second point: If your profile—warts and all—is pegged to a string of numbers in cookie files, then, in theory, a Web site could manage your request for access by matching it to that same string. Authentication would be far from perfect, but perfection is rare in cyberspace. "We need a button we can push that says 'show me the profile you have on me,'" says personal privacy detective Richard Smith in Boston. "That should be relatively straightforward, because they already have an account mechanism, the sign-in." And if companies refuse? People could take it to the Fair Trade Commission.

The FTC, by the way, is on the case. It established an advisory committee on online access and security that began meeting on Feb. 4. It's made up of 40 people, including lawyers, professors, industry representatives and privacy advocates. And it plans to provide recommendations to the FTC on a range of options by May 15.

Not all the modes of online behavior that come before this committee will be so terribly controversial. Few argue against letting consumers see—and correct if necessary—sensitive data such as financial records and medical data. But many execs say providing access to routine info would be a costly nuisance of dubious benefit to consumers. "Do you really need to see that Banana Republic says you bought five shirts when you bought four, and do you really need to correct that?" says a lobbyist for one Web company.

But even where it's a nuisance to business, consumers should see more of what goes on behind the curtain. If you're being hounded by a direct marketer who is convinced you are interested in sex toys, you should be able to see whose data generated this profile. The marketer will probably argue that the data are culled from too many places. But there's an easy answer to that, too: Make the marketers keep a source list. Computers excel at keeping track of such things. If they were bad at it, this privacy morass never would have happened.

4—Play Fair or Pay

Better warnings. More choice. Access to your personal records. These things will go a long way toward protecting your privacy. But they won't be enough. After passing the broad laws that we are proposing, Congress will have to take extra steps to ensure that companies honor them.

The reason: Privacy laws are unusually hard to enforce. Say, for example, that you plug information about your stock portfolio into a financial Web site but deny permission for this information to be shared. Say that the site ignores your request and sells the data to a charity anyway. Most likely, you'll never find out about the privacy breach. And even if you do, the infraction didn't cause you any economic harm. That means you wouldn't have much financial incentive to sue the offender—and you'd no doubt have a hard time getting a lawyer to take your case. "Only people with a real privacy vendetta are going to sue," says Jonathan Zittrain, executive director of Harvard University's Berkman Center for the Internet & Society.

Because enforcement is chancy, unethical Web sites will be tempted to cheat on the rules. So, to ensure that crime does not pay, Congress will have to shell out a lot of money for privacy cops. Which agency should handle the job? Some experts have suggested creating a brand-new federal privacy commission—but that would be a political nightmare. Others have suggested a government-authorized, industry-run group such as the Internet Corporation for Assigned Names & Numbers (ICANN). This type of quasigovernmental organization would probably move faster than a typical agency, but it also would be vulnerable to becoming the pawn of the very people they're supposed to regulate.

We favor giving the job to the Federal Trade Commission, which has begun moving aggressively on the issue of Internet privacy and which already enforces the Children's Online Privacy Protection Act, the Truth in Lending Act, and the Fair Credit Reporting Act. The agency should be empowered to impose stiff penalties for violations.

Private Protection Of course, any privacy laws will need to evolve. As the Internet makes its way onto cell phones, watches, and other devices, some of the privacy rules that make sense in a world of deskbound PCs may become irrelevant. And the long-term prospect of biometric authentication—where fingerprints and retinal scans may be used as New Age passwords to Web sites—will certainly raise serious new privacy issues. Such a scheme would require nothing less than a national database of identifying biological data, raising the spectre of abuse by both outlaw hackers and Big Brother prosecutors.

Meanwhile, new technologies will certainly emerge to help consumers safeguard their own privacy. This summer may see the launch of the long-awaited P3P software standard, which will provide the means for consumers to set privacy preferences in their browsers and allow them to be automatically alerted when the Web sites they click on have privacy policies that differ from their choices. But this technology won't be a panacea. Privacy isn't just about fancy software. It's also about making sure that information is being used in the ways companies had promised. Technology won't protect people from privacy invasions. Only people can do that.

Privacy in an Age of Terror

MIKE FRANCE, HEATHER GREEN,
JIM KERSTETTER, JANE BLACK,
ALEX SALKEVER, AND DAN CARNEY

To track terrorists, government snoops will have to track you, too.

Khalid Al-Midhar came to the attention of federal law enforcers about a year and a half ago. As the Saudi Arabian strolled into a meeting with some of Osama bin Laden's lieutenants at a hotel in Kuala Lumpur in December, 1999, he was videotaped by a Malaysian surveillance team. The tape was turned over to U.S. intelligence officials and, after several months, Al-Midhar's name was put on the Immigration & Naturalization Service's "watch list" of potential terrorists. When the INS discovered in August that Al-Midhar was already in the U.S., the FBI assigned agents to track him down.

By the time the FBI figured out where Al-Midhar was, downtown Manhattan was in flames, part of the Pentagon had been destroyed, and more than 5,000 people were dead. Racing to reconstruct the disaster, agents pulled the manifest of hijacked American Airlines Flight 77—and discovered that Al-Midhar had bought a ticket for the flight using his real name.

As politicians, businesspeople, and terrorism experts try to prevent the horror of September 11 from ever being repeated, they are taking a closer look at the story of Khalid Al-Midhar. Could the tiny shred of information about him—his name and his image—have been used to thwart the attack? The answer may be yes. Technology exists that, had it been far more aggressively deployed, might have tracked down Al-Midhar before he stepped on board the plane. The FBI's list of potential terrorists, for instance, could have been linked to commercial databases so that he might have been apprehended when he used his Visa card days before the attack.

The videotape of Al-Midhar also could have been helpful. Using biometric profiling, it would have been possible to make a precise digital map of his face. This data could have been hooked up to airport surveillance cameras. When the cameras captured Al-Midhar, an alarm would have sounded, allowing cops to take him into custody.

The aim of these technologies is simple: to make it harder for terrorists to hide. That's top priority now—and it's likely to drive a broad expansion of the use of intrusive security measures. Polls taken since September 11 show that 86% of Americans are in favor of wider use of facial-recognition systems; 81% want closer monitoring of banking and credit-card transactions; and 68% support a national ID card. But the quest for safety is also going to come at an incalculable cost to personal privacy. Any tool that is powerful enough to strip away the anonymity of Khalid Al-Midhar—one dangerous traveler among millions of innocents—will do the same thing to ordinary citizens. Their faces will have to be scanned by the same cameras, their spending habits studied by the same computers.

The war on terrorism is still in its early days, but one thing is already clear: In the future, information about what you do, where you go, who you talk to, and how you spend your money is going to be far more available to government, and perhaps business as well. "September 11 changed things," says former Federal Trade Commissioner Robert Pitofsky, one of the most forceful privacy advocates in recent decades. "Terrorists swim in a society in which their privacy is protected. If some invasions of privacy are necessary to bring them out into the open, most people are going to say, 'O.K., go ahead.'"

Across a wide range of battlefields, privacy is on the retreat. Many high-tech surveillance tools that were deemed too intrusive before September 11, including the FBI's "Carnivore" Internet eavesdropping system, are being unleashed. Pre-attack legislation aimed at protecting people from unwanted privacy invasions has been shelved, while Congress is on the verge of passing an anti-terrorism law giving cops broad new powers to wiretap, monitor Internet activity, and peer into personal bank accounts. The notion of forcing citizens to carry a national identity card—once anathema to America's open culture—is getting more serious consideration than ever in U.S. history.

These developments could wind up having profound implications for our democracy. Privacy involves the most fundamental issue in governance: the relationship of the individual to the state. Since the forefathers, Americans have been committed to the idea that people have the right to control how much information about their thoughts, feelings, choices, and political beliefs is disclosed. It's a matter, first and foremost, of dignity—creating a boundary that protects people from the prying eyes of the outside world. That, in turn, helps to shield religious minorities, political fringe groups, and other outsiders from persecution by the majority.

By reducing our commitment to privacy, we risk changing what it means to be Americans. To the extent that ID cards, databases, and surveillance cameras help the government track ordinary citizens, they may make people marginally less willing to exercise basic freedoms—to travel, to assemble, to speak their minds. "It's possible that through a tyranny of small decisions, we could make a nightmare society," says Harvard Law School Professor Laurence H. Tribe.

Of course, we're still a long way from that point. Although many civil libertarians worry that the era of Big Brother is dawning, polls show that Americans are still committed to personal privacy and are unwilling to give law enforcers a blank check. President George W. Bush quickly dismissed the notion of a national ID card. And a coalition of left- and right-wing libertarians gave the Anti-Terrorism Act far rougher going than most commentators initially expected. Furthermore, none of the proposals currently on the table—such as installing facial-recognition systems at airports or linking the FBI's databases to those run by the airlines—fundamentally threatens civil liberties.

But this is a rapidly evolving issue. We have already abandoned a number of old privacy taboos. If new attacks come and the U.S. is powerless to stop them, a mandate could develop for greater levels of surveillance. Here are some of the key areas in which personal privacy could begin to erode:

▮▮▮ What You Do

No matter how hard terrorists try to keep a low profile, they live in the real world. The team that attacked the World Trade Center had to buy plane tickets, take flying lessons, communicate with one another, and draw money from bank accounts.

All of these moves leave traces on widely dispersed computer databases. That's why the tool that probably has the most potential to thwart terrorism is data-mining. Think of it as a form of surveillance that casts its eye on computer networks. If cops could survey the nation's computer systems and discover that a member of an extremist group also bought explosives and visited a Web site about building demolition, they might be able to halt a potential attack. Or if someone tried to purchase anthrax, the seller could run an instant background check.

Today, those databases aren't linked. The FBI's watch list of suspected terrorists hasn't even been connected to the INS or the State Dept., much less the private sector. A wide variety of laws and taboos has prevented the government from hooking up its files with those of airlines, credit-card companies, and private data-collection organizations. But that's already changing: On Oct. 11, INS chief James Ziglar told a Congressional committee that he is moving to link the agency's computers to the FBI's central database of bad guys. He also wants to require air carriers to submit passenger lists to the INS to prevent suspected terrorists from boarding U.S.-bound planes.

Some people, including Oracle Corp. CEO Lawrence J. Ellison, are recommending the creation of even broader databases. Other industry experts, all of whom stand to profit from such a plan, argue that such vast systems are already feasible. For example, Wal-Mart Stores Inc. and Kmart Corp. have databases containing over 100 terabytes of information about everything from sales to inventory to deliveries. That's the equivalent of about 200 billion documents—some 100 times larger than the Internal Revenue Service's commercial tax-filing database. "There are real-life data warehouses that absorb information in near real time, process it, and issue alerts within seconds or minutes," says Richard Winter, an independent expert on large database systems.

A key challenge will be developing sophisticated software to sift through the databases, pinpointing likely terrorists and suspicious behavior. Working together, a team of criminologists and software developers would need to design profiles of potential evildoers. That has been done in the past to track down serial killers and to thwart hijackings with mixed results. The airline industry's Computer Assisted Passenger Screening system (CAPS) failed to pick out almost all of the September 11 terrorists. But there's good reason to believe the technology can improve. Software maker Sybase Inc.'s new mining software can already analyze up to 1,000 variables, vastly increasing cops' ability to find the needle in a haystack of personal data.

Of course, there are huge political and legal hurdles to launching such systems. For one thing, government officials have a long history of abusing their power to collect personal information. Remember J. Edgar Hoover and Richard M. Nixon? For another, databases created for one purpose have a way of being reused in unintended ways. Files that Massachusetts accumulated about citizen health insurance claims, for example, had to be turned over to the tobacco industry when the state sued cigarette makers (though the state took steps to ensure that individuals' identities were masked). Over the long term, widespread deployment of data-mining will depend in large part on the ability of law enforcers to persuade the public that effective guidelines can be designed—and followed.

▪▪▪ Who You Are

One of the most controversial issues on the privacy landscape is that of national ID cards. Many Americans are instinctively repulsed by the idea. Passion runs so strong on this issue that the government has repeatedly blocked efforts to use Social Security numbers for drivers' licenses, voter registration, and prison records. The fear is that the Social Security number would become the equivalent of a national ID card.

More than 100 other countries, many of them democracies, disagree. They come in many varieties. Germany, after the human rights abuses of the Nazis, takes a minimal approach. Cards contain basic information, including name, place of birth, and eye color. Malaysia, on the other hand, this year launched a project to issue 2 million "multi-purpose" cards in Kuala Lumpur. A computer chip allows the card to be used as a combination drivers' license, cash card, national health service card, and passport.

That's only the beginning of what's theoretically possible. Given the power of digital technology, criminal records, immigration data, and more could be packed onto ID cards. In fact, they could contain so much data that they become the equivalent of portable personal files.

That's still a long way off. From a cop's perspective, ID cards are desirable because they make anticrime databases work better. As things stand now, one typing error at the airline check-in counter—say, John Smiht—and all the fancy efforts to unite Delta Air Lines Inc.'s database with the INS watch list don't add up to much. Forged drivers' licenses or passports—not to mention legitimate alternative spellings, such as John Smith or John K. Smith—produce the same problem.

A national ID card solves this by turning every person into a reliable data point for entry into larger databases. Once national ID cards are in place, airlines, explosives manufacturers, and border-crossing guards will know exactly which John Smith they are dealing with. So terrorists will have a harder time passing themselves off as ordinary citizens. True, ID cards can be forged. But that problem can largely be managed via "smart" cards equipped with computer chips that can store the cardholders' fingerprints or iris scans as biometric authentication devices.

The concern, of course, is that ID cards could lead the country down a slippery slope. Over the long run, say critics, they might be used as a platform for creating new databases. Starting with a card like, say, the one Malaysia just launched, governments could require the ID cards to be swiped into electronic readers every time people shopped, traveled, or surfed the Web and could accumulate an unprecedented quantity of information on their citizens.

For now, though, the question of a national ID card appears to be off the agenda, though it's nowhere near dead. Even some longtime civil libertarians are reevaluating. On Sept. 10, "I was a knee-jerk opponent of ID cards," says Harvard University law professor Alan M. Dershowitz. "Now, I've had to rethink the whole thing."

▪▪▪ Where You Go

In recent years, scientists have made enormous advances in location-tracking tools. Surveillance cameras with facial-recognition software can pick out criminals in public places. Global positioning satellite (GPS) transponders in cars, boats—and one day, in handheld devices such as phones—send out signals identifying people's latitude and longitude to within 10 feet. Both of these technologies will flourish in an environment free of many of the privacy concerns that clouded their future before September 11.

So far, facial-recognition systems are used primarily in highly controlled situations as authentication devices, to vouch for the identities of workers entering, say, a nuclear power plant. They are not often used, especially in the U.S., as a general surveillance device in public places. Tampa police use them in high-crime districts. A few casinos have also installed them. But in the wake of the terror attacks, a security committee formed by Secretary of Transportation Norman Y. Mineta has recommended the aggressive rollout of facial-recognition systems in airports. But it's still unclear how useful they will be. They can still be tricked by people wearing fake beards. And they tend to generate too many false alarms. Unless these glitches get fixed, the devices may never be appropriate for high-traffic settings such as tunnels and bridges.

GPS is a different story. The technology works—and it has been rapidly spreading to new places. Before September 11, privacy groups and some legislators had been working to limit the ability of companies to collect location data from customers surreptitiously and to raise the legal standards for enforcement officials to subpoena this material. Those battles, for the time being, are lost causes. If GPS information helps track down terrorists, it will be collected.

▬ ▪ ▪ Whom You Talk To

Law enforcers need the ability to find out with whom suspected terrorists are talking and what they are saying. That's why the government lobbied for the Anti-Terrorism Act, which gives the feds increased powers to eavesdrop on telephone calls and digital communications made through e-mail, online service providers, and digital devices.

Unlike facial surveillance, ID cards, or data-mining—which invade everybody's privacy—the government's new eavesdropping powers will primarily target known suspects. So they don't raise as many issues for the public at large.

There's one major exception: Carnivore, a technology the FBI uses to monitor e-mails, instant messages, and digital phone calls. Carnivore generated widespread controversy before September 11 for being too powerful. When installed on a suspect's Internet service provider, it searched through not only the suspect's Web activities but also those of people who used the same ISP. After privacy advocates complained, the FBI scaled back its deployment. Now, the brakes are off. There are widespread reports that the government has hooked up Carnivore to ISPs with minimal oversight. The government will probably soon demand that ISPs and digital wireless providers design networks to make them easier to tap. Just a few months ago, the FBI wouldn't have dared to ask. Now, such a move would barely make the papers.

Facial-recognition software. Data mining. National ID cards. Carnivore. For the near future, these technologies are going to be deployed as stand-alone systems, if at all. But we live in a digital age. All of these technologies are built on ones and zeros. So it is possible to blend them together—just as TVs, computers, video games, and CD players are converging—into one monster snooping technology. In fact, linking them together makes each one exponentially more effective.

A national ID card, for example, could be used to launch a new unified database that would track everybody's daily activities. Information culled from Carnivore could be stored in the same place. This super database, in turn, could be linked to facial-recognition cameras so that an all-points bulletin could go out for a potential terrorist the second the data-mining program detected a suspicious pattern of conduct.

Other, more futuristic new technologies could be added to the mix. Scientists will be able to make much more powerful surveillance devices if they're freed of the privacy concerns that have restrained them in recent years. Already, researchers are working on satellites that can read the unique color spectrums emitted by people's skin and cameras that can tell whether people are lying by how frequently they blink. Left unchecked, technologists could eventually create a nearly transparent society, says

David J. Farber, a pioneering computer scientist who helped develop the Net. "All the technology is there," he says. "There is absolutely nothing to stop that scenario—except law."

To be sure, nobody is proposing such systems. And they are a long, long way from technical feasibility. But they are within sight—and no more far-fetched than, say, eBay Inc.'s auction-everything Web site was a generation ago. Indeed, unifying the various surveillance systems makes sense from a technological standpoint, and there's likely to be strong pressure, once the tools are in place, to try to make them work better.

As the U.S. enters the next phase of the war on terror, it is useful to keep this Orwellian scenario in mind, if only as a warning beacon of some of the hazards ahead. It is also reassuring to know that privacy principles developed in the past still apply in this new world. Surveillance can be checked by laws that require regular audits, that call for citizens to be notified when they're investigated, and that give people the right to correct information collected about them. That's the best way of guaranteeing that, in our efforts to catch the next Khalid Al-Midhar, we don't wind up with Big Brother instead.

PART III

Ethics

Introduction

Few issues demand as much attention as ethics. Most people agree that a strong sense of ethics is important in life, but few agree on appropriate ethical standards for any given situation. Ethics are not the same as morality, and ethics also differ from what is legal, although both morality and legality may be taken into account in any particular situation where ethics need to be applied.

As with privacy issues, concerns over ethics wax and ebb over time. As this introductory section is being written, ethics is once again an important issue in the United States. In 2001 and 2002, the country watched as one corporate scandal after another was exposed to public view and as investors lost their money and employees lost jobs. Most of the names of the companies involved are very well-known now: Adelphia, Enron, Tyco, WorldCom. Many now are calling for a reemphasis on the teaching of ethics in business schools, as if business schools have not been teaching ethics all along. Ethics is so much a part of the business school curriculum that the particular approach to ethical teaching in business schools is distinguished as "business ethics." And while the focus on ethics, business or otherwise, intensifies, it is rare to hear anyone in the press or in political office talk about the ethics of design or the ethics of systems development. Yet, as students of engineering or computer science or MIS, the brand of ethics that applies most to you is that which governs design and development.

What kind of issues are we concerned with when we talk about an ethics of design and development? One of the key concepts integral to such an approach is the recognition that those who design and develop do so for someone else. Designers and developers work to produce a product that someone else will buy and use. This implies that the designer must look beyond technical issues about the elegance and functionality and ease of use of the product to questions like: What will this be used *for?* Could the product be *misused?* Could someone be hurt through proper use of the product? Could someone be hurt through misuse of the product? Could someone use the product to exploit others?

For information systems designers and developers, understanding the ethical issues involved in systems development requires recognition of the pervasiveness of computing in modern Western society. A software component or object could be used in a car or an automated teller machine or a missile.

▪▪▪ The Articles in Part 3

Leveson, N., and C. S. Turner. 1993. "An investigation of the Therac-25 accidents." *IEEE Computer* 26(7): 18–41.

> Few events in the history of software-controlled medical devices have been as dramatic as those surrounding the use of the Therac-25. In this article, computer safety experts Leveson and Turner use publicly available materials to extensively document the accidents associated with the Therac-25. They conclude with a set of lessons learned from the accidents and their investigation.

Smith, H. J., and J. Hasnas. 1999. "Ethics and information systems: The corporate domain." *MIS Quarterly* 23(1): 109–127.

> Smith and Hasnas provide three normative theories of business ethics: the stockholder theory, the stakeholder theory, and the social contract theory. They then use a celebrated business strategy announced by Blockbuster Video in 1990 to show what the differences in business action would be based on each of the different theories of ethics.

Oz, E. 2002. "Ethical issues." *Encyclopedia of Information Systems.* San Diego, CA: Academic Press.

> Oz provides an overview of the ethical issues relevant to today's information systems professional, from the invasion of privacy to ethical issues related to the Internet to the violation of intellectual property.

Excerpts from Weiss, E. A. (ed). 1990. "Self-assessment procedure XXII: Ethical values in computer professions." *Communications of the ACM* 33(11): 110–132.

> Many professions, including accounting, provide tests of ethical behavior as part of their certification processes. A proposed self-test for information systems professionals was published by the Association of Computing Machinery in 1990, and excerpts from this test are reprinted here. The excerpts consist of a series of scenarios, which ask the reader to place himself or herself in the position of the information systems professional facing an ethical (or not) dilemma.

▪▪▪ Related Places to Go on the Web

Many professional organizations have codes of ethics and codes of professional conduct. For people who will be working in the information technology field, one of the most visible professional organizations is the Association for Computing Machinery (ACM). The ACM Code of Ethics is available at www.acm.org/constitution/code.html. This version was first adopted in 1992.

Other professional codes of ethics or conduct that you might be interested in looking at include the following.

Academy of Management www.aomonline.org/
    Code of Ethical Conduct: www.aomonline.org/aom.asp?ID=&page_ID=54
American Psychological Association (APA) www.apa.org
    Ethics Office: www.apa.org/ethics/homepage.html
    2002 Code of Ethics: www.apa.org/ethics/code 2002.html

British Computer Society (BCS) www.bcs.org
Code of Conduct: www1.bcs.org.uk/portal/showSection.asp?contentid=
    3224&link=/DocsRepository/03200/3224/default.htm
Code of Practice: www1.bcs.org.uk/portal/showSection.asp?contented=
    3223&link=/DocsRepository/03200/3223/default.htm
Institute of Electrical and Electronic Engineers (IEEE) www.ieee.org
Code of Ethics: www.ieee.org/portal/index.jsp?pageID=corp_
    level1&path=about/whatis&file=code.xml&xsl=generic.xsl

ADDITIONAL READING

Davison, R. M. 2000. "Professional ethics in information systems: A personal perspective." *Communications of the AIS* 3(8): 1–34.

Dejoie, R. M., Fowler, G. C., and Paradice, D. B. (eds.) 1991. *Ethical Issues in Information Systems: A Book of Readings*. Boston: Boyd & Fraser Publishing Company.

Langford, D. 1996. "Ethics and the Internet: Appropriate behavior in electronic communication." *Ethics and Behavior* 6(2): 91–106.

Mason, R. O. 1986. "Four ethical issues of the Information Age." *MIS Quarterly* 10(1): 4–12.

Mason, R. O., Mason, F. M., and Culnan, M. J. 1995. *Ethics of Information Management*. Thousand Oaks, CA: Sage Publications.

Oz, E. 1992. "Ethical standards for information systems professionals: A case for a unified code." *Management Information Systems Quarterly* 16(4): 423–433.

Oz, E. 1994. *Ethics for the Information Age*. Boston, MA: McGraw-Hill.

Taylor, G. S., and Shim, J. P. 1993. "A comparative-examination of attitudes toward software piracy among business professors and executives." *Human Relations* 46(4): 419–433.

Walsham, G. 1996. "Ethical theory, codes of ethics and IS practice." *Information Systems Journal* 6(1): 69–81.

An Investigation of the Therac-25 Accidents

NANCY G. LEVESON
CLARK S. TURNER

Computers are increasingly being introduced into safety-critical systems and as a consequence, have been involved in accidents. Some of the most widely cited software-related accidents in safety-critical systems involved a computerized radiation therapy machine called the Therac-25. Between June 1985 and January 1987, six known accidents involved massive overdoses by the Therac-25—with resultant deaths and serious injuries. They have been described as the worst series of radiation accidents in the 35-year history of medical accelerators.[1]

With information for this article taken from publicly available documents, we present a detailed accident investigation of the factors involved in the overdose and the attempts by the users, manufacturers, and the US and Canadian governments to deal with them. Our goal is to help others learn from this experience, not to criticize the equipment's manufacturer or anyone else. The mistakes that were made are not unique to this manufacturer but are, unfortunately, fairly common in other safety-critical systems. As Frank Houston of the US Food and Drug Administration (FDA) said, "A significant amount of software for life-critical systems comes from small firms, especially in the medical device industry; firms that fit the profile of those resistant to or uninformed of the principles of either system safety or software engineering."[2]

Furthermore, these problems are not limited to the medical industry. It is still common belief that any good engineer can build software, regardless of whether he or she is trained in state-of-the-art software-engineering procedures. Many companies building safety-critical software are not using proper procedures from a software-engineering and safety-engineering perspective.

Most accidents are system accidents; that is, they stem from complex interactions between various components and activities. To attribute a single cause to an accident is usually a serious mistake. In this article, we hope to demonstrate the complex nature of accidents and the need to investigate all aspects of system development and operation to understand what has happened and to prevent future accidents.

Despite what can be learned from such investigations, fears of potential liability or loss of business make it difficult to find out the details behind serious engineering mistakes. When the equipment is regulated by government agencies, some information may be available. Occasionally, major accidents draw the attention of the US Congress or President and result in formal accident investigations (for instance, the Rogers commission investigation of the Challenger accident and the Kemeny commission investigation of the Three Mile Island incident).

The Therac-25 accidents are the most serious computer-related accidents to date (at least nonmilitary and admitted) and have even drawn the attention of the popular press. (Stories about the Therac-25 have appeared in trade journals, newspapers, *People Magazine,* and on television's *20/20* and *McNeil/Lehrer News Hour.*) Unfortunately, the previous accounts of the Therac-25 problems have been oversimplified, with misleading omissions.

In an effort to remedy this, we have obtained information from a wide variety of sources, including lawsuits and the US and Canadian government agencies responsible for regulating such equipment. We have tried to be very careful to present only what we could document from original sources, but there is no guarantee that the documentation itself is correct. When possible, we looked for multiple confirming sources for the more important facts.

We have tried not to bias our description of the accidents, but it is difficult not to filter unintentionally what is described. Also, we were unable to investigate firsthand or get information about some aspects of the accidents that may be very relevant. For example, detailed information about the manufacturer's software development, management, and quality control was unavailable. We had to infer most information about these from statements in correspondence or other sources.

As a result, our analysis of the accidents may omit some factors. But the facts available support previous hypotheses about the proper development and use of software to control dangerous processes and suggest hypotheses that need further evaluation. Following our account of the accidents and the responses of the manufacturer, government agencies, and users, we present what we believe are the most compelling lessons to be learned in the context of software engineering, safety engineering, and government and user standards and oversight.

▪▪▪ Genesis of the Therac-25

Medical linear accelerators (linacs) accelerate electrons to create high-energy beams that can destroy tumors with minimal impact on the surrounding healthy tissue. Relatively shallow tissue is treated with the accelerated electrons; to reach deeper tissue, the electron beam is converted into X-ray photons.

In the early 1970s, Atomic Energy of Canada Limited (AECL) and a French company called CGR collaborated to build linear accelerators. (AECL is an arms-length entity, called a crown corporation, of the Canadian government. Since the time of the incidents related in this article, AECL Medical, a division of AECL, is in the process of being privatized and is now called Theratronics International Limited. Currently, AECL's primary business is the design and installation of nuclear reactors.) The products of AECL and CGR's cooperation were (1) the Therac-6, a 6 million electron volt (MeV) accelerator capable of producing X-rays only and, later, (2) the Therac-20, a 20-MeV dual-mode (X-rays or electrons) accelerator. Both were versions of older CGR machines, the Neptune and Sagittaire, respectively, which were augmented with computer control using a DEC PDP 11 minicomputer.

Software functionality was limited in both machines: The computer merely added convenience to the existing hardware, which was capable of standing alone. Industry-standard hardware safety features and interlocks in the underlying machines were retained. We know that some old Therac-6 software routines were used in the Therac-20 and that CGR developed the initial software.

The business relationship between AECL and CGR faltered after the Therac-20 effort. Citing competitive pressures, the two companies did not renew their cooperative agreement when scheduled in 1981. In the mid-1970s, AECL developed a radical new "double-pass" concept for electron acceleration. A double-pass accelerator needs much less space to develop comparable energy levels because it folds the long physical mechanism required to accelerate the electrons, and it is more economic to produce (since it uses a magnetron rather than a klystron as the energy source).

Using this double-pass concept, AECL designed the Therac-25, a dual-mode linear accelerator that can deliver either photons at 25 MeV or electrons at various energy levels (see Figure 1). Compared with the Therac-20, the Therac-25 is notably more compact, more versatile, and arguably easier to use. The higher energy takes advantage of the phenomenon of "depth dose": As the energy increases, the depth in the body at which maximum dose buildup occurs also increases, sparing the tissue above the target area. Economic advantages also come into play for the customer, since only one machine is required for both treatment modalities (electrons and photons).

Several features of the Therac-25 are important in understanding the accidents. First, like the Therac-6 and the Therac-20, the Therac-25 is controlled by a PDP 11. However, AECL designed the Therac-25 to take advantage of computer control from the outset; AECL did not build on a stand-alone machine. The Therac-6 and Therac-20 had been designed around machines that already had histories of clinical use without computer control.

In addition, the Therac-25 software has more responsibility for maintaining safety than the software in the previous machines. The Therac-20 has independent protective

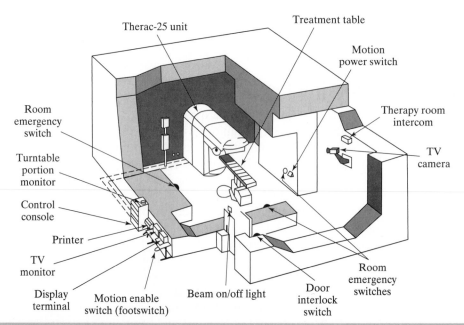

▪▪▪▪▪▪▪▪▪▪▪▪ **FIGURE 1 Typical Therac-25 Facility**

circuits for monitoring electron-beam scanning, plus mechanical interlocks for policing the machine and ensuring safe operation. The Therac-25 relies more on software for these functions. AECL took advantage of the computer's abilities to control and monitor the hardware and decided not to duplicate all the existing hardware safety mechanisms and interlocks. This approach is becoming more common as companies decide that hardware interlocks and backups are not worth the expense, or they put more faith (perhaps misplaced) on software than on hardware reliability.

Finally, some software for the machines was interrelated or reused. In a letter to a Therac-25 user, the AECL quality assurance manager said, "The same Therac-6 package was used by the AECL software people when they started the Therac-25 software. The Therac-20 and Therac-25 software programs were done independently, starting from a common base." Reuse of Therac design features or modules may explain some of the problematic aspects of the Therac-25 software (see the sidebar "Therac-25 Software Development and Design"). The quality assurance manager was apparently unaware that some Therac-20 routines were also used in the Therac-25; this was discovered after a bug related to one of the Therac-25 accidents was found in the Therac-20 software.

AECL produced the first hardwired prototype of the Therac-25 in 1976, and the completely computerized commercial version was available in late 1982. (The sidebars provide details about the machine's design and controlling software, important in understanding the accidents.)

In March 1983, AECL performed safety analysis on the Therac-25. This analysis was in the form of a fault tree and apparently excluded the software. According to the final report, the analysis made several assumptions:

1. Programming errors have been reduced by extensive testing on a hardware simulator and under field conditions on teletherapy units. Any residual software errors are not included in the analysis.
2. Program software does not degrade due to wear, fatigue, or reproduction process.
3. Computer execution errors are caused by faulty hardware components and by "soft" (random) errors induced by alpha particles and electromagnetic noise.

The fault tree resulting from this analysis does appear to include computer failure, although apparently, judging from these assumptions, it considers only hardware failures. For example, in one OR gate leading to the event of getting the wrong energy, a box contains "Computer selects wrong energy" and a probability of 10^{-11} is assigned to this event. For "Computer selects wrong mode," a probability of 4×10^{-9} is given. The report provides no justification of either number.

▮▮▮ Accident History

Eleven Therac-25s were installed: five in the US and six in Canada. Six accidents involving massive overdoses to patients occurred between 1985 and 1987. The machine was recalled in 1987 for extensive design changes, including hardware safeguards against software errors.

Related problems were found in the Therac-20 software. These were not recognized until after the Therac-25 accidents because the Therac-20 included hardware safety interlocks and thus no injuries resulted.

In this section, we present a chronological account of the accidents and the responses from the manufacturer, government regulatory agencies, and users.

Kennestone Regional Oncology Center, 1985 Details of this accident in Marietta, Georgia, are sketchy since it was never carefully investigated. There was no admission

Therac-25 Software Development and Design

We know that the software for the Therac-25 was developed by a single person, using PDP 11 assembly language, over a period of several years. The software "evolved" from the Therac-6 software, which was started in 1972. According to a letter from AECL to the FDA, the "program structure and certain subroutines were carried over to the Therac 25 around 1976."

Apparently, very little software documentation was produced during development. In a 1986 internal FDA memo, a reviewer lamented, "Unfortunately, the AECL response also seems to point out an apparent lack of documentation on software specifications and a software test plan."

The manufacturer said that the hardware and software were "tested and exercised separately or together over many years." In his deposition for one of the lawsuits, the quality assurance manager explained that testing was done in two parts. A "small amount" of software testing was done on a simulator, but most testing was done as a system. It appears that unit and software testing was minimal, with most effort directed at the integrated system test. At a Therac-25 user group meeting, the same quality assurance manager said that the Therac-25 software was tested for 2,700 hours. Under questioning by the users, he clarified this as meaning "2,700 hours of use."

The programmer left AECL in 1986. In a lawsuit connected with one of the accidents, the lawyers were unable to obtain information about the programmer from AECL. In the depositions connected with that case, none of the AECL employees questioned could provide any information about his educational background or experience. Although an attempt was made to obtain a deposition from the programmer, the lawsuit was settled before this was accomplished. We have been unable to learn anything about his background.

AECL claims proprietary rights to its software design. However, from voluminous documentation regarding the accidents, the repairs, and the eventual design changes, we can build a rough picture of it.

The software is responsible for monitoring the machine status, accepting input about the treatment desired, and setting the machine up for this treatment. It turns the beam on in response to an operator command (assuming that certain operational checks on the status of the physical machine are satisfied) and also turns the beam off when treatment is completed, when an operator commands it, or when a malfunction is detected. The operator can print out hard-copy versions of the CRT display or machine setup parameters.

The treatment unit has an interlock system designed to move power to the unit when there is a hardware malfunction. The computer monitors this interlock system and provides diagnostic messages. Depending on the fault, the computer either prevents a treatment from being started or if the treatment is in progress, creates a pause or a suspension of the treatment.

The manufacturer describes the Therac-25 software as having a stand-alone, real-time treatment operating system. The system is not built using a standard operating system or executive. Rather, the real-time executive was written especially for the Therac-25 and runs on a 32K PDP 11/23. A preemptive scheduler allocates cycles to the critical and noncritical tasks.

The software, written in PDP 11 assembly language, has four major components: stored data, a scheduler, a set of critical and noncritical tasks, and interrupt services. The stored data includes calibration parameters for the accelerator setup as well as patient-treatment data. The interrupt routines include

- a clock interrupt service routine,
- a scanning interrupt service routine,
- traps (for software overflow and computer-hardware-generated interrupts),
- power up (initiated at power up to initialize the system and pass control to the scheduler),
- treatment console screen interrupt handler,
- treatment console keyboard interrupt handler,
- service printer interrupt handler, and
- service keyboard interrupt handler.

(continued)

The scheduler controls the sequences of all noninterrupt events and coordinates all concurrent processes. Tasks are initiated every 0.1 second, with the critical tasks executed first and the noncritical tasks executed in any remaining cycle time. Critical tasks include the following:

- The treatment monitor (Treat) directs and monitors patient setup and treatment via eight operating phases. These are called as subroutines, depending on the value of the phase control variable. Following the execution of a particular subroutine, Treat reschedules itself. Treat interacts with the keyboard processing task, which handles operator console communication. The prescription data is cross-checked and verified by other tasks (for example, the keyboard processor and the parameter setup sensor) that inform the treatment task of the verification status via shared variables.

- The servo task controls gun emission, dose rate (pulse-repetition frequency), symmetry (beam steering), and machine motions. The servo task also sets up the machine parameters and monitors the beam-tilt-error and the flatness-error interlocks.

- The housekeeper task takes care of system-status interlocks and limit checks, and puts appropriate messages on the CRT display. It decodes some information and checks the setup verification.

Noncritical tasks include

- Check sum processor (scheduled to run periodically).

- Treatment console keyboard processor (scheduled to run only if it is called by other tasks or by keyboard interrupts). This task acts as the interface between the software and the operator.

- Treatment console screen processor (run periodically). This task lays out appropriate record formats for either displays or hard copies.

- Service keyboard processor (run on demand). This task arbitrates non-treatment-related communication between the therapy system and the operator.

- Snapshot (run periodically by the scheduler). Snapshot captures preselected parameter values and is called by the treatment task at the end of a treatment.

- Hand-control processor (run periodically).

- Calibration processor. This task is responsible for a package of tasks that let the operator examine and change system setup parameters and interlock limits.

It is clear from the AECL documentation on the modifications that the software allows concurrent access to shared memory, that there is no real synchronization aside from data stored in shared variables, and that the "test" and "set" for such variables are not indivisible operations. Race conditions resulting from this implementation of multitasking played an important part in the accidents.

---

that the injury was caused by the Therac-25 until long after the occurrence, despite claims by the patient that she had been injured during treatment, the obvious and severe radiation burns the patient suffered, and the suspicions of the radiation physicist involved.

After undergoing a lumpectomy to remove a malignant breast tumor, a 61-year-old woman was receiving follow-up radiation treatment to nearby lymph nodes on a Therac-25 at the Kennestone facility in Marietta. The Therac-25 had been operating at Kennestone for about six months; other Therac-25s had been operating, apparently without incident, since 1983.

On June 3, 1985, the patient was set up for a 10-MeV electron treatment to the clavicle area. When the machine turned on, she felt a "tremendous force of heat . . . this red-hot sensation." When the technician came in, the patient said, "You burned me." The technician replied that that was not possible. Although there were no marks on the patient at the time, the treatment area felt "warm to the touch."

It is unclear exactly when AECL learned about this incident. Tim Still, the Kennestone physicist, said that he contacted AECL to ask if the Therac-25 could operate in electron mode without scanning to spread the beam. Three days later, the engineers at AECL called the physicist back to explain that improper scanning was not possible.

In an August 19, 1986, letter from AECL to the FDA, the AECL quality assurance manager said, "In March of 1986, AECL received a lawsuit from the patient involved . . . This incident was never reported to AECL prior to this date, although some rather odd questions had been posed by Tim Still, the hospital physicist." The physicist at a hospital in Tyler, Texas, where a later accident occurred, reported, "According to Tim Still, the patient filed suit October 1985 listing the hospital, manufacturer, and service organization responsible for the machine. AECL was notified informally about the suit by the hospital, and AECL received official notification of a lawsuit in November 1985."

Because of the lawsuit (filed on November 13, 1985), some AECL administrators must have known about the Marietta accident—although no investigation occurred at this time. Further comments by FDA investigators point to the lack of a mechanism in AECL to follow up reports of suspected accidents. The lack of follow-up in this case appears to be evidence of such a problem in the organization.

The patient went home, but shortly afterward she developed a reddening and swelling in the center of the treatment area. Her pain had increased to the point that her shoulder "froze" and she experienced spasms. She was admitted to West Paces Ferry Hospital in Atlanta, but her oncologists continued to send her to Kennestone for Therac-25 treatments. Clinical explanation was sought for the reddening of the skin, which at first her oncologist attributed to her disease or to normal treatment reaction.

Major event time line

	1985	
JUN	3rd: Marietta, Georgia, overdose.	
	Later in the month, Tim Still calls AECL and asks if overdose by Therac-25 is possible.	
JUL	26th: Hamilton, Ontario, Canada, overdose, AECL notified and determines microswitch failure was the cause.	
SEP	AECL makes changes to microswitch and notifies users of increased safety.	
	Independent consultant (for Hamilton Clinic) recommends potentiometer on turntable.	
OCT	Georgia patient files suit against AECL and hospital.	
NOV	8th: Letter from CRPB to AECL asking for additional hardware interlocks and software changes.	
DEC	Yakima, Washington, clinic overdose.	
	1986	
JAN	Attorney for Hamilton clinic requests that potentiometer be installed on turntable.	
	31st: Letter to AECL from Yakima reporting overdose possibility.	
FEB	24th: Letter from AECL to Yakima saying overdose was impossible and no other incidents had occurred.	
MAR	21st: Tyler, Texas, overdose. AECL notified; claims overdose in impossible and no other accidents had occurred previously. AECL suggests hospital might have an electrical problem.	
APR	7th: Tyler machine put back in service after no electrical problem could be found.	
	11th: Second Tyler overdose. AECL again notified. Software problem found.	
	15th: AECL files accident report with FDA.	

MAY	2nd: FDA declares Therac-25 defective. Asks for CAP and proper renotification of Therac-25 users.
JUN	13th: First version of CAP sent to FDA.
JUL	23rd: FDA responds and asks for more information.
AUG	First user group meeting.
SEP	26th: AECL sends FDA additional information.
OCT	30th: FDA requests more information.
NOV	12th: AECL submits revision of CAP.
DEC	Therac-20 users notified of a software bug.
	11th: FDA requests further changes to CAP.
	22nd: AECL submits second revision of CAP.

1987

JAN	17th: Second overdose at Yakima.
	26th: AECL sends FDA its revised test plan.
FEB	Hamilton clinic investigates first accident and concludes there was an overdose.
	3rd: AECL announces changes to Therac-25.
	10th: FDA sends notice of adverse findings to AECL declaring Therac-25 defective under US law and asking AECL to notify customers that it should not be used for routine therapy. Health Protection Branch of Canada does the same thing. This lasts until August 1987.
MAR	Second user group meeting.
	5th: AECL sends third version of CAP to FDA.
APR	9th: FDA responds to CAP and asks for additional information.
MAY	1st: AECL sends fourth revision of CAP to FDA.
	26th: FDA approves CAP subject to the testing and safety analysis.
JUN	5th: AECL sends final test plan and draft safety analysis to FDA.
JUL	Third user group meeting.
	21st: Fifth (and final) revision of CAP sent to FDA.

1988

JAN	29th: Interim safety analysis report issued.
NOV	3rd: Final safety analysis report issued.

About two weeks later, the physicist at Kennestone noticed that the patient had a matching reddening on her back as though a burn had gone through her body, and the swollen area had begun to slough off layers of skin. Her shoulder was immobile, and she was apparently in great pain. It was obvious that she had a radiation burn, but the hospital and her doctors could provide no satisfactory explanation. Shortly afterward, she initiated a lawsuit against the hospital and AECL regarding her injury.

The Kennestone physicist later estimated that she received one or two doses of radiation in the 15,000- to 20,000-rad (radiation absorbed dose) range. He does not believe her injury could have been caused by less than 8,000 rads. Typical single therapeutic doses are in the 200-rad range. Doses of 1,000 rads can be fatal if delivered to the whole body; in fact, the accepted figure for whole-body radiation that will cause death in 50 percent of the cases is 500 rads. The consequences of an overdose to a smaller part of the body depend on the tissue's radiosensitivity. The director of radiation oncology at the Kennestone facility explained their confusion about the accident as due to the fact that they had never seen an overtreatment of that magnitude before.

Eventually, the patient's breast had to be removed because of the radiation burns. She completely lost the use of her shoulder and her arm, and was in constant pain. She had suffered a serious radiation burn, but the manufacturer and operators of the machine refused to believe that it could have been caused by the Therac-25. The treatment prescription printout feature was disabled at the time of the accident, so there was no hard copy of the treatment data. The lawsuit was eventually settled out of court.

From what we can determine, the accident was not reported to the FDA until *after* the later Tyler accidents in 1986 (described in later sections). The reporting regulations for medical device incidents at that time applied only to equipment manufacturers and importers, not users. The regulations required that manufacturers and importers report deaths, serious injuries, or malfunctions that could result in those consequences. Health-care professionals and institutions were not required to report incidents to manufacturers. (The law was amended in 1990 to require health-care facilities to report incidents to the manufacturer and the FDA.) The comptroller general of the US Government Accounting Office, in testimony before Congress on November 6, 1989, expressed great concern about the viability of the incident-reporting regulations in preventing or spotting medical-device problems. According to a GAO study, the FDA knows of less than 1 percent of deaths, serious injuries, or equipment malfunctions that occur in hospitals.[3]

At this point, the other Therac-25 users were unaware that anything untoward had occurred and did not learn about any problems with the machine until after subsequent accidents. Even then, most of their information came through personal communication among themselves.

Ontario Cancer Foundation, 1985   The second in this series of accidents occurred at this Hamilton, Ontario, Canada, clinic about seven weeks after the Kennestone patient was overdosed. At that time, the Therac-25 at the Hamilton clinic had been in use for more than six months. On July 26, 1985, a 40-year-old patient came to the clinic for her 24th Therac-25 treatment for carcinoma of the cervix. The operator activated the machine, but the Therac shut down after five seconds with an "H-tilt" error message. The Therac's dosimetry system display read "no dose" and indicated a "treatment pause."

Since the machine did not suspend and the control display indicated no dose was delivered to the patient, the operator went ahead with a second attempt at treatment by pressing the "P" key (the proceed command), expecting the machine to deliver the proper dose this time. This was standard operating procedure and, as described in the sidebar "The Operator Interface" on p. 232, Therac-25 operators had become accustomed to frequent malfunctions that had no untoward consequences for the patient. Again, the machine shut down in the same manner. The operator repeated this process four times after the original attempt—the display showing "no dose" delivered to the patient each time. After the fifth pause, the machine went into treatment suspend, and a hospital service technician was called. The technician found nothing wrong with the machine. This also was not an unusual scenario, according to a Therac-25 operator.

After the treatment, the patient complained of a burning sensation, described as an "electric tingling shock" to the treatment area in her hip. Six other patients were treated later that day without incident. The patient came back for further treatment on July 29 and complained of burning, hip pain, and excessive swelling in the region of treatment. The machine was taken out of service, as radiation overexposure was suspected. The patient was hospitalized for the condition on July 30. AECL was informed of the apparent radiation injury and sent a service engineer to investigate. The FDA, the then-Canadian Radiation Protection Bureau (CRPB), and the users were informed that there was a problem, although the users claim that they were never informed that a patient injury had occurred. (On April 1, 1986, the CRPB and the

Bureau of Medical Devices were merged to form the Bureau of Radiation and Medical Devices or BRMD.) Users were told that they should visually confirm the turntable alignment until further notice (which occurred three months later).

The patient died on November 3, 1985, of an extremely virulent cancer. An autopsy revealed the cause of death as the cancer, but it was noted that had she not died, a total hip replacement would have been necessary as a result of the radiation overexposure. An AECL technician later estimated the patient had received between 13,000 and 17,000 rads.

Manufacturer response.   AECL could not reproduce the malfunction that had occurred, but suspected a transient failure in the microswitch used to determine turntable position. During the investigation of the accident, AECL hardwired the error conditions they assumed were necessary for the malfunction and, as a result, found some design weakness and potential mechanical problems involving the turntable positioning.

The computer senses and controls turntable position by reading a 3-bit signal about the status of three microswitches in the turntable switch assembly (see the sidebar "Turntable Positioning" on p. 234). Essentially, AECL determined that a 1-bit error in the microswitch codes (which could be caused by a single open-circuit fault on the switch lines) could produce an ambiguous position message for the computer. The problem was exacerbated by the design of the mechanism that extends a plunger to lock the turntable when it is in one of the three cardinal positions: The plunger could be extended when the turntable was way out of position, thus giving a second false position indication. AECL devised a method to indicate turntable position that tolerated a 1-bit error: The code would still unambiguously reveal correct position with any one microswitch failure.

In addition, AECL altered the software so that the computer checked for "in transit" status of the switches to keep further track of the switch operation and the turntable position, and to give additional assurance that the switches were working and the turntable was moving.

As a result of these improvements, AECL claimed in its report and correspondence with hospitals that "analysis of the hazard rate of the new solution indicates an improvement over the old system by at least five orders of magnitude." A claim that safety had been improved by five orders of magnitude seems exaggerated, especially given that in its final incident report to the FDA, AECL concluded that it "cannot be firm on the exact cause of the accident but can only suspect . . ." This underscores the company's inability to determine the cause of the accident with any certainty. The AECL quality assurance manager testified that AECL could not reproduce the switch malfunction and that testing of the microswitch was "inconclusive." The similarity of the errant behavior and the injuries to patients in this accident and a later one in Yakima, Washington, (attributed to software error) provide good reason to believe that the Hamilton overdose was probably related to software error rather than to a microswitch failure.

Government and user response.   The Hamilton accident resulted in voluntary recall by AECL, and the FDA termed it a Class II recall. Class II means "a situation in which the use of, or exposure to, a violative product may cause temporary or medically reversible adverse health consequences or where the probability of serious adverse health consequences is remote." Four users in the US were advised by a letter from AECL on August 1, 1985, to visually check the ionization chamber to make sure it was in its correct position in the collimator opening before any treatment and to discontinue

The Operator Interface

In the main text, we describe changes made as a result of an FDA recall, and here we describe the operator interface of the software version used during the accidents.

The Therac-25 operator controls the machine with a DEC VT100 terminal. In the general case, the operator positions the patient on the treatment table, manually sets the treatment field sizes and gantry rotation, and attaches accessories to the machine. Leaving the treatment room, the operator returns to the VT 100 console to enter the patient identification, treatment prescription (including mode, energy level, dose, dose rate, and time), field sizing, gantry rotation, and accessory data. The system then compares the manually set values with those entered at the console. If they match, a "verified" message is displayed and treatment is permitted. If they do not match, treatment is not allowed to proceed until the mismatch is corrected. Figure A shows the screen layout.

When the system was first built, operators complained that it took too long to enter the treatment plan. In response, the manufacturer modified the software before the first unit was installed so that, instead of reentering the data at the keyboard, operators could use a carriage return to merely copy the treatment site data.[1] A quick series of carriage returns would thus complete data entry. This interface modification was to figure in several accidents.

The Therac-25 could shut down in two ways after it detected an error condition. One was a *treatment suspend*, which required a complete machine reset to restart. The other, not so serious, was a *treatment pause*, which required only a single-key command to restart the machine. If a treatment pause occurred, the operator could press the "P" key to "proceed" and resume treatment quickly and conveniently. The previous treatment parameters remained in effect, and no reset was required. This convenient and simple feature could be invoked a maximum of five times before the machine automatically sus-

(continued)

PATIENT NAME: TEST			A 1
TREATMENT MODE: FIX	BEAM TYPE: X ENERGY (KeV):		25

	ACTUAL	PRESCRIBED	
UNIT RATE/MINUTE	0	200	
MONITOR UNITS	50 50	200	
TIME (MIN)	0.27	1.00	

GANTRY ROTATION (DEG)	0.0	0	VERIFIED
COLLIMATOR ROTATION (DEG)	359.2	359	VERIFIED
COLLIMATOR X (CM)	14.2	14.3	VERIFIED
COLLIMATOR Y (CM)	27.2	27.3	VERIFIED
WEDGE NUMBER	1	1	VERIFIED
ACCESSORY NUMBER	0	0	VERIFIED

DATE : 84-OCT-26	SYSTEM: BEAM READY	OP. MODE: TREAT	AUTO
TIME : 12:55. 8	TREAT: TREAT PAUSE	X-RAY	173777
OPR ID: T25VO2-RO3	REASON: OPERATOR	COMMAND:	

▐ ▐ ▐ ▐ ▐ ▐ ▐ ▐ ▐ ▐ ▐ **FIGURE A** Operator Interface Screen Layout

pended treatment and required the operator to perform a system reset.

Error messages provided to the operator were cryptic, and some merely consisted of the word "malfunction" followed by a number from 1 to 64 denoting an analog/digital channel number. According to an FDA memorandum written after one accident

> The operator's manual supplied with the machine does not explain nor even address the malfunction codes. The [Maintenance] Manual lists the various malfunction numbers but gives no explanation. The materials provided give *no* indication that these malfunctions could place a patient at risk.
>
> The program does not advise the operator if a situation exists wherein the ion chambers used to monitor the patient are saturated, thus are beyond the measurement limits of the instrument. This software package does not appear to contain a safety system to prevent parameters being entered and intermixed that would result in excessive radiation being delivered to the patient under treatment.

An operator involved in an overdose accident testified that she had become insensitive to machine malfunctions. Malfunction messages were commonplace—most did not involve patient safety. Service technicians would fix the problems or the hospital physicist would realign the machine and make it operable again. She said, "It was not out of the ordinary for something to stop the machine . . . It would often give a low dose rate in which you would turn the machine back on . . . They would give messages of low dose rate, V-tilt, H-tilt, and other things; I can't remember all the reasons it would stop, but there [were] a lot of them." The operator further testified that during instruction she had been taught that there were "so many safety mechanisms" that she understood it was virtually impossible to overdose a patient.

A radiation therapist at another clinic reported an average of 40 dose-rate malfunctions, attributed to underdoses, occurred on some days.

Reference

[1]E. Miller, "The Therac-25 Experience," *Proc. Conf. State Radiation Control Program Directors*, 1987.

treatment if they got an H-tilt message with an incorrect dose indicated. The letter did not mention that a patient injury was involved. The FDA audited AECL's subsequent modifications. After the modifications, the users were told that they could return to normal operating procedures.

As a result of the Hamilton accident, the head of advanced X-ray systems in the CRPB, Gordon Symonds, wrote a report that analyzed the design and performance characteristics of the Therac-25 with respect to radiation safety. Besides citing the flawed microswitch, the report faulted both hardware and software components of the Therac's design. It concluded with a list of four modifications to the Therac-25 necessary for minimum compliance with Canada's Radiation Emitting Devices (RED) Act. The RED law, enacted in 1971, gives government officials power to ensure the safety of radiation-emitting devices.

The modifications recommended in the Symonds report included redesigning the microswitch and changing the way the computer handled malfunction conditions. In particular, treatment was to be terminated in the event of a dose rate malfunction, giving a treatment "suspend." This would have removed the option to proceed simply by pressing the "P" key. The report also made recommendations regarding collimator test procedures and message and command formats. A November 8, 1985 letter signed by Ernest Létourneau, M.D., director of the CRPB, asked that AECL make changes to the Therac-25 based on the Symonds report "to be in compliance with the RED Act."

Although, as noted above, AECL did make the microswitch changes, it did not comply with the directive to change the malfunction pause behavior into treatment

Turntable Positioning

The Therac-25 turntable design is important in understanding the accidents. The upper turntable (see Figure B) is a rotating table, as the name implies. The turntable rotates accessory equipment into the beam path to produce two therapeutic modes: electron mode and photon mode. A third position (called the field-light position) involves no beam at all; it facilitates correct positioning of the patient.

Proper operation of the Therac-25 is heavily dependent on the turntable position; the accessories appropriate to each mode are physically attached to the turntable. The turntable position is monitored by three microswitches corresponding to the three cardinal turntable positions: electron beam, X ray, and field light. These microswitches are attached to the turntable and are engaged by hardware stops at the appropri-

ate positions. The position of the turntable, sent to the computer as a 3-bit binary signal, is based on which of the three microswitches are depressed by the hardware stops.

The raw, highly concentrated accelerator beam is dangerous to living tissue. In electron therapy, the computer controls the beam energy (from 5 to 25 MeV) and current while scanning magnets spread the beam to a safe, therapeutic concentration. These scanning magnets are mounted on the turntable and moved into proper position by the computer. Similarly, an ion chamber to measure electrons is mounted on the turntable and also moved into position by the computer. In addition, operator-mounted electron trimmers can be used to shape the beam if necessary.

(continued)

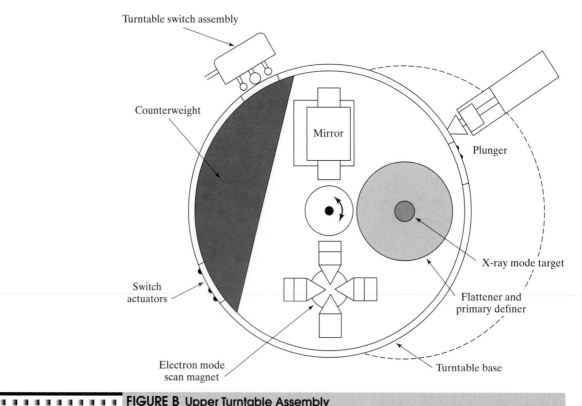

▪▪▪▪▪▪▪▪▪▪▪▪ **FIGURE B** Upper Turntable Assembly

For X-ray therapy, only one energy level is available: 25 MeV. Much greater electron-beam current is required for photon mode (some 100 times greater than that for electron therapy)[1] to produce comparable output. Such a high dose-rate capability is required because a "beam flattener" is used to produce a uniform treatment field. This flattener, which resembles an inverted ice-cream cone, is a very efficient attenuator. To get a reasonable treatment dose rate out, a very high input dose rate is required. If the machine produces a photon beam with the beam flattener not in position, a high output dose rate results. This is the basic hazard of dual-mode machines: If the turntable is in the wrong position, the beam flattener will not be in place.

In the Therac-25, the computer is responsible for positioning the turntable (and for checking turntable position) so that a target, flattening filter, and X-ray ion chamber are directly in the beam path. With the target in the beam path, electron bombardment produces X rays. The X-ray beam is shaped by the flattening filter and measured by the X-ray ion chamber.

No accelerator beam is expected in the field-light position. A stainless steel mirror is placed in the beam path and a light simulates the beam. This lets the operator see precisely where the beam will strike the patient and make necessary adjustments before treatment starts. There is no ion chamber in place at this turntable position, since no beam is expected.

Traditionally, electromechanical interlocks have been used on these types of equipment to ensure safety—in this case, to ensure that the turntable and attached equipment are in the correct position when treatment is started. In the Therac-25, software checks were substituted for many traditional hardware interlocks.

Reference

[1] J.A. Rawlinson, "Report on the Therac-25," OCTRF/OCI Physicists Meeting, Kingston, Ont., Canada, May 7, 1987.

suspends, instead reducing the maximum number of retries from five to three. According to Symonds, the deficiencies outlined in the CRPB letter of November 8 were still pending when subsequent accidents five months later changed the priorities. If these later accidents had not occurred, AECL would have been compelled to comply with the requirements in the letter.

Immediately after the Hamilton accident, the Ontario Cancer Foundation hired an independent consultant to investigate. He concluded in a September 1985 report that an independent system (beside the computer) was needed to verify turntable position and suggested the use of a potentiometer. The CRPB wrote a letter to AECL in November 1985 requesting that AECL install such an independent upper collimator positioning interlock on the Therac-25. Also in January 1986, AECL received a letter from the attorney representing the Hamilton clinic. The letter said there had been continuing problems with the turntable, including four incidents at Hamilton, and requested the installation of an independent system (potentiometer) to verify turntable position. AECL did not comply: No independent interlock was installed on the Therac-25s at this time.

Yakima Valley Memorial Hospital 1985   As with the Kennestone overdose, machine malfunction in this accident in Yakima, Washington, was not acknowledged until after later accidents were understood.

The Therac-25 at Yakima had been modified in September 1985 in response to the overdose at Hamilton. During December 1985, a woman came in for treatment with the Therac-25. She developed erythema (excessive reddening of the skin) in a parallel striped pattern at one port site (her right hip) after one of the treatments. Despite, this, she continued to be treated by the Therac-25 because the cause of her reaction was not determined to be abnormal until January or February of 1986. On January 6, 1986, her treatments were completed.

The staff monitored the skin reactions closely and attempted to find possible causes. The open slots in the blocking trays in the Therac-25 could have produced such a striped pattern, but by the time the skin reaction had been determined to be abnormal, the blocking trays had been discarded. The blocking arrangement and tray striping orientation could not be reproduced. A reaction to chemotherapy was ruled out because that should have produced reactions at the other ports and would not have produced stripes. When it was discovered that the woman slept with a heating pad, a possible explanation was offered on the basis of the parallel wires that deliver the heat in such pads. The staff x-rayed the heating pad and discovered that the wire pattern did not correspond to the erythema pattern on the patient's hip.

The hospital staff sent a letter to AECL on January 31, and they also spoke on the phone with the AECL technical support supervisor. On February 24, 1986, the AECL technical support supervisor sent a written response to the director of radiation therapy at Yakima saying, "After careful consideration, we are of the opinion that this damage could not have been produced by any malfunction of the Therac-25 or by any operator error." The letter goes on to support this opinion by listing two pages of technical reasons why an overdose by the Therac-25 was impossible, along with the additional argument that there have "apparently been no other instances of similar damage to this or other patients." The letter ends, "In closing, I wish to advise that this matter has been brought to the attention of our Hazards Committee, as is normal practice."

The hospital staff eventually ascribed the skin/tissue problem to "cause unknown." In a report written on this first Yakima incident after another Yakima overdose a year later (described in a later section), the medical physicist involved wrote:

> At that time, we did not believe that the patient was overdosed because the manufacturer had installed additional hardware and software devices to the accelerator.
>
> In a letter from the manufacturer dated 16-Sep-85, it is stated that "Analysis of the hazard rate resulting from these modifications indicates an improvement of at least five orders of magnitude"! With such an improvement in safety (10,000,000 percent) we did not believe that there could have been any accelerator malfunction. These modifications to the accelerator were completed on 5,6-Sep-85.

Even with fairly sophisticated physics support, the hospital staff, as users, did not have the ability to investigate the possibility of machine malfunction further. They were not aware of any other incidents, and, in fact, were told that there had been none, so there was no reason for them to pursue the matter. However, it seems that the fact that three similar incidents had occurred with this equipment should have triggered some suspicion and investigation by the manufacturer and the appropriate government agencies. This assumes, of course, that these incidents were all reported and known by AECL and by the government regulators. If they were not, then it is appropriate to ask why they were not and how this could be remedied in the future.

About a year later (in February 1987), after the second Yakima overdose led the hospital staff to suspect that the first injury had been due to a Therac-25 fault, the staff investigated and found that this patient had a chronic skin ulcer, tissue necrosis (death) under the skin, and was in constant pain. This was surgically repaired, skin grafts were made, and the symptoms relieved. The patient is alive today, with minor disability and some scarring related to the overdose. The hospital staff concluded that the dose accidentally delivered to this patient must have been much lower than in the second accident, as the reaction was significantly less intense and necrosis did not develop until six to eight months after exposure. Some other factors related to the place on the body where the overdose occurred also kept her from having more significant problems as a result of the exposure.

East Texas Cancer Center, March 1986   More is known about the Tyler, Texas, accidents than the others because of the diligence of the Tyler hospital physicist, Fritz Hager, without whose efforts the understanding of the software problems might have been delayed even further.

The Therac-25 was at the East Texas Cancer Center (ETCC) for two years before the first serious accident occurred; during that time, more than 500 patients had been treated. On March 21, 1986, a male patient came into ETCC for his ninth treatment on the Therac-25, one of a series prescribed as follow-up to the removal of a tumor from his back.

The patient's treatment was to be a 22-MeV electron-beam treatment of 180 rads over a 10×17-cm field on the upper back and a little to the left of his spine, or a total of 6,000 rads over period of 6 1/2 weeks. He was taken into the treatment room and placed face down on the treatment table. The operator then left the treatment room, closed the door, and sat at the control terminal.

The operator had held this job for some time, and her typing efficiency had increased with experience. She could quickly enter prescription data and change it conveniently with the Therac's editing features. She entered the patient's prescription data quickly, then noticed that for mode she had typed "x" (for X ray) when she had intended "e" (for electron). This was a common mistake since most treatments involved X rays, and she had become accustomed to typing this. The mistake was easy to fix; she merely used the cursor up key to edit the mode entry.

Since the other parameters she had entered were correct, she hit the return key several times and left their values unchanged. She reached the bottom of the screen where a message indicated that the parameters had been "verified" and the terminal displayed "beam ready," as expected. She hit the one-key command "B" (for "beam on") to begin the treatment. After a moment, the machine shut down and the console displayed the message "Malfunction 54." The machine also displayed a "treatment pause," indicating a problem of low priority (see The Operator Interface sidebar). The sheet on the side of the machine explained that this malfunction was a "dose input 2" error. The ETCC did not have any other information available in its instruction manual or other Therac-25 documentation to explain the meaning of Malfunction 54. An AECL technician later testified that "dose input 2" meant that a dose had been delivered that was either too high or too low.

The machine showed a substantial underdose on its dose monitor display: 6 monitor units delivered, whereas the operator had requested 202 monitor units. The operator was accustomed to the quirks of the machine, which would frequently stop or delay treatment. In the past, the only consequences had been inconvenience. She immediately took the normal action when the machine merely paused, which was to hit the "P" key to proceed with the treatment. The machine promptly shut down with the same "Malfunction 54" error and the same underdose shown by the display terminal.

The operator was isolated from the patient, since the machine apparatus was inside a shielded room of its own. The only way the operator could be alerted to patient difficulty was through audio and video monitors. On this day, the video display was unplugged and the audio monitor was broken.

After the first attempt to treat him, the patient said that he felt like he had received an electric shock or that someone had poured hot coffee on his back: He felt a thump and heat and heard a buzzing sound from the equipment. Since this was his ninth treatment, he knew that this was not normal. He began to get up from the treatment table to go for help. It was at this moment that the operator hit the "P" key to proceed with the treatment. The patient said that he felt like his arm was being shocked by electricity and that his hand was leaving his body. He went to the treatment room door and pounded on it. The operator was shocked and immediately opened the door for him. He appeared shaken and upset.

The patient was immediately examined by a physician, who observed intense erythema over the treatment area, but suspected nothing more serious than electric shock. The patient was discharged with instructions to return if he suffered any further reactions. The hospital physicist was called in, and he found the machine calibration within specifications. The meaning of the malfunction message was not understood. The machine was then used to treat patients for the rest of the day.

In actuality, but unknown to anyone at that time, the patient had received a massive overdose, concentrated in the center of the treatment area. After-the-fact simulations of the accident revealed possible doses of 16,500 to 25,000 rads in less than 1 second over an area of about 1 cm.

During the weeks following the accident, the patient continued to have pain in his neck and shoulder. He lost the function of his left arm and had periodic bouts of nausea and vomiting. He was eventually hospitalized for radiation-induced myelitis of the cervical cord causing paralysis of his left arm and both legs, left vocal cord paralysis (which left him unable to speak), neurogenic bowel and bladder, and paralysis of the left diaphragm. He also had a lesion on his left lung and recurrent herpes simplex skin infections. He died from complications of the overdose five months after the accident.

User and manufacturer response. The Therac-25 was shut down for testing the day after this accident. One local AECL engineer and one from the home office in Canada came to ETCC to investigate. They spent a day running the machine through tests but could not reproduce a Malfunction 54. The AECL home office engineer reportedly explained that it was not possible for the Therac-25 to overdose a patient. The ETCC physicist claims that he asked AECL at this time if there were any other reports of radiation overexposure and that the AECL personnel (including the quality assurance manager) told him that AECL knew of no accident involving radiation overexposure by the Therac-25. This seems odd since AECL was surely at least aware of the Hamilton accident that had occurred seven months before and the Yakima accident, and, even by its own account, AECL learned of the Georgia lawsuit about this time (the suit had been filed four months earlier). The AECL engineers then suggested that an electrical problem might have caused this accident.

The electric shock theory was checked out thoroughly by an independent engineering firm. The final report indicated that there was no electrical grounding problem in the machine, and it did not appear capable of giving a patient an electrical shock. The ETCC physicist checked the calibration of the Therac-25 and found it to be satisfactory. The center put the machine back into service on April 7, 1986, convinced that it was performing properly.

East Texas Cancer Center, April 1986 Three weeks after the first ETCC accident, on Friday, April 11, 1986, another male patient was scheduled to receive an electron treatment at ETCC for a skin cancer on the side of his face. The prescription was for

10 MeV to an area of approximately 7×10 cm. The same technician who had treated the first Tyler accident victim prepared this patient for treatment. Much of what follows is from the deposition of the Tyler Therac-25 operator.

As with her former patient, she entered the prescription data and then noticed an error in the mode. Again she used the cursor up key to change the mode from X ray to electron. After she finished editing, she pressed the return key several times to place the cursor on the bottom of the screen. She saw the "beam ready" message displayed and turned the beam on.

Within a few seconds the machine shut down, making a loud noise audible via the (now working) intercom. The display showed Malfunction 54 again. The operator rushed into the treatment room, hearing her patient moaning for help. The patient began to remove the tape that had held his head in position and said something was wrong. She asked him what he felt, and he replied "fire" on the side of his face. She immediately went to the hospital physicist and told him that another patient appeared to have been burned. Asked by the physicist to describe what he had experienced, the patient explained that something had hit him on the side of the face, he saw a flash of light, and he heard a sizzling sound reminiscent of frying eggs. He was very agitated and asked, "What happened to me, what happened to me?"

This patient died from the overdose on May 1, 1986, three weeks after the accident. He had disorientation that progressed to coma, fever to 104 degrees Fahrenheit, and neurological damage. Autopsy showed an acute high-dose radiation injury to the right temporal lobe of the brain and the brain stem.

User and manufacturer response.   After this second Tyler accident, the ETCC physicist immediately took the machine out of service and called AECL to alert the company to this second apparent overexposure. The Tyler physicist then began his own careful investigation. He worked with the operator, who remembered exactly what she had done on the occasion. After a great deal of effort, they were eventually able to elicit that Malfunction 54 message. They determined that data-entry speed during editing was the key factor in producing the error condition: If the prescription data was edited at a fast pace (as is natural for someone who had repeated the procedure a large number of times), the overdose occurred.

It took some practice before the physicist could repeat the procedure rapidly enough to elicit the Malfunction 54 message at will. Once he could do this, he set about measuring the actual dose delivered under the error condition. He took a measurement of about 804 rads but realized that the ion chamber has become saturated. After making adjustments to extend his measurement ability, he determined that the dose was somewhere over 4,000 rads.

The next day, an engineer from AECL called and said that he could not reproduce the error. After the ETCC physicist explained that the procedure had to be performed quite rapidly, AECL could finally produce a similar malfunction on its own machine. AECL then set up its own set of measurements to test the dosage delivered. Two days after the accident, AECL said they had measured the dosage (at the center of the field) to be 25,000 rads. An AECL engineer explained that the frying sound heard by the patient was the ion chambers being saturated.

In fact, it is not possible to determine the exact dose each of the accident victims received; the total dose delivered during the malfunction conditions was found to vary enormously when different clinics simulated the faults. The number of pulses delivered in the 0.3 second that elapsed before interlock shutoff varied because the software adjusted the start-up pulse-repetition frequency in very different values on different machines. Therefore, there is still some uncertainty as to the doses actually received in the accidents.[1]

In one lawsuit that resulted from the Tyler accident, the AECL quality control manager testified that a "cursor up" problem had been found in the service mode at the Kennestone clinic and one other clinic in February or March 1985 and also in the summer of 1985. Both times, AECL thought that the software problems had been fixed. There is no way to determine whether there is any relationship between these problems and the Tyler accidents.

Related Therac-20 problems. After the Tyler accidents, Therac-20 users (who had heard informally about the Tyler accidents from Therac-25 users) conducted informal investigations to determine whether the same problem could occur with their machines. As noted earlier, the software for the Therac-25 and Therac-20 both "evolved" from the Therac-6 software. Additional functions had to be added because the Therac-20 (and Therac-25) operates in both X-ray and electron mode, while the Therac-6 has only X-ray mode. The CGR employees modified the software for the Therac-20 to handle the dual modes.

When the Therac-25 development began, AECL engineers adapted the software from the Therac-6, but they also borrowed software routines from the Therac-20 to handle electron mode. The agreements between AECL and CGR gave both companies the right to tap technology used in joint products for their other products.

After the second Tyler accident, a physicist at the University of Chicago Joint Center for Radiation Therapy heard about the Therac-25 software problem and decided to find out whether the same thing could happen with the Therac-20. At first, the physicist was unable to reproduce the error on his machine, but two months later he found the link.

The Therac-20 at the University of Chicago is used to teach students in a radiation therapy school conducted by the center. The center's physicist, Frank Borger, noticed that whenever a new class of students started using the Therac-20, fuses and breakers on the machine tripped, shutting down the unit. These failures, which had been occurring ever since the center had acquired the machine, might appear three times a week while new students operated the machine and then disappear for months. Borger determined that new students make lots of different types of mistakes and use "creative methods of editing" parameters on the console. Through experimentation, he found that certain editing sequences correlated with blown fuses and determined that the same computer bug (as in the Therac-25 software) was responsible. The physicist notified the FDA, which notified Therac-20 users.[4]

The software error is just a nuisance on the Therac-20 because this machine has independent hardware protective circuits for monitoring the electron-beam scanning. The protective circuits do not allow the beam to turn on, so there is no danger of radiation exposure to a patient. While the Therac-20 relies on mechanical interlocks for monitoring the machine, the Therac-25 relies largely on software.

The software problem. A lesson to be learned from the Therac-25 story is that focusing on particular software bugs is not the way to make a safe system. Virtually all complex software can be made to behave in an unexpected fashion under certain conditions. The basic mistakes here involved poor software-engineering practices and building a machine that relies on the software for safe operation. Furthermore, the particular coding error is not as important as the general unsafe design of the software overall. Examining the part of the code blamed for the Tyler accidents is instructive, however, in showing the overall software design flaws. The following explanation of the problem is from the description AECL provided for the FDA, although we have tried to clarify it somewhat. The description leaves some unanswered questions, but it is the best we can do with the information we have.

As described in the sidebar on "Therac-25 software development and design," the treatment monitor task (Treat) controls the various phases of treatment by executing its eight subroutines (see Figure 2). The treatment phase indicator variable (Tphase) is used to determine which subroutine should be executed. Following the execution of a particular subroutine, Treat reschedules itself.

One of Treat's subroutines, called Datent (data entry), communicates with the keyboard handler task (a task that runs concurrently with Treat) via a shared variable (Date entry completion flag) to determine whether the prescription data has been entered. The keyboard handler recognizes the completion of data entry and changes the Data-entry completion variable to denote this. Once the Data-entry completion variable is set, the Datent subroutine detects the variable's change in status and changes the value of Tphase from 1 (Data Entry) to 3 (Setup Test). In this case, the Datent subroutine exits back to the Treat subroutine, which will reschedule itself and begin execution of the Set-Up Test subroutine. If the Data-entry completion variable has not been set, Datent leaves the value of Tphase unchanged and exits back to Treat's main line. Treat will then reschedule itself, essentially rescheduling the Datent subroutine.

The command line at the lower right corner of the screen is the cursor's normal position when the operator has completed all necessary changes to the prescription. Prescription editing is signified by cursor movement off the command line. As the program was originally designed, the Data-entry completion variable by itself is not sufficient since it does not ensure that the cursor is located on the command line. Under the

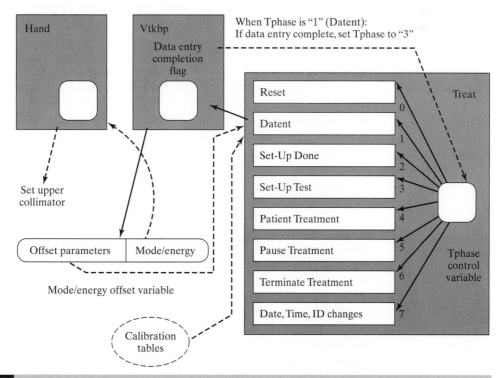

FIGURE 2 Tasks and Subroutines in the Code Blamed for the Tyler Accidents

right circumstances, the date-entry phase can be exited before all edit changes are made on the screen.

The keyboard handler parses the mode and energy level specified by the operator and places an encoded result in another shared variable, the 2-byte mode/energy offset (MEOS) variable. The low-order byte of this variable is used by another task (Hand) to set the collimator/turntable to the proper position for the selected mode/energy. The high-order byte of the MEOS variable is used by Datent to set several operating parameters.

Initially, the data-entry process forces the operator to enter the mode and energy, except when the operator selects the photon mode, in which case the energy defaults to 25 MeV. The operator can later edit the mode and energy separately. If the keyboard handler sets the data-entry completion variable before the operator changes the data in MEOS, Datent will not detect the changes in MEOS since it has already exited and will not be reentered again. The upper collimator, on the other hand, is set to the position dictated by the low-order byte of MEOS by another concurrently running task (Hand) and can therefore be inconsistent with the parameters set in accordance with the information in the high-order byte of MEOS. The software appears to include no checks to detect such an incompatibility.

The first thing that Datent does when it is entered is to check whether the mode/energy has been set in MEOS. If so, it uses the high-order byte to index into a table of preset operating parameters and places them in the digital-to-analog output. The contents of this output table are transferred to the digital-analog converter during the next clock cycle. Once the parameters are all set, Datent calls the subroutine Magnet, which sets the bending magnets. Figure 3 is a simplified pseudocode description of relevant parts of the software.

Setting the bending magnets takes about 8 seconds. Magnet calls a subroutine called Ptime to introduce a time delay. Since several magnets need to be set, Ptime is entered and exited several times. A flag to indicate that bending magnets are being set is initialized upon entry to the Magnet subroutine and cleared at the end of Ptime. Furthermore, Ptime checks a shared variable, set by the keyboard handler, that indicates the presence of any editing requests. If there are edits, then Ptime clears the bending magnet variable and exits to Magnet, which then exits to Datent. But the edit change variable is checked by Ptime only if the bending magnet flag is set. Since Ptime clears it during its first execution, any edits performed during each succeeding pass through Ptime will not be recognized. Thus, an edit change of the mode or energy, although reflected on the operator's screen and the mode energy offset variable, will not be sensed by Datent so it can index the appropriate calibration tables for the machine parameters.

Recall that the Tyler error occurred when the operator made an entry indicating the mode/energy, went to the command line, then moved the cursor up to change the mode/energy, and returned to the command line all within seconds. Since the magnet setting takes about 8 seconds and Magnet does not recognize edits after the first execution of Ptime, the editing had been completed by the return to Datent, which never detected that it had occurred. Part of the problem was fixed after the accident by clearing the bending-magnet variable at the end of Magnet (after all the magnets have been set) instead of at the end of Ptime.

But this was not the only problem. Upon exit from the Magnet subroutine, the data-entry subroutine (Datent) checks the data-entry completion variable. If it indicates that data entry is complete, Datent sets Tphase to 3 and Datent is not entered again. If it is not set, Datent leaves Tphase unchanged, which means it will eventually be rescheduled. But the data-entry completion variable only indicates that the cursor has been down to the command line, not that it is still there. A potential race condition is

```
Datent:
    if mode/energy specified then
        begin
            calculate table index
            repeat
                fetch parameter
                output parameter
                point to next parameter
            until all parameters set
            call Magnet
            if mode/energy changed then return
        end
    if data entry is complete then set Tphase 3
    if data entry is not complete then
        if reset command entered then set Tphase to 0
    return


Magnet:
    Set bending magnet flag
    repeat
        Set next magnet
        Call Ptime
        if mode/energy has changed, then exit
    until all magnets are set
    return


Ptime:
    repeat
        if bending magnet flag is set then
            if editing taking place then
                if mode/energy has changed then exit
    until hysteresis delay  has expired
    Clear bending magnet flag
    return
```

▪ ▪ ▪ ▪ ▪ ▪ ▪ ▪ ▪ ▪ ▪ ▪ **FIGURE 3** Datent, Magnet, and Ptime Subroutines

set up. To fix this, AECL introduced another shared variable controlled by the keyboard handler task that indicates the cursor is not positioned on the command line. If this variable is set, then prescription entry is still in progress and the value of Tphase is left unchanged.

Government and user response.   The FDA does not approve each new medical device on the market. All medical devices go through a classification process that determines the level of FDA approval necessary. Medical accelerators follow a procedure called pre-market notification before commercial distribution. In this process, the firm must establish that the product is substantially equivalent in safety and effectiveness to a product already on the market. If that cannot be done to the FDA's satisfaction, a pre-market approval is required. For the Therac-25, the FDA required only a pre-market notification.

The agency is basically reactive to problems and requires manufacturers to report serious ones. Once a problem is identified in a radiation-emitting product, the FDA must approve the manufacturer's corrective action plan (CAP).

The first reports of the Tyler accidents came to the FDA from the state of Texas health department, and this triggered FDA action. The FDA investigation was well under way when AECL produced a medical device report to discuss the details of the radiation overexposures at Tyler. The FDA declared the Therac-25 defective under the Radiation Control for Health and Safety Act and ordered the firm to notify all purchasers, investigate the problem, determine a solution, and submit a corrective action plan for FDA approval.

The final CAP consisted of more than 20 changes to the system hardware and software, plus modifications to the system documentation and manuals. Some of these changes were unrelated to the specific accidents but were improvements to the general machine safety. The full implementation of the CAP, including an extensive safety analysis, was not complete until more than two years after the Tyler accidents.

AECL made its accident report to the FDA on April 15, 1986. On that same date, AECL sent a letter to each Therac user recommending a temporary "fix" to the machine that would allow continued clinical use. The letter (shown in its complete form) read as follows:

> **SUBJECT: CHANGES IN OPERATING PROCEDURES FOR THE THERAC 25 LINEAR ACCELERATOR**
> Effective immediately, and until further notice, the key used for moving the cursor back through the prescription sequence (i.e., cursor "UP" inscribed with an upward pointing arrow) must not be used for editing or any other purpose.
>
> To avoid accidental use of this key, the key cap must be removed and the switch contacts fixed in the open position with electrical tape or other insulating material. For assistance with the latter you should contact your local AECL service representative.
>
> Disabling this key means that if any prescription data entered is incorrect then [an] "R" reset command must be used and the whole prescription reentered.
>
> For those users of the Multiport option, it also means that editing of dose rate, dose, and time will not be possible between ports.

On May 2, 1986, the FDA declared the Therac defective, demanded a CAP, and required renotification of all the Therac customers. In the letter from the FDA to AECL, the director of compliance, Center for Devices and Radiological Health, wrote:

> We have reviewed Mr. Down's April 15 letter to purchasers and have concluded that it does not satisfy the requirements for notification to purchasers of a defect in an electronic product. Specifically, it does not describe the defect nor the hazards associated with it. The letter does not provide any reason for disabling the cursor key and the tone is not commensurate with the urgency for doing so. In fact, the letter implies the inconvenience to operators outweighs the need to disable the key. We request that you immediately re-notify purchasers.

AECL promptly made a new notice to users and also requested an extension to produce a CAP. The FDA granted this request.

About this time the Therac-25 users created a user group and held their first meeting at the annual conference of the American Association of Physicists in Medicine. At the meeting, users discussed the Tyler accident and heard an AECL representative present the company's plans for responding to it. AECL promised to send a letter to all users detailing the CAP.

Several users described additional hardware safety features that they had added to their own machines to provide additional protection. An interlock (that checked gun current values), which the Vancouver clinic had previously added to its Therac-25, was labeled as redundant by AECL. The users disagreed. There were further discussions of poor design and other problems that caused 10-to-30 percent underdosing in both modes.

The meeting notes said

> . . . there was a general complaint by all users present about the lack of information propagation. The users were not happy about receiving incomplete information. The AECL representative countered by stating that AECL does not wish to spread rumors and that AECL has no policy to "keep things quiet." The consensus among the users was that an improvement was necessary.

After the first user group meeting, there were two user group newsletters. The first, dated fall 1986, contained letters from Still, the Kennestone physicist, who complained about what he considered to be eight major problems he had experienced with the Therac-25. These problems included poor screen refresh subroutines that left trash and erroneous information on the operator console, and some tape-loading problems upon start-up, which he discovered involved the use of "phantom tables" to trigger the interlock system in the event of a load failure instead of using a check sum. He asked the question "Is programming safety relying too much on the software interlock routines?" The second user group newsletter, in December 1986, further discussed the implication of the "phantom table" parameterization.

AECL produced the first CAP on June 13, 1986. It contained six items.

1. Fix the software to eliminate the specific behavior leading to the Tyler problem.
2. Modify the software sample-and-hold circuits to detect one pulse above a nonadjustable threshold. The software sample-and-hold circuit monitors the magnitude of each pulse from the ion chambers in the beam. Previously, three consecutive high readings were required to shut off the high-voltage circuits, which resulted in a shutdown time of 300 ms. The software modification results in a reading after each pulse, and a shutdown after a single high reading.
3. Make Malfunctions 1 through 64 result in treatment *suspend* rather than *pause*.
4. Add a new circuit, which only administrative staff can reset, to shut down the modulator if the sample-and-hold circuits detect a high pulse. This is functionally equivalent to the circuit described in item 2. However, a new circuit board is added that monitors the five sample-and-hold circuits. The new circuit detects ion-chamber signals above a fixed threshold and inhibits the trigger to the modulator after detecting a high pulse. This shuts down the beam independently of the software.
5. Modify the software to limit editing keys to cursor up, backspace, and return.
6. Modify the manuals to reflect the changes.

FDA internal memos describe their immediate concerns regarding the CAP. One memo suggests adding an independent circuit that "detects and shuts down the system when inappropriate outputs are detected," warnings about when ion chambers are saturated, and understandable system error messages. Another memo questions "whether all possible hardware options have been investigated by the manufacturer to prevent any future inadvertent high exposure."

On July 23 the FDA officially responded to AECL's CAP submission. They conceptually agreed with the plan's direction but complained about the lack of specific information necessary to evaluate the plan, especially with regard to the software. The FDA requested a detailed description of the software development procedures and documentation, along with a revised CAP to include revised requirements documents, a detailed description of corrective changes, analysis of the interactions of the modified software with the system, and detailed descriptions of the revised edit modes, the changes made to the software setup table, and the software interlock interactions. The FDA also made a very detailed request for a documented test plan.

AECL responded on September 26 with several documents describing the software and its modification but no test plan. They explained how the Therac-25 software evolved from the Therac-6 software and stated that "no single test plan and report exists for the software since both hardware and software were tested and exercised separately and together over many years." AECL concluded that the current CAP improved "machine safety by many orders of magnitude and virtually eliminates the possibility of lethal doses as delivered in the Tyler incident."

An FDA internal memo dated October 20 commented on these AECL submissions, raising several concerns:

> Unfortunately, the AECL response also seems to point out an apparent lack of documentation on software specifications and a software test plan.
>
> . . . concerns include the question of previous knowledge of problems by AECL, the apparent paucity of software QA [quality assurance] at the manufacturing facility, and possible warnings of information dissemination to others of the generic type problems.
>
> . . . As mentioned in my first review, there is some confusion on whether the manufacturer should have been aware of the software problems prior to the [accidental radiation overdoses] in Texas. AECL had received official notification of a lawsuit in November 1985 from a patient claiming accidental over-exposure from a Therac-25 in Marietta, Georgia . . . If knowledge of these software deficiencies were known beforehand, what would be the FDA's posture in this case?
>
> . . . The materials submitted by the manufacturer have not been in sufficient detail and clarity to ensure an adequate software QA program currently exists. For example, a response has not been provided with respect to the software part of the CAP to the CDRH [FDA Center for Devices and Radiological Health] request for documentation on the revised requirements and specifications for the new software. In addition, an analysis has not been provided, as requested, on the interaction with other portions of the software to demonstrate the corrected software does not adversely affect other software functions.
>
> The July 23 letter from the CDRH requested a documented test plan including several specific pieces of information identified in the letter. This request has been ignored up to this point by the manufacturer. Considering the ramifications of the current software problem, changes in software QA attitudes are needed at AECL.

On October 30, the FDA responded to AECL's additional submissions, complaining about the lack of a detailed description of the accident and of sufficient detail in flow diagrams. Many specific questions addressed the vagueness of the AECL response and made it clear that additional CAP work must precede approval.

AECL, in response, created CAP Revision 1 on November 12. This CAP contained 12 new items under "software modifications," all (except for one cosmetic change) designed to eliminate potentially unsafe behavior. The submission also contained other relevant documents including a test plan.

The FDA responded to CAP Revision 1 on December 11. The FDA explained that the software modifications appeared to correct the specific deficiencies discovered as a result of the Tyler accidents. They agreed that the major items listed in CAP Revision 1 would improve the Therac's operations. However, the FDA required AECL to attend to several further system problems before CAP approval. AECL had proposed to retain treatment pause for some dose-rate and beam-tilt malfunctions. Since these are dosimetry system problems, the FDA considered the safely interlocks and believed treatment must be suspended for these malfunctions.

AECL also planned to retain the malfunction codes, but the FDA required better warnings for the operations. Furthermore, AECL had not planned on any quality assurance testing to ensure exact copying of software but the FDA insisted on it. The FDA further requested assurances that rigorous testing would become a standard part of AECL's software modification procedures:

> We also expressed our concerns that you did not intend to perform the protocol in future modifications to software. We believe that the rigorous testing must be performed each time a modification is made in order to ensure the modification does not adversely affect the safety of the system.

AECL was also asked to draw up an installation test plan to ensure both hardware and software changes perform as designed when installed.

AECL submitted CAP Revision 2 and supporting documentation on December 22, 1986. They changed the CAP to have dose malfunctions suspend treatment and included a plan for meaningful error messages and highlighted dose error messages. They also expanded diagrams of software modifications and expanded the test plan to cover hardware and software.

On January 26, 1987, AECL sent the FDA their "Component and Installation Test Plan" and explained that their delays were due to the investigation of a new accident on January 17 at Yakima.

Yakima Valley Memorial Hospital, 1987   On Saturday, January 17, 1987, the second patient of the day was to be treated at the Yakima Valley Memorial Hospital for a carcinoma. This patient was to receive two film-verification exposures of 4 and 3 rads, plus a 79-rad photon treatment (for a total exposure of 86 rads).

Film was placed under the patient and 4 rads were administered with the collimator jaws opened to 22×18 cm. After the machine paused, the collimator jaws opened to 35×35 cm automatically, and the second exposure of 3 rads was administered. The machine paused again.

The operator entered the treatment room to remove the film and verify the patient's precise position. He used the hand control in the treatment room to rotate the turntable to the field-light position, a feature that let him check the machine's alignment with respect to the patient's body to verify proper beam position. The operator then either pressed the set button on the hand control or left the room and typed a set command at the console to return the turntable to the proper position for treatment; there is some confusion as to exactly what transpired. When he left the room, he forgot to remove the film from underneath the patient. The console displayed "beam ready," and the operator hit the "B" key to turn the beam on.

The beam came on but the console displayed no dose or dose rate. After 5 or 6 seconds, the unit shut down with a pause and displayed a message. The message "may have disappeared quickly"; the operator was unclear on this point. However, since the machine merely paused, he was able to push the "P" key to proceed with treatment.

The machine paused again, this time displaying "flatness" on the reason line. The operator heard the patient say something over the intercom, but couldn't understand him. He went into the room to speak with the patient, who reported "feeling a burning sensation" in the chest. The console displayed only the total dose of the two film exposures (7 rads) and nothing more.

Later in the day, the patient developed a skin burn over the entire treatment area. Four days later, the redness took on the striped pattern matching the slots in the blocking tray. The striped pattern was similar to the burn a year earlier at this hospital that had been attributed to "cause unknown."

AECL began an investigation, and users were told to confirm the turntable position visually before turning on the beam. All tests run by the AECL engineers indicated that the machine was working perfectly. From the information gathered to that point, it was suspected that the electron beam had come on when the turntable was in the field-light position. But the investigators could not reproduce the fault condition that produced the overdose.

On the following Thursday, AECL sent an engineer from Ottawa to investigate. The hospital physicist had, in the meantime, run some tests with film. He placed a film in the Therac's beam and ran two exposures of X-ray parameters with the turntable in field-light position. The film appeared to match the film that was left (by mistake) under the patient during the accident.

After a week of checking the hardware, AECL determined that the "incorrect machine operation was probably not caused by hardware alone." After checking the software, AECL discovered a flaw (described in the next section) that could explain the erroneous behavior. The coding problems explaining this accident differ from those associated with the Tyler accidents.

AECL's preliminary dose measurements indicated that the doses delivered under these conditions—that is, when the turntable was in the field-light position—was on the order of 4,000 to 5,000 rads. After two attempts, the patient could have received 8,000 to 10,000 instead of the 86 rads prescribed. AECL again called users on January 26 (nine days after the accident) and gave them detailed instructions on how to avoid this problem. In an FDA internal report on the accident, an AECL quality assurance manager investigating the problem is quoted as saying that the software and hardware changes to be retrofitted following the Tyler accident nine months earlier (but which had not yet been installed) would have prevented the Yakima accident.

The patient died in April from complications related to the overdose. He had been suffering from a terminal form of cancer prior to the radiation overdose, but survivors initiated lawsuits alleging that he died sooner than he would have and endured unnecessary pain and suffering due to the overdose. The suit was settled out of court.

The Yakima software problem. The software problem for the second Yakima accident is fairly well established and different from that implicated in the Tyler accidents. There is no way to determine what particular software design errors were related to the Kennestone, Hamilton, and first Yakima accidents. Given the unsafe programming practices exhibited in the code, it is possible that unknown race conditions or errors could have been responsible. There is speculation, however, that the Hamilton accident was the same as this second Yakima overdose. In a report of a conference call on January 26, 1987, between the AECL quality assurance manager and Ed Miller of the FDA discussing the Yakima accident, Miller notes

> This situation probably occurred in the Hamilton, Ontario, accident a couple of years ago. It was not discovered at that time and the cause was attributed to intermittent interlock failure. The subsequent recall of the multiple microswitch logic network did not really solve the problem.

The second Yakima accident was again attributed to a type of race condition in the software—this one allowed the device to be activated in an error setting (a "failure" of a software interlock). The Tyler accidents were related to problems in the data-entry routines that allowed the code to proceed to Set-Up Test before the full prescription had been entered and acted upon. The Yakima accident involves problems encountered later in the logic after the treatment monitor Treat reaches Set-Up Test.

The Therac-25's field-light feature permits very precise positioning of the patient for treatment. The operator can control the Therac-25 right at the treatment site using a small hand control offering certain limited functions for patient setup, including setting gantry, collimator, and table motions.

Normally, the operator enters all the prescription data at the console (outside the treatment room) before the final setup of all machine parameters is completed in the treatment room. This gives rise to an "unverified" condition at the console. The operator then completes the patient setup in the treatment room, and all relevant parameters now "verify." The console displays the message "Press set button" while the turntable is in the field-light position. The operator now presses the set button on the hand control or types "set" at the console. That should set the collimator to the proper position for treatment.

In the software, after the prescription is entered and verified by the Datent routine, the control variable Tphase is changed so that the Set-Up Test routine is entered (see Figure 4). Every pass through the Set-Up Test routine increments the upper collimator position check, a shared variable called Class3. If Class3 is nonzero, there is an inconsistency and treatment should not proceed. A zero value for Class3 indicates that the relevant parameters are consistent with treatment, and the beam is not inhibited.

After setting the Class3 variable, Set-Up Test next checks for any malfunctions in the system by checking another shared variable (set by a routine that actually handles the interlock checking) called F\$mal to see if it has a nonzero value. A nonzero value in F\$mal indicates that the machine is not ready for treatment, and the Set-Up Test subroutine is rescheduled. When F\$mal is zero (indicating that everything is ready for treatment), the Set-Up Test subroutine sets the Tphase variable equal to 2, which results in next scheduling the Set-Up Done subroutine, and the treatment is allowed to continue.

The actual interlock checking is performed by a concurrent Housekeeper task (Hkeper). The upper collimator position check is performed by a subroutine of Hkeper called Lmtchk (analog/digital limit checking). Lmtchk first checks the Class3 variable. If Class3 contains a nonzero value, Lmtchk calls the Check Collimator (Chkcol) subroutine. If Class3 contains zero, Chkcol is bypassed and the upper collimator position check is not performed. The Chkcol subroutine sets or resets bit 9 of the F\$mal shared variable, depending on the position of the upper collimator (which in turn is checked by the Set-Up Test subroutine of Datent so it can decide whether to reschedule itself or proceed to Set-Up Done).

During machine setup, Set-Up Test will be executed several hundred times since it reschedules itself waiting for other events to occur. In the code, the Class3 variable is incremented by one for each pass through Set-Up Test. Since the Class3 variable is 1 byte, it can only contain a maximum value of 255 decimal. Thus, on every 256th pass

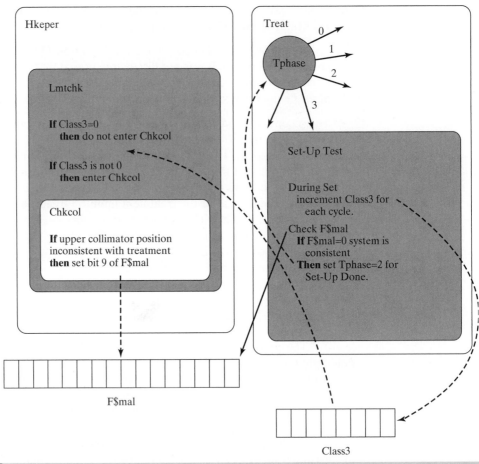

FIGURE 4 Yakima Software Flaw

through the Set-Up Test code, the variable overflows and has a zero value. That means that on every 256th pass through Set-Up Test, the upper collimator will not be checked and an upper collimation fault will not be detected.

The overexposure occurred when the operator hit the "set" button at the precise moment that Class3 rolled over to zero. Thus Chkcol was not executed and F$mal was not set to indicate the upper collimator was still in field-light position. The software turned on the full 25 MeV without the target in place and without scanning. A highly concentrated electron beam resulted, which was scattered and deflected by the stainless steel mirror that was in the path.

AECL described the technical "fix implemented for this software flaw as simple: The program is changed so that the Class3 variable is set to some fixed nonzero value each time through Set-Up Test instead of being incremented.

Manufacturer, government, and user response. On February 3, 1987, after interaction with the FDA and others including the user group, AECL announced to its customers

- a new software release to correct both the Tyler and Yakima software problems,
- a hardware single-pulse shutdown circuit,
- a turntable potentiometer to independently monitor turntable position, and
- a hardware turntable interlock circuit.

The second item, a hardware single pulse shutdown circuit, essentially acts as a hardware interlock to prevent overdosing by detecting an unsafe level of radiation and halting beam output after one pulse of high energy and current. This provides an independent safety mechanism to protect against a wide range of potential hardware failures and software errors. The turntable potentiometer was the safety device recommended by several groups, including the CRPB, after the Hamilton accident.

After the second Yakima accident, the FDA became concerned that the use of the Therac-25 during the CAP process, even with AECL's interim operating instructions, involved too much risk to patients. The FDA concluded that the accidents had demonstrated that the software alone cannot be relied upon to assure safe operation of the machine. In a February 18, 1987, internal FDA memorandum, the director of the Division of Radiological Products wrote the following:

> It is impossible for CDRH to find all potential failure modes and conditions of the software. AECL has indicated the "simple software fix" will correct the turntable position problem displayed at Yakima. We have not yet had the opportunity to evaluate that modification. Even if it does, based upon past history, I am not convinced that there are not other software glitches that could result in serious injury.
>
> For example, we are aware that AECL issued a user's bulletin January 21 reminding users of the proper procedure to follow if editing of prescription parameters is desired after entering the "B" (beam on) code but before the CR [carriage return] is pressed. It seems that the normal edit keys (down arrow, right arrow, or line feed) will be interpreted as a CR and initiate exposure. One must use either the backspace or left arrow key to edit.
>
> We are also aware that if the dose entered into the prescription tables is below some present value, the system will default to a phantom table value unbeknownst to the operator. This problem is supposedly being addressed in proposed interim revision 7A, although we are unaware of the details.
>
> We are in the position of saying that the proposed CAP can reasonably be expected to correct the deficiencies for which they were developed (Tyler). We cannot say that we are [reasonably] confident about the safety of the entire *system* to prevent or minimize exposure from other fault conditions.

On February 6, 1987, Miller of the FDA called Pavel Dvorak of Canada's Health and Welfare to advise him that the FDA would recommend all Therac-25s be shut down until permanent modifications could be made. According to Miller's notes on the phone call, Dvorak agreed and indicated that they would coordinate their actions with the FDA.

On February 10, 1987, the FDA gave a Notice of Adverse Findings to AECL declaring the Therac-25 to be defective under US law. In part, the letter to AECL reads:

> In January 1987, CDRH was advised of another accidental radiation occurrence in Yakima, which was attributed to a second software defect related to the "Set" command. In addition, the CDRH has become aware of at least two other software features that provide potential for unnecessary or inadvertent patient exposure. One of these is related to the method of editing the prescription after the "B" command is entered and the other is the calling of phantom tables when low doses are prescribed.
>
> Further review of the circumstances surrounding the accidental radiation occurrences and the potential for other such incidents has led us to conclude that in addition to the items in your proposed corrective action plan,

hardware interlocking of the turntable to insure its proper position prior to beam activation appears to be necessary to enhance system safety and to correct the Therac-25 defect. Therefore, the corrective action plan as currently proposed is insufficient and must be amended to include turntable interlocking and corrections for the three software problems mentioned above.

Without these corrections, CDRH has concluded that the consequences of the defects represent a significant potential risk of serious injury even if the Therac-25 is operated in accordance with your interim operating instructions. CDRH, therefore, requests that AECL immediately notify all purchasers and recommend that use of the device on patients for routine therapy be discontinued until such time that an amended corrective action plan approved by CDRH is fully completed. You may also advise purchasers that if the need for an individual patient treatment outweighs the potential risk, then extreme caution and strict adherence to operating safety procedures must be exercised.

At the same time, the Health Protection Branch of the Canadian government instructed AECL to recommend to all users in Canada that they discontinue the operation of the Therac-25 until "the company can complete an exhaustive analysis of the design and operation of the safety systems employed for patient and operator protection." AECL was told that the letter to the users should include information on how the users can operate the equipment safely in the event that they must continue with patient treatment. If AECL could not provide information that would guarantee safe operation of the equipment, AECL was requested to inform the users that they cannot operate the equipment safely. AECL complied by letters dated February 20, 1987, to Therac-25 purchasers. This recommendation to discontinue use of the Therac-25 was to last until August 1987.

On March 5, 1987, AECL issued CAP Revision 3, which was a CAP for both the Tyler and Yakima accidents. It contained a few additions to the Revision 2 modifications, notably

- changes to the software to eliminate the behavior leading to the latest Yakima accident,
- four additional software functional modifications to improve safety, and
- a turntable position interlock in the software.

In their response on April 9, the FDA noted that in the appendix under "turntable position interlock circuit" the descriptions were wrong. AECL had indicated "high" signals where "low" signals were called for and vice versa. The FDA also questioned the reliability of the turntable potentiometer design and asked whether the backspace key could still act as a carriage return in the edit mode. They requested a detailed description of the software portion of the single-pulse shutdown and a block diagram to demonstrate the PRF (pulse repetition frequency) generator, modulator, and associated interlocks.

AECL responded on April 13 with an update on the Therac CAP status and a schedule of the nine action items pressed by the users at a user group meeting in March. This unique and highly productive meeting provided an unusual opportunity to involve the users in the CAP evaluation process. It brought together all concerned parties in one place so that they could decide on and approve a course of action as quickly as possible. The attendees included representatives from the manufacturer (AECL); all users, including their technical and legal staffs; the US FDA; the Canadian BRMD; the

Canadian Atomic Energy Control Board; the Province of Ontario; and the radiation Regulations Committee of the Canadian Association of Physicists.

According to Symonds of the BRMD, this meeting was very important to the resolution of the problems since the regulators, users, and the manufacturer arrived at a consensus in one day.

At this second users meeting, the participants carefully reviewed all the six known major Therac-25 accidents and discussed the elements of the CAP along with possible additional modifications. They came up with a prioritized list of modifications that they wanted included in the CAP and expressed concerns about the lack of independent software evaluation and the lack of a hard-copy audit trail to assist in diagnosing faults.

The AECL representative, who was the quality assurance manager, responded that tests had been done on the CAP changes, but that the tests were not documented, and independent evaluation of the software "might not be possible." He claimed that two outside experts had reviewed the software, but he could not provide their names. In response to user requests for a hard-copy audit trail and access to source code, he explained that memory limitations would not permit including an audit option, and source code would not be made available to users.

On May 1, AECL issued CAP Revision 4 as a result of the FDA comments and users meeting input. The FDA response on May 26 approved the CAP subject to submission of the final test plan results and an independent safety analysis, distribution of the draft revised manual to customers, and completion of the CAP by June 30, 1987. The FDA concluded by rating this a Class I recall: a recall in which there is a reasonable probability that the use of or exposure to a violative product will cause serious adverse health consequences or death.[5]

AECL sent more supporting documentation to the FDA on June 5, 1987, including the CAP test plan, a draft operator's manual, and the draft of the new safety analysis (described in the sidebar "Safety Analysis of the Therac-25"). The safety analysis revealed four potentially hazardous subsystems that were not covered by CAP Revision 4:

1. electron-beam scanning,
2. electron-energy selection,
3. beam shutoff, and
4. calibration and/or steering.

AECL planned a fifth revision of the CAP to include the testing and safety analysis results.

Referring to the test plan at this, the final stage of the CAP process, an FDA reviewer said

Amazingly, the test data presented to show that the software changes to handle the edit problems in the Therac-25 are appropriate prove the exact opposite result. A review of the data table in the test results indicates that the final beam type and energy (edit change) [have] no effect on the initial beam type and energy. I can only assume that either the fix is not right or the data was entered incorrectly. The manufacturer should be admonished for this error. Where is the QC [quality control] review for the test program? AECL must: (1) clarify this situation, (2) change the test protocol to prevent this type of error from occurring, and (3) set up appropriate QC control on data review.

Safety Analysis of the Therac-25

The Therac-25 safety analysis included (1) failure mode and effect analysis, (2) fault-tree analysis, and (3) software examination.

Failure mode and effect analysis An FMEA describes the associated system response to all failure modes of the individual system components, considered one by one. When software was involved, AECL made no assessment of the "how and why" of software faults and took any combination of software faults as a single event. The latter means that if the software was the initiating event, then no credit was given for the software mitigating the effects. This seems like a reasonable and conservative approach to handling software faults.

Fault-tree analysis An FMEA identifies single failures leading to Class I hazards. To identify multiple failures and quantify the results, AECL used fault-tree analysis. An FTA starts with a postulated hazard—for example, two of the top events for the Therac-25 are high dose per pulse and illegal gantry motion. The immediate causes for the event are then generated in an AND/OR tree format, using a basic understanding of the machine operation to determine the causes. The tree generation continues until all branches end in "basic events." Operationally, a basic event is sometimes defined as an event that can be quantified (for example, a resistor fails open).

AECL used a "generic failure rate" of 10^{-4} per hour for software events. The company justified this number as based on the historical performance of the Therac-25 software. The final report on the safety analysis said that many fault trees for the Therac-25 have a computer malfunction as a causative event, and the outcome of quantification is therefore dependent on the failure rate chosen for software.

Leaving aside the general question of whether such failure rates are meaningful or measurable for software in general, it seems rather difficult to justify a single figure of this sort for every type of software error or software behavior. It would be equivalent to assigning the same failure rate to every type of failure of a car, no matter what particular failure is considered.

The authors of the safety study did note that despite the uncertainty that software introduces into quantification, fault-tree analysis provides valuable information in showing single and multiple failure paths and the relative importance of different failure mechanisms. This is certainly true.

Software examination Because of the difficulty of quantifying software behavior, AECL contracted for a detailed code inspection to "obtain more information on which to base decisions." The software functions selected for examination were those related to the Class I software hazards identified in the FMEA: electron-beam scanning, energy selection, beam shutoff, and dose calibration.

The outside consultant who performed the inspection included a detailed examination of each function's implementation, a search for coding errors, and a qualitative assessment of its reliability. The consultant recommended program changes to correct shortcomings, improve reliability, or improve the software package in a general sense. The final safety report gives no information about whether any particular methodology or tools were used in the software inspection or whether someone just read the code looking for errors.

Conclusions of the safety analysis The final report summarizes the conclusions of the safety analysis.

The conclusions of the analysis call for 10 changes to Therac-25 hardware; the most significant of these are interlocks to back up software control of both electron scanning and beam energy selection.

Although it is not considered necessary or advisable to rewrite the entire Therac-25 software package, considerable effort is being expended to update it. The changes recommended have several distinct objectives: improve the protection it provides against hardware failures; provide additional reliability via cross-checking; and provide a more maintainable source package. Two or three software releases are anticipated before these changes are completed.

The implementation of these improvements including design and testing for both hardware and software is well under way. All hardware modifica-

(continued)

tions should be completed and installed by mid 1989, with final software updates extending into late 1989 or early 1990.

The recommended hardware changes appear to add protection against software errors, to add extra protection against hardware failures, or to increase safety margins. The software conclusions included the following:

> The software code for Beam Shut-Off, Symmetry Control, and Dose Calibration was found to be straightforward and no execution path could be found which would cause them to perform incorrectly. A few improvements are being incorporated, but no additional hardware interlocks are required.
>
> Inspection of the Scanning and Energy Selection functions, which are under software control, showed no improper execution paths; however, software inspection was unable to provide a high level of confidence in their reliability. This was due to the complex nature of the code, the extensive use of variables, and the time limitations of the inspection process. Due to these factors and the possible clinical consequences of a malfunction, computer-independent interlocks are being retrofitted for these two cases.

Given the complex nature of this software design and the basic multitasking design, it is difficult to understand how any part of the code could be labeled "straightforward" or how confidence could be achieved that "no execution paths" exist for particular types of software behavior. However, it does appear that a conservative approach—including computer-independent interlocks—was taken in most cases. Furthermore, few examples of such safety analyses of software exist in the literature. One such software analysis was performed in 1989 on the shutdown software of a nuclear power plant, which was written by a different division of AECL.[1] Much still needs to be learned about how to perform a software-safety analysis.

Reference

[1] W.C. Bowman et al., "An Application of Fault Tree Analysis to Safety-Critical Software at Ontario Hydro," *Conf. Probabilistic Safety Assessment and Management*, 1991.

A further FDA memo said the AECL quality assurance manager

> . . . could not give an explanation and will check into the circumstances. He subsequently called back and verified that the technician completed the form incorrectly. Correct operation was witnessed by himself and others. They will repeat and send us the correct data sheet.

At the American Association of Physicists in Medicine meeting in July 1987, a third user group meeting was held. The AECL representative gave the status of CAP Revision 5. He explained that the FDA had given verbal approval and he expected full implementation by the end of August 1987. He reviewed and commented on the prioritized concerns of the last meeting. AECL had included in the CAP three of the user-requested hardware changes. Changes to tape-load error messages and check sums on the load data would wait until after the CAP was done.

Two user-requested hardware modifications had not been included in the CAP. One of these, a push-button energy and selection mode switch, AECL would work on after completing the CAP, the quality assurance manager said. The other, a fixed ion chamber with dose/pulse monitoring, was being installed at Yakima, had already been installed by Halifax on their own, and would be an option for other clinics. Software documentation was described as a lower priority task that needed definition and would not be available to the FDA in any form for more than a year.

On July 6, 1987, AECL sent a letter to all users to inform them of the FDA's verbal approval of the CAP and delineated how AECL would proceed. On July 21, 1987,

AECL issued the fifth and final CAP revision. The major features of the final CAP are as follows:

- All interruptions related to the dosimetry system will go to a treatment suspend, not a treatment pause. Operators will not be allowed to restart the machine without reentering all parameters.
- A software single-pulse shutdown will be added.
- An independent hardware single-pulse shutdown will be added.
- Monitoring logic for turntable position will be improved to ensure that the turntable is in one of the three legal positions.
- A potentiometer will be added to the turntable. It will provide a visible signal of position that operators will use to monitor exact turntable location.
- Interlocking with the 270-degree bending magnet will be added to ensure that the target and beam flattener are in position if the X-ray mode is selected.
- Beam on will be prevented if the turntable is in the field-light or an intermediate position.
- Cryptic malfunction messages will be replaced with meaningful messages and highlighted dose-rate messages.
- Editing keys will be limited to cursor up, backspace, and return. All other keys will be inoperative.
- A motion-enable foot switch will be added, which the operator must hold closed during movement of certain parts of the machine to prevent unwanted motions when the operator is not in control (a type of "dead man's switch").
- Twenty-three other changes to the software to improve its operation and reliability, including disabling of unused keys, changing the operation of the set and reset commands, preventing copying of the control program on site, changing the way various detected hardware faults are handled, eliminating errors in the software that were detected during the review process, adding several additional software interlocks, disallowing changing to the service mode while a treatment is in progress, and adding meaningful error messages.
- The known software problems associated with the Tyler and Yakima accidents will be fixed.
- The manuals will be fixed to reflect the changes.

In a 1987 paper, Miller, director of the Division of Standards Enforcement, CDRH, wrote about the lessons learned from the Therac-25 experiences.[6] The first was the importance of safe versus "user-friendly" operator interfaces—in other words, making the machine as easy as possible to use may conflict with safety goals. The second is the importance of providing fail-safe designs:

> The second lesson is that for complex interrupt-driven software, timing is of critical importance. In both of these situations, operator action within very narrow time-frame windows was necessary for the accidents to occur. It is unlikely that software testing will discover all possible errors that involve operator intervention at precise time frames during software operation. These machines, for example, have been exercised for thousands of hours in the factory and in the hospitals without accident. Therefore, one must provide for prevention of catastrophic results of failures when they do occur.
>
> I, for one, will not be surprised if other software errors appear with this or other equipment in the future.

Miller concluded the paper with

FDA has performed extensive review of the Therac-25 software and hardware safety systems. We cannot say with absolute certainty that all software problems that might result in improper dose have been found and eliminated. However, we are confident that the hardware and software safety features recently added will prevent future catastrophic consequences of failure.

▪▪▪ Lessons Learned

Often, it takes an accident to alert people to the dangers involved in technology. A medical physicist wrote about the Therac-25 accidents:

In the past decade or two, the medical accelerator "industry" has become perhaps a little complacent about safety. We have assumed that the manufacturers have all kinds of safety design experience since they've been in the business a long time. We know that there are many safety codes, guides, and regulations to guide them and we have been reassured by the hitherto excellent record of these machines. Except for a few incidents in the 1960s (e.g., at Hammersmith, Hamburg) the use of medical accelerators has been remarkably free of serious radiation accidents until now. Perhaps, though, we have been spoiled by this success.[1]

Accidents are seldom simple—they usually involve a complex web of interacting events with multiple contributing technical, human, and organizational factors. One of the serious mistakes that led to the multiple Therac-25 accidents was the tendency to believe that the cause of an accident had been determined (for example, a microswitch failure in the Hamilton accident) without adequate evidence to come to this conclusion and without looking at all possible contributing factors. Another mistake was the assumption that fixing a particular error (eliminating the current software bug) would prevent future accidents. There is always another software bug.

Accidents are often blamed on a single cause like human error. But virtually all factors involved in accidents can be labeled human error, except perhaps for hardware wear-out failures. Even such hardware failure could be attributed to human error (for example, the designer's failure to provide adequate redundancy or the failure of operational personnel to properly maintain or replace parts): Concluding that an accident was the result of human error is not very helpful or meaningful.

It is nearly as useless to ascribe the cause of an accident to a computer error or a software error. Certainly software was involved in the Therac-25 accidents, but it was only one contributing factor. If we assign software error as *the* cause of the Therac-25 accidents, we are forced to conclude that the only way to prevent such accidents in the future is to build perfect software that will never behave in an unexpected or undesired way under any circumstances (which is clearly impossible) or not to use software at all in these types of systems. Both conclusions are overly pessimistic.

We must approach the problem of accidents in complex systems from a system-engineering point of view and consider all possible contributing factors. For the Therac-25 accidents, contributing factors included

- management inadequacies and lack of procedures for following through on all reported incidents,
- overconfidence in the software and removal of hardware interlocks (making the software into a single point of failure that could lead to an accident)

- presumably less-than-acceptable software-engineering practices, and
- unrealistic risk assessments along with overconfidence in the results of these assessments.

The exact same accident may not happen a second time, but if we examine and try to ameliorate the contributing factors to the accidents we have had, we may be able to prevent different accidents in the future. In the following sections, we present what we feel are important lessons learned from the Therac-25. You may draw different or additional conclusions.

System engineering   A common mistake in engineering, in this case and many others, is to put too much confidence in software. Nonsoftware professionals seem to feel that software will not or cannot fail; this attitude leads to complacency and overreliance on computerized functions. Although software is not subject to random wear-out failures like hardware, software design errors are much harder to find and eliminate. Furthermore, hardware failure modes are generally much more limited, so building protection against them is usually easier. A lesson to be learned from the Therac-25 accidents is not to remove standard hardware interlocks when adding computer control.

Hardware backups, interlocks, and other safety devices are currently being replaced by software in many different types of systems, including commercial aircraft, nuclear power plants, and weapon systems. Where the hardware interlocks are still used, they are often controlled by software. Designing any dangerous system in such a way that one failure can lead to an accident violates basic system-engineering principles. In this respect, software needs to be treated as a single component. Software should not be assigned sole responsibility for safety, and systems should not be designed such that a single software error or software-engineering error can be catastrophic.

A related tendency among engineers is to ignore software. The first safety analysis on the Therac-25 did not include software (although nearly full responsibility for safety rested on the software). When problems started occurring, investigators assumed that hardware was the cause and focused only on the hardware. Investigation of software's possible contribution to an accident should not be the last avenue explored after all other possible explanations are eliminated.

In fact, a software error can always be attributed to a transient hardware failure, since software (in these types of process-control systems) reads and issues commands to actuators. Without a thorough investigation (and without online monitoring or audit trails that save internal state information), it is not possible to determine whether the sensor provided the wrong information, the software provided an incorrect command, or the actuator had a transient failure and did the wrong thing on its own. In the Hamilton accident, a transient microswitch failure was assumed to be the cause, even though the engineers were unable to reproduce the failure or find anything wrong with the microswitch.

Patient reactions were the only real indications of the seriousness of the problems with the Therac-25. There were no independent checks that the software was operating correctly (including software checks). Such verification cannot be assigned to operators without providing them with some means of detecting errors. The Therac-25 software "lied" to the operators, and the machine itself could not detect that a massive overdose had occurred. The Therac-25 ion chambers could not handle the high density of ionization from the unscanned electron beam at high-beam current; they thus became saturated and gave an indication of a low dosage. Engineers need to design for the worst case.

Every company building safety-critical systems should have audit trails and incident-analysis procedures that they apply whenever they find any hint of a problem that might lead to an accident. The first phone call by Still should have led to an extensive investigation of the events at Kennestone. Certainly, learning about the first lawsuit should have triggered an immediate response. Although hazard logging and tracking is required in the standards for safety-critical military projects, it is less common in non-military projects. Every company building hazardous equipment should have hazard logging and tracking as well as incident reporting and analysis as parts of its quality control procedures. Such follow-up and tracking will not only help prevent accidents, but will easily pay for themselves in reduced insurance rates and reasonable settlement of lawsuits when they do occur.

Finally, overreliance on the numerical output of safety analyses is unwise. The arguments over whether very low probabilities are meaningful with respect to safety are too extensive to summarize here. But, at the least, a healthy skepticism is in order. The claim that safety had been increased five orders of magnitude as a result of the microswitch fix after the Hamilton accident seems hard to justify. Perhaps it was based on the probability of failure of the microswitch (typically 10^{-5})ANDed with the other interlocks. The problem with all such analyses is that they exclude aspects of the problem (in this case, software) that are difficult to quantify but which may have a larger impact on safety than the quantifiable factors that are included.

Although management and regulatory agencies often press engineers to obtain such numbers, engineers should insist that any risk assessment numbers used are in fact meaningful and that statistics of this sort are treated with caution. In our enthusiasm to provide measurements, we should not attempt to measure the unmeasurable. William Ruckelshaus, two-time head of the US Environmental Protection Agency, cautioned that "risk assessment data can be like the captured spy; if you torture it long enough, it will tell you anything you want to know."[7] E.A. Ryder of the British Health and Safety Executive has written that the numbers game in risk assessment "should only be played in private between consenting adults, as it is too easy to be misinterpreted."[8]

Software engineering   The Therac-25 accidents were fairly unique in having software coding errors involved—most computer-related accidents have not involved coding errors but rather errors in the software requirements such as omissions and mishandled environmental conditions and system states. Although using good basic software-engineering practices will not prevent all software errors, it is certainly required as a minimum. Some companies introducing software into their systems for the first time do not take software engineering as seriously as they should. Basic software-engineering principles that apparently were violated with the Therac-25 include:

- Documentation should not be an afterthought.
- Software quality assurance practices and standards should be established.
- Designs should be kept simple.
- Ways to get information about errors—for example, software audit trails—should be designed into the software from the beginning.
- The software should be subjected to extensive testing and formal analysis at the module and software level; system testing alone is not adequate.

In addition, special safety-analysis and design procedures must be incorporated into safety-critical software projects. Safety must be built into software, and, in addition, safety must be assured at the system level despite software errors.[9,10] The Therac-20 contained the same software error implicated in the Tyler deaths, but the machine included hardware interlocks that mitigated its consequences. Protection against software errors can also be built into the software itself.

Furthermore, important lessons about software reuse can be found here. A naive assumption is often made that reusing software or using commercial off-the-shelf software increases safety because the software has been exercised extensively. Reusing software modules does not guarantee safety in the new system to which they are transferred and sometimes leads to awkward and dangerous designs. Safety is a quality of the system in which the software is used; it is not a quality of the software itself. Rewriting the entire software to get a clean and simple design may be safer in many cases.

Taking a couple of programming courses or programming a home computer does not qualify anyone to produce safety-critical software. Although certification of software engineers is not yet required, more events like those associated with the Therac-25 will make such certification inevitable. There is activity in Britain to specify required courses for those working on critical software. Any engineer is not automatically qualified to be a software engineer—an extensive program of study and experience is required. Safety-critical software engineering requires training and experience in addition to that required for noncritical software.

Although the user interface of the Therac-25 has attracted a lot of attention, it was really a side issue in the accidents. Certainly, it could have been improved, like many other aspects of this software. Either software engineers need better training in interface design, or more input is needed from human factors engineers. There also needs to be greater recognition of potential conflicts between user-friendly interfaces and safety. One goal of interface design is to make the interface as easy as possible for the operator to use. But in the Therac-25, some design features (for example, not requiring the operator to reenter patient prescriptions after mistakes) and later changes (allowing a carriage return to indicate that information has been entered correctly) enhanced usability at the expense of safety.

Finally, not only must safety be considered in the initial design of the software and its operator interface, but the reasons for design decisions should be recorded so that decisions are not inadvertently undone in future modifications.

User and government oversight and standards   Once the FDA got involved in the Therac-25, their response was impressive, especially considering how little experience they had with similar problems in computerized medical devices. Since the Therac-25 events, the FDA has moved to improve the reporting system and to augment their procedures and guidelines to include software. The problem of deciding when to forbid the use of medical devices that are also saving lives has no simple answer and involves ethical and political issues that cannot be answered by science or engineering alone. However, at the least, better procedures are certainly required for reporting problems to the FDA and to users.

The issues involved in regulation of risky technology are complex. Overly strict standards can inhibit progress, require techniques behind the state of the art, and transfer responsibility from the manufacturer to the government. The fixing of responsibility requires a delicate balance. Someone must represent the public's needs, which may be subsumed by a company's desire for profits. On the other hand, standards can have the undesirable effect of limiting the safety efforts and investment of companies that feel their legal and moral responsibilities are fulfilled if they follow the standards.

Some of the most effective standards and efforts for safety come from users. Manufacturers have more incentive to satisfy customers than to satisfy government agencies. The American Association of Physicists in Medicine established a task group to work on problems associated with computers in radiation therapy in 1979, long before the Therac-25 problems began. The accidents intensified these efforts, and the association is developing user-written standards. A report by J.A. Rawlinson of the Ontario Cancer Institute attempted to define the physicist's role in assuring adequate safety in medical accelerators:

> We could continue our traditional role, which has been to provide input to the manufacturer on safety issues but to leave the major safety design decisions to the manufacturer. We can provide this input through a number of mechanisms. . . These include participation in standards organizations such as the IEC [International Electrotechnical Commission], in professional association groups . . . and in accelerator user groups such as the Therac-25 user group. It includes also making use of the Problem Reporting Program for Radiation Therapy Devices . . . and it includes consultation in the drafting of the government safety regulations. Each of these if pursued vigorously will go a long way to improving safety. It is debatable however whether these actions would be sufficient to prevent a future series of accidents.
>
> Perhaps what is needed in addition is a mechanism by which the safety of any new model of accelerator is assessed independently of the manufacturer. This task could be done by the individual physicist at the time of acceptance of a new machine. Indeed many users already test at least the *operation* of safety interlocks during commissioning. Few however have the time or resources to conduct a comprehensive assessment of safety *design*.
>
> A more effective approach might be to require that prior to the use of a new type of accelerator in a particular jurisdiction, an independent safety analysis is made by a panel (including but not limited to medical physicists). Such a panel could be established within or without a regulatory framework.[1]

It is clear that users need to be involved. It was users who found the problems with the Therac-25 and forced AECL to respond. The process of fixing the Therac-25 was user driven—the manufacturer was slow to respond. The Therac-25 user group meetings were, according to participants, important to the resolution of the problems. But if users are to be involved, then they must be provided with information and the ability to perform this function. Manufacturers need to understand that the adversarial approach and the attempt to keep government agencies and users in the dark about problems will not be to their benefit in the long run.

The US Air Force has one of the most extensive programs to inform users. Contractors who build space systems for the Air Force must provide an Accident Risk Assessment Report (AFAR) to system users and operators that describes the hazardous subsystems and operations associated with that system and its interfaces. The AFAR also comprehensively identifies and evaluates the system's accident risks; provides a means of substantiating compliance with safety requirements; summarizes all system safety analyses and testing performed on each system and subsystem; and identifies design and operating limits to be imposed on system components to preclude or minimize accidents that could cause injury or damage.

An interesting requirement in the Air Force AFAR is a record of all safety-related failures or accidents associated with system acceptance, test, and check-out, along with an assessment of the impact on flight and ground safety and action taken to prevent recurrence. The AFAR also must address failures, accidents, or incidents from previous missions of this system or other systems using similar hardware. All corrective action taken to prevent recurrence must be documented. The accident and correction history must be updated throughout the life of the system. If any design or operating parameters change after government approval, the AFAR must be updated to include all changes affecting safety.

Unfortunately, the Air Force program is not practical for commercial systems. However, government agencies might require manufacturers to provide similar information to users. If required for everyone, competitive pressures to withhold information might be lessened. Manufacturers might find that providing such information actually increases customer loyalty and confidence. An emphasis on safety can be turned into a competitive advantage.

Most previous accounts of the Therac-25 accidents blamed them on a software error and stopped there. This is not very useful and, in fact, can be misleading and dangerous: If we are to prevent such accidents in the future, we must dig deeper. Most accidents involving complex technology are caused by a combination of organizational, managerial, technical, and, sometimes, sociological or political factors. Preventing accidents requires paying attention to *all* the root causes, not just the precipitating event in a particular circumstance.

Accidents are unlikely to occur in exactly the same way again. If we patch only the symptoms and ignore the deeper underlying causes or we fix only the specific cause of one accident, we are unlikely to prevent or mitigate future accidents. The series of accidents involving the Therac-25 is a good example of exactly this problem: Fixing each individual software flaw as it was found did not solve the device's safety problems. Virtually all complex software will behave in an unexpected or undesired fashion under some conditions—there will always be another bug. Instead, accidents must be understood with respect to the complex factors involved. In addition, changes need to be made to eliminate or reduce the underlying causes and contributing factors that increase the likelihood of accidents or loss resulting from them.

Although these accidents occurred in software controlling medical devices, the lessons apply to all types of systems where computers control dangerous devices. In our experience, the same types of mistakes are being made in nonmedical systems. We must learn from our mistakes so we do not repeat them.

ACKNOWLEDGMENTS

Ed Miller of the FDA was especially helpful, both in providing information to be included in this article and in reviewing and commenting on the final version. Gordon Symonds of the Canadian Government Health Protection Branch also reviewed and commented on a draft of the article. Finally, the referees, several of whom were apparently intimately involved in some of the accidents, were also very helpful in providing additional information about the accidents.

REFERENCES

The information in this article was gathered from official FDA documents and internal memos, lawsuit depositions, letters, and various other sources that are not publicly available. *Computer* does not provide references to documents that are unavailable to the public.

1. J. A. Rawlinson, "Report on the Therac-25," OCTRF/OCI Physicists Meeting, Kingston, Ont., Canada, May 7, 1987.
2. F. Houston, "What Do the Simple Folk Do?: Software Safety in the Cottage Industry," *IEEE Computers in Medicine Conf.*, 1985.

3. C. A. Bowsher, "Medical Devices: The Public Health at Risk," US Gov't Accounting Office Report GAO/T-PEMD-90-2, 046987/139922, 1990.

4. M. Kivel, ed., *Radiological Health Bulletin,* Vol. XX, No. 8, US Federal Food and Drug Administration, Dec. 1986.

5. *Medical Device Recalls, Examination of Selected Cases,* GAO/PEMD-90-6, 1989.

6. E. Miller, "The Therac-25 Experience," *Proc. Conf., State Radiation Control Program Directors,* 1987.

7. W. D. Ruckelshaus, "Risk in a Free Society," *Risk Analysis,* Vol. 4, No. 3, 1984, pp. 157–162.

8. E. A. Ryder, "The Control of Major Hazards: The Advisory Committee's Third and Final Report," *Transcript of Conf. European Major Hazards,* Oyez Scientific and Technical Services and Authors, London, 1984.

9. N.G. Leveson, "Software Safety: Why, What, and How," *ACM Computing Surveys,* Vol. 18, No. 2, June 1986, pp. 25–69.

10. N.G. Leveson, "Software Safety in Embedded Computer Systems," *Comm. ACM,* Feb. 1991, pp.34–46.

Ethics and Information Systems: The Corporate Domain

JOHN HASNAS

⠿ Introduction

> Despite the explosion in information technology . . . in the last 20 years, scholars, students, and practitioners would be hard-pressed to claim similar progress in ethical thinking about information technology. There is an ethical vacuum in cyberspace (Laudon 1995, p. 33).

Information systems (IS) are enabling an increasing number of corporate initiatives—efforts aimed at improved efficiency, effectiveness, or strategic advantage of the firm (Cash et al. 1992). However, many of these applications are being embraced in an ethical environment that harbors vast areas of ambiguity—spaces in which there are often no explicit or agreed-upon rules with respect to appropriate and inappropriate behaviors (Johnson 1989). Consider, for example, a quandary faced by one company in the early 1990s.

Blockbuster's Quandary

On December 26, 1990, an article in the *Wall Street Journal,* titled "Coming Soon to Your Local Video Store: Big Brother," castigated the Blockbuster Entertainment Corporation chain for a reported plan to categorize its 30 million customers according to the types of movies they rented and to "sell information from the data base . . . to direct mailers, for planning target-marketing campaigns." The article explained:

> Many businesses commonly sell their customer lists, but Blockbuster is one of a small fraction using sophisticated computers to keep records of each individual's transactions. Its data base promises to raise some especially difficult pri-

---

"Ethics and Information Systems: The Corporate Domain" by H. J. Smith and J. Hasnas, *MIS Quarterly,* Vol. 23, No. 1, September 1999, pp. 109–127. Copyright © 1999 by the Management Information Systems Research Center (ISRC) of the University of Minnesota. Reprinted by permission.
[1]Allen Lee was the accepting senior editor for this paper.

vacy issues, for the same reason it should be such a gold mine for direct mailers: Video choices are among the most revealing decisions a consumer makes.

A . . . federal law forbids video stores to disclose the names of movies its customers rent. But the law permits stores to tell direct marketers "the subject matter" of movies a customer has rented.

Blockbuster, whose members represent one out of six American households, says its data base will be legal because it will only monitor video categories, not specific titles. The chain currently organizes its shelves by 37 categories, and plans to add as many as 30 to 40 more. . . .

Direct-marketers are ravenous for information about consumers' taste and life styles, because such data help pinpoint targets for expensive mail campaigns. Blockbuster envisions selling lists of mystery movie renters to mystery book clubs, kids movie renters to toy stores, classics renters to senior-citizen marketers, and many such other matches.

"I can turn around and promote all the John Wayne names to the national Republican Party," says Allan Caplan, the Blockbuster vice president overseeing the database project. "We not only will know their tastes in movies—we'll know their frequency and that will give us a little more information about their life style" (Miller 1990, p. 9).

While the technical question of *legality* seemed moot in this case—indeed, the law seemed to allow such a sale of customer data, categorized by movie type—many indicated concerns about the *ethical* issues involved. "The basic principle is that information collected for one purpose shouldn't be used for another purpose without an individual's consent," noted one observer (Miller 1990, p. 10). Confronted with negative publicity about the endeavor, Blockbuster's executives might well have asked: what are our ethical obligations with respect to this database? As will be seen later in this paper, there are three different theoretical answers to this question.

Ethical Ambiguity in the IS Domain

Just as the Blockbuster executives discovered, there is a vast terrain of unexplored ethical territory through which many IS applications must travel. Such ambiguity is often rebounding against well-intentioned, strategic initiatives, and Blockbuster is not the only company to have encountered a negative response (see Culnan and Smith 1995). In addition, IS professionals have been taken to task for their behavior in well-publicized systems development failures. Greyhound's attempt to re-engineer its reservation and tracking systems with a complex software tool, "Trips," ended in abject failure, has driven the company into a financial tailspin, and has resulted in the departure of many senior executives. Perhaps the most troubling aspect of the story is that some IS executives were aware of the problems with the project but, when senior executives dismissed their concerns, the IS executives did not pursue the issue further, even though the system was being touted in support of a major stock offering (Tomsho 1994). Similarly, it was noted that the very visible failure of the CONFIRM project at AMR Information Services (a subsidiary of the American Airlines Corporation)—which ultimately resulted in a 125 million dollar writeoff—was in some measure the result of IS developers' reluctance to raise their concerns about the project to an appropriate level in the corporation:

In a letter to employees, Max Hopper, American Airlines Information Services chief, wrote: "Some people who have been part of CONFIRM management did not disclose the true status of the project in a timely manner. This has created more difficult problems—of both business ethics and finance—than would have existed if those people had come forward with accurate information. Honesty is an imperative in our business—it is an ethical and technical imperative" (Oz 1994b, p. 29).

Ethical Leadership: Previous Perspectives

It is becoming apparent that the ethical dimensions of IS-related business decisions cannot be safely ignored. Against this backdrop, growing attention is being paid to ethics in IS curricula, and major IS journals are devoting an increasing amount of space to deeper analysis of such issues (see, for example, Collins et al. 1994; Culnan 1993; Loch et al. 1992; Loch and Conger 1996; Milberg et al. 1995; Oz 1992, 1994b; Smith 1993; Straub and Collins 1990; Weisband and Reinig 1995). A number of authors have addressed various subsets of the domain of IS ethics by assessing which actions are perceived by various subjects as ethical or unethical in a series of behavioral vignettes (e.g., see Brookshire et al. 1994; Parker 1979; Parker et al. 1990). Others have developed or inferred theoretical frameworks which have guided ethical assessments in either laboratory or field settings (e.g., Culnan 1993; Smith 1993).

Another group of pioneering works includes appeals to traditional philosophical theories as a framework for ethical decision making in IS environs (for example, see Johnson 1994; Kallman and Grillo 1996; Laudon 1995; Mason et al. 1995; Milberg et al. 1995; Oz 1994a; Smith 1994). These approaches, which often include references to "deontological" and "teleological" theories,[2] utilize perspectives on ethical decision making that have been honed by philosophers through centuries of debate. While there is no consensus with respect to the correctness of these opposing theories, their use by IS ethicists has certainly increased the rigor of analysis and provided a substantive framework for debate.

A thorough reading of the major IS ethical works to date reveals a consistent theme: Most of the IS ethical quandaries are set in *corporate business environs,* in which the decision maker is forced to make an ethical decision not as a free agent but, instead, as an agent of a corporate body. The same boundary is adopted in this paper by focusing on those quandaries and decisions that occur in a corporate domain and that, therefore, can be addressed by the field of business ethics.

Focus of This Paper

This paper has as its goal the examination and critique of the normative theories of business ethics as applied to the IS arena. The paper has as its primary audience those in the business community who are confronting IS-related ethical quandaries. Secondarily, the paper may also provide insights to those in the IS academic community who are conducting research into IS ethical issues. In this light, the specific goals of this paper are threefold: (1) to clearly explain the competing normative theories of business ethics, (2) to link these theories to IS ethical issues and show, by examining the Blockbuster situation in depth, how they can be applied, and (3) to consider the challenges managers and the IS community face in confronting ethical quandaries. Managerial challenges include not only the selection of an existing theory of business ethics or the formulation of a new theory of business ethics, but also the application of theory. The IS community faces the additional challenge of creating systemic mechanisms to increase consistency with theoretical proscriptions. The following sections and subsections correspond to these major goals and the subordinate issues.

---

[2]The deontological approach holds that the ethical quality of an action is determined, at least in part, by what type of action it is, and not exclusively on the basis of its consequences. The teleological approach holds that the ethical quality of an action is determined solely on the basis of its consequences.

▪▪▪ Normative Theories of Business Ethics[3]

Many of the ethical quandaries in the IS domain are complex ones, filled with apparently conflicting responsibilities on the part of a professional, manager, or executive. Traditional philosophical approaches to ethics (e.g., deontology and teleology) can be directly applied to the quandaries, but it is generally argued by business ethicists that this strategy has significant weaknesses for those quandaries that occur within the boundaries of a corporation (see, for example, Stark 1993). To some extent, this is due to the defects in the philosophical theories themselves. However, to a much greater extent, the problem with attempting to apply these theories directly to ethical issues in business is that they are expressed in language not easily accessible to non-philosophers. As has been observed,

> People who have been trained in engineering, computer science, and management information systems, frequently have little training in ethics, philosophy, and moral reasoning. Without a vocabulary with which to think and talk about what constitutes an ethical computing issue, it is difficult to have the necessary discussions to develop social norms (Conger and Loch 1995, p. 36).

Unfortunately, the doctrines of philosophical ethics are highly abstract and are essentially meaningless to one with little or no philosophical training.

These problems with the traditional approach have led business ethicists to develop "normative theories of business ethics" (NTBEs) (Hasnas 1998). These theories attempt to derive what might be called "intermediate level" ethical principles—principles expressed in language accessible to the ordinary business person and which can be applied to the concrete moral quandaries of the business domain. The NTBEs focus exclusively upon interactions that involve *business* relationships. Because they are *normative,* they define obligations that managers "should" or "ought" to fulfill, and they can be distinguished from *descriptive* statements, which describe how the world "is."

The three leading NTBEs are the stockholder, stakeholder, and social contract theories. Each specifies a different set of responsibilities for managers, and these accounts of one's ethical obligations are ultimately incompatible. Thus, no more than one of them can be correct. In what follows, each of these theories is briefly described, its supporting rationale is commented upon, and some common objections to the theory are examined. (See Figure 1 and the "Ethical Obligations" section of Table 1.)

Stockholder Theory

The first NTBE is the stockholder theory. According to this theory, the stockholders advance capital to the managers, who act as their agents in realizing specified ends. Under this view, managers are agents of the stockholders. In this role, they are required to spend corporate funds only in ways that have been authorized by the stockholders. Of course, managers may spend their *personal* funds on any socially beneficial project they wish, but *when functioning in their corporate capacity,* managers have a duty to expend funds only as authorized by the stockholders (Friedman 1997; see also Bowie

---

[3]These theories are also referred to as "theories of corporate social responsibility" by some authors (e.g., Jones 1980). This paper adopts the clearer moniker "normative theories of business ethics" as embraced by Hasnas (1998), who targets business ethicists and philosophers as his primary audience and who concentrates on the derivations of the theories at an abstract level. The present effort goes beyond Hasnas by focusing on the IS ethical domain, embracing a much more practical perspective toward the theories by targeting IS professionals as its audience (and, in the process, making the theories more accessible to non-philosophers), and addressing the challenges associated with the theories.

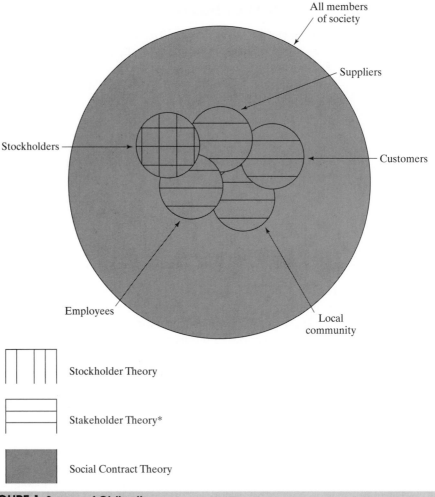

Stockholder Theory

Stakeholder Theory*

Social Contract Theory

▪▪▪▪▪▪▪▪▪▪▪▪ **FIGURE 1** Scope of Obligation

*There could be other stakeholders for whom obligations also exist; shown above are those who are specifically denoted as being vitally affected by Even and Freeman (1988).

and Freeman 1992, pp. 3–21). Since stockholders normally purchase shares so as to maximize their return on investment, the stockholder theory is often considered simply as a managerial obligation to maximize the financial returns to the stockholders. As Milton Friedman wrote,

> There is one and only one social responsibility of business—to use its resources and engage in activities designed to increase its profits so long as it stays within the rules of the game, which is to say, engages in open and free competition, without deception or fraud (Friedman 1962, p. 133).

There are two points that are important to keep in mind when considering the stockholder theory. First, the stockholder theory obligates managers to increase corporate profitability only through *legal, non-deceptive means* (Friedman 1997, pp. 56, 61). Second, although not specifically codified by Friedman, the stockholder theory is generally viewed as having a *long-term* orientation. It directs managers not to seek short-term financial health but to maximize corporate profits in the long run.

TABLE 1 Summary of Theories

	Stockholder Theory	Stakeholder Theory	Social Contract Theory
Ethical Obligations	* Conform to laws and regulations * Avoid fraud and deception * Maximize profits	* Determine who are relevant stakeholders * Determine rights of each; reject options that violate these * Accept remaining option that best balances interest of stakeholders	* Reject actions that are fraudulent/deceptive, dehumanize employees, or involve invidious discrimination * Eliminate options that reduce welfare of society's members * Choose remaining option that maximizes probability of financial success
Challenges to Managers	* Keep up with legal landscape in light of shifting technological trends * Determine mechanisms for avoiding fraud and deception * Predict outcomes of alternatives	* Determine who "stakeholders" are in internetworked, distributed environment * Determine legal and moral rights for each stakeholder * Create mechanisms for defining and respecting stakeholders' interests * Determine algorithm for balancing stakeholder interest	* Determine mechanisms for avoiding fraud and deception * Determine which options might dehumanize employees (a subjective concept) * Determine which options are truly discriminatory * Assess both tangible and intangible concepts of well-being * Create projects that meet other criteria but are still profitable

There are two different moral arguments associated with the stockholder theory. First, there is a teleological argument that is often used by free market economists. If individuals pursue profits, according to Adam Smith's theory, they will also be promoting the interests of society (see Evan and Freeman 1988; Quinn and Jones 1995). However, critics argue that because the market tends to produce coercive monopolies and damaging externalities and is beset by instances of market failure, the private pursuit of profit simply cannot be relied upon to secure the common good (Evan and Freeman 1988).

Second, there is another moral argument, which is deontological in nature, that we believe to be more compelling. If managers accept the stockholders' money and then proceed to spend it to accomplish goals not authorized by the stockholders, they would be spending other people's money without their consent, which is wrong (Friedman 1962, p. 135). Such an action would violate Kant's (1804/1981, p. 35) principle that persons have "absolute worth," which holds that one who breaches an agreement that induced another to deal with him or her is treating the other merely as a means to his or her own ends rather than as an end in himself or herself (Kant 1804/1981, p. 37). The most common objection to this moral argument is that it can be morally appropriate to spend other people's money without their consent as long as it is done to promote the public interest (Donaldson 1982, 1989). However, it appears that the supporters of the stockholder theory could reasonably claim that this objection misses the point of their argument.

Stakeholder Theory

The second main NTBE is the stakeholder theory. This theory asserts that managers have a fiduciary duty not merely to the corporation's stockholders, but to the corporation's stakeholders—anyone who has "a stake in or claim on the firm" (Evan and Freeman 1988, p. 97). Although the term "stakeholder" has been defined in the past to include any group or individual who can affect or is affected by the corporation, it is currently understood in a narrower sense as referring only to those groups that are either *vital* to the survival and success of the corporation or whose interests are *vitally* affected by the corporation. Such groups typically include stockholders, customers, employees, suppliers, and the local community,[4] although in many instances it may include others who are vitally concerned as well. According to the stakeholder theory, managers have a fiduciary duty to give equal consideration to the legitimate interests of all such stakeholders and to adopt corporate policies which produce the optimal balance among them without violating the rights of any stakeholder (Even and Freeman 1988).

Ironically, the stakeholder theory claims to be based on the same Kantian principle of respect for persons as was the stockholder theory—that every human being is entitled to be treated as an end in himself or herself rather than merely as a means to some other end. To respect someone as an end is to recognize that he or she is an autonomous moral agent, with desires of his or her own and the free will to act upon those desires. Thus, the principle of respect for persons requires respect for the autonomy of others. Stakeholder theory applies this principle by claiming that corporate managers are bound to respect it as much as anyone else. This means that managers may not treat their corporation's stakeholders merely as means to corporate ends but must recognize that all stakeholders are entitled to "agree to and hence participate (or choose not to participate) in the decisions to be used as such" (Evan and Freeman

---

[4]Obviously, there could be some overlap among these stakeholder groups, although the theory does not explore this point or offer any algorithm for addressing it.

1988, p. 100). Stakeholder theorists argue that this implies that all stakeholders are entitled to "participate in determining the future direction of the firm in which they have a stake" (Evan and Freeman 1988, p. 97). However, because all of the firm's stakeholders cannot be consulted for every decision, the firm's management has an obligation to "act in the interests of the stakeholders as their agent" (Evan and Freeman 1988, p. 103) by giving equal consideration to the interests of all stakeholder groups in corporate decision making and to choose a course of action that will achieve an optimal balance among the conflicting claims of these groups.

Although the stakeholder theory currently enjoys a great deal of popularity, the adequacy of its supporting argument has been questioned (Donaldson and Preston 1995), and we must agree that there is a gap in the reasoning. Even if one concedes that corporations are ethically bound to treat all stakeholders as ends in themselves and, hence, that all stakeholders are entitled to "agree to and hence participate (or choose not to participate) in the decisions to be used" (Evan and Freeman 1988, p. 100) by the corporation, this claim appears to imply only that no stakeholder may be forced to deal with the corporation without his or her consent. It seems incorrect to assert that respect for another's autonomy requires that he or she have a say in any decision that affects his or her interests. For example, a student's interests may be crucially affected by what grade he or she receives in a course, but the student's autonomy is not violated when he or she is denied a say in that decision. Until contemporary stakeholder theorists can close this gap in their supporting argument, we believe the adequacy of the stakeholder theory will remain an open question.

Social Contract Theory

The third NTBE is the social contract theory,[5] which derives the social responsibilities of corporate managers from what people would agree to in a society with no corporations or other complex business arrangements (i.e., a state of "individual production;" Donaldson 1982, p. 44). Social contract theorists ask what conditions would have to be met for the members of such a society to agree to allow corporations to be formed. The ethical obligations toward the individual members of society are then derived from the terms of this agreement.

In granting corporations the right to exist, the members of society give them legal recognition as a single agent and authorize them to own and use land and natural resources and to hire the members of society as employees. Social contract theorists argue that the minimum the members of society would demand in return is "that the benefits from authorizing the existence of productive organizations outweigh the detriments of doing so" (Donaldson 1982, p. 44). In general, this would mean that corporations would be required to "enhance the welfare of society through the satisfaction of consumer and worker interests, in a way which relies on exploiting corporations' special advantages and minimizing disadvantages" (Donaldson 1982, p. 54) while *remaining* "within the bounds of the general canons of justice" (Donaldson 1982, p. 57).

This hypothetical agreement may be thought of as giving rise to social contracts with two terms: the social welfare term and the justice term. The social welfare term recognizes that the members of society will be willing to authorize corporate existence

---

[5]The social contract theory is really a family of closely related theories and, in some ways, is still in process of formation. A complex and highly sophisticated version of the theory called Integrative Social Contracts Theory (Donaldson and Dunfee 1994) has recently been introduced, and those authors are presently in the process of developing a book-length exposition of the theory. Because any attempt to address this recent work would be well beyond the scope of the present enterprise, consideration is being restricted to the more basic and widely accepted version of social contract theory.

only if they gain by doing so. Thus, managers are obligated to pursue corporate profit only in ways likely to enhance the material well-being of society as a whole, specifically, in ways likely to enhance the material well-being of the members of society in their capacity as consumers and employees.

The justice term recognizes that the members of society will be willing to authorize corporate existence only if corporations agree to remain within the bounds of the general canons of justice. Although what these canons are is far from settled, social contract theorists assert that there is general agreement that the least they require is that corporate managers "avoid fraud and deception . . . show respect for their workers as human beings, and . . . avoid any practice that systematically worsens the situation of a given group in society," i.e., refrain from invidious discrimination (Donaldson 1982, p. 53).

The social contract theory is criticized on the ground that the "social contract" is not a contract at all (Kultgen 1985). There has been no true meeting of the minds between those who decide to incorporate and the other members of the society, and most people who form corporations would be surprised to learn that they had contractually agreed to serve society's interests in ways that can reduce the profitability of their firm. Since to enter into a contractual arrangement one must at least be aware one is doing so, the critics of the theory maintain that the social contract is a fiction rather than a true contract.

Social contract theorists freely admit that the social contract is a fictional or hypothetical contract, but they claim that this is precisely what is required: "If the contract were something other than a fiction it would be inadequate for the purpose at hand: namely revealing the moral foundations of productive organizations" (Donaldson 1989, p. 56). They argue that the moral force of the social contract is not derived from the consent of the parties but from its underlying moral theory (Donaldson 1989, p. 61). The problem with this response is that it merely pushes the inquiry back one level. The acceptability of the social contract theory now turns on the acceptability of the underlying moral theot to be clearly articulated and defended. Therefore, until this defense is provided, we believe that the adequacy of the social contract theory remains an open question.

Looking Across the Theories

The three NTBEs—stockholder, stakeholder, and social contract—have distinct and, for the most part, incompatible perspectives on issues of normative business ethics. Even so, the theories are consistent on two important dimensions.

Consider the first such dimension: their domain of application. These theories were specifically designed to provide ethical guidance to individuals working for profit-seeking businesses in a market environment. They can be relied upon to provide the proper resolution to ethical quandaries *only in this context*. These theories cannot be properly applied to corporate entities such as government agencies, non-profit companies, or other organizations such as universities or hospitals whose primary function is not to earn a profit. They certainly cannot be applied to any organization functioning in a non-market, communal, or socialistic environment. One might think of the theories as ethical "lenses" designed to focus the principles of philosophical ethics exclusively on for-profit businesses in capitalist societies.

The three NTBEs are also consistent on a second dimension: the essential purpose of the theories. These theories are designed to provide ethical guidance to *individuals* functioning in the business environment. This means that their purpose is to give business people an *independent* standard by which they may not only decide how to act themselves, but also to assess the ethical quality of the orders of their business superiors as well as the firm's policies, culture, and code of conduct.

By thus functioning as a guide to individual conscience, the theories are external to any value system the company intentionally or unintentionally attempts to instill in its employees. In fact, each theory may be viewed as an attempt to supply the ethical standard by which any such value system should itself be judged. Of course, in many cases, a particular manager's ethical conclusions may not match those of an organization's senior managers or its cultural norms. In such situations, the manager must resolve the inconsistency by prodding the organization and its executives to modify the norms by exercising "voice" procedures (see Bies and Shapiro 1988) or, in more extreme situations, by "blowing the whistle" (see Miceli and Near 1992) or exiting the organization (see Farrell 1983).

With these points in mind, the paper now examines how these theories would be applied to IS-related ethical quandaries.

▪▪▪ Applying the Theories: Blockbuster Revisited

The Blockbuster scenario is now considered as an illustration of the theories' applicability. Each NTBE prescribes a different ethical response and presents a different set of challenges for the Blockbuster executives.

Stockholder Theory

Under the stockholder theory, Blockbuster should probably *market personal data about its customers.* As long as the sale (1) is legal, (2) involves no deceptive practices, and (3) is likely to increase Blockbuster's profits, Blockbuster's management would not only be ethically permitted to sell the information, but is under an ethical obligation to do so. Since the proposed sale does not violate the federal statute prohibiting the disclosure of the names of the movies rented by Blockbusters' customers (and because very few state or local ordinances apply to this case), it does not appear to run afoul of the stockholder theory's constraint against illegal activity. Furthermore, as long as Blockbuster employs no deceptive or misleading practices in acquiring the information, it will not violate the theory's constraint against fraud and deception. Finally, if the stockholders have neither explicitly nor implicitly instructed the management not to engage in such behavior and if the sale is, in fact, likely to increase the corporation's long-term financial health, it would appear to be precisely the type of action that would help realize the goal of the stockholder theory. Hence, Blockbuster's management would have an ethical obligation to market the information.

Stakeholder Theory

If the stakeholder theory is applied, the answer regarding ethical obligations is *it depends on the particular facts of the situation.* Functioning once again under the assumption that Blockbuster structures the sale so that it is neither deceptive nor misleading, it would not seem to violate the constraint of the stakeholder theory, which prohibits violating the rights of any stakeholder.[6] The question then becomes whether pursuing the sale would produce the optimal balance among the legitimate interests of all of Blockbuster's stakeholders. This, however, will turn on certain empirical considerations that cannot be determined in the abstract.

To make this determination, Blockbuster's management must begin by identifying the stakeholders whose interests would be affected by the proposed sale. In this case,

---

[6]While it could be argued that individuals have a general right to control what others know about them, such a right does not have wide support among ethicists (see Schoeman 1984).

neither Blockbuster's suppliers, employees, nor the local communities served by its stores appear to have anything significant at stake.[7] Thus, the only stakeholders whose interests must be considered are Blockbuster's stockholders, who stand to benefit financially from the sale, its ordinary customers, whose preferences comprise the information to be sold, and its potential new customers, who are interested in purchasing this information. Giving each of these groups equal consideration, Blockbuster's management must now attempt to choose the course of action that produces the optimal balance among their legitimate interests. This, of course, will depend on the particular benefits and costs the sale will impose upon each.

For example, assume the proposed sale will (1) marginally increase Blockbuster's profits, slightly enhancing returns to the stockholders, (2) provide a small benefit to the purchasers of the information, but (3) seriously inconvenience or even offend Blockbuster's ordinary customers while providing them little control over their personal information. Under such circumstances, it is extremely likely that the sale would not be ethically justified. However, assume that the sale (1) will significantly increase the company's profitability, greatly enhancing returns to the stockholders, (2) represents a major business innovation of great value to the purchasers of the information, and (3) is structured to produce only minor inconveniences to Blockbuster's ordinary customers while allowing them to retain what they themselves would deem to be sufficient control over how the information is used. Under these circumstances, it is extremely likely that the sale would be ethically acceptable. Thus, under the stakeholder theory, the ethical quality of the sale will depend upon an empirical evaluation of the nature and intensity of the costs it imposes on Blockbuster's ordinary customers relative to the nature and intensity of the benefits it provides to Blockbuster's stockholders and potential customers for the information.

Social Contract Theory

In contrast, if the social contract theory is applied, Blockbuster would almost certainly have to *refrain from marketing the information*. This is because even if the transaction were structured so as to satisfy the justice term of the social contract, it still could not meet the social welfare term. If, as described above, care was taken to ensure that Blockbuster's actions were neither deceptive nor misleading to their customers, it would not violate the justice term since it would not involve fraudulent or deceptive behavior, the dehumanization of Blockbuster's employees, or invidious discrimination against a particular social group. However, it is difficult to see how the sale could be construed as meeting the social welfare term, which instructs managers to pursue corporate profits solely in ways that tend to enhance the material welfare of the members of society in their capacity as consumers and employees. The sale seems to provide no material benefit to Blockbuster's customers,[8] many of whom may greatly prefer that

---

[7]Obviously, the local community does include the Blockbuster customers. However, per our reading of Evan and Freeman (1988), the local community should be considered as a *whole* rather than as a collection of disparate units. In that light, it is unlikely that the overall community would suffer in any substantive way—certainly, it would not be harmed in the context often associated with a plant closing, for example.

[8]Some might argue that, since customers could receive information about other goods and services because their names are sold on the Blockbuster list, such improved information would constitute a "material benefit." The counter-argument, however, is that a customer might just as easily be excluded as included in new information flows based on the list's categorizations; that the customer might likely receive the same information eventually through some other channel; and that the receipt of such information, from whatever channel, would be unlikely to yield a *significant* improvement in the customer's well-being. In any event, no monetary advantage would accrue to the customer due to the sale of their information, since a system such as that described by Laudon (1996) and Hagel and Rayport (1997) does not yet exist.

information about their preferences remain secret, and is unlikely to affect the material well-being of Blockbuster's employees in any significant way. Unless there was good reason to believe that the information would be used only in ways that would produce material benefits to Blockbuster's customers or that the sale would have such a profound impact on the company's profitability that its employees would directly benefit, the social contract theory would hold that the sale is unethical.

Blockbuster in Context

As can be seen in the Blockbuster case, the three NTBEs will often prescribe very different ethical responses to a given set of facts. In the Blockbuster scenario, the stockholder theory would demand that the data be marketed, while the social contract theory would prohibit such marketing efforts. The stakeholder theory would require a much deeper assessment that included the calculation of costs and benefits.

The Blockbuster case provides an illustrative example of some of the ethical complexities facing managers who deal with the collection, use, and sharing of information. The next section moves to a more general exploration of managers' challenging ethical domain in the information age.

▪▪▪ Challenges to Managers

Managers who grapple with IS-related ethical quandaries face a number of challenges, explored in this section. First to be discussed is the overarching challenge that extends across the entire domain of IS ethics: choosing the right theory—a non-trivial endeavor for which there exist three different options. The challenges to managers in applying the specific theories that have been described are then considered. Finally, some special challenges for the IS community as it grapples with codes of ethical behavior are examined.

Choosing a Normative Theory of Business Ethics

The stockholder, stakeholder, and social contract theories each purport to provide an absolute standard of ethical behavior in the business environment. This paper has described all three because there is as yet no consensus as to which, if any, of the three is correct in a philosophical sense. Further, in a more descriptive sense, societal norms have not yet coalesced around a single vision of corporate social responsibility. Thus, individual managers must evaluate these arguments for themselves in order to determine which theory, if any, they will adopt as their *own* NTBE.

A common question from managers is: "Can my NTBE allow me the flexibility to embrace different perspectives (stockholder, stakeholder, or social contract) at different times, depending on the immediate issues under consideration?" Unfortunately for managers asking this question, the stockholder, stakeholder, and social contract theories' authors all adopt an absolutist perspective, in that they expect their theory to be viewed as a manager's NTBE for *all* the ethical quandaries faced in the business environment. The scope and specifics of obligation (Figure 1 and Table 1) apply to all ethical quandaries; a manager who embraces one of these theories as his or her NTBE is "locked in" to applying it without exception. To do anything else would be to violate the most valued philosophical principle of all: logical consistency (see Kant 1804/1981, pp. 30–33).

For example, were a manager to claim the stockholder theory as his or her NTBE, this would preclude the manager from making *any* decision that held no reasonable long-term expectation of benefits to the stockholders. As an illustration, this would preclude a manager from making a plant location decision that was grounded in "community interests" rather than in returns to stockholders. Similarly, were a manager to claim the social contract theory as his or her NTBE, this would preclude the manager from sidestepping the obligation to avoid actions that dehumanize employees—even if this led to a significant reduction in profits.

Thus, managers cannot logically view the stockholder, stakeholder, and social contract theories as entries on a menu, from which they simply choose one as their NTBE on certain occasions and a different one as their NTBE on others. Similarly, managers cannot logically embrace certain clauses of the theories while ignoring others, *unless they can proffer a logical argument that defends their choices in a theoretically consistent fashion.*

But, in light of this italicized condition, there are three legitimate options managers can consider as they formulate their own NTBEs: embracing an existing theory; modifying an existing theory; or creating an original NTBE.

Embracing an Existing Theory

Obviously, a manager may be quite convinced that the stockholder, stakeholder, or social contract theory is correct as presented and may adopt that theory as his or her own NTBE. If so, the manager's obligations are clear: to consistently apply that theory when resolving ethical quandaries in the business world.

Modifying an Existing Theory

A manager may be convinced that the fundamental arguments underlying either the stockholder, stakeholder, or social contract theory are correct, but certain components of the theory may not be consistent with the manager's philosophical perspective. If so, a manager can credibly modify the theory before adopting it as his or her NTBE *as long* as the manager can provide a logical defense of the modification.

For example, many managers find the stakeholder theory to be compelling, but they nevertheless disagree with the assertion that all stakeholder groups should have equal standing when interests are balanced. A manager might credibly argue that interests should be weighted according to some predetermined and defended criteria: as an illustration, one might claim that interests should be weighted according to the proportion of business risk that is borne by each stakeholder group. In such a case, stockholders would probably be seen as bearing the greatest risk, perhaps employees might be second, and so on. Similarly, a manager might argue that the present boundaries on the definition of a "stakeholder" are either too wide or too narrow: in the former case, one or more of the five stakeholder units in the current definition might lose their standing; in the latter case, additional stakeholder units (e.g., debt-holders) might be added. In our view, all of these modifications to the stakeholder theory can be logically defended almost as easily as the original theory, and a manager who embraced and articulated such defenses would be on sound philosophical footing in adopting a modified stakeholder theory as his or her NTBE.

Creating an Original NTBE

Finally, managers can move beyond the current domain of business ethics by crafting their own, original NTBEs, which may be unrelated to the stockholder, stakeholder, and social contract theories. There is no reason to believe that philosophers or business ethicists have a monopoly on the articulation or defense of normative theories.

For example, a manager might posit that normative obligations emanate from neither Kantian assertions regarding humanity nor from a contract between corporations and society. Rather, obligations might be grounded solely in what philosophers refer to as "virtue ethics"—that we should take those actions that make us more virtuous as individuals.[9] To date, none of the theories of normative business ethics has relied on this philosophical stream, but there is nothing to prohibit this approach. From this premise, a manager might develop a set of guiding principles that would lead to decisions, in a business context, that would in turn lead to a more virtuous life. Admittedly, this approach is much more abstract in its current form than are the previously articulated theories. However, a manager would be on a solid philosophical path in pursuing it—and this path is only one of many that could be followed.

A Broad Domain

The above examples of a modification and an original NTBE are intended as just that: examples. Obviously, to exhaustively list or defend all the possible options would be well beyond the scope of this paper and, indeed, would extend well beyond the existing boundaries of business ethics literature. Much work remains to be done by philosophers and business ethicists, and managers are well within their rights to challenge the ethicists' theories and to bring their own perspectives to the debates.

Applying the Specific Theories

As the previous section showed, managers have numerous options in choosing their own NTBE. However, at present, only the stockholder, stakeholder, and social contract theories have been clearly articulated in the business ethics literature. Thus, for the moment, the discussion returns to those three theories and considers the challenges associated with their application to IS-related quandaries. (See "Challenges to Managers" section of Table 1.)

Stockholder Theory

The challenges associated with the stockholder theory are threefold. First, with respect to the legal requirement, a manager will likely find it necessary to enlist corporate or outside counsel to review all federal, state, and local legislation and administrative mandates that may bear upon the proposed business activity. Such a challenge is particularly problematic for many IS activities, since the law is changing quickly—albeit in a reactive fashion—as the technological landscape shifts (Smith 1996), and new legislative mandates, particularly at the state level, seem to emerge almost daily.

Second, managers face a challenge in determining exactly *how* they will avoid deception and fraud in IS-related activities. In some cases, it might be argued that simply giving notice of intent to affected parties (e.g., telling customers that data would be used in a certain way after collection) might be enough. But how should such messages be communicated? This remains an area of ambiguity. To the extent that contractual negotiations surround a transaction, the terms could be spelled out clearly in the contract. However, in situations where no true negotiations take place, managers must decide between options such as placing notices on an application form, posting notices in a place of business, printing qualifications on the back of software packages, etc. Note, however, that managers have no ethical obligation, under the stockholder theory, to give affected parties any *control* over the terms of the relationship.

Third, managers face a tremendous challenge in many situations in predicting the outcomes that will ensue from the alternatives they are facing. Since the ultimate objective is to maximize long-term returns to shareholders, the manager must predict which actions will lead to the greatest revenue gains and/or smallest losses. This often

---

[9]This philosophical stream is most often associated with Aristotle (384 b.c./1985).

requires stochastic predictions regarding the probability of negative media attention, competitor reactions, customer backlashes, or legislative responses. While some amount of research can be undertaken to improve the estimation process, the cost of such research would, of course, also be a factor in the manager's decision making.

Stakeholder Theory

When the challenges associated with the stakeholder theory are considered, it becomes apparent why it often proves particularly problematic when applied to IS quandaries. First, it is often unclear just who constitute the "stakeholders" for an IS initiative. Certainly, the five traditional stakeholder groups often apply, but the stakeholder theory also provides for consideration of the interests of other parties who are "vital to the survival and success of the corporation" (Evan and Freeman 1988, p. 100). Trends in two technological areas—telecommunications and distributed databases—are enabling many new IS applications that cross organizational boundaries in complex patterns. As these interorganizational systems proliferate, data flow in new and unpredictable paths, which can often lead to the identification of new stakeholders who previously had not been considered as such. Managers confront many new challenges in identifying all the stakeholders in such complicated webs.

Second, it is often a challenge to establish just which rights exist for each stakeholder in an IS-related context. At issue are not just *legal* rights, which can be determined as under the stockholder theory, but also *moral* rights, which can in many cases be quite distinct. For example, consider the rights that accrue to the author of a copyrighted work. That author has a legal right to the document's contents, which should not be copied and resold. But another writer could paraphrase the author's ideas without violating this legal right. Still, the second writer has a moral (though not a legal) duty to give the first author credit for the ideas. Particularly when managers work in organizations that deal with ownership of ideas and written codifications thereof (e.g., in maintaining pages on the World Wide Web), they must be very aware not only of legal rulings but also the rights that accrue to each stakeholder under the ethical rubric.

Third, the stakeholder theory requires managers to consider stakeholders' interests, which can often be ill-defined and subject to interpretation. In many ways, the requirements for satisfactorily addressing stakeholders' concerns are considerably more stringent than under the stockholder theory. For example, with respect to use of customer data, a reasonable interpretation of the stakeholder theory would require that customers not only be informed of potential data uses (the stockholder theory requirement) but also be given the opportunity to "opt out" (or, arguably, to "opt in") of the uses (Smith 1994, pp. 241–243).

Fourth, the stakeholder theory holds a particularly problematic challenge for managers in that it does not specify *how* the optimal balancing of stakeholder interests should be achieved. This challenge is not unique to the IS domain, of course, but it is a significant weakness of the stakeholder theory in its general form. Managers must contemplate a myriad of possibilities, calculate a number of cost-benefit analyses (with attention to each stakeholder's gain or loss), and balance these in some rational fashion.

Social Contract Theory

The social contract theory holds five important challenges for managers grappling with IS quandaries. First, as under the stockholder theory, a mechanism for avoiding fraud and deception must be implemented. Second, managers must carefully consider whether an action dehumanizes employees—a real constraint for many IS applications, which are often argued to reduce the necessary skills for certain jobs. Concomitant with this challenge, managers must confront the fact that dehumanization is a somewhat subjective concept: some employees might view a system as freeing them to perform more challenging tasks, while others might view the same system with disdain.

Third, the extent to which a technological application causes invidious discrimination must be considered. This is a real societal concern for many IS projects, as it has been argued that many newer technologies enable "information redlining" (Cespedes and Smith 1993, p. 14) that bypasses certain socio-economic strata and ethnic communities. But how can a manager distinguish between inappropriate discrimination and a rational business decision to target information flows to those most likely to make use of, and respond to, the information? This analysis continues to stand as a major challenge for many IS projects.

Fourth, and related, managers must determine how particular IS initiatives will impact the material well-being of society's members as employees or consumers. From the perspective of employee well-being, it would appear that projects which have a reasonable potential of raising employees' eventual remuneration would be preferred. However, a manager still might have to confront complex situations in which overall headcount would be reduced due to a new system's effects, but the remaining employees would earn more afterward. Such situations are still open to evaluation and judgment. As for consumers' material well-being, managers must often consider both tangible and intangible benefits; for example, automated teller machines (ATMs) provide more intangible than tangible benefits to consumers (primarily convenience), but few would deny that they have improved consumers' well-being. In many cases, identification of such benefits will be a challenging task, however.

Fifth, in light of the significant constraints on alternatives imposed by the social contract theory's provisions, managers face the difficulty of identifying profitable projects that, in fact, are consistent with their other ethical obligations under the theory—to reject actions that are fraudulent/deceptive or that dehumanize employees and to eliminate options that reduce the welfare of society's members. This is particularly problematic within the IS domain, since some applications might appear to meet the terms of the social contract in their original formulation, but eventual usage of the systems might well diverge from the intended purpose. While profitable projects that meet the requirements of the social contract theory—both in their original design and in their eventual usage—do exist, the rather stringent demands of the social contract theory will no doubt scuttle many projects that would be deemed "ethical" under one of the other theories.

Challenges of Application

It is obvious that the stockholder, stakeholder, and social contract theories are far from "cookbook" theories with respect to applicability. All require substantial and nontrivial evaluation from a managerial perspective; in addition, managers may have to do some amount of fact-gathering before entering the cognitive phase of theory application. While these theories—or other NTBEs that managers might articulate and defend—have great worth in enabling more consistent ethical decisions, the challenges that accompany their application must be acknowledged. And, while we would not argue that the issues faced by the IS community are inherently more complex than those faced by the business community as a whole, we would nevertheless note some specific focus items for those who are associated with IS investments and applications.

Special Considerations for the IS Community

So far, the discussion has been targeted to managers in *all* corporate roles as they confront ethical quandaries, but there are also some special considerations for members of the corporate IS community—mechanisms that may increase the probability that decisions made during the development and implementation of information systems will be consistent with those of the respective theories.

At the outset, it should be noted that, because "ethics is essentially an individual matter" (Mason et al. 1995, p. 149), the normative theories of business ethics are stated in their pristine form at the individual (micro) level as obligations for human beings who are employed in corporations. But the inference to collective (macro) level[10] obligations are rather direct and can be reasonably extrapolated to the corporation as a whole. "Hovering between the individual and collective levels of ethics is the institution of professions" (Mason et al. 1995, p. 149).

Unfortunately, the professional codes being proffered by various IS organizations (e.g., ACM, BCS, CIPS, DPMA, ICCP; see Oz 1992, 1994a) remain somewhat of a patchwork quilt, with many areas of ambiguity remaining unaddressed. Even in situations where the codes do address similar issues, they are often in conflict with respect to the duties and responsibilities assigned to IS professionals by a corporation (Mason et al. 1995; Oz 1992). Further, it is becoming increasingly common for corporations to define their own codes for corporate IS ethics, and there is no guarantee that such codes will coincide with those proffered by the professional organizations. Thus, simple reliance on professional or corporate codes to ensure ethical behavior in corporate environs, as defined by the normative theories of business ethics, will be foolhardy. Instead, IS professionals should focus on a systematic approach that will raise ethical issues at the appropriate times. Three specific steps can be taken.

First, *before ethical quandaries occur*, professionals can engage others in their own corporation in dialogue regarding which theoretical perspective will be embraced by the corporate body as a whole. Admittedly, this dialogue is more easily effected by senior management than by those lower in the corporate hierarchy, but even those at the programmer or systems analyst level can prod others to consider the different perspectives.

Second, assuming that a collective (macro) level theory has been derived from the individual (micro) level theory and has been agreed upon, an additional period of scrutiny for each prospective IS project before it is implemented will be helpful in identifying misalignments between that theory's perspective on ethical obligations and how those obligations are being met as systems are rolled out. If the social contract theory is believed to be correct, for example, all IS proposals should be evaluated to ensure that they are consistent with the demands of that theory (see Donaldson 1982). If a proposed system were likely to dehumanize workers, for example, this would violate one of the terms of the theoretical "contract" and the system should therefore be modified. Such scrutiny can be considered a regular part of the systems development process by, for example, adding an ethics checkpoint during certain phases of the systems development life cycle. Some organizations may even appoint an audit professional to evaluate the projects' consistency with the collective (macro) level theory. We believe that such systematic scrutiny of projects will lead to appropriate timing of ethical analysis.

Third, it may be helpful for organizations to appoint an ombudsperson (sometimes called an "ethics officer") to which IS professionals can bring their concerns about ethically questionable activities. With respect to the two items above, we acknowledge that it may sometimes be difficult for IS professionals to convince others to change direction in light of ethical concerns during the systems development life

---

[10]See Laudon (1995) and Mason et al. (1995) for a discussion of these terms.

cycle will likely address only those issues that surface during the process of software development. Thus, to the extent that ethical quandaries are still evident even in light of these mechanisms, the option of bringing issues to an ombudsperson—reporting outside the normal management channels—could enhance the ability of IS professionals to raise ethical concerns at a senior management level.

CONCLUSION

While the IS field has paid great attention to strategic uses of technology over the past two decades, the growing number of ethical quandaries with which corporate managers must grapple, which also grew during this same time frame, have received much less attention. It is encouraging that many practitioners and researchers are beginning to pay more attention to information ethics; however, many of the discussions are occurring in a theoretical vacuum. While this paper represents some amount of forward movement in adding rigor to the debate, much work remains to be done. In particular, the NTBEs are clearly bounded by their applicability to the corporate domain, and individuals in non-profit or public sector organizations may also encounter quandaries. Obviously, future research efforts should clarify obligations for individuals in these other domains. In addition, as became obvious in the previous sections, the application of these theories is often a non-trivial endeavor. Indeed, much work remains on the parts of both researchers and practitioners to clarify the specific obligations of each theory at a granular level. Even so, we believe that—for IS-related quandaries that occur in corporate contexts—NTBEs offer helpful guidance that surpasses even that of the traditional philosophical theories.

In the end, of course, ethics relates to an individual's expression of his or her free will. Any ethical theory is only as helpful as human beings and their organizational and societal contexts will allow it to be. As perceptions of ethical lapses—such as those that were allegedly encountered in the Blockbuster, Greyhound, and AMR cases—continue, ethical issues will become more prominent in IS discourse. As expressed in earlier research,

> Everyone who develops applications, designs equipment, performs any kind of testing, uses methodologies, analyzes jobs, designs human interfaces, writes documentation, or prescribes the use of computers, will have ethical dilemmas on every project; they just might not recognize them (Conger and Loch 1995, p. 32).

Whether as managers, IS professionals, or academic researchers, we ignore these ethical dilemmas and their theoretical assessment at the risk of our community's own credibility.

ACKNOWLEDGMENTS

We gratefully acknowledge the Georgetown School of Business; the Georgetown University Center for Business-Government Relations; and the Babcock Graduate School of Management, Wake Forest University, Research Fellowship Program for their support of this research. Mary Culnan, the late Ernest Kallman, and Allen Lee provided helpful comments on an earlier draft of this paper.

REFERENCES

Aristole. *Nicomachean Ethics* (trans. by T. Irwin), Hackett Publishing Company, Indianapolis, IN, 384 b.c./1985.

Bies, R. J., and Shapiro, D. L. "Voice and Justification: Their Influences on Procedural Fairness Judgments," *Academy of Management Journal* (31:3), 1988, pp. 676–685.

Bowie, N. E., and Freeman, R. E. "Ethics and Agency Theory: An Introduction," in *Ethics and Agency Theory*, N. E. Bowie and R. E. Freeman (eds.), Oxford University Press, Oxford, 1992.

Branscomb, A. W. *Who Owns Information?* Basic Books, New York, 1994.

Brookshire, R. G., Stevens, S. P., and Forcht, K. A. "The Computer Ethics of University Students: An International Exploratory Study," presented at the Third National Computer Ethics Conference, Washington, DC, April 29, 1994.

Cash, J. I., McFarlan, F. W., and McKenney, J. L. *Corporate Information Systems Management: The Issues Facing Senior Executives* (3rd ed.), Irwin, Homewood, IL, 1992.

Cespedes, F. V., and Smith, H. J. "Database Marketing: New Rules for Policy and Practice," *Sloan Management Review* (34), Summer 1993, pp. 7–22.

Collins, W. R., Miller, K. W., Spielman, B. J., and Wherry, P. "How Good Is Good Enough?*" Communications of the ACM* (37:1), January 1994, pp. 81–91.

Conger, S., and Loch, K. D. "Ethics and Computer Use," *Communications of the ACM* (38:12), December 1995, pp. 31, 32.

Culnan, M. J. "How Did They Get My Name? An Exploratory Investigation of Consumer Attitudes Toward Secondary Information Use," *MIS Quarterly* (17:3), September 1993, pp. 341–363.

Culnan, M. J., and Smith, H. J., "Lotus Marketplace: Households—Managing Information Privacy Concerns" in *Computer Ethics and Social Values,* D. G. Johnson and H. Nissenbaum (eds.), Prentice-Hall, Englewood Cliffs, NJ, 1995, pp. 269–277.

Donaldson, T. J. *Corporations and Morality,* Prentice-Hall, Englewood Cliffs, NJ, 1982.

Donaldson, T. J. *The Ethics of International Business,* Oxford University Press, New York, 1989.

Donaldson, T., and Dunfee, T. W. "Toward a Unified Conception of Business Ethics: Integrative Social Contracts Theory," *Academy of Management Review* (19:2), 1994, pp. 252–284.

Donaldson, T., and Preston, L. E. The Stakeholder Theory of the Corporation: Concepts, Evidence, and Implications," *Academy of Management Review* (20:1), 1995, pp. 65–91.

Evan, W. M., and Freeman, R. E. "A Stakeholder Theory of the Modern Corporation: Kantian Capitalism," in Ethical Theory and Business (3rd ed.), T. L.

Beauchamp, and N. E. Bowie (eds.), Prentice-Hall, Englewood Cliffs, NJ, 1988, pp. 97–106.

Farrell, D. "Exit, Voice, Loyalty, and Neglect as Responses to Job Dissatisfaction: A Multidimensional Scaling Study," *Academy of Management Review* (26:4), 1983, pp. 596–607.

Friedman, M. *Capitalism and Freedom*, University of Chicago Press, Chicago, 1962, p. 133.

Friedman, M. "The Social Responsibility of Business Is to Increase its Profits," in *Ethical Theory and Business* (5th ed.), T. L. Beauchamp, and N. E. Bowie (eds.), Prentice-Hall, Englewood Cliffs, NJ, 1997, pp. 56–61.

Hagel, J., and Rayport, J. F. "The Coming Battle for Customer Information," *Harvard Business Review* (75:1), January-February 1997, pp. 53–65.

Hasnas, J. "The Normative Theories of Business Ethics: A Guide for the Perplexed," *Business Ethics Quarterly* (8:1), January 1998, pp. 19–42.

Johnson, D. G. "The Public-Private Status of Transactions in Computer Networks," in *The Information Web: Ethical and Social Implications of Computer Networking,* C. C. Gould (ed.), Westview Press, Boulder, CO, 1989, pp. 37–55.

Johnson, D. G. *Computer Ethics*, 2nd ed., Prentice-Hall, Englewood Cliffs, NJ, 1994.

Jones, T. M. "Corporate Social Responsibility: Revisited, Redefined," *California Business Review* (22), 1980, pp. 59ff.

Kallman, E. A., and Grillo, J. P. *Ethical Decision Making and Information Technology,* 2nd ed., McGraw-Hill, New York, 1996.

Kant, I. *Grounding for the Metaphysics of Morals* (trans. by J. W. Ellington), Hackett Publishing, Indianapolis, IN, 1804/1981.

Kultgen, J. "Donaldson's Social Contract for Business," *Business and Professional Ethics Journal* (5:1), 1985, pp. 28–39.

Laudon, K. C. "Ethical Concepts and Information Technology," *Communications of the ACM* (38:12), December 1995, pp. 33–39.

Laudon, K. C. "Markets and Privacy," *Communications of the ACM* (39:9), September 1996, pp. 92–104.

Loch, K. D., Carr H. H., and Warkentin, M. E. "Threats to information Systems: Today's Reality, Yesterday's Understanding," *MIS Quarterly* (16:2), June 1992, pp. 173–186.

Loch, K. D., and Conger, S. "Evaluating Ethical Decision Making and Computer Use," *Communications of the ACM* (9:7), July 1996, pp. 74–83.

Mason, R. O. "Four Ethical Issues of the Information Age," *MIS Quarterly* (10:1) March 1986, pp. 4–12.

Mason, R. O., Mason, F. M., and Culnan, M. J. *Ethics of Information Management*, Sage Publications, Thousand Oaks, CA, 1995.

Miceli, M. P. and Near, J. P. *Blowing the Whistle: The Organizational and Legal Implications for Companies and Employees*, Lexington Books, New York, 1992.

Milberg, S. J., Burke, S. J., Smith, H. J., and Kallman, E. A. "A Cross-Cultural Study of Relationships Between Values, Personal Information Privacy Concerns, and Regulatory Approaches," *Communications of the ACM* (38:12), December 1995, pp. 65–74.

Miller, M. W. "Coming Soon to Your Local Video Store: Big Brother," *The Wall Street Journal,* December 26, 1990, pp. 9, 10.

Oz, E, "Ethical Standards for Information Systems Professionals: A Case for a Unified Code," *MIS Quarterly* (16:4), December 1992, pp. 423–433.

Oz, E. *Ethics for the Information Age,* Irwin/McGraw-Hill, New York 1994a.

Oz, E. "When Professional Standards Are Lax: The CONFIRM Failure and Its Lessons," *Communications of the ACM* (37:10), October 1994b, pp. 29–36.

Parker, D. B. *Ethical Conflicts in Computer Science and Technology*, AFIPS Press, New York, 1979.

Parker, D. B., Swope, S., and Baker, B. *Ethical Conflicts in Information and Computer Science, Technology, and Business,* QED Information Sciences, Inc., Wellesley, MA, 1990.

Quinn, D. P. and Jones, T. M. "An Agent Morality View of Business Policy," *Academy of Management Review* (20:1), pp. 22–42.

Schoeman, F. *Philosophical Dimensions of Privacy,* Cambridge University Press, Cambridge, 1984.

Smith, H. J. "Legal Lag Time," *Beyond Computing* (5:6), July/August 1996, pp. 12 & 13.

Smith, H. J. "Privacy Policies and Practices: Inside the Organizational Maze," *Communications of the ACM* (36:12), December 1993, pp. 105–122.

Smith, H. J. *Managing Privacy: Information Technology and Corporate America,* University of North Carolina Press, Chapel Hill, NC, 1994.

Smith, H. J. and Kallman, E. A. "Defining Ethical Feasibility," *Beyond Computing (*4:2) March/April 1995, pp. 12 & 13.

Stark, A. "What's the Matter With Business Ethics?" *Harvard Business Review (*71:3), 1993, pp. 38–48.

Straub, D. W., and Collins, R. W. "Key Information Liability Issues Facing Managers: Software Piracy, Proprietary Databases, and Individual Rights to Privacy," *MIS Quarterly* (14:2), June 1990, pp. 142–156.

Sviokla, J. J. and Gentile, M. "Information Technology in Organizations: Emerging Issues in Ethics and Policy," Harvard Business School Note (#9-190-130), 1990.

Tomsho, R. "Real Dog: How Greyhound Lines Re-Engineered Itself Right Into a Deep Hole," *Wall Street Journal,* October 20, 1994, pp. Al, A6.

Weisband, S. P., and Reinig, B. A. "Understanding Users' Perceptions of Electronic Mail Privacy," *Communications of the ACM* (38:12), December 1995, pp. 40–47.

Ethical Issues

Effy Oz

Ethics is a branch in philosophy that studies morality. It deals with right and wrong acts. *Ethical* is often synonymous with *right,* while *unethical* is often synonymous with *wrong.* However, there is hardly any absolute ethical and unethical behavior in terms of time and location. What might once have been considered ethical (e.g., polygamy) is now unethical. What is considered ethical in some countries (copying someone's creative work) is considered unethical in others. Although we do not elaborate on ethical theories in this article, the reader is encouraged to review the major ethical theories, utilitarian as well as deontological. However, modern means of communication and transportation have gradually eroded national and cultural differences and, therefore, the differences in ethical approach to ethical issues.

Historically, every major technological change has prompted discussion of the adequacy of current social and ethical norms. Often, these discussions have resulted in new political doctrines, social agreements, ethical codes, and legislation. One need only look back and see what happened in the Industrial Revolution: A sense of injustice produced an ongoing public debate on employer–employee relations, socialist movements, and social legislation that stemmed out of a feeling that the world we were used to yesterday is no longer our world today. Similar discussions and debates have taken place since information technology (IT) started to permeate our lives in the mid-1980s. Ethical norms have been created; legislation followed; and the debates are still going on. The rapid development of a global information network, the Internet, has only intensified calls for ethical norms and legislation regarding privacy, freedom of speech, and intellectual property rights. This article surveys the major ethical issues relating to IT. Undoubtedly, as the technology develops, new issues will arise.

I. The Need for Ethical Norms in the Information Age

In broad terms, we can see several major changes in human history during the past 5000 years. In the Western World, more than two-thirds of the workforce is engaged in work that either produces information or relies on information and does not produce any tangible goods. Education relies on information systems and computer networks. At home, we spend an increasing amount of time with computers for entertainment and communication. A growing number of working people rely on IT to work from home rather than in organizational offices.

The growing reliance on IT has brought up grave issues: Employees and consumers are losing control of information that reveals much of their private lives; it is relatively easy to steal information in digital form; free speech can be supported by the technology, but there are concerns about unrestricted transmission of violent, racist, and sexual material on the Internet; violation of intellectual property rights has increased; and other crimes, popularly referred to as computer crimes, are proliferating. These issues have prompted some countries to pass laws specifically dealing with acts performed with IT. The laws include prohibition of certain uses of computers, such as unauthorized access to computer systems; limits on collection, maintenance, and dissemination of personal data; rules for duplication of digital intellectual property; and other rules whose purpose is generally to limit our use of IT for purposes that do not harm the well-being of other people.

As often happens with ethical issues, we strive to resolve the collision of interests of two or more parties. For instance, employers want to monitor their employees to ensure productivity and security while employees resist infringement on their privacy rights. Governments want to be able to monitor communication of people suspected of illegal activities, while citizens resist government attempts to gain access to their communication, much of which is now executed through computer networks. Individuals pursue free speech and want to be able to post on the World Wide Web any material they wish to post, while other individuals are concerned that some people, especially children, may be harmed by certain information. Meanwhile, millions of IT professionals have a tremendous impact on our lives but do not have to comply with any mandatory code of ethics as other professionals do. Clearly, it has created situations that call for reconsideration of current ethical codes and initiation of new ones to deal with the issues. In many cases, the public debate on an IT ethical issue has found its way to legislatures, which pass laws to address concerns.

▬▬▬ II. Cultural Differences

Ethical conflicts often occur when two cultures encounter each other. Cultures have different social values and therefore promote acts that may be deemed ethical in one culture but unethical in another. One such example is the difference in approach to intellectual property. In the West, intellectual property is simply that: the property of the person or organization that created it, be it a book, a painting, musical piece, or a software application. In many Asian countries, the concept is relatively new, because for many centuries artistic creations were not the property of the person who created them. So, while in the United States the painter of a new piece of art is entitled to royalties from those who copy her work, in China the greatest honor a painter can receive is to have many people copy his work; for many centuries painters did not expect any material compensation for the copying. The introduction of software in countries with this culture has created friction between old traditions and new realities, whereby software authors (who are mainly Western organizations) demand financial compensation for copies of their work. While governments in these countries yielded to Western pressure and passed intellectual property laws similar to the Western ones, old habits die hard and pose a challenge both to the authors and the local governments.

Similar cultural differences exist with regard to privacy and free speech. While Americans treasure their personal privacy in dealings with governments, they have largely accepted violation of privacy by private organizations. This is probably the result of a long promotion of personal freedom while at the same time espousing free markets and competition of commercial enterprises. In Western Europe, the quest for privacy progressed regardless of who the potential violator might be; privacy laws treat all organizations equally, whether governmental or private.

Free speech is sanctioned in the constitutions of many Western countries, but is not regarded as a supreme value in many other countries. In Asian, Arab, and some African countries, values such as harmony of the family and the community far supercede the value of free speech, which is individualistic in essence. Thus, when means such as the Internet became available, Westerners took advantage of them to voice their opinions more than individuals in other nations. Of course, political systems also have a major role in the measure of how much free speech citizens are allowed; however, the political systems themselves are often the result of cultures that allow them to exist.

▪ ▪ ▪ III. Invasion of Privacy

In the context of information, privacy is the ability of individuals to control information about themselves. In the past, collection, maintenance, and dissemination of any information, let alone, personal information, was expensive, labor intensive, and paper based. Nowadays, it is inexpensive, involves little labor, and is digital. Huge amounts of personal information, such as credit card numbers and Internet activities, can be automatically collected via digital means, fed into databases, manipulated, duplicated, and transmitted using IT. The threat to privacy has increased greatly since the introduction of computers into the business world in the 1950s and 1960s, but it intensified even more in the mid-1990s with the opening of the Internet to commercial activity.

A. Violation of Consumer Privacy

Consumers are often asked to return warranty cards of the products they purchased with much more information than is required for ensuring warranty of the product. Questions such as "What is your favorite hobby" and "How many alcoholic beverages do you consume per week" are not unusual. The same questions are asked of people who log on to a Web site and wish to participate in sweepstakes, download software, or receive information. The data are channeled into large databases. Database management systems are used to manipulate the data in almost any manner imaginable. It can be sorted by demographic and geographic characteristics, matched with other data that the individual provided in the past to another organization, and practically produce an elaborate personal dossier of the individual. Such dossiers may include credit history, employment history, medical profile, buying patterns, religious and professional affiliations, and even social relationships and political inclinations. Telecommunications technology lets the owner of such a database transmit millions of personal records to other organizations, usually for a fee, within minutes.

Commercial organizations claim that they need information about consumers to compete in a free market. The information can help them produce products that the consumers need and market them to the individuals most likely to purchase them. This helps not only the organizations, which can save costs when "target marketing," but also provides consumers with better products and services. Civil rights advocates, on the other hand, argue that personal dossiers held by organizations violate privacy. They argue that when an organization collects personal information, it should disclose several items to the individual: the purpose of collecting the information, the intended use, the length of time the information will be held, whether the information may be communicated to other organizations, and what security measures will be taken to ensure that only people with a "need to know" will access it. In addition, many privacy advocates demand that organizations give individuals an opportunity to scrutinize their records and ensure that proper corrections are made when the individual legitimately asks for corrections. Some advocates also insist that organizations should pay individuals every time they sell the individual's record to another party.

In countries that are members of the European Union, many of these demands have been met by laws. The 15 members have enacted privacy laws that conform to the European Directive on Data Protection *(Directive 95/46/EC of the European Parliament and of the Council of 24 October 1995 on the protection of individuals with regard to the processing of personal data and on the free movement of such data)*. The directive requires any organization, whether a government agency or a commercial enterprise, to tell individuals how the data will be stored and used, and for how long. It guarantees them scrutiny of their records and that they will be notified whenever the organization intends to transfer the data to another organization. Furthermore, no decision based solely on automated processing of personal data may be made regarding credit or employment.

The Internet, and especially the commercialization of the Web, have intensified the issue of consumer privacy. Cookie technologies help companies collect personal information even if the surfer is not aware of it. *Cookies* are information files kept on the hard disk of the user. They accumulate information such as access codes, Web pages to which the user logged on, and the mouse's click stream. Over time, a cookie may collect enough information to describe the shopping habits and other characteristics of the user. While the idea is to make the Web experience of the user more efficient (no need to reenter access codes and account numbers) and effective (automatically taking the user to pages of greater interest), privacy advocates argue that they expose much of a person's private life to commercial organizations.

Software technologies such as data warehousing and data mining exacerbate the privacy problem. Companies channel millions of records from transactional databases to large archival databases. Some companies, especially large retail chains and financial institutions, have amassed several terabytes of data each. Special applications that combine artificial intelligence and statistical methods "mine" the data for shopping patterns, fraud patterns and other patterns. To minimize identification of individuals when using such data, corporations have tried to develop privacy-enhancing technologies. However, the possibility of identification always exists.

Almost all of the information accumulated about consumers comes from the consumers themselves. Often, they are notified that they must provide information to receive a service. If they agree, the act is called "informed consent"; they know how the information will be used, and they give it out of their free will in return for something, such as a product, a service, or participation in a sweepstakes. Many Web sites also let consumers choose not to allow the organization to transmit the information to any other party. Yet, concern is growing about privacy on the Web, especially regarding information provided by minors.

B. Violation of Employee Privacy

Employers have two main purposes for monitoring workers: ensuring productivity and enforcing security. For many years the two purposes were pursued by supervisors who were physically present at the place where work was performed. The television era ushered in the ubiquitous closed-circuit camera, which allows managers to visually monitor their subordinates from a distance with or without an early warning. As of the mid-1980s, when millions of workers started using personal computers for their daily work, the PC itself has become a means of monitoring. By connecting the PCs to an organizational network, supervisors can monitor everything that an employee does with a computer, from the number of keystrokes per minute to electronic mail messages to Web pages viewed by the worker.

Business leaders keep arguing that they must ensure productivity by monitoring without prior warning. They argue that a prior warning defeats the purpose, because it changes the workers' behavior. Workers have claimed that unannounced electronic monitoring causes stress, fear, and tension. Attempts in the U.S. Congress to legislate against monitoring without early warning have failed. Employee claims that employers violate their privacy when supervisors monitor their e-mail messages have been rejected by U.S. courts. The courts maintain that since the equipment belongs to the employer, the employer is entitled to enforce organizational policies as to the content of e-mail and Internet information that the employees send and receive.

▪▪▪ IV. Ethical Issues on the Internet

The Internet has connected millions of people the world over. It is not limited to any national territory, and hence provides opportunities to improve education, commercial activities, and the quality of work life. However, it has also generated phenomena of questionable ethicality.

A. Free Speech

The Internet, especially its most popular application—the Web, became a new means of mass communications in the 1990s. Unlike most television transmission, Web pages can be received globally, rather than within a limited territory. Anyone who has a computer with access to the Internet can post Web pages with any content in the form of text, still pictures, animation, sound, and streaming video. This may include materials that are offensive to some people, such as virulent racist slurs, pornographic images, and images of extreme violence. In some countries such posting is limited. For example, the German state of Bavaria threatened America Online (AOL), the Internet service provider and information service company, that its service would be banned in that state unless it blocked Web pages with pornographic content. The Chinese government systematically blocks access to sites that post "unacceptable" materials, including pornography and political information that government officials regard as offensive.

Free speech is sanctioned in the constitutions of some countries, including the United States and West European states. Yet, large parts of the populations of these countries have demanded that information posted on the Internet be censored. In 1996, the Decency in Communication Act was passed by the U.S. Congress but was later struck down by the Supreme Court as unconstitutional. The court placed the responsibility at the receiving end: If a person does not wish to receive such information, he or she should not log on to the Web site. Claims that children may have access to violent or pornographic Web pages did not sway the court, which insisted that it is parents' responsibility to monitor what their children do. Yet, in other Western countries censorship has been applied to the Internet. For instance, a French court found an Internet service provider (ISP) responsible for pornographic images that his clients posted. In protest, the ISP shut down the service and dissolved the firm.

One must understand that any censorship of the Internet is limited. It is practically impossible to block access to every Web site that transmits unacceptable information. As an increasing number of Internet lines become unguided, that is, use satellites, setting a control office that monitors all transmission via guided (cables, optical fibers, and the like) lines will become impossible, because an increasing number of people will receive information using satellite antennas.

B. Spamming

Soon after facsimile (fax) machines became commonplace in many households, legislatures rushed to pass laws against broadcasts of fax advertisements. However, there is no law that forbids commercial enterprises to advertise through electronic mail. E-mail advertising is one of the least costly means of advertising. Many businesses broadcast daily advertisements to people whose e-mail address they obtained either directly, mainly through the Web, or purchased from companies that sell e-mail address lists.

Massive broadcast of e-mail, especially for commercial purposes, is popularly called *spamming*. Many people resent the phenomenon of "junk e-mail," masses of e-mailed advertisements. Such e-mail clogs their e-mail boxes, wastes their times trying to separate useful e-mail from spam, and takes up disk space and CPU time that could otherwise be used for useful work. Several states in the United States have proscribed spamming, but the majority of states and other countries allow it.

C. Cybersquatting

For several years after the Internet was opened for commercial activities, anyone could receive a Web domain name (such as http://www.mycompany.com) free of charge. Now, domain names are sold on a first-come, first-served basis. Some people saw an opportunity to capitalize on the opportunity and purchased domain names containing the names of commercial organizations or generic names that might be attractive to Internet entrepreneurs, and then offered them for sale. Reportedly, some domain names, such as http://www.drugs.com have been sold for hundreds of thousands of dollars.

As long as the names were generic, there were no complainers. However, commercial organizations claim that domain names should be treated the same way as trademarks: They uniquely associate products and services with a specific company, and therefore should not be used without permission by anyone except the company. People or organizations that register domain names with intention to sell them later are popularly called *cybersquatters*.

American courts have accepted the argument. If the domain name is generic, the party that registered it is entitled to it. However, if someone registered a name that had been the trademark of a business, the business is entitled to it. In such a case, the business must only pay the holder back the registration fee and can then begin using it. Some people claim that the Web is a new business frontier and should not be ruled by traditional conventions and laws; thus, trademark law should not be applied to the Web. The debate is likely to continue.

D. Gambling

Gambling, in itself, has been the topic of ethical debate for many years. It is legal in some states, illegal in others, and pronounced immoral by many people regardless of its legal status. The Internet poses serious challenges to communities that control gambling. There is no practical way to stop people from gambling online. All they have to do is provide a credit card number to the online casino and then play the games online. The social danger may be greater than gambling from locations where gambling is prohibited; it is the ability of anyone with access to the Internet to gamble from the comfort of one's home or office at any time of the day. This may lure more people to gamble with larger amounts of money and result in a greater number of ruined families. Proponents of online gambling argue that it simply provides a choice, and that the choice should remain with individuals, not governments.

E. Daytrading

Online trading of securities, especially stocks, has gained huge popularity. However, it does not only replace human brokers. It allows small investors to buy and sell stocks within minutes. Indeed, thousands of individuals engage in what has become known as *day-trading:* buying and selling the same stock multiple times on the same day to profit from tiny fluctuations in the stock's price. The media have reported that some people resigned from their jobs to devote all their time to daytrading. With the opening of "off-hours" trading to the public, small investors could potentially devote 24 hours per day to such activity.

Experts argue that only a few people can earn a living from daytrading, let alone become rich from it. Daytrading is practically gambling, especially in light of the fact that many daytraders are not knowledgeable investors. Some sociologists fear that daytrading, along with online gambling, will ruin families. Civil libertarians argue that daytrading should be subject to individual choice and that governments should not intervene in the matter. As with online gambling, there is no practical way to control daytrading.

■ ■ ■ V. Violation of Intellectual Property

Software has always been available in digital form, stored on magnetic disks and tapes and optical disks and tapes. Artistic works, such as books, pictures, and sounds, are also available, or can be made available, in digital form. The ease, small cost, and small chance of being caught make illegal copying of such work tempting.

A. Software

Two organizations have kept tabs on illegal copying of software, also called software piracy: the Software and Information Industry Association (SIIA) and Business Software Alliance (BSA). According to both organizations, the financial damage of illegal copying of software worldwide is $10–15 billion annually. Software piracy seems to be the most pervasive crime in which people of all walks of life engage. The problem seems to be worse in countries where material compensation for artistic work has not been the norm for many centuries, such as Asian and African societies. Under Western pressure, especially from the United States, the majority of the world's countries now have copyright laws similar to the American one, forbidding copying of software and other artistic work without permission from the owners.

B. Artistic Works

Artistic works such as books, music, photos, and paintings can be easily digitized. Once digitized, they can be copied to another computer storage medium within seconds or minutes, or transmitted to another computer thousands of miles away. Unlike other copies (such as from a copy machine or an analog music tape), digital copies of artistic work are as good as the original. Digital copying is also easy. It is extremely difficult to pinpoint someone who copied digital work unless the copies are openly offered for sale. This is the reason why leaders in the music industry are looking for means to protect their copyrights against infringement.

The Internet offers an effective means to publish music and distribute it. This gives new artists an opportunity to publish their work, but the same technology enables people with little regard for the law to post at Web sites copyrighted music that can then be downloaded by anyone. Attempts by the music industry to outlaw the sale of special devices that download music from the Web have failed. In a way, this is a repetition of the attempt to prohibit the sale of videocassette recorders, which failed. Leaders in the music industry have been looking for innovative means to protect the industry from mass violation of copyright laws. Some observers opine that this industry will have to change dramatically because of the new technologies.

▪▪▪ VI. Computer Crime

The advent of computers in government and business organizations in the 1960s ushered in some types of crime that either did not exist before, or took a turn for the worse because of the new technology. The following sections provide a brief review of the major types of what is popularly referred to as computer crime.

A. Unauthorized Access

Unauthorized access to a computer system is any logging on to a system directly or through communications lines without permission of the owner or operator of the system. Popularly, the act is often called hacking or cracking. Some countries do not have laws that forbid such acts, but it is considered unethical. Where there are laws, some prohibit only uninvited access to security systems. A *security system* is one that specifically requires an access code (such as a password) or automatically identifies the person who tries to log on. Under these laws, access to a system that is not a security system is not an offense.

Unauthorized access alone may not cause any damage. The reason why unauthorized access is regarded as unethical or is illegal is simple: Hacking is often the prelude to other illegal or, at least, unethical acts, such as fraud and money theft, information theft, service theft, data alteration, and the launching of computer viruses.

When the culprits are caught, they often argue that the intrusion helped the organization realize that its security measures were flawed, and hence they provided a good service. This argument would not withstand any ethical doctrine. It is akin to burglars claiming they helped the owners realize their home could be invaded.

B. Fraud and Money Theft

While we still use cash for transactions, much of the money that exchanges hands is actually electrical impulses and magnetic fields. Billions of dollars are transferred daily from one bank account to another by way of simple instructions to computers and transmission of electrical signals via computer networks. By either illegally obtaining access codes or by circumventing them, criminals can transfer millions of dollars from one bank account to another from a remote computer. Contrary to popular belief, the majority of online fraud and money theft is carried out by "insiders," that is employees of the victim organizations.

C. Information Theft

While several decades ago much of industrial espionage was done by searching paper folders and waste-baskets, modern theft of information for industrial espionage or other purposes is done by accessing computer systems either directly or via networks such as the Internet. The ease with which this can be done, and the difficulty involved in tracing the culprits has led some countries to change their laws; information is now considered property like any physical property. These laws were also modified to define theft of information as copying information without permission. Thus, culprits are considered thieves even if they do not remove anything physically, and even if they do not mean to deprive the lawful owner of the information or the use of information. The mere copying is criminal.

D. Data Alteration and Data Destruction

Data alteration and data destruction in corporate databases have been the nightmare of information systems executives. As long as a system is connected to a public network such as the Internet, it is potentially subject to uninvited intrusion. Once the system has been invaded, the hackers often find ways to either destroy or alter data. Cases have been reported of intrusion into hospital databases and alteration of medication doses that could result in killing patients. Thus, the risk may not be only material, but also a matter of life and death.

In recent years, the most common data alteration and destruction incidences involved corporate Web pages. The home pages of many companies and government agencies have been defaced either "for fun" or because the hackers resent the policies or activities of the organization. As the Internet is growing in size and use, this type of crime, although not outlawed by all countries, seems to be the greatest threat to electronic commerce and dissemination of information.

E. Computer Viruses

A computer virus is any rogue computer program that can spread by using computer networks or exchange of storage devices such as magnetic disks. The early computer viruses appeared in 1988. Some estimates put the number of new viruses at 3000 per year. A computer virus may cause damage in several ways: It may over-occupy the CPU, thereby slowing down productive work; it may over-occupy network servers, thereby not allowing reasonably fast data communications; or it may simply destroy data files or applications. The growing popularity of e-mail fostered the worldwide spread of destructive viruses such as the Melissa and I LOVE YOU viruses in the late 1990s and 2000.

Interestingly, some people claim that viruses should be considered a form of free speech and therefore should not be banned. Indeed, not all viruses are malicious, but the consternation that even the benign ones cause makes them unethical, if not criminal, in the eyes of the majority of people.

Another interesting point is the legality of computer viruses. The majority of countries (including most states in the United States) do not prohibit computer viruses per se. An attempt to modify the U.S. federal act against computer crimes (Computer Fraud and Abuse Act of 1986) failed not because of objection from any interested party, but because of a problematic situation. The launchers of viruses often are not aware of the launch, because they simply transfer contaminated files received innocently from other people. Thus, legislating against people who launch viruses may miss the real culprit. Legislating against creating a virus violates civil rights, because the mere creation of the virus does not cause any damage. Legislation against viruses must include creation as well as knowingly launching. Many legislatures seem to have had a serious challenge with the language of proposed bills and have thus decided against passing antivirus laws. In the meantime, countries that have computer crime laws prosecute under laws that forbid unauthorized access, because often the person who launches a virus does so by accessing a computer system without permission. Most laws regard the mere reach of the virus into a system as unauthorized access.

F. Service Theft

Service theft occurs when an employee or another person uses the resources of a computer system without permission. This may include use of the computer's CPU, disk space, and applications. Unauthorized use of computing resources is often the result of a lack of clear organizational policies rather than deliberate theft of service. Companies that have clear policies which are communicated often to workers suffer less from such acts. Organizations vary in their official or unofficial policies regarding worker use of computers. Some allow use only for work. Others allow use of such resources outside paid time. Some further restrict use for educational purposes only.

G. Denial of Service

Online businesses depend on reliable and prompt availability of the information and services they provide via the Internet. By flooding a site with inquiries, perpetrators clog servers with illegitimate requests and deny access to many legitimate ones, since servers can respond to only a limited number of requests at a time. Several denial-of-services attacks have forced, for example, online brokerages, auction sites, and other online businesses to shut down service for several hours at a time. No effective remedy to this type of attack has been found.

H. Internet Terrorism

Hackers often seize confidential information. Sometimes they use credit card information to make illegal purchases, but in some cases they have tried to extort money. They threaten the victim businesses with publication of the stolen information if the organization does not pay the requested ransom.

▪▪▪ VII. Codes of Ethics and Professional Standards

Information systems (IS) professionals perform work that has as much impact as civil engineers, certified public accountants, lawyers, and often physicians, but do not have a mandatory code of ethics and professional standards like these and many other professionals have. In fact, the only codes that IS professionals honor, voluntarily, are those of some professional organizations. The major international organizations include Association for Computing Machinery (ACM), Association for Information Technology Professionals (AITP), Institute of Electrical and Electronics Engineers (IEEE) Computer Society, and the Institute for Certification of Computer Professionals (ICCP). Several countries have their own, national organizations, such as the British Computer Society (BCS), Canadian Information Processing Society (CIPS), and German Gesellschaft für Informatik. Some of these organizations accept members from any country.

A. Obligations

The breadth and depth of the codes of ethics of IS professional organizations vary from no codes at all to terse codes of several lines (such as the code of AITP) to very detailed codes (such as the codes of ACM and IEEE Computer Society). The organization of the principles of these codes varies, too. However, some core elements appear in almost all of the codes. Here, we list them by the constituency to which the IS professional has an ethical obligation. Many of the ethics principles apply to several constituencies.

1. To Society

Educate the public about information technology; protect the privacy and confidentiality of information; avoid misrepresentation of the member's qualifications; avoid misrepresentation of information technology; obey laws; and do not take credit for other people's achievements.

2. To Employers

Update own knowledge in the field of information technology; accept responsibility for own work; present work-related information to the employer in an objective manner; and respect confidentiality.

3. To Clients

Protect confidential information and privacy; give comprehensive opinion regarding information systems; do not diminish the effectiveness of a system through commission or omission.

4. To Colleagues

Some of the codes of ethics mention colleagues, the profession, and the professional organization itself as a party toward which the member has ethical obligations. The principles are not different from those of other professions and include respect for colleagues' work and not denigrating the profession or the organization.

B. Remaining Issues

It is important to recognize that unlike in other professions, none of the IS codes of ethics clearly prefers a certain party. Physicians always have the interest of their patients (clients) above those of other parties. The same principle applies to attorneys: They always defer to the interests of their clients as opposed to those of any other party. IS professionals do not have such clear guidance either during their education or in codes of ethics. A simple case illustrates the dilemma they may face.

Suppose an IS professional is called to fix the hard disk of a university professor. The computer belongs to the professor, but it is linked to the Internet via a server that is owned by the university. The IS professional finds that the professor downloaded pornographic images from the Web. Should the professional report this fact to his employer, namely, the university? Should the professional limit himself only to fixing the problem, disregarding the information he found on the disk? None of the codes of ethics of any professional organization gives clear guidance to the professional. The lack of ranking of constituencies in importance for professionals' consideration in cases of ethical dilemmas seems to be their greatest weakness. Perhaps the codes will grow to resemble those of more established professions as the IS profession matures.

The huge loss of financial and other resources due to failure of information systems often points to lack of ethics and professional standards of the people who build and maintain the systems. In some of the largest failures of IS development projects, there were clear violations of ethical principles as simple as telling the truth about the status of a project or disclosing a lack of skill or technical capability.

C. Certification

Few of the professional organizations and societies also serve as certification institutions; one exception is the ICCP. The need for certification is a controversial issue. Certification of professionals is often expected of people with expertise above the norm who are also in a position to make decisions that affect clients, the clients' stake-holders, and the public at large. Mandatory certification could guarantee a minimum level of skill so that employers better know what to expect from a new hire and clients know what to expect from IS professionals who offer to develop and maintain information systems for them. However, the IS profession (a controversial term in itself) has been characterized by lack of mandatory standards in general, let alone standardization of ethical principles and professional standards. Thus, despite the great impact of IS professionals on our physical and financial well-being, work, and educational systems, none is subject to mandatory certification.

VIII. Conclusion

The proliferation of information systems and their use throughout the world and the growth of public computer networks have raised issues about ethical conduct with information systems. Predominantly, the issues involve privacy, unauthorized access to and use of information systems, free speech, protection of digitized intellectual property, and lack of professional ethics. Legislation has addressed some of the issues. However, as information technology progresses and continues to invade many facets of our lives, we should expect more questions about the ethics of development and use of information systems to emerge.

BIBLIOGRAPHY

Johnson, D. G., Nissenbaum, H. F. (eds.). (1995). *Computers, ethics, and social values.* Englewood Cliffs, NJ: Prentice Hall.

Kling, R. (1996). *Computerization and controversy: Value conflicts and social choices,* 2nd ed. San Diego: Academic Press.

Oz, E. (1994). *Ethics for the information age.* Dubuque, IA: Wm. C. Brown.

Rothfeder, J. (1992). *Privacy for sale.* New York: Simon and Schuster.

Wecket, J., and Douglas, A. (1997). *Computer and information ethics.* Westport, CT: Greenwood Publishing Group.

Self-Assessment*

EDITED BY ERIC A. WEISS

Scenario II.5

Computer Scientist: Accepting a Grant on a Possibly Unachievable Program

A professor of computer science applied for and received a grant from the Strategic Defense Initiative Program (SDI) to engage in a software assurance research project of a theoretical nature. The goal was to determine the methods by which error-free software might be produced on a large-scale basis. The professor does not believe that SDI is a viable Department of Defense program. She does believe, however, that her work could add measurably to the body of scientific knowledge concerning the development of error-free software. Thus, she accepted the grant money.

Pause, deliberate. Is there an ethics issue involved? Were the professors' actions unethical or not unethical? What general principles apply?

Scenario II.6

Software Developer: Relying on Questionable Inputs

A software professional was assigned the task of developing software to control a particular units of a large system. Preliminary analysis indicated that the work was well within the state of the art, and no difficulties were anticipated with the immediate task.

To function properly, or to function at all, however, the software to be developed required inputs from other units in the system. Someone gave the professional an article by an eminent software specialist that convinced him that the inputs could not be trusted. Thus, neither the software he was designing nor the unit his company was providing could correctly accomplish the task. The professional showed the article to his supervisor and explained its significance. The supervisor's response was, "That's not our problem; let's just be sure that our part of the system functions properly." The software professional continued to work on the project.

Pause, deliberate. Is there an ethics issue involved? Was the software professional's action unethical or not unethical? Was the supervisor's attitude unethical or not unethical? What general principles apply?

▮▮▮ Scenario II.II

Software Company: Ignoring Voting Machine Malfunctions

Company XYZ has developed software for a computerized voting machine. Company ABC, which manufactured the machine, has persuaded several cities and states to purchase it: On the strength of these orders, ABC is planning a major purchase from XYZ. XYZ engineer software Smith is visiting ABC one day and learns that problems in the construction of the machine mean that one in ten is likely to miscount soon after installation. Smith reports this to her superior, who informs her that that is ABC's problem. Smith does nothing further.

Pause, deliberate. Is there an ethics issue involved? Was Smith's action unethical or not unethical? Was her superior's action unethical or not unethical? What general principles apply?

▮▮▮ Scenario III.I

Computer Hacker ("Breaker"): Accessing Commercial Computer Services

Without malicious intent, a computer hacker was scanning telephone numbers with his microcomputer and identifying those numbers that responded with a computer tone. He accessed one of these computers, using a telephone number he had acquired. Without entering any identification, he received a response welcoming him to an expensive and exclusive service offered by a large bank. He was offered free of charge a sample use of some of the services if he would give his name and address. He provided someone else's name and address and used the free promotional services. This stimulated his interest in the services that the bank charged for and gave him sufficient knowledge of access protocols to attempt to use the services without authorization. He gained access to and examined the menus of services offered and instructions for use. However, he did not use the services. By examining the logging audit file and checking with the impersonated customer, bank officials identified the computer hacker and claimed that he had used their services without authorization.

Pause, deliberate. Is there an ethics issue involved? Were the hacker's actions unethical or not unethical? Consider the following actions:

- Scanning telephone numbers for computer tone
- Accessing a computer system after being "invited" to do so
- Using someone else's name and address

Consider the ethicality of the bank's contention that the hacker had used its services without authorization. What general principles apply?

▮▮▮ Scenario III.5

Programmer: Producing New Software Built on an Existing Program

Searching for new product ideas, an independent commercial programmer purchased a highly popular copyrighted software package and studied it thoroughly. He concluded that he could produce a new package that would be faster, have greater capacity, and offer additional features. He also concluded that the market would be users of the commercial package that he had studied; his new product would replace the older one. The programmer realized that in some respects he could not improve the existing product and that compatibility between his product and the existing one would attract users and minimize the transition to his new product.

The programmer went ahead and developed the new product, meeting the higher performance and new feature capabilities that he had envisioned. The keyboard codes and screen formats (except for the additional features) for the new product were the same as those for the existing product. The computer program, however, was different and independently produced. The new manual was also entirely different from the existing product manual in content and style. The programmer gave his product a new name but advertised the value of its compatibility with the existing product.

The new product was highly successful. The company that produced the existing product, however, complained that the programmer had acted unethically in producing the new product. Although the company threatened criminal and civil and legal action, it never followed through with litigation.

Pause, deliberate. Is there an ethics issue involved? Were the actions of the programmer unethical or not unethical? What general principles apply?

▮▮▮ Scenario IV.6

Programmer: Developing Marketing Profiles from Public Information

An enterprising programmer used publicly available information stored in a variety of places or available by purchase from the Department of Motor Vehicles, mail-order firms, and other sources to compile "profiles" of people (shopping habits, likely income level, whether the family was likely to have children, etc.). He sold the profiles to companies interested in marketing specialized products to niche markets. Some of his profiles were inaccurate, and the families received a large volume of unsolicited, irrelevant mail and telephone solicitations. They did not know why this increase in their junk mail and calls had occurred and found it annoying and bothersome. Other profiles were accurate, and families benefited from receiving the sales materials.

Pause, deliberate. Is there an ethics issue involved? Were the programmer's actions unethical or not unethical? What general principles apply?

▮▮▮ Scenario IV.7

Instructor: Using Students as Subjects of Experiments

An instructor of a logic course decided to test a computer-assisted instruction (CAI) system under development. The large class was divided randomly into two groups. The instructor arranged a controlled experiment in which one group was taught in the traditional manner with a textbook, lectures, and tests, but with no CAI. The other group used the same textbook, lectures, and tests, but in addition used CAI. The grading practices were the same for both groups.

By the middle of the term, the instructor realized that the students in the experimental group who had access to CAI were doing much better than the students in the control group. Some students in the control group sensed this difference and complained that, although they paid the same tuition, they were being denied an educational opportunity offered to others. These students insisted that the instructor allow them to use the CAI package for the remainder of the term. The instructor refused the students' request on the grounds that ending the experiment prematurely would vitiate the results of the experiment. The instructor pointed out that only by chance were they in the group and, because free inquiry and research are the nature of the academic world, students should take part willingly in such experiments for the sake of advancing knowledge. At the end of term, the grades in the experimental group were significantly higher than the grades in the control group.

Pause, deliberate. Is there an ethics issue involved? Were the instructor's actions unethical or not unethical? Consider the following actions:

- Using students as subjects of experiments
- Refusing students' requests to discontinue the experiment

What general principles apply?

▮▮▮ Scenario V.7

President of a Software Development Company: Marketing a Software Product Known to Have Bugs

A software development company has just produced a new software package that incorporates the new tax laws and figures taxes for both individuals and small businesses. The president of the company knows that the program probably has a number of bugs. He also believes that the first firm to put this kind of software on the market is likely to capture the largest market share. The company widely advertises the program. When the company actually ships a disk, it includes a disclaimer of responsibility for errors resulting from use of the program. The company expects it will receive a certain number of complaints, queries, and suggestions for modification. The company plans to use these to make changes and eventually issue updated, improved, and debugged versions. The president argues that this is general industry policy and that anyone who buys version 1.0 of a program knows this and will take proper precautions. Because of bugs, a number of users filed incorrect tax returns and were penalized by the IRS.

Pause, deliberate. Is there an ethics issue involved? Were the president's actions unethical or not unethical? Consider the following actions:

- Marketing a product with a disclaimer of responsibility
- Arguing that his action is general industry policy

What general principles apply?

▮▮▮ Scenario VI.6

Information Security Manager: Monitoring Electronic Mail

The information security manager in a large company was also the access control administrator of a large electronic mail system operated for company business among its employees. The security manager routinely monitored the contents of electronic correspondence among employees. He discovered that a number of employees were using the system for personal purposes; the correspondence included love letters, disagreements between married partners, plans for homosexual relations, and a football betting pool. The security manager routinely informed the human resources department director and the corporate security officer about these communications and gave them printed listings of them. In some cases, managers punished employees on the basis of the content of the electronic mail messages. Employees objected to the monitoring of their electronic mail, claiming that they had the same right of privacy as they had using the company's telephone system or internal paper interoffice mail system.

Pause, deliberate. Is there an ethics issue involved? Were the information security manager's, the employees,' and top management's actions unethical or not unethical?

▮▮▮ Scenario VI.7

Employer: Monitoring Worker's Computer Usage

An information worker in a large company performed her assignments on a workstation connected to the company's mainframe system. The company had a policy of allowing employees to use the computer services for personal purposes as long as they had the explicit approval of management. The woman had such approval to use the system for the extracurricular activities of the employees in her department.

The company suspected a rising amount of employee unrest because of its potential acquisition by another company. Management had the security department monitor all computer service activities of the information worker. Memos, letters, email messages, bulletin board notices, collections and expenditures of money, and budgets were all carefully scrutinized for evidence of employee unrest. In addition, the security department prepared reports detailing the information worker's use of the computer services—both her regular work and her employee recreation work. These reports were read and analyzed by a wide range of company managers and were stored in company vital records facilities. All of this took place unknown to the information worker.

Pause, deliberate. Is there an ethics issue involved? Were the actions unethical or not unethical? Consider the following actions:

- Allowing employees to use computer services for approved personal purposes
- Directing security departments to monitor computer services activities

What general principles apply?

PART IV

The Internet

▦ Introduction

The Internet. A decade ago, few outside of academia and government had heard of it. Now it is as common to most Americans, even if they have never experienced it directly, as newspapers and television. The Internet seems to have come out of nowhere, but now that it is here to stay, it causes changes in our lives on a regular basis. However, the Internet is not static. It changes as time goes on and as more people log on. People do not surf anymore; they log on, perform very targeted tasks, and they log off. Shopping was not the killer application—the bursting of the stock market bubble showed us that. The "new economy" only lasted for a few years. No, the killer app was not e-commerce or m-commerce; instead, it was e-mail, something we knew but did not want to believe. Yet as the Internet spreads to new demographic groups and to new countries, the first thing people use it for is e-mail. The Internet is not so much a commercial technology as it is a social technology. Pornography was (and continues to be) a financial success long before (and after) online trading became popular. Gambling, fraud, and other human vices thrive online. However, the same technology also is used by parents sending photos of children to relatives, teenagers using instant messaging, and virtual communities who gather online to say things and be things they would never be or say in person. Who can predict how will it change again as more people move to broadband? How long will it take for the Internet to remake itself again? Five years? Two years? One?

For these reasons, no book purporting to be about computers and society can *not* focus on the Internet. Even though this fourth part of the book is supposed to be devoted to the Internet, you will notice that the Internet seeps into the other parts of the book as well.

▦ The Articles in Part 4

The Internet in the United States and the World

Excerpts from Barua, A., and A. Whinston. 2001. *Measuring the Internet Economy*. Center for Research in Electronic Commerce, Graduate School of Business, University of Texas at Austin, TX. Available at www.internetindicators.com.

When the results of this study were first made public, they were considered to be remarkable. The "new economy," the Internet economy, as measured by

Barua and Whinston, was larger than many had anticipated. These excerpts provide various economic indicators and show how the Internet economy can be thought of as consisting of four different layers.

Wolcott, P., L. Press, W. McHenry, S. E. Goodman, and W. Foster. 2001. "A framework for assessing the global diffusion of the Internet." *Journal of the AIS* 2.

As Wolcott and his colleagues note, no other technical innovation has diffused throughout the world as quickly as the Internet. The authors have created a framework that allows for the measurement of Internet diffusion at the national level. After explaining the framework, they use Cuba as an example of how the framework can be applied.

Social Implications of Internet Use

Kraut, R., V. Lundmark, M. Patterson, S. Kiesler, T. Mukopadhyay, and W. Scherlis. 1998. "Internet paradox: A social technology that reduces social involvement and psychological well-being?" *American Psychologist* 53(9): 1017–1031.

The authors studied 93 families in the Pittsburgh, Pennsylvania area as part of their HomeNet project in 1995 and 1996. The families that participated did not have Internet access in their homes, and most did not have access to powerful computers in their homes prior to the study. Analyzing their data longitudinally, the authors found Internet use to be associated with declines in family communication and social-circle size and increases in loneliness and depression.

Kraut, R., S. Kiesler, B. Boneva, J. Cummings, V. Helgeson, and A. Crawford. 2002. "Internet paradox revisited." *Journal of Social Issues* 58: 49–74.

Three years after the original HomeNet data were collected, the authors conducted a follow-up study with the original participants. They found that, among the original participants, many of the negative effects of Internet use, found in the first year or two of the study, had disappeared 3 years later. The authors also found generally positive effects of Internet use in a new sample they studied in 1998–1999.

The Internet, Government, and the Law

Excerpts from Branscomb, A. W. 1996. "Cyberspaces: Familiar Territory or Lawless Frontiers," *Journal of Computer-Mediated Communication* 2(1).

The image of the Internet as a lawless frontier has become common, yet as Branscomb demonstrates in this abridged version of her article, many have worked to bring some sort of order to the frontier.

Thompson, K. M., C. R. McClure, P. T. Jaeger. "Evaluating Federal Web sites: Improving E-Government for the People."

E-government has grown alongside e-commerce. More and more government agencies in the United States and around the world are establishing Web sites to provide information and government services. Thompson, McClure, and

Jaeger discuss the need for evaluating U.S. federal government Web sites and their implications for e-democracy.

Digital Divides

Hoffman, D. L., and T. P. Novak. 1998. "Bridging the digital divide on the Internet." *Science*, April 17, 390–391.

> In this 1998 article, Hoffman and Novak investigated the differences in computer and Internet access and use between white Americans and African Americans. Their work supports the existence of a substantial gap, in favor of white Americans, even when income is factored into the equation.

Eastin, M. S., and R. LaRose. 2000. "Internet self-efficacy and the psychology of the digital divide." *Journal of Computer-Mediated Communication* 6(1).

> Eastin and LaRose developed a scale for Internet self-efficacy and found that it was related to experience with the Internet, with Internet use, and with outcome expectations. They reason that giving computer and Internet access alone to people may not necessarily close the digital divide unless the psychological effects of low self-efficacy are also considered.

Boneva, B., R. Kraut, and D. Frohlich. 2001. "Using e-mail for personal relationships: The difference gender makes." *American Behavioral Scientist. Special issue on The Internet and Everyday Life* 45(3): 530–549.

> Boneva, Kraut, and Frohlich found differences in e-mail use, depending on gender. Women were more likely than men to use e-mail to maintain relationships with family and to find contact with family and friends gratifying. Women are also more likely than men to use e-mail to support distant relationships.

Free Speech and the Internet

Davenport, D. 2002. "Anonymity on the Internet: Why the price may be too high." *Communications of the ACM* 45(4): 33–35.

> Some believe that anonymous communication on the Web is a key part of the Internet culture and a guarantor of truly free speech. Davenport argues that anonymity is actually a threat to society and that more openness and accountability are to be preferred.

American Library Association. 1948. "Library Bill of Rights."

> First adopted in 1948, the Library Bill of Rights lays out seven principles the American Library Association believes should guide the services provided by libraries.

Lessig, L. 1999. *Code and Other Laws of Cyberspace*, Chap 12. New York: Basic Books.

> In "Free Speech," a chapter from his celebrated book *Code*, Lessig writes about the regulation of and the protection of speech in cyberspace.

▮▮▮ Related Places to Go on the Web

In many ways, the Internet is a self-documenting system. Many, many Web sites are devoted solely to the Internet. Just about anything one would want to know about the Internet is documented somewhere on the Web, most likely in dozens or even hundreds of sites. The best way to start is just to find a favorite search engine, enter some key words, and start surfing.

All I can do here is provide you with a few sites related to the Internet topics introduced in this section that I have found useful over the years.

For finding out the latest in who is using the Internet and for what, I have found few better general sites that www.nua.net/surveys/.

If you are interested in reading more by Hoffman and Novak and their colleagues, go to http://elab.vanderbilt.edu/, the official site of their research group, eLab.

You can also find out more about Carnegie Mellon University's HomeNet project by going to their Web site, http://homenet.andrew.cmu.edu/progress/.

The American Library Association (ALA) has many materials on its Web site (www.ala.org) that relate to privacy and free speech issues that involve the Internet. You will also find information on free speech on some of the Web sites provided in the introduction to the section on privacy, such as www.cdt.org/.

The GVU Center at the Georgia Institute of Technology (Georgia Tech) conducted a series of 10 celebrated Web surveys between 1994 and 1998. Just about everything you would want to know about these surveys is at www.gvu.gatech.edu/user_surveys/.

ADDITIONAL READING

Brown, J. S., and P. Duguid. 2000. *The Social Life of Information*. Boston: Harvard Business School Press.

Gates, W. 2000. *Business @ the Speed of Thought: Succeeding in the Digital Economy*. New York: Warner Books.

Hagel, J., and A. G. Armstrong. 1997. *Net Gain*. Boston: Harvard Business School Press.

Hoffman, D. L., and T. P. Novak. 2000. "The growing digital divide: Implications for an open research agenda." In E. Brynjolffson and B. Kahin (eds.), *Understanding the Digital Economy: Data, Tools and Research*, pp. 245–260. Cambridge: MIT Press.

Katz, J., and R. Rice. 2002. *Social Consequences of Internet Use: Access, Involvement, and Interaction*. Cambridge: MIT Press.

Lessig, L. 2001. *The Future of Ideas*. New York: Random House.

Margolis, J., and A. Fisher. 2001. *Unlocking the Clubhouse: Women in Computing*. Cambridge: MIT Press.

Negroponte, N. 1996. *Being Digital*. New York: Vintage Books.

Norris, P. 2001. *Digital Divide: Civic Engagement, Information Poverty, and the Internet Worldwide*. Cambridge, UK: Cambridge University Press.

Press, L. 1997. "Tracking the global diffusion of the Internet." *Communications of the ACM* 40(11): 11–17.

Scherlis, W. L., and J. Eisenburg. 2003. "IT research, innovation, and e-government." *Communications of the ACM* 46(1): 67–68.

Schneier, B. 2000. *Secrets & Lies: Digital Security in a Networked World*. New York: John Wiley & Sons, Inc.

Schwartau, W. 2000. *Cybershock*. New York: Thunder Mouth's Press.

Shapiro, C., and H. R. Varian. 1999. *Information Rules*. Boston: Harvard Business School Press.

Measuring the Internet Economy

ANITESH BARUA

ANDREW WHINSTON

▪▪▪ Executive Summary

The Internet Economy force has become a more integral part of the U.S. economy than ever before, creating jobs and increasing productivity in companies across the economy. The impact goes far beyond dot coms, as Internet Economy forces are transforming traditional companies and jobs.

Seven of every 10 of these jobs are traditional, rather than high-tech, jobs, according to a new study by the University of Texas' Center for Research in Electronic Commerce. Of the Internet-related jobs, only 28 percent are in Information Technology, which ranks below sales and marketing (33 percent) as the job function generating the most Internet-related employment. Dot com companies are a very small part (about 9.6 percent) of the overall Internet Economy.

The research is contained in the fourth report measuring the Internet Economy commissioned by Cisco Systems and covers the first half of 2000.

It shows the Internet is transforming the economy and the way people work, to an extent few people would have imagined just a few years ago.

According to the study, the Internet Economy now directly supports more than 3.088 million workers, including an additional 600,000 in the first half of 2000. This is about 60,000 more than the number employed in insurance industry and double the real estate industry. These jobs were created both by the explosion of the Internet and by companies shifting workers to take advantage of the benefits created by embracing the Internet.

Employment in Internet Economy companies is growing much faster than employment in the overall economy. Total employment at Internet Economy companies grew 10 percent between the first quarter of 1999 and the first quarter of 2000. Internet-related jobs at Internet Economy companies grew 29 percent during the same period. Both of these figures far exceed the growth of non-Internet related jobs in these same Internet Economy companies, which grew 6.9 percent during the same period.

The Internet Economy generated an estimated $830 billion in revenues in 2000, a 58 percent increase over 1999. The $830 billion in revenues is a 156 percent increase from 1998, when the Internet accounted for $323 billion in revenues.

Internet Economy revenue is growing twice as fast as Internet Economy employment. In 2000, for example, second quarter revenue grew 58.8 percent over the second quarter of 1999. Meanwhile second quarter employment grew 22.6 percent over 1999. Internet-related revenue is a growing piece of corporate revenue as a whole. For Internet Economy companies, Internet revenue is one-fifth the size of non-Internet revenue—but growing three times as fast as corporate revenue as a whole. Revenue grew by $23 billion between the first quarter of 1999 and first quarter of 2000. Internet-related revenue grew $68 billion during the same period.

Internet Economy employees are increasingly productive employees. Revenue per employee increased an estimated 11.5 percent in the first half of 2000—a key indication of the productivity gains generated by the Internet.

In the first half of 2000, Internet Economy companies generated $1 of every $5 in revenue from the Internet.

Even as the overall economy experiences fluctuations, Internet Economy forces continue to reshape the economy in unprecedented ways, producing savings for businesses and consumers alike. And reports of strong online holiday spending levels in 2000 (a study by Goldman Sachs and PC Data, for example, said total Internet holiday spending rose to $8.7 billion from $4.2 billion in 1999) provide yet another sign of the way customers and retailers now routinely use the Internet.

The Internet is increasingly becoming part of the basic business model for many companies, laying the groundwork for even more impressive growth during strong economic conditions. The Internet is rapidly becoming an integral part of the traditional economy—like telephones, elevators and personal computers over the years—leading to the day when there will be no separate measure of the Internet Economy.

▮▮▮ Key Findings

The Internet Economy Supported an Additional 612,375 Jobs in the First Half of 2000 and Directly Supports Three Million Workers

The addition of 612,375 jobs in the Internet Economy in the first six months of 2000 was nearly as much as all of 1999 (when 650,000 jobs were added). Overall, Internet Economy employment jumped 25 percent during the first half of 2000 from the end of 1999. As an example of its growing role in the economy, the Internet Economy now employs more workers than the insurance industry (2.36 million workers) and the real estate industry (1.5 million).[1] The largest provider of Internet jobs is now the Internet Commerce layer, which added over a quarter million jobs in the first six months of 2000.

---

[1] Bureau of Labor Statistics, "Employees on nonfarm payrolls by industry," August, 2000.

Internet Economy Indicators
Quarterly Employment Figures
Summary by Layer and Total Internet Economy

	Quarter 1, 2000	Growth over Q1 1999	Quarter 2, 2000	Growth over Q2 1999
Layer 1—Infrastructure Indicator	877,245	51.8%	932,484	37.7%
Layer 2—Application Indicator	711,396	62.3%	740,673	51.9%
Layer 3—Intermediary Indicator	457,876	5.5%	468,689	3.9%
Layer 4—Internet Commerce Indicator	1,020,416	12.6%	1,033,159	8.2%
The Internet Economy (After removing overlap)	2,986,913	29.1%	3,088,497	22.6%

Source: Center for Research in Electronic Commerce, Graduate School of Business, University of Texas at Austin, © 2001

The Internet Economy Is Projected to Produce $830 Billion in Revenues in 2000, a 58 Percent Increase over 1999

If the technology sector and the U.S. economy remain relatively healthy, the Internet Economy generated an estimated $830 billion in revenues in 2000, a 58 percent increase over 1999. To understand how far the Internet Economy has come in a short period of time, the $830 billion is a 156 percent increase from 1998 when the Internet accounted for $323 billion in revenues in 1998.

Internet Economy Indicators
Quarterly Revenue
Summary by Layer and Total Internet Economy (in $ Millions)

	Quarter 1, 2000	Growth over Q1 1999	Quarter 2, 2000	Growth over Q2 1999
Layer 1—Infrastructure Indicator	$67,656	69.3%	$75,211	57.4%
Layer 2—Application Indicator	$33,930	73.5%	$38,925	58.9%
Layer 3—Intermediary Indicator	$27,295	63.8%	$36.704	84.6%
Layer 4—Internet Commerce Indicator	$60,341	66.7%	$66,956	57.8%
The Internet Economy (After removing overlap)	$173,601	64.2%	$200,219	58.8%

Source: Center for Research in Electronic Commerce, Graduate School of Business, University of Texas at Austin, © 2001

Internet-Related Jobs Are Not Just in Information Technology

Of the Internet-related jobs, only 28 percent are in Information Technology, which ranks below Sales and Marketing (33 percent) as the job function generating the most Internet-related employment. What this reflects is the impact the Internet is having on traditional businesses and jobs—from sales and manufacturing to finance and accounting positions.

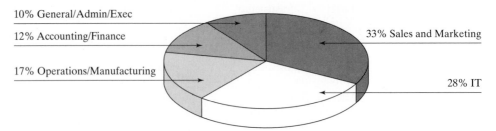

The "Dot Coms" Versus the Overall Internet Economy

While "dot com" companies have often been the face of the Internet Economy, interestingly they make up a very small part of it. Only 9.6 percent of the revenue was generated by "dot coms"—firms with 95 percent or more of their revenue derived from the Internet.

Internet Economy Indicators
"dot com" Summary

	Quarter 1 2000	Percent of Total Internet Economy	Quarter 2 2000	Percent of Total Internet Economy	Growth Q1–Q2
"dot com" Revenue (in $ Millions)	$16,114	9.3%	$19,125	9.6%	18.7%
"dot com" Employees	362,487	12.1%	360,718	11.7%	−.5%

Employment in Internet Economy Companies Is Growing Much Faster Than Employment in the Overall Economy

Total employment at Internet Economy companies grew 10 percent between the first quarter of 1999 and the first quarter of 2000. Internet-related jobs at Internet Economy companies grew 29 percent during the same period. Both of these figures far exceed the growth of non-Internet related jobs in these same Internet Economy companies, which grew 6.9 percent during the same period.

Internet Economy Indicators
Internet Employees vs. Non-Internet Employees
Percentage and Growth

	Quarter 1, 1999 Employment/ Percent	Quarter 1, 2000 Employment/ Percent	Growth Q1, 1999– Q1, 2000	Quarter 2, 2000 Employment/ Percent
Total Employees (Internet and Non-Internet)	21,783,949/ 100%	23,792,169/ 100%	10.3%	24,639,520/ 100%
Internet Employees	2,313,280/ 11%	2,986,913/ 13%	29%	3,088,497/ 13%
Non-Internet Employees	19,470,669/ 89%	20,805,256/ 87%	6.9%	21,551,023/ 87%

Source: Center for Research in Electronic Commerce, Graduate School of Business, University of Texas at Austin, © 2001

Internet Economy Revenue Is Growing Twice As Fast As Internet Economy Employment

The fact that revenues are growing at such a significant pace above employment strongly suggests that the Internet is enabling substantial efficiency gains. What also bears this out is the growth in productivity for the overall business sector in the United States. The Bureau of Labor Statistics reports 2.7 percent growth in 1998 and 3.1 percent growth in 1999 for the business sector, which indicates a substantial increase in productivity in the broader U.S. economy. During the same period, unemployment remained at historic lows.

The Internet Has Become an Indispensable Revenue Stream—One in Every Five Dollars in Revenue Is Generated from the Internet

Internet-related revenue is a growing piece of the corporate revenue pie. Despite the fact it only accounts for a fraction of the overall revenue base, it is driving the vast majority of revenue gains. For example, Internet Economy companies' Internet-related revenue grew $68 billion from the first quarter of 1999 to the first quarter of 2000—an astounding 64 percent. That compares to a $23 billion growth in non-Internet revenue during the same period—a growth rate of 3.6 percent.

Internet Economy Indicators
Internet Revenue vs. Non-Internet Revenue
Percentage and Growth (in $ Millions)

	Quarter 1, 1999 Revenue/ Percent	Quarter 1, 2000 Revenue/ Percent	Growth Q1, 1999– Q1, 2000	Quarter 2, 2000 Revenue/ Percent
Total Revenue (Internet and Non-Internet)	$775,814/ 100%	$867,473/ 100%	11.8%	$906,806/ 100%
Internet Revenue	$105,751/ 14%	$173,601/ 20%	64%	$200,219/ 22%
Non-Internet Revenue	$670,063/ 86%	$693,872/ 80%	3.6%	$706,587/ 78%

Source: Center for Research in Electronic Commerce, Graduate School of Business, University of Texas at Austin, © 2001

The Internet Economy Is Highly Productive, with Quarterly Revenue Per Employee Increasing 11.5 Percent Through the First Two Quarters of 2000

Overall, revenue per employee increased 11.5 percent from the first quarter to second quarter of 2000 alone. The Intermediary Layer alone increased 31.4 percent through the first two quarters of the year.

Internet Economy Indicators
Quarterly Revenue per Employee and Growth Summary
by Layer and Total Internet Economy

	Quarter 1, 2000	Quarter 2, 2000	Growth Q1–Q2
Layer 1— Infrastructure Indicator	$77,123	$80,657	4.6%
Layer 2— Application Indicator	$47,695	$52,554	10.2%
Layer 3— Intermediary Indicator	$59,612	$78,312	31.4%

(continued)

	Quarter 1, 2000	Quarter 2, 2000	Growth Q1–Q2
Layer 4— Internet Commerce Indicator	$59,134	$64,807	9.6%
The Internet Economy (after removing overlap)	$58,121	$64,827	11.5%

Source: Center for Research in Electronic Commerce, Graduate School of Business, University of Texas at Austin, © 2001

Internet Intermediaries Take Off in First Half of 2000

The Internet Intermediary Layer grew an impressive 34.5 percent between the first and second quarters of 2000, generating almost $64 billion in revenues in the first half of the year. Year over year, Layer Three first quarter revenues grew 63.8 percent in relation to the first quarter of 1999. But the real story came in the second quarter, when revenues increased an amazing 84.6 percent over the second quarter of last year.

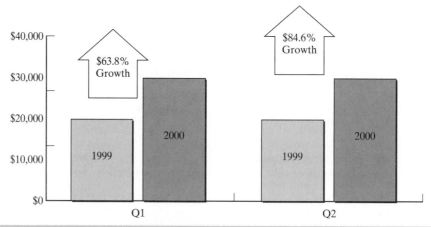

▪▪▪▪▪▪▪▪▪▪▪▪ **Layer Three Quarterly Revenue Growth Comparison 1999–2000**

▪▪▪ Overview—The Big Picture

It has often been said that the personal computer industry's growth from zero to $100 billion in ten years was "the greatest legal accumulation of wealth in history." While the PC has played a significant role in the adoption of the Internet, the Internet economy will cross $800 billion in five years. Today, the Internet has enabled a new business model that Forester Research calls "Dynamic Trade," which is fundamentally altering the creation, delivery and pricing of products and services.

In the third wave of the Internet Economy Indicators research (June 2000), we documented an impressive growth of both revenues and jobs associated with the emerging Internet economy. Despite the failure of some highly publicized dot coms during the last two quarters, numbers from this research suggest that this new economy keeps growing rapidly and continues to create opportunities for all types of companies. This report shows that the Internet economy constitutes much more than dot coms, and is pervasive across all business sectors. Smart, traditional companies are embracing the Internet and "digitizing" their business models and processes to leverage this ubiquitous electronic infrastructure in every aspect of their business operations. Such companies are observing significant increases in revenue and revenue per employee. Their contribution to the Internet economy revenue and job estimates far exceeds that of dot com companies, suggesting that the Internet economy is creating a real, measurable impact on the physical economy. Furthermore, the demise of some large names in dot coms does not imply that all dot coms will turn out to be failures. Our research identifies a large number of such dot com companies, most of which are not publicly held. While they constitute a small percentage of the Internet economy in terms of revenues, as a group these dot coms have had a healthy revenue growth in the first two quarters of 2000, and have held up an impressive gross profit margin. More importantly, they are improving their financial performance rapidly over time, indicating the presence of a strong learning effect.

The unprecedented rate of growth of this new economy calls for an analysis of the tremendous changes that are brought about by the Internet. More specifically, how do we understand a technological breakthrough such as the Internet? What are some key differences between the Internet economy and the bricks-and-mortar economy? How do we understand the wide range of consequences that the Internet has across various sections of the economy? Is there a historical precedent for the major technological innovations to go through a period of experimentation before they gain widespread acceptance? How can we obtain an accurate assessment of the consumer value of the Internet? How is the growth of the Internet different from that predicted by economic growth theories? To what extent do traditional bricks-and-mortar and dot coms contribute to the growth and productivity of the new economy? Who are the beneficiaries of the Internet revolution? In this report, we document another two quarters of record growth of revenues and jobs in the Internet economy, and begin to address a wide range of questions involving potential economic impacts. Welcome to the fourth wave of the Internet Economy Indicators research.

IIII The Internet Economy Indicators

Due to the complexity and inter-relatedness of the companies that contribute to the Internet Economy, a classification system was developed to separate associated revenues and employees into distinct segments. The most logical approach for this classification system was to break apart the Internet Economy into layers based upon the unique elements necessary to facilitate the ultimate revenue producer on the Internet: sales transactions. This diverse range of elements underscores that the Internet Economy is much more than just online retail sales. The Internet has become a

Internet backbone providers
Internet service providers
Networking hardware and software companies
PC and Server manufacturers
Security vendors
Fiber optics makers
Line acceleration hardware manufacturers

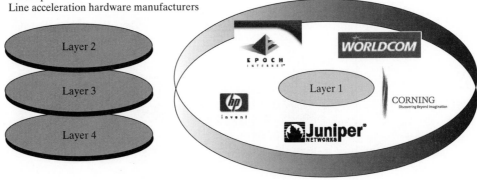

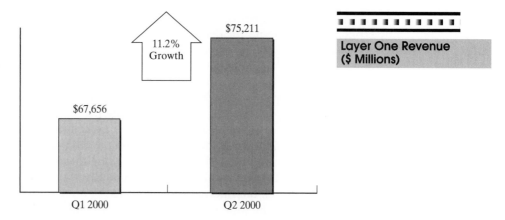

Layer One Revenue ($ Millions)

medium through which a wide variety of goods and services are traded between businesses, businesses and consumers, and even between private individuals.

Layer One—The Internet Infrastructure Indicator

The Internet Infrastructure Layer consists of the telecommunications companies, Internet Service Providers, Internet backbone carriers, "last mile" access companies and manufacturers of end-user networking equipment—all of which are a prerequisite for the Web and the proliferation of Internet-based electronic commerce.

- The Internet Infrastructure Layer generated $142.8 billion in revenues in the first half of the year 2000, growing 11.2 percent between the first and second quarters.
- Year over year, Layer One first quarter revenues grew 69.3 percent when compared to the same quarter in 1999. Second quarter revenues increased by 57.4 percent over the same quarter last year.
- The Internet Infrastructure Layer employed over 932,000 individuals at the end of the first half of 2000, growing just under 6 percent between the first and second quarters.
- Layer One employment in the first quarter grew almost 52 percent over the same quarter of last year. Second quarter growth slowed in comparison with the same quarter of 1999, growing 37.7 percent year over year.

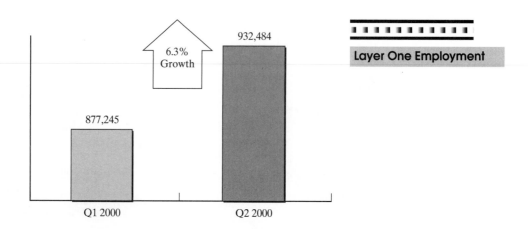

Layer One Employment

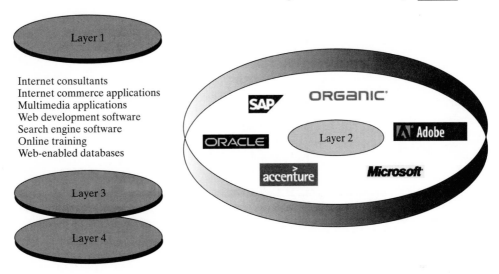

Layer 1

Internet consultants
Internet commerce applications
Multimedia applications
Web development software
Search engine software
Online training
Web-enabled databases

Layer 3

Layer 4

- Layer One provides the platform for growth for the remainder of the Internet Economy. Quarterly revenue per employee is the highest of all the layers, reaching over $80,000 for the second quarter alone. This healthy figure indicates continued high productivity among infrastructure players.
- It is important to consider that many of the largest Internet Infrastructure companies contribute not only to Layer One, but also generate significant e-commerce revenues. In many cases, they also provide Layer Two products and services.

Layer Two—The Internet Applications Infrastructure Indicator

The Internet Applications Infrastructure involves software products and services necessary to facilitate Web transactions as well as transaction intermediaries. In addition to the software products and platforms that help facilitate Web transactions, this layer of the Internet Economy includes the consultants and service companies that design, build and maintain all types of Web sites, from portals to full e-commerce sites. While the output of this layer may not be tangible to the average user of the Internet, it is the fundamental basis for e-commerce and other functionality on the Internet.

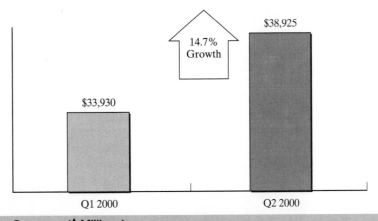

Layer Two Revenue ($ Millions)

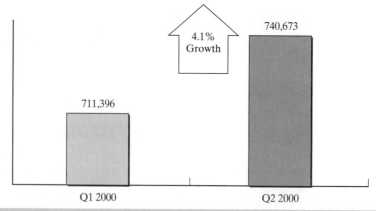

- The Internet Applications Infrastructure Layer grew 14.7 percent between the first and second quarters of 2000, generating $72.8 billion in revenues.
- Year over year, Layer Two first quarter revenues grew 62.3 percent in relation to the first quarter of 1999. Second quarter revenues increased by 51.9 percent over the same quarter last year.
- Layer Two employment in the first quarter grew over 62 percent when compared with the first quarter of last year. Second quarter employment growth was almost 52 percent in comparison with the same quarter of 1999.
- The Internet Applications Infrastructure Layer employed over 740,000 individuals at the end of the first half of 2000, growing just over 4 percent between the first and second quarters.
- Layer Two has the lowest quarterly revenue per employee at $52,554 for the second quarter of 2000. This lower revenue is reasonable, however, when seen in the context of applications, integration, and consulting—two major components of the Internet Applications Infrastructure layer. These components of Layer Two

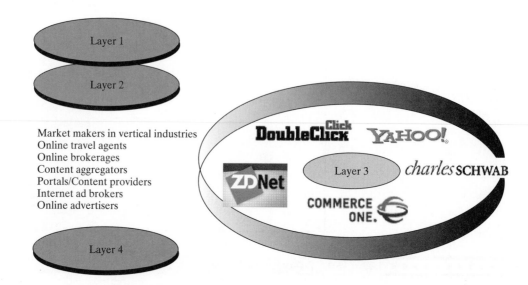

Market makers in vertical industries
Online travel agents
Online brokerages
Content aggregators
Portals/Content providers
Internet ad brokers
Online advertisers

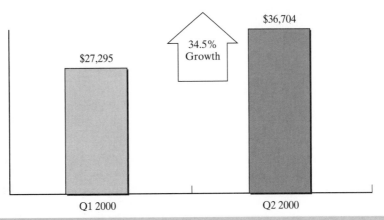

▪▪▪▪▪▪▪▪▪▪▪ **Layer Three Revenue ($ Millions)**

are very human capital intensive, requiring more employees to generate revenue than other layers.

Layer Three—The Internet Intermediary Indicator

When looking at businesses conducting transactions on the Web, it was recognized that there was a class of business that did not generate transaction-related revenues in the same way as companies in the Internet Commerce Layer (Layer Four). Therefore, it was determined that a category would be added for these types of companies and this layer is called the Internet Intermediary Indicator.

A distinct type of company operates in Layer Three, one that is predominantly an Internet pure-play. While not directly generating revenues from transactions, their Web-based business generates revenues through advertising, membership subscription fees, and commissions. Many of the Layer Three companies are purely Web content providers, while others are market makers or market intermediaries. This is an important

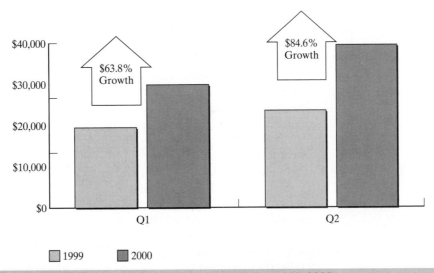

▪▪▪▪▪▪▪▪▪▪▪ **Layer Three Quarterly Revenue Growth Comparison 1999–2000**

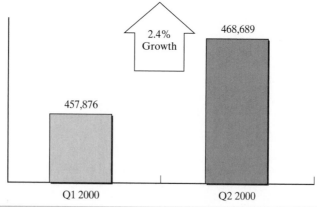

▪▪▪▪▪▪▪▪▪▪▪▪ **Layer Three Employment**

group of companies that is likely to have a significant impact over time on the efficiency and performance of electronic markets.

- The Internet Intermediary Layer grew an impressive 34.5 percent between the first and second quarters of 2000, generating almost $64 billion in revenues in the first half of the year.
- Year over year, Layer Three first quarter revenues grew 63.8 percent in relation to the first quarter of 1999. But the real story came in the second quarter, when revenues increased an amazing 84.6 percent over the second quarter of last year.
- The Internet Intermediary Layer employs the fewest individuals of any of the layers, yet employment at the end of the first half of 2000 approached half a million employees (468,689), growing just over 2 percent between the first and second quarters.
- Layer Three employment in the first quarter grew just 5.5 percent when compared with the first quarter of last year. Second quarter employment growth was just 3.2 percent in comparison with the same quarter of 1999. These low growth rates reflect the nature of the Internet Intermediary Layer, where infrastructure investments and automated processes can be most leveraged to produce revenue. For example, airlines can process ticket sales online and grow their revenue from the Internet without adding additional employees. Customers can compare ticket prices and book online without the use of a travel agent. This layer is efficient by nature, because in many cases it removes the employee from the transaction between the company and the customer.
- Quarterly revenue per employee for the Intermediaries is the second highest of all the layers at $78,312 for the second quarter alone, again reflecting the potential for leveraging technology infrastructure to raise the productivity of employees and processes.
- The majority of the impressive growth that we see in the Intermediary Layer was generated by smaller companies, which seem to be maturing and beginning to produce revenues as they move from the "build-out" to the "operational" stage of the corporate life cycle. At the same time, several large companies achieved respectable double-digit growth over this period. Examples include DoubleClick, 24/7, OmniCom, and Interpublic in advertising; Yahoo!, Lycos, Disney and USA Networks in content; E-Bay, Cheap Tickets, HomeStore, and Hotel Reservations in other areas of intermediary commerce.

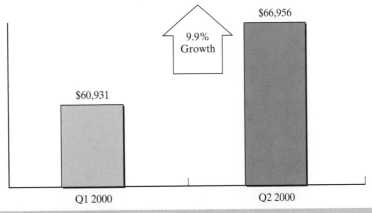

E-tailers
Manufacturers selling online
Fee/Subscription-based companies
Airlines selling online tickets
Online entertainment and professional services

Layer Four—The Internet Commerce Indicator

The companies that are included in Layer Four are only those companies that are conducting Web-based commerce transactions. While many other studies of e-commerce have included intermediary companies such as VerticalNet or eBay, we included those companies in Layer Three.

The companies that we have included in Layer Four cross a wide variety of vertical industries. In addition, the commerce layer contains quite a few "mom and pop" shops generating a respectable revenue stream. This layer also includes the e-commerce revenue of retailers with significant "brick-and-mortar" or catalog presence.

It is important to note that Layer Four can include Business-to-Business e-commerce as well as Business-to-Consumer online sales. The distinction between "B2B" and "B2C" is not always easy to make and many companies play in both arenas. Clearly, some companies sell only to other businesses, as in the case of cocoexchange. com (which leases and rents equipment to companies over the Internet). Others, such as Target.com, are clearly in the consumer market. At the same time, many Layer Four companies sell both to consumers and to businesses of all sizes. Examples include the airlines (selling to business and leisure passengers), Dell and other online computer retailers (who sell to enterprises through customized Web portals and to consumers through Dell.com), and even office supplies retailers such as Office Depot, Office Max,

Layer Four Revenue ($ Millions)

and Staples (which have consumer e-commerce but also allow their business customers to order from their contract stationer arms over the Internet).

- Internet Commerce Layer grew 11 percent between the first and second quarters of 2000, generating over $127 billion in revenues in the first half of 2000.
- Year over year, Layer Four first quarter revenues grew 66.7 percent in relation to the first quarter of 1999. Second quarter revenues were 57.8 percent higher than those produced in the second quarter of 1999.
- The Internet Commerce Layer has the highest employment of any of the layers, topping 1 million in the first half of 2000. It is not surprising, given current trends such as the shakeout in business-to-consumer dot coms, that employment growth between the first and second quarters was just over 1 percent.
- Layer Four employment in the first quarter grew 12.6 percent when compared with the first quarter of last year. Second quarter employment growth was 8.2 percent in comparison with the same quarter of 1999.
- Quarterly revenue per employee for the second quarter came in at just under $65,000—reflecting slow employment growth combined with respectable revenue growth.

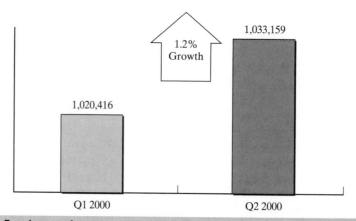

▪ ▪ ▪ ▪ ▪ ▪ ▪ ▪ ▪ ▪ ▪ **Layer Four Employment**

A Framework for Assessing the Global Diffusion of the Internet

PETER WOLCOTT
LARRY PRESS
WILLIAM MCHENRY
SEYMOUR GOODMAN
WILLIAM FOSTER

I. Introduction

With a jump in the user base from tens of thousands at the beginning of the 1990s to over 300 million at the end, the Internet has undoubtedly diffused faster than almost any other technical innovation in modern times. And yet, trying to characterize the nature of this diffusion beyond some obvious, first order statistics such as number of hosts, is exceedingly difficult. Even the definition of what constitutes a true "user" or host is difficult to pin down. How any given user experiences the Internet depends on a wide variety of factors. The Internet topology is constantly changing, and is a delivery mechanism for a constantly evolving array of software applications and information. At the same time numerous Internet "factoids," such as the Nov., 2000 estimate of 407 Million Internet users, are constantly being introduced by a barrage of press releases and web sites (Nua Internet Surveys, 2001). The underlying methodologies for these studies are often obscure. This leads both to confusion and to a false sense that we know what is going on.

The purpose of this paper is to set forth a framework by which Internet diffusion may be measured at the national level. This framework was developed by the MOSAIC Group as part of the Global Diffusion of the Internet Project (GDI). Parts of it have been explained in previous papers (Goodman et al., 1998a; Press et al., 1998) or in studies of specific countries, but this is the first time it is being published in full. The framework is based on an ongoing inductive study of the Internet in a wide representation of countries around the world.[1] This paper does not try to set forth a general theory of why the Internet diffuses as it does, but may be considered a necessary precursor to the development of such a theory.

The need for well-justified country-level diffusion metrics is strong. The recent proliferation of various "e-readiness" and similar indexes, and a recently announced initiative by the World Bank's InfoDev unit to fund such studies (Infodev, 2001), underscores the strong interest of policy makers and business people alike. Researchers who are studying how the Internet is influencing and changing the economic, political, and social systems of various countries have been limited by the absence of measures that are more accurate, descriptive, and sophisticated than the simple number of Internet hosts in a country (Menou, 1999; Wilson, Daly and Griffiths, 1998).

Interest in national level metrics is well-founded. Miller and Slater (2000, 1), in justifying their ethnographic approach, point out: "contrary to the first generation of Internet literature—the Internet is not a monolithic or placeless 'cyber-space'; rather, it is numerous new technologies, used by diverse people, in diverse real-world locations." To *what* a user has access and *why* depends on the specific legal, economic, political, and social conditions that surround that user. In spite of claims that the Internet and other trends related to globalization are subverting the sovereignty of national governments and blurring national boundaries, governments still make policies that can have a dramatic effect on the diffusion and absorption of the Internet (Greenberg and Goodman, 1996). Furthermore, users are located within a particular National System of Innovation, which also strongly influences the diffusion process and the absorptive capacity of a country.[2]

Authors who write papers that are primarily concerned with metrics always face a dilemma. If we begin by examining prior work and the theory behind the measures, we must ask readers to accept the justification without fully understanding the measures. If we put the measures first, we must ask the reader to temporarily accept that they do, in fact, have sufficiently strong justifications. We have chosen to present the measures first in Section II, referring only to aspects of justification that are essential in directly describing the measures.

Classification systems reduce more complex phenomena to simpler representations that are easier to understand and to manipulate in the formulation and testing of hypotheses. Classification systems should be "natural," meaning that they represent real underlying properties and relationships—the way the world actually works (Ridley, 1986). They also should be practical, based on data that can be collected with reasonable accuracy, timeliness, and cost. We accordingly break the justification section into two parts. Section III concerns underlying theories and other work on Internet diffusion. We will consider the relationship of the GDI methodology to the National Systems of Innovation work, to evolutionary analogies, and to Diffusion of Innovations theory. Section IV concerns how the framework may be applied in practice, and presents a brief summary of one of the GDI studies. Section V presents conclusions, contributions, and directions for future research.

---

[1]Goodman et al. (1994) took an early look at Internet diffusion. See Table 11, Section IV for a list of GDI studies and references. Check Wolcott (2001) for new GDI work.

[2]Edquist (1997) and Archibugi (1999) provide excellent introductions to the National Systems of Innovation (NSI) literature. The GDI methodology can also be applied to a region larger than a country or to sub-units within a country, and throughout this paper readers may substitute region for country with no loss of generality. This is in keeping with similar extensions to the NSI approach (Howells, 1999). We return to the NSI approach in Section III.

▪▪▪ ## II. A Framework for Analyzing Internet Diffusion Within a Country

Traditional diffusion studies typically stop at the point at which a user has chosen to adopt a single innovation, and thus have a single dependent variable (Rogers, 1995). For the Internet, this variable has often been "number of hosts" or "users." We will argue, however, that the Internet is not a single innovation but is a cluster of related technologies that must be present together to support adoption decisions by end users. The Internet cannot work unless there are servers, communication links, software, end user devices, content to transmit, etc. For interactive technologies such as the Internet, network externalities influence the critical mass needed for widespread adoption (Mahler and Rogers, 1999). Using a single measurement variable does not capture the richness of what is happening and in fact may be misleading.

The GDI framework therefore consists of six *dimensions,* each of which describe an important, somewhat intuitive, and measurable feature of the presence of the Internet in a country. In a rough sense, these dimensions form a complete set in that they collectively cover most things that might reasonably be of interest, and each dimension offers something to the overall picture that the others do not. They have been chosen to reflect the full cluster of constituent technologies from infrastructure to end user applications, thus capturing the multifaceted diversity of experiences that countries have with the Internet. At the same time, the number of dimensions is small enough that they can easily be kept in mind. The values assigned to each dimension are discrete and proceed from less to more in an ordered way. Each discrete level maps to a relatively broad range of underlying values or conditions, a breadth that is sufficient to reflect the fact that much of the information available about the Internet changes rapidly, is incomplete, and varies in credibility. The conciseness of the dimension definitions should allow different people looking at the same raw data to assign the same values to them.

The framework also includes *determinants,* which may be thought of as proximate causes that led to the current conditions. Understanding how the determinants influence the dimensions in a given country can lead to prescriptive statements, and GDI studies typically include thorough analyses of both the dimensions and the determinants (cf. Wolcott and Goodman, 2000). While the determinants are discussed to a certain extent in Sections III and IV, the focus of this paper is on the dimensions.

The results are presented on a Kiviat Diagram (cf. Kolence and Kiviat, 1973) with six "spokes" representing each of the dimensions. Values for one or more countries at one or more times can be plotted on the same diagram or compared side-by-side on several diagrams. Figure 1, for example, shows the status of Internet diffusion in Turkey and Pakistan in 1999. Figure 2 shows the rapid growth of the Internet in Finland from 1994 to 1997.

The dimensions, determinants and their intervals were developed by a team of six members of the MOSAIC Group, including most of the authors, with expertise about the Internet in a wide variety of countries including the United States, China, Finland, Chile, Cuba, the Gulf States, and India among others. We have since applied the framework to Internet diffusion in about 25 countries (see Table 11 in Section IV). Though we have made a few modifications in the framework based on accumulated experience, we have found it to be an excellent tool for analyzing the Internet in each of these countries. In the rest of this section, we first examine the nature of the Internet technology cluster and how this led to the selection of the dimensions, and then we present the dimensions in complete detail. In Section III we return to the more theoretical questions of why these dimensions should depict Internet diffusion and other work that has been done along these lines.

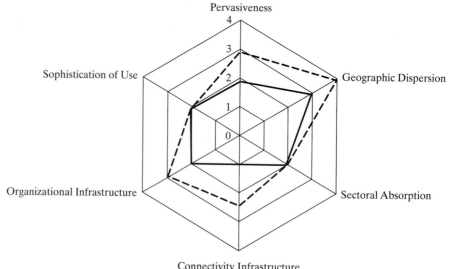

FIGURE 1 Dimensions for Turkey and Pakistan, 1999

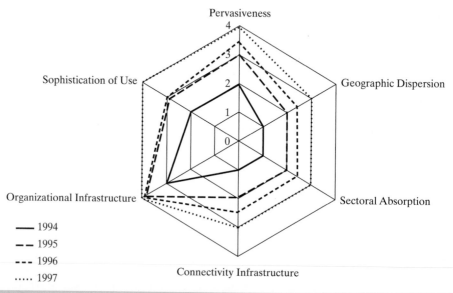

FIGURE 2 Dimensions for Finland, 1994–1997

Framework Dimensions—Overview of the Cluster

A simple model of the Internet technology cluster depicts three levels (Figure 3).[3] At the bottom level is the underlying network infrastructure, without which there can be no Internet in practice. We have created a corresponding dimension called *"Connectivity Infrastructure."* At the top level are the technologies needed by end users in order to adopt and make use of the Internet. We have chosen to depict this level with two dimensions. *Pervasiveness* is an overall measure that reflects the raw number of individual Internet users in a country. *Sectoral Absorption,* on the other hand, considers Internet use from the viewpoint of adoption at an organizational level.

Next, there has to be some sort of mechanism to bring services from the telecommunications infrastructure to the users. We have depicted this Internet services infrastructure layer in two dimensions. The first, *Organizational Infrastructure,* is primarily focused on the number and robustness of the organizations that provide these services. The second, *Geographic Dispersion,* reflects the extent to which these organizations, along with the supporting telecommunications infrastructure, is distributed across the entire territory of a country.

Both the pervasiveness and sectoral adoption measures are similar to the constructs of traditional diffusion studies in that they simply consider whether or not the technology has been adopted, and do not try to distinguish among various intensities of adoption or various uses. A third user-oriented dimension, therefore, is *Sophistication of Use,* which tries to plug this gap. It recognizes that the adoption of the leading edge applications depends not only on what the users want, but also on what the Internet services infrastructure is able and willing to provide. Figure 3 shows all six dimensions along with the single or multiple levels in the technology cluster to which they correspond. In the next section, we consider the definitions of the dimensions in complete detail.

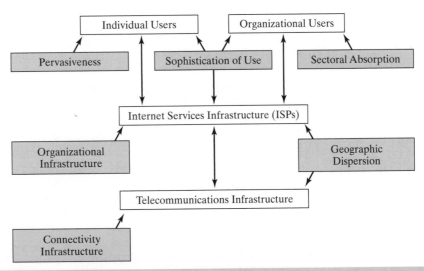

FIGURE 3 Constituents of the Internet Technology Cluster

---

[3]A much more complete map of the information industries is provided by Houghton (1999), who defines 16 segments divided on the horizontal axis by conduits to content (form to substance), and on the vertical axis by products to services.

Framework Dimensions—Defined in Detail

Pervasiveness

Pervasiveness (Table 1) is a function principally of the number of users per capita. It differs from commonly used Internet growth metrics only in that the final measure of Pervasiveness is not an absolute number, but a ranking of that number in one of five levels. The intent is to depict the portion of a population that uses the Internet.[4] Accurate user counts are not readily available. However, it is often possible to obtain or reasonably estimate the number of users accessing the Internet through switched (dial-up) and fixed (LAN) connections by extrapolating from numbers of subscribers. In some countries one user may access the Internet in numerous ways (including wireless, Internet cafes and kiosks, and home, work and/or school accounts), while in others single accounts may be shared by many users. Some users are heavy and others light; some started long ago while others started recently. Estimates based on samples therefore may provide more accurate results when available, and the authors of GDI studies often discuss these subtleties when examining the evidence for assigning this parameter. Ultimately, reports on users usually are in the same order of magnitude, and therefore get the same rating under the GDI definitions.

Traditional diffusion studies make no assumption about the total number of potential users, and typically divide the adopters into innovators (first 2.5%), early adopters (next 13.5%), early majority (next 34%), late majority (next 34%), and laggards (last 16%) (Rogers, 1995, p.252ff). The GDI framework uses a logarithmic scale. Why?

In order to measure Internet diffusion in a country, which has a known population and therefore a known upper limit on the number of adopters, it only makes sense to measure against the country's population. A "per capita" scale allows comparisons among countries. The discrete logarithmic levels makes it possible to consider the very early stages in much greater detail than is revealed by the traditional adopter categories. We are interested in understanding at what point the Internet has "taken hold," as well as the point at which it has become common. Our scale therefore provides for comparisons between developing and developed nations.

TABLE 1 The Pervasiveness of the Internet

Level 0	*Non-existent*: The Internet does not exist in a viable form in this country. No computers with international IP connections are located within the country. There may be some Internet users in the country; however, they obtain a connection via an international telephone call to a foreign ISP.
Level 1	*Embryonic*: The ratio of users per capita is on the order of magnitude of less than one in a thousand (less than 0.1%).
Level 2	*Nascent*: The ratio of Internet users per capita is on the order of magnitude of at least one in a thousand (0.1% or greater).
Level 3	*Established*: The ratio of Internet users per capita is on the order of magnitude of at least one in a hundred (1% or greater).
Level 4	*Common*: The ratio of Internet users per capita is on the order of magnitude of at least one in 10 (10% or greater).

---

[4]When data are available to do so, we exclude those who have only UUCP, Fido or any store and forward accounts.

Geographic Dispersion

Geographic Dispersion (Table 2) describes the physical dispersion of the Internet within a country. In addition to just having the network accessible throughout the country, there are benefits to having multiple points-of-presence within an area, redundant transmission paths, and multiple international access points. In many countries the Internet has only been accessible in the capital city. Widespread geographic dispersion is a requirement for the Internet to transform the country as a whole and not just a few isolated cities.

Two problems typically arise in interpreting this dimension. First, the analyst must determine what counts as a "first-tier political subdivision." In most countries, the state, province, or governate constitutes the first-tier political sub-division. Some countries have a small number of large divisions, such as the Philippines' division into three main island groups of Luzon, Visayas, and Mindanao. In this case using the next level division of the province makes more sense (Connally, 2000).

Second, there is the question of how dial-up access is available. Users obviously can get Internet access by making long distance calls, but usually the extra cost of doing so is prohibitive for all but occasional use. Effective rural access means, at the very least, that long distance charges need not be paid, and perhaps that unlimited local calls may be made for a single charge.

Sectoral Absorption

Sectoral Absorption (Tables 5, 6, and 7) focuses on the extent to which organizations in four major sectors have made a tangible commitment to Internet use. They are: academic, commercial, health, and public (government).[5] The subsectors describe the major social and economic divisions in society as depicted in Table 3. Personal use is not considered in this metric.

Internet use within each sector is rated as "non-existent," "minimal," "medium," or "great majority," using the guidelines in Table 4. To rate the country as a whole, each sector where there is no use of the Internet is assigned zero points, each "minimal" sector is assigned one point, each "medium" sector two points, and each "great majority"

TABLE 2 The Geographic Dispersion of the Internet

Level 0	*Non-existent.* The Internet does not exist in a viable form in this country. No computers with international IP connections are located within the country. A country may be using UUCP connections for email and USENET.
Level 1	*Single location*: Internet points-of-presence are confined to one major population center.
Level 2	*Moderately dispersed*: Internet points-of-presence are located in multiple first-tier political subdivisions of the country.
Level 3	*Highly dispersed*: Internet points-of-presence are located in at least 50% of the first-tier political subdivisions of the country.
Level 4	*Nationwide*: Internet points-of-presence are located in essentially all first-tier political sub-divisions of the country. Rural access is publicly and commonly available.

▪▪▪▪▪▪▪▪▪

---

[5]Health, commercial and academic were initially selected because they corresponded to categories in the UNDP human development index. The public sector is obviously a very important user potentially comparable in size to the others. See www.undp.org/.

TABLE 3 Major Internet-Using Sectors of the Economy

Sector	Subsectors
Academic	Primary and Secondary Education, University Education
Commercial	Distribution, Finance, Manufacturing, Retail, Service
Health	Hospitals, Clinics, Research Centers, Physicians/Practitioners
Public	Central Government, Regional and Local Governments, Public Companies

sector three points. These points are added together and then reduced to a single number using Table 5.

Sectoral absorption paints an important picture of how the Internet is perceived in different countries. In some, there may be considerable commercial use but little use in the public sector. In others, this pattern may be reversed. Typically the health sector is one of the last to adopt the Internet, so that rating a country at Level 4 is very indicative of widespread diffusion. We explicitly chose not to include non-governmental organizations, religious organizations, and other organizations (e.g. organized crime) that do not fall under these definitions either because they play a relatively small role in the economy or because information about them is even harder to obtain. In determining the ratings within each sector, we chose to map the "medium" value to a rather wide range of underlying conditions because we are interested in distinguishing the state where only innovators and some early adopters have embraced the Internet (on the order of 10%) from the state when even the late majority have adopted the innovation (on the order of 85–90%). Having such a wide definition increases the likelihood that different analysts will reach the same conclusions about the same or different countries, making it more robust when these data are difficult to obtain. The presence of a server or use of a server co-hosted elsewhere represents a serious commitment by an organization to the Internet. Similarly, paying for leased lines indicates a considerable amount of use. We chose to focus on servers for commercial and public organizations, and leased lines for educational and health organizations because these better represent the types of information flows in and out of these organizations, but they are both surrogates for indicating commitment to the Internet, and may be used interchangeably.

TABLE 4 Sectoral Use of the Internet

Sector	Minimal	Medium	Great Majority
Academic	>0–10% have leased-line Internet connectivity	10–90% have leased-line Internet connectivity	>90% have leased-line Internet connectivity
Commercial	>0–10% have Internet servers	10–90% have Internet servers	>90% have Internet servers
Health	>0–10% have leased-line Internet connectivity	10–90% have leased-line Internet connectivity	>90% have leased-line Internet connectivity
Public	>0–10% have Internet servers	10–90% have Internet servers	>90% have Internet servers

TABLE 5 The Sectoral Absorption of the Internet Scale

Sectoral Point Total	Sectoral Absorption	Dimension Rating
0	Level 0	*Non-existent*
1–3	Level 1	*Rare*
4–6	Level 2	*Moderate*
7–9	Level 3	*Common*
10–12	Level 4	*Widely used*

Connectivity Infrastructure

Connectivity infrastructure (Table 6) assesses the extent and robustness of the physical structure of the network, and comprises four components: the aggregate bandwidth of the domestic backbone(s), the aggregate bandwidth of the international IP links, the number and type of inter-connection exchanges, and the type and sophistication of local access methods being used. Table 6 depicts how these factors are related to the assessment of the level of infrastructure development, with Level 0 assigned to a country with no Internet presence (and hence, no infrastructure) and Level 4 assigned to a country with a robust domestic infrastructure, multiple high-speed international links, many bilateral ("peering") and open Internet exchanges—facilities where two or more IP networks exchange traffic—and multiple access methods in use.

Estimating the aggregate capacity of both the domestic backbone and international links has been problematical. Some of the GDI authors have added together the capacity of all the lines found and called that the aggregate capacity, an approach similar to that taken by TeleGeography (Abramson, 2000). This approach is most attractive for international links, where it makes sense that each additional line going out of a country adds to the overall throughput of traffic that can flow in and out of the country at any given time. Such an aggregated measure, however, does not begin to answer the question of where the traffic needs to go and what are the costs associated with specific flows. TeleGeography (Abramson, 2000) reported that aggregate bandwidth from

TABLE 6 The Connectivity Infrastructure of the Internet

		Domestic Backbone	International Links	Internet Exchanges	Access Methods
Level 0	*Non-existent*	None	None	None	None
Level 1	*Thin*	≤2 Mbps	≤128 Kbps	None	Modem
Level 2	*Expanded*	>2–200 Mbps	>128 Mbps–45 Mbps	1	Modem 64 Kbps leased lines
Level 3	*Broad*	>200 Mbps–100 Gbps	>45 Mbps–10 Gbps	More than 1; Bilateral or Open	Modem >64 Kbps leased lines
Level 4	*Extensive*	>100 Gbps	>10 Gbps	Many; Both Bilateral and Open	<90% modem >64 Kbps leased lines

Africa to Europe (as of Sept., 1999) was 68.5 MBps, but Africa to the U.S. was 170 MBps. Traffic may flow from Africa to the U.S. via Europe and vice versa, so is it really accurate to say that total bandwidth to the U.S. is only 170 MBps and not 238.5 MBps? Nevertheless, major backbone providers have adopted this measure, and it seems to be a reasonable way to characterize countries. Wilson, Daly and Griffiths (1998) use total bandwidth to outside countries.

Using such an approach for the domestic backbone is more problematical, because the patterns of connectivity among backbone components influence overall throughput and performance. Fiber-miles or fiber-kilometers is often used to describe capacity, but does not capture the fact that different devices at either end will change the throughput of the fiber. Therefore some researchers just focus on measured performance. The Center for International Development at Harvard focuses largely on the services provided from the end-user's point of view (Information Technologies Group, 2000). Boardwatch also focuses on end-user delivered performance, testing download times for files from various vantage points at various times (Martin, 2001; Muellar and Erickson, 1999). Despite outlining a promising method for examining network capacity based on mathematical depictions of network connections as graphs,[6] Gorman and Malecki aggregate "the total bandwidth available to each network . . . to give a measure of the . . . gross capacity of each network" (Gorman and Malecki, 2000, 122). We have used this approach in most GDI studies. The levels that we have outlined in Table 6 refer to adding up the capacity of all the links in the backbone(s) in the country. Given the rapidly changing levels of capacity around the world, the thresholds in Table 6 need frequent scrutiny and revision.

Without domestic Internet exchange points, traffic from one ISP to another within the same country must first travel outside the country to a global connection point. Domestic Internet exchanges presumably reduce costs and increase speeds. The presence of such exchanges often indicates a certain level of maturity among backbone providers, and provision of ancillary services that facilitate the development of the Internet as a whole. Open exchanges allow any qualified backbone provider to join, while bilateral connections may be private. Our cutoff point on this parameter is somewhat vague, leaving it to the analyst to distinguish the point at which more than one exchange becomes many.

The access methods column tracks two different forms of access. One is the "last mile" connections, mainly into homes, that have traditionally used modems but may now be adopting cable, xDSL, or even other forms of access (e.g. fixed wireless or satellite). These newer forms of access appear in our framework at Level 4, where the rating of >90% using modems assumes that the rest use one or more of these methods. The second form of access is via a leased line, and here we have made a distinction between those that are no greater than 64 Kbps (older ISDN technologies), and those that are. The higher speeds of cable, xDSL, and other methods may soon blur distinctions between slow, home access and fast, work access, although the rate of broadband adoption around the world has been much slower than expected.

Though it would be possible to imagine a country in which one of these four constituents of the telecommunications infrastructure was at Level 4 and another at Level 1, our experience has shown that when the constituents diverge, they tend to cluster around two levels. Choosing a particular level depends on there being three out

---

[6]For each network, they derive the cyclomatic number, and the alpha, beta, and gamma, which are all ratios derived using various formulas from the number of nodes and connections between nodes (edges) in a graph. This is the underlying structure that comprises a computer network. Gorman and Malecki (2000, 120) provide more precise definitions.

of four ratings on a particular level. When a country is clearly in between levels, we have sometimes evaluated it as halfway between, but have generally stayed away from half ratings because this changes the framework from five levels to ten.

Organizational Infrastructure

The Internet Services Infrastructure is the "middleware" between the basic telecommunications infrastructure and users that makes the raw "pipes" useable. Our measure, Organizational Infrastructure (Table 7), is centered on the number of Internet Service Providers (ISPs) and their competitive environment. It tries to assess the robustness of the market and services themselves, and recognizes that when strong competition is present, more services will probably be offered. ISPs may be transforming themselves into Internet Content Providers (ICPs) and Application Service Providers (ASPs), and the array of services offered at this level is expanding. Some countries will permit this evolution and some will not. The definition for Level 4 includes the concept that a group of ISPs has begun to gel as an industry, and is therefore creating mechanisms that will enhance its professional standing. Public exchanges signify that ISPs are working together. Collaborative organizations, such as industry associations, can lobby on behalf of the ISPs, ICPs, and ASPs. Emergency response teams cut across organizations and may require joint funding. These are examples, and other indications of robustness may be found in various countries.

Sophistication of Use

To truly understand the Internet capability of a country, it is necessary to understand not only how many people use the services and where, but also how the Internet is employed. As noted above, the Internet comprises a technology cluster, and various specific technologies are being adopted by different user groups at different rates. For example, one might study the demographics of the adoption of MP3 files for the distribution of music, or the diffusion of EDI-over-Internet use. Our measure (Table 8) attempts to synthesize sophistication in terms of what leading-edge groups of users are doing, while recognizing that to characterize a whole country by a small number of advanced users is not particularly useful. Part of the motivation of looking at leading

---

TABLE 7 The Organizational Infrastructure of the Internet

Level 0	*None:* The Internet is not present in this country.
Level 1	*Single:* A single ISP has a monopoly in the Internet service provision market. This ISP is generally owned or significantly controlled by the government.
Level 2	*Controlled:* There are only a few ISPs and the market is closely controlled through high barriers to entry. All ISPs connect to the international Internet through a monopoly telecommunications service provider. The provision of domestic infrastructure is also a monopoly.
Level 3	*Competitive:* The Internet market is competitive. There are many ISPs and low barriers to market entry. The provision of international links is a monopoly, but the provision of domestic infrastructure is open to competition, or vice versa.
Level 4	*Robust:* There is a rich service provision infrastructure. There are many ISPs and low barriers to market entry. International links and domestic infrastructure are open to competition. There are collaborative organizations and arrangements such as public exchanges, industry associations, and emergency response teams.

TABLE 8 The Sophistication of Use of the Internet

Level 0	*None:* The Internet is not used, except by a very small fraction of the population that logs into foreign services.
Level 1	*Minimal:* The user community struggles to employ the Internet in conventional, mainstream applications.
Level 2	*Conventional:* The user community changes established practices somewhat in response to or in order to accommodate the technology, but few established processes are changed dramatically. The Internet is used as a substitute or straightforward enhancement for an existing process (e.g. e-mail vs. post). This is the first level at which we can say that the Internet has "taken hold" in a country.
Level 3	*Transforming:* The use of the Internet by certain segments of users results in new applications, or significant changes in existing processes and practices, although these innovations may not necessarily stretch the boundaries of the technology's capabilities.
Level 4	*Innovating:* Segments of the user community are discriminating and highly demanding. These segments are regularly applying, or seeking to apply the Internet in innovative ways that push the capabilities of the technology. They play a significant role in driving the state-of-the-art and have a mutually beneficial and synergistic relationship with developers.

edge groups is to see what is possible in a given social, political, and economic system; the trailblazers show that it can be done and lead the way for the others.

Of particular interest is the point that is reached when the Internet attracts interest and use outside of a narrow community of technicians. Although there will be many "chasms" to cross for many sub-technologies (Moore and McKenna, 1999), a country must first deal with adopting the basic services of the Internet. This is reflected in going from Level 1 to Level 2.

A second major milestone (Level 3) is reached when user communities integrate the Internet into business processes in such a way that significant changes are made in them. For example, the adoption of user-determined pricing mechanisms such as auctions may require substantial changes in the way a business operates. At an individual level, changing a "business process" may refer to shopping on-line, spending more time on-line than watching television, etc.

A third milestone is reached (Level 4) when user communities transition from only using the Internet to creating new applications, often eventually having an impact on the Internet elsewhere in the world. In the diffusion literature this is called "reinvention," and has received only moderate attention from diffusion researchers (Rogers, 1995, 174). It can be argued that very few countries are in this category, with the United States being the leading example.

Table 8 depicts the development stages that reflect these increasing levels of sophistication in the use of the Internet. Not all users may ever reach the high water mark, especially with respect to Level 4, but knowing that a country is capable of being there is quite significant.

Table 9 illustrates some examples of usage of the Internet at various levels of sophistication by individuals and organizations at the time of this writing. This dimension is also subject to frequent scrutiny and possible revision, as yesterday's innovations become today's routine applications.

TABLE 9 Examples of Sophistication of Use of the Internet (circa 1999–2000)

Level	Individual Use	Organizational Use
Level 0 None	No use of the Internet	No use of the Internet
Level 1 Minimal	E-mail communication or Web browsing is an infrequent, and novel experience.	E-mail is available, but is not used as an alternative to traditional inter-personal communications (memos, telephone, meetings). Web sites consist of a very small number of static pages reflecting a "minimalist brochure."
Level 2 Conventional	E-mail may be a preferred means of communicating with people in an individual's circle of acquaintances. Web surfing is a regular activity. Some individuals maintain Web sites to post personal interest information. Individuals may listen to broadcast programming on the Web rather than on the radio or television. Online Chat is an advanced form of Level 2, or possibly a Level 3, depending on whether it is primarily entertainment or results in changes in the individual's social network.	E-mail is widely used for both official and unofficial communication. Listservs or their equivalent are used to disseminate information or solicit feedback. Web sites are largely static, but are extensive and provide customers with in-depth information about products and services, utilization of those services, comparative information, etc. The content is more than just advertisement.
Level 3 Transforming	On-line communities proliferate around shared interests. These communities bring together people who otherwise would not have contact with each other. Interaction between members of such communities is substantive and often interactive. Examples include on-line Bridge clubs, use of ICQ ("I seek you") to create communities, Individuals' Web-cams (e.g. Jenni-Cam knock-offs).	One strong indicator of business process re-engineering is that a significant number (over 5%) of Web sites, both government and business, are interactive. Web sites are dynamic, becoming an alternative distribution channel. On-line ordering is possible. Customer service functions expand to permit customers to conduct transactions that formerly involved employees (e.g. home banking, FedEx package tracking, etc.) International companies use the Internet as a substitute for business trips, enabling round-the-clock collaborative product development. E-Commerce/E-business has taken hold.
Level 4 Innovating	Highly sophisticated forms of technology supporting inter-personal interaction and access to content are not only used by, but developed for, a demanding customer base. Principal examples include the development (not just use) of highly-interactive on-line games, ICQ ("I seek you"), Napster, etc.	The fundamental structure of organizations and their external relations with other organizations is altered. Examples include Egghead Software, which no longer has a bricks-and-mortar presence, and Amazon.com, the on-line bookseller. Business to Business (B2B) vertical exchanges continue to add more and more value as they integrate enterprise information systems.

▪▪▪▪▪▪▪▪▪

▪▪▪ III. Internet Diffusion: Theory and Other Work

Any classification system has a strong relationship to the purpose for which it was conceived. To study Internet diffusion in a country, we first need measures that reflect the nature and actual adoption of the Internet. In Section II we have already satisfied the need to reflect the nature of the Internet by crafting measures that capture the underlying technology cluster that comprises it.[7] Pervasiveness and Sectoral Absorption are directly related to adoption, attempting to count numbers of things—like saying there are so many wolves in Alaska. They make use of the simplest possible characteristic: presence or absence.

If we were to stop with just these two adoption dimensions, we could say that we have captured diffusion within some geographical boundary, but we would be hard pressed to say that we have reflected the elements of a country in our analysis. The other four GDI dimensions are based implicitly on underlying theories of National Systems of Innovation, on evolutionary analogies (i.e. Evolutionary Economics), and on Diffusion of Innovations theory. The literatures on these subjects are vast, and it is beyond the scope of this paper to do justice to any of them. We can only make suggestive analogies and point to representative references.

The National Systems of Innovation (NSI) literature is primarily about how country- and region-specific institutions provide the necessary support for the development and diffusion of innovations within that country and/or region. Particularly over the last decade, this literature has examined key issues such as the role of multinational corporations in the development and diffusion of innovations and whether or not globalization is rendering the concept of the NSI obsolete. The overwhelming conclusion is that it is not (cf. Pavitt and Patel, 1999).

Germane to our task is the kinds of measures the NSI approach uses. Patel and Pavitt (1994), for example, use multiple, complex measures such as dollar volume of R&D activity by firms, research and educational institutions; patents; published papers and citations to them; and census-based data on the population. These measures look both at inputs (e.g. the level of R&D investment), and outputs (e.g. the number of patents produced). Both are important: R&D investment stands as an indicator of the importance with which the nation views innovation, and the response of institutions to this challenge, but is also an input that may or may not produce new innovations. Complex measures such as these are justified because "innovations are generated not only by individuals, organizations, and institutions, but by their, often complex, patterns of interactions" (Saviotti, 1997, 180).

Connectivity Infrastructure, Organizational Infrastructure, and Geographic Dispersion are similarly complex measures that incorporate both inputs and outputs and their interrelationships. Within this technology cluster (Figure 3), the amount of capacity and available services present in the bottom two levels determine the upper limit of the extent of Internet diffusion. Investments in these areas may be driven by demand, and depend on many interacting decisions by organizations and governmental bodies. Governmental policy may range from acknowledgment of the importance of the Internet in public pronouncements to policies that encourage, support, or mandate its use (King et al.,1994). By incorporating an institutional focus, these three dimensions represent three broad ways to characterize the Internet-related NSI of a country, and give a sense of how the NSI is shaping Internet diffusion.[8]

---

[7]Van Slyke (1998) traces the concept of technology clusters to Silverman and Baily (1961), whereas LaRose and Hoag (1996) cite Rogers (1986) as the primary source. Technology clusters in information technology have been examined for a least a decade (cf. Chin and Moore, 1991). King et al. (1994) discuss clusters in the broader context of institutions and their role in innovation diffusion. Prescott and Van Slyke (1997) recommended treating the Internet as a cluster and summarize some evidence in support of this approach. Hahn and Schoch (1997) emphasize that a cluster entails adoption of some, but not necessarily all, of the constituent technologies.

[8]Institutional views have been taken by Daly (1999) and the "Internet Counts" project with which he has been affiliated (Wilson et al., 1998). The Leland Initiative Telematics for Africa project at the Center for International Development and Conflict Management (CIDCM) at the University of Maryland is developing an instrument for Internet assessment that is highly focused on institutions and uses qualitative data gathering techniques (bridges.org, 2001).

Another stream of NSI research concerns the NSI as a "learning economy" (Lundvall, 1999). Our Sophistication of Use dimension reflects this learning ability or absorptive capacity of users within the country by giving a sense of the extent to which they have learned to use (and create) increasingly sophisticated aspects of the Internet and the applications it provides. This dimension compensates, to a certain extent, for the inability to survey every use of every Internet-based technology in all countries of the world. It also reflects the NSI, as the NSI is very much concerned with education and training, and also influences the climate of innovation that can make innovations available to sophisticated users.

Standing behind our dimensions, and helping to establish their values, are determinants that reflect the nature of the NSI of a country. These determinants are consistent with work by Nelson (1993), Porter (1998) and others, but do not represent a general theory of Internet diffusion.[9] Section IV of this paper takes up the question of how to apply the GDI scales and lists determinants that we find particularly useful to consider.

Partly because NSI researchers themselves do not consider the systems of innovation approach to be a fully developed theory, but more of "conceptual framework" (Edquist, 1997, 2), considerable work has been done to relate the NSI approach to evolutionary theory by using biological analogies.[10] In this formulation, innovations arise not because of a direct need for survival, but because of an innate pleasure taken by humans in novelty (Basalla, 1988). Concepts of diversity, variation, and natural selection must be adapted to study human innovations.

> In economic systems variation is essentially created by search activities, all those activities that scan the environment searching for alternatives to existing routines. Variation creates a large number of potential species/ technologies, accompanied by new routines, only some of which are sufficiently adapted to the environment. The less adapted ones are eliminated by selection. Selection is the result of a series of processes, like competition and several forms of regulation (Saviotti, 1997, 188).

Evolutionary theories predict that National Systems of Innovation will exhibit characteristics of path dependence, whereby variations in technologies and routines will largely be dependent on what has existed previously; irreversibility, whereby countries are unlikely to revert to previous states; and multistability, whereby it is posited that more than one stable state may arise from the existence of similar outcomes (Saviotti, 1997). Path dependence and irreversibility are fundamental principles that underlie the development of evolutionary systems of classification, and lead to the use of common characteristics to make inferences about which entities evolved from which other entities (Ridley, 1986). When applied to technologies, these principles support the idea that measurement scales should reflect increasing sophistication and complexity. An evolutionary

---

[9]The GDI work grew out of a similar approach to measuring the information systems capability of a nation, developed by Wolcott, Goodman, and Burkhart (1996). Sharif (1988) provided an important example of technology assessment measurement, and Liff, He and Steward (1993) provided an important example of devising dimensions. It is beyond the scope of this paper to formulate an overarching theory of Internet diffusion and to relate it to other general models of Internet diffusion which have already been developed. Daly (2000) has proposed a conceptual framework that interrelates Internet penetration, utilization, and impacts. His model includes many of the same dimensions and determinants as contained in our model. Bazar and Boalch (1997) also put forth a general model of Internet diffusion that has some similarities with our model. Abramson (2000) characterizes our methodology as a "sophisticated adjunct" to "country-by-country Internet user counts," which of course does not capture the full richness of our dimensions and determinants (Abramson, 2000, 70).

[10]A somewhat different focus was taken by Basalla (1988), who related evolutionary analogies to the history of technology. The growing field of evolutionary economics represents another application of evolutionary analogies (cf. Nelson and Winter, 1982).

explanation was proposed, for example, by Ein-Dor and Segev (1993) in their examination of the development of information system types.[11] The GDI dimension scales specifically embody these concepts of increasing sophistication and complexity. They are consistent with broad, underlying theories of how National Systems of Innovation work.

A third body of theory, Diffusion of Innovations (DOI), has been most extensively elaborated by Everett Rogers (1986, 1995). Although not a universal theory, the Rogers model is based on examination of thousands of studies which span a large number of fields of human endeavor, and "has quite rightly had a profound role in shaping the basic concepts, terminology, and scope of the field" (Fichman, 2000, 107). Innovation diffusion is "the process by which an innovation is communicated through certain channels over time among the members of a social system. It is a special type of communication, in that the messages are concerned with new ideas" (Rogers, 1995, 5). DOI theory is concerned with the mechanisms by which innovations are communicated and selected. It may be seen as one of the constituent processes within a more general evolutionary explanation, although this proposition has not yet been examined in detail.

According to Rogers (1995),[12] an innovation is something perceived as new by potential adopters, who may be divided into categories such as innovators, early adopters, early and late majority, and laggards depending on how willing they are to take a risk with something new. The rate of adoption depends on the characteristics of the innovation, and we therefore examine various aspects of the technology cluster in assigning several dimension values. Adoption also depends on communication channels by which information is transmitted, and the social system of potential adopters, which again emphasizes that the country level is appropriate. Adoption decisions may be made by individuals (optional), within organizations (collective), or by some authority such as the state (authority). Pervasiveness and Sectoral Absorption measures represent use at these levels. Adoption may be understood as trying the innovation out (implementation) and deciding to continue using it (confirmation), an insight that is incorporated in our Sophistication of Use measure (Rogers, 1995).

Within the I/S field there is a sizeable body of literature that uses the DOI approach. Because Rogers' model does not apply equally well in all cases, I/S researchers have developed "middle range" range theories that are oriented towards specific technologies and/or adoption contexts (Fichman, 2000). Prescott and Conger (1995) have usefully classified this literature by the "locus of technology impact" and "the research approach." Technology impacts have been studied at the level of I/S departments themselves, within organizations more generally, or across organizations. Research approaches have focused on the relationships of various factors (i.e. what determines diffusion), or on understanding what happens during the diffusion process at various stages (the stage approach). Research taking the factor approach resembles typical diffusion studies by using some form of adoption, generally by individuals, as the dependent variable (Prescott and Conger, 1995).

This literature supports our framework in two ways. First, studies of the impact of inter-organizational systems within this tradition found critical mass (i.e. network externalities) to be an important explanatory variable for their diffusion, and thus indirectly support our treatment of the Internet as a technology cluster (Prescott and Conger, 1995).

---

[11]Their work differs from ours, however, in that they were trying to characterize information systems themselves. We are trying to find characteristics that reflect the extent of adoption of an innovation (not the innovation *per se*). In examining properties, functions, and the timing of the introduction of new systems, Ein-Dor and Segev (1993) adopted a combination of phenetic, teleological, and phylogenetic approaches that mirror the traditional methods of evolutionary taxonomy. See Ridley (1986).

[12]An easily accessible summary of his theory may be found in Rogers and Scott (1997).

Second, this literature supports our use of a qualitative, process-oriented research approach. I/S researchers taking the stage approach have studied the processes by which new systems are created and incorporated into business processes or organizations. Using qualitative methods, adoption is understood as a multifaceted phenomenon that takes place in a variety of ways over time. The qualitative approach does not constrain the analysis to any pre-determined variables. It allows the researcher to examine the "rich organizational and political processes whereby a given set of information technology is instantiated" (Lee, 1999). Furthermore, it has long been recognized that interpretive methods, along with surveys and possibly field experiments and case studies, are most appropriate for studying information systems phenomena at the level of a society (cf. Galliers and Land, 1987).

Thus we find in the I/S literature itself strong justification for viewing adoption as a multifaceted construct and taking a qualitative approach in determining the value of the dimensions. Our measures, particularly Sophistication of Use, view Internet diffusion as a process that passes through typical and definable stages. GDI studies have often been exploratory, in countries where little or no exhaustive research on the Internet has yet been done. Countries comprise many people and numerous organizations, so to try to understand the general level of Internet diffusion in a country, we must be cognizant of multiple instantiation processes in differing circumstances even within one country. Rather than constraining or prescribing the use of any particular data, the GDI framework encourages researchers to consider any available sources.

Other Internet Diffusion Work

We are now in a position to characterize other research work that has tried to measure the status of Internet diffusion in various countries (Table 10). These may be grouped into four categories: (1) studies grounded in traffic patterns and data collection from the net itself, (2) studies based on survey research and statistical samples, (3) estimates and derived indexes that are based on self-assessment or syntheses of other studies, and (4) quantitative modeling approaches. Table 10 is a representative but not necessarily exhaustive list of these approaches and references where more information may be found about them. Press (1997a) presented one of the first survey articles about ongoing measurement techniques. Daly (1999) and Abramson (2000) have also characterized and provided references to a number of these approaches, and Bridges.org (2001) has compared a number of them.[13]

The principle contribution of the net-based collections techniques is to establish and determine the actual extent of Internet diffusion. Sending and receiving e-mails to and from a country, for example, was an easy way to see which countries were connected. While these techniques can, to a certain extent, tell us what is where, they are most useful as input to more complete diffusion studies. Most quantitative Internet studies have used one single dependent variable, adoption.[14] Most are variance studies in that they try to relate a variety of exogenous factors to this decision. They have generally used the number of hosts as the surrogate for Internet diffusion in a country, and thus the conclusions which may be drawn from them have been limited. Hargittai (1999), for example, acknowledges that qualitative factors are needed to enhance the conclusions that can be drawn from quantitative studies, while pointing out that quantitative studies help define

---

[13]Larry Press provides a web page with links to many of the Internet measurement efforts. See http://som.csudh.edu/fac/lpress/GDIFF/GDIFF projects.htm. Hal Varian also maintains a page about Internet metrics at www.slms.berkeley.edu/resources/infoecon/Accounting.html. An extensive list of references to all aspects of Internet measurement is maintained by Martin Dodge (2000) at www.cybergeography.org. See also Dodge (1998).

[14]Buselle (1999) discuss various approaches to Internet diffusion studies, but all involve adoption as the dependent variable. One typical example of such a study is Teo and Tan (1998).

TABLE 10 Other Research on Internet Diffusion

Technique	*Representative Users and References*
1. Net-Based Collection	
Sending/Receiving Emails	Larry Landweber (ftp://ftp.cs.wisc.edu/connectivity_table/); Olivier Crepin-Leblond (http://www.nsrc.org/oclb/)
Automated Discovery of Number and Location of Hosts	Network Wizards' Internet Domain Survey (Internet Software Consortium, 2001); Matrix.Net (Matrix.Net, 2000); Netcraft Web Server Survey (Netcraft, 2000); RIPE NCC (2000)
WWW Pages	Lawrence and Giles (2000)
Topology and Internet "Weather Reports"	Cooperative Association for Internet Data Analysis (CAIDA, www.caida.org/); Claffy (1996, 1999); Monk and Claffy (1996); Monk (2000); Burch and Cheswick (1999); TeleGeography (Staple, 1999); Andover Advanced Technologies, Inc. (2000)
2. Survey Research and Samples	
Internet Size based on IP Address Samples	Telcordia Technologies (2000a, 2000b)
Panels of Representative WWW Users	Media Metrix, A.C. Neilsen, other marketing research firms. (See Rood (1999) for a cautionary view.)
Surveys with convenience/non-representative samples	Graphics, Visualization and Usability (GVU) Center at Georgia Institute of Technology (Georgia Institute of Technology, 1999)
Other surveys	WITSA (2000)
3. Syntheses/Indexes	
Survey of available other statistics	Nua Internet Surveys (2000); Nua Internet Surveys (2001); Cyberatlas (www.cyberatlas.com)
Indexes/Self-Assessments	CSPP Readiness Guide for Living in the Networked World (CSPP, 1998); Internet Counts Project (Wilson, Daly and Griffiths, 1998); The IDC/World Times Index (IDC, 2001); Meta Group Global New E-Economy Index (GNEI) (Foley, 2000; Meta Group, 2000); The Economist Intelligence Unit E-Readiness Index (Foley, 2000); Readiness for the Networked World (CID, 2000); McConnell International E-Readiness Index (McConnell International, 2000); APEC E-Commerce Readiness Guide (APEC, 2000)
4. Quantitative Modeling	
Fitting Number of Hosts to S-Curves	Gurbaxanl (1990); Rai, Ravichandran and Samadar (1998)
Using Regression Analysis	Hargittai (1999); Kedzie (1997), Maitland and Bauer (2001); Robinson and Crenshaw (1999)
Using "Coupled Hazard" Approach	Dekimpe, Marnik, and Savary (2000)

▪ ▪ ▪ ▪ ▪ ▪ ▪ ▪ ▪

the most important variables of interest. However, finding suitable statistics for measuring these exogenous variables has been problematic (e.g. Hargittai (1999) was only able to include 18 countries in her analysis). Maitland and Bauer (2001) contend that because DOI theory is centered on users' perceptions of technology, it must be modified when considering such national level characteristics as infrastructure, which do not depend on individual adoption decisions. They would see teledensity as exogenous to Internet adoption, whereas we see it as a part of the Internet technology cluster. The development of the telecommunications infrastructure is, after all, intimately tied to demand spurred by Internet use.

A very large number of surveys have been done, some using representative samples and others using convenience samples. Similarly, other forms of indexes have been used, some which sound rather similar to our approach.[15] While a detailed examination of these measures is beyond the scope of this paper, we assert that, when taken alone, they are problematical because they may be too narrow in scope or unrepresentative, they may use questionable methodologies, or they may involve too many assumptions to be useful in practice. GDI studies often make careful use of data derived from many of these approaches, and appear to be most comprehensive in this regard (bridges.org, 2001).

▮▮▮ ## IV. Applying the Framework and a Brief Case Study

The GDI framework has been applied by MOSAIC Group members and others to study the status of the Internet in about 25 countries (see Table 11). As noted in Section III, the GDI methodology is fundamentally qualitative, permitting the researcher to gather data from as many diverse sources as possible.[16] The following non-exhaustive list represents the types of sources we frequently consult. Many of these activities are carried out in parallel, and sources may be revisited as new information becomes available:

- collecting any available data from existing sources, including other studies, press reports, net-based collections methods, etc.
- collecting primary data from the Internet/WWW itself. For example, surfing web pages of ISPs can be quite helpful
- gathering expert opinions using Delphi-type processes or asking for self-assessment using the GDI scales
- interviewing stakeholders face-to-face in country, at conferences, etc., and via e-mail communications with them
- consulting universities, regulatory agencies, governmental bodies, NGOs, development agencies, etc.
- carrying out focus groups and/or mounting actual larger-sample surveys on or off the Internet. Collection of quantitative data is not excluded, and GDI studies may give rise to increasingly quantitative approaches (not excluding testable hypotheses) at some point in the future.

Though a considerable amount of data is sometimes available from published and/or Internet sources, it is often incomplete and sometimes contradictory. As a hypothetical example, if one source claims 50% of the population uses the Internet, yet another says that only 10% has access to computers at home or work, further information is needed to resolve this discrepancy. We do not simply average the two numbers to get 30%.

We therefore find it highly useful to visit a country in the course of preparing a country study. Interviews with a cross section of decision-makers drawn from government, academia, and the Internet business community are invaluable for understanding not only the dimensions, but particularly the determinants of Internet diffusion (Table 12). The interview format often allows us to present a picture of the determinants and to get valuable feedback and insights. In doing interviews, collecting existing information from secondary

---

[15]For example, the IDC/World Times Information Society Index (ISI) aggregates available national-level indicators by category into four measures: computer infrastructure, information infrastructure, Internet infrastructure, and social infrastructure. The social infrastructure, consists of "Civil liberties, Newspaper readership per capita, Press freedom, Secondary school enrollment, and Tertiary school enrollment." Sources include IDC, UNESCO, ITU, World Bank, and Freedom House. These are aggregated to form a single index. See World Times/IDC (2000). This is a good example of a method that does not directly measure Internet diffusion.

[16]Sudweeks and Simoff (1999) provide a means for integrating quantitative and qualitative approaches in Internet research that is similar to the GDI methodology. Both ultimately make interpretation central.

TABLE 11 Country Studies Done Using the GDI Methodology as of mid-2000[18]

Country/Region	Reference(s)
Bahrain	Goodman, et al. (1998a)
Bangladesh	Press and Goodman (1999)
Bosnia and Herzegovina	Goodman, et al. (1998a)
China	Goodman, et al. (1998a); Goodman, et al. (1998b); Press, Foster and Goodman (1999); Foster, Goodman and Tan (1999); Foster, Goodman, Tan and Burkhart (1999); Foster and Goodman (2000)
Cuba	Press (1998); Goodman, et al. (1998a)
Finland	Goodman, et al. (1998a)
Historical Palestine	Ein-Dor, Goodman, and Wolcott (2000)
Hong Kong	Foster, et al. (1999)
India	Goodman, et al. (1998b); Press (1999); Wolcott (1999c)
Iran	Goodman, et al. (1998a)
Iraq	Goodman, et al. (1998a)
Israel	Ein-Dor, Goodman, and Wolcott (1999a)
Jordan	Ein-Dor, Goodman, and Wolcott (1999b)
Kingdom of Saudi Arabia	Goodman, et al. (1998a)
Kuwait	Goodman, et al. (1998a)
Nepal	Goodman, et al. (2000)
Oman	Goodman, et al. (1998a)
Pakistan	Wolcott (1999b); Wolcott and Goodman (2000)
Qatar	Goodman, et al. (1998a)
Singapore	Press (1997b)
Taiwan	Foster, et al. (1999)
Turkey	Wolcott (1999a), Wolcott and Goodman (2000)
Uganda	Minges, et al. (2000)
United Arab Emirates	Goodman, et al. (1998a)
Yemen	Goodman, et al. (1998a)

sources, guiding self-assessments, etc. researchers applying the GDI methodology typically develop a mental model of which factors play the most important role in determining how and why the Internet is diffusing. We then can present our conceptualization to new interviewees to see if they have a different perspective or anything to add. As each additional interviewee (and information source) begins to add less and less new information, we begin to have confidence in our evaluation of the dimensions and determinants for that particular country. In this sense we are applying the concept of the hermeneutic circle as expounded by Lee (1999). Our interviewing methodology draws on qualitative interviewing (Rubin and Rubin, 1995).

Can the GDI methodology be applied by other researchers?[17] Certainly, we consider the dimensions and their definitions to be clear enough that they can easily be

---

[17]The GDI methodology has been used by other researchers studying Iran (Adibi et al. 1999), and Uganda (Minges et al., 2000). Numerous master's level papers have been written as well by various students of some of the authors.

[18]Preliminary studies have also been done of Russia (Perov and McHenry, 2000), the Philippines (Connally, 2000), and other countries. Work derived from and related to this project includes Burkhart and Goodman (1998), Burkhart et al. (1998), Tan et al. (1999), and Wolcott and Cagiltay (2001).

TABLE 12 Determinants of Internet Diffusion

Qualities of the Technology Itself

1. Perceived Value	Similar to relative advantage in traditional diffusion studies
2. Ease of Use of the Internet	Similar to complexity and compatibility, this may also entail looking at literacy and availability of local-language content
3. Cost of Internet Access	Having to do with relative advantage and trialability, it may also entail looking at Internet costs relative to income levels

Inter-Relationships Within the Technology Cluster

4. Access to Constituent Technologies	Looks at the balance between all the technologies that must be present for various levels of use
5. Demand for Capacity, Multiplicity of ISPs, Services Provided	How demand at various levels of the cluster is driving the connectivity infrastructure development

External/Surrounding Forces

6. Geography	How physical geography influences Internet development
7. Adequacy and Fluidity of Resources	A broad category considering financial, informational, human, technological or capital, and material resources and the ease with which they can flow from where they are to where they are needed
8. Ability to Execute	The ability to develop a sound strategy and a suitable design given opportunities and constraints, and the ability to manage plans through to completion
9. Culture of Entrepreneurship	How entrepreneurship is rewarded, both at the organizational and individual level
10. Regulatory/Legal Framework	Specific laws and regulations influencing Internet diffusion
11. Forces for Change	Such things as competitive environment, presence of demanding domestic customers, rate of creation of new organizations, presence of champions
12. Enablers of Change	Conditions that allow a community to accept and incorporate change, including institutional, historical, cultural, and educational factors

assigned when the necessary information is available. The more ambiguous and obscure the source information, the more necessary it may be to fill in the gaps by examining determinants. There is no doubt that experience helps the researcher using the GDI methodology to ask the necessary questions and essentially look in the right places for the needed information.

As noted in Section III, we do not claim that the set of determinants we typically investigate represents a general theory of Internet diffusion. Our process of observing and deriving these determinants has been an inductive one, carried out on the basis of choosing and studying a widely diverse set of countries. These studies confirmed the importance of this set of determinants, and this set that we list here is obviously a subset of all possible factors that might influence innovation decisions. We do not view them as primary causal forces, nor are they all completely independent of one another. We present them as useful guidelines (a checklist) for thorough data collection and analysis, and leave the development of grounded theory on the basis of these studies for future work (Glasser and Strauss, 1967). It may not be necessary to examine these determinants in detail before assigning some of the dimension values.

These determinants highlight three central elements of Rogers' Diffusion of Innovation model: the innovation/technology cluster's characteristics, adopters and adoption decisions, and the surrounding social/economic/regulatory system. Important characteristics of the innovation are whether or not it offers advantages relative to other innovations or existing ways of doing things (relative advantage); how compatible it is with existing values, beliefs, needs, and previously adopted ideas (compatibility); how complex it is to understand and use (complexity); how easy it is to try it out (trialability); and how easy it is to observe (observability) (Rogers, 1995). Our model does not start, as Rogers' does, with the elements that directly influence the adoption decision, but looks one or more levels back in the chain of determination in order to find which factors make the most difference in any given country. Thus, as elaborated in Section III, our analyses are strongly influenced by the National Systems of Innovation approach (Edquist, 1997), and pay particular attention to the role of government policies that may encourage or mandate Internet development and adoption (King et al., 1994).

Rather than providing extensive definitions and examples of these determinants, we provide a small example that illustrates some of their application in practice. Our first analysis of the state of the Internet in Cuba was performed in 1997 (Press, 1998). Figure 4 shows the ease with which the reader can quickly grasp the status of the Internet in Cuba using the Kiviat diagram. Succinct justifications for the dimension assessments (as of 1997) supplement the diagram (the numbers in parentheses refer to Table 12).

Pervasiveness: Cuban IP connectivity was at the embryonic level, with perhaps as few as 100 users. Even if we had included UUCP e-mail accounts, less than 1/1,000 population used them. However, it was noteworthy that e-mail use extended well beyond the network technician community. Home use essentially did not exist, and access everywhere was limited by high cost (3) and absence of telephone infrastructure (4). This was partially determined by the absence of resources (7); the difficulty of attracting capital to an impoverished communist nation that the U.S. was embargoing might be interpreted as an inability to execute (8). Most important was value as perceived by the government (1). On the one hand, use at work could be justified in an atmosphere in which the government saw positive value in the promotion of cultural values such as

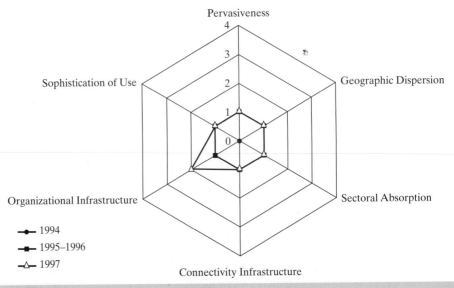

FIGURE 4 GDI Analysis of Cuba, 1994–1997

health care, education and urban-rural equality. It also recognized the economic value of the Net in the promotion of hard-currency generating industries such as medical instruments, and health and leisure tourism. On the other hand, it wished to restrict content and the potential use of networks for U.S. propaganda and/or by subversive elements (1). This dichotomy slowed the development of the Internet between 1995 and 1997, influencing all the other dimensions.

Geographic Dispersion: The only IP point of presence offering network connectivity in Cuba was at the Center for Automated Exchange of Information (CENIAI) in Havana. However, taking into account e-mail connectivity, we found access in every province and nearly every municipality. So, while Cuba was rated at the single location level because of limited IP connectivity, there was considerable interest in geographic dispersion. This could be considered an enabler of change (12), and represented cultural values noted under pervasiveness. Such dispersion was atypical of poor nations.

Sectoral Absorption: IP connectivity was minimal in the health and government sectors, and nonexistent in education and commerce, giving Cuba a rare overall ranking. On the other hand, UUCP-based e-mail was used in the health sector throughout the nation, more than 10% of the ministries had e-mail accounts, and the Youth Computer Clubs (education sector) were nationwide (1). The absence of an entrepreneurial culture (9) in a planned economy and the absence of a business sector inhibited commercial use, while emphasis on the education and health sectors was a force in favor of change (11).

Connectivity Infrastructure: While Cuba had an international IP link, it had no domestic backbone and barely any leased line access, placing it at the low end of Level 1 (thin) on this dimension. Cuba was severely hampered here by its poor telephone infrastructure and its historical concentration on the X.25 protocol (4,12). Low levels of investment in telecommunications reflect different government priorities, but also the overall inadequacy and lack of fluidity of resources (7). However, the populist history of Cuba influenced decisions to expand the infrastructure outside the capital, thus serving as a force for change (11).

Organizational Infrastructure: While not independent businesses, CENIAI and Teledatos[19] both provided connectivity to organizations with networks, and there was some evidence of competition between them (either by design or historical development(12)). There was also a degree of coordination provided by the Interministerial Commission for Networking. On this basis, we ranked Cuba at the controlled level. Prospects for allowing a more competitive environment seemed slim (9), given concerns about political stability, the recent Soviet experience being foremost in mind (12).

Sophistication of Use: As there was little IP connectivity, Cuba had to be ranked at the minimal level; however, e-mail and information retrieval from e-mail-driven servers reached the conventional level in the health care and biotechnology communities. We felt that the poor telephone network (4) and absence of private enterprise (7) would inhibit sophisticated uses of the Internet for some time to come. On the other hand, uses in the social sphere, e.g. for enabling lower cost health care, represented positive perceived value (1) and the possibility of some transformation in business processes (11).

The most significant determinants, therefore, were the perceived value and cost (1,3), access to constituent technologies (4), resources (7), entrepreneurship (9), forces for/against change (11), and enablers/inhibitors of change (12). These policies, which

---

[19]Teledatos mainly offered UUCP connections over an X.25, but was upgrading their X.25 backbone in late 1997 so that they could run IP over X.25.

ultimately stemmed from the decision to be a Communist nation and concerns about the recent Soviet experience, also led to an unusual emphasis on the use of the Internet in the social sphere. This was a counterbalancing force that could somewhat offset these inhibitors. It is also interesting to note that at this level of use by a mainly technical community, ease of use (2) had not begun to play much of a role. Drivers of demand for capacity (5) had started to appear as the CENIAI international link had become badly overloaded, but were dampened by a lack of critical mass and the role of centralized planning. Physical geography (6) played a large role in the political fortunes of Cuba, but not in the deployment of the Internet *per se*. Finally, the Cuban government exercised control less through formal regulations and laws (10) than through controlling access and through more pervasive, less transparent means of inhibiting socially risky communication.

The GDI methodology helped us to sift through the enormous amount of available data in order to weight which dimensions were most important and what factors played the most significant roles in determining them. Even this brief Cuba analysis represents a sizeable amount of underlying research and analytical work.

▮▮▮ V. Conclusion

The most common means for comparing the status of the Internet in various countries has been to use "number of users" or "number of hosts." The GDI methodology provides a measurement scale that captures the status of the principle components of the technology cluster that comprises the Internet. Since it encompasses all major parts of the cluster, it provides a much better picture of Internet status than any single-valued measure. The significance of the measures are easy to grasp when graphed on a Kiviat diagram. The GDI scale can be applied over time to paint a picture of the speed with which the Internet is being diffused. When enough countries have been characterized using this method, we will have a much clearer picture of global Internet diffusion.

Having been used for about 25 countries so far, the GDI measures have proven to be sufficiently robust for widespread application. The nation-state is an appropriate unit of analysis for diffusion. While a learning curve will be necessary for some other researchers to apply the methodology in full, including full-blown exploration of the determinants, the measures themselves are sufficiently clear that they may be understood and applied by a wide variety of potential users. A concerted effort by many interested parties around the world could result in the rapid characterization of the Internet status in many countries.

Results of the GDI studies will prove useful for several stakeholder groups. Those in business should get a clearer picture of what they can expect to find when investing and doing business in a given country. Internal and external policymakers can get a better idea of what needs to be done to eliminate bottlenecks and push Internet development and use forward. Studies done using this framework contribute to the debate over what levers are available to policy-makers at the national and international level to influence, shape, and positively (or negatively) influence the Internet's development, use, and growth.

Researchers can deepen their understanding of diffusion in general and the diffusion of the Internet in particular. The more the researcher understands and applies the determinants, the deeper and better justified that analysis can be. We hope to write an extensive companion paper to this one about the determinants. Having a uniform set of metrics for Internet diffusion that can be used on a global scale will immensely facilitate empirical diffusion studies.

Other plans for the GDI group include doing more studies of other countries and updating some studies we have already done, continuing to review the scales while taking into account the need for longitudinal consistency, working on the development of a grounded theory of Internet diffusion, and working towards a synthesis of the results to date.

REFERENCES

Editor's Note: The following reference list contains hyperlinks to World Wide Web pages. . . . Readers are warned, however, that

1. these links existed as of the date of publication but are not guaranteed to be working thereafter.
2. the contents of Web pages may change over time. Where version information is provided in the References, different versions may not contain the information or the conclusions referenced.
3. the author(s) of the Web pages, not AIS, is (are) responsible for the accuracy of their content.
4. the author(s) of this article, not AIS, is (are) responsible for the accuracy of the URL and version information.

Abramson, B. (2000) "Internet Globalization Indicators" *Telecommunications Policy* 24, 69–74.

Adibi, I. et al. (1999, June 15) *Iran's Telecom and Internet Sector: A Comprehensive Survey*. Open Research Network Document Number 102–101–01/105–101–01 Release 1.0, www.science-arts.org/internet/ (Accessed May 2, 2001).

Andover Advanced Technologies, Inc. (2000) "Internet Traffic Report" www.internettrafficreport.com/ (current Aug. 2, 2000, decommissioned March 31, 2001).

APEC (2000) *E-Commerce Readiness Guide*, Electronic Commerce Steering Group, Asian Pacific Economic Cooperation (APEC), V 5.0, www.ecommerce.gov/ apec/docs/readiness_guide_files/readiness_guide_5.pdf (Current April 26, 2001).

Archibugi, D., J. Howells, and J. Michle (1999) "Innovation systems and policy in a global economy" in *Innovation Policy in a Global Economy*, Archibugi, D., J. Howells, and J. Michie, eds. Cambridge: Cambridge University Press, 1–18.

Basalla, G. (1988) *The Evolution of Technology* Cambridge: Cambridge University Press.

Bazar, B., and G. Boalch (1997) "A Preliminary Model of Internet Diffusion within Developing Countries" Proceedings of AUSWEB-97, The Third Australian World Wide Web Conference, 5–9 July, 1997, Gold Coast, Australia http://ausweb.scu.edu.au/ proceedings/boalch/paper.html (Current April 26, 2001).

Bridges.org (2001) Comparison of E-Readiness Assessment Models, v8.13f, www.bridges.org/ereadiness/ report.html (Current April 26, 2001).

Burch, Hal, and B. Cheswick (1999, April) "Mapping the Internet" *Computer* pp. 97–98, 102.

Burkhart, G. E., and S. E. Goodman (1998) "The Internet gains acceptance in the Persian Gulf" *Communications of the ACM* 41(3), 19–25.

Burkhart, G. E., et al. (1998) "The Internet in India: better times ahead?" *Communications of the ACM* 41(11), 21–26.

Busselle, R., J. Reagan, B. Pinkleton, and J. Jackson (1999) "Factors affecting Internet use in a saturated-access population" *Telematics and Informatics* 16, 45–58.

Chin, W., and G. Moore (1991) "Technology Clusters: An Empirical Investigation of the Adoption of Information Technology Applications by End Users." *Proceedings of the Annual Conference of the Administrative Sciences Association of Canada Information Systems Division*, May 30–June 2, 1991, Niagara Falls, Ontario, Canada, 80–89.

CID (2000) *Readiness for the Networked World*, Center for International Development, Harvard University, http://www.readinessguide.org/ (Current April 26, 2001).

Claffy, K. C. (1996, Aug. 17) "'But Some Data Is Worse Than Others': Measurement Of The Global Internet" http://www.caida.org/outreach/papers/telegeog96.html (Current April 26, 2001).

Claffy, K. C. (1999) "Internet Measurement And Data Analysis: Topology, Workload, Performance And Routing Statistics" NAE'99 Workshop, 1999, http://www.caida.org/outreach/papers/Nae/ (Current April 26, 2001).

Connally, B. (2000) *Status Of The Internet in the Philippines: A Case Study*. Master's Thesis, Communication, Culture and Technology Program, Georgetown University.

CSPP (1998) Computer Systems Policy Project Readiness Guide for Living in the Networked World, http://206.183.2.91/projects/readiness/ (Current April 26, 2001).

Daly, J. (1999, May) "Measuring Impacts of the Internet in the Developing World" *IMP Magazine*, http://www.cisp.org/imp/may_99/daly/05_99daly.htm (Current April 26, 2001).

Daly, J. (2000) "A Conceptual Framework for the Study of the Impacts of the Internet," http://www.bsos.umd.edu/ cidcm/papers/jdaly/concept.htm (Current April 26, 2001).

Dekimpe, M., P. Parker, and M. Sarvary (2000, Feb.) "Global Diffusion of Technological Innovations: A Coupled-Hazard Approach" *Journal of Marketing Research* XXXVII, 47–59.

Dodge, M. (1998) "The Geographies of Cyberspace" Proceedings of the Association of American Geographers, Boston, March, 1998, http://www.geog.ucl.ac.uk/casa/martin/aag/aag.html (current April 26, 2001).

Dodge, M. (2000) "About Cyber Geography Research," http://www.cybergeography.org/about.html (Current April 26, 2001).

Dunning, J. H. (1993) *Multinational Enterprises and the Global Economy*, Wokingham: Addison-Wesley.

Edquist, C. (1997) "Systems of Innovation Approaches — Their Emergence and Characteristics" in *Systems of Innovation: Technologies, Institutions and Organizations*, Edquist, C., ed., London: Pinter, 1–29.

Ein-Dor, P., S. E. Goodman, and P. Wolcott (1999a) "The Global Diffusion of the Internet Project: The State of Israel" (November, 1999), http://mosaic.unomaha.edu/Israel_1999.pdf (Current April 26, 2001).

Ein-Dor, P., S. E. Goodman, and P. Wolcott (1999b) "The Global Diffusion of the Internet Project: The Hashemite Kingdom of Jordan," http://mosaic.unomaha.edu/Jordan_1999.pdf (Current April 26, 2001).

Ein-Dor, P., S. E. Goodman, and P. Wolcott (2000) "From Via Maris to Electronic Highway: The Internet in Canaan" *Communications of the ACM*, 43(7), 19–23.

Ein-Dor, P., and E. Segev (1993, June) "A Classification of Information Systems: Analysis and Interpretation" *Information Systems Research* 4(2), 166–204.

Fichman, Robert (2000) "The Diffusion and Assimilation of Information Technology Innovations," in Zmud, R. (ed.), *Framing the Domains of IT Management: Projecting the Future Through the Past*, Cincinnati, OH: Pinnaflex Education Resources, Inc., 105–127.

Foley, K. (2000, July 10) "Indexing the Internet" *NUA Analysis*, http://www.nua.ie/nkb/index.cgi?f=VA&art_type=NISA&art_id=471 (Current May 2, 2000).

Foster, W., S. Goodman, and Z. (Alex) Tan (1999) "The Internet and E-Commerce in Greater South China" http://mosaic.unomaha.edu/shina.pdf (Current January 11, 2000).

Foster, W., S. Goodman, Z. (Alex) Tan, and G. Burkhart (1999) "The Internet and Greater South China (Taiwan, Hong Kong, Fujian, and Guangdong)" http://mosaic.unomaha.edu/schina.pdf (Current April 26, 2001).

Foster, W., and S. E. Goodman (2000, Nov.) *The Diffusion of the Internet in China*. Stanford University: Center for International Security and Cooperation.

Galliers, R. D., and F. F. Land (1987) "Choosing Appropriate Information Systems Research Methodologies" *Communications of the ACM*, 30(11), 900–902.

Georgia Institute of Technology. Graphics, Visualization and Usability Center. (1999, Oct.) "GVU's WWW User Surveys," http://www.gvu.gatech.edu/user_surveys/ (Current April 26, 2001).

Glasser, B. G., and A. L. Strauss (1967) *The Discovery of Grounded Theory: Strategies for Qualitative Research*, Chicago: Aldine Publishing.

Goodman, S., et al. (1994) "The Global Diffusion of the Internet. Patterns and Problems" *Communications of the ACM* 37(8), 27–31.

Goodman, S., G. Burkhart, W. Foster, L. Press, Z. (Alex) Tan, and J. Woodard (1998a) *The Global Diffusion of the Internet Project: An Initial Inductive Study*. Fairfax, VA: SAIC, Available at: http://www.istis.unomaha.edu/isqa/wolcott/gdi/GDI1998/GDI1998.html (Current April 26, 2001).

Goodman, S., G. Burkhart, W. Foster, A. Mittal, L. Press, and Z. (Alex) Tan (1998b) *Asian Giants On-Line*, Fairfax, VA: SAIC, http://mosaic.unomaha.edu/gdi.html (Current April 26, 2001).

Goodman, S., and T. Kelly, M. Minges, L. Press (2000, Nov.) *The Internet from the Top of the World: Nepal Case Study*. Geneva: ITU http://www.itu.int/ti/casestudies/nepal/material/nepal.pdf (Current April 26, 2001).

Gorman, S. P., and E. J. Malecki (2000) "The Networks of the Internet: An Analysis of Provider Networks in the USA" *Telecommunications Policy* 24, 113–134.

Greenberg, L. T., and S. E. Goodman (1996) "Is Big Brother Hanging by His Bootstraps?" *Communications of the ACM* 39(7), 11–15.

Gurbaxani, V. (1990) "Diffusion in Computer Networks: The Case of BITNET" *Communications of the ACM* 33(12), 65–75.

Hahn, K. L., and N. A. Schoch (1997). "Applying diffusion theory to electronic publishing: A conceptual framework for examining issues and outcomes" *Proceedings of the American Society for Information Science Conference ASIS-97*, Washington, DC, November 1–6, 1997, http://www.asis.org/annual-97/hahnk.htm (Current April 26, 2001).

Hargittai, E. (1999) "Weaving the Western Web: Explaining Differences in Internet Connectivity Among OECD Countries" *Telecommunications Policy* 23, 701–718.

Houghton, J. W. (1999) "Mapping Information Industries and Markets" *Telecommunications Policy* 23, 689–699.

Howells, J. (1999) "Regional systems of innovation?" in *Innovation Policy in a Global Economy*, Archibugi, D., J. Howells, and J. Michie, eds. Cambridge: Cambridge University Press, pp. 67–93.

IDC (2001) "Sweden Remains the World's Dominant Information Economy While the United States Slips, According to the 2001 IDC/World Times Information Society Index," IDC Press Release, http://www.idc.com/ITOver/press/020801pr.stm (Current April 26, 2001).

Infodev (2001) "ICT Infrastructure and E-Readiness Assessment Initiative" http://www.infodev.org/ereadiness/ (Current April 26, 2001).

Information Technologies Group. Center for International Development at Harvard University (2000) "Readiness for the Networked World. A Guide for Developing Countries," http://www.readinessguide.org (current April 26, 2001).

Internet Software Consortium (2001) "Internet Domain Survey," http://www.isc.org/ds/ (Current April 26, 2001).

Kedzie, C. (1997) *Communication and Democracy: Coincident Revolutions and the Emergent Dictator's Dilemma*, RGSD-127, RAND Corporation, Santa Monica, CA., Abstract at: http://www.rand.org/cgibin/Abstracts/ordi/getabbydoc.pl?doc=RGSD−127 (Current April 26, 2001).

King, J. L., et al. (1994) "Institutional Factors in Information Technology Innovation" *Information Systems Research* 5(2), 139–169.

Kolence, K., and P. Kiviat (1973, Sept.) "Software Unit Profiles and Kiviat Figures" *ACM SIGMETRICS: Performance Evaluation Review*, pp. 2–12.

LaRose, R., and A. Hoag (1996) "Organisational Adoptions of the Internet and the Clustering of Innovations" *Journal of Telematics and Informatics* 13(1), 49–61.

Lawrence, S., and C. Giles (2000) "How Big Is the Web?" http://www.neci.nj.nec.com/homepages/lawrence/websize.html (Current April 26, 2001).

Lee, A. S. (1999) "Researching MIS" in W. Currie and B. Galliers (eds.) *Rethinking Management Information Systems*, New York: Oxford, pp. 7–27.

Liff, S., J. He, and F. Steward (1993) "Technology Content and Competitive Advantage: Strategic Analysis in the Steel Processing and Watch Manufacturing Sectors in the People's Republic Of China" *International Journal of Technology Management* 8(3–5), 309–332.

Lundvall, B. (1999) "Technology policy in the learning economy" in *Innovation Policy in a Global Economy*, Archibugi, D., J. Howells, and J. Michie, eds. Cambridge: Cambridge University Press, pp. 19–34.

Mahajan, V., E. Muller, and F. M. Bass (1990, January) "New product diffusion models in marketing: a review and directions for research" *Journal of Marketing* 54, 1–26.

Mahler, A. and E. Rogers (1999). "The diffusion of interactive communication innovations and the critical mass: the adoption of telecommunications services by German banks" *Telecommunications Policy* 23, 719–740.

Maitland, C., and J. Bauer (2001, in press) "National Level Culture and Global Diffusion: The Case of the Internet" in *Culture, Technology, Communication: Towards An Intercultural Global Village*, Ess, C., ed., Albany, NY: State University of New York Press.

Martin, L. (2001) "Backbone Web Hosting Measurements" *ISPworld*, http://www.ispworld.com/isp/Performance_Test.htm (Accessed May 2, 2001).

Matrix.net (2000, April 28) "LA Firm Funds Matrix.net," Press Release, http://www.mids.org/press/funding.html (Current Aug. 14, 2000).

McConnell International (2000, Aug.) Risk E-Business: Seizing the Opportunity of Global E-Readiness, http://mcconnellinternational.com/ereadiness/default.cfm (Current April 26, 2001).

Menou, M. J. (1999) "Impact Of The Internet: Some Conceptual and Methodological Issues, or How to Hit a Moving Target Behind the Smoke Screen" in D. Nicholas and I. Rowlands (eds.). *The Internet: Its Impact and Evaluation. Proceedings Of An International Forum Held At Cumberland Lodge, Windsor Park*, 16–18 July 1999, Aslib.

Meta Group (2000) "The META Group Global New E-Economy Index. Facts about the Methodology," http://www.metagroup.com/global/factsheet.htm (Current April 26, 2001).

Miller, D., and D. Slater (2000) *The Internet: An Ethnographic Approach*, New York: New York University Press.

Minges, M., W. Brown, and T. Kelly (2000) *Uganda Internet Case Study* Geneva: ITU http://www.itu.int/ti/casestudies/uganda/uganda.htm (Current April 26, 2001).

Monk, T. (2000, April 26). "Network Measurement Tools. Presentation at ESnet Site Coordinators Meeting," http://www.caida.org/outreach/presentations/esnet0004/index.htm (Current April 26, 2001).

Monk, T., and K. C. Claffy (1996, June 18) "A Survey of Internet Statistics/Metrics Activities" http://www.caida.org/outreach/papers/metricsurvey.html (April 26, 2001).

Moore, G. A., and R. McKenna (1999) *Crossing the Chasm: Marketing and Selling High-Tech Products to Mainstream Customers*. Revised edition, New York: Harper-Business.

Muellar, Fritz, and T. J. Erickson (1999, Summer) "Backbone Web Hosting Measurements" *Directory of Internet Service Providers*, http://www.boardwatch.com/isp/summer99/measure.html (Current June 6, 2000).

Nelson, R., and S. Winter (1982) *An Evolutionary Theory of Economic Change* Cambridge, MA: Harvard University Press.

Nelson, R. R. (ed.) (1993) *National Innovation Systems: A Comparative Analysis* New York: Oxford University Press.

Netcraft (2000) "The Netcraft Web Server Survey," http://www.netcraft.com/Survey/ (Current April 26, 2001).

Nua Internet Surveys (2000) "Methodology," http://www. nua.ie/surveys/how_many_online/methodology.html (Current April 26, 2001).

Nua Internet Surveys (2001) "How Many Online?" http://www.nua.ie/surveys/how_many_online/index. html (Current April 26, 2001).

Paltridge, S. (1998) "Internet Infrastructure Indicators" Paris: OECD, http://www.oecd.org/dsti/sti/it/cm/ prod/tisp98-7e.pdf (Current April 26, 2001).

Patel, P., and K. Pavitt (1994) "National Innovation Systems: Why They Are Important, and How They Might Be Measured and Compared" *Economics, Innovations, and New Technology*, v. 3, pp. 77–95.

Pavitt, K., and P. Patel (1999) "Global corporations and national systems of innovation: who dominates whom?" in *Innovation Policy in a Global Economy*, Archibugi, Daniele, Howells, Jeremy, Michie, Jonathan, eds. Cambridge: Cambridge University press, pp. 94–119.

Perov, E., and W. K. McHenry (2000) "Measuring the Russian Internet" *Proceedings of the First Annual Global Information Technology World Conference*, June 11–13, 2000, Memphis, TN, pp. 192–195.

Porter, M. E. (1998) *The Competitive Advantage of Nations: With a New Introduction*. New York: The Free Press.

Prescott, M., and S. Conger (1995, May/August) "Information Technology Innovations: A Classification by IT Lotus of Impact and Research Approach" *Data Base Advances* 26(2–3), 20–41.

Prescott, M., and C. Van Slyke (1996). "The Internet as Innovation." *Proceedings of the Association of Information Systems Conference, ACIS-96*. Phoenix, Arizona August 16–18, 1996. http://hsb.baylor.edu/ ramsower/ais.ac.96/papers/PRESCOTT.htm (Current April 26, 2001).

Press, L. (1997a) "Tracking the Global Diffusion of the Internet" *Communications of the ACM* 40(11), 11–17.

Press, L. (1997b) "The Internet in Singapore: A Benchmark Report," http://mosaic.unomaha.edu/ SINGAPORE_2000.pdf (Current April 26, 2001).

Press, L. (1998) "Cuban Computer Networks and their Determinants" DRR-1814-OSD, RAND Corporation, Santa Monica, CA, February, 1998, 49 pp.

Press, L. (1999) "The Second Internet Diffusion Survey" *OnTheInternet* 5(6), 34–37, http://som.csudh.edu/fac/ lpress/GDIFF/otidevnations.htm (April 26, 2001).

Press, L. (2000, July) "The State of the Internet," *Proceedings of INET 2000, International Networking Conference*, Yokohama, Japan, July, 2000. Reston, VA: Internet Society, http://www.isoc.org/inet2000/ cdproceedings/8e/8e_4.htm (Current April 26, 2001).

Press, L., and L. G. Rodriguez (1996) "Toward an Internet Census for Developing Nations," *Proceedings of INET '96, International Conference of the Internet*

Society, Montreal, June, 1996, http://www.isoc.org/inet96/ proceedings/f2/f2_3.htm (Current April 26, 2001).

Press, L., G. Burkhart, W. Foster, S. Goodman, P. Wolcott, and J. Woodard (1998) "An Internet Diffusion Framework" *Communications of the ACM* 41(10), 21–26.

Press, L., W. A. Foster, and S. E. Goodman (1999) "The Internet in China and India" *Inet '99 Proceedings*, Internet Society.

Press, L., and S. E. Goodman (1999) "Against All Odds, The Internet in Bangladesh," http://som.csudh.edu/fac/ lpress/devnat/nations/Bangladesh/bdmosaic.htm (Current April 26, 2001).

Rai, A., T. Ravichandran, and S. Samadar, (1998) "How to Anticipate the Internet's Global Diffusion" *Communications of the ACM* 41(10), 97–106.

Ridley, M. (1986) *Evolution and Classification*, London: Longman.

RIPE NCC (Réseaux IP Européens Network Coordination Center) (2000) "Internet Statistics. The RIPE Region Hostcount," http://www.ripe.net/ripencc/ pub-services/stats/hostcount/ (Current April 26, 2001).

Robinson, K. K., and E. M. Crenshaw (1999, Dec.) "Cyber-Space and Post-Industrial Transformations: A Cross-National Analysis of Internet Development," Working Paper, Ohio State University Dept. of Sociology.

Rogers, E. (1986). *Communication Technology: The New Media in Society*. New York: The Free Press.

Rogers, E. M. (1995) *Diffusion of Innovations*, 4th ed., New York: The Free Press.

Rogers, E., and Scott, K. (1997) "The Diffusion of Innovations Model and Outreach from the National Network of Libraries of Medicine to Native American Communities" Draft paper prepared for the National Network of Libraries of Medicine, Pacific Northwest Region, Seattle, http://www.nnlm.nlm.nih.gov/pnr/ eval/rogers.html (Current April 26, 2001).

Rood, H. (1999) "A Word About Internet Statistics" *Telecommunications Policy* 23, 687–688.

Rubin, H. J., and I. S. Rubin (1995) *Qualitative Interviewing: The Art of Hearing Data*. Thousand Oaks, CA: Sage Publications.

Saviotti, P. (1997) "Innovation Systems and Evolutionary Theories" in *Systems of Innovation: Technologies, Institutions and Organizations*, Edquist, C., ed., London: Pinter, pp. 180–199.

Sharif, M. N. (1988, August) "Basis For Techno-Economic Policy Analysis" *Science and Public Policy*, pp. 217–229.

Silverman, L. J., and W. C. Bailey (1961) *Trends in the Adoption of Recommended Farm Practices*, State College, Mississippi Agricultural Experiment Station Bulletin 617.

Staple, G. (1999) *Global Telecommunications Traffic Statistics & Commentary*, Washington, D.C.: TeleGeography.

Sudweeks, F., and S. Simoff (1999) "Complementary Explorative Data Analysis: The Reconciliation of Quantitative and Qualitative Principles" in Jones, S., Ed. *Doing Internet Research*. Thousand Oaks: Sage Publications, pp. 29–56.

Tan, Z. (Alex), W. Foster, and S. Goodman (1999) "China's State-Coordinated Internet Infrastructure" *Communications of the ACM* 42(6), 44–52.

Telcordia Technologies (2000a) "How many computer hosts in the Internet?" http://www.netsizer.com/ (Current April 26, 2001).

Telcordia Technologies (2000b) "Telcordia Applied Research," http://www.telcordia.com/products_services/appliedresearch/index.html (Current April 26, 2001).

Teo, Thompson S. H., and M. Tan (1998). "An empirical study of adopters and non-adopters of the Internet in Singapore" *Information & Management* 34, 339–345.

Van Slyke, C. (1998) Technology Cluster Innovations: Impacts Of Adding A Technology To An Existing Cluster, Ph.D. Dissertation, College of Business Administration, University of South Florida.

Wilson, E., J. Daly, and J.-M. Griffiths (1998) "Internet Counts: Measuring the Impacts of the Internet" Washington, D.C.: National Academy Press, http://www.bsos.umd.edu/cidcm/wilson/xnasrep2.htm (Current April 26, 2001).

WITSA (2000). International Survey Of E-Commerce 2000, World Information Technology and Services Alliance, http://www.witsa.org/papers/EComSurv.pdf (Current April 26, 2001).

Wolcott, P. (1999a) "The Diffusion of the Internet in the Republic of Turkey," http://mosaic.unomaha.edu/TURK_PUB.pdf (Current April 26, 2001).

Wolcott, P. (1999b) "The Diffusion of the Internet in Pakistan," http://mosaic.unomaha.edu/GD199Pakistan.pdf (current April 26, 2001).

Wolcott, P. (1999c). "The Diffusion of the Internet in the Republic of India: An Update," http://mosaic.unomaha.edu/India_new.pdf (Current May 2, 2001).

Wolcott, P. (2001) "Global Diffusion of the Internet Project Webpage," http://mosaic.unomaha.edu/gdi.html (Current April 26, 2001).

Wolcott, P., and S. E. Goodman (2000, Dec.) *The Internet in Turkey and Pakistan: A Comparative Analysis*. Stanford University: Center for International Security and Cooperation.

Wolcott, P., and K. Cagiltay (to appear, 2001) "Telecommunications, Liberalization, and the Growth of the Internet in Turkey" *The Information Society* 17/2.

Wolcott, P., S. Goodman, and G. Burkhart (1996) "The Information Technology Capability of Nations: A Framework for Analysis," http://mosaic.unomaha.edu/ITC_1996.pdf (Current April 26, 2001).

World Times/IDC (2000, Jan. 6) "Information Society Index. Measuring the Global Impact of Information Technology and Internet Adoption," http://www.idc.com:8080/Data/Global/ISI/ISIMain.htm (Current May 2, 2001).

Internet Paradox

A Social Technology That Reduces Social Involvement and Psychological Well-Being?

ROBERT KRAUT, VICKI LUNDMARK,
MICHAEL PATTERSON, SARA KIESLER,
TRIDAS MUKOPADHYAY,
AND WILLIAM SCHERLIS

Fifteen years ago, computers were mainly the province of science, engineering, and business. By 1998, approximately 40% of all U.S. households owned a personal computer; roughly one third of these homes had access to the Internet. Many scholars, technologists, and social critics believe that these changes and the Internet, in particular, are transforming economic and social life (e.g., Anderson, Bikson, Law, & Mitchell, 1995; Attewell & Rule, 1984; King & Kraemer, 1995). However, analysts disagree as to the nature of these changes and whether the changes are for the better or worse. Some scholars argue that the Internet is causing people to become socially isolated and cut off from genuine social relationships, as they hunker alone over their terminals or communicate with anonymous strangers through a socially impoverished medium (e.g., Stoll, 1995; Turkle, 1996). Others argue that the Internet leads to more and better social relationships by freeing people from the constraints of geography or isolation brought on by stigma, illness, or schedule. According to them, the Internet allows people to join groups on the basis of common interests rather than convenience (e.g., Katz & Aspden, 1997; Rheingold, 1993).

Arguments based on the attributes of the technology alone do not resolve this debate. People can use home computers and the Internet in many different ways and for many purposes, including entertainment, education, information retrieval, and communication. If people use the Internet mainly for communication with others through email, distribution lists, multiuser dungeons (MUDs), chats, and other such applications, they might do so to augment traditional technologies for social contact, expanding their number of friends and reducing the difficulty of coordinating interaction with them. On the other hand, these applications disproportionately reduce the costs of communication with geographically distant acquaintances and strangers; as a result, a smaller proportion of people's total social contacts might be with family and close friends. Other applications on the Internet, particularly the World Wide Web, provide asocial entertainment that could compete with social contact as a way for people to spend their time.

Whether the Internet is increasing or decreasing social involvement could have enormous consequences for society and for people's personal well-being. In an influential article, Putnam (1995) documented a broad decline in civic engagement and social participation in the United States over the past 35 years. Citizens vote less, go to church less, discuss government with their neighbors less, are members of fewer voluntary organizations, have fewer dinner parties, and generally get together less for civic and social purposes. Putnam argued that this social disengagement is having major consequences for the social fabric and for individual lives. At the societal level, social disengagement is associated with more corrupt, less efficient government and more crime. When citizens are involved in civic life, their schools run better, their politicians are more responsive, and their streets are safer. At the individual level, social disengagement is associated with poor quality of life and diminished physical and psychological health. When people have more social contact, they are happier and healthier, both physically and mentally (e.g., S. Cohen & Wills, 1985; Gove & Geerken, 1977).

Although changes in the labor force participation of women and marital breakup may account for some of the declines in social participation and increases in depression since the 1960s, technological change may also play a role. Television, an earlier technology similar to the Internet in some respects, may have reduced social participation as it kept people home watching the set. By contrast, other household technologies, in particular, the telephone, are used to enhance social participation, not discourage it (Fischer, 1992). The home computer and the Internet are too new and, until recently, were too thinly diffused into American households to explain social trends that originated over 35 years, but, now, they could either exacerbate or ameliorate these trends, depending on how they are used.

The goal of this article is to examine these issues and to report early empirical results of a field trial of Internet use. We show that within a diverse sample during their first year or two on-line, participants' Internet use led to their having, on balance, less social engagement and poorer psychological well-being. We discuss research that will be needed to assess the generality of the effects we have observed and to track down the mechanisms that produce them. We also discuss design and policy implications of these results, should they prove stable.

▮▮▮ Current Debate

Since the introduction of computing into society, scholars and technologists have pondered its possible social impact (e.g., Bell, 1973; Jacobson & Roucek, 1959; Leavitt & Whisler, 1958; Short, Williams, & Christie, 1976). With its rapid evolution, large numbers of applications, wealth of information sources, and global reach to homes, the Internet has added even more uncertainty. People could use the Internet to further privatize entertainment (as they have purportedly done with television), to obtain previously inaccessible information, to increase their technical skills, and to conduct commercial transactions at home—each are somewhat asocial functions that would make it easier for people to be alone and to be independent. Alternatively, people could use the Internet for more social purposes, to communicate and socialize with colleagues, friends, and family through electronic mail and to join social groups through distribution lists, newsgroups, and MUDs (Sproull & Faraj, 1995).

Internet for Entertainment, Information, and Commerce

If people use the Internet primarily for entertainment and information, the Internet's social effects might resemble those of television. Most research on the social impact of television has focused on its content; this research has investigated the effects of TV violence, educational content, gender stereotypes, racial stereotypes, advertising, and portrayals of family life, among other topics (Huston et al., 1992). Some social critics have argued that television reinforces sociability and social bonds (Beniger, 1987, pp. 356–362; McLuhan, 1964, p. 304). One study comparing Australian towns before and after television became available suggests that the arrival of television led to increases in social activity (Murray & Kippax, 1978). However most empirical work has indicated that television watching reduces social involvement (Brody, 1990; Jackson-Beeck & Robinson, 1981; Neuman, 1991; Maccoby, 1951). Recent epidemiological research has linked television watching with reduced physical activity and diminished physical and mental health (Andersen, Crespo, Bartlett, Cheskin, & Pratt, 1998; Sidney et al., 1998).

If watching television does indeed lead to a decline in social participation and psychological well-being, the most plausible explanation faults time displacement. That is, the time people spend watching TV is time they are not actively socially engaged. Basing their estimates on detailed time diaries, Robinson and Godbey (1997; see also Robinson, 1990) reported that a typical American adult spends three hours each day watching TV; children's TV watching is much higher (Condry, 1993). Although a large percentage of TV watching occurs in the presence of others, the quality of social interaction among TV viewers is low. People who report they are energetic and happy when they are engaged in active social interaction also report they are bored and unhappy when they are watching TV (Kubey & Csikszentmihalyi, 1990). Lonely people report watching TV more than others (Canary & Spitzberg, 1993), and people report using TV to alleviate loneliness (Rubinstein & Shaver, 1982; Rook & Peplau, 1982). Although we cannot disentangle the direction of causation in this cross-sectional research, a plausible hypothesis is that watching TV causes both social disengagement and worsening of mood.

Like watching television, using a home computer and the Internet generally imply physical inactivity and limited face-to-face social interaction. Some studies, including our own, have indicated that using a home computer and the Internet can lead to increased skills and confidence with computers (Lundmark, Kiesler, Kraut, Scherlis, & Mukopadhyay, 1998). However, when people use these technologies intensively for learning new software, playing computer games, or retrieving electronic information, they consume time and may spend more time alone (Vitalari, Venkatesh, & Gronhaug, 1985). Some cross-sectional research suggests that home computing may be displacing television watching itself (Danko & McLachlan, 1983; Kohut, 1994) as well as reducing leisure time with the family (Vitalari et al., 1985).

Internet for Interpersonal Communication

The Internet, like its network predecessors (Sproull & Kiesler, 1991), has turned out to be far more social than television, and in this respect, the impact of the Internet may be more like that of the telephone than of TV. Our research has shown that interpersonal communication is the dominant use of the Internet at home (Kraut, Mukhopadhyay, Szczypula, Kiesler, & Scherlis, 1998). That people use the Internet mainly for interpersonal communication, however, does not imply that their social interactions and relationships on the Internet are the same as their traditional social interactions and relationships (Sproull & Kiesler, 1991), or that their social uses of the Internet will have effects comparable to traditional social activity.

Whether social uses of the Internet have positive or negative effects may depend on how the Internet shapes the balance of strong and weak network ties that people maintain. Strong ties are relationships associated with frequent contact, deep feelings of affection and obligation, and application to a broad content domain, whereas weak ties are relationships with superficial and easily broken bonds, infrequent contact, and narrow focus. Strong and weak ties alike provide people with social support. Weak ties (Granovetter, 1973), including weak on-line ties (Constant, Sproull, & Kiesler, 1996), are especially useful for linking people to information and social resources unavailable in people's closest, local groups. Nonetheless, strong social ties are the relationships that generally buffer people from life's stresses and that lead to better social and psychological outcomes (S. Cohen & Wills, 1985; Krackhardt, 1994). People receive most of their social support from people with whom they are in most frequent contact, and bigger favors come from those with stronger ties (Wellman & Wortley, 1990).

Generally, strong personal ties are supported by physical proximity. The Internet potentially reduces the importance of physical proximity in creating and maintaining networks of strong social ties. Unlike face-to-face interaction or even the telephone, the Internet offers opportunities for social interaction that do not depend on the distance between parties. People often use the Internet to keep up with those whom they have preexisting relationships (Kraut et al., 1998). But they also develop new relationships on-line. Most of these new relationships are weak. MUDs, listservs, newsgroups, and chat rooms put people in contact with a pool of new groups, but these on-line "mixers" are typically organized around specific topics, activities, or demographics and rarely revolve around local community and close family and friends.

Whether a typical relationship developed on-line becomes as strong as a typical traditional relationship and whether having on-line relationships changes the number or quality of a person's total social involvements are open questions. Empirical evidence about the impact of the Internet on relationships and social involvement is sparse. Many authors have debated whether the Internet will promote community or undercut it (e.g., Rheingold, 1993; Stoll, 1995; Turkle, 1996) and whether personal relationships that are formed on-line are impersonal or as close and substantial as those sustained through face-to-face interaction (Berry, 1993; Heim, 1992; Walther, Anderson, & Park, 1994). Much of this discussion has been speculative and anecdotal, or is based on cross-sectional data with small samples.

▮▮▮ Current Data

Katz and Aspden's national survey (1997) is one of the few empirical studies that has compared the social participation of Internet users with nonusers. Controlling statistically for education, race, and other demographic variables, these researchers found no differences between Internet users' and nonusers' memberships in religious, leisure, and community organizations or in the amount of time users and nonusers reported spending communicating with family and friends. From these data, Katz and Aspden concluded that "[f]ar from creating a nation of strangers, the Internet is creating a nation richer in friendships and social relationships" (p. 86).

Katz and Aspden's (1997) conclusions may be premature because they used potentially inaccurate, self-report measures of Internet usage and social participation that are probably too insensitive to detect gradual changes over time. Furthermore, their observation that people have friendships on-line does not necessarily lead to the inference that using the Internet increases people's social participation or psychological well-being; to draw such a conclusion, one needs to know more about the quality of their on-line relationships and the impact on their off-line relationships. Many studies show unequivocally that people can and do form on-line social relationships (e.g., Parks & Floyd, 1995). However, these data do not speak to the frequency, depth, and impact of on-line relationships compared with traditional ones or whether the existence of on-line relationships changes traditional relationships or the balance of people's strong and weak ties.

Even if a cross-sectional survey were to convincingly demonstrate that Internet use is associated with greater social involvement, it would not establish the causal direction of this relationship. In many cases, it is as plausible to assume that social involvement causes Internet use as the reverse. For example, many people buy a home computer to keep in touch with children in college or with retired parents. People who use the Internet differ substantially from those who do not in their demographics, skills, values, and attitudes. Statistical tests often under-control for the influence of these factors, which in turn can be associated with social involvement (Anderson et al., 1995; Kraut, Scherlis, Mukhopadhyay, Manning, & Kiesler, 1996; Kohut, 1994).

▪▪▪ A Longitudinal Study of Internet Use

The research described here uses longitudinal data to examine the causal relationship between people's use of the Internet, their social involvement, and certain likely psychological consequences of social involvement. The data come from a field trial of Internet use, in which we tracked the behavior of 169 participants over their first one or two years of Internet use. It improves on earlier research by using accurate measures of Internet use and a panel research design. Measures of Internet use were recorded automatically, and measures of social involvement and psychological well-being were collected twice, using reliable self-report scales. Because we tracked people over time, we can observe change and control statistically for social involvement, psychological states, and demographic attributes of the trial participants that existed prior to their use of the Internet. With these statistical controls and measures of change, we can draw stronger causal conclusions than is possible in research in which the data are collected once.

Method

Sample

The HomeNet study consists of a sample of 93 families from eight diverse neighborhoods in Pittsburgh, Pennsylvania. People in these families began using a computer and the Internet at home either in March 1995 or March 1996. Within these 93 families, 256 members signed consent forms, were given email accounts on the Internet, and logged on at least once. Children younger than 10 and uninterested members of the households are not included in the sample.

Each year's subsample was drawn from four school or neighborhood groups so that the participants would have some preexisting communication and information interests in common. The first year's participants consisted of families with teenagers participating in journalism classes in four area high schools. The second year's participants consisted of families in which an adult was on the Board of Directors of one of four community development organizations.

Families received a computer and software, a free telephone line, and free access to the Internet in exchange for permitting the researchers to automatically track their Internet usage and services, for answering periodic questionnaires, and for agreeing to an in-home interview. The families used Carnegie Mellon University's proprietary software for electronic mail, MacMail II, Netscape Navigator 2 or 3 for web browsing, and Claris Works Office. At least two family members also received a morning's training in the use of the computer, electronic mail, and the World Wide Web.

None of the groups approached about the study declined the invitation, and over 90% of the families contacted within each group agreed to participate. Because the recruitment plan excluded households or individuals with active Internet connections, the data represent people's first experiences with Internet use, and for all but a few of the households, their first experience with a powerful home computer.

Some participants left the study to attend college, because they moved, or for other reasons. Of the 256 individuals who completed the pretest questionnaire, 169 (66%) from 73 households also completed the follow-up questionnaire. Table 1 provides descriptive statistics on the sample that completed both a pretest and posttest questionnaire. Compared with participants who completed only the pretest questionnaire, participants who completed both were wealthier ($53,300 vs. $43,600 annual household income, $r = .20, p < .01$), more likely to be adults (74% vs. 55%, $r = .16, p < .01$), and less lonely (1.98 vs. 2.20 on a 5-point scale, $r = -.13, p < .05$). *They did not differ on other measures.*

TABLE 1 Description of the Sample

Variable	N	M
Household income (dollars in thousands)	164	54.46
Race (White = 1, minority = 0)	167	0.75
Age (teen = 1, adult = 0)	169	0.28
Gender (female = 1, male = 0)	169	0.56
Social extraversion (1–5 scale)	169	3.66
Household size (individuals in household at pretest)	231	4.08
Family communication T1 (mean hours per day)	231	4.29
Family communication T3 (mean hours per day)	231	4.51
Local social network T1 (number of people)	166	23.94
Local social network T3 (number of people)	166	22.90
Distant social network T1 (number of people)	166	25.43
Distant social network T3 (number of people)	166	31.73
Social support T1 (1–5 scale, 16 items)	164	3.97
Social support T3 (1–5 scale, 16 items)	166	3.97
Loneliness T1 (1–5 point scale, 3 items)	165	1.99
Loneliness T3 (1–5 point scale, 3 items)	163	1.89
Stress T1 (mean of hassles reported of 49 items)	169	0.23
Stress T3 (mean of hassles reported of 49 items)	169	0.23
Depression T1 (0–3 scale, 15 items)	167	0.73
Depression T3 (0–3 scale, 15 items)	164	0.62
Internet usage T2 (mean hours per week)	169	2.43

Note. The units of the means and standard deviations for Internet hours and family communication are weekly hours.

Because estimates of communication within the family were based on reports from multiple family members, we have data for 231 individuals for this measure.

Data Collection

We measured demographic characteristics, social involvement, and psychological well-being of participants in the HomeNet trial on a pretest questionnaire, before the participants were given access to the Internet. After 12 to 24 months, participants completed a follow-up questionnaire containing the measures of social involvement and psychological well-being. During this interval, we automatically recorded their Internet usage using custom-designed logging programs. The data reported here encompass the first 104 weeks of use after a HomeNet family's Internet account was first operational for the 1995 subsample and 52 weeks of use for the 1996 subsample.

Demographic and Control Variables   In previous analyses of this sample, we found that the demographic factors of age, gender, and race were associated empirically with Internet usage (Kraut et al., 1998). Others have reported that household income is associated with Internet usage (Anderson et al., 1995). We used those demographic factors as control variables in our equations. Also, as a control variable that might influence participants' family communication, social network, social support, and loneliness, we included a measure of social extraversion in those analyses (e.g., "I like to mix socially with people"; Bendig, 1962). A few other controls used in single analyses are described below.

Internet Usage   Software recorded the total hours in a week in which a participant connected to the Internet. Electronic mail and the World Wide Web were the major applications that participants used on the Internet and account for most of their time on-line. Internet hours also included time that participants read distribution lists such as listservs or Usenet newsgroups and participated in real-time communication using Web chat lines, MUDs, and Internet Relay Chat. For the analyses we report here, we averaged weekly Internet hours over the period in which each participant had access to the Internet, from the pretest up to the time he or she completed the follow-up questionnaire. Our analyses use the log of the variable to normalize the distribution.

Personal Electronic Mail Use   We recorded the number of e-mail messages participants sent and received. To better distinguish the use of the Internet for interpersonal communication rather than for information and entertainment, we excluded e-mail messages in which the participant was not explicitly named as a recipient in our count of received mail. These messages typically had been broadcast to a distribution list to which the participant had subscribed. We believe these messages reflect a mix of interpersonal communication and information distribution.

World Wide Web Use   We recorded the number of unique World Wide Web domains or sites accessed per week (a domain or site is an Internet protocol address, such as www.disney.com). Our metric for total volume of World Wide Web use is the number of different domains accessed during the week. The average number of weekly domains visited and the average number of weekly hypertext mark-up language (html) pages retrieved were very highly correlated ($r = .96$).

Social Involvement and Psychological Well-Being   Before participants gained access to the Internet and again (depending on sample) approximately 12 to 24 months later, they completed questionnaires assessing their social involvement and psychological well-being. We used four measures of social involvement: family communication, size of local social network, size of distant social network, and social support. To measure family communication, we asked participants to list all the members of their household and to estimate the number of minutes they spent each day communicating with each member. Pairs reported similar estimates ($r = .73$), and their estimates were averaged. The total amount of family communication for each participant is the sum of the minutes communicating with other family members. Extreme values (greater than 400 minutes) were truncated to 400 minutes. Because the measure was skewed, we took its log in the analyses that follow, to make the distribution more normal. Family communication is partly determined by the number of family members and is interdependent within households, so we controlled statistically for these group effects by including family as a dummy variable in the analyses involving family communication.

To measure the size of participants' local social network, we asked them to estimate the "the number of people in the Pittsburgh area . . . whom you socialize with at least once a month." The size of their distant social network was defined as "the number of people outside of the Pittsburgh area whom you seek out to talk with or to visit at least once a year." Because both measures had some outliers, they were truncated (at 60 for the local circle and 100 for the distant circle); because they were skewed, we took their log in the analyses that follow.

Social support is a self-report measure of social resources that theoretically derive from the social network. To measure participants' levels of social support, we asked them to complete 16 items from S. Cohen, Mermelstein, Kamarck, and Hoberman's (1984) Interpersonal Support Evaluation List (Cronbach's $\alpha = .80$), which asks people to report how easy it is to get tangible help, advice, emotional support, and companionship, and how much they get a sense of belonging from people around them (e.g., "There is someone I could turn to for advice about changing my job or finding a new one").

We used three measures of psychological well-being that have been associated with social involvement: loneliness, stress, and depression. Participants completed three items (Cronbach's $\alpha = .54$) from the UCLA Loneliness Scale (Version 2), which asks people about their feelings of connection to others around them (e.g., "I can't find companionship when I want it" (Russell, Peplau, & Cutrona, 1980). To measure stress we used Kanner, Coyne, Schaefer, and Lazarus' (1981) Hassles Scale. Participants reported whether they experienced one or more of 49 possible daily life stressors in the preceding month; the stressors ranged from having one's car break down, to not liking school, to illness in the family. Because stress is often a trigger for depression, this measure was also included as a control variable in analyses involving depression. Participants completed 15 items from the Center for Epidemiologic Studies Depression (CESD; Radloff, 1977) Scale (Cronbach's $\alpha = .86$) measuring depression in the general population. The scale asks respondents to report feelings, thoughts, symptoms, and energy levels associated with mild depression (e.g., "I felt that everything I did was an effort," "I felt I could not shake off the blues, even with help from family and friends").

Analysis

Our data analysis examined how changes in people's use of the Internet over 12 to 24 months was associated with changes in their social involvement and psychological well-being. We statistically controlled their initial levels of social involvement and psychological well-being, as well as certain demographic and control variables. Figure 1 describes the logic of our analysis as a path model (Bentler, 1995).

We used path analysis to test the relationships among variables measured at three time periods: pretest questionnaire at Time 1 (T1), Internet usage during Time 2 (T2), and posttest questionnaire at Time 3 (T3). The statistical associations among demographic

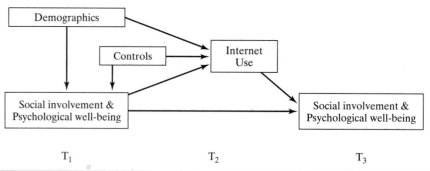

characteristics, social involvement, and psychological well-being measured at T1 and Internet use measured at T2 provide an estimate of how much preexisting personal characteristics led people to use the Internet. The link between social involvement and psychological well-being at T1 and T3 reflects stability in involvement and well-being. Evidence that using the Internet changes social involvement and psychological well-being comes from the link between Internet use at T2 and social involvement and psychological well-being at T3. Because this analysis controls for a participant's demographic characteristics and the initial level of the outcome variables, one can interpret the coefficients associated with the link between Internet use at T2 and outcomes at T3 as the effect of Internet use on changes in social involvement and psychological well-being (J. Cohen & Cohen, 1983). By using longitudinal data, measuring Internet use over an extended period, and measuring the outcome variables at two time periods, we can evaluate the possibility that initial social involvement or psychological well-being led to Internet use. We explicitly tested this possibility in the link between involvement and well-being at T1 and Internet use at T2; this link is controlled when we test the link between Internet use at T2 and outcome link at T3.

Results

Table 1 presents the means and standard deviations of the demographic variables, measures of Internet use, social involvement, and psychological well-being used in this study. Table 2 presents a correlation matrix showing the relationships among these variables.

All the path models are summarized in Table 3. When these models are complex, we also show these relationships graphically, in Figures 2–4.

Social Involvement

Family Communication   Figure 2 documents a path model in which the amount of time participants communicated with other members of their households is the dependent variable. Coefficients in the model are standardized beta weights showing the relationships among variables linked by arrows, when variables measured earlier have been controlled. Because communication within a single household is interdependent, we included a dummy variable for each family in the analysis. For purposes of clarity, only links with coefficients significant at the .05 level or less are included in Figure 2, although the full set of coefficients is included in Model 1 in Table 3.

The analysis of family communication showed that teenagers used the Internet more hours (T2) than did adults, but Whites did not differ from minorities, and female participants did not differ from male participants in their average hours of use. Different families varied in their use of the Internet (the family dummy variable), but

TABLE 2 Correlations Among Variables

Variable	1	2	3	4	5	6	7	8	9	10	11	12	13	14	15	16	17	18	19	20	21
1. Household income (dollars in thousands)	—																				
2. Race (White = 1, minority = 0)	.28	—																			
3. Age (teen = 1, adult = 0)	-.03	.08	—																		
4. Gender (female = 1, male = 0)	-.14	-.20	.03	—																	
5. Social extraversion (1–5 scale)	.11	.00	.12	.19	—																
6. Household size (people in household at pretest)	.27	.16	.16	-.07	.17	—															
7. Family communication T1 (mean hours per day)	-.14	-.01	-.07	.18	.09	.28	—														
8. Family communication T3 (mean hours per day)	-.03	-.10	-.28	.14	-.09	.01	.40	—													
9. Local social network T1 (number of people)	-.05	-.02	.27	.03	.07	.13	.09	.01	—												
10. Local social network T3 (number of people)	-.06	-.02	.24	.04	.12	.17	.20	.01	.56	—											
11. Distant social network T1 (number of people)	.14	.14	.02	.02	.06	.00	.09	.01	.30	.17	—										
12. Distant social network T3 (number of people)	.18	.27	.16	-.17	.06	.07	.06	.03	.16	.36	.38	—									
13. Social support T1 (1–5 scale, 16 items)	.12	.05	.05	.22	.34	.04	.25	.05	.16	.08	.06	.10	—								
14. Social support T3 (1–5 scale, 16 items)	.14	.13	.05	.18	.30	.14	.12	.04	.10	.14	.19	.13	.57	—							
15. Loneliness T1 (1–5 scale, 3 items)	-.09	-.07	-.18	-.08	-.37	-.12	-.25	-.10	-.21	-.19	-.08	-.18	-.61	-.48	—						
16. Loneliness T3 (1–5 scale, 3 items)	.07	-.08	-.05	-.21	-.36	-.07	-.15	-.05	-.30	-.23	-.15	-.12	-.49	-.67	.55	—					
17. Stress T1 (mean of hassles reported of 49 items)	-.01	-.01	-.15	.09	.04	.07	.06	.10	.03	.00	.07	-.09	-.08	-.01	.13	.09	—				
18. Stress T3 (mean of hassles reported of 49 items)	-.02	.13	.01	.05	.01	-.01	-.05	-.03	.07	.06	.00	.08	-.09	.10	.05	.01	.60	—			
19. Depression T1 (0–3 scale, 15 items)	.07	.05	.33	.10	-.14	.14	-.07	.03	.16	.12	.04	.08	-.26	-.12	.22	.24	.37	.30	—		
20. Depression T3 (0–3 scale, 15 items)	-.07	-.15	.14	.03	.00	-.06	-.08	-.20	-.07	-.06	-.13	-.11	-.12	-.36	.25	.36	.21	.31	.32	—	
21. Internet usage T2 (mean hours per week)	.06	.17	.23	-.07	-.10	-.07	-.09	-.08	-.07	-.11	-.08	-.05	-.01	-.04	-.09	.15	-.14	.04	.07	.15	—

Note. N for household size and family communication = 231. Other *N*s vary between 163 and 169. Family communication, social networks, and Internet use have been logged before computing correlations. When $r = .15, p = .05$; when $r = .17, p = .025$; when $r = 20, p = .01$.

TABLE 3 Effects of the Internet on Social Involvement and Psychological Well-being

Independent Variable	Model 1		Model 2		Model 3		Model 4		Model 5		Model 6		Model 7	
	Family Communication, T3	Internet Hours	Local Social Circle, T3	Internet Hours	Distant Social Circle, T3	Internet Hours	Social Support, T3	Internet Hours	Loneliness, T3	Internet Hours	Stress, T3	Internet Hours	Depression, T3	Internet Hours
Intercept	.00	-.17	-.03	.00	-.03	-.01	-.02	-.01	.02	.00	-.01	.00	.03	-.01
Household Income (dollars in thousands)	.10	.02	-.01	.05	.08	.06	.07	.04	.13†	.04	-.06	.02	-.04	-.01
Race (White = 1, minority = 0)			.03	.14	.19	.16†	.11	.12	-.16*	.12	.11	.15		.12
Age (teen = 1, adult = 0)	-.09*	.18**	.10	.25**	.13†	.21**	.00	.23*	.02	.20**	.11	.18*	-.21*	.15
Gender (female = 1, male = 0)	.09*	-.01	.06	.01	-.11	.02	.07	-.01	-.14*	.00	.07	-.01	.09	.15
Social extraversion (5-point scale)		.15	.03	-.16*			.09	-.18*	-.16*	-.20	.01		-.03	-.02
Family	—****													
Family communication T1 (mean hours per day)	.40***	-.16*												
Local social circle T1 (number of people)			.53***	-.14†										
Distant social circle T1 (number of people)					.33***	-.12								
Social support T1 (5-point scale, 16 items)							.51***	.04						
Loneliness T1 (5-point scale, 3 items)									.50***	-.11			-.03	.01
Stress T1 (mean of hassles reported of 49 items)											.65***	-.11	.17†	-.13
Depression T1 (0–3 scale, 15 items)													.22*	.06
Internet usage (mean hours per week)	-.08*		-.14*		-.14†		-.05		.15*		.11†		.19*	
R^2	.84	.42	.34	.10	.09	.10	.35	.09	.38	.10	.41	.08	.19	.07
N	231	231	155	158	156	158	152	156	152	157	161	161	150	155

Note. Entries are standardized beta coefficients from ordinary least squares regressions. T1 = time 1; T3 = time 3.
*Family was represented by 72 dummy variables differentiating the unique families, and therefore does not have a single estimate.
†p < .10 (marginally significant). *p < .05. **p < .01. ***p < .001.

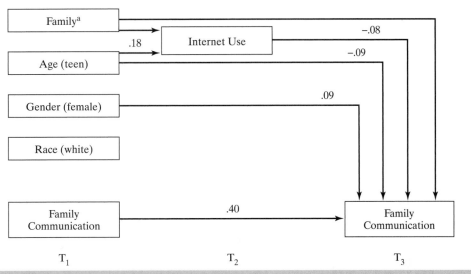

FIGURE 2 Influence of Internet Use on Family Communication

the amount of communication that an individual family member had with other members of the family did not predict subsequent Internet use. Family communication was stable over the period from T1 to T3. Whites increased their family communication more than minorities did. Adults increased their communication more than teens, and women/girls increased their communication in the family more than men/boys did. For our purposes, the most important finding is that greater use of the Internet was associated with subsequent declines in family communication.

Size of Participants' Social Networks   Models 2 and 3 in Table 3 present analyses involving the size of participants' local and distant social circles, respectively. Because social extroversion may influence the number of friendships that an individual

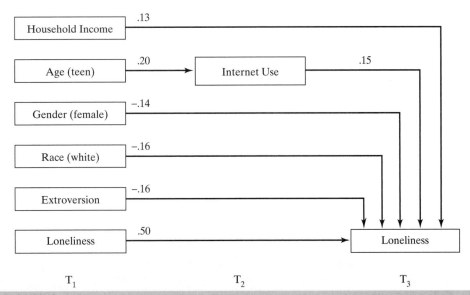

FIGURE 3 Influence of Internet Use on Loneliness

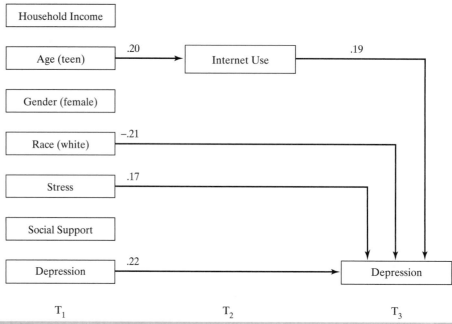

▪ ▪ ▪ ▪ ▪ ▪ ▪ ▪ ▪ ▪ ▪ ▪ **FIGURE 4** Influence of Internet Use on Depression

maintains and because preliminary analyses showed that more extroverted individuals subsequently used the Internet less, we included social extroversion as a control variable.

Greater social extroversion and having a larger local social circle predicted less use of the Internet during the next 12 or 24 months. Whites reported increasing their distant social circles more than minorities did, and teens reported increasing their distant circles more than adults did; these groups did not differ in changes to their local circles. Holding constant these control variables and the initial sizes of participants' social circles, greater use of the Internet was associated with subsequent declines in the size of both the local social circle ($p < .05$) and, marginally, the size of the distant social circle ($p < .07$).

Social Support   The social-circle measures ask respondents to estimate the number of people with whom they can exchange social resources. However, the definition provided to participants may have focused their attention primarily on people with whom they had face-to-face contact, thus leading to a biased view of social resources if the Internet allowed for the substitution of on-line contacts for face-to-face ones. The social support and loneliness measures are more direct measures of the consequences of having social contact and are not inherently biased by the medium of communication.

The social support measure and the loneliness measure have some items with comparable content (e.g., "I can find companionship when I want it" is on the loneliness scale and "When I feel lonely, these are several people I can talk to" is on the social support scale). Also, the two measures are correlated ($r = .60$). However, whereas the loneliness scale focuses on psychological feelings of belonging, the social support scale includes components measuring the availability of tangible resources from others (e.g., a loan), intangible resources from others (e.g., advice), and reflected esteem (e.g., respect for abilities).

Model 4 in Table 3 is a path analysis in which social support was the dependent variable. We included the extroversion scale at T1 as a covariate. Although the association between Internet use and subsequent social support was negative, the effect did not approach statistical significance ($p > .40$).

Psychological Well-Being

Loneliness Model 5 in Table 3 is the path analysis involving the loneliness scale. We included the extroversion scale at T1 as a covariate. Figure 3 summarizes the results. Note that initial loneliness did not predict subsequent Internet use. Loneliness was stable over time. People from richer households increased loneliness more than did those from poorer households, men increased loneliness more than did women, and minorities increased loneliness more than did Whites. Controlling for these personal characteristics and initial loneliness, people who used the Internet more subsequently reported larger increases in loneliness. The association of Internet use with subsequent loneliness was comparable to the associations of income, gender, and race with subsequent loneliness.

Stress Model 6 in Table 3 describes the analysis involving self-reports of daily "hassles," an index of the extent of daily life stress. The occurrence of these stressors was stable over the interval we studied. People who used the Internet more reported experiencing a greater number of daily life stressors in a subsequent period, an increase that is marginally significant ($p = .08$). The Hassle Scale (S. Cohen et al., 1984) is a simple mean of a large number of stressors. We tried to gain more insight into the detailed changes that were occurring in participants' lives by conducting an exploratory, post hoc analysis to identify the particular stressors that increased with Internet use. We conducted separate analysis for each potential stressor, regressing it on its occurence at the pretest time and the other variables from Model 6, and we used the Bonferroni correction to guard against capitalizing on chance in reporting results. Under this analysis, no single stressor changed reliably from its baseline. The implication is that even though use of the Internet may increase aggregate stress, it does not do so through a common route across the sample.

Depression Model 7 in Table 3 presents the path analysis involving depression; Figure 4 shows the significant variables. Because stress often triggers depression, and social support is often a buffer protecting against depression, we included both the hassle and social support measures at T1 as covariates. The stability of depression in this sample was lower than the stability of other outcomes measured, but was comparable to its stability in other general populations (Radloff, 1977). Initial depression did not predict subsequent Internet use. Minorities reported more increases in depression than did Whites, and those with higher initial stress also reported greater increases in depression. For the purposes of this analysis, the important finding is that greater use of the Internet was associated with increased depression at a subsequent period, even holding constant initial depression and demographic, stress, and support variables that are often associated with depression. This negative association between Internet use and depression is consistent with the interpretation that use of the Internet caused an increase in depression. Again, it is noteworthy that depression at T1 did not predict using the Internet subsequently.

▪▪▪ Discussion

Evaluating the Causal Claim

The findings of this research provide a surprisingly consistent picture of the consequences of using the Internet. Greater use of the Internet was associated with small, but statistically significant declines in social involvement as measured by communication within the family and the size of people's local social networks, and with increases in loneliness, a psychological state associated with social involvement. Greater use of the Internet was also associated with increases in depression. Other effects on the size of the distant social circle, social support, and stress did not reach standard significance levels but were consistently negative.

Our analyses are consistent with the hypothesis that using the Internet adversely affects social involvement and psychological well-being. The panel research design gives us substantial leverage in inferring causation, leading us to believe that in this case, correlation does indeed imply causation. Initial Internet use and initial social involvement and psychological well-being were included in all of the models assessing the effects of Internet use on subsequent social and psychological outcomes. Therefore, our analysis is equivalent to an analysis of change scores, controlling for regression toward the mean, unreliability, contemporaneous covariation between the outcome and the predictor variables, and other statistical artifacts (J. Cohen & Cohen, 1983). Because initial social involvement and psychological well-being were generally not associated with subsequent use of the Internet, these findings imply that the direction of causation is more likely to run from use of the Internet to declines in social involvement and psychological well-being, rather than the reverse. The only exception to this generalization was a marginal finding that people who initially had larger local social circles were lighter users of the Internet.

The major threat to the causal claim would arise if some unmeasured factor varying over time within individuals were to simultaneously cause increases in their use of the Internet and declines in their normal levels of social involvement and psychological well-being. One such factor might be developmental changes in adolescence, which could cause teenagers to withdraw from social contact (at least from members of their families) and to use the Internet as an escape. Our data are mixed regarding this interpretation. In analyses not reported in Table 3, statistical interactions of Internet use with age showed that increases in Internet use were associated with larger increases in loneliness ($ß = -.16, p < .02$) and larger declines in social support ($ß = -.13, p < .05$) for teenagers than for adults. On the other hand, increases in Internet use were associated with smaller increases in daily stress for teenagers than adults ($ß = -.16, p < .02$). There were no statistical interactions between Internet use and age for family communication, depression, or size of social circle.

Although the evidence is strong that using the Internet caused declines in social participation and psychological well-being within this sample, we do not know how generalizable the findings are across people, time, or outcomes. The sample examined here was selected to be diverse, but it was small and not statistically representative of any particular geographic region or population. In addition, the sample consisted of families with at least one member engaged in a preexisting face-to-face group (students working on a high school newspaper or adults on the board of a community development organization). If the sample had consisted of those who were already isolated (e.g., homeless or elderly people), social interaction on the Internet might have increased social participation and psychological well-being rather than decreased them.

Moreover, the sample examined people in their first one or two years on-line, starting in 1995 or 1996; whether results would have been the same at different points in their experience or at different points in the history of the Internet is unclear. Some of the teenagers, for example, reported that the Internet lost its appeal as they became immersed in the more serious work of college. The Internet itself changed during the course of this research. For example, group-oriented software, like America Online's Instant Messenger or Mirabilis' ICQ, which allow people to monitor the availability of selected individuals and to immediately swap messages with them when they go on-line, was not available during the early days of this trial.

Finally, we can generalize our results only to outcomes related to social behavior. In particular, we are not reporting effects of the Internet on educational outcomes or on self-esteem related to computer skill learning. Participants gained computer skills with more Internet usage. Several parents of teenagers who had spent many hours on-line judged that their children's positive educational outcomes from using the Internet outweighed possible declines in their children's social interaction. Future research will be needed to evaluate whether such trade-offs exist.

Possible Causal Mechanisms

To this point, we have attempted to establish the existence of a phenomenon-that Internet use causes declines in social involvement and psychological well-being. We have not, however, identified the mechanisms through which this phenomenon occurs. There are at least two plausible and theoretically interesting mechanisms, but we have little evidence from our current research to establish which, if either, is correct.

Displacing Social Activity   The time that people devote to using the Internet might substitute for time that they had previously spent engaged in social activities. According to this explanation, the Internet is similar to other passive, nonsocial entertainment activities, such as watching TV, reading, or listening to music. Use of the Internet, like watching TV, may represent a privatization of entertainment, which could lead to social withdrawal and to declines in psychological well-being. Putnam (1995) made a similar claim about television viewing.

The problem with this explanation is that a major use of the Internet is explicitly social. People use the Internet to keep up with family and friends through electronic mail and on-line chats and to make new acquaintances through MUDs, chats, Usenet newsgroups, and listservs. Our previous analyses showed that interpersonal communication was the dominant use of the Internet among the sample studied in this research (Kraut et al., 1998). They used the Internet more frequently for exchanging electronic mail than for surfing the World Wide Web and, within a session, typically checked their mail before looking at the Web; their use of electronic mail was more stable over time than their use of the World Wide Web; and greater use of e-mail relative to the Web led them to use the Internet more intensively and over a longer period (Kraut et al., 1998). Other analyses, not reported here, show that even social uses of the Internet were associated with negative outcomes. For example, greater use of electronic mail was associated with increases in depression.

Displacing Strong Ties   The paradox we observe, then, is that the Internet is a social technology used for communication with individuals and groups, but it is associated with declines in social involvement and the psychological well-being that goes with social involvement. Perhaps, by using the Internet, people are substituting poorer quality social relationships for better relationships, that is, substituting weak ties for strong ones (e.g., Granovetter, 1973; Krackhardt, 1994). People can support strong ties electronically. Indeed, interviews with this sample revealed numerous instances in which participants kept up with physically distant parents or siblings, corresponded with children when they went off to college, rediscovered roommates from the past, consoled distant friends who had suffered tragedy, or exchanged messages with high school classmates after school.

However, many of the on-line relationships in our sample, and especially the new ones, represented weak ties rather than strong ones. Examples include a woman who exchanged mittens with a stranger she met on a knitting listserv, a man who exchanged jokes and Scottish trivia with a colleague he met through an on-line tourist website, and an adolescent who exchanged (fictional) stories about his underwater exploits to other members of a scuba diving chat service. A few participants met new people on-line and had friendships with them. For instance, one teenager met his prom date on-line, and another woman met a couple in Canada whom she subsequently visited during her summer vacation. However, interviews with participants in this trial suggest that making new friends on-line was rare. Even though it was welcomed when it occurred, it did not counteract overall declines in real-world communication with family and friends. Our conclusions resonate with Katz and Aspden's (1997) national survey data showing that only 22% of the respondents who had been using the Internet for two or more years had ever made a new friend on the Internet. Although neither we nor Katz and Aspden provide comparison data, we wonder whether, in the real world, only a fifth of the population make a friend over a two-year period.

On-line friendships are likely to be more limited than friendships supported by physical proximity. On-line friends are less likely than friends developed at school, work, church, or in the neighborhood to be available for help with tangible favors, such as offering small loans, rides, or baby-sitting. Because on-line friends are not embedded in the same day-to-day environment, they will be less likely to understand the context for conversation, making discussion more difficult (Clark, 1996) and rendering support less applicable. Even strong ties maintained at a distance through electronic communication are likely to be different in kind and perhaps diminished in strength compared with strong ties supported by physical proximity (Wellman & Wortley, 1990). Both frequency of contact and the nature of the medium may contribute to this difference. For example, one of our participants who said that she appreciated the e-mail correspondence she had with her college-aged daughter also noted that when her daughter was homesick or depressed, she reverted to telephone calls to provide support. Although a clergyman in the sample used e-mail to exchange sermon ideas with other clergy, he phoned them when he needed advice about negotiating his contract. Like that mother and clergyman, many participants in our sample loved the convenience of the Internet. However, this convenience may induce people to substitute less involving electronic interactions for more involving real-world ones. The clergyman in the sample reported that his involvement with his listserv came at the expense of time with his wife.

Implications for Policy and Design

The negative effects of Internet use that we have documented here are not inevitable. Technologies are not immutable, especially not computing ones. Their effects will be shaped by how they are constructed by engineers, how they are deployed by service providers, and how they are used by consumers.

Designing technology and policy to avoid negative outcomes will depend on a more complete understanding of the mechanisms through which use of the Internet influences social involvement and psychological well-being. If we assume, for example, that the negative consequences of using the Internet occur at least partly because people spend more time and attention on weak ties and less time and attention on strong ties, then some design and policy solutions come easily to mind.

Most public policy discussion of the Internet has focused on its potential benefits as an information resource and as a medium for commercial exchange. Research funding also heavily favors the development of better resources for efficient information delivery and retrieval.

Both policy and technology interventions to better support the Internet's uses for interpersonal communication could right this imbalance. For example, recent legislation to limit taxes on the Internet favored the Internet for commercial transactions. There are no comparable policy initiatives to foster use of the Internet as an interpersonal communications medium (see Andersen et al., 1998). At the technological level, services for finding people are far less common, sophisticated, or accurate than services for finding information and products. On-line directories of e-mail addresses are far less comprehensive than on-line directories of telephone numbers. Search services on the Internet, such as Yahoo, Alta Vista, InfoSeek, and Lycos, grew from sophisticated industrial and government-funded research programs in information retrieval. The initiative on digital libraries, funded by the National Science Foundation and the Defense Advanced Research Projects Agency, has a goal of making pictures, graphs, and video images as easy to search and retrieve as text. Comparable search capabilities for finding people based on their attributes are far less well-supported. (See the research on collaborative filtering, e.g., Resnick & Varian, 1997, for an interesting exception.)

The interpersonal communication applications currently prevalent on the Internet are either neutral toward strong ties or tend to undercut rather than promote them. Because most websites, Usenet news groups, and listservs are topically organized, strangers are encouraged to read each others' messages and exchange communication on the basis of their common interests in soap operas, civil rights, stamp collecting, or other narrow topics. This communication is dominated by the designated topic, and people are frequently discouraged by social pressure from straying from the topic. Although some of these groups are formed explicitly to provide support, and a few even encourage real-world friendships and tangible help, these are relatively few in comparison to the thousands of groups focused on professional advice, hobbies, and entertainment. Information and communication services that are geographically based and designed to support people who already know and care about each other are even rarer. Some successful experiments at community-based on-line communication do exist (e.g., Carroll & Rosson, 1996) along with some successful commercial services that support preexisting social groups (e.g., "buddy lists" in America OnLine's Instant Messenger product). We believe these are valuable directions.

More intense development and deployment of services that support preexisting communities and strong relationships should be encouraged. Government efforts to wire the nation's schools, for example, should consider on-line homework sessions for students rather than just on-line reference works. The volunteers in churches, synagogues, and community groups building informational websites might discover that tools to support communication among their memberships are more valuable.

Both as a nation and as individual consumers, we must balance the value of the Internet for information, communication, and commerce with its costs. Use of the Internet can be both highly entertaining and useful, but if it causes too much disengagement from real life, it can also be harmful. Until the technology evolves to be more beneficial, people should moderate how much they use the Internet and monitor the uses to which they put it.

REFERENCES

Andersen, R. E., Crespo, C. J., Bartlett, S. J., Cheskin, L. J. & Pratt, M. (1998). Relationship of physical activity and television watching with body weight and level of fatness among children. *Journal of the American Medical Association, 279,* 938–942.

Anderson, R. H., Bikson, T. K., Law, S. A. & Mitchell, B. M. (1995). *Universal access to e-mail: Feasibility and societal implications.* Santa Monica, CA: Rand Corporation.

Attewell, P. & Rule, J. (1984). Computing and organizations: What we know and what we don't know. *Communication of the ACM, 27,* 1184–1192.

Bell, D. (1973). *The coming of post-industrial society: A venture in social forecasting.* New York: Basic Books.

Bendig, A. W. (1962). The Pittsburgh scales of social extraversion, introversion and emotionality. *The Journal of Psychology, 53,* 199–209.

Beniger, J. R. (1987). Personalization of mass media and the growth of pseudocommunity. *Communication Research, 14,* 352–371.

Bentler, P. M. (1995). *EQS: Structural equations program manual.* Encino, CA: Multivariate Software, Inc.

Berry, W. (1993). *Sex, economy, freedom, and community.* New York: Pantheon.

Brody, G. H. (1990, April). Effects of television viewing on family interactions: An observational study. *Family Relations, 29,* 216–220.

Canary, D. J. & Spitzberg, B. H. (1993). Loneliness and media gratification. *Communication Research, 20,* 800–821.

Carroll, J. & Rosson, M. (1996). Developing the Blacksburg electronic village. *Communications of the ACM, 39* (12), 68–74.

Clark, H. H. (1996). *Using language.* New York: Cambridge University Press.

Cohen, J. & Cohen, P. (1983). *Applied multiple regression/correlation analysis for the behavioral sciences.* Hillsdale, NJ: Erlbaum.

Cohen, S., Mermelstein, R., Kamarck, T. & Hoberman, H. (1984). Measuring the functional components of social support. In I. G. Sarason & B. R. Sarason (Eds.), *Social support: Theory, research and applications* (pp. 73–94). The Hague, Holland: Martines Niijhoff.

Cohen, S. & Wills, T. A. (1985). Stress, social support, and the buffering hypothesis. *Psychological Bulletin, 98,* 310–357.

Condry, J. (1993, Winter). Thief of time, unfaithful servant: Television and the American child. *Daedalus, 122,* 259–278.

Constant, D., Sproull, L. & Kiesler, S. (1996). The kindness of strangers: On the usefulness of weak ties for technical advice. *Organization Science, 7,* 119–135.

Danko, W. D. & MacLachlan, J. M. (1983). Research to accelerate the diffusion of a new invention. *Journal of Advertising Research, 23* (3), 39–43.

Fischer, C. S. (1992). *America calling.* Berkeley, CA: University of California Press.

Gove, W. R. & Geerken, M. R. (1977). The effect of children and employment on the mental health of married men and women. *Social Forces, 56,* 66–76.

Granovetter, M. (1973). The strength of weak ties. *American Journal of Sociology, 73,* 1361–1380.

Heim, M. (1992). The erotic ontology of cyberspace. In M. Benedikt (Ed.), *Cyberspace: First steps* (pp. 59–80). Cambridge, MA: MIT Press.

Huston, A. C., Donnersteinf, E., Fairchild, H., Feshbach, N., Katz, P., Murray, J., Rubinstein, E., Wilcox, B. & Zuckerman, D. (1992). *Big world, small screen: The role of television in American society.* Lincoln: University of Nebraska Press.

Jackson-Beeck, M. & Robinson, J. P. (1981). Television nonviewers: An endangered species? *Journal of Consumer Research, 7,* 356–359.

Jacobson, H. B. & Roucek, J. S. (1959). *Automation and society.* New York: Philosophical Library.

Kanner, A. D., Coyne, J. C., Schaefer, C. & Lazarus, R. S. (1981). Comparisons of two modes of stress measurement: Daily hassles and uplifts versus major life events. *Journal of Behavioral Medicine, 4,* 1–39.

Katz, J. E. & Aspden, P. (1997). A nation of strangers? *Communications of the ACM, 40* (12), 81–86.

King, J. L. & Kraemer, K. L. (1995). Information infrastructure, national policy, and global competitiveness. *Information Infrastructure and Policy, 4,* 5–28.

Kohut, A. (1994). *The role of technology in American life.* Los Angeles: Times Mirror Center for the People and the Press.

Krackhardt, D. (1994). The strength of strong ties: The importance of Philos in organizations. In N. Nohria & R. Eccles (Eds.), *Networks and organizations: Structure, form, and action.* Boston, MA: Harvard Business School Press.

Kraut, R., Mukhopadhyay, T., Szczypula, J., Kiesler, S. & Scherlis, W. (1998). Communication and information: Alternative uses of the Internet in households. *In Proceedings of the CHI 98* (pp. 368–383). New York: ACM.

Kraut, R., Scherlis, W., Mukhopadhyay, T., Manning, J. & Kiesler, S. (1996). The HomeNet field trial of residential Internet services. *Communications of the ACM, 39,* 55–63.

Kubey, R. & Csikszentmihalyi, M. (1990). *Television and the quality of life: How viewing shapes everyday experience.* Hillsdale, NJ: Erlbaum.

Leavitt, H. J. & Whisler, T. L. (1958, November-December). Management in the 1980s. *Harvard Business Review, 36,* 41–48.

Lundmark, V., Kiesler, S., Kraut, R., Scherlis, W. & Mukhopadhyay, T. (1998). *How the strong survive: Patterns and significance of competence, commitment, and requests for external technical support in families on the Internet.* Unpublished manuscript.

Maccoby, E. E. (1951). Television: its impact on school children. *Public Opinion Quarterly, 15,* 421–444.

McLuhan, M. (1964). *Understanding media.* New York: McGraw-Hill.

Murray, J. P. & Kippax, S. (1978). Children's social behavior in three towns with differing television experience. *Journal of Communication, 28,* 18–29.

Neuman, S. B. (1991). *Literacy in the television age: The myth of the TV effect.* Norwood, NJ: Ablex.

Parks, M. R. & Floyd, K. (1995, month day). Making friends in cyberspace. *Online Journal of Computer Mediated Communication, I* (4). Available: www.ascusc.org/jcmc/vol1/issue4/vol1no4.html

Putnam, R. (1995, January). Bowling alone: America's declining social capital. *Journal of Democracy, 6*, 65–78.

Radloff, L. (1977). The CES-D Scale: A self-report depression scale for research in the general population. *Applied Psychological Measurement, 1*, 385–401.

Resnick, P. & Varian, H. (1997). Recommender systems: Introduction to the special section. *Communications of the ACM, 40* (3), 56–58.

Rheingold, H. (1993). *The virtual community: Homesteading on the electronic frontier.* Reading, MA: Addison Wesley.

Robinson, J. P. (1990). Television's effects on families' use of time. In J. Bryant (Ed.), *Television and the American family* (pp. 195–209). Hillsdale, NJ: Erlbaum.

Robinson, J. P. & Godbey, G. (1997). *Time for life: The surprising ways Americans use their time.* University Park: The Pennsylvania State University Press.

Rook, K. S. & Peplau, L.A. (1982). Perspectives on helping the lonely. In L. A. Peplau & D. Perlman (Eds.), *Loneliness: A sourcebook of current theory, research and therapy* (pp. 351–378). New York: Wiley.

Rubinstein, C. & Shaver, P. (1982). *In search of intimacy.* New York: Delcorte.

Russell, D., Peplau, L. & Cutrona, C. (1980). The revised UCLA loneliness scale: Concurrent and discriminant validity evidence. *Journal of Personality and Social Psychology, 39*, 472–480.

Short, J., Williams, E. & Christie, B. (1976). *The social psychology of telecommunications.* London: Wiley.

Sidney, S., Sternfeld, B., Haskell, W.L., Jacobs, D.R., Chesney, M. A. & Hulley, S. B. (1998). Television viewing and cardiovascular risk factors in young adults: The CARDIA study. *Annals of Epidemiology, 6* (2), 154–159.

Sproull, L. & Faraj, S. (1995). Atheism, sex, and databases: The Net as a social technology. In B. Kahin & J. Keller (Eds.), *Public access to the Internet* (pp. 62–81). Cambridge, MA: MIT Press.

Sproull, L. & Kiesler, S. (1991). *Connections: New ways of working in the networked organization.* Cambridge, MA: MIT Press.

Stoll, C. (1995). *Silicon snake oil.* New York: Doubleday.

Turkle, S. (1996, Winter). Virtuality and its discontents: Searching for community in cyberspace. *The American Prospect, 24*, 50–57.

Vitalari, N. P., Venkatesh, A. & Gronhaug, K. (1985). Computing in the home: Shifts in the time allocation patterns of households. *Communications of the ACM, 28* (5), 512–522.

Walther, J. B., Anderson, J. F. & Park, D. (1994). Interpersonal effects in computer-mediated interaction: A meta-analysis of social and anti-social communication. *Communication Research, 21*, 460–487.

Wellman, B. & Wortley, S. (1990). Different strokes for different folks: Community ties and social support. *American Journal of Sociology, 96*, 558–588.

Internet Paradox
Revisited

ROBERT KRAUT, SARA KIESLER,
BONKA BONEVA, JONATHON CUMMINGS,
VICKI HELGESON, AND ANNE CRAWFORD

With the rapidly expanding reach of the Internet into everyday life, it is important to understand its social impact. One reason to expect significant social impact is the Internet's role in communication. From the early days of networked mainframe computers to the present, interpersonal communication has been the technology's most frequent use (Sproull & Kiesler, 1991). Over 90% of people who used the Internet during a typical day in 2000, sent or received email (Pew Internet Report, 2000), far more than used any other online application or information source. Using email leads people to spend more time online and discourages them from dropping Internet service (Kraut, Mukhopadhyay, Szczpula, Kiesler, & Scherlis, 2000). Other Internet communication services are increasingly popular—instant messaging, chat rooms, multi-user games, auctions, and myriad groups comprising "virtual social capital" on the Internet (Putnam, 2000, pg. 170).

If communication dominates Internet use for a majority of its users, there is good reason to expect that the Internet will have positive social impact. Communication, including contact with neighbors, friends, and family, and participation in social groups, improves people's level of social support, their probability of having fulfilling personal relationships, their sense of meaning in life, their self-esteem, their commitment to social norms and to their communities, and their psychological and physical well-being (e.g., Cohen & Wills, 1985; Diener, Sul, Lucas, & Smith, 1999; Thoits, 1983; Williams, Ware, & Donald, 1981).

Through its use for communication, the Internet could have important positive social effects on individuals (e.g., McKenna & Bargh, 2000; McKenna, Green, & Gleason, this issue), groups and organizations (e.g., Sproull & Kiesler, 1991), communities (e.g., Wellman, Quan, Witte & Hampton, 2001; Borgida, Sullivan, Oxendine, Jackson, Riedel, & Gang, 2002), and society at large (e.g., Hiltz & Turoff, 1978). Because the Internet permits social contact across time, distance, and personal circumstances, it allows people to connect with distant as well as local family and friends, co-workers, business contacts, and with strangers who share similar interests. Broad social access could increase people's social involvement, as the telephone did in an early time (e.g., Fischer, 1992). It also could facilitate the formation of new relationships (Parks & Roberts, 1998), social identity and commitment among otherwise isolated persons (McKenna & Bargh, 1998), and participation in groups and organizations by distant or marginal members (Sproull & Kiesler, 1991).

Whether the Internet will have positive or negative social impact, however, may depend upon the quality of people's online relationships and upon what people give up to spend time online. Stronger social ties generally lead to better social outcomes than do weaker ties (e.g., Wellman & Wortley, 1990). Many writers have worried that the ease of Internet communication might encourage people to spend more time alone, talking online with strangers or forming superficial "drive by" relationships, at the expense of deeper discussion and companionship with friends and family (e.g., Putnam, 2000, pg. 179). Further, even if people use the Internet to talk with close friends and family, these online discussions might displace higher quality face-to-face and telephone conversation (e.g., Cummings, Butler & Kraut, in press; Thompson & Nadler, this issue).

Research has not yet led to consensus on either the nature of social interaction online or its effects on social involvement and personal well-being. Some survey research indicates that online social relationships are weaker than off-line relationships (Parks & Roberts, 1998), that people who use email regard it as less valuable than other modes of communication for maintaining social relationships (Cummings et al., in press; Kraut & Attewell, 1996), that people who use email heavily have weaker social relationships than those who do not (Riphagen & Kanfer, 1997) and that people who use the Internet heavily report spending less time communicating with their families (Cole, 2000). In contrast, other survey research shows that people who use the Internet heavily report more social support and more in-person visits with family and friends than those who use it less (Pew Internet Report, 2000). Because this research has been conducted with different samples in different years, it is difficult to identify central tendencies and changes in these tendencies with time. Further, the cross-sectional nature of the research makes it impossible to distinguish self-selection (in which socially engaged and disengaged people use the Internet differently) from causation (in which use of the Internet encourages or discourages social engagement).

A longitudinal study by Kraut, Patterson, Lundmark, Kiesler, Mukophadhyay, and Scherlis (1998) was one of the first to assess the causal direction of the relationship between Internet use and social involvement and psychological well-being. The HomeNet field trial followed 93 households in their first 12–18 months online. The authors had predicted that the Internet would increase users' social networks and the amount of social support to which they had access. The consequence should be that heavy Internet users would be less lonely, have better mental health, and be less harmed by the stressful life events they experienced (Cohen & Wills, 1985). The sample as a whole reported high well-being at the start of the study. Contrary to predictions, however, the association of Internet use with changes in the social and psychological variables showed that participants who used the Internet more heavily became less socially involved and more lonely than light users and reported an increase in depressive symptoms. These changes occurred even though participants' dominant use of the Internet was communication.

These findings were controversial. Some critics argued that because the research design did not include a control group without access to the Internet, external events or statistical regression could have been responsible for participants' declines in social involvement and psychological well-being (e.g., Gross, Juvonen, & Gable, 2002; Shapiro, 1999). However, these factors would have affected heavy and light Internet users similarly, so could not account for the differences in outcomes between them.

A more pertinent problem noted in the original HomeNet report is the unknown generalizability of the results over people and time. The participants in the original study were an opportunity sample of families in Pittsburgh. In 1995 and 1996, when they began the study, they initially had higher community involvement and more social ties than the population at large. In addition, they had little experience online, and few of their family and friends had Internet access. One possibility is that using the Internet disrupted this group's existing social relationships. Had the study begun with a more socially deprived sample or more recently, when more of the population was online, the group's use of the Internet for social interaction might have led to more positive effects. In addition, some critics questioned the particular measures of social involvement and well-being deployed in this study (e.g., Shapiro, 1999).

The present article addresses these issues of generalizability through a follow up of the original HomeNet sample and a new longitudinal study. The rationale for both studies is similar. If use of the Internet changes the amount and type of interpersonal communication people engage in and the connections they have to their friends, family, and communities, then it should also influence a variety of psychological outcomes, including their emotions, self-esteem, depressive symptoms and reactions to stressors (e.g., Cohen & Wills, 1985; Diener, Sul, Lucas, & Smith, 1999; Thoits, 1983; Williams, Ware, & Donald, 1981). The follow-up study examined the longer-term impact of Internet use on those in the original HomeNet sample, providing a second look at a group for whom initial Internet use had poor effects. It retained the outcome measures collected in original HomeNet study.

The second study followed a new sample in the Pittsburgh area, from 1998 and 1999. It compared an explicit control-group of those who had recently purchased a television set with those who purchased a computer. It also examines the impact of the Internet on a broader variety of social and psychological outcome measures than did the original HomeNet study. The goal was not to make differentiated predictions for each measure, but to see if using the Internet had similar consequences across a variety of measures of social involvement and psychological well-being. The sample was sufficiently large to permit an analysis of the impact of individual differences in personality and social resources on Internet usage and outcomes. In particular, the research examines whether using the Internet had different consequences for people differing in extraversion and in social support. As discussed further in the introduction to Study 2, people differing in extraversion and social support are likely use the Internet in different ways. In addition, they are likely to have different social resources available in their off-line lives, which could change the benefits they might gain from social resources they acquire online.

▪▪▪ Study 1: Follow-Up of the Original HomeNet Sample

The data are from 208 members of 93 Pittsburgh families, to whom we provided a computer and access to the Internet in 1995 or 1996. The families were recruited through four high school journalism programs and four community development organizations in 8 Pittsburgh neighborhoods. The sample was more demographically diverse than was typical of Internet users at the time. Details of the sampling and research protocol are described in Kraut et al. (1996).

The analyses of social impact reported in Kraut et al. (1998) were drawn from Internet usage records and from surveys given just before participants began the study and again in May 1997. Server software recorded participants' use of the Internet—hours online, email volume, and Web sites visited per week. The surveys included four measures of social involvement (time spent in family communication, size of local social network, size of distant social network, and perceived social support [Cohen, Mermelstein, Kamarck, & Hoberman, 1984]), and three well-established measures of psychological well-being: the UCLA Loneliness Scale (Russell, Peplau, & Cutrona, 1980), the Daily Life Hassles Scale, a measure of daily-life stress (Kanner, Coyne, Schaefer, & Lazarus, 1981), and the Center for Epidemiological Studies' Depression Scale (Radloff, 1977). It included the demographic characteristics of age, gender, household income, and race as control variables, because there is evidence that these factors influence both the amount of Internet use and the social and psychological outcomes (e.g., Von Dras & Siegler, 1997; Magnus, Diener, Fujita, Payot, 1993). We also included the personality trait of extraversion (Bending, 1962) as a control variable, because extraversion is often associated with well-being (Diener, et al, 1999) and may also influence the way people use the Internet. However, the sample was too small to examine statistical interaction involving the extraversion measure. See Table 1 for basic statistics and other information about these variables.

Kraut et al. (1998) used a regression analysis of the effect of hours of Internet use on social involvement and psychological well-being in 1997 (Time 2), controlling for scores on these outcome measures at the pretest (Time 1) and the demographic and personality control variables. The follow-up study re-examines the impact of use of the Internet by adding a third survey, administered in February 1998 (Time 3). For about half the participants, the final survey came nearly 3 years after they first used the Internet; for the other half, the final survey came nearly 2 years later.

Method

All longitudinal research faces the potential of participant attrition. Our research was especially vulnerable because we had not planned initially to follow the participants for more than one year. Many of the high school students in the original sample graduated and moved to college. Further, technology changed rapidly during this period, and some participants changed Internet providers, ending our ability to monitor their Internet use. Of the 335 people who qualified for participation in the original study, 261 returned a pretest survey at Time 1 (78%), 227 returned a survey at Time 2 (68%), and 154 returned a survey at Time 3 (46%). Because this research is fundamentally about changes in social and psychological outcomes, we limit analysis to 208 participants who completed a minimum of 2 out of 3 surveys.

We used a longitudinal panel design to examine the variables that influenced changes in social involvement and psychological well-being from Time 1 to Time 2, and from Time 2 to Time 3. The measure of Internet use is the average hours per week a participant spent online between any two surveys, according to automated usage records (i.e., weekly use between Times 1 and 2 and between Time 2 and 3). Because this variable was highly skewed, we used a log transformation. When assessing the impact of Internet use on social involvement and psychological well-being at one time, we statistically controlled for the prior level of social involvement and psychological well-being by including the lagged dependent variable as a control variable in the model. Since this analysis controls for participants' demographic characteristics and the lagged outcome, one can interpret the coefficients associated with Internet use as the effect of Internet use on changes in these outcomes (Cohen & Cohen, 1983, p. 417–422). (For example, when examining the effect of Internet use on loneliness at Times 2 and 3, we included the lagged variable for loneliness at Times 1 and 2, respectively, in the model to control for the effects of prior loneliness on Internet use and on subsequent loneliness.)

As demographic control variables, we included adult status (0 if age $< = 18$; 1 if age > 18), gender (0 = female; 1 = male), race (0 = non-white; 1 = white) and household

TABLE 1 Descriptive Statistics for Variables in Studies 1 and 2

	Study 1			Study 2			
Variable	Mean	Std	N	Alpha	Mean	Std	N
Adult[a]	.66	.48	208	NA	.88	.32	446
Male[a]	.42	.50	208	NA	.47	.50	446
White[a]	.72	.45	208	NA	.92	.27	438
Income[b]	5.53	1.27	197	NA	4.91	1.55	443
Education[c]				NA	4.06	1.23	446
Computer sample[a]				NA	.72	.45	446
Extraversion[g]	3.54	.77	204	.80	3.22	.65	389
Social support[g]	4.02	.57	206	.81	3.80	.54	389
Internet use[h]	.72	.76	206	.86	.00	.78	406
Local circle (log)[d]	3.01	.81	206	NA	2.56	.79	375
Distant circle (log)[e]	3.01	1.15	206	NA	2.21	1.05	361
Family communication (log)[f]	4.31	.78	193	NA	4.10	1.63	389
Face-to-face communication[h]				.55	−.01	1.00	406
Phone communication[g]				.83	4.69	1.15	387
Closeness near friends[g]				NA	3.54	.76	434
Closeness distant friends[g]				NA	2.94	1.10	286
Community involvement[g]				.70	2.83	.75	390
Stay in Pittsburgh[g]				NA	3.69	1.38	388
Trust[g]				.74	3.17	.83	391
Anomie[g]				.57	2.66	.63	391
Stress[j]	.24	.17	208	.88	.22	.14	382
Loneliness[g]	1.93	.68	204	.75	2.10	.66	389
Depression[i]	.65	.40	205	.88	.53	.47	389
Negative affect[g]				.88	1.67	.64	390
Positive affect[g]				.88	3.49	.72	388
Time pressure[g]				.82	3.02	.76	390
Self-esteem[g]				.85	3.70	.62	389
Computer skill[g]				.90	3.26	.93	389
US knowledge[k]				.41	.71	.33	388
Local knowledge[k]				.34	.68	.26	388

Note: All variables are coded so that higher numbers indicate more of the variable.
[a]Dicotomous variable (0/1)
[b]6 categories, from under $10,000 to over $75,000
[c]6 categories, from less than 11th grade to graduate-level work
[d]Truncated at 60 and logged
[e]Truncated at 100 and logged
[f]Sum of minutes communicating with other household members, logged
[g]5-point Likert response scale, with endpoints 1 and 5, where 5 is highest score.
[h]Hours per week using the Internet (logged) in Study 1; Mean of standardized variables in Study 2
[i]4-point Likert scales, with endpoint 0 and 3, where 3 is highest score.
[j]Mean of dicotomous response scales (0/1)
[k]Proportion correct on multiple choice questions

income. Because teens use the Internet substantially more than adults and in different ways (Kraut et al., 1998), we included the generation X Internet use interaction to determine whether the Internet had similar effects on both generations. Because the personality trait of extraversion is likely to influence social involvement, Bendig's (1962) measure of extraversion was included as a control variable when predicting social support and the size of local and distant social circles. Because daily-life stress is a risk factor for psychological depression, we included Kanner, Coyne, Schaefer, & Lazarus' (1981) hassles scale as a control variable when predicting depressive symptoms.

The analyses were conducted using the xtreg procedure in Stata (StataCorp, 2001) for cross-sectional time series analyses with independent variables modeled as a fixed effects and participant modeled as a random effect. For the dependent measures listed in Table 2, the basic model is Dependent Variable$_{Tn}$ = Intercept + Demographic Characteristics$_{T1}$ + Time Period + Dependent Variable$_{Tn-1}$ + Control Variables$_{Tn}$ + Log Internet Hours$_{Tn-1}$ + Log Internet Hours$_{Tn-1}$ × Time Period + Log Internet Hours$_{Tn-1}$ × Generation$_{T1}$. In the model, Dependent Variable$_{Tn}$ is a measure of social involvement or psychological well-being at the end of the first or second time period and Dependent Variable$_{Tn-1}$ represents the same measure administered in the previous time period. The analyses of particular interest are the main effects of Internet use on subsequent measures of social involvement and psychological well-being and the statistical interactions of Internet use and time period on these outcomes. The main effect of Internet use assesses the cumulative impact of Internet use over the two or three years of the study, and the interaction of Internet use with time period assesses whether this impact is the same in the early period (previously reported in Kraut et al., 1998) and in the more recent period.

Results

Table 2 shows results from the analyses. Kraut et al. (1998) showed Internet use was associated with declines in family communication, in the number of people in participants' local and distant social circles, and with increases in loneliness, depressive symptoms, and daily-life stress. Of these effects, Internet use over the longer period tested in the current analyses is associated only with increases in stress. Two significant Internet use × time period interactions suggest that Internet use had different effects early and late in respondents' use of the Internet. In particular, depressive symptoms significantly increased with Internet use during the first period but significantly declined with Internet use during the second period (for the interaction, $p < .05$). Loneliness significantly increased with Internet use during the first period but was not associated with Internet use during the second period (for the interaction, $p < .01$). Whether these differences in results over time reflect participants' learning how to use the Internet as they gain more experience or whether they reflect changes in the Internet itself over this period is a topic we will return to in the discussion.

Because teenagers use the Internet more than their parents and because teens and adults differed on several of the outcomes reported in Table 2, we tested the differential effects of Internet use with age. There was only one marginally significant interaction: Adults' stress increased more than teens' stress with more Internet use ($p < .10$).

▮▮▮ Study 2: A Longitudinal Study of Computer and Television Purchasers

Study 2 is a replication of the original HomeNet research design in a sample of households that had recently purchased new home technology—either a computer or TV. We added controls to the design and new measures. First, we attempted to manipulate

TABLE 2 Analysis of the Original HomeNet Study After 3 Years (n = 208)

Independent Variables	Social Support[a]			Local Social Circle[b]			Distant Social Circle[c]			Family Communication (log)[d]			Stress[e]			Depression[f]			Loneliness[g]		
	beta	se	p	beta	se	p	beta	se	p	beta	se	p	beta	se	p	beta	se	p	beta	se	p
Intercept	0.00	0.04		3.76	3.37		8.85	6.74		-0.03	0.05		0.01	0.01		-0.01	0.03		0.03	0.04	
Adult (0 = teen; 1 = adult)	-0.13	0.09		-19.37	7.41	**	-49.02	14.70	***	0.34	0.11	**	0.00	0.02		-0.14	0.06	*	0.04	0.09	
Male (0 = female; 1 = male)	-0.16	0.08	*	-2.74	6.89		6.57	13.70		-0.08	0.10		0.00	0.02		0.02	0.05		0.27	0.08	**
Household income	0.00	0.00		-0.20	0.15		0.14	0.29		0.00	0.00		0.00	0.00		0.00	0.00		0.00	0.00	
White (0 = other; 1 = white)	0.15	0.09		-8.26	8.23		-6.74	16.38		0.11	0.13		0.04	0.02	*	-0.14	0.07	*	-0.22	0.10	*
Time period[h]	0.10	0.06		0.97	2.52		-4.04	4.66		-0.34	0.10	***	0.06	0.01	***	0.01	0.04		0.12	0.06	+
Stress[e]																0.61	0.17	***			
Extraversion[i]	0.07	0.05		1.04	2.74		-5.28	5.21		0.37	0.08	***	0.54	0.06	***	0.18	0.06	***	0.44	0.05	***
Lagged dependent variable	0.45	0.07	***	0.21	0.06	***	0.33	0.10	***	0.05	0.07		0.03	0.01	*	-0.01	0.03		0.00	0.05	
Internet hours (log)	0.02	0.05		-1.15	3.29		-5.14	6.27		0.16	0.12		-0.01	0.02		-0.13	0.05	*	-0.21	0.08	**
Internet * period	0.10	0.08		-0.37	3.06		2.88	5.62		-0.02	0.13		0.04	0.02	+	-0.08	0.06		-0.09	0.10	
Internet * adult	0.06	0.09		5.44	6.08		7.52	11.57													
n	189			189			187			177			195			187			186		
R²	0.29			0.26			0.17			0.15			0.46			0.20			0.36		

Note. +p < .10, *p < .05, **p < .01, ***p < .001; variables were centered before analyses.
[a]Cohen, et al., 1984;
[b]number kept up with monthly, living in the Pittsburgh area;
[c]number kept up with annually, living outside of the Pittsburgh area;
[d]log of the minutes communicating per day;
[e]Kanner et al., 1981;
[f]Radloff, 1977;
[g]Russell, et al, 1980;
[h]period 1 is 12–18 months, from 1995 or 1996 to 1997 and period 2 is from the first posttest in 1997 to the second posttest in 1998;
[i]Bendig, 1962; [j]the dependent variable measured approximately 12–18 month previously.

Internet use to create a true experiment, with participants randomly assigned to condition. We recruited households who recently bought a new home computer and randomly offered half free Internet service; households in the control condition received an equivalent amount of money ($225) to participate. Unfortunately, this experimental procedure failed when, by the end of 12 months, 83% of the control households obtained Internet access on their own (versus 95% of the experimental households who took advantage of free Internet service). Because this attempt to conduct a true experiment failed, we combined the groups for analyses of the effects of using the Internet.

Another design change was to add a comparison group—recent purchasers of a new television set. Study 1 had only compared heavier and lighter users of the Internet, all of whom had access to it. The addition of a TV-purchaser comparison group in Study 2 (of whom just 29% obtained Internet access after 12 months) provides a sample that was unlikely to use the Internet and helps to rule out explanations of change based on external events. In analyses of the effects of Internet use, we included participants from the television purchaser group, but controlled for sample selection bias by creating a dummy variable indicating whether participants were recruited for buying a television or computer.

We also increased the number of dependent variables, to examine the generalizability of the effects of using the Internet across outcomes and measures. The original study contained four measures of personal social involvement and three of psychological well-being. We added measures of personal social involvement (spending time with family and friends, use of the telephone, perceived closeness to a random sample from of the respondents' social networks). In response to Putnam's (2000) concerns that the Internet might undercut community participation as well as interpersonal contact, we added measures of involvement with and attitudes toward the community at large. To measure psychological well-being, we added scales measuring the experience of negative and positive affect, perceived time pressure, and self-esteem. Because the Internet is a source of information as well as social contact, we added knowledge tests and a scale to measure computing skill. To test whether the distance-minimizing properties of the Internet blur traditional distinctions between geographically close and distant regions, our measures of social involvement and knowledge differentiated between these, for example, asking separately about local and distant social circles and about knowledge of the Pittsburgh region and broader areas.

Finally, we extended the HomeNet study conceptually by examining the differential effects of individual differences in extraversion and perceived social support on the effects of Internet use. Extraversion is the tendency to like people, to be outgoing, and to enjoy social interaction; it is a highly stable personality trait, predictive of social support, social integration, well-being, and positive life events (e.g., Von Dras & Siegler, 1997; Magnus, Diener, Fujita, Payot, 1993). The perception of social support refers to feelings that others are available to provide comfort, esteem, assistance, and information or advice; perceived social support buffers the effects of stress (e.g., Cohen, 1988).

We offer two opposing models of the relationship between extraversion and social support and Internet use. A "rich get richer" model predicts that those who are highly sociable and have existing social support will get more social benefit from using the Internet. Highly sociable people may reach out to others on the Internet and be especially likely to use the Internet for communication. Those who already have social support can use the Internet to reinforce ties with those in their support networks. If so, these groups would gain more social involvement and well-being from using the Internet than those who are introverted or have limited networks. They can gain these benefits both by adding members to their social networks and by strengthening existing ties.

By contrast, a "social compensation" model predicts that those who are introverted or lack social support would profit most from using the Internet. People with fewer social resources could use the new communication opportunities online to form connections with people and obtain supportive communications and useful information otherwise missing locally (see McKenna & Bargh, 1998). At the same time, for those who already have satisfactory relationships, using the Internet might interfere with their real-world relationships, if they swap strong real world ties for weaker ones online. Analogous to the finding that cancer patients with emotionally-supportive spouses can be harmed by participating in peer-discussion support groups (Helgeson, Cohen, Schulz, & Yasko, 2000), it is possible that people with strong local relationships might turn away from family and friends if they used the Internet for social interaction.

Method

Sample   We recruited participants through advertisements placed in local newspapers, soliciting people for a study of household technology who purchased a new computer or new television within the previous six months. We obtained agreement from all adults and children in the family above age 10 to complete surveys. Half of the computer purchaser households were randomly offered free Internet access to participate in the study; the other participants were offered payments to complete surveys. After the initial telephone contact, we mailed consent forms and pretest surveys with return envelopes. Unlike the procedures used in Study 1, we did not encourage Internet use or provide technology support.

Measures   We administered surveys three times during the study, in February 1998, 6 months later, and a year later, February 1999. Because we had automated measures of Internet usage only for the group randomly given Internet access, our main independent variable is an index of self-reported Internet use (e.g.," I use the world wide web very frequently"; "Time per day spent using email"; "Frequency per month of using a computer at home." The full text of unpublished measures is available at http://HomeNet.hcii.cs.cmu.edu/progress/research.html.) Within the group randomly given Internet access, the Pearson correlations between the self-report index of Internet use and the automated count of the number of sessions logged into the Internet in the 8 weeks surrounding the questionnaires was moderate ($r(112) = .55$ at Time 2 and $r(104) = 42$ at Time 3). These correlations reflect moderate validity of the self-report measure, although they are far from perfect because there is error in both the self-reports and in the server data (e.g., the usage records do not include Internet use at work and include cases where one family member uses another's account).

We used self-report measures to assess demographic characteristics of the participants and measures from the original HomeNet study, including perceived social support (Cohen et al., 1984), size of local and distant social circles, and time talking with other family members. We used the same measure of extraversion (Bendig, 1962). We added new measures of anomie (Srole, 1956), trust in people (Rosenberg, 1957, revised from Survey Research Center, 1969), community involvement (adapted from Mowday and Speers' 1979 measure of organizational commitment; e.g., "I spend a lot of time participating in community activities"; "I feel part of the community in Pittsburgh"), and intentions to stay in the Pittsburgh area ("Even if I had a chance to move to another city, I would very much want to stay in the Pittsburgh area"). We also assessed respondents' relationships with specific family and friends by asking them "How close do you feel?" to five individuals living in the Pittsburgh area and five living outside of the area who were closest to them in age. Participants described closeness to each nominee using 5-point Likert scales.

To assess well-being, we again used the CES-D to measure depressive symptoms (Radloff, 1977), the daily life stresses scale (Kanner, Coyne, Schaefer, & Lazarus, 1981), and the UCLA Loneliness Scale (Russell, Peplau, & Cutrona, 1980) from the original HomeNet study. We added measures of self-esteem (Heatherton & Polivy, 1991), positive and negative affect (Watson, Clark, & Tellegen, 1988), perceived time pressure (adapted from Kraut & Attewell, 1997) and physical health (subscale from the SF-36; Ware, Snow, Kosinski, & Gandek, 1993).

Finally, because the Internet is a source of information as well as communication, we added measures of knowledge. We included a self-report measure of skill using computers, expanded from the original HomeNet study (e.g., "I am very skilled at using computers"; "I don't know much about using computers," (R)). We also added a test of knowledge, including multiple choice items on national current events, Pittsburgh current events, and general knowledge from a high school equivalency test (Research & Education Association, 1996). The knowledge test contained different items at different time periods.

Analyses Data come from 216 households. Of the 446 individuals who were eligible to be in the sample, 96% completed survey 1, 83% completed survey 2, and 83.2% completed survey 3. Analyses are based on 406 respondents (91% of the original sample) who completed at least two surveys. The analyses were similar to those for Study 1. We used Stata's xtreg procedure with participant as a random effect, (StataCorp, 2001) to analyze the panel design. In the Study 2 models, social involvement, well-being, and knowledge outcomes at the second and third time period were regressed on self-reported Internet use during that period, controlling for demographic characteristics and the lagged dependent variables. The models control for whether the respondent came from the TV purchaser or computer purchaser sub-sample and whether the dependent variables were collected at the second or third time period. To test whether levels of extraversion and social support moderated the effects of using the Internet, we included the main effects for the Bendig (1962) measure of extraversion and Cohen et al.'s (1984) measure of social support and the interaction of these variables with Internet use. We included adult status, gender, race, education, and household income as demographic controls. Because teenagers use the Internet quite differently from adults, we also included the interaction of generation with Internet use.

Results

Table 2 shows scale reliabilities and descriptive statistics for variables in the sample, averaged over the three time periods. A table of correlations is available at http://HomeNet.hcii.cs.cmu.edu/progress/research.html.

Effects on Interpersonal and Community Social Involvement Models testing the effects of using the Internet on interpersonal communication and community involvement are shown in Tables 3 and 4, respectively. The main effects of Internet use on these measures of social involvement were generally positive. As Table 3 shows, participants who used the Internet more had larger increases in the sizes of their local social circle ($p < .01$) and distant social circle ($p < .01$) and their face-to-face interaction with friends and family increased ($p < .05$). As Table 4 shows, they also reported becoming more involved in community activities ($p < .10$) and felt greater trust in people ($p < .05$). The only significant reversal to the positive trend is that those who used the Internet more became less committed to living in the Pittsburgh area ($p < .05$).

TABLE 3 Predicting Interpersonal Social Involvement as a Function of Use of the Internet Over Time and Individual Difference Variables. Study 2.

Independent Variables	Social Support[a]			Local Social Circle (log)[b]			Distant Social Circle (log)[c]			Family Communication (log)[d]			Face-to-Face Communication[e]			Phone Communication[e]			Closeness to Local Friends[e]			Closeness to Distant Friends[e]		
	beta	se	p	beta	se	p	beta	se	p	beta	se	p	beta	se	p	beta	se	p	beta	se	p	beta	se	p
Intercept	-0.01	0.02		-0.02	0.03		0.01	0.04		0.29	0.01	***	0.02	0.03		-0.02	0.03		-0.01	0.06		-0.01	0.04	
Adult (0 = teen; 1 = adult)[a]	0.18	0.05	***	-0.04	0.10		0.31	0.12	*	0.00	0.03		-0.55	0.11	***	0.12	0.10		0.27	0.17		0.15	0.16	
Male (0 = female; 1 = male)	-0.09	0.03	**	0.03	0.06		-0.08	0.07		-0.01	0.02		-0.19	0.07	**	-0.30	0.07	***	-0.29	0.12	*	-0.02	0.09	
Household income	0.15	0.06	*	0.37	0.12	**	0.28	0.15	+	-0.03	0.04		-0.11	0.13		-0.04	0.13		-0.41	0.25	+	-0.16	0.20	
White (0 = other; 1 = white)	0.02	0.01	*	-0.01	0.02		0.01	0.03		-0.01	0.01		-0.01	0.02		0.03	0.02		-0.09	0.04	*	0.01	0.03	
Education	0.01	0.01		0.00	0.03		0.06	0.03	+	0.00	0.01		-0.04	0.03		-0.02	0.03		0.00	0.05		-0.01	0.04	
Computer sample (0 = no; 1 = yes)	0.02	0.04		0.12	0.07		0.07	0.09		-0.01	0.02		-0.22	0.08	**	-0.03	0.08		-0.10	0.13		-0.10	0.10	
Time period (0 = 1st 6 months; 1 = 2nd 6 months)	0.01	0.02		-0.05	0.04		-0.12	0.05	*	0.00	0.01		0.03	0.05		0.08	0.04	+	0.00	0.00		-0.04	0.06	
Lagged dependent variable	0.53	0.03	***	0.33	0.04	***	0.46	0.03	***	3.86	0.04	***	0.28	0.03	***	0.50	0.03	***	-0.99	0.00	***	0.50	0.04	***
Extraversion[f]	0.15	0.03	***	0.09	0.05	*	0.09	0.06		0.02	0.01		0.14	0.05	**	0.16	0.05	**	0.00	0.00		0.01	0.07	
Social support[a]				0.17	0.05	***	0.13	0.07	+	0.04	0.02	*	0.28	0.07	***	0.11	0.06	+	0.00	0.00		0.30	0.08	***
Internet use[e]	-0.01	0.02		0.12	0.04	**	0.15	0.05	**	0.00	0.01		0.09	0.04	*	0.05	0.04		0.00	0.00		0.07	0.06	
Internet * extraversion	0.01	0.03		0.02	0.06		-0.05	0.07		-0.01	0.02		-0.02	0.07		0.10	0.06		0.00	0.00		0.01	0.08	
Internet * support				0.01	0.07		0.02	0.09		0.05	0.02	**	-0.11	0.08		-0.08	0.07		0.00	0.00		0.15	0.10	
Internet * adult	-0.11	0.06	+	-0.13	0.11		-0.02	0.15		-0.06	0.03	+	0.30	0.13	*	0.04	0.12		0.00	0.00		0.35	0.18	*
n	406			385			365			373			406			391			351			285		
R^2	.51			.42			.47			.95			.31			.51			.16			.44		

Note. + $p < .10$, * $p < .05$, ** $p < .01$, *** $p < .001$; variables were centered before analyses.
[a]Cohen, et al., 1984;
[b]Number kept up with monthly, living in the Pittsburgh area;
[c]number kept up with annually, living outside of the Pittsburgh area;
[d]minutes communicating per day;
[e]see Table 2;
[f]Bendig, 1962.

TABLE 4 Predicting Community Social Involvement as a Function of Use of the Internet Over Time and Individual Difference Variables. Study 2.

Independent Variables	Community Involvement[a]			Stay in Pittsburgh[b]			Trust[c]			Anomie[d]		
	beta	se	p	beta	se	p	beta	se	p	beta	se	p
Intercept	0.00	0.02		−0.02	0.04		−0.01	0.02		0.00	0.02	
Adult (0 = teen; 1 = adult)	0.11	0.07		−0.01	0.14		0.30	0.08	***	−0.24	0.06	***
Male (0 = female; 1 = male)	−0.09	0.04	*	0.11	0.08		−0.01	0.05		0.07	0.04	*
Household income	−0.10	0.09		0.47	0.18	**	0.22	0.10	*	−0.12	0.08	
White (0 = other; 1 = white)	−0.05	0.02	**	−0.06	0.03	*	−0.02	0.02		−0.03	0.01	+
Education	0.05	0.02	**	0.01	0.04		0.04	0.02	+	−0.03	0.02	*
Computer sample (0 = no; 1 = yes)	0.09	0.05	+	0.11	0.10		0.07	0.06		−0.07	0.05	
Time period (0 = 1st 6 months; 1 = 2nd 6 months)	0.01	0.04		−0.07	0.06		−0.01	0.04		0.04	0.03	
Lagged dependent variable	0.51	0.03	***	0.55	0.03	***	0.51	0.03	***	0.43	0.03	***
Extraversion[f]	0.17	0.04	***	0.13	0.07	*	0.07	0.04	+	−0.06	0.03	+
Social support[g]	0.17	0.04	***	0.19	0.08	*	0.21	0.05	***	−0.16	0.04	***
Internet use[c]	0.05	0.03	+	−0.13	0.06	*	0.07	0.03	*	−0.01	0.03	
Internet * extraversion	0.10	0.05	*	0.09	0.09		0.00	0.05		−0.01	0.04	
Internet * support	0.02	0.05		−0.08	0.10		0.02	0.06		0.02	0.05	
Internet * adult	−0.01	.09		0.10	0.17		−0.12	0.10		−0.04	0.08	
n	403			402			405			405		
R²	.50			.49			.48			.47		

Note. + p < .10, *p < .05, **p < .01, ***p < .001; variables were centered before analyses.
[a]See Table 2;
[b]see Table 2;
[c]Srole, 1956;
[d]Rosenberg, 1957;
[e]Bendig, 1962;
[f]Cohen et al., 1984.

The interaction with extraversion shows that the association of Internet use with changes in community involvement was positive for extraverts and negative for introverts. Figure 1a illustrates these effects. Holding constant respondents' prior community involvement, extraverts who used the Internet extensively reported more community involvement than those who rarely used it; on the other hand, introverts who used the Internet extensively reported less community involvement than those who rarely used it. Interactions of Internet use with social support show that Internet use was associated with larger increases in family communication for those who initially had more social support. Each of these interaction effects supports the "rich get richer" hypothesis.

Finally, interactions of age with Internet use suggest different positive effects for adults and teens. Teens, as compared with adults, increased their social support and family communication with more Internet use, whereas adults increased their face-to-face interaction with family and friends and their closeness to distant relatives and friends with more Internet use.

Effects on Psychological and Physical Well-Being Table 5 shows the effects of Internet use on psychological well-being. These results are mixed, showing that, overall, both stress and positive affect increased with Internet use. The several interactions of Internet use with extraversion indicate that Internet use was associated

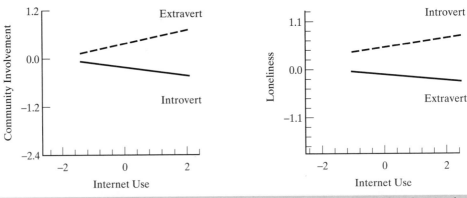

FIGURE 1 Interaction of Internet Use and Extraversion on Community Involvement and Loneliness

Note: The plot shows the effects on community involvement and loneliness of Internet use for people differing in extraversion. The plots show predictions from the models reported in Tables 4 and 5 as Internet use and extraversion move through the range appearing in the sample. Internet use varied from 1.12 standard deviations units less than the mean to 2.54 standard deviation units greater than the mean. The Introvert line represents the most introverted respondent, with an extraversion score −2.12 units below the mean, corresponding to a value of 1.10 on the original 5-point Bendig extraversion scale (1962). The Extravert line represents the extraverted respondent, with a score 1.78 units greater than the mean, corresponding to a 5 on the original scale.

with better outcomes for extraverts and worse outcomes for introverts. In particular, extraverts who used the Internet more reported increased well-being, including decreased levels of loneliness, decreased negative affect, decreased time pressure, and increased self-esteem. In contrast, these same variables showed declines in well-being for introverts. Figure 1b illustrates these effects. Holding constant prior loneliness, extraverts who used the Internet extensively were less lonely than those who rarely used it, while introverts who used the Internet extensively were more lonely than those who rarely used it. There were no interactions with social support or with age, and no effects on measures of physical health (not shown in the table).

Effects on Skill and Knowledge Table 6 shows the effects of Internet use on self-reported computer skill and multiple choices tests of world knowledge. Computer skill increased with more Internet use ($p < .001$); this increase was larger among those with more social support ($p < .05$). Knowledge of general knowledge (not shown in the table) and national current events did not change with Internet use. In contrast, those who used the Internet more became less knowledgeable about the local Pittsburgh area ($p < .05$).

Different Uses of the Internet Because the way people choose to use the Internet could strongly influence its effects, we asked participants to report how often they used the Internet for various purposes. We conducted an exploratory factor analysis of these items to create four scales reflecting different uses of the Internet: (a) for communication with friends and family; (b) for acquiring information for school, work, news, and other instrumental purposes such as shopping; (c) for entertainment such as playing games, downloading music, and escape, and (d) for meeting new people and socializing in chat rooms. These uses of the Internet were moderately interrelated (mean $r = .51$). Using the Internet for communication with family and friends ($r = .69$) and for information ($r = .62$) had the highest association with the Internet use index in reported in Table 2, followed by use for entertainment ($r = 51$) and meeting new people ($r = 38$). Those with more extraversion were more likely than those with less

TABLE 5 Predicting Psychological Well Being as a Function of Use of the Internet Over Time and Individual Difference Variables. Study 2.

Independent Variables	Stress[a]			Loneliness[b]			Depression[c]			Negative affect[d]			Positive affect[e]			Time pressure[f]			Self-esteem[g]		
	beta	se	p	beta	se	p	beta	se	p	beta	se	p	beta	se	p	beta	se	p	beta	se	p
Intercept	0.00	0.00		0.00	0.02		0.01	0.01		0.01	0.02		0.00	0.02		0.00	0.02		-0.01	0.02	
Adult (0 = teen; 1 = adult)	0.04	0.02	**	0.08	0.06		0.01	0.05		-0.12	0.07	+	0.05	0.08		0.23	0.09	**	0.06	0.05	
Male (0 = female; 1 = male)	-0.01	0.01		-0.01	0.03		0.02	0.03		-0.02	0.04		0.07	0.05		-0.18	0.05	***	0.11	0.03	***
Household income	0.00	0.02		-0.10	0.07		0.01	0.06		-0.03	0.09		-0.15	0.09	+	0.12	0.10		-0.01	0.07	
White (0 = other; 1 = white)	0.00	0.00		-0.01	0.01		-0.02	0.01	+	-0.03	0.02	*	0.02	0.02		0.03	0.02		0.01	0.01	
Education	0.01	0.00		0.01	0.02		-0.01	0.01		0.03	0.02		0.00	0.02		-0.02	0.02		-0.01	0.01	
Computer sample (0 = no; 1 = yes)	-0.02	0.01	+	-0.06	0.04		-0.03	0.04		-0.08	0.05		-0.02	0.06		-0.03	0.06		0.07	0.04	+
Time period (0 = 1st 6 months; 1 = 2nd 6 months)	0.01	0.01		-0.04	0.03		-0.04	0.02	+	-0.04	0.03		0.07	0.03	*	-0.06	0.04	+	0.03	0.02	
Lagged dependent variable	0.54	0.03	***	0.27	0.03	***	0.48	0.03	***	0.39	0.03	***	0.32	0.03	***	0.41	0.03	***	0.58	0.03	***
Extraversion[f]	0.00	0.01		-0.21	0.03	***	0.03	0.02		0.01	0.04		0.09	0.04	*	-0.15	0.04	***	0.05	0.03	+
Social support[g]	-0.02	0.01	*	-0.59	0.04	***	-0.21	0.03	***	-0.23	0.04	***	0.41	0.05	***	-0.12	0.05	*	0.28	0.03	***
Internet use[e]	0.01	0.01	*	0.03	0.02	*	0.01	0.02		0.04	0.03		0.14	0.03	***	0.05	0.03		0.02	0.02	
Internet * extraversion	-0.01	0.01		-0.08	0.03		-0.05	0.03		-0.12	0.04	**	0.04	0.05		-0.14	0.05	**	0.09	0.03	**
Internet * support	0.01	0.01		0.01	0.04		0.01	0.04		-0.08	0.05		-0.08	0.06		0.06	0.06		0.04	0.04	
Internet * adult	-0.02	0.02		-0.10	0.07		-0.09	0.06		-0.13	0.09		0.10	0.09		-0.06	0.10		0.01	0.07	
n	398			406			405			405			405			406			406		
R^2	.51			.66			.48			.40			.43			.42			.63		

Note. + $p < .10$, *$p < .05$, **$p < .01$, ***$p < .001$; variables were centered before analyses.
[a]Kanner, Coyne, Schaefer, & Lazarus, 1981;
[b]Russell, Peplau, & Cutrona, 1980;
[c]Radloff, 1977;
[d]Watson, Clark, & Tellegen, 1988;
[e]Watson, et al., 1988;
[f]see Table 2;
[g]Heatherton & Polivy, 1991;
[h]Bendig, 1962;
[i]Cohen et al., 1984.

TABLE 6 Predicting Knowledge as a Function of Use of the Internet Over Time and Individual Difference Variables. Study 2.

Independent Variables	Computer Skill[a]			U. S. Knowledge[a]			Local Knowledge[a]		
	beta	se	p	beta	se	p	beta	se	p
Intercept	0.02	0.02		0.00	0.01		0.00	0.01	
Adult (0 = teen; 1 = adult)	−0.11	0.07		0.18	0.04	***	0.13	0.03	***
Male (0 = female; 1 = male)	0.05	0.04		0.04	0.02	+	0.04	0.02	*
Household income	−0.01	0.08		0.09	0.04	*	0.06	0.04	
White (0 = other; 1 = white)	−0.01	0.02		0.00	0.01		0.00	0.01	
Education	0.03	0.02		0.03	0.01	***	0.03	0.01	***
Computer sample (0 = no; 1 = yes)	−0.10	0.05	+	0.01	0.03		0.02	0.02	
Time period (0 = 1st 6 months; 1 = 2nd 6 months)	0.04	0.03		−0.04	0.02	*	−0.09	0.01	***
Lagged DV	0.65	0.03	***	0.22	0.04	***	0.11	0.04	**
Extraversion[f]	0.02	0.03		−0.02	0.02		0.00	0.01	
Social support[g]	0.03	0.04		0.05	0.02	*	0.01	0.02	
Internet use[e]	0.31	0.03	***	0.00	0.01		−0.03	0.01	*
Internet * extraversion	−0.02	0.04		0.01	0.02		0.03	0.02	
Internet * support	0.10	0.05	*	0.00	0.03		0.00	0.02	
Internet * adult	0.14	0.08		−0.01	0.04		0.01	0.04	
n	400			403			403		
R^2	.71			.15			.15		

Note: $+ p < .10$, $*p < .05$, $**p < .01$, $***p < .001$; variables were centered before analyses.
[a]See Table 2;
[b]Russell, Peplau, & Cutrona, 1980;
[c]Radloff, 1977;
[d]Watson, Clark, & Tellegen, 1988;
[e]Watson, et al., 1988;
[f]see Table 2;
[g]Heatherton & Polivy, 1991;
[h]Bendig, 1962;
[i]Cohen et al., 1984.

extraversion to use the Internet to keep up with friends and family ($r = .10, p < .05$) and to meet new people online and frequent chat rooms ($r = .12$, $p < .05$), but the associations were weak. Those with stronger initial social support were less likely than those with weaker support to use the Internet to meet new people or use chat rooms online ($r = .11, p < .05$) or for entertainment ($r = −.14, p < .05$). Adults were more likely than teens to use the Internet for meeting new people ($r = −.41, p < .001$) and for entertainment ($r = −.29, p < .001$).

To test whether particular ways of using the Internet were more beneficial than others, we conducted a mediation analysis by adding the measures of specific Internet use to the models in Tables 3–6. These additions did not significantly affect the interactions between overall Internet use and extraversion or social support.

▮▮▮ **Discussion**

The original HomeNet sample began using the Internet in 1995 or 1996. Our follow-up of participants remaining in the sample in 1998 showed that most of the negative outcomes initially associated with use of the Internet dissipated, except for its association with increased stress. The statistical interactions of loneliness and depressive symptoms with time period suggest that use of the Internet led to negative outcomes during the first phase of the study and more positive outcomes later.

In Study 2, conducted from 1998 to 1999, more use of the Internet was associated with positive outcomes over a broad range of dependent variables measuring social involvement and psychological well-being—local and distant social circles, face-to-face communication, community involvement, trust in people, positive affect, and unsurprisingly, computer skill. On the other hand, heavier Internet use was again associated with increases in stress. In addition, it was associated with declines in local knowledge, and declines in the desire to live in the local area, suggesting lowered commitment to the local area.

Having more social resources amplified the benefits that people got from using the Internet on several dependent variables. Among extraverts, using the Internet was associated with increases in community involvement and self-esteem, and declines in loneliness, negative affect, and time pressure; it was associated with the reverse for introverts. Similarly, among people with more rather than less social support, using the Internet was associated with more family communication and greater increases in computer skill. Adults and teens gained somewhat different benefits from more Internet use, with adults more likely to increase their face-to-face interactions locally and their closeness to geographically distant relatives and friends.

What accounts for the differences between the original HomeNet research, showing generally negative consequences of using the Internet, and the follow-ups, showing generally positive consequences? Maturation of participants between the early and late phases of Study 1, differences in samples between Studies 1 and 2, and changes in the Internet itself are all potential explanations for this shift in results. Although our research cannot definitely choose among these explanations, a change in the nature of the Internet is the most parsimonious explanation.

Maturation of participants and changes in the way they used the Internet could potentially account for the shift in results between the early and later phases of Study 1. For example, as the novelty of using the Internet wore off, participants may have jettisoned unrewarding Internet activities and adopted or increased their use of more personally rewarding ones. However, the first phase of Study 1, with its negative outcomes, occurred during participants' first year on line. Study 2, with its positive outcomes, also occurred during a one-year period, when most participants' were new to the Internet. Thus, while maturation could account for differences between the early and late phases of Study 1, it cannot account for differences between Studies 1 and 2.

Participants in Studies 1 and 2 came from separate opportunity samples. These sample differences make comparisons between the two studies problematic and could potentially account for differences in results between them. For example, the original sample included a larger proportion of teens and minorities. Although teenagers and adults gained somewhat different benefits from using the Internet, teenagers did not fare worse overall than adults from using the Internet. Similarly, supplementary analyses (not shown in Tables 3–6) do not reveal racial differences in outcomes that can account for difference between the two studies.

Participants in Study 1 had more social support and were more extraverted than those in Study 2, probably because they were recruited from families with organizational memberships. However, the statistical interactions with extraversion and social support reported in Study 2 would lead one to expect that outcomes would be more positive in Study 1 than Study 2, but this was not the case. While other, unmeasured differences in the samples might account for the differences in results between Study 1 and Study 2, differences in age, race, and social resources do not appear to do so.

The similarity of findings comparing the early and later phases of Study 1 and comparing Studies 1 and 2 suggest that changes in the Internet environment itself might be more important to understanding the observed effects than maturation or differences between samples. Simply put, the Internet may have become a more hospitable place over time. From 1995 to 1998, the number of Americans with access to the Internet at home more than quadrupled. As a result, many more of participants' close family and friends were likely to have obtained Internet access. Similarly, the services offered online changed over this period, increasing the ease with which people could communicate with their strong ties. For example, new communication services, such as American Online's instant messaging allow users to subscribe to a list of family and friends and be notified when members of their "buddy lists" came online. In addition to these changes to the online social environment, over the span of this research, the Internet provided a richer supply of information, with more news, health, financial, hobby, work, community, and consumer information available. It began to support financial and commercial transactions. Together, these changes could have promoted better integration of participants' online behavior with the rest of their lives.

Our finding from Study 2, that extraverts and those with more support benefited more from their Internet use, is consistent with this idea. That is, the Internet may be more beneficial to individuals to the extent they can leverage its opportunities to enhance their everyday social lives. Those who are already effective in using social resources in the world are likely to be well positioned to take advantage of a powerful new technology like the Internet.

Research shows that people can form strong social bonds online, and relationships formed online can carry over to the off-line world (e.g., Parks & Roberts, 1998; McKenna, Green, & Gleason, 2002). However, research also suggests that strong relationships developed online are comparatively rare. Most studies show that people use the Internet more to keep up with relationships formed off line than to form new ones (e.g, Kraut et al., 1996; Pew Internet and American Life Project, 2000). In addition, online relationships are weaker on average than those formed and maintained off-line (e.g., Cummings, Butler, & Kraut, in press; Gross, Juvonen, & Gable, 2002). Gross, Juvonen, and Gable (2002) also report that adolescents who feel socially anxious and/or lonely are especially likely to communicate online with people with whom they do not feel close. Thus one would expect that a diet filled with online relationships would be harmful to the social and psychology health of Internet users. Fortunately, people don't seem to use the Internet this way. Rather they mingle their online and off-line worlds, using the Internet to keep up with people from their off-line lives and calling and visiting people they initially met online (Kraut et al., 1996; McKenna et al., 2002).

Although the impact of using the Internet across the two studies was generally positive, some negative outcomes remained. Across both studies, as people used the Internet more, they reported increases in daily life stress and hassles. Supplementary analyses did not identify any single stressor that occurred more frequently with Internet use, even though the cumulative increase with Internet use was statistically significant. One explanation is that the time spent online leaves less for many other activities, and that this time drought may lead to a generalized perception of stress.

In addition to increases in stress, heavier Internet use was also associated with declining commitment to living in the local area and less knowledge about it. These declines may come about because the Internet makes available an abundance of online information (and social relationships) outside of the local area. Unlike regional newspapers, for example, the Internet makes news about distant cities as accessible as news about ones hometown.

The mechanisms by which the Internet has its impact on social involvement and psychological well-being remain unclear. One possibility is that the effects of using the Internet depend upon what people do online. For example, one might expect that interpersonal communication with friends and family would have more beneficial effects than using the Internet for downloading music, playing computer games, or communicating with strangers. Another possibility is that all uses of the Internet are equivalent in this regard, and that the important factor is not how people use the Internet, but what they give up to spend time online. Thus the effects of using the Internet might be very different if it substituted for time spent watching TV or time spent conversing with close friends. No research to date, however, including our own, can distinguish between these two possibilities. Our own attempts to identify the unique effects of using the Internet for different functions were unsuccessful. Self-report measures may be too insensitive to track true differences in use.

Understanding the mechanisms for the Internet's impact is essential for informing private, commercial, and public policy decisions. People need better information to know whether to ration their time online or to decide which uses of the Internet are in their long-term interests. As experience with television suggests, enjoyable uses of new technology may be harmful in the long term (e.g., Huston et al, 1992; Putnam, 2000). Service providers need to decide what applications to offer online. School and libraries need to decide whether to offer email and chat capabilities along with their information-oriented services.

Experiments are a standard way to assess the impact of an intervention. While laboratory experiments can identify short-term consequences of Internet use, they are too limited to illuminate how the Internet affects slowly emerging phenomena, such as social relationships, community commitment, or psychological well-being (Rabby & Walther, in press). Unfortunately, it is probably late in the evolution of the Internet to carry out true long-term experiments, at least in North America. We tried to conduct such an experiment on Internet use for Study 2, but in less than 12 months, 83% of the households in the control group had acquired Internet access on their own.

Nonetheless, researchers should continue to attempt to discern how using the Internet is affecting people's lives with the best designs possible. Although cross-sectional designs are most common in research on the impact of the Internet (e.g., Cole, 2000; Parks, & Roberts, 1981; The Pew Internet & American Life Project, 2000; Riphagen & Kanfer, 1997), they cannot distinguish pre-existing differences among people who use the Internet from consequences of using it. Therefore, we believe longitudinal designs are essential to understanding the effects of Internet use and the differences in these effects as the Internet changes. In addition, we need better and more detailed descriptions of how people spend their time, both online and off, to relate these detailed descriptions to changes in important domains of life. The diary measures used by Gross, Juvonen, and Gable, (2002) are a step in this direction.

REFERENCES

Bendig, A. W. (1962). The Pittsburgh scales of social extraversion, introversion and emotionality. *The Journal of Psychology, 53,* 199–209.

Cohen J., & Cohen, P. (1983). *Applied multiple regression/correlation analysis for the behavioral sciences.* Hillsdale, NJ: Lawrence Erlbaum Associates.

Cohen, S., & Wills, T. A. (1985). Stress, social support, and the buffering hypothesis. *Psychological Bulletin, 98,* 310–357.

Cohen, S., Mermelstein, R., Kamarck, T., & Hoberman, H. (1984). Measuring the functional components of social support. In I. G. Sarason & B. R. Sarason (Eds.), *Social support: Theory, research and applications* (pp. 73–94). The Hague, Holland: Martines Niijhoff.

Cole, J. (2000). Surveying the digital future: The UCLA Internet report. Downloaded from http://WWW.CCP.UCLA.EDU/pages/internet-report.asp. November 17, 2000.

Cummings, J., Butler, B., & Kraut, R. (In press). The quality of online social relationships. *Communications of the ACM*.

Diener, E., Suh, E. M., Lucas, R. E., & Smith, H. (1999). Subjective well-being: Three decades of progress. *Psychological Bulletin, 125*, 276–302.

Fischer, C. S. (1992). *America calling*. Berkeley, CA: University of California Press.

Heatherton, T. F., & Polivy, J. (1991). Development and validation of a scale for measuring state self-esteem. *Journal of Personality and Social Psychology, 60*, 895–910.

Helgeson, V. S., Cohen, S., Schulz, R., & Yasko, J. (2000). Group support interventions for people with cancer: Who benefits from what? *Health Psychology, 19*, 107–114.

Hiltz, S. R., & Turoff, M. (1978). *Network nation: Human communication via computer*. Reading, MA: Addison Wesley.

Huston, A. C., Donnerstein, E., Fairchild, H., Feshbach, N. D., Katz, P. A., Murray, J. P., Rubinstein, E. A., Wilcox, B., & Zuckerman, D. (1992). *Big world, small screen: The role of television in American society*. Lincoln, NE: University of Nebraska Press.

Kanner, A. D., Coyne, J. C., Schaefer, C., & Lazarus, R. S. (1981). Comparisons of two modes of stress measurement: Daily hassles and uplifts versus major life events. *Journal of Behavioral Medicine, 4*, 1–39.

Kiesler, S., Lundmark, V., Zdaniuk, B., Kraut, R. Scherlis, W., & Mukhopadhyay, T. (2000). Troubles with the Internet: The dynamics of help at home. *Human-Computer Interaction, 15* (4), 223–352.

Kraut, R. E., & Attewell, P. (1997). Media use in a global corporation: Electronic mail and organizational knowledge. In S. Kiesler (Ed.), *Culture of the Internet* (pp. 323–342). Mahwah, NJ: Lawrence Erlbaum Associates.

Kraut, R., Mukhopadhyay, T., Szczypula, J., Kiesler, S., & Scherlis, B. (2000). Information and communication: Alternative uses of the Internet in households. *Information Systems Research, 10*, 287–303

Kraut, R. E., Patterson, M., Lundmark, V., Kiesler, S., Mukhopadhyay, T., & Scherlis, W. (1998). Internet paradox: A social technology that reduces social involvement and psychological well-being? *American Psychologist, 53*, (9), 1017–1032.

Kraut, R., Scherlis, W., Mukhopadhyay, T., Manning, J., & Kiesler, S. (1996). The HomeNet field trial of residential Internet services. *Communications of the ACM, 39*, 55–63.

Magnus, K., Diener, E., Fujita, F., Payot, W. (1993). Extraversion and neuroticism as predictors of objective life events: A longitudinal analysis. *Journal of Personality and Social Psychology, 65*, 1046–1053.

McKenna, K. Y. A., & Bargh, J. A. (1998). Coming out in the age of the Internet: Identity "demarginalization"

through virtual group participation. *Journal of Personality and Social Psychology, 75*, 681–694.

McKenna, K. Y. A., & Bargh, J. A. (2000). Plan 9 from cyberspace: The implications of the Internet for personality and social psychology. *Personality and Social Psychology Review, 4*, 57–75.

Parks, M., & Roberts, L. (1998). Making MOOsic: The development of personal relationships on line and a comparison to their off-line counterparts. *Journal of Social and Personal Relationships, 15*, 517–537.

The Pew Internet & American Life Project (2000, May 10). Tracking online life: How women use the Internet to cultivate relationships with family and friends. Downloaded May 15, 2000, at http://www.pewinternet.org/reports/

Putnam, R. D. (2000). *Bowling alone*. New York: Simon & Schuster.

Rabby, M., & Walther, J. B. (in press). Computer-mediated communication impacts on relationship formation and maintenance. In D. Canary & M. Dainton (Eds.), *Maintaining relationships through communication: Relational, contextual, and cultural variations*. Mahwah, NJ: Lawrence Erlbaum Associates.

Radloff, L. (1977). The CES-D Scale: A self-report depression scale for research in the general population. *Applied Psychological Measurement, 1*, 385–401.

Research & Education Association (1996). The best test preparation for the GED (General Educational Development). Piscataway, NJ: Author.

Riphagen, J., & Kanfer, A. (1997) How does e-mail affect our lives? Champaign-Urbana Illinois: National Center for Supercomputing Applications. Retrieved October 15, 1999 from the World Wide Web: http://www.ncsa.uiuc.edu/edu/trg/e-mail/index.html.

Rosenberg, M. (with the assistance of E. A. Suchman & R. K. Goldsen) (1957). *Occupations and values*. Glencoe, IL: Free Press.

Russell, D., Peplau, L., & Cutrona, C. (1980) The revised UCLA loneliness scale: Concurrent and discriminant validity evidence. *Journal of Personality and Social Psychology, 39* (3), 472–480.

Shapiro, J. S. (1999). Loneliness: Paradox or artifact? *The American Psychologist, 54* (9), 782–783.

Sproull, L., & Kiesler, S. (1991). *Connections: New ways of working in the networked organization*. Cambridge, MA: MIT Press.

Srole, L. (1956). Social integration and certain corollaries. *American Sociological Review, 21*, 709–716.

StataCorp (2001). Stata Statistical Software: Release 7.0. College Station, TX: Stata Corporation.

Survey Research Center (1969). *1964 election study*. Ann Arbor, Michigan: Inter-University Consortium for Political Research, University of Michigan.

Thoits, P. (1983). Multiple identities and psychological well-being: A reformulation and test of the social isolation hypothesis. *American Sociological Review, 48,* 174–187.

Von Dras, D. D., & Siegler, I. C. (1997). Stability in extraversion and aspects of social support at midlife. *Journal of Personality and Social Psychology, 72,* 233–241

Ware, J. E., Snow, K. K., Kosinski, M., & Gandek, B. *SF-36 Health Survey: Manual and interpretation guide.* Boston: Nimrod, 1993.

Watson, D., Clark, L. A., & Tellegen, A. (1988). Development and validation of brief measures of positive and negative affect: The PANAS scales. *Journal of Personality and Social Psychology, 54,* 1063–1070.

Wellman, B., Haase, A., Witte, J., & Hampton, K. (2001). Does the Internet increase, decrease or supplement social capital?: Social networks, participation, and community commitment. *American Behavioral Scientist 45.* (3), 436–455

Wellman, B., & Wortley, S. (1990). Different strokes for different folks: Community ties and social support. *American Journal of Sociology, 96* (3), 558–588.

Williams, A. W., Ware, J. E., & Donald, C. A. (1981). A model of mental health, life events, and social supports applicable to general populations. *Journal of Health and Social Behavior, 22,* 324–333.

Cyberspaces: Familiar Territory or Lawless Frontiers

▤ Introduction

In 1995, the World Wide Web burst into view on the journalistic scene like a rocket ship headed for outer space. Reporters surfed the Web (while their editors wondered whether they were really working) and wrote volumes about the wonders of "the net" and this new electronic frontier. Meanwhile many of their readers shook their heads with doubt that this strange new world of graphics, text, and sound emanating from computers would change their lives in the manner in which the commentators suggested that it might. Was this the real "information revolution," long predicted but slow to materialize, or just another ho-hum passing phase in the evolution of communications technology from smoke signals to satellites?

No one knew the answer, but almost everyone tested the waters for fear of being left behind in the dust bins of an outmoded age. Corporations were quick to allocate funds to hire young gurus skilled in the intricacies of hypertext markup language (HTML) to design "home pages" that would attract the new computer literati to these new virtual estates in what was called, for lack of a better description, cyberspace.[1] There is not just one cyberspace but many cyberspaces, populated by and already regulated by the many computer users who have come to spend time there. The pioneers of these spaces are rapidly becoming settlers and establishing proprietary rights within the spaces of the Networld that they are using.

In 1995, Java became the hottest topic, not the coffee but a new, easy-to-deploy computer language that allegedly anybody could master. It promised to provide "applets," or little applications that could be downloaded from web servers and temporarily installed, rather than requiring the user to purchase expensive, memory-hogging shrink-wrapped software. This promise, if fulfilled, would facilitate a "user-

"Cyberspaces: Familiar Territory or Lawless Frontiers" by A. W. Branscomb, *Journal of Computer Mediated Communication*, Vol. 2, No. 1, 1996. Copyright © 1996.

friendly" computing environment—a utopia thought by most, except the most sophisticated computer gurus, to be just beyond almost everyone's grasp.

In that case anyone could become a publisher, a producer, or an information provider as well as an information user. In other words, the media moguls who controlled much of the world's commerce, news, politics, and entertainment would be challenged by an endless number of smaller players offering products within these new computer-mediated spaces—a veritable marketplace of information. Those in the know rushed to post personal home pages; others held back, not from lack of competence but from an awareness that a certain amount of autonomy was being lost in this rush to bare all about oneself to the electronically sophisticated world.

Lawyers, who for the most part had been reluctantly drawn out of their fax-based, print-prone world, decided that they, too, needed to learn how to navigate the new electronic backwoods and multimedia malls. After all, herein lived the litigants of tomorrow. There were two schools of thought among the lawyers rushing helter-skelter into the new Networld of computer-mediated communication. One group assumed that whatever skills they had acquired in the real world would serve them well in the virtual world. The other group saw a new electronic frontier free from real-world restrictions, where their skills would be challenged to tame cyberspaces, whether or not the natives wanted to be tamed.

The computer literati—the console cowboys of the electronic frontier—preferred an anarchical but benign electronic environment, in which everyone would behave more or less civilly because it was the right and proper way to use the new capabilities efficiently. However, experienced users (called "netizens") who came to inhabit these new cyberspaces sought to regularize civilized behavior in this new Networld by establishing their own "netiquette."[2] These new rules of etiquette were posted in FAQs (frequently asked questions) by the various discussion groups that popped up spontaneously on the Usenet group—more than 10,000 by 1996—and countless more in self-generated groups called Listservs. Only a year ago, but these were days of delirium for both journalists and lawyers who saw their futures inextricably entwined in computer-mediated communication as a tool and as a working environment.

▪▪▪ The History of the Internet

The Internet evolved from the ARPAnet, established by the Department of Defense in 1968, as a device for load sharing among the large computers serving research facilities around the country. Its design specifications called for providing secure communications in the advent of an outbreak of war, so that no centralized node would be vulnerable to destroying the entire network. As a consequence, the worldwide interconnection of networks, now known as the Internet, is a decentralized conglomeration of many different networks. Although it was, and remains, a system built by and for computer sophisticates rather than for widespread public use, it has come to be perceived as the potential backbone of worldwide interconnection for digital data.

The first general interest publication to spotlight cyberspace was *Scientific American*, which came out with a special issue on computer networking in September 1991.[3] In 1993, the Internet made its debut as a top priority news story, first in Gary Trudeau's "Doonesbury," then in a *New Yorker* cartoon, which pictured two dogs at their personal computer, one saying to the other, "On the Internet no one knows you're a dog!"[4] By December 7, 1993, *Time* carried an article about the Internet entitled, "First Nation in Cyberspace"[5] and the *Wall Street Journal* published Santa's Internet addresses for

Santa Claus (santa@north.pole.org or elves@north.pole.org).[6] By Christmas 1995, even the Pope had decided to post his Christmas message on the Internet.[7]

What all this publicity translated to was a spurt of activity by users signing up for access to the Internet through various gateways, commercial as well as nonprofit. The Internet, now expanding at 20% per month according to some estimates, is "the place to be." Access to it was reported to be established for 37 million computer owners in the United States and Canada by late 1995.[8] Subscribers to commercial Information Service Providers increased from 5 million in winter of 1994 to 12 million by June 1995.[9] America Online (AOL), with some 5.5 million subscribers in 1996,[10] became the most successful of the ISP's, fast outstripping its competitors. CompuServe lagged with 4.7 million, and Prodigy with fewer than an estimated million subscribers was looking for a buyer.[11] The Microsoft Network, a late starter, claimed to have signed up a million subscribers in less than a year.[12] Genie and Delphi were far behind. The News Corporation sold Delphi with only 50,000 subscribers back to its former owners in 1996.[13]

Who could resist the lure of this new globally interconnected Networld? By Spring 1996 there were, for example, two dozen individuals linking their Web pages to the Concord, Massachusetts, home page. Unsophisticated users joined the computer literati, transforming a little-known and less-noticed electronic exchange of information by academics into an electronic agora of many commercial netmalls. According to one fanciful extrapolation, based upon the 1995 rate of newcomers to ISP's, the entire world population could be online by the turn of the century.

By May 1996, 89% of the domain names on the Internet were commercial,[14] and the pioneers began to fear that what they had thought was their very own anarchical domain was being invaded by business interests that did not share their vision of the future of computer-mediated communication networks.

▪ ▪ ▪ The History of Legal Concerns

Lawyers were not the least or last to sign up for access to the Internet. Despite a singular lack of interest in the early days of online communication, by 1995 law firms were flocking to establish Web pages. As they saw the Internet developing into a full-service, computer-mediated communications system, replicating activities of the real world, lawyers began to see "cyberspace" and "cybercommerce" beckon with promises of new business tasks. Some also saw the development of "cyberlaw" in "cybercommunities" as not only a daunting task but also as a challenging opportunity.[15]

What is developing, as Benjamin Wittes noticed in his online discussion group, is a new system of governance:

> Suppose you wanted to witness the birth and development of a legal system.
> You would need a large, complex social system that lies outside of all other
> legal authorities. Moreover, you would need that system somehow to accelerate
> the seemingly millennial progress of legal development, so you could witness
> more than a mere moment of the process. The hypothetical system might seem
> like a social scientist's fantasy, but it actually exists. It's called the Internet.[16]

This flurry of interest is something new. Back in the early seventies, activity among lawyers representing large multinational corporations was modest. Lawyers were apprehensive that the data privacy initiatives in the Europe might inhibit internal "transborder data flows" of these octopus-like companies whose arms reached into many legal jurisdictions. Special conferences were organized. A special newsletter was started to keep lawyers, policy makers, and corporate executives informed.[17] Alarms were sounded to protect the U.S. multinationals from excessive regulatory actions that might interfere with corporate autonomy over computerization of company activities.

Many large special-purpose global networks were formed to serve airlines (SITA) and banks (SWIFT) and large corporations. IBM, Hewlett Packard, and Citibank were among the first to organize their own global interconnections.[18] A group of lawyers within the Science and Technology Section of the American Bar Association, who represented such companies, or were interested in doing so, organized a study group to teach themselves and their peers what global telecommunications and computers were all about. They hoped to serve the growing number of companies involved in this activity and to lead the U.S. efforts in coping with policy initiatives. Such pioneering work explored the many ways in which global communications networks were serving the needs of management, research, education, politics.[19]

Of minor interest was the Internet, primarily serving the research communities of large universities, compared with the visibly significant dedicated networks of large multinationals. In the late 1970s IBM supported the establishment of BITNET as a peer network among universities around the world. The BITNET was a noncommercial venture, however, which was eventually absorbed into the Internet.

All global networks initially were largely dependent upon mainframes accessed by professionals specially trained to manage these big computers and their work flows. This reliance upon mainframes preceded the advent of the personal computer—Apple made its debut in the latter half of the 1970s and the IBM-PC in the early '80s. In the days when a bunch of nerdie kids experimented with puny home-made Altairs, or the commercially assembled Commodore PET or Tandy's TRS-80, no one anticipated that use of personal computers would someday bypass these powerful computers with a widely distributed and highly decentralized system interconnecting thousands of servers and multi-millions of individual computer users. Indeed, the Internet had evolved unnoticed even by the mass media. The first controversy to attract general public interest came in early November 1988, when a young computer science student at Cornell tested his wings with a computer program that would, according to his side of the story, demonstrate the vulnerabilities of the Internet. Unfortunately, the student was not quite as skilled as he had hoped nor was the "back door" as unknown as he thought. Robert Morris's "worm" ate up so much space on the Internet that the entire system, of mainly educational networked communities, was brought to a halt within twenty-four hours, and the outside world discovered the Internet.

Concerns About Rogue Behavior and Security

Thus, the first legal concerns on the electronic frontier were focused on security. What constitutes criminal behavior? Should computer files be considered "property" for the purposes of "theft" in existing laws? Could the essential elements of traditional "takings" take place with intangible bits and bytes of data that were "stolen" by copying, but which left the original owners in possession of what was already theirs?

By the late 1980s most of the states had something called computer laws in place. Congress had enacted a federal statute making it a felony to interfere with computers connected through interstate commerce.[20] Although Morris and his attorney argued that he had no intention to bring down the government-supported network, he was, nonetheless, convicted under this statute, the court holding that malintent was not a necessary finding, only the intent to insert the virus that caused the damage.[21] The miscreant behavior of Morris having attracted the interest of the federal agents as well as state law enforcement officers, abusive behavior online attracted a spate of activity seeking to curb it.

One of the more widely publicized incidents was the distribution over the Internet of Apple Computer source code, by the NuPromutheus League, as a protest against the company's policy of maintaining a closed and proprietary architecture. After having been independently approached by federal investigators seeking to track down the culprits, Mitch Kapor and John Perry Barlow decided that the agents hadn't the foggiest notion of what they were up against and were perhaps overstepping the bounds of propriety in their eagerness to locate the perpetrators. As a consequence, Kapor and Barlow joined forces to establish an organization to fight for the preservation of basic constitutional protection and civil rights in cyberspace.[22]

Thus the Electronic Frontier Foundation was formed with the stated mission to assist in defending the accused in cases where it appeared that law enforcement agents were overstepping their authority and infringing constitutionally guaranteed rights. EFF also intended to lobby for sensible policies adapted to the unique qualities of computer uses and networking behavior. The EFF efforts were spectacularly successful in chastising federal agents for overstepping constitutional bounds in their raid on the premises of a publisher of books, magazines, and computer games, whose computers were seized in March of 1990 bringing his business to an abrupt halt.[23] Nonetheless, federal prosecutors were more successful in gaining conviction of members of a group called the Legion of Doom, some of whose members pleaded guilty of stealing the BellSouth software used for the 911 emergency telephone system.[24]

Mitch Kapor was also a member of the Computer Sciences and Telecommunication Board (CSTB) of the National Research Council (NRC). In this capacity he was instrumental in stimulating the CSTB to study the rights and responsibilities of users of online communications. This study resulted in two rather remarkable conferences in November 1992 and February 1993 to which an assortment of lawyers, technical experts, and entrepreneurs of bulletin boards, community freenets, and commercial information providers were invited to explore mutual interests in seeing networking develop in a rational, responsible, and legally manageable manner. Although the CSTB report illuminated many of the issues perplexing users—freedom of speech, electronic vandalism, intellectual property interests, and privacy—it did not come out with any recommendations for resolution of the conflicts among various competing interests.[25]

Paralleling the CSTB study, the National Conference of Lawyers and Scientists (NCLS), a professional group of appointees of the American Bar Association and the American Association for the Advancement of Science organized its own study of similar issues. The group is mandated to seek the resolution of issues that overlap interests of these two professions and where computer network abuses and uses would seem logically to reside. NCLS brought together yet a different (although some of the same participants) group interested in exploring legal, technical, and ethical aspects of computer networking, which met at the National Academy of Sciences, Beckman Center, in Irvine, California, December 17–19, 1993, and at Wye Plantation of the Aspen Institute in Queenstown, Maryland, October 7–9, 1994.

No publication came out of these conferences, but a short report on the December 1993 conference was posted on the Web.[26] Many op-ed pieces written by participants in the October 1994 conference, as well as a consultant's summary of the conference discussions, appear on the Web.[27] The op-ed pieces are organized around three themes: (1) Defining and Attributing Accountability/Liability for the Content of Networked Communications; (2) Defining What is "Public" and What is "Private" on Computer Networks, *and* (3) Determining the kinds of ethical, legal, and administrative frameworks that should be constructed for the global information infrastructure. The

NCLS also fell short of developing consensus on the direction the law should take in part because participants represented divergent, often conflicting concerns. Nonetheless, the NCLS study produced a wealth of material, as did the CSTB study for those seeking to determine how best to deal with problems arising in computer-mediated communication.

By the early 1990s even a few lawyers were hanging up shingles as "cyberlawyers" and more than a few were hanging out on the "cyberia" conference (its name had been changed from "cyberlaw" when a lawyer claimed to have trademarked that word for the name of his news column). Both Counsel Connect and Westlaw, online legal services, set up special forums for lawyers to exchange musings about the future of Netlaw.

Newsletters and conferences and online journals began spreading like wildfire in the early 1990s.[28] Lyonette Louis-Jacques compiled the most authoritative and comprehensive list of legal sites on the Internet.[29] Trotter Hardy, the moderator and instigator of the online Cyberia Listserv legal discussion digested much of the online chat into an article entitled *The Proper Legal Regime for "Cyberspace."*[30] A title a bit presumptuous, perhaps, but Hardy provided a sound summary of the relevant legal issues.

Other lawyers, such as Lance Rose and Jonathan Wallace, authored an aid to managers of bulletin board systems in 1992,[31] and two young Texas console cowboys ostentatiously entitled their 1994 work *The Law of Cyberspace*.[32] Henry Perritt, Jr., an early pioneer in the law of databases, organized a conference of like-minded lawyers in 1993[33] and published one of the most ambitious and comprehensive legal tomes in early 1996.[34] The *National Law Journal* organized special conferences for lawyers interested in online services in fall 1994 and again in 1995.[35] The Fall Internet World '95 featured a special session on "The Law of Cyberspace: An Overview." By spring 1996 law schools all over the country were organizing seminars for lawyers interested in obtaining credit for continuing legal education by pursuing interests in "the law of cyberspace."[36] Computer-mediated communication had become a hot subject for lawyers throughout the United States as their clients rushed to explore opportunities on the World Wide Web.

Why Is Law Important?

Despite the stated desire of many pioneer netizens to keep the lawyers and laws out of their cyberspaces[37], this is not always possible. Very simply, law and lawyers are important, because when something goes wrong aggrieved parties turn to lawyers for help. To determine what they can do to obtain redress for their clients' grievances, lawyers look to existing law for precedent. U.S. citizens are very litigious, so the courts have vast experience sorting out demands for justice. The judges themselves turn to existing law to determine how to seek fair and equitable solutions to problems presented in court. Policy analysts always use existing precedents to see what works and what doesn't. Users too rely upon the existing law, because they carry their expectations from one environment to another. Netizens frustrated with online procedures often look to the law for guidance or to seek redress, if the grievance is substantial, in the courts.

Expectations of Privacy in Email Traffic

A good example of this carry over from one environment to another occurs with corporate email. Because we expect to have privacy in the U.S. Postal Service, we expect it in online email. Indeed, the Electronic Communications Privacy Act was passed specifically to apply privacy protection to traffic in public messaging systems. Because we expect such privacy in private email traffic on public systems, we expect it also in corporate email, even though there is no legal basis for such an expectation. Indeed, cases addressing this issue have confirmed that corporations may dictate how corporate resources should be used.[38]

Thoughtful corporations and nonprofit institutions are well advised to have a clear policy so that their employees may understand what expectations are reasonable. Even if employees understand that their email may be monitored and should be restricted to business use, might they not understandably be confused if they are permitted access to corporate servers from home using their own computers? "Surfing the Web" for personally useful information or sending email messages to friends might seem a reasonable "perq" that incurs little incremental cost and is perhaps no more reprehensible than taking home a company pencil or making a few copies of personal letters on the corporate copier.

Interestingly enough, some lawyers are themselves confused about the existing state of the law and advise corporate clients that corporate email may come under the Electronic Communications Privacy Act even though it was the intent of the Act only to cover messages in transit within public messaging systems.[39] Legislation has been proposed to require companies to notify employees of their practices, but to date no legal requirement that corporations respect the privacy of corporate email has been imposed despite confusion when corporate employees use their company LANs from home computers or use the corporate LAN to access the Internet. Indeed, many corporations do honor a privacy code for internal email messages just as most companies do not monitor voice telephonic traffic unless these messages relate to a business function such as making airline reservations.

If there is confusion concerning the applicability of privacy protocols within corporate email, either by its lawyers or its employees, the advice that privacy should be honored will become a self-fulfilling prophecy. As the expectations of users rise, the foundations of what may become customary law will be erected.

▪▪▪ Metaphors Available from Existing Law

Another way in which the expectations of users is important is in the use of metaphors to describe behavior online.[40] Why are such metaphors important? Because they serve as a map for sorting out what is similar and what is different when confronting a new problem. Litigants as well as lawyers, judges, juries, legislators, and policy analysts all look to the familiar in attempting to understand the unfamiliar. They seek to cope with the unknown through known circumstances and prior experiences.

The following models reflect only a few metaphors that might be applied to computer-mediated communication: (1) Publishers, such as newspapers, as Prodigy has been characterized;[41] (2) Distributors, such as newsstands and bookstores, as CompuServe was characterized;[42] (3) Libraries and Information Providers such as LEXIS, Dialog, and Medlars; (4) Private, Corporate, Nonprofit Networks; (5) Personal and Club Bulletin Boards; (6) Common Carriers—traditionally government-operated postal services and today such telecommunications services as Deutsche Telecomm, Cable & Wireless, Regional Bell Operating Companies (RBOCs), MCI, AT&T, and SPRINT; (7) Mixed or Hybrid Systems, such as cable television; (8) Cooperatives, such as EduNet, NearNet, FarNet; (9) Trusteeship—Broadcasters licensed to operate "in the public interest" as trustees for publicly owned airwaves; (10) Marketplaces—the real world malls are replicated in aggregations of Information Providers such as found in the commercial malls on the World Wide Web or the search engines such as Yahoo, Lycos, or Alta Vista; (11) Information Utilities, like the electric or gas companies—community systems, such as the Santa Monica Public Information Network and the Cleveland FreeNet.

Clearly, many metaphors and much existing law are associated with each one. Enterprising lawyers enjoy a rich heritage of legal precedents to apply to activities in computer-mediated communications. To attempt to write omnibus laws that would apply equitably across all of the Networld would be frustrating at best and destructive at worst. The online practices are as rich and varied as the existing metaphors and some would not fit comfortably into any of the available legal boundaries.

Existing legal models are designed to enforce laws within a given technology, e.g., broadcast or cable, telephone or mail. When the message traffic is mixed in a digital bit stream it becomes more difficult to sort out which kind of legal model applies, so we are never entirely sure which one we are drawing upon. On the computer monitor we find mixed text, video, data, and even new types of texts called "hypertext" and new conglomerated forms called "multimedia." Indeed, some bulletin boards purport to be private communications among a discrete group of friends. Yet they may deliver email far and wide. At first blush they may resemble a personal bulletin board, like the one on your refrigerator, so you may say the long arm of the law should not touch them at all. But when these private systems operators start delivering mail, they enter a legal domain where public interest in protecting the mail may come into play. Private email between two parties or even a multiple distribution to a few chosen friends is unlike the distribution into a public discussion group to hundreds or even thousands of readers and participants, many of whom are unknown to the poster of the message. Indeed, even to call this email is a misnomer and confusing to the legal mind. Some more rational analysis must be devised to comprehend, much less attempt to regulate, online message traffic.

▪▪▪ Property Rights in Information

At a round table discussion in Washington, D.C., on October 4, 1995, cyberspace experts met in the First Amendment room of the National Press Club to discuss "The Internet and Property Rights: What's Mine Is Yours?" The discussion centered on the unique legal problems of intellectual property rights on the Networld. David Post, Georgetown law professor and cofounder of the Cyberspace Law Institute equated the Internet with a "a giant, worldwide copying machine"—where online theft of a book, article or manuscript occurs too rapidly for the damaged party to prevent incalculable damage before the perpetrator can be brought into court. Such a situation occurred in France when the full manuscript of a book by Mitterrand's doctor, disclosing the former President's long fight against cancer, was posted online after the book had been withdrawn by the publisher as an invasion of Mitterrand's privacy.

David Johnson, the other cofounder of the Institute, proposed a scheme for Virtual Magistrates, who might be empowered to resolve such conflicts involving intellectual property rights rapidly—without resorting to litigation. The online magistrates might arbitrate disputes in the prelitigation stage, thus relieving overburdened courts and expediting resolution of the problem. Access providers or system operators, such as America Online, Prodigy, and CompuServe, might turn to the arbitrators for fast rulings on alleged copyright violations.

This proposal has been developed into a full-fledged system going online in March 1996. Virtual Magistrates, if users and providers decide to use them, can handle all manner of online disputes other than the potential copyright infringements. They intend to provide rapid resolution of disputes involving users of online systems, especially those who claim to be wrongfully affected by postings, and to expedite decisions concerning the appropriate action to be taken by systems operators. [http://vmag/.law.vill.edu:8080/]

In 1991, the U.S. Supreme Court clarified the outer boundaries of the copyright law, holding explicitly that facts may not be copyrighted regardless of the amount of labor expended in collecting them.[61] The implication is that no proprietary claims may be made concerning personal attributes or behavior that may be considered to be factual in nature. The "sweat of the brow" is not to be considered in granting protection, nor is the value to the person about which the facts are concerned. The decision may create tremendous turmoil for computer-mediated communication, because facts are now what most concern users of online services—telephone numbers, names and addresses, health records, and physical movements, or even sites "surfed" on the World Wide Web. These are called transaction generated information—data about what you purchase or where you travel. "Data mining" by companies seeking to know more about individuals has become a major growth industry.

The legal system currently does not protect a right to personal autonomy over information about oneself except in very few instances, such as credit histories and viewing of videotapes rented from video stores or programs viewed on cable television.[62] In Europe and Canada there exists a long tradition of protection of personal data dating back several decades to concerns about the computerization of society and big governments intruding upon the lives of its citizens. Today, it is not so much the intrusion of big government agencies (although the paranoia has not disappeared) but the intrusiveness of commercial interests in computer-mediated communication that creates concern.[63] Many people are apprehensive about the ability of computers to extract information about them from a variety of sources and to compile valuable dossiers of information which they offer for sale to an unknown and unauthorized multiplicity of users. Recent polls show that 63 percent of those questioned feel that "technology has almost gotten out of control."[64]

▪▪▪ Obscenity and Indecency Online

Many "cyberspaces" are segmented into separate channels of message use, where different communities of interested users congregate and discuss all manner of topics from the most sophisticated scientific research to the most erotic "cybersex" encounters.[66] The Usenet conferences on the Internet in spring 1996 numbered more than 10,000 discussion groups. A fair sprinkling include images that may be quite objectionable to many viewers. Whether children might be exposed to harmful images and sexually explicit stories became a subject of much concern as the public interest in the Internet accelerated.

The year 1996 marked a milestone in the history of the Internet when local authorities and national governments discovered behavior that they thought transgressed local laws. Many nations, e.g., Germany, Saudi Arabia, and China took steps either to block access to the Internet altogether or to crack down on behavior they thought objectionable.[67] The U.S. Congress passed legislation[68] purporting to curb not only obscenity (content already illegal and unprotected by the First Amendment of the Constitution) but also "indecency," a term difficult to define, that had been upheld for broadcast media but was immediately challenged as an unconstitutional restriction on freedom of speech as well as unworkable and undesirable for online communications.[69]

REFERENCES

[1] "Cyberspace" refers to the electronic environment in which users relay their messages and establish electronic linkages or cybercommunities. I prefer the terms "electronic environments and networked communities." However, the press has popularized "cyberspace" and it has come to be accepted by a large number of users. Cyberspace in the singular is innaccurate. There are numerous cyberspaces. "Cyberspace" was popularized by William Gibson in his classic science fiction novel, *Neuromancer*, in 1984. What Gibson meant by "cyberspace" was more like what we now call "virtual reality," the convergence of sight, sound, and other senses in electronic experiences, which would replicate reality.

[2] For more about "NETiquette" see Virginia Shea, *NETiquette* (San Francisco: Albion Books, 1994).

[3] Ironically, when this author suggested to her husband that the article she had written for this issue on legal issues be entitled "Common Law for Cyberspace," her husband rebuked her saying the word was too "nerdy" for such a sophisticated magazine. Although the editors changed the name of my article to "Common Law for the Electronic Frontier," they nevertheless splashed across the cover that this issue was all about "cyberspace." This special issue, vol. 265, No. 3, September 1991, was re-issued in 1994.

[4] July 1993.

[5] Philip Elmer-DeWitt, "First Nation in Cyberspace," *Time*, December 6, 1993, p. 62.

[6] Teri Agins, "An Santa's Reindeer Will Take The Information Superhighway," *Wall Street Journal*, Dec. 16, 1993, B-1, c.1.6.

[7] URL: [http://www.vatican.va].

[8] The Commercenet/ Nielsen Internet Demographics Survey, Executive Summary, Oct. 30, 1995.

[9] Times Mirror Center for The People and The Press. "Technology in the American Household: Americans Going Online . . . Explosive Growth, Uncertain Destinations." News Release, Oct. 16, 1995. Clearly some of these subscribers are duplications, For example, the author of this article subscribes to several online services. This is a common practice for many long-time users in order to preserve redundancy, to take advantage of different technical capabilities, or to sort different message streams.

[10] Reuters, BC cycle, May 7, 1996, NEXIS. AOL was reported to be signing up 66 percent of the new subscribers to online services, "Total online households in the U.S. to reach 35 million by the year 2000," Information Access Company, M2 Communications, M2 Presswire, April 30, 1966, NEXIS.

[11] Reuters, BC cycle, May 7, 1996, NEXIS.

[12] Denise Caruso, Microsoft Morphs Into a Media Company, *Wired*, June 1996, pp. 188, 190; This, however, represents only 5 percent of the 20 million purchasers of Windows 95 with which the MSN software was included.

[13] *Communications Daily*, vol. 16, no. 87, p. 5.

[14] TIG Internet Domain-Name Data Base. URL: [http://home.tig.com/cgi-bin/genobobject/domaindb].

[15] A new book on cybercommunities is being published, Peter Kollock and Marc Smith, eds., *Communities in Cyberspace* (Berkeley, CA: University of California Press, 1996). The table of contents is available at URL: [http://www.scnet.ucla.edu/soc/csoc/cinc]"; see also, Mike Godwin, *Cyber Rights: Free Speech and Society in the Digital Era* (New York, NY: Random House, 1996).

[16] B. Wittes, "Witnessing the Birth of a Legal System," Feb. 27, 1995, *The Connecticut Law Tribune*, Supplement, Special Section: Technology; p. 8A.

[17] *Transnational Data and Communications Report*.

[18] Many large corporations now have intra-corporate networks (called LANS or Intranets) for electronic mail and access to outside information resources. Corporate email is growing at about 18 percent per year. Such industrywide networks now abound, serving florists, hotel reservations, and sundry other purposes. This figure was reported by David Whitten of the Gartner Group, of Stamford, Connecticut in "Electronic Mail: What Hath Samuel Morse Wrought!" *Beyond Computing*, November–December 1993, p. 24–26. Hughes Aircraft, for example, has 45,000 workstations interconnected throughout its decentralized organization.

[19] Anne W. Branscomb, editor, *Toward A Law of Global Communications Networks* (New York and London: Longman 1984). For a more recent academic analysis of policy issues online, see Linda Harasim, editor, *Global Networks* (Cambridge, MA: MIT Press, 1993).

[20] The federal statute in effect at the time of the incident and under which Morris was convicted was Title 18 U.S.C. Section 1030 (a) (5). For a full discussion of the "hacker" mentality, rogue programs, and existing laws, see Anne W. Branscomb, "Rogue Computer Programs and Computer Rogues: Tailoring the Punishment to Fit the Crime," *Rutgers Computer Technology and Law Journal* 1–16, vol. 1, 1990. See also Edward A. Cavazos and Gavino Morin, *Cyberspace and the Law: Your Rights and Duties in the On-line World* (Cambridge, MA: MIT Press, 1994) Appendixes, G, H, & I.

[21] *U.S. v. Robert Tappan Morris*, 928 F. 2d 504 (2nd Cir. 1991).

[22] Barlow and Kapor recounted their experiences at a seminar at Harvard University Law School on April 1, 1996; they were also recounted by Barlow in "Crimes and Puzzlement," *Whole Earth Review*.

[23] *Steve Jackson Games, Inc. v. U.S. Secret Service*, 36 3d 457 (5th Cir. 1994); see also, Mike Godwin, "The Feds and the Net: Closing the Culture Gap," *Internet World*, May 1994.

[24] *U.S. v. Robert J. Riggs, et al.,* 2 CCH Computer Cases 46, 389 (N.D. GA 1990).

[25] Computer Science and Telecommunications Board, National Research Council, *Rights and Responsibilities of Participants in Networked Communities* (Washington, D.C.: National Academy Press, 1994).

[26] The NCLS is planning a follow-up study of Anonymity on the Internet, according to a communication from a staff member at the AAAS, April 17, 1996.

[27] "Envisioning a Global Information Infrastructure: The Ethical, Legal, and Technological Aspects of Network Use and Abuse." Some of the material in this article is taken from an unpublished presentation prepared by this author as a background paper for the first conference in December 1993.

[28] At least three specialized print publications are dedicated to cyberspace issues, one offered by Leader Publications (e-mail: ran@ljx.com), *Internet Newsletter: Legal & Business Practices*, one by Glasser Legal Works (legalwks@aol.com) called *The Cyberspace Lawyer*, and one by GoAhead Publications entitled *The Internet Lawyer*. Online legal journals were set up by the University of Richmond Law School, the *Richmond Journal of Law & Technology* [URL: http://www.urich.edu/~jol]; the William and Mary Law School in Williamsburg, *Journal of Online Law* [URL: http//www.wm.edu/law/publications/jol]; and the *Michigan Telecommunications & Technology Journal* [URL: http://www.umich.edu/~mttlr].

[29] Available by contacting mailer@lawlib.slu.edu orgopher://lawnext.uchicago.edu/hh/.web/lists.html.

[30] I. Trotter Hardy, "The Proper Legal Regime for 'Cyberspace,'" 55 *U. Pitt. L. Rev.* 993 (1994).

[31] *Syslaw* (LOL Productions 1992).

[32] Cavazos and Morin, note 20, infra.

[33] See, e.g. Henry H. Perritt, Jr., "Dispute Resolution in Electronic Network Communities," 38 *Vill. L. Rev.* 349 (1993).

[34] Henry H. Perritt, Jr., *Law and the Information Superhighway* (New York, NY: John Wiley, 1996).

[35] See, e.g. *Business & Legal Aspects of the Internet and Online Services*, Readings for Conference held on September 14–15, 1995.

[36] See, e.g. Seventh Annual Advanced Computer Law Seminar, Computer and Cyberspace Law, sponsored by the University of Dayton School of Law, June 14, 1996, Dayton, Ohio.

[37] See, e.g. Bob Berger, "The Circuit Rider," *Netguide*, September 1995, p. 10–12, quoting John Perry Barlow, ". . . the law itself may actually go away;" John Perry Barlow's "Cyberindependence Declaration" can be found at [URL: http://www.eff.org/~barlow].

[38] *Alana Shoars v. Epson America, Inc.,* No. SWC112749 (Los Angeles Superior Court 1990) and *Flanagan v. Epson America, Inc.,* No. BC007036 (Los Angeles Superior Court 1990).

[39] See, e.g. *Internet Commerce*, 1995, Gordon & Glickson, P.C., Barry D. Weiss, "Implementing Sound Corporate Internet Policies," p. 4–6 and Diana J.P. McKenzie, "Doing Business in Cyberspace: How to Minimize The Legal Costs of Doing Business on the Information Superhighway," p. 15–16.

[40] For a law review article on this subject, see, e.g. David R. Johnson & Kevin Marks, "Mapping Electronic Data Communications Onto Existing Legal Metaphors: Should We Let Our Conscience (and Our Contracts) Be Our Guide? 38 *Vill. L. Rev.* 487 (1993).

[41] *Stratton Oakmont, Inc. v. Prodigy Services Co.,* 23 Media L. Rep (BNA)1794 (N.Y. Sup. Ct. 1995).

[42] *Cubby, Inc. v. CompuServe, Inc.,* 776 F.Supp. 135 (S.D.N.Y. 1991).

[61] *Feist v. Rural Telephone*, 499 U.S. 340 (1991).

[62] For a fuller discussion of these issues, see Anne W. Branscomb, *Who Owns Information?* (New York, NY: Basic Books 1994).

[63] See, e.g. Bruce Horowitz, "Marketers Tap Data We Once Called Our Own," *USA Today*, December 19, 1995, p. 1A: "Suppose everything you bought was monitored. Very closely. So closely that the grocer knows that your dog prefers canned food to dry or that you recently switched from roll-on deodorant to spray. So closely that the hotel you stayed at last week knows what your favorite candy bar is and how many Kleenex boxes you want in your room—even though no one asked. Or that the last time you signed onto the Internet, someone could have watched what you did, what you said or what you bought, and then shared the information with a curious marketer who wanted to know. . . . It has gotten so out of hand, some experts say, that the right to privacy has all but disappeared, sacrificed on the altar of customer service and corporate profits."

[64] *Equifax-Harris Mid-Decade Consumer Privacy Survey 5* (New York, NY: Louis Harris & Associates 1995).

[66] Not everyone is as enthusiastic about the Internet as some of its most ardent proponents. See, for example, "Internot[sic]," *The New York Times Magazine*, Dec. 19, 1993, p. 18. "Yes, C-sex exists. It's like phone sex, except you have to keep typing. The sad truth is that your friend the Net troller spent last night in front of a monitor just as you

did. Except while you were watching the Duke deck the bad guys, he was plowing through acres of 'uupsi alt.internet-.services:3258 comp.org.eff.talk: 14065.' Odds are you had more fun."

[67] In Germany authorities ordered CompuServe to shut some sites offering images that contravened German law. Although CompuServe first complied, the outcry from users in other countries was so great that it eventually restored access to its subscribers. China sought to restrict access to the Internet to a small number of gateways that could be monitored

for objectionable traffic, and Saudi Ara offered a couple of gateways to the Inte

[68] Communications Decency Act of 1996.

[69] Full information concerning the court acti found at the following locations on the Web www.epic.org/free_speech/bills/censorship/la http://www.eff.org/pub/censorship/Internet censorship/;http://www.eff.org/pub/legal/cases/ EFFACLU v DoJ/; and http://www.cdt.org/. See also for news articles from the *New York Times*: http:// www.nytimes.com/.

Evaluating Federal Web Sites: Improving E-Government for the People

KIM M. THOMPSON
CHARLES R. MCCLURE
PAUL T. JAEGER

Introduction

Electronic government, commonly known as e-government, is a strategy for government to deliver services and information through technology to citizens, businesses, and to other governments. By applying information technology to federal government activities, e-government has become "a dynamic concept" that "has arisen within a very brief period of time" (Reylea 2002, p. 31). The portal Firstgov.gov[1] is an emerging effort by the federal government of the United States to put basic public services online such as tax forms and filing services, social security and unemployment benefits, and student grant applications.

E-government also extends to the state and local level. Pennsylvania, for example, is creating a portal that gives citizens instant access to government agency information and services, and Chicago is in the process of creating an online city hall.[2] These e-services are a way for the government to better meet the needs of citizens, businesses, and other government agencies. They also enable government agencies to respond in a more timely manner to user requests for information. Agency Web managers have seen Web page usage increase steadily as people access a wider range of federal agency Web sites on a more frequent basis. At this point in its evolution, e-government means "the use of technology, particularly the Internet, to enhance access to and delivery of government infor-

[1]FirstGov: Your first click to the U.S. government, available at www.firstgov.gov.
[2]PA PowerPort, available, at www.state.pa.us/. City of Chicago, available at www.cityofchicago.org/.

mation and services to citizens, businesses, government employees, and other agencies at the federal and state levels" (Hernon, Reylea, Dugan, and Cheverie 2002, p. 388).

In his 2002 *Presidential Memo on the Importance of E-government*, President George W. Bush stated the administration's goal to make e-government more "citizen-centered, results-oriented and business-based" (White House 2002). This business-modeled focus entails not only an increase in the number of services available online, but also an evaluation of current federal Web sites and services to better meet user needs. However, examining the quality of the services rendered online and evaluating agency Web sites is difficult. With 22,000 Web sites totaling more than 33 million Web pages belonging to the federal government alone, the quantity of sites needing evaluation is daunting (Bednarz 2002). In addition, evaluative methods are limited and funding for assessment of Web sites and services is relatively uncommon (Robinson 2002).

This chapter will address the need for evaluation of federal agency Web sites and what kinds of evaluation are especially useful for such an assessment. We will begin with a look at federal information policy that affects Web site development and will then provide an overview of evaluation and Web site evaluation measures currently used for assessing the efficiency and effectiveness of online sites and services. Finally, we will discuss the importance of evaluation of federal agency Web sites and online services in furthering the goals of creating a fully inclusive e-democracy.

A key theme of this chapter is the importance of ongoing evaluation of information technologies—such as federal Web sites—if such technology and applications are to meet user needs. E-government information and services will only reach their full potential if they are usable in an effective and efficient manner. Poor usability can cause a Web site to be underused or completely disregarded (Nielsen 2000). E-government Web sites, therefore, must be designed to account for the needs of the users, and the evaluation of e-government needs to focus on the usability of the sites.

Federal Information Policy

Policy at any level directs the decisions and actions of organizations and individuals in those organizations. With federal policy, guidelines are set forth to structure the decision making of governments and societies. As stated in the *Encyclopedia of Library and Information Science*:

> Society both affects and is affected by government information policies developed at the national and local level. Information policies in turn affect the degree to which people have access to the expanding universe of traditional and electronic information. A nation's information policies provide a framework for how that country provides the information services and products. (McClure 1999, p. 306)

Information policy, then, is the statement of a specific goal set by the federal government to regulate information-related activities—both in the government and in society. Policy statements can appear in legislation, guidelines, court decisions, presidential statements, agency circulars, and other official statements.

Policy is essentially a socially agreeable way to solve problems. *Stakeholders*, the people affected by a social problem or *issue*, recognize that policies may be developed to deal with a particular social problem. Stakeholders often have conflicting value systems and have differing objectives in the resolution of an issue. Policy issues are usually the subject of ongoing debate and long-term discussion (McClure 1999).

Representative issues related to e-government and online information resources and services that federal agencies need to consider include:

- Electronic records management
- Information access
- Intellectual property
- Information security
- Information privacy

Electronic records management policy instruments concern issues regarding the creation, maintenance, use, and disposal of federal records. Internet access policy instruments are concerned with ensuring the equitable access for U.S. citizens to electronic information contained on federal government Web sites. Intellectual property policy instruments include a wide variety of ownership rights in intangible products, such as copyrights, patents, trademarks, and trade secrets. Information security instruments concern risks to the ongoing operation of government computer systems, their integrity, and the protection of classified or confidential materials they contain. Information privacy instruments seek to protect personal information collected from agency Web site users.

No single body of law describes and coordinates federal information policy. Because of this decentralization, when the input of multiple agencies is necessary for a complete solution but agency information cannot be shared due to discrepancies in data formatting or software compatibility, we have what are known as *stovepipe* information systems. This lack of coordination between agency information compatibility invariably gets in the way of efficient and effective e-government.

The Office of Management and Budget (OMB) reports directly to the president's office and is responsible for implementation and oversight of federal information policies. At the September 2002 Interagency Resources Management Conference (IRMCO), OMB official Mark Forman (2002) stated that the next step for the development of e-government would be "breakthrough performance," which is based on:

- A citizen-centered strategy
- Concrete outcomes, measures, and statistics
- Real-time data collection
- Cross-agency collaboration and partnerships
- Simplifying services (three clicks to service)
- Standardizing technology and eliminating stovepipe applications

He also reiterated the stated goal of the administration to effectively implement e-government in order to make the federal government "more responsive and cost-effective" (White House 2002). This effort provides specific strategies and techniques to help agencies facilitate these goals and develop "breakthrough performance" in the delivery of e-government through federal Web sites.

I I I Key Policies Affecting Federal Web Site Development and Management

Thus, it is through federal information policy that the legal and procedural framework in which government agencies make information and services available to the public is established. An information policy instrument "describes how information will be collected, managed, protected, accessed, disseminated, and used" (McClure 1999, p. 307). Following is an introductory list of selected U.S. federal information policy instruments that affect the development and management of federal Web sites.

Electronic Record Management

- *Government Performance and Results Act of 1993*—Sets forth performance plans, goals, and measures for agency programs.
- *Paperwork Reduction Act of 1995*—Makes federal agencies publicly accountable for reducing the burden of federal paperwork on the public.
- *Electronic Freedom of Information Act of 1996*—Amends the Freedom of Information Act of 1967 to provide for public access to information in an electronic format.
- *Government Paperwork Elimination Act of 1998*—Establishes that Web sites are to be interoperable and standardized across agencies of the federal government.

Information Access

- *Section 508 of the Rehabilitation Act*—Mandates that information technology that is acquired or produced by the federal government, including e-government Web sites, must be accessible to individuals with disabilities.
- *National Information Infrastructure (NII) Agenda for Action*—Establishes government responsibility to make government information more easily and equitably accessible.

Intellectual Property

- *NII Copyright Protection Act of 1995*–Adapts copyright law to include digital and networked information.
- *Digital Millennium Copyright Act of 1998*—Protects copyright in electronic media.

Information Security

- *Computer Security Act of 1987*—Establishes standards and security guidelines for the protection of sensitive information in federal computer systems.
- *Electronic Signatures in Global and National Commerce Act of 2000* (ESIGN)—Recognizes e-signatures as legal across the United States.

Information Privacy

- *Privacy Act of 1974*—Establishes federal guidelines for the protection of personal information.
- *USA Patriot Act of 2001*—Describes the rights of citizens to information privacy, particularly with regard to criminal or financial records.

This listing, though not comprehensive, offers a general sense of the range of existing federal policies relevant to the development, management, and evaluation of Web sites.

Federal information policy and agency Web site development occur in a dynamic environment. Stakeholder issues and technological changes affect information policy, having a rapid impact on established information policies and the creation of new ones. Federal agencies often must adjust their operations almost immediately. Policy tends to follow technology and practice. Sometimes the lag between policy and practice can be significant, causing agencies to construct their own policies to rationalize practices before Congress has the opportunity to enact new laws.

Evaluation of federal Web sites and online services is the key to creating better regulations and to maintaining a high standard of e-government. The *Government Performance Results Act of 1993* mentioned earlier is one policy that focuses attention on the evaluation and accountability of federal agency information access and dissemination. The Bush administration has signaled its support for the various e-government programs and assessments. The administration in its 2002 budget notes the importance of accountability and performance assessment of e-government initiatives.

In late 2002, the Congress and the Senate passed the *E-government Act of 2002* (H.R. 2458), which is intended to improve the quality of the federal e-government. Though the Act has a wide array of purposes, one of its main goals is to make e-government more focused on the needs of the citizen. The stated purposes of the Act include using e-government to "provide increased opportunities for citizen participation in the Government," to "provide citizen-centered Government information and services," and to "promote access to high quality government information and services" (H.R. 2458, § 2). This focus on increasing citizen use of and participation in e-government emphasizes the importance of the holistic evaluation of e-government Web sites.

▪▪▪ Evaluation

Web site evaluation is the use of research or investigative procedures to systematically determine the effectiveness of a Web-based information system on an ongoing basis. Evaluation plays a key role in organizational planning, monitoring Web site activities and services, and modifying goals and objectives on an ongoing basis. This is "formative" evaluation. In contrast, "summative" evaluation determines the degree to which the Web site is meeting set goals and user needs. Figure 1 illustrates this dual role. On the left side of the diagram, information discovered as part of the evaluation process feeds back into goal setting and planning. Ongoing evaluation is a vital source of information for agencies' planning processes. For example, an evaluation of current Web site user satisfaction may reveal usability issues with the current page design or information architecture. Planners may choose to change or modify goals based upon newly discovered problems or the achievement of previously set goals.

On the right side of the diagram, evaluation determines the degree to which the organization has met stated goals. Developing goals and objectives with no follow-up effort to determine how well those objectives were actually accomplished significantly reduces the overall value of both planning and the use of assessment techniques. Based on the previous evaluation, if the organization had created a goal to improve site usability, they would then use evaluation to determine the degree to which the site's usability had improved.

Both formative and summative evaluation efforts are important, although most organizations tend to concentrate on summative approaches. For purposes of monitoring and continually improving services, formative evaluation (intended to improve, not prove) is essential.

Information Systems Evaluation

Information systems (IS) evaluation has become an increasingly important topic within the competitive online environment in the United States. Several factors have contributed to the growing importance of IS evaluation:

- IS projects historically have had low success rates; some researchers have suggested success rates as low as 30 to 40 percent (Willcocks and Margetts 1994). Many organizations, in government and in business, that attempt to restructure around the online environment do not succeed because online success often has more to do with relationships and organization than with information technology. This increases pressure on managers to both justify their projects and show how their projects can and will succeed.

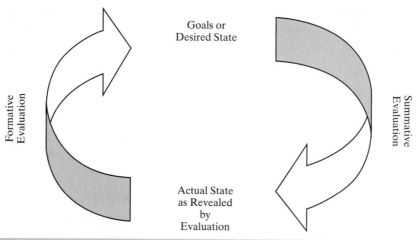

Goals or
Desired State

Formative
Evaluation

Summative
Evaluation

Actual State
as Revealed
by
Evaluation

▮▮▮▮▮▮▮▮▮▮▮▮ **FIGURE 1** Formative and Summative Evaluation

- Vendors inundate mangers with dizzying hype surrounding new products and information technology trends. Managers need evaluation tools to help them determine the actual usefulness of these products and trends for their organizations.
- Although organizations' budgets have generally increased allocations for information technology, downsizing and streamlining demands require information technology managers to show how increased information technology spending is adding value to the organization.

Guidance for addressing these issues related to IS evaluation in government can be found in reports such as:

- The National Research Council report *More Than Screen Deep: Toward Every-Citizen Interfaces to the Nation's Information Infrastructure*, www.nap.edu/readingroom/books/screen.
- *Performance-Based Management: Eight Steps to Developing and Using IT Measures Effectively* by the GSA Office of Governmentwide Policy, www.gsa.gov/attachments/GSA_PUBLICATIONS/extpub/prnfinal.doc.

Readers should note that the many resources developed for general IS evaluation can be adapted for use in Web site evaluation.

Web IS Evaluation

Since the mid-1990s, interest in Web site evaluation has surged. One result has been the publication of a range of Web "do-it-yourself" books that include advice on both design and evaluation (e.g., see Nielsen 2000; Jacobson 1999). At the same time, researchers from the business, education, and information science fields have sought to evaluate Web sites based on many different criteria, including:

- Web metrics (Sterne 2002)
- Interface design (Kopak and Cherry 1998; Van House, Butler, Ogle, and Schiff 1996)
- Usability (Benbunan-Fich 1999)
- Comparison to peer organizations—benchmarking (Johnson and Misic 1999)
- Fit with theoretical models (e.g., marketing model: von Dran, Zhang, and Small 1999; motivational model: Zhang and von Dran 2000)

- Web site strategy (Auger 1997)
- Information quality (McMurdo 1998)
- Hypertext structure (Bauer and Scharl 2000)

Web site evaluation has also become a popular topic within the trade press (e.g., Dugan 2000). A significant amount of Web evaluation emphasis focuses on log analysis techniques (Rubin 2001) and use of specific log analysis software such as WebTrends and Webtracker.

Readers should keep in mind that information on general Web site evaluation is applicable to the federal Web environment with certain key allowances made for design restraints imposed by regulation or statute.

Web Site Evaluation in Federal Agencies

Federal Web site evaluation has been ongoing since the inception of federal Web sites. One early landmark was the World Wide Web Federal Consortium publication of suggested guidelines for federal Web site development (draft 1996).[3] These guidelines have been periodically updated in recent years.[4] Many federal agencies conduct periodic evaluations to maintain and enhance the quality of their sites. A substantial and increasingly sophisticated academic evaluation research stream has also been produced. Current Web evaluation research has examined federal Web sites in terms of a variety of evaluation criteria, including information content and ease of use (e.g., Eschenfelder et al. 1997; McClure and Wyman 1997; Hert and Marchionini 1997) and compliance with federal records guidelines (McClure and Sprehe 1999).

Further, some studies have looked at specific aspects of Web sites. For instance, Hert (1998) evaluated Web site-finding aids and Moen and McClure (1997) examined the government information locator service (GILS). Other evaluation efforts have taken a more holistic approach. For instance, Hert, Eschenfelder, and McClure (1999) included techniques of usability, management, technical, and policy analysis. Finally, these studies vary in methodologies, with some relying on mainly one method (e.g., log file analysis, Redalen and Miller 2000; Bertot et al. 1997), whereas others have taken a multimethod approach (e.g., Hert, Escenfelder, and McClure 1999).

Many federal agencies are struggling with the development of Web site evaluation techniques, the development of statistics and performance measures, the integration of assessment into Web site planning and development, and the incorporation of user-based feedback that can assist them in evaluating the performance and impact of their Web sites (Hert, Eischenfelder, and McClure 1999; McClure, Sprehe, and Eschenfelder 2000; McClure et al. 2002). Anecdotal information and site usage statistics are often used as the basis for assessment—if assessment occurs at all.

Citizen input and feedback are also vital components of the delivery of meaningful e-government services; however, much more could be done to effectively and systematically collect and use this input and feedback if standardized tools and mechanisms were in place. Using criteria relevant to service enhancement, these tools could formally assess user data to improve services and to provide summaries to agencies to help them refine their public services.

Such evaluation tools are essential if federal agencies are to have measures and statistics to assist them in program development and planning of Web site services. They are also necessary in order to determine the degree to which Web-based program plans are successfully integrated into overall agency goals, to enable agencies to com-

---

[3]The original guidelines are available at www.dtic.mil/staff/cthomps/guidelines. Accessed October 2002.
[4]Updated July 1999, available at www.ojp.usdoj.gov/oa/fedWebguide/welcome.html. Accessed October 2002.

ply with accountability requirements as outlined in the *Government Performance and Results Act* (and other federal mandates), to demonstrate the use and impact of particular services and resources provided via the Web site, and to respond to public needs for access, content, and services.

Federal Web Site Evaluation Approaches

Web sites can be evaluated based on a number of different approaches. (McClure and Bertot 2001; Menascé and Almeida 2002; Sterne 2002). In addition, a number of recent reports have offered "assessments" of federal Web sites. Unfortunately, their methods are suspect or nonexistent, and they offer a "report card" mentality of assessment (Stowers 2002). To make federal Web sites and services more customer/citizen-centered, Web masters and agency chief information officers (CIOs) must realize that there is no "one size fits all" template for success in online service. The following is a selection of only a few of the myriad evaluative approaches available for holistic assessment of Web services.

Approaches for incorporating public comments and concerns about Web site content and access or comparing the success of their efforts to other Web sites are quite limited. Generally, such approaches rely on a "comments" or "suggestions" icon strategically placed on various Web site pages. Bertot and McClure (1999) experimented with "pop up" questionnaires on selected pages with some success. Surveys, focus groups, and other types of usability assessment can also collect user input (Sterne 2002). Difficulties with the various approaches for user input include coordinating the data from the various sources, ensuring that the responses are representative of the Web site user population, and obtaining adequate response rates.

Log analysis techniques provide a great deal of data about Web user activity (Yonaitis 2001). Current Web or e-metrics typically used for determining the success of a Web site include such log files as page impressions (the number of pages viewed), the number of visitors to a site, the length of time they spent on a particular page, and the number of screens downloaded or printed from a site (Nicholas, Huntington, and Williams 2002). However, the data captured by log files is more useful for determining the burden placed on the Web server, the success of search engines in locating a site, or the way users navigate the Web in general than they are evaluating the needs of users of the Web sites (Zawitz 1998; Fieber 1999; Nicholas, Huntington, and Williams 2001; Garofalakis, Kappos, and Markris 2002). Statistical measurements based on this logged data, such as the Velocity, Stickiness, and Personalization Index, better tailor Web site services to meet the dynamic and highly personalized needs of the individual user (Cutler and Sterne 2000).

User satisfaction can be measured through a number of methods. Federal agencies have considered a wide range of approaches that address issues of evaluation of Web site user satisfaction and usage data. One proposed approach, Value Measuring Methodology (VMM) encourages the assessment of the value and usage of e-government Web sites and projects based on a multidimensional analysis of the cost/benefit, social, and political factors (Mechling and Booz Allen Hamilton 2002). Another approach involves the use of digital guides as a part of federal e-government Web sites and services (Hoening 2001). Commercial firms such as ForeSee Results also have developed products of this nature to assess user satisfaction.[5] No matter what approach or combination of approaches employed, there is a pressing need for the creation of a practical and more holistic approach to determine user satisfaction and general usage of federal agency Web sites.

---

[5]ForeSee Results available at www.forseeresults.com/.

Technical assessment of the Web site in terms of hardware, software, and network connectivity is another crucial area that affects overall Web performance. This key component affects the overall success of the Web site and the degree to which the technology infrastructure adequately supports the objectives, activities, and resource/ services provisions from the Web site. Although there are a number of guides to direct assessment development in this area, recent work by Menascé and Almeida (2002) and Sterne (2002) provides a very useful summary and practical guide for technically oriented measures and assessment techniques.

A management and policy perspective considers the manner in which the agency is organized to design, provide, administer, evaluate, and plan for the Web site. Previous work by Hert, Eischenfelder, and McClure (1999) suggests that a range of managerial and organizational issues can affect the quality and usefulness of an agency Web site. A policy perspective is especially important in assessing federal Web sites given the range of privacy, security, access, records management, and accessibility issues that affect the successful operation of an agency website.

Federal information policy areas such as security, privacy, records management, and accessibility (among others) affect federal Web site development and implementation. For example, Section 508 of the Rehabilitation Act establishes accessibility standards for federal government information technology to provide equal access to individuals with disabilities, whether they are federal government employees or citizens using federal government information technologies (29 U.S.C.A. § 794d). Section 508 compels federal government agencies and vendors to comply with accessibility standards.[6] These guidelines are issued by the Architectural and Transportation Barriers Compliance board, commonly known as the Access Board, which "is the primary federal agency for creating accessibility standards, including the standards for Section 508" (Jaeger 2002).

Evaluation tools are essential if federal agencies are to have measures and statistics to assist them in program development and planning of Web site services. They are also necessary to determine the degree to which Web-based program plans are successfully integrated into overall agency and e-government goals, to enable agencies to comply with Web site accountability requirements, to demonstrate the use and impact of particular services and resources provided via the Web site, and to respond to public needs for access, content, and services.

Usability Assessment of Federal Government Web Sites

Some agencies maintain a range of statistics describing Web services, whereas others have undertaken only minimal or no data collection and analysis efforts; some have devoted substantial resources to "one-stop shopping" for information; many have developed "frequently asked questions" to assist visitors to agency Web sites. Most agencies already use Web log statistics and other software-based measures (i.e., e-metrics) to examine aspects of their Web sites' performance. However, agencies still need a flexible approach that goes beyond Web statistics such as transaction logs to offer a variety of techniques by which agencies can determine whether their Web sites are successfully achieving the information dissemination missions for which they are intended.

Usability is immensely important for Web sites, because the first element of a site that a user experiences is usability (Nielsen 2000). Holistic usability assessment employs the range of evaluation approaches described previously. Usability is formally defined as "the effectiveness, efficiency, and satisfaction with which specified users can

---

[6]Standards for Section 508 of the Rehabilitation Act are available at *www.section508.gov*.

Phase 1: Usability Assessment

The evaluator conducts a review of user needs and usability issues, such as error frequencies, user complaints, and other potential problem areas. In this phase, the evaluator creates an outline of the scope of the project, associated timelines and deliverables, costs, the users to be tested, and basic evaluation methods. This phase also includes the identification of representative tasks and users to assist in the usability evaluation.

Phase 2: Usability Evaluation

The use of both empirical and nonempirical methods is preferred and recommended.

EXPERT ANALYSIS

- Heuristic Evaluations—Usability professionals evaluate the environment for compliance to standard design and usability heuristics.
- Cognitive Walkthroughs—Usability professionals test the environment using typical scenarios designed around expected user behavior.

USABILITY METRICS

- Interviews—Users reflect about their use of a site and are questioned regarding their opinions, insights, and attitudes.
- Focus Groups—A small group of representative users are asked to discuss the usability of a particular Web site from the perspective of their own information needs.
- Log Analysis—Specialized software collects statistics about the users' interactions with a Web site, providing accurate data on the users' specific actions.
- User Feedback—Users provide feedback as they use a particular system, providing valuable data on user satisfaction, changing needs, and critical concerns.
- Questionnaires—User demographics, previous experience, attitude, and pre- and posttesting information are collected.

REPRESENTATIVE USER TESTING

- Formal Empirical Observations—Individual users complete specific tasks and are observed as they interact wit the environment.
- The "Think-aloud" Approach—Individual users provide a running commentary on their thoughts as they perform particular tasks.
- Constructive Interactions—Pairs or small groups of users work on particular tasks while discussing the Web site's features and characteristics aloud.

▪▪▪▪▪▪▪▪▪▪▪▪ **FIGURE 2** Usability Assessment Processes

achieve specified goals in particular environments" (International Standards Organization, ISO DIS 9241-11). For practical purposes, however, a broader meaning for usability including log analysis, policy analysis, Web site management and organization, and user satisfaction is typically employed. Observation, a well-known usability approach, is only one component of usability testing. Figure 2 offers a general overview for conducting usability assessments.

Usability experts stress the importance of an holistic approach to user-centered design in the process of designing and evaluating a system (Mayhew 1999; Landauer 1997). However, most usability testing focuses exclusively on formal, empirical methods, which primarily can be performed only after a useable system is nearly complete (Nielsen 1993). These post hoc usability assessments generally do not reveal usability problems with the same proficiency as assessments that use a variety of inspection methods throughout the use of the system (Nielsen and Mack 1994). Thus, usability assessment should include both formative and summative evaluation approaches.

The federal Web site Usability.gov, created and maintained by the National Cancer Institute, is a starting point for usability assessment, providing good usability resources, Web design checklists, and basic usability guidelines.[7] The key to usability is not only how well the Web site works, but also the degree to which the Web site meets user needs. Figure 2 provides details on this approach, stressing the importance of IS in meeting user needs and engaging in an ongoing process to regularly determine if, in fact, users' needs are being met. Developing information systems and services (such as Web sites) without such ongoing assessment techniques is likely to result in applications that are not used or are largely ineffective. If the usability of an e-government Web site is problematic, the usage of the services and information offered by the site may be limited by the usability problems, defeating much of the potential value of government online.

▐▐▐ Improving Federal Web Sites and E-Government

Abundant evidence indicates that federal Web sites need to be improved in terms of usability in order to meet federal policy guidelines, such as accessibility requirements for individuals with disabilities, and to support e-government initiatives (Robinson 2002). Helping agencies to understand and implement evaluation methods will make their Web sites and Web-related services as useable and useful as possible, which furthers the government's goal of making Web-based digital government available to all citizens. Ongoing evaluation can address these and related problems with federal Web sites and can facilitate the growth of federal e-government into a federal e-democracy. When agencies understand and implement evaluation methods that will make their Web sites and Web-related services as useable and useful as possible, citizens can better use and access the digital government information services and resources those Web sites provide.

Interest in evaluation of Web-based services continues to increase, though few comprehensive approaches assess federal Web sites on an ongoing basis. As agencies continue to be encouraged to provide additional Web-based services with limited resources and as implementation of the *Government Performance and Results Act* presses forward, ongoing evaluation and use of performance measures are likely to take on increased importance.

REFERENCES

Auger, P. (1997). *Marketing on the World Wide Web: An Empirical Investigation of the Relationship Between Strategy and the Performance of Corporate Web Sites.* Unpublished dissertation. Syracuse University, Syracuse, NY.

Bauer, C., and A. Scharl. 2000. "Quantitative evaluation of Web site content and structure." *Internet Research* 10: 31–44.

Bednarz, A. 2002. "Getting plugged into e-government." *Network World.* Available: www.nwfusion.com/supp/government2002/authentication.html. Accessed April 2003.

Benbunan-Fich, R. 1999. "Methods for evaluating the usability of Web based systems. *AMCIS Americas Conference on Information Systems*, August, Milwaukee, WI.

---

[7]Usability.gov Web site available at *www.usability.gov/*.

Bertot, J. C., and C. R. McClure. 1999. *Assessment of Del-AWARE statewide website*. Dover, DE: State Library of Delaware.

Bertot, J. C., C. R. McClure, W. E. Moen, and J. Rubin. 1997. "Web usage statistics: Measurement issues and analytical techniques." *Government Information Quarterly* 14(4): 373–395.

Cutler, M., and J. Sterne 2000. *E-metrics: Business Metrics for the New Economy*. Cambridge, MA: NetGenesis.

Dugan, S. 2000. "Where will e-business take you?" *Infoworld.com*. Available: www.infoworld.com/articles/hn/xml/00/04/03/000403hnresearch.xml. Accessed April 2003.

Eschenfelder, K. R., J C. Beachboard, C. R. McClure, and S. K. Wyman. 1997. "Assessing U.S. federal government websites." *Government Information Quarterly* 14(2): 173–189.

Fieber, J. 1999. *Browser caching and Web log analysis*. Available: http://ella.slis.indiana.edu/~jfieber/papers/bcwla/bcwla.html.

FirstGov: Your first click to the U.S. government. Available: http://firstgov.gov. Accessed April 2003.

Forman, M. *Developing E-government strategies*. Hershey, PA: Interagency Resources Management (IRMCO) Annual Conference. (September 4, 2002). (Speech).

Garafalakis, J., P. Kappos, and C. Markis. 2002. "Improving the performance of Web access by bridging global ranking with local page popularity metrics." *Internet Research: Electronic Networking Applications and Policy* 12: 43–54.

General Services Administration (GSA) Office of Governmentwide Policy. 2002. *Performance-based management: Eight steps to develop and use IT performance measures effectively*. Available: www.gsa.gov/attachments/GSA_PUBLICATIONS/extpub/pmfinal.doc. Accessed April 2003.

Hernon, P., H. C. Reylea, R. E. Dugan, and J. F. Cheverie. 2002. *United States Government Information: Polices and Sources*. Westport, CT: Libraries Unlimited.

Hert, C. A. 1998. Facilitating statistical information seeking on websites: Intermediaries, organizational tools and other approaches. *Final Report to the Bureau of Labor Statistics*. Available: http://istWeb.syr.edu/~hert/BLSphase2.html.

Hert, C. A., K. R. Eschenfelder, and C. R. McClure. 1999. *Evaluation of selected websites at the U.S. Department of Education: Increasing access to Web-based resources*. Syracuse, NY: Information Institute of Syracuse.

Hert, C. A., and G. Marchionini. 1997. *Seeking statistical information on federal websites: Users, tasks, strategies, and design recommendations. Final Report to the Bureau of Labor Statistics*. Available: http://ils.unc.edu/~march/blsreport/mainbls.html. Accessed April 2003.

Hoenig, C. 2001. "Beyond e-government: Building the next generation of public services." *Government Executive* 33(14): 49–58.

Information Infrastructure Task Force. *The National Information Infrastructure: An agenda for action*. Washington D.C.: Department of Commerce, 1993.

Jacobson, R. 1999. *Information Design*. Cambridge, MA: MIT Press.

Jaeger, P. T. 2002. "Section 508 goes to the library: Complying with federal legal standards to produce accessible electronic and information technology in libraries." *Information Technology and Disabilities* 8(2). Available: www.rit.edu/~easi/itd/itdv08n2/jaeger.html.

Johnson, K. L., and M. M. Misic. 1999. "Benchmarking: A tool for Web site evaluation and improvement". *Internet Research* 9:383–392.

Kopak, R. W., and J. M. Cherry. 1998. "Bibliographic displays and Web catalogues: User evaluations of three prototype displays." *Electronic Library* 16: 309–323.

Landauer, T. 1997. *The Trouble with Computers: Usefulness, Usability, and Productivity*. Cambridge, MA: MIT Press.

Mayhew, D. 1999. *The Usability Engineering Lifecycle: A Practitioner's Handbook for User Interface Design*. San Francisco: Morgan Kaufman.

McClure, C. R. 1999. "United States information policy." In A. Kent (Ed.), *Encyclopedia of Library and Information Science* Vol. 65, Supp. 28. (pp. 306–314). New York: Marcel Dekker.

McClure, C. R., and J. C. Bertot. (Eds.). 2001. *Evaluating Networked Information Services: Techniques, Policy, and Issues*. Medford, NJ: Information Today.

McClure, C. R., R. D. Lankes, M. Gross, and B. Choltco-Devlin. 2002. *Statistics, Measures, and Quality Standards for Assessing Digital Reference Library Services: Guidelines and Procedures*. Syracuse, NY: Information Institute of Syracuse.

McClure, C. R., and J. T. Sprehe. 1999. *Analysis and Development of Model Quality Guidelines for Electronic Records Management on State and Federal Websites: Final Report*. Washington, D.C.: The National Historical Publications and Records Commission.

McClure, C. R., J. T. Sprehe, and R. Eschenfelder. 2000. *Performance measures for agency websites: Final report*. Sponsored by the U.S. Energy Information Administration, the Government Printing Office, and the Defense Technical Information Center.

McClure, C. R., and S. Wyman. 1997. *Quality Criteria for Evaluating Information Resources and Services Available from Federal Websites Based on User Feedback Online*. Dublin, OH: Computer Library Center.

McMurdo, G. 1998. "Evaluating Web information and design." *Journal of Information Science* 24: 192–204.

Mechling, J., and Booz Allen Hamilton. 2002. *Building a Methodology for Measuring the Value of E-Services*. Washington, D.C.: Booz Allen Hamilton.

Menascé, D. A., and V. A. F. Almeida. 2002. *Capacity Planning for Web Services: Metrics, Models, and Methods*. New York: Prentice Hall.

Moen, W. E., and C. R. McClure. 1997. *An Evaluation of the Federal Government's Implementation of the Government Information Locator Service (GILS): Final Report*. Available: www.unt.edu/wmoen/publications/gilseval/titpag.htm. Accessed April 2003.

National Research Council. *More than screen deep: Toward every-citizen interfaces to the nation's information infrastructure*. Washington D.C.: National Academy Press. Available: http://search.nap.edu/readingroom/books/screen/. Accessed April 2003.

Nielsen, J. 1993. *Usability Engineering*. Boston: Academic Press.

Nielsen, J. 2000. *Designing Web Usability: The Practice of Simplicity*. Indianapolis, IN: New Riders.

Nielsen, J., and R. Mack. (Eds.). 1994. *Usability Inspection Methods*. New York: Wiley.

Nicholas, D., P. Huntington, and P. Williams. 2001. "Establishing metrics for the evaluation of touch screen kiosks." *Journal of Information Science* 27: 61–72.

Nicholas, D., P. Huntington, and P. Williams. 2002. "Evaluating metrics for comparing the use of Web sites: A case study of two consumer health Web sites." *Journal of Information Science* 28: 63–76.

PA PowerPort. Available: www.state.pa.us/. Accessed April 2003.

Redalen, A., and N. Miller. 2000. "Evaluating website modifications at the National Library of Medicine through search log analysis." *D-Lib Magazine* 6.

Relyea, H. C. 2002. "E-gov: Introduction and overview." *Government Information Quarterly* 19(1): 9–35.

Robinson, B. 2002. "Making do: Agencies' efforts to design usable websites slowed by lack of resources, training." *Federal Computer Week* 16 (October 14, 2002): 24–28. Available: www.fcw.com/fcw/articles/2002/1014/mgt-web-10-14-02.asp.

Rubin, J. H. 2001. "Introduction to log analysis techniques: Methods for evaluating networked services." In C. R. McClure and J. C. Bertot (Eds.), *Evaluating Networked Information Services: Techniques, Policy, and Issues*. Medford, NJ: Information Today.

Sterne, J. 2002. *Web Metrics: Proven Methods for Measuring Web Site Success*. New York: John Wiley.

Stowers, G. N. L. 2002. *The State of Federal Websites: The Pursuit of Excellence*. San Francisco, CA: Public Administration Program. [E-government Series of the PricewaterhouseCoopers Endowment for the Business of Government.]

Usability.gov. 2002. *National Cancer Institute: Improving the communication of cancer research*. Available: http://usability.gov/. Accessed April 2003.

Van House, N. A., M. H. Butler, V. Ogle, and L. Schiff. 1996. "User-centered iterative design for digital libraries: The cypress experience." *D-Lib Magazine* 2(2).

von Dran, G., P. Zhang, and R. Small. 1999. "Quality websites: An application of the Kano model to website design." *Americas Conference on Information Systems*. Milwaukee, WI.

White House. 2002. *Presidential memo on the importance of E-government: Memorandum for the heads of executive departments and agencies*. Available: www.whitehouse.gov/news/releases/2002/07/20020710-6.html. Accessed April 2003.

World Wide Web Federal Consortium. 1999. *Guidelines and best practices*. Available: www.dtic.mil/staff/cthomps/guidelines.

World Wide Web Federal Consortium. 1996. *Federal World Wide Web guidelines and best practices*. Available: www.ojp.usdoj.gov/oa/fedwebguide/welcome.html.

Willcocks, L., and H. Margetts. 1994. "Risk assessment and information systems." *European Journal of Information Systems* 3: 127–138.

Yonaitis, R. B. 2001. *Understanding Internet Traffic: Using Your Web Server Log Files*. Concord, NH: Hiawatha Publishing.

Zawitz, W. 1998. *Web Statistics—Measuring User Activity*. Available: www.ojp.usdoj.gov/bjs/pub/ascii/wsmua.txt. Accessed April 2003.

Zhang, P., and G. von Dran. 2000. "Satisfiers and dissatisfiers: A two-factor model for website design and evaluation." *Journal of the American Society for Information Science* 51: 1253–1268.

Bridging the Racial Divide on the Internet

DONNA L. HOFFMAN

THOMAS P. NOVAK

The Internet is expected to do no less than transform society(1); its use has been increasing exponentially since 1994(2). But are all members of our society equally likely to have access to the Internet and thus participate in the rewards of this transformation? Here we present findings both obvious and surprising from a recent survey of Internet access and discuss their implications for social science research and public policy.

Income and education drive several key policy questions surrounding the Internet(3),(4). These variables are the ones most likely to influence access to and use of interactive electronic media by different segments of our society. Looming large is the concern that the Internet may be accessible only to the most affluent and educated members of our society, leading to what Morrisett has called a "digital divide" between the information "haves" and "have-nots(5)."

Given these concerns, we investigated the differences between whites and African Americans in the United States with respect to computer access and Web use. We wished to examine whether observed race differences in access and use can be accounted for by differences in income and education, how access affects use, and when race matters in access.

Our analysis is based on data provided by Nielsen Media Research, from the Spring 1997 CommerceNet/Nielsen Internet Demographic Study (IDS), conducted from December 1996 through January 1997(6). This nationally projectable survey of Internet use among Americans collected data on race and ethnicity(7).

Computer Access and Web Use

Our survey results (Table 1, column 1) show that overall whites were significantly more likely than African Americans to have a home computer in their household(8). Whites were also slightly more likely to have access to a PC at work.

TABLE 1 Percentage (Weighted) of Individuals in Each Group Responding Positively Concerning the Variable Specified in That Row. Asterisk Indicates That the Difference Between Whites and Blacks Is Statistically Significant ($P < 0.05$); Larger Number in Bold.

| | (1) Full Sample | | NON-STUDENTS | | | | | | | | STUDENTS | | | |
| | | | (2) $40,000 Income | | (3) $40,000+ Income | | (4) High School or Less | | (5) Some College | | (6) All Students | | (7) Have Home PC | | (8) No PC at Home | |
	Whites N = 4906	Blacks N = 493	Whites N = 1833	Blacks N = 213	Whites N = 1916	Blacks N = 131	Whites N = 1794	Blacks N = 210	Whites N = 2776	Blacks N = 219	Whites N = 336	Blacks N = 64	Whites N = 247	Blacks N = 22	Whites N = 89	Blacks N = 42
Own home computer	**44.3***	29.0*	**27.5***	13.3*	61.2	65.4	**27.0***	16.4*	**57.7***	49.3*	**73.0***	31.9*	100	100	0.0	0.0
PC access at work	38.5	33.8	25.9	20.7	59.1*	**76.7***	24.2	18.4	55.0*	**63.9***	27.0	24.0	30.1	32.3	18.6	20.1
Buy PC in 6 months	16.7*	**27.2***	14.3*	**23.4***	20.4*	**35.7***	12.6*	**23.3***	19.4*	**28.5***	26.3	40.3	22.3	9.3	37.1	54.8
Internet TV interest	11.8	14.9	9.2	9.4	15.0*	**23.9***	8.2	12.3	13.6	16.8	23.5	21.4	26.7	26.6	14.9	19.0
Ever used Web	26.0	22.0	**13.0***	7.5*	36.7	38.8	10.1	11.5	36.5	29.2	**65.8***	48.6*	72.1	63.8	48.8	41.5
... in past 6 months	**22.4***	16.6*	**10.4***	4.7*	32.5	36.2	8.2	7.4	31.6	26.5	**58.9***	31.1*	66.7	63.8	**37.8***	15.9*
... in past 3 months	**20.6***	14.9*	**9.5***	4.3*	29.9	33.8	7.6	5.9	29.2	24.7	**51.9***	28.8*	58.9	56.5	32.8	15.9
... in past month	**17.8***	9.7*	**8.1***	2.5*	26.5	24.3	**6.7***	3.3*	**25.3***	16.6*	**44.9***	19.8*	51.8	35.4	26.2	12.4
... in past week	**12.9***	5.8*	**5.9***	1.1*	19.2	17.1	**4.7***	1.4*	**18.6***	11.6*	**31.9***	9.9*	38.0	20.8	**15.5***	4.8*
... at home	**14.7***	9.0*	**6.4***	2.4*	22.3	22.8	5.3	3.4	21.6	16.9	**33.3***	13.0*	43.6	36.8	5.5	1.9
... at work	11.1	8.4	4.9	3.7	19.8	24.5	3.6	5.0	19.2	16.8	**8.8***	2.0*	11.4	6.3	1.9	0.0
... at school	7.2	10.9	2.8	2.6	6.6	8.5	1.9*	**5.9***	6.9	6.9	45.5	42.8	48.3	49.9	38.1	39.5
... at other locations	7.3	5.3	**4.4***	1.8*	8.8	12.8	2.8	3.3	9.4	9.0	**23.5***	4.2*	**24.0***	5.5*	**22.1***	3.7*

Nearly twice as many African Americans as whites stated that they planned to purchase a home computer in the next 6 months. African Americans were also slightly more interested in purchasing a set-top box for Internet television access.

The racial gap in Web use was proportionally larger the more recently the respondent stated that he or she had last used the Web. Proportionally, more than twice as many whites as African Americans had used the Web in the past week. As of January 1997, we estimate that 5.2 million ($\pm$1.2 million) African Americans and 40.8 million whites ($\pm$2.1 million) have ever used the Web, and that 1.4 million ($\pm$0.5 million) African Americans and 20.3 million ($\pm$1.6 million) whites used the Web in the past week.

Whites and African Americans also differed in terms of where they had ever used the Web. Whites were significantly more likely to have ever used the Web at home, whereas African Americans were slightly more likely to have ever used the Web at school.

Possible Causes

Because students behave quite differently from the rest of the respondents with respect to computer access and Internet use, we treat them separately later.

We used the national median household income of $40,000 to divide respondents. For household incomes under $40,000, whites were proportionally twice as likely as African Americans to own a home computer and slightly more likely to have computer access at work (Table 1, columns 2 and 3).

However, for household incomes of $40,000 or more, a slightly greater proportion of African Americans owned a home computer, and a significantly greater proportion had computer access at work.

We adjusted race differences in home computer ownership for income and found, as one would expect, that increasing levels of income corresponded to an increased likelihood of owning a home computer, regardless of race. In contrast, adjusting for income did not eliminate the race differences with respect to computer access at work. African Americans were more likely than whites to have access to a computer at work after taking income into account.

What accounts for this result? African Americans with incomes of $40,000 or more in our sample were more likely to have completed college, were younger, and were also more likely to be working in computer-related occupations than whites. These factors led to greater computer access at work.

At lower incomes, the race gap in Web use was proportionally larger the more recently the respondent stated that he or she had last used the Web. Whites were almost six times more likely than their African American counterparts to have used the Web in the past week and also significantly more likely to have used the Web at home and in other locations. Notably, as indicated above, race differences in Web use vanish at household incomes of $40,000 and higher.

Regardless of educational level, whites were significantly more likely to own a home computer than were African Americans and to have used the Web recently (Table 1, columns 4 and 5). These differences persisted even after statistically adjusting for education. Thus, although income explains race differences in home computer ownership and Web use, education does not: Whites are still more likely to own a home computer than are African Americans and to have used the Web recently, despite controlling for differences in education.

However, greater education corresponded to an increased likelihood of work computer access, regardless of race.

Thus, race matters to the extent that societal biases have either (i) required African Americans to obtain higher levels of education in order to achieve the same income as whites, or (ii) resulted in older African Americans not being able to achieve high incomes.

Students Are Special: Race Almost Always Matters

Higher education translates into an increased likelihood of Web use. Students were more likely than any other income or educational group to have used the Web (Table 1, column 6). Students exhibited the highest levels of Web use because, even without home computer ownership or access at work, they presumably had access at school.

The most dramatic difference between whites' and African Americans' home computer ownership was among current students (including both high school and college students). Whereas 73% of white students owned a home computer, only 32% of African American students owned one. This difference persisted when we statistically adjusted for students' reported household income. Thus, in the case of students, household income does not explain race differences in home computer ownership. This is the most disturbing instance yet of when race matters in Internet access.

Our analysis also revealed (Table 1, column 6) that white students were significantly more likely than African American students to have used the Web, especially in the past week. However, there were no differences in use when students had a computer at home.

White students without a computer in the home (Table 1, column 8), were more than twice as likely as similar African American students to have used the Web in the past 6 months and more than three times as likely to have used the Web in the past week. Thus, white students lacking a home computer, but not African American students, appear to be accessing the Internet from locations such as homes of friends and relatives, libraries, and community centers.

Policy Points

Five million African Americans have used the Web in the United States as of January 1997, considerably more than the popular press estimate of 1 million. This means that African Americans are already online in impressive numbers and that continued efforts to develop online content targeted to African Americans, commercial or otherwise, are likely to be met with success.

Overall, students enjoy the highest levels of Web use. However, white students were proportionally more likely than African Americans to own a home computer, and this disquieting race difference seems to result from factors other than income.

Also, white students who lacked a home computer were more likely to use the Web at places other than home, work, or school than were African Americans. Thus, it is important to create access points for African Americans in libraries, community centers, and other nontraditional places where individuals may access the Internet and to encourage use at these locations.

Overall, increasing levels of education are needed to promote computer access and Web use. Education explains race differences in work computer access, although our findings for African Americans with household incomes above the national median suggest the presence of a powerful bias that could restrict Internet use to a narrow segment of African Americans.

The policy implication is obvious: To ensure the participation of all Americans in the information revolution, it is critical to improve educational opportunities for African Americans.

Finally, access translates into usage. Whites were more likely than African Americans to have used the Web because they were more likely to have access, whereas African Americans in our survey were more likely to want access. This may explain in part the recent commercial success of computers priced below $1000. It follows that programs that encourage home computer ownership and the adoption of inexpensive devices that enable Internet access through the television should be aggressively pursued.

The consequences to U.S. society of a persistent racial divide on the Internet may be severe. If a significant segment of our society is denied equal access to the Internet, U.S. firms will lack the technological skills needed to remain competitive. Employment opportunities and income differences among whites and African Americans may be exacerbated, with further negative consequences to the nation's cities. As Liebling observed regarding the freedom of the press(9), the Internet may provide equal opportunity and democratic communication, but only for those with access.

REFERENCES AND NOTES

1. W. J. Clinton, *State of the Union Address*. Given at the United States Capitol, 4 February 1997 [www.whitehouse.gov/WH/SOU97/].
2. Network Wizards, "Internet Domain Survey," January 1998 [www.nw.com/zone/WWW/report.html].
3. D. L. Hoffman, W. Kalsbeek, T. P. Novak, *Comm. ACM* **39**, 36 (1996).
4. J. Katz and P. Aspden, "Motivations for and Barriers to Internet Usage: Results of a National Public Opinion Survey," Paper presented at the 24th Annual Telecommunications Policy Research Conference, Solomons, MD, 6 October 1996.
5. J. Keller, in *Public Access to the Internet*, B. Kahin and J. Keller, Eds. (MIT Press, Cambridge, MA, 1996), pp. 34–45; T. P. Novak, D. L. Hoffman, A. Venkatesh, paper presented at the Aspen Institute forum on Diversity and the Media, Queenstown, MD, 5 November 1997; P. Burgess, "Study Explores 'Digital Divide'," *Rocky Mountain News*, 11 March 1997, p. F31A.
6. Nielsen Media Research, "The Spring 1997 CommerceNet/Nielsen Media Internet Demographic Survey," Full Report, Volume I of II (1997).
7. The IDS is based on an unrestricted, random-digit, dial sampling frame and used a computer-assisted telephone interviewing system to obtain 5813 respondents. Weighted, these respondents represent and allow projection to the total population of 199.9 million individuals in the United States aged 16 and over.
8. All significance tests were obtained with Research Triangle Institute's SUDAAN software and incorporate sampling weights provided by Nielsen Media Research (6).
9. A. J. Liebling, *The New Yorker* **36**, 105 (14 May 1960).

Internet Self-Efficacy and the Psychology of the Digital Divide

MATTHEW S. EASTIN
ROBERT LAROSE

Introduction

The digital divide that separates predominantly white, middle-class Internet users from predominantly minority, lower-income non-users has attracted the attention of both policy makers (NTIA, 1999) and social scientists (Hoffman & Novak, 1998), is undoubtedly one of the most important social equity issues facing the information society (Benton Foundation, 1999; Hoffman, Novak, & Slosser, 2000), and is international in scope (Van Dijk & Hacker, 2000). The digital divide has been conceptualized primarily in terms of patterns of race and class discrimination that are reflected in unequal access to computers and the Internet. While the importance of class and ethnicity cannot be denied, all novice Internet users face psychological as well as socio-economic and racial barriers. New Internet users are less comfortable using the Internet, are less satisfied with their Internet skills and are more likely to encounter stress-inducing problem situations (GVU, 1999, q11, q101, q102). Uncertainty about how to get started and the perception that computers are too complicated are nearly as important as cost and lack of access as barriers to getting started on the Internet (Katz & Aspden, 1996).

Complexity, knowledge barriers to initial Internet adoption, and comfort and satisfaction issues faced by new users may be construed as self-efficacy deficits. Self-efficacy is the belief "in one's capabilities to organize and execute the courses of action required to produce given attainments" (Bandura, 1997, p. 3). People who have little confidence in their ability to use the Internet, who are dissatisfied with their Internet skills or who are uncomfortable using the Internet may be said to have weak self-efficacy beliefs. Those with low self-efficacy should be less likely to perform related behaviors in the future (Bandura, 1982), in this case, adopt and use the Internet, than those with high degrees of self-efficacy.

Within social cognitive theory (Bandura, 1982; 1997) self-efficacy is a form of self-evaluation that influences decisions about what behaviors to undertake, the amount of effort and persistence put forth when faced with obstacles, and finally, the mastery of the behavior. Self-efficacy is not a measure of skill; rather, it reflects what individuals believe they can do with the skills they possess. For example, in discussing computer self-efficacy, Compeau and Higgins (1995) distinguished between component skills such as formatting disks and booting up the computer and behaviors individuals can accomplish with such skills, such as using software to analyze data. Thus, Internet self-efficacy focuses on what a person believes he or she can accomplish online now or in the future. It does not refer to a person's skill at performing specific Internet-related tasks, such as writing HTML, using a browser, or transferring files, for example. Instead, it assesses a person's judgment of his or her ability to apply Internet skills in a more encompassing mode, such as finding information or troubleshooting search problems.

The relationship between self-efficacy and personal computer use is perhaps intuitively obvious. Personal computers represent a complex and somewhat troublesome technology, requiring considerable skill and extensive training to operate successfully. Self-efficacy is essential to overcome the fear many novice users experience. Compeau and Higgins (1995) empirically verified the relationship between computer self-efficacy and computer use. Staples, Hulland, and Higgins (1998) found that those with high levels of self-efficacy in remote computing situations were more productive and satisfied, and better able to cope when working remotely.

The Internet requires development of a further set of skills that, to the novice user, at least, may be daunting. These include establishing and maintaining a stable Internet connection, learning how to navigate on the Internet, and searching it for relevant information. Internet self-efficacy may be distinguished from computer self-efficacy as the belief that one can successfully perform a distinct set of behaviors required to establish, maintain and utilize effectively the Internet over and above basic personal computer skills.

Social cognitive theory offers an alternative to socio-economic explanations of the Digital Divide (e.g., Hoffman, et al., 2000; NTIA, 1999); the latter are less convincing now that personal computer prices have fallen to the levels of VCRs and Internet services to the level of cable television subscriptions, expenditures that over half of US households manage. "Don't want it" rivals cost as a factor explaining non-use of the Internet in minority equipped with computers (NTIA, 1999), suggesting that users must experience the benefits of the Internet for themselves to close the Digital Divide. This realization, the formation of positive outcome expectations in social cognitive terms, occurs only if Internet use persists long enough for the benefits to become apparent. For that to happen, self-efficacy beliefs must first be established.

Early research on Internet self-efficacy focused on the performance of specific tasks such as entering World-Wide Web addresses, creating folders and bookmarks, mailing pages, using File Transfer Protocol (FTP) and telnet, constructing a hypertext index, and moving bookmarks (Nahl, 1996, 1997). Ren (1999) reported a measure of self-efficacy specific to searching for government information sources. Results were consistent with previous self-efficacy literature, with self-efficacy perceptions positively related to task performance (Nahl, 1996, 1997) and the amount of use (Ren, 1999).

The prior studies did not yield a measure of self-efficacy suitable for studying overall Internet usage, and reported no information about reliability and validity. In Nahl (1997), scale items confounded distinct behaviors; a single item asked about e-mail, hypertext mark-up language (HTML) scripting, telnet, and file transfer protocol. Nahl's measure referred to specific subsidiary tasks (e.g., creating bookmarks) instead of overall attainments (e.g., obtaining useful information) and thus did not properly reflect the constructive definition of self-efficacy. Ren (1999) operationalized self-efficacy in a manner more consistent with its conceptual definition (e.g., search the Internet by yourself), but a single item measure was employed so its reliability could not be determined. Ren's measure applied to a specific behavioral domain (i.e., seeking government information) rather than overall Internet use, limiting its future application.

In an effort to further understand psychological aspects of the Digital Divide, the present study builds on past research to develop a new measure of Internet self-efficacy. It assesses reliability and analyzes the construct validity of Internet self-efficacy by comparing it to measures of other constructs thought to be positively related, negative related or unrelated on theoretical grounds (Anastasi, 1988).

▪▪▪ Hypotheses

Prior experience is an antecedent of self-efficacy (Lewis, 1985). For example, math skills are needed in computer programming and math skills and number of math courses taken play an important role in an individual's judgments about his or her programming ability (Bandura, 1977; Oliver & Shapiro 1993). Prior experience with the Internet hones related skills and should be positively related to Internet self-efficacy.

H1: Internet self-efficacy will be positively correlated with prior Internet experience.

Self-efficacy judgments are in turn related to outcome expectations. Outcome expectations are estimates that a behavior will produce particular outcomes (Oliver & Shapiro, 1993) but depend upon how well one thinks her or she can perform the behavior (Bandura, 1977). Oliver and Shapiro (1993) found that the stronger a person's self-efficacy beliefs, the more likely he or she was to try to achieve the desired outcome. In the present context this means that Internet self-efficacy should be positively related to the expectation of positive outcomes of Internet use, such as meeting new people on the Internet.

Compeau & Higgins (1995) found that computer self-efficacy influenced expectations about the future outcomes of computer use such as job performance and personal accomplishment. In terms of the Internet, social outcomes would derive from social encounters on-line. Personal outcomes are what we can achieve personally through using the Internet, such as being entertained or obtaining information. Internet self-efficacy should be positively related to positive outcome expectations.

H2: Internet self-efficacy will be positively related to expected positive outcomes of Internet use.

Past research on computer self-efficacy indicated a significant positive relationship between computer efficacy and computer usage (Burkhart & Brass, 1990; Compeau & Higgins, 1995; Compeau & Higgins, 1999; Oliver & Shapiro, 1993). Internet use and Internet self-efficacy should also be directly related since we are more likely to attempt and persist in behaviors that we feel capable of performing.

H3: Internet self-efficacy will be positively related to Internet use.

The amount of stress a person feels performing a task is negatively related to self-efficacy (Bandura, 1977). Individuals experienced an increase in stress when attempting to perform behaviors they didn't feel confident performing (Stumpf, Brief, & Hartman, 1989). As stress increased, efficacy beliefs decreased due to self-doubt and emotional arousal when performing the behavior (Oliver & Shapiro, 1993). Performing a task successfully increased self-efficacy and decreased stress; conversely, failure or difficulty experienced in performing a task decreased self-efficacy and increased stress (Hancock, 1990).

Stress encountered while using the Internet can be understood in terms of the number of stressors encountered while online. Having trouble getting on the Internet or having the computer freeze up are common examples. When such problems are encountered they lower expectations about successful interactions with the Internet in the future. As the number of stressors encountered online increase, perceptions of success decrease and self-efficacy along with it.

H4: Internet stress will be negatively correlated with Internet self-efficacy.

Self-efficacy is one type of self-monitoring mechanism, but there are others. Self-disparagement occurs when an individual judges his or her performances as inferior to other performances. Self-disparaging people misrepresent their performance attainments or distort their recollection of past events as negative experiences (Bandura, 1977; Bandura, 1997). Self-disparaging people are depression-prone and typically dwell on their failures as evidence of their personal deficiencies while attributing their successes to external factors. In contrast, individuals with a high sense of efficacy accept success as an indication of their ability and attribute failure to external causes. Based on this relationship:

H5: Self-efficacy will be negatively related to self-disparagement.

The hypothesized relationships also fit into a causally ordered theoretical framework. Self-efficacy beliefs are continually re-formed based on experience. Internet users therefore continually modify their Internet self-efficacy beliefs based on their experiences online. Using Internet self-efficacy as an antecedent to use (Bandura, 1997), the following relationships between Internet self-efficacy, Internet use, social, informational, and entertainment outcomes, and online stressors is proposed. While increased levels of self-efficacy increase Internet use, both self-efficacy and Internet use increase perceived social, informational, and entertainment outcome expectancies. Furthermore, while increased levels of self-efficacy will decrease perceptions of Internet stress, perceptions of stress will increase feeling of self-disparagement, and thus, decrease use.

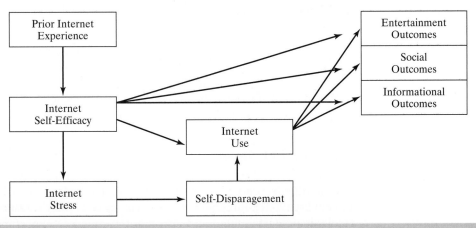

▪▪▪▪▪▪▪▪▪▪▪▪ **FIGURE 1** Initial Path Model

Finally, to complete the construct validity argument, Internet self-efficacy should be unrelated to theoretically distinct concepts. It is conceptually important to distinguish self-efficacy from general measures of psychological well-being since a competing hypothesis would be that self-efficacy merely reflects a generally positive outlook on life, feeling good about oneself and one's social environment. Therefore, Internet self-efficacy should not be related to such general indicators of psychological well being such as depression, loneliness, perceived social support and general life stress.

H6: Internet self-efficacy will be unrelated to depression, loneliness, perceived social support and life stress.

▪▪▪ Methods

Participants

The participants were 171 undergraduate students from an introductory communication class at a large Midwestern university. A convenience sample was deemed appropriate for the purposes of scale construction and validation since college students are a population with wide variation in Internet experience, including both heavy Internet users and many novice users. Of those who participated in the survey, 35 percent were freshman, 22 percent were sophomores, 18 percent were juniors, and 25 percent were seniors. Of these, 60 percent were male, 40 percent were female, and the mean age was 21 years old.

Questionnaires were administered in class at two separate times to maximize participation in the survey. Respondents picked up the questionnaire on the first day of class each week and returned it the second day of class that same week. Respondents were offered extra credit for participating in the study. An alternative form of extra credit was provided for those who chose not to participate.

Self-Efficacy Scale Development

Items for the Internet self-efficacy scale were suggested by Compeau and Higgins (1995), the GVU 10th survey (GVU, 1999), and Nahl (1996). Items from these scales were adapted to the conceptual definition of Internet self-efficacy by phrasing them as individuals' judgments of their ability to use the Internet to produce overall attainments, as opposed to accomplishing specific sub-tasks. An eight-item measure of Internet self-efficacy was developed. A Likert-type agree-disagree scale was used to assess the participants' confidence that they could use the Internet in each of the ways specified, where 7 corresponded to "strongly agree" and 1 to "strongly disagree." Confirmatory Factor Analysis (CFA) was conducted on the eight items to assess internal consistency and factor loadings using program PACKAGE (Hunter & Gerbing, 1982).

Substantial factor loadings and a standardized Cronbach alpha of .93 were obtained (Table 1), indicating internal consistency. Each of the scale items, factor loadings, means, and standard deviations can be found in Table 1.

Operational Measures

First, *Previous Internet Experience* was measured with one item ranging from less than two months (scored 1) to over 24 months (scored 5). Borrowing from Charney & Greenberg (2001), three *outcome expectancy constructs* measuring social and personal (including entertainment and information) outcome expectancies were created. The five-item Social Outcome ($\alpha = .86$) scale assessed the perceived likelihood of developing

TABLE 1 Factor Loadings of the Internet Self-Efficacy Scale

Scale Item	Factor Loadings	Mean(SD)
I feel confident . . .		
1 . . . understanding terms/words relating to Internet hardware.	.86	5.05(1.83)
2 . . . understanding terms/words relating to Internet software.	.91	4.94(1.78)
3 . . . describing functions of Internet hardware.	.93	4.63(1.85)
4 . . . trouble shooting Internet problems.	.85	4.14(1.86)
5 . . . explaining why a task will not run on the Internet.	.81	3.87(1.72)
6 . . . using the Internet to gather data.	.65	5.47(1.46)
7 . . . confident learning advanced skills within a specific Internet program.	.79	4.62(1.83)
8 . . . turning to an on-line discussion group when help is needed.	.60	3.39(1.89)
Standardized Alpha = .93		

relationships over the Internet.[1] A four-item Personal Entertainment Outcome ($\alpha = .87$) scale measured the likelihood finding entertainment on the Internet.[2] The six-item Personal Information Outcome ($\alpha = .83$) measure assessed the likelihood of finding immediate information on the Internet.[3] For each of these measures, the likelihood (rated as very likely (7) to very unlikely (1)) of an expected outcome was multiplied by the corresponding evaluation of that outcome (rated very good (+3) to very bad (–3)), following the expectancy-value formulation recommended by Ajzen and Fishbein (1980).

Internet Stress was a four-item measure ($\alpha = .61$) developed for this study from previous work evaluating Internet frustrations (Charney & Greenberg, 2001) and problems encountered on the Internet (GVU, 1999). Respondents were asked to rate their likelihood of experiencing each type of stressful Internet behavior (e.g., trouble getting on the Internet)[4] on a seven-point scale that ranged from very likely (7) to very unlikely (1). *Self-disparagement* consisted of three Likert-type items rated from strongly agree (7) to strongly disagree (1) ($\alpha = .71$).[5] This measure assessed self-perceptions of Internet-related performance.

Internet Use was measured with four items. Two items, ranging from no use (1) to more than five hours of use (5) assessed Internet use on a typical weekend and weekday, respectively. One item, scored from 0 to 7, assessed the number of days the respondent went online during a typical week; and one item ranging from no hours (1) to over 20 hours (7) assessed time spent surfing during a typical week.

Life Stresses were measured with 49 items drawn from the Kanner, Coyne, Schafer, and Lazarus (1981) Hassles Scale ($\alpha = .93$). Subjects reported on the frequency with which they had encountered the daily life stresses (e.g., car maintenance, crime) in the

---

[1]Find companionship, meet new friends, maintain relationships, get in touch with people I know, and meet someone in person whom I met on the Internet.
[2]Feel entertained; Find a way to pass time; Relieve boredom; Have fun.
[3]Find current information like time, weather, stock prices and sports scores; Get information about products and services; Get immediate knowledge of big news events; Get information I can trust; Find information that is new to me; Encounter controversial information; Find information to complete a course assignment.
[4]The other items were have trouble finding what I am looking for, have my computer freeze up, and get blocked by password protection
[5]I feel my computer skills are inadequate; The things I can do on the Internet really don't amount to much; I can never accomplish what I want on the Internet.

previous month, on a four-point scale (None, Somewhat severe, Moderately severe, Extremely severe). Depression was measured with the 20-item Center for Epidemiological Studies Depression (CES-D) scale (Radloff, 1977) (α = .91). The 20-item UCLA Loneliness Scale (Russell, Peplau, & Cutrona, 1980) was used to assess general *loneliness* (α = .90). Finally sixteen (out of 40) representative items from the Interpersonal Support Evaluation List[6] (Cohen, et al., 1985, α = .81) were used as a measure of *social support*.

Analyses

Zero order correlations were used to test each of the hypothesized relationships. LISREL 8.3 was used to test the proposed path model (Jöreskog & Sörbom, 2000).

▬▬ Results

A matrix of Pearson product-moment correlation coefficients is shown in Table 2. Hypothesis 1 was supported. Internet self-efficacy had a significant relationship to prior Internet experience (r = .36, p < .01). Social outcome expectations (r = .36, p < .01), personal information outcome expectations (r = .31, p < .01), and personal entertainment outcome expectations (r = .32, p < .01) were also found to be significantly related to Internet self-efficacy, supporting Hypothesis 2. Internet self-efficacy was also significantly related to Internet use (r = .63, p < .01). Both Internet stress (r = −.25, p < .01) and self-disparagement (r = −.61, p < .01) exhibited a significant negative relationship to Internet self-efficacy, supporting Hypotheses 4 and 5, respectively. In summary, Internet stress and self-disparagement were negatively related to efficacy beliefs, while prior Internet experience, outcome expectancies and Internet use were significantly and positively correlated to Internet self-efficacy judgments.

Finally, Hypothesis 6 was supported. Life hassles (r = −.06, p = .381), depression (r = −.12, p = .122), loneliness (r = −.06, p = .418) and perceived social support (r = .09, p = .240) were not related to Internet self-efficacy (Table 2).

The initial model which specified the development of self-efficacy through use and outcome expectations was not consistent with the data ($\chi^2(17)$ = 78.94, p < .001). A revised model shown in Figure 2 was found to be consistent with the data ($\chi^2(7)$ = 13.27, p > .05). In it, prior experience was related to Internet self-efficacy (β = .36) which in turn was related to use (β = .54), self disparagement (β = −.61) as well as social (β = .13) and informational (β = .18) outcome expectancies. Use was related to both social (β = .35) and informational (β = .21) outcome expectations and self-disparagement (β = −.15).

The predictive power of this model is indicated by the **R**^{2} statistics shown in Figure 2. From this model, 13 percent of the variance in Internet self-efficacy was explained. Further, 41 percent of the variance in Internet use was explained, while 20 percent and

---

[6]Scored 1 for True and 0 for false with items indicating a lack of social support reflected. The items were: There is at least one person I know whose advice I really trust; There is really no one who can give me objective feedback on how I'm handling my problems; There is someone whom I feel comfortable going to for advice about sexual problems; I feel that there is no one with whom I can share my most private worries and fears; No one I know would throw a birthday party for me; There are several different people with whom I enjoy spending time; Most people I know don't enjoy the same things that I do; I feel that I'm on the fringe in my circle of friends; If I were sick and needed someone to drive me to the doctor, I would have trouble finding someone; There is no one I could call on if I needed to borrow a car for a few hours; If I needed a quick emergency loan of $100, there is someone could get it from; If I needed some help in moving to a new home, I would have a hard time finding someone to help me; In general, people don't have much confidence in me; Most of my friends are more successful at making changes in their lives than I am; I think that my friends feel that I'm not very good at helping them solve problems; I am closer to my friends than most other people.

TABLE 2 Pearson Product-Moment Correlation Coefficients

	1	2	3	4	5	6	7	8	9	10	11	12	Mean	SD
1 Internet Self-Efficacy													36.11	11.76
2 Internet Experience	.36**												4.66	.67
3 Social Outcome Expectancy	.35**	.26**											13.02	24.84
4 Personal Information Outcome Expectancy	.31**	.25**	.15										58.19	41.49
5 Personal Entertainment Outcome Expectancy	.32**	.13	.40**	.55**									31.23	27.37
6 Internet Use	.63**	.22**	.43**	.32**	.46**								14.21	4.31
7 Internet Stress	-.25**	-.12	-.10**	-.10	-.09	-.18*							14.73	4.76
8 Self Disparagement	-.61**	-.33**	-.25**	-.24**	-.25**	-.48**	.33**						9.29	4.24
9 Life Stress	-.06	-.11	.01	.04	-.14	-.03	.29**	-.03					85.01	19.61
10 Depression	-.12	-.18*	.00	-.19	-.11	-.02	.23**	.00	.43**				35.71	9.79
11 Loneliness	-.06	-.15	.02	-.24**	-.22**	.03	.22**	.01	.45**	.63**			35.83	9.76
12 Social Support	.09	.15	-.14	.13	.28	-.04	-.20**	-.27**	-.36**	-.58**	-.64**		13.50	2.84

**p < .001 *p < .05

425

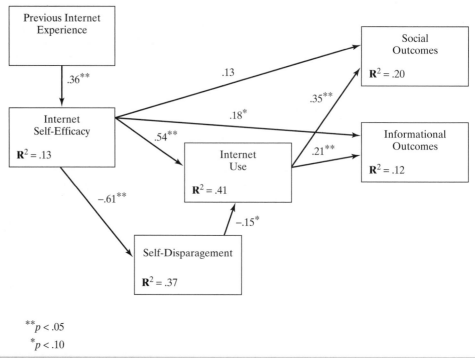

**p < .05
*p < .10

▮▮▮▮▮▮▮▮▮▮▮ FIGURE 2 Final Path Model

12 percent of the variance was explained in social and informational outcome expectancies, respectively. Thirty-seven percent of the variance in self-disparagement was explained.

▀▀▀ Discussion

Overall, there was consistent evidence of the construct validity of Internet self-efficacy. Internet self-efficacy was positively correlated to Internet usage, prior Internet experience, and outcome expectancies, as Social Cognitive theory suggests it should be, and negatively correlated with measures it should be inversely related to, such as Internet stress and self-disparagement. Internet self-efficacy was also unrelated to measures of general psychological well-being, including depression, loneliness, perceived social support and life stress, ruling out the competing hypothesis that self-efficacy merely reflects a generally positive outlook.

Prior Internet experience was the strongest predictor of Internet self-efficacy. Up to two years' experience may be required to achieve sufficient self-efficacy. Prior research showed that new users who had been on the Internet for two years or less encountered more stressful problems online and were also less satisfied with their Internet skills than veteran users (GVU, 1999). In the present research there was also a demarcation at the two-year point, Internet self-efficacy was much lower in the first two years than later ($t = -2.37, p < .027$).

The path model (see Figure 2) supported a theoretical model constructed from Bandura (1997). The model demonstrated that Internet use was directly affected by self-efficacy judgments. Usage and self-efficacy subsequently increased outcome expectations.

However, while self-efficacy was found to affect outcome expectations directly, the relationships were not as powerful as those found with usage. The specificity of the Internet self-efficacy measure could be at issue. The measure included only single items representing the achievement of social or informational outcomes on the Internet, such as using it to gather data or to obtain help from a discussion group. It appears that the ability to obtain these types of outcome expectancies through the Internet is something that gradually develops over time (Pew Research Center, 2000), so Internet self-efficacy specific to relationship formation and management may play a role in its attainment.

Likewise, there were no items in the self-efficacy measure referring to the use of the Internet for entertainment purposes. It also may be that the entertainment outcomes of the Internet are so easily attained that they do not require special skills, so that no mediation through self-efficacy is required. That said, the relationship between Internet self-efficacy and Internet outcome expectancies has provided researchers with new areas from which to begin validating and expanding this self-efficacy measure.

The expected relationship among self-efficacy, Internet stress, self-disparagement and Internet use was not observed. The revised model presented self-disparagement as an antecedent to Internet use. Given the low reliability obtained for Internet stress, researchers should continue to explore this relationship as presented in Figure 1.

For Future Research

Further research should explore self-efficacy measures specific to achieving particular types of outcomes through the use of the Internet. The importance of distinguishing general and task-specific self-efficacy has been discussed with respect to computer usage (Marakas, Yi & Johnson, 1998) and can be expected to be an important issue in Internet-related studies as well. Social cognitive theory also distinguishes coping self-efficacy, or beliefs in one's ability to deal with specific stress-inducing problems. In this case, these would be the various technical (e.g., inability to establish a connection) and socio-technical (e.g., receiving unwanted e-mail) difficulties that result from Internet use. The process of initially establishing Internet access, whether through one's own computer or a public access node, is also a distinct skill set that is beyond the scope of the Internet self-efficacy measure developed in the present study.

Further research should investigate the interplay among Internet self-efficacy, stress and on-line support. Social support should relieve stress (Cutrona & Russell, 1987). The amount of perceived and actual technical support available has been found to increase computer self-efficacy (Compeau & Higgins, 1995).

Social cognitive theory recognizes instances of reciprocal causation that cannot be assessed through one-time cross-sectional surveys. For example, perceived outcomes of behavior directly affect the future performance of behavior, so a reciprocal causation path from behavior to expected outcomes should be examined. Likewise, the successful performance of a behavior should have a direct reciprocal effect on self-efficacy perceptions. Longitudinal research would supply the time series data needed to test predictive validity and the reciprocal causality that should exist between Internet self-efficacy and Internet use.

Internet Self-Efficacy and Closing the Digital Divide

Our measure and conceptualization of Internet self-efficacy should help guide future efforts to close the digital divide. Social cognitive theory suggests four mechanisms that can be used to formulate and understand intervention strategies. The sources of self-efficacy that should be investigated include enactive mastery, vicarious experience, verbal persuasion and physiological responses (Bandura, 1997; Oliver & Shapiro, 1993).

Enactive mastery, gained by reflecting upon one's own successful past performances, is by far the most powerful source of self-efficacy. Enactive mastery of complex behaviors such as Internet use can be bolstered by steadily building upon the successful attainment of subskills that are relatively easy to master. However, infrequent trips to standalone computer labs or short-term immersion courses are unlikely to be effective.

Vicarious experience gained by observing others as they master the Internet can be both positive and negative. Vicarious experience is generally thought to be less effective than direct (enactive) experience with one important exception: the observation of failure on the part of similar others can have a particularly devastating effect on self-efficacy judgments. So, when testing intervention strategies aimed as closing the digital divide, research should pair novice users with Internet experienced peer tutors (including online); this could be an effective method to increase Internet self-efficacy judgments and subsequent use. The common practices of holding group computer labs in educational settings and using the "buddy system" to share computer resources can have a negative effect on self-efficacy in populations where Internet skills are generally low. Here, observing the failures of peers is likely to discourage (i.e., decrease self-efficacy judgments) those struggling with Internet use and may also negatively affect those who have achieved early success. Individualized instruction would thus be preferable for new Internet users. Failing that, labs could be redesigned with partitions or staggered seating to restrict information about the failures of peers. Novice Internet users can also be persuaded to have greater self-efficacy through verbal feedback about their performance, if delivered by competent and credible evaluators. Feedback about the capability of the novice user is highly effective. However, verbal feedback must be constructive in order to increase self-efficacy. Telling new Internet users that they can succeed only through hard work or that they need to work harder is likely to lower self-efficacy in the long run since that conveys the message that the user must have been deficient to begin with to require such hard work to succeed.

Our alternative formulation of the digital divide problem is by no means intended to minimize the role played by race and class discrimination in creating unequal access to the Internet. Indeed, there are likely to be race and class differences in Internet self-efficacy as well. Research that examines the suggested intervention strategies within specific ethnic and socioeconomic groups is needed. We hope that our self-efficacy conceptualization will alert reformers to the possibility that although providing computers and network connections eliminates the physical barriers to access, psychological barriers may still remain.

However, by vigorously publicizing the Digital Divide as an important social problem while simultaneously defining it in terms of race and class, there is the risk that deficient computer skills will come to be viewed as stereotypical of the groups that are presently below the divide. Social cognitive theory warns us that when this happens the stereotyped group tends to adopt the stereotype as a standard for their own self-comparisons (Bandura, 1997), lowering their self-efficacy and imposing a further psychological barrier to successful Internet use. Thus, as researchers attempt to uncover the underlying barriers influencing the divide, it might be more productive to conceptualize the divide in terms of the barriers shared by all novice users of the Internet.

Limitations

The validity of a construct cannot be established by a single study. Without longitudinal data it is hard to distinguish cause and effect ordering (Pedhazur, 1982) and the reciprocal causation mechanisms specified by social cognitive theory could not be examined. The convenience sample used restricts the generalizability of the results. Prior Internet experience was a single item measure and the Internet stress measure had a marginal level of internal consistency, calling into question the reliability of those results. Finally, only a single measure of Internet self-efficacy was employed. Construct validation procedures following the multi-trait multi-method approach (Anastasi, 1988) require the development and comparative analysis of multiple measurement methods using alternative approaches to self-efficacy measurement (Lee & Bobko, 1994).

Conclusion

The present study represents a further step in understanding the role that Internet self-efficacy plays in the use of the Internet. Finally, research suggested on the development of self-efficacy judgments (e.g., enactive mastery, vicarious experience, verbal persuasion and physiological responses) would help to further validate the Internet self-efficacy scale presented in this study as well as increase our overall understanding of Internet use.

REFERENCES

Ajzen, I., & Fishbein, M. (1980). *Understanding attitudes and predicting social behavior*. Englewood Cliffs, NJ: Prentice-Hall.

Anastasi, A. (1988). *Psychological testing*. New York, New York: Macmillan Publishing Company.

Bandura, A. (1977). Self-efficacy:Toward a unifying theory of behavioral change. *Psychological Review, 84*, 191–215.

Bandura, A. (1997). *Self-efficacy: The exercise of control*. New York: W.H. Freeman.

Bandura, A. (1982). Self-efficacy mechanisms in human agency. *American Psychologist, 37*, 122–147.

Benton Foundation (1999). Digital Divide Network. [Online] Available: http://www.digitaldividenetwork.org/.

Burkhart, M., & Brass, D. (1990). Changing patterns of patterns changing:The effects of a change in technology on social network structure and power. *Administrative Science Quarterly, 35*, 104–127.

Charney, T. & Greenberg, B. S. (2001). Uses and gratification of the Internet Communication, technology and science. In C. Lin & D. Atkin (Eds.), *Communication technology and society: Audience adoption and uses of the new media*. Creskkill, NJ: Hampton Press. 379–407.

Cohen, S., Mermelstein, R., Kamarck T., & Hoberman, H. (1985). Measuring the functional components of social support. In I. G. Sarason & B. R. Sarason (Eds.), *Social support: Theory, research and applications* (pp. 73–94). The Hague, Holland: Martines Niijhoff.

Compeau, D., & Higgins, C. (1995). Computer self-efficacy: Development of a measure and initial test. *MIS Quarterly, 19*, 189–211.

Compeau, D., & Higgins, C. (1999). Social Cognitive Theory and individual reactions to computing technology: A longitudinal study. *MIS Quarterly, 23*, 145–158.

Cutrona, C. E., & Russell, D. W. (1987) The provisions of social support and adaptations to stress. *Advances in Personal Relationships, 1*, 37–67.

GVU (Graphic, Visualization and Usability Center). (1999) *GVU's Tenth Annual WWW User's Survey*, Atlanta, GA: Georgia Institute of Technology. [Online] http://www.cc.gatech.edu/gvu/user_surveys/.

Hancock, V. (1990). Overcoming technophobia. *Educational Leadership, 47*, 81–85.

Hoffman, D. L., & Novak, T. P. (1998). Bridging the racial divide on the Internet. *Science*, April 17: 390–391.

Hoffman, D. L., Novak, T. P., & Schlosser, A. E. (2000). The evolution of the digital divide: How gaps in Internet access may impact electronic commerce. *Journal of Computer Mediated Communication* [Online] *5* (3). Available: http://www.ascusc.org/jcmc/vol5/issue3/hoffman.html.

Hunter, J. E., & Gerbing, D. W. (1982). Machiavellian beliefs and personality: Construct invalidity of the Machavellianism dimension. *Journal of Personality and Social Psychology, 43*, 1293–1305.

Jöreskog, K., & Sörbom, D. (2000). *LISREL 8.30*. Scientific Software International Inc.

Kanner, A. D., Coyne, J. C., Schaefer, C., & Lazarus, R. S. (1981). Comparisons of two modes of stress measurement: Daily hassles and uplifts versus major life events. *Journal of Behavioral Medicine, 4*, 1–39.

Katz, J. E., & Aspeden, P. (1996, October). *Motivations for and barriers to Internet usage: Results of a national public opinion survey*. Paper presented to the 24th Annual Telecommunications Policy Research Conference, Solomons, MD.

Katz, J. E., & Aspden, P. (1997). A nation of strangers? *Communications of the ACM, 40* (12), 81–86.

Lee, C., & Bobko, P. (1994). Self-efficacy beliefs: Comparison of 5 measures. *Journal of Applied Psychology, 79*, 364–369.

Lewis, C. (1985). An exploratory study of the influences of self-efficacy on the personal computer learner. *Dissertation Abstracts International, 46*. Cited in Oliver, T. A., & Shapiro, F. (1993). Self-efficacy and computers. *Journal of Computer-Based Interactions, 20*, 81–85.

Nahl, D. (1996). Affective monitoring of Internet learners: Perceived self-efficacy and success. *Journal of American Society for Information Sciences, 33*, 100–109.

Nahl, D. (1997). User-centered assessment of two Web browsers: Errors, perceived self-efficacy, and success. *Journal of American Society for Information Sciences, 34*, 89–97.

National Telecommunications and Information Administration (NTIA). (1999). *Falling through the Net: Defining the digital divide.* [Online] http://www.ntia.doc.gov/ntiahome/fttn99/contents.html

Nielsen NetRatings. (1999). Nielsen NetRatings. [Online] http://www.nielsennetratings.com/.

Oliver, T. A., & Shapiro, F. (1993). Self-efficacy and computers. *Journal of Computer-Based Interactions, 20*, 81–85.

Pedhazur, E. (1982). *Multiple regression in behavioral research.* Fort Worth: Harcourt Brace College Publishers.

Pew Research Center. (2000). *Tracking online life: How women use the Internet to cultivate relationships with family and friends.* Retrieved May 10, 2000 from the World Wide Web: http://www.pewinternet.org/reports/toc.asp?Report=11.

Radloff, L. (1977). The CES-D Scale: A self-report depression scale for research in the general population. *Applied Psychological Measurement, 1*, 385–401.

Ren, W. (1999). Self-efficacy and the search for government information. *Reference & User Service Quarterly, 38*, 283–291.

Russell, D., Peplau, L., & Cutrona, C. (1980). The revised UCLA Loneliness Scale: Concurrent and discriminant validity evidence. *Journal of Personality and Social Psychology, 39*, 472–480.

Staples, D. S., Hulland, J. S., & Higgins, C. A. (1998). A self-efficacy theory explanation for the management of remote workers in virtual organizations. *Journal of Computer-Mediated Communication* [Online], *3* (4). Available: http://www.ascusc.org/jcmc/vol3/issue4/staples.html.

Stumpf, S. A., Brief, A. P., & Hartman, K. (1989). Self-efficacy expectations and coping with career-related events. *Journal of Vocational Behavior, 31*, 91–108.

Van Dijk, J., and Hacker, K. (2000, June). *The digital divide as a complex and dynamic phenomenon.* Paper presented at the 50th Annual Conference of the International Communication Association, Acapulco, Mexico, 1–5 June.

Wellman, B., & Gulia, M. (1999). Virtual communities as communities: Net surfers don't ride alone. In Smith, M. A. & Kollock, P. (Eds.), *Communities in Cyberspace* (pp. 167–194). New York: Routledge.

Using E-Mail for Personal Relationships: The Difference Gender Makes

BONKA BONEVA
ROBERT KRAUT
DAVID FROHLICH

Interpersonal communication remains the dominant use of the Internet, even though the Internet supports a rich array of other services, from information retrieval, to electronic commerce and entertainment (Kraut, Mukhopadhyay, Szczypula, Kiesler, & Scherlis, 1999; Stafford, Kline, & Dimmick, 1999). According to a survey conducted by the Pew Internet and American Life Project (2000b), 78% of those who went online in a typical day in 2000 sent e-mail—more than double the number of those who used the Internet for any other single activity. Between 1995 and 1998, there was an almost 50% growth in the use of e-mail for personal relationships, whereas there was virtually no growth in the work-related use of e-mail (Cummings & Kraut, 2000). The Internet has been largely praised as a tool that allows people from around the world to communicate. However, very few studies have examined how already existing personal relationships are maintained online (e.g., Cummings, Butler, & Kraut, 2001; Pew Internet Report, 2000; Stafford, Kline, & Dimmick, 1999).

The current article examines how women and men use the Internet, and e-mail in particular, to sustain their personal relationships. We illustrate how the use of new technologies perpetuates traditional gender roles in communication behavior. Previous research suggests that women are more likely than men to define themselves through their social relations and to act as the communication hub between the household and kin and friends. Women, we argue, have now appropriated the Internet for these purposes. Further, we explore the specific ways in which the new communication technologies influence their social networks.

431

Personal relationships require significant investments in energy and time if they are to be maintained (Duck, 1988; Canary & Stafford, 1994; Stafford & Canary, 1991). Whatever initial factors brought two people together—blood ties, common interests, beauty, or charm—lose power with time (Berg & Clark, 1986). They must be supplemented with behavioral exchanges, which influence whether the relationship will be valued and retained, or, devalued and dropped. The Internet provides a new mechanism for contact and a new tool to enact personal relationships, and does so in a way that saves both time and money.

However, women and men tend to value relationships differently and to have different styles in sustaining them (e.g., Deaux & Major, 1987; Duck & Wright, 1993; Eagle & Steffen, 1984; Spence & Buckner, 1995). As a result, one would expect to see differences in the way they use the Internet for interpersonal communication. Some indications of such differences have started to appear in the research literature (e.g., Kraut et al., 1998; Pew Internet & American Life Project, 2000a). The present article examines in more detail potential gender differences in using the Internet for personal relationships. In order to provide a context for examining gender-specific patterns of using the Internet to communicate with family and friends, we first review some of the previously found gender differences in relating to others.

▮▮▮ Gender Differences in Relating to Others

Many authors have identified differences in the way men and women relate to others and manage their relationships. Spence and Helmreich (1978) proposed the term *expressiveness* to indicate a set of attitudes and behaviors associated with emotional intimacy and sharing in personal relationships, and the term *instrumentality* to indicate a more agentic style of relationship oriented around common activities. Even though women and men vary widely from one person to another on these styles, there is evidence that women are, on average, more relationally oriented and less agentic than men (e.g., Deaux & Major, 1987; Eagle & Steffen, 1984). Consequently, women have been found to be more expressive and men to be more instrumental in maintaining their relationships. Women tend to engage in intimate conversation with their good friends, whereas men tend to spend time in common activities with theirs (e.g., Caldwell & Peplau, 1982; Davidson & Duberman, 1982; Duck & Wright, 1993; Spence & Buckner, 1995; Twenge, 1997; Walker, 1994; Wright & Scanlon, 1991). It has also been suggested that women tend more to communicate in order to avoid isolation and gain community, whereas men tend more to communicate to gain and keep social position (e.g., Tannen, 1992).

Other authors have emphasized that men and women differ in their conversation styles. For example, Hauser and colleagues (1987) distinguish between *enabling* or *facilitative* styles of communication, which help to 'ramp up' a conversation, and *restricting* styles that tend to dampen the interaction. Women are socialized into using the facilitative styles and men the restricting styles (Maccoby, 1990). In communication, women tend to seek dialogue, whereas men tend to interrupt the communication process at an early stage.

Since women, on average, invest more in personal relationships, some studies have found that women have more extensive social networks (e.g., Moore, 1990; Walker, 1994; Wellman, 1992). Other studies, however, indicate that men report more same-sex friendships than women, although male friendships tend to be less intimate than female friendships (e.g., Claes, 1992). More specific role obligations are consistent with the general tendency of women to connect to others: women are expected to be the maintainers of family ties (Di Leonardo, 1987; Rosenthal, 1985) and of their family's connections to friends (Wellman, 1992).

Such gender differences, first observed in face-to-face behavior, have already been found to carry over to ways in which men and women use the telephone (Noble, 1987). Women, for example, are more frequent users of the telephone than men (e.g., Brandon, 1980; Lacohée & Andreson, 2001; Walker, 1994). Men use the phone more instrumentally than women do. Small talk and emotional sharing are not considered legitimate motives for men to initiate phone contact, and men may not call if they do not have an instrumental reason to call (Lacohée & Anderson, 2001; Walker, 1994). Because technology makes it easier to share thoughts and feelings at a distance than to engage in common activities at a distance, women use the telephone more often than men to sustain a larger circle of distant friendships (Lacohée & Anderson, 2001; Walker, 1994).

Do these gender differences in communication and relationship styles hold for computer-mediated communication? Do women embrace computers as a new means of connecting to others? If so, we may expect more use of the Internet for communication by women than men, and more expressive communication by women, and more instrumental communication by men. On the other hand, do the technological features of e-mail somehow interfere with women's expressive communication style? Some studies indicate that the text-based communication format of e-mail makes it less suitable for maintaining relationships than face-to-face communication or the phone (Cummings, Butler, & Kraut, 2001; Walther, 1996). Other studies suggest it is, instead, more suitable for management and coordination of activities (Sproull & Kiesler, 1986). That is, the text-based format of e-mail may facilitate an instrumental communication style more commonly associated with men.

A recent national survey of Internet use (Pew Internet and American Life Project, 2000a) showed that women use the Internet more for communication than do men. Of those who use e-mail, more women than men use it to communicate with both family and friends. Women, for example, were more likely than men to have sent e-mail to their parents or grandparents and to have reached out electronically to their extended families — aunts, uncles or cousins. Women were more likely than men to use e-mail to sustain distant friendships; 73% of women who use e-mail said they had sent e-mail to friends who lived far away, compared to 65% of men. More women than men e-mailers liked e-mail, mostly because they find it more efficient than other forms of communication (Pew Internet and American Life Project, 2000a). Other studies have also suggested quantitative, and possibly qualitative, differences in how men and women use computers to communicate (e.g., Kraut et al., 1998).

The current article examines in more detail how men and women use e-mail to maintain their personal relationships. Guided by previous findings about gender differences in relational maintenance, we investigate how type of relationships, distance between communication partners and type of message influence women's and men's e-mail use. This exploratory study is based on qualitative data analysis. In addition, we draw upon survey data from 1998–1999, collected within the HomeNet project — a long-term investigation of how the Internet is influencing the lives of Americans (see Kraut et al., 1998; 2000 for more details).

Method

Sample

The HomeNet survey data were collected from two samples. The first consisted of 220 members of 93 Pittsburgh households recruited during the spring of 1995 and 1996 and followed for two to three years (Kraut et al., 1998). The second sample consisted of 446 individuals from 237 households in the Pittsburgh area who had recently purchased either a computer or a television during the spring of 1998. They were followed for one year

(Kraut et al., 2002). Within the HomeNet Project, 41 interviews were conducted between 1996–1999 in four sub-samples: 10 households in 1996, 14 in 1997, 5 in 1998 and 12 in 1999. We selected households where at least one member was in the top quartile in time online.

Qualitative Data

The present study is mainly based on analyses of interviews with adult women and men from these 41 households. All interviewees were Internet neophytes. The interview sub-sample includes 32 women (mean age 47) and 28 men (mean age 48.8). The sample comprises highly educated and high income adults, with 77.5% having at least some college education and 35.2% a graduate degree; 27.3% had a household income of $35,000 or less, 36.4% between $35,000–$50,000 and 36.3% $50,000 or over. Ninety-eight percent were Caucasian.

Interviews were semi-structured and lasted two to three hours. We attempted to interview all household members (including children), first as a group around the kitchen or dining room table and then individually in front of the family computer. All interviews were tape recorded and transcribed. The portion in front of the computer was videotaped as well.

The analyses of the interviews followed standard guidelines for structured thematic analyses (e.g., Silverman, 2000; Taylor & Bogdan, 1998), using NUD*IST software (QSR, 1999). Coding was first done for three major types of relationships (relatives, friends and acquaintances) and for three major Internet applications (e-mail, chat rooms and instant messaging) separately for the adult men and women in the four inter-view sub-samples. We gathered eighteen collections of excerpts from the transcripts, nine referring to women's and nine to men's communication with relatives, or friends, or acquaintances by e-mail, or chat rooms, or instant messaging. For the final analyses, we compared women's and men's communication within each type of relationship for each modality and for each sub-sample. However, we do not report our findings for each sub-sample separately, because, with very few exceptions, we did not see changes in the way men and women where using the Internet to maintain relationships over time.[1]

Quantitative Data

We also draw upon cross-sectional quantitative data from the second HomeNet survey sample (Kraut et al., 2000).[2] Respondents completed survey questionnaire three times: in the spring of 1998, the fall of 1998 and the spring of 1999. Several measures of com-munication by e-mail were consistently used in the three questionnaire surveys. For the purposes of the present report, analyses include only adult participants who had Internet access during the time of the surveys (N = 253). Because the first question-naire was administered before many of the households had Internet access, the analy-ses here are done only on data from the second and the third questionnaires, with scores averaged across the two surveys.

For this study, the quantitative analyses are based on questionnaire items related to using the computers in personal relationships: self-reports on actual behaviors, and

---

[1]Exploratory interviews that we conducted in 2000 and 2001 suggest that instant messaging applications are now being used much more frequently than in the earlier periods, and that they seem to be used in a differ-ent manner to sustain relationships than e-mail. However, we do not have enough data about the use of instant messaging or chat rooms to investigate it separately. Consequently, this article focuses on communi-cation by e-mail. National survey research shows that as of 2000, e-mail dominated use of instant messaging.
[2]We also conducted analyses on the basis of questionnaire items from the first HomeNet sample (Kraut et al., 1998). However, measures differ somewhat across the two samples—from the wording of the items to the range of scales used—which makes combining the two data sets problematic. In the separate analyses of the 1995–1998 HomeNet survey data, we found similar gender-related tendencies associated with e-mail use in personal communication. For lack of space and because the focus of this study is our quantitative data analyses, we only report here the more recent survey data analyses.

attitudes about how useful and how much fun computers are in sustaining personal relationships (for details on the measures used, see Kraut et al., 2002). The following self-reported behaviors are of particular interest here: (a) frequency of e-mail use; (b) frequency of keeping in touch with a friend or relative far away and with people in the Pittsburgh area; and (d) time (measured in minutes) spent on the most recent weekday on each of the following activities: communicating with friends, communicating with family, using e-mail and using the World Wide Web. Frequency of e-mail use was measured on an four-item index (Cronbach's alpha = .91). For the analysis, this variable was centered, with a mean of 0. When measures had outliers, they were truncated. Because the distributions of the time measures were skewed, we took their log in the analyses that follow.

Another set of questions asked about attitudes toward using computers to communicate with others. Respondents were asked to rate how useful and how much fun computers were for sending e-mail, keeping up with family and friends, finding new people to communicate with from all over the world, keeping up with music and entertainment, playing computer games and searching the World Wide Web for hobby information. All items were measures on a 5-point scale, where one meant not at all useful (or fun) and five meant extremely useful (or fun).

▌▌▌ Does E-Mail Perpetuate Gender Differences in Relational Maintenance?

Quantitative Data Results

To place the interview data findings in context, we first present the results from the 1998–1999 survey data. An analysis of covariance was conducted, to test for the effect of gender on frequency of e-mail use, controlling for educational level and household income. Since 98 percent of the sample were Caucasian, we did not control for race in the present analyses. Women were marginally more likely than men to report using e-mail frequently ($p = .11$). (See Table 1).

Since three of the self-report time measures of communicating with others were theoretically and statistically related, a multivariate analysis of covariance was conducted to test for gender effects on time spent on a weekday communicating with family, communicating with friends and using e-mail, controlling for education and household income. There was a significant multivariate (Hotelling's test) gender effect ($F(3, 238) = 4.59$; $p = .004$). The univariate tests showed significant gender effects on all three measures (See Table 1). Women reported spending more minutes than men communicating with family. They spent more time communicating with friends. Finally, they spent more time using e-mail. In contrast, there was no gender effect on time spent using the World Wide Web.

A multivariate analysis of covariance was conducted to test for gender effects on frequency of Internet communication with friends in the local area and with people far away, controlling for education and household income. The multivariate test was significant for gender ($F(2, 239) = 3.31$; $p = .038$). Univariate tests showed no gender differences in frequency of people's use of the Internet to communicate with local friends, but women were more likely than men to use the Internet to keep up with people far away. (See Table 1). To test for the interaction of gender by geographic distance of the partner, a 2 (gender) × 2 (e-mail locally versus far away) ANOVA was conducted. The interaction was not statistically significant ($F(1, 240) = 1.78$; $p = .18$). There was an overall gender effect ($F(1, 240) = 5.41$; $p = .02$) on frequency of communication locally and far away, with women scoring higher than men.

TABLE 1 Means and Standard Deviations for Women and Men on Measures of Internet Use for Personal Relationships.

Time Spent Using the Internet			
	Women	*Men*	*F*[A]
Frequency of using e-mail[¥]	.24	.09	2.62
	(.81)	(.77)	
Communicating with friends (minutes)	110.31***	77.53***	10.41***
	(95.53)	(89.67)	
Communicating with family (minutes)	169.54*	123.92*	4.47*
	(144.34)	(111.99)	
Using the World Wide Web (minutes)	32.20	33.99	.20
	(50.25)	(48.81)	
Using e-mail (minutes)	24.32*	16.07*	3.95*
	(37.49)	(23.89)	

Frequency of Using the Internet for Different Purposes[‡]			
	Women	*Men*	*F*
For communicating with friends in the Pittsburgh area	2.48[†]	2.36[†]	2.76[†]
	(1.30)	(1.24)	
For keeping in touch with someone far away	2.98*	2.55*	6.62**
	(1.41)	(1.29)	

Attitudes toward Internet Use for Specific Activities[‡‡]						
	How useful			*How much fun*		
Software that allows to . . .	*Women*	*Men*	*F*	*Women*	*Men*	*F*
Send e-mail	4.17	3.94	.98	3.98**	3.48**	9.34**
	(1.12)	(1.11)		(1.15)	(1.08)	
Keep in touch with family and friends	4.09**	3.63**	8.95**	4.01**	3.56**	7.66**
	(1.02)	(1.10)		(1.07)	(1.09)	
Find new people to communicate with from all over the world	2.95*	2.53*	6.38**	3.18*	2.78*	4.91**
	(1.21)	(1.02)		(1.21)	(1.06)	
Keep up with music and entertainment	2.76	2.59	.05	2.99	2.82	.35
	(1.15)	(1.16)		(1.20)	(1.13)	
Play new computer games	2.59	2.52	.55	3.07	3.05	.07
	(1.20)	(1.06)		(1.34)	(1.18)	
Search the Internet or the World Wide Web for hobby information	3.82	3.80	.46	3.80	3.69	.001
	(1.18)	(1.04)		(1.22)	(.98)	

▪▪▪▪▪▪▪▪▪

[A]F-values are based on the multivariate analyses of covariance described in the text. Df for the numerator is 1 and df for the denominator varies between 233 and 245 for different dependent variables. [†]p < 10; * p < 05; **p < .01; ***p < .001
[¥]This variable was centered with a mean of 0.
[‡]Measured on a 5-point scale (1 = never and 5 = often).
[‡‡]Measures on a 5-point scale (1 = not at all useful (or fun) and 5 = useful (or fun).

Similarly, we used multivariate analyses to test for gender differences in attitudes about how useful and how much fun it is to use computers for five different activities, controlling for education, household income and e-mail usage. The multivariate analysis showed significant gender effect on the dependent variables measuring how useful computers were ($F(6, 233) = 4.12$; $p = .001$). Univariate tests indicated that women more than men believed the Internet was useful for keeping up with family and friends. (See Table 1). Again, women scored higher than men on usefulness of computers in finding communication partners. In contrast, there was no significant of gender differences on non-social items, such as keeping up with music and entertainment, playing computer games, or searching the Internet for hobby information. However, although women scored higher on the usefulness of useful sending e-mail is, this difference was not statistically significant.

A comparable pattern was found for the effect of gender on the set of dependent variables measuring how much fun computers were for certain activities. The multivariate analysis showed significant gender effect on the dependent variables measuring how much fun computers are ($F(6, 229) = 4.12$; $p = .007$). Univariate tests indicated that women more than men though computers were fun for sending e-mail, for keeping up with family and friends, and for finding communication partners. In contrast, there was no significant effect of gender on the items that were not associated with personal relationships, namely, keeping up with music and entertainment, playing computer games, or searching the Internet for hobby information. (See Table 1.)

Qualitative Data Results

The survey data analyses describe gender-related pattern of sustaining personal relationships using computers, but they provide no detail about differences in communication between friends and family, or why women use the Internet more than men for distant partners but not for local ones. They provide no information about the substance of the communication online. To explore these issues, we turn to the interview data.

In general, more women than men interviewees reported using e-mail for personal relationships. Of the 32 women who were interviewed, 29 reported using e-mail at home to communicate with others they know, whereas of the 28 interviewed men, only 14 used e-mail. Of those who did not use e-mail, all three women, but only two of the 14 men attributed it to lack of time and/or knowledge about how to use e-mail or to having difficulty typing. None of the women and five men in the sample reported lack of interest in using e-mail to communicate with others, illustrated in the following comments of two men who did not use e-mail.

JIM:[3]   I utilize the computer for entertainment and information. I don't e-mail or any . . . I don't e-mail at all.

MARC: I don't e-mail friends or relatives . . . I don't know why . . . I'm not one to communicate often with friends, you know, like, I communicate with them once a month and that's fine with me.

In the context of these findings—that ninety-one percent of the women and only half of the men in our sample use e-mail to communicate with others—we further examine what specific relationships are sustained by this mode of communication.

---

[3]For considerations of confidentiality, we use pseudonyms throughout the text.

Types of Relationships Sustained by E-Mail

Communication with Family and Kin

Interviewees conducted little communication within the household by e-mail. Only two families reported using e-mail among themselves. In one case, a family used e-mail to communicate with each other in different parts of the house. In another case, a husband at work exchanged messages with his wife at home—on topics ranging from how their day was going to making shopping lists.

Communication by e-mail with other family and more distant kin perpetuates the gender-role pattern described earlier. One of the female interviewees described explicitly such a gender-related pattern in her family.

BARBARA: In our family . . . I'm much more of the communicator and my husband is not. It's a typical, I guess, gender division, and it happens to be true in our case. I'm the one who, you know, talks on the phone to the other family members and makes social arrangements and all kinds of things like that, and when we got the e-mail, that trend just stayed. I mean I am the one who e-mails our son, who's at college and I e-mail other family members and my husband really has no interest in e-mail. And he was never one who would talk on the phone, either. He occasionally has used it [the computer] to pursue a few of his, you know, hobby interests on the Internet, but other than that he doesn't use it. So, I don't know, it's not because he's shy, I just think people who aren't that interested in communicating they're not going to do it with e-mail either.

The interview data suggest that women in the recent cohort were more likely to use the Internet to communicate with family and kin than those in the earlier subsample. Only 12 out of 20 women who used e-mail between 1996–1998 reported extensively using it to contact their family and kin, while all nine women interviewed in 1999 did so. We did not see similar cohort effects in men's e-mail use.

Women reported communicating by e-mail most frequently with their siblings and with their parents. Of the 29 women who used email, ten corresponded with their siblings and six with their parents. Communication with family was less common among the 14 men e-mailers—only four reported staying in touch with siblings by e-mail, and none with parents. When women failed to use e-mail with siblings or parents, their most common explanation was that the relatives did not have Internet access. Men were less likely to give this explanation. We also found weak evidence that e-mail supplemented women's telephone conversations with their parents, whereas it substituted for telephone calls with their siblings. For example, some of the women who communicated with both elderly parents and siblings by e-mail explained that they also called their parents as before, but did not call their brothers and/or sisters as often, since having the e-mail connection.

Ten of the female interviewees and three of the male interviewees reported communicating by e-mail with other kin—namely, cousins, aunts and uncles, a niece and a nephew, or, with their in-laws. One case is of particular interest because it presents a nontraditional way of meeting future in-laws. After their wedding date was announced, Jean started communicating with her future in-laws online before she even met them in person. For example, she developed a relationship with her sister-in-law online long before she met her in person on the wedding day.

Our interviews do not contain adequate information on the e-mail communication between the parents and their children who do not live at home, because our sample contained only four children (two daughters and two sons) away in college. Mothers reported staying in touch with all four by e-mail, whereas only one father reported occasionally corresponding with his son. Three more women, who expected their daughters to be leaving for college soon, expressed enthusiasm about using e-mail in the future to stay in touch with daughters in college. One family kept a common e-mail account that they could use to keep in touch with their son in college, but only the mother regularly checked the account. With one exception (when a son regularly did not answer e-mail), mothers found e-mail connections with their children in college to be useful and satisfying.

As a whole, our qualitative data findings do not indicate that e-mail usage introduced any dramatic changes in the gender-specific pattern of communication with family and kin. There was, however, one case when using e-mail resulted in redefining a traditional communication pattern. One participant, Barbara took advantage of e-mail to change dramatically her relationships with both her father and her son. From the beginning of her marriage, she had long, weekly phone conversations with her mother; her father would get on the line only briefly to say "hi". She had hardly ever exchanged personal thoughts and emotions with him before he started using e-mail. With e-mail, they started a regular correspondence and her father shared his feelings, thoughts and personal history with her. Still, when Barbara would call home, it would be only her mother, but not her father, who would talk to her. "If it were not for the e-mail, I wouldn't have talked to my father . . ." Barbara also found e-mail communication with her son in college more gratifying than phone communication with him.

> BARBARA: I e-mail him [my son] a lot. And I enjoy that and I feel that we have a much better communication on e-mail than we would on the phone. And if we didn't have e-mail I wonder what our communication would be, because somehow when I call, it's like, you know, he's busy, or he's tired, or he's studying, or whatever.

Such cases suggesting that e-mail is radically changing relationships with friends and kin, however, were only exceptions in our data. Despite this, we believe it is important to investigate in depth such cases in the future in order to better understand why this is happening and how gender and other social and personal factors influence this process.

Communication with Friends

In our interview sample, women and men differed in the size of the circle of friends they sustained by e-mail. Twenty-three women, or 72% of the women interviewed (79% of the e-mail users) and nine men, or 32% of the men interviewed (64% of the e-mail users) reported staying in touch with friends using e-mail. Our interviews suggest that, like communication with family and kin, women have the responsibility for sustaining relationships with common family friends by e-mail. Irene and Tom, a husband and wife that we interviewed, described this pattern in their family. It seemed natural to them that Irene was the one who communicated directly with family and common friends by e-mail, thus leaving Tom feeling that he did not need to duplicate the activity.

> IRENE: [talking about relatives and friends]. . . people e-mail me stuff and I'll send it to him [her husband].
>
> TOM: . . . rather than both sending [e-mail] . . . I mean, she talks [by e-mail] to them and then she e-mails me anything I need to know, so I don't really communicate directly with them, but indirectly, through her routing me the e-mails.

Communication with Local Friends   Women and men did not seem to differ much in their use of e-mail to communicate with geographically local friends. Seven men (25%

of those interviewed and half of the male e-mailers) and 10 women (31% of those interviewed and 34% of the female e-mailers) reported using e-mail to communicate locally with friends. Both men and women emphasized the convenience of e-mail for organizing activities and arranging events with friends and acquaintances. Neither women nor men seemed to use e-mail just to chat with local friends. An exception is Jane, who reported preferring e-mail over phone to chat with her closest friend locally.

JANE: I have a friend that lives 10 minutes away and we e-mail back and forth [just to chat] . . . I could pick up the phone and talk, but we don't.

Jane explained that they e-mail instead of talking by phone, because "it is painless," each of them could do it at their convenience.

Communication with Geographically Distant Friends In contrast to its use for local relationships, e-mail was more central to distant relationships, and women used it more extensively than men.

E-mail made it easier for both men and women to sustain personal friendships with people far away in at least three different ways. First, e-mail helped people to retain relationships despite geographic mobility. Interviewees reported that after moving to a new location or job, e-mail kept them in touch with people from the old location—former colleagues, friends from college, and neighbors. While geographic relocation frequently interrupts regular contacts with extended less close family and non-intimate friends, e-mail counters this disruption with low cost communication.

Second, e-mail provides a low-cost means of reinvigorating previously dormant relationships. A combination of e-mail and the World Wide Web allowed some interviewees to actively search for friends they had lost contact with and to re-initiate contact with them. Thus, through e-mail, people intensified their communication with dormant friends and acquaintances. Jill, for example, explained how she was able to keep in touch with some friends, with whom in the past she had only exchanged Christmas cards.

JILL: On Christmas cards I sent out the e-mail address and I did discover I had some surprising contacts . . . I did find again some long lost friends . . .

Finally, and more rarely, e-mail allowed people to develop relationships with others they would not maintain otherwise. Irene, for example, described being able to build strong relationships communicating frequently by e-mail.

IRENE: [T]here are people I never talk to, like my friends in Alaska, I never talk to him on the phone, we just e-mail each other. Also, my friend in Ireland, we never talk, we just e-mail, so, that's really nice because . . . My friend in Alaska I've only seen him three times ever and we . . . basically our whole relationship for the three or four years has been over the Internet and e-mailing, so, that's kind of interesting.

Without computer-mediated communication, Irene and other interviewees would not have been able to develop satisfying relationships with people far away with whom they shared common interests.

The interviews suggest that e-mail expands the circle of geographically distant friends more for women than for men. Eleven women (38% of e-mailer and 34% of all women with Internet access) and four men (29% of e-mailers and 14% of all men with Internet access) reported keeping in touch with more geographically distant friends because of e-mail. Women, it seems, are not just using e-mail as another modality to supplement already existing distant ties; they are taking advantage of the low cost communication to revive lost connections and to stay in touch with friends who would otherwise be lost through geographic mobility.

Message Types and Patterns of Message Traffic

To better understand how e-mail builds and sustains relationships, we analyzed interviewees' descriptions of their e-mail content and a limited sample of e-mail messages that they made available to us. These data suggest that there are three types of e-mail messages—boilerplate messages, messages for coordination and messages for personal sharing—which have different roles in developing and sustaining relationships. Because of the small sample of messages, we do not even speculated here on possible gender differences.

Message Types

Boilerplate Messages   Boilerplate messages include jokes, stories, sayings, greeting cards, pointers to music sites, and other pre-fabricated messages copied by the sender from one source and then forwarded, often to more than one recipient. For example, one of the women in the sample received the following note addressed to her and nine other recipients, most of whom she did not even know:

> Feminist saying, circa 1968–1972: "The hand that rocks the cradle can also cradle a rock."

Like conventional greeting cards, these boilerplate messages serve to remind partners of each other's existence and, as such, preserve a relationship as a potential resource for companionship, advice, or social support at some later time. It is also important to emphasize that these are messages often addressed to a group of receivers—the circle of sender's friends and/or relatives. Whether and how this could affect the "density" of one's social network needs to be studied further.

Coordination Messages   A second type is a coordination message. It is used to set up a joint activity or other occasion where the participants share companionship and other social resources. This excerpt from a message of one woman to another illustrates this second type:

> JULIE: I don't know how your plans are working out for tomorrow night, but it's no problem with me if we have to reschedule it for next week or whenever. I will be out of the house most of tomorrow, so you probably won't be able to get me on the phone then anyway.

Other examples of messages for coordination included organizing a group of friends to play golf over the weekend, arranging monthly board-game nights with 20 other family friends, and managing activities of a local community committee on families and education.

Messages for Personal Sharing   The third type of messages have personal content that directly supports the relationship. Such messages have an expressive nature, and in themselves they provide companionship and social support by allowing communicators to share thoughts and feelings with one another. Contrast, for example, the coordination e-mail from Julie above with the following message Alice sent. Alice's message has substantive content, which enacts the relationship.

Long time no hear from! How are you? I'm getting by. I'm still
working at the law firm as a receptionist but I am bored!!! And I
was turned down for two jobs this week. I had second interviews
for both. I thought at least one would be good! I really feel like I
suck!!! Anyway, I came across your address and thought I'd write
you. Hope all is better for you. I'm glad spring is coming!!

Dorothy, a creative writer, exchanges with her artist mother, along with regular phone
calls and occasional visits. They talk about family gossip and the events of the day, and in
particular, what her mother has been working on that day. These messages also serve to
enact the relationship, by themselves providing companionship and social support.

DOROTHY: For her [my mother], talking about work in progress is very inter-
             esting to her and can get her going. So, she'll be telling me she's
             working on something and ask for my ideas on it and I'll send
             ideas back and so, back and forth, that kind of thing, and then fam-
             ily gossip . . . you know, this sister is coming to dinner, or you
             know, this nephew said this funny thing. There's certain amount of
             family chit chat in there, too.

We have some preliminary evidence that women may not consider e-mail very
suitable for sharing of emotions and personal thoughts. Six women reported that they
restricted their e-mail contacts to light conversation, reserving deep conversations
involving social support for more interactive media—the phone or, in more recent
times, instant messaging. Kathleen described media choice when communicating with
her daughter this way:

KATHLEEN: [W]hen times were stressful, she [my daughter] would call up . . .
             you know, that upset does not necessarily come through on an
             e-mail. And so, I was there for emotional support . . . So, a lot of it
             was not conversational . . . While, just here [in her e-mail mes-
             sages] is some information . . . what are you doing, Mom, and I
             would write back and you know, those kind of things . . . it's likely
             to be much longer and in depth if we're on the phone.

However, at least two women judged e-mail more appropriate than the phone for
deep, emotionally laden topics with someone far away. In one case, a female family
friend was terminally ill and her husband used e-mail to keep friends informed bout
her physical and emotional state. In another case, e-mail communication supplied
indispensable emotional support for two sisters after their mother died.

CYNTHIA: My Mom had died a while ago and . . . we were talking about that
             through e-mail and you know, she [my sister] said stuff about my
             Mom and everything, and . . . the way we were talking, I'm think-
             ing, I probably never would have said that to her . . .

Although these examples may only be exceptions, they suggest some of the conditions under which e-mail may be preferred over the telephone for sharing deep emotions. E-mail is more efficient than interactive media for broadcasting messages to a
group of recipients. In addition, e-mail is a more reflective medium than the phone or
instant messaging, and allows the writer to more carefully choose and review message
content before sending it.

Patterns of Message Traffic   The interview data suggest two differing styles of e-mail
use for maintaining personal relationships: *facilitating dialogue* (enacting the relation-

ship in intense bursts of e-mail communication) and *restricting dialogue* (interrupting the communication in an early stage). Several women emphasized that they e-mailed others "in spurts," activating a dormant relationship through an intensive communication exchange for a few days, then allowing it to die back. The following excerpt is an example of how initiating communication with another stimulates further communication for women.

JILL: For a short spurt I'll e-mail her back and we'll e-mail for a couple of days and then we sort of fade out for a while until the next spurt . . . [Once we get in touch,] I usually get excited about e-mailing the person, it just makes me want to talk to them more . . .

In contrast, men seemed more apt to accept substantial delay between messages. One of the interviewees, Jim described this pattern in some detail. When he would get an e-mail message from a friend, he would almost never respond to it right away. He would get back to him in some future communication session.

JIM: I don't see much use [in e-mail] unless it's something important. If it's something [important], I'd like to get to it later, like, I won't answer right then. Like, say, if I'm just checking e-mail, but if I really want to write [back] something. I'll leave it [the message] there, so the next time I can come back and write whatever it is.

Harry emphasized that intensive e-mail message exchange with another person was not something 'men do.'

HARRY: For me, it [e-mail] usually has a point of giving him [his friend] information, asking him questions: are you available for that . . . Not back and forth simultaneously in chains. Not for me, maybe for [Elizabeth] [his daughter].

As in the case of telephone use, gender-role expectations seem to channel e-mail behavior. Our findings also suggest that instant messaging, by facilitating dialogue, may be more appealing to women than to men. Melanie, interviewed in 1999, describes below why she prefers instant messaging to e-mail.

MELANIE: Well, first of all, an e-mail message . . . it's a one-sided conversation, you have to get a response before you can type anymore, but on instant chat we use a split screen all the time, so you can chat constantly. It's just like talking on the telephone except that you're using a printed word instead, [which is] much better.

However, because instant messaging did not exist when we started to collect interview data, its use is underrepresented in our sample.

▪▪▪ Discussion and Conclusions

Several studies have found that, controlling for overall Internet use, women are heavier users of e-mail than men (e.g. Kraut et al., 1998; Pew Internet & American Life Project, 2000a). The current article suggests that the different role obligations men and women have towards relationships, the different value they place on personal relationships, the precise ways they use the Internet for developing and sustaining relationships may account for these differences in e-mail use. Our qualitative and quantitative data analyses show gender differences in both behavior and attitudes toward computer-mediated communication with family and friends.

Our findings, of course, are conditional on the limitations of our survey and interview samples. For example, data were collected with relatively small samples only in the city of Pittsburgh. Our survey and interview samples are not directly comparable, since interviews were accumulated gradually between 1995 to 1999, while the surveys reported here were collected in 1998 and 1999. Most of the participants in our samples were middle class, highly educated, white Americans, married, between 35 and 55 years old. Men and women other than middle class and white appear to have different gender ideologies and different patterns of personal relationship maintenance and styles of relating to others (e.g., Franklin, 1992; Hensen, 1992). Only one author coded the interviews. Our conclusions about message content are based on interviewees' comments as much as they are on the text of the messages. Also, we do not compare e-mail to other modes of communication, nor do we consider the gender of the corresponding partner. Previous studies, for example, show differences in communication patterns between same-gender and different-gender friends (e.g., Parker & de Vries, 1993).

Despite these limitations, our study shows that some pre-existing differences between men and women in their beliefs and behaviors in maintaining personal relationships are being perpetuated in e-mail communication. For example, women in the United States have been traditionally responsible for maintaining relationships among family and friends, and we find that they have appropriated e-mail as a new tool for this traditional role obligation. Women were more likely than men to report sending e-mail to their elderly parents and siblings. They also reported more often than men sending e-mail to extended family. These findings of gender differences using e-mail replicate gender differences using the phone, greeting cards, and letters. In all these modes of communication, women do most of the "work of kin" (cf. Di Leonardo, 1987).

Proximity—a major factor in relationship maintenance—seems to interact with gender in e-mail use. Both our survey and interview data suggest that women are more likely than men to use e-mail to communicate with family and friends who live far away, and women are more interested in actively seeking communication by e-mail with someone far away. Being socialized in connectedness and seeking closeness in dialogue, women seem to have embraced e-mail as a less costly way to connect to others far away. Locally, however, men and women use e-mail similarly, mainly for coordination of joint activities.

We speculate that these differences come about because of the different way women and men generally enact relationships. E-mail fits better women's expressive style of relationship maintenance, with its emotional intimacy and sharing of personal information, because e-mail allows women to carry out this style with distant friends and family. In contrast, men's more instrumental style of relationship maintenance, with its emphasis on joint activities, is hard to accomplish with distant partners through computer mediated communication. Men seem to be less willing to use e-mail to sustain geographically distant relationships, possibly because it would be difficult to sustain these relationships without sharing personal thoughts and feelings. Instead, e-mail is useful for setting up joint activities with local partners, and both men and women use it for coordinating social activities with local partners. These findings are consistent with recent reports on a narrowing gap between women and men on instrumentality but not on expressiveness (Duck & Wright, 1993; Spence & Buckner, 2000; Twenge, 1997; Wright & Scanlon, 1991).

Our survey data show that women have more positive attitudes toward using e-mail as a tool to connect to others. They find sending e-mail to family and friends more useful and more enjoyable than men do. Other studies have come to a similar conclusion—e-mail is more psychologically gratifying to women than to men (see e.g., Pew Internet & American Life Project, 2000a; Stafford, Kline, & Dimmick, 1999).

Since women tend to use a facilitative communication style, seeking dialogue, they seem to communicate by e-mail "in spurts", enacting their relationships in intense bursts of communication. In contrast men, being more prone to a restricting style of communication, seem to tolerate considerable delays between communication sessions. These findings suggest that instant messaging may differentially appeal to women than men, because it better supports highly interactive communication sessions.

In addition to finding that e-mail perpetuates some gender-related behaviors and attitudes, our study indicates that certain types of personal relationships may be changing as a consequence of computer-mediated communication. For example, while previous studies—based on more traditional modes of communication—report that, of all family ties, the mother-daughter relationship is the closest and most frequently enacted (e.g., Schütze, 1996), we found that e-mail exchanges with siblings was most frequent. One reason may be that availability drives frequency. Because elderly parents have less access to the Internet than their adult children, the middle-aged adults can't send e-mail to them. However, our data also suggest that women are using e-mail to supplement telephone conversations with their parents, whereas they are substituting it for telephone calls with their siblings.

Thus, our study suggests, women are using the new technologies to expand their distant social networks and to intensify certain family and kin relationships. Both men and women are using it to keep up with siblings and with local friends. The interview data imply that e-mail is having a generally beneficial effect on personal relationships, but more so for women than for men.

While our study focuses on e-mail, Internet services for real-time communication has been spreading rapidly, especially among the younger population. We do not have enough observations on the role of more recent communication technologies (for example, instant messaging), since we stopped collecting data in mid-1999. Future research on the issues of how the new technologies are used to sustain personal relationships should include all these modalities, and more diverse demographic groups.

REFERENCES

Berg, J. H., & Clark, M. S. (1986). Differences in social exchange between intimate and other relationships: Gradually evolving or quickly apparent? In V. J. Derlega and B. A. Winstead (Eds.). *Friendship and Social Interaction*. New York: Springer-Verlag.

Brandon, B. (1980). *The effects of the demographics of individual households on their telephone usage*. Cambridge, MA: Ballinger.

Caldwell, M. A., & Peplau, L. A. (1982). Sex differences in same-sex friendships. *Sex Roles*, 8, 721–732.

Canary, D. J., & Stafford, L. (1994). Maintaining relationships through strategic and routine interactions. In D. J. Canary & L. Stafford (Eds.), *Communication and relationship maintenance.* (pp. 3–22). NY: Academic Press.

Cancian, F. M. (1987). *Love in America: Gender and self-development*. Cambridge: Cambridge University Press.

Claes, M. E. (1992). Friendship and personal adjustment during adolescence. *Journal of Adolescence*, 15(1), 39–55.

Cummings, J. N., Butler, B., & Kraut, R. (in press, 2001). The quality of online relationships. *Communications of the ACM*.

Davidson, L. R., & Duberman, L. (1982). Friendship: Communication and interactional patterns in same-sex dyads. *Sex Roles*, 8, 809–822.

Deaux, K., & Major, B. (1987). Putting gender into context: An interactive model of gender-related behavior. *Psychological Review*, 94, 369–389.

Di Leonardo, M. (1987). The female world of cards and holidays: Women, families and the work of kinship. *Signs: Journal of Women in Culture and Society*, 12, 440–453.

Duck, S. W. (1988). *Relating to others*. Chicago: Dorsey.

Duck, S., & Wright, P. H. (1993). Reexamining gender differences in friendships: A close look at two kinds of data. *Sex Roles*, 28, 709–727.

Eagle, A. H., & Steffen, V. J. (1984). Gender stereotypes stem from the distribution of women and men into social roles. *Journal of Personality and Social Psychology*, 46, 735–754.

Fox, M., Gibbs, M., & Auerbach, D. (1985). Age and gender dimensions of friendships. *Psychology of Women Quarterly*, 9, 489–502.

Hauser, S. T., Powers, S. I., Weiss-Perry, B., Follansbee, D. J., Rajapak, D., & Greene, W. M. (1987). *The constraining and enabling coding system manual*. Unpublished manuscript.

Kraut, R., Kiesler, S., Boneva, B., Cummings, J., & Helgeson, V. (2002). Internet Paradox Revisited. *Journal of Social Issues*, 58(1), 49–74.

Kraut, R., Mukhopadhyay, T., Szczypula, J., Kiesler, S., Scherlis, W. (1999). Communication and Information: Alternative Uses of the Internet in Households. *Information Systems Research*, 10(4), 287–303.

Kraut, R., Patterson, M., Lundmark, V., Kiesler, S., Mukopadhyay, T., & Scherlis, W. (1998). Internet Paradox. A Social Technology that Reduces Social Involvement and Psychological Well-being? *American Psychologist*, 53(9), 1017–1031.

Kraut, R., Scherlis, W., Mukhopadhyay, T., Manning, J., & Kiesler, S. (1996). The HomeNet field trial of residential Internet services. *Communications of the ACM*, 39, 55–63.

Lacohée, H., & Anderson, B. (2001). Interacting with the telephone. *International Journal of Human-Computer Studies*, 54(5), 665–699.

Maccoby, E. E. (1990). Gender and relationships: A developmental account. *American Psychologist*, 45(4), 513–520.

Moore, G. (1990). Structural determinants of men's and women's personal networks. *American Sociological Review*, 55, 726–735.

Noble, G. (1987). Individual differences, psychological neighbourhoods and use of the domestic telephone. *Media Information Australia*, 44, 37–41.

Parker, S., & de Vries, B. (1993). Patterns of friendship for women and men in same- and cross-sex relationships. *Journal of Social and Personal Relationships*, 10(4), 617–626.

The Pew Internet & American Life Project (2000a, May 10). Tracking online life: How women use the Internet to cultivate relationships with family and friends. Downloaded May 15, 2000, at http://www.pewinternet.org/reports/.

Pew Internet and American life project (2000b). Daily Internet Activities. Downloaded January 9, 2001, at http://www.pewinternet.org/reports/chart.asp?img=5_Daily_Activities.gif.

Rosenthal, C. (1985). Kinkeeping in the familial division of labor. *Journal of Marriage and the Family*, 47, 965–974.

QSR NUD*IST software. (1999). SCILARI. SAGE Publications Software.

Schütze, Y. (1996). Relationships between adult children and their parents. In A. E. Auhagen, & M. von Salisch (Eds.), *The diversity of human relationships*. (pp. 106–119). Cambridge: Cambridge University Press.

Silverman, D. (2000). Analyzing talk and text. In N. K. Denzin, & Y. S. Lincoln (Eds.), *Handbook of qualitative research*. Thousand Oaks, CA: Sage Publications.

Spence, J. T., & Buckner, C. E. (2000). Instrumental and expressive traits, trait stereotypes, and sexist attitudes: What do they signify? *Psychology of Women Quarterly*, 24, 44–62.

Spence, J. T., & Buckner, C. (1995). Masculinity and femininity: Defining the undefinable. In P. J. Kalbfleisch, & M. J. Cody (Eds.), *Gender, power, and communication in human relationships*. (pp. 105–140). Hillsdale, NJ. Lawrence Erlbaum Associates, Publishers.

Sproull, L., & Kiesler, S. (1986). Reducing social context cues: E-mail in organizational communication. *Management Science*, 32, 1492–1512.

Stafford, L., & Canary, D. J. (1991). Maintenance strategies and romantic relationship type, gender and relational characteristics. *Journal of Social and Personal Relationships*, 8, 217–242.

Stafford, L., Kline, S. L., & Dimmick, J. (1999). Home e-mail: Relational maintenance and gratification opportunities. *Journal of Broadcasting & Electronic Media*, 43(4), 659–669.

Tannen, D. (1992). *You just don't understand. Women and men in conversation*. London: Virago Press.

Twenge, J. M. (1997). Changes in masculine and feminine traits across time: A meta-analysis. *Sex Roles*, 36, 305–327.

Walker, K. (1994). "I'm no friends the way she's friends": Ideological and behavioral constructions of masculinity in men's friendships. *Masculinities*, 2, 38–55.

Walther, J. B. (1996). Computer-mediated communication: Impersonal, interpersonal, and hyperpersonal Interaction. *Communication Research*, 23(1), 3–43.

Wellman, B. (1992). Men in Networks: Private Communities, Domestic Friendships. In P. M. Nardi (Ed.). *Men's friendships*. (pp. 74–114). London: SAGE.

Wellman, B., & Wortley, S. (1989). Brothers' keepers. *Sociological Perspectives*, 23, 273–306.

Wright, P. H., & Scanlon, M. B. (1991). Gender role orientations and friendship: Some attenuation but gender differences abound. *Sex Roles*, 24, 551–566.

Anonymity on the Internet: Why the Price May Be too High

DAVID DAVENPORT

▦ Introduction

Anonymous communication is seen as the cornerstone of an Internet culture that promotes sharing and free speech and is overtly anti-establishment. Anonymity, so the argument goes, ensures that governments cannot spy on citizens and thus guarantees privacy and free speech. The recommendations of the American Association for the Advancement of Science's conference on "Anonymous Communication Policies for the Internet"[1] support this view. Among the findings were that "online anonymous communication is morally neutral" and that "it should be considered a strong human and constitutional right."

I believe this view is fundamentally mistaken and that by allowing anonymous communication we actually risk an incremental breakdown of the fabric of our society. The price of our freedoms is not, I believe, anonymity, but accountability. Unless individuals and, more importantly, governments can be held accountable, we lose all recourse to the law and hence risk our very freedom. The following sections argue this in more detail and suggest that the only real solution is more openness, not less.

▦ Social Justice Requires Accountability

Individuals living in a free society reap benefits in terms of sustenance, shelter and protection, and in return are expected to contribute to the community. Problems occur due to imbalances in this relationship. If individuals or groups acquire excessive wealth or power, or, conversely, do not receive just rewards, tension is inevitable. Small groups, e.g. villages or family units, where people know and depend more directly upon each other, tend to be reasonably stable despite significant imbalances. In larger communities, e.g. cities or countries, however, such differences can quickly lead to crime, social unrest, protests and even revolution. In circumstances where people can be largely anonymous, and the threat of punishment is thus minimal, they find it easier to justify to themselves actions against those they see as outsiders or enemies.

Large social groupings necessitate some sort of decision-making mechanism (monarch, government, etc.) to guide them, and a system of controls (police and judiciary) to ensure fairness and compliance. In a democratic society, citizens "consent" to such bodies resolving any problems or conflicts that may arise, rather than taking action themselves. By punishing misconduct, society aims to deter repetition of such offenses and send a clear warning to those who may be similarly tempted to violate the rights of others. The democratic system also incorporates controls (elections and laws) that ensure that governing bodies cannot abuse their position. Obviously, resolving any unfairness, whether involving individuals, groups or the state, requires that those responsible for the problems can be held accountable. In a free and fair society, justice must exist, and be seen to exist.

Experience suggests that a society relying solely on the good will and conscience of its citizens would be unlikely to succeed in ensuring justice. Similarly, attempting to guarantee justice by adopting measures that would prevent the very possibility of wrongdoing is unfeasible since there is little hope of covering all eventualities. We should, of course, attempt to raise individuals to be good and conscientious citizens, and take precautions in an attempt to make misbehavior impossible, but we would surely be foolish not to also retain the safety net of accountability.

▪▪▪ The Consequences of Anonymity

Accountability requires that those responsible for any misconduct can be identified and brought to justice. However, if people remain anonymous, by definition, they cannot be identified, making it impossible to hold them accountable. Proponents of anonymous communications on the Internet thus open the door to many forms of criminal and anti-social behavior, while leaving victims and society helpless. Internet-based crimes, such as hacking, virus writing, denial of service attacks, credit card fraud, harassment and identity theft are on the increase. Already, damage estimates are measured in billions of dollars per year, but the human cost, in terms of ruined reputations, loss of trust and a general deterioration in morals, is immeasurable.

While all this is dangerous enough, there is a much more ominous aspect to anonymity. Were anonymous communication to become the default, then, it would be available, not just to the private citizen, but to the state and to those individuals that comprise it. Highly sensitive material could be leaked, paybacks could be made to secure lucrative deals, pressure could be placed on officials, elections could be rigged and arrangements could be made for political opponents to be attacked or even eliminated, all with impunity. Distrusting a government that is accountable to the people is one thing, facilitating a government that is completely unaccountable is quite another. Some may argue that governments already employ anonymity to cloak clandestine operations, so it would make no difference. However, where governments do currently use it, they do so illegally. Those involved know it is wrong and know the penalties if they are caught, thus deterring all but the most desperate or naïve.

▪▪▪ Free Speech

The right to freedom of speech is a fundamental aspect of the democratic tradition. The rationale for it is simple. Ideas transform society, and any idea, no matter how bizarre it may appear initially, might ultimately prove beneficial. Citizens should thus not be unduly restricted from or punished for expressing their views, however unpalatable they may seem. The very notion of free speech under law means protecting the speaker from prosecution and persecution, thus the speaker's identity is known. While anonymous communication is not necessary for there to be free speech, it clearly ensures that no restrictions or punishments can be imposed on anyone, whatever they may say. Does this apparent benefit outweigh its costs, as advocates claim?

Freedom of speech is concerned primarily with protecting the individual against the might of the establishment, be it the political or religious authorities, or the moral majority. Anonymous communication, however, is likely to be singularly ineffective in this regard. In dictatorships and undemocratic countries where free speech is most needed, it is unlikely that the regime would make such communication available at all. Even in circumstances where anonymous communication was allowed, unless it was pervasive, its use might easily be detected and taken as an indication of wrongdoing. Besides, messages sent anonymously are unlikely to have much impact on their own. Only if the recipient of a message knows and trusts its writer, is action likely to ensue. Trust is built up as a result of numerous encounters, but if the communications are truly anonymous then it is difficult to establish such a relationship. Messages sent anonymously are thus unlikely to have much impact on their own and hence reliance on anonymous communications for whistle blowing, informing the world of human rights violations or promulgating a political platform would seem to be misplaced.

History is made by those brave enough to speak out, despite the serious personal risks involved. Reform may take longer to come about, but surely bravery, honesty and openness should be encouraged as a means of effecting change. Cowering behind a cloak of anonymity hardly seems an auspicious basis for profound social upheavals. Anonymity seems to offer a cheap and easy way to speak out against authority and promote change, in reality it is ineffectual and may ultimately prove to be very costly.

When it comes to more mundane personal communications, anonymity is said to have the advantage of promoting free and open exchanges, unhampered by prejudices often formed by race, gender or religion. Text-only communications certainly remove most, though not all, such clues, but this is a transitory situation. Once voice and video-conferencing technology become widespread, few people will exchange its convenience for such nebulous gains. Of course, enabling open discussion, particularly of medical, psychological or legal problems, is undoubtedly something valuable. It is quite natural for people to be reticent about talking openly of such personal matters, so when they need advice they either turn to professionals in such areas (who guarantee to hold client conversations in the strictest of confidence), confide in close friends (whom they trust to keep the conversation private) or turn to complete strangers (who they hope will not learn their identity.) On the Internet however, even assuming that one's identity never accidentally slipped out (to be linked with all the intimate details poured out over the months or years) and that one could trust the advice of a totally unknown confidant, anonymity can be seriously misused. There are legitimate restrictions to the right to free speech, in particular, it does not apply to libelous remarks or ones intended to defraud, or to incite hatred or violence. In order to protect the innocent, all communications must be subject to the rule of law and this, as argued above, implies that their originators must be accountable and hence not anonymous.

That communication must be subject to law should not be taken to mean that the government has the right to track, intercept or read them. All that is necessary is that the courts, as opposed to the government, be able to establish the source of a communication, when, and only if, it becomes the subject of legal dispute. The need for accountability requires that all communication be traceable and that this information be available to courts subject to due process. It does not entail that others, even the recipient, need know the source. Authors could thus hide their identity if they wish, but on the understanding that they can still be held accountable under law.

▮▮▮ The Way Forward

Advocates of anonymous communication claim that anonymity is essential to ensure free speech on the Internet, and that this outweighs any harm that might result from drug barons, Mafia and other criminals being untouchable. I have argued that this view is mistaken. Accountability lies at the very heart of the democratic tradition and is crucial to the continued stability of a free and fair society. Removing its safety net would only encourage deceit, and lead to more crime and increasing numbers of victims unable to obtain justice. More significantly, those in power could use anonymity to their own ends, making governments unaccountable. It was distrust of government that led to calls for anonymous communications as a means to ensure free speech. The end result of anonymity, however, plays right into their hands and has little real impact in terms of free speech.

The way forward is clear, embrace accountability and reject anonymous communications. The concerned citizen can use the improved communications offered by the Internet to participate more fully than ever before in the functioning government. Our freedom comes at the price of vigilance. If we abdicate our responsibilities we have only ourselves to blame. Moving to a more open, participatory form of democratic government, is a better, safer, more stable option than that offered by the quicksand of anonymity.

Accountability, openness and honesty may sound like old-fashioned morality, but they have stood us in good stead. They are the price of our freedoms, a small price to pay, surely, for the right to life, liberty and the pursuit of happiness.

REFERENCES

1. Teich A., Frankel M. S., Kling R., and Ya-ching L., "Anonymous Communication Policies for the Internet: Results and recommendations of the AAAS conference," *The Information Society*, Vol 15, No. 2, 1999.

This paper has been shaped and reshaped over the course of many heated discussions. I am particularly indebted to Selim Erdoğan, Robin Turner, Will Sayer, Eray Özküral, David Grünberg & Erdine Sayan, for their insightful comments and suggestions.

Library Bill of Rights

The American Library Association affirms that all libraries are forums for information and ideas, and that the following basic policies should guide their services.

I. Books and other library resources should be provided for the interest, information, and enlightenment of all people of the community the library serves. Materials should not be excluded because of the origin, background, or views of those contributing to their creation.

II. Libraries should provide materials and information presenting all points of view on current and historical issues. Materials should not be proscribed or removed because of partisan or doctrinal disapproval.

III. Libraries should challenge censorship in the fulfillment of their responsibility to provide information and enlightenment.

IV. Libraries should cooperate with all persons and groups concerned with resisting abridgment of free expression and free access to ideas.

V. A person's right to use a library should not be denied or abridged because of origin, age, background, or views.

VI. Libraries which make exhibit spaces and meeting rooms available to the public they serve should make such facilities available on an equitable basis, regardless of the beliefs or affiliations of individuals or groups requesting their use.

Free Speech

L. Lessig

The Right to Free Speech is not The Right to Speak for Free. It is not the Right to free access to television, or the right that people not hate you for what you have to say. Strictly speaking—legally speaking—the right to free speech in the United States means the right to be free from punishment by the government in retaliation for at least some (probably most) speech. You cannot be jailed for criticizing the president, though you can be jailed for threatening him; you cannot be fined for promoting segregation, though you will be shunned if you do; you cannot be stopped from speaking in a public place, though you can be stopped from speaking with an FM transmitter. Speech in the United States is protected—in a complex, and at times convoluted, way—but its constitutional protection is a protection against the government.

Nevertheless, a constitutional account of free speech that thought only of government would be radically incomplete.[1] Two societies could have the same "First Amendment"—the same protections against government's wrath—but if within one dissenters are tolerated while in the other they are shunned, the two societies would be very different free speech societies. More than government constrains speech, and more than government *protects* free speech. A complete account of this—and any—right must consider the full range of burdens and protections.

Consider, for example, the "rights" of the disabled to protection against discrimination. The law protects the disabled; social norms don't, neither does the market, and until the law intervened, neither did architectures. The net of these four modalities would describe the protection, in any particular context, that the disabled have. Law might intervene to strengthen the protection—regulating architecture, for example, so that it better protects against discrimination in access. But for any given mix we could understand these four modalities working together to protect (however slightly) the disabled from discrimination.

In the terms of chapter 7, we could then use the same four modalities to consider within each context the protection *from* constraint, as well as the imposition *of* regulatory constraints. Modalities of constraint (powers) function as a sword against the object regulated; modalities of protection (rights) function as a shield for the regulated against constraint. The following figure captures the point.

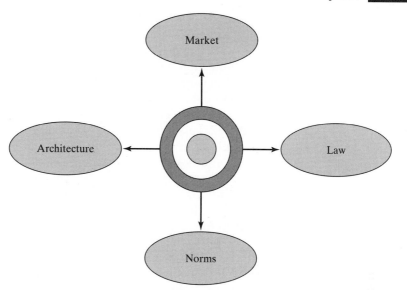

In the center is the object regulated—the pathetic dot from chapter 7. Surrounding the individual now is a shield of protection, the net of law/norms/market/architecture that limits the constraints these modalities would otherwise place on the individual. I have not separated the four in the sphere of the shield because obviously there is no direct match between the modality of constraint and the modality of protection. When law as protector conflicts with law as constraint, constitutional law overrides ordinary law.

These modalities function together. Some might undercut others, meaning that the sum of protections might seem to be less significant than the parts. The "right" to promote the decriminalization of drugs in the present context of the war on drugs is an example. The law protects your right to advocate the decriminalization of drugs. The state cannot lock you up if, like George Soros, you start a campaign for the decriminalization of marijuana or if, like the Nobel Prize–winning economist Milton Friedman or the federal judge Richard Posner, you write articles suggesting it. If the First Amendment means anything, it means that the state cannot criminalize speech about law reform.

But that legal protection does not mean that I would suffer no consequences for promoting legalization of drugs. My neighbors would be appalled at the idea, and some no doubt would shun me. Nor would the market necessarily support me. It would be quite difficult to buy time on television for a speech advocating such a reform. Television stations have the right to select their ads (within some limits); they do not like controversial or tasteless ads.[2] Mine would most likely be deemed too controversial. Stations also have the FCC—an active combatant in the war on drugs—looking over their shoulders. And even if I were permitted to advertise, I am not George Soros. I do not have millions to spend on such a campaign. I might manage a few off-hour spots on a local station, but I could not afford, for instance, a campaign on the networks during prime time.

Finally, architecture wouldn't protect my speech very well either. In the United States at least, there are few places where you can stand before the public and address them about some matter of public import without most people thinking you a nut or a nuisance. There is no speakers' corner in every city; most towns do not have a town meeting. "America offline," in this sense, is very much like America Online—not designed to give individuals access to a wide audience to address public matters. Only professionals get to address Americans on public issues—politicians, scholars, celebrities, journalists, and activists, most of whom are confined to single issues. The rest of us have a choice—listen, or be dispatched to the gulag of social lunacy.

Thus, the protection for controversial speech is more conditional than a narrow legal view would suggest. The right to be a dissenter is on balance less protected than it could be when more than law is reckoned.

Let's take this example now to cyberspace. How is the "right" to promote the legalization of drugs in cyberspace protected? Here too, of course, the law protects my right of advocacy—at least in the United States. It is quite possible that the same speech would be illegal elsewhere and that perhaps I could be prosecuted for uttering such speech in cyberspace "in" another country. Speech promoting the Nazi Party, for example, is legal in the United States but not in Germany.[3] Uttering such speech in cyberspace may make one liable in German space as well.

The law therefore is an imperfect protection. Do norms help to protect speech? With the relative anonymity of cyberspace and its growing size, norms do not function well there to restrain controversial speech. Even in cyberspaces where people know each other well, they are likely to be more tolerant of dissident views when they know (or believe, or hope) the dissident lives thousands of miles away.

The market provides a major protection to speech—relative to real space, market constraints on speech in cyberspace are tiny. Recall how easily Jake Baker became a publisher, with a potential readership greater than the readership of all law books (like this one) published in the last decade.

But on top of this list of protectors of speech in cyberspace is architecture. Relative anonymity, decentralized distribution, multiple points of access, no necessary tie to geography, no simple system to identify content, tools of encryption[4]—all these features and consequences of the Internet protocol make it difficult to control speech in cyberspace. The architecture of cyberspace is the real protector of speech there; it is the real "First Amendment in cyberspace," and this First Amendment is no local ordinance.[5]

Just think about what this means. For over fifty years the United States has been the exporter of a certain political ideology, at its core a conception of free speech. Many have criticized this conception: some found it too extreme, others not extreme enough. Repressive regimes—China, North Korea—rejected it directly; tolerant regimes—France, Hungary—complained of cultural decay; egalitarian regimes—the Scandinavian countries—puzzled over how we could think of ourselves as free when only the rich can speak and pornography is repressed.

This debate has gone on at the political level for a long time. And yet, as if under cover of night, we have now wired these nations with an architecture of communication that builds within their borders a far stronger First Amendment than our ideology ever advanced. Nations wake up to find that their telephone lines are tools of free expression, that e-mail carries news of their repression far beyond their borders, that images are no longer the monopoly of state-run television stations but can be transmitted from a simple modem. We have exported to the world, through the architecture of the Internet, a First Amendment *in code* more extreme than our own First Amendment *in law*.

This chapter is about the regulation of speech and the protection of speech in cyberspace—and therefore also in real space. My aim is to obsess about the relationship between architecture and the freedom it makes possible, and about the significance of law in the construction of that architecture. It is to get you to see how this freedom is built—the constitutional politics in the architectures of cyberspace.

I say "politics" because this building is not over. As I have argued (over and over again), there is no single architecture for cyberspace; there is no given or necessary structure to its design. The first-generation Internet might well have breached walls of control. But there is no reason to believe that architects of the second generation will do so, or not to expect a second generation to build in control. There is no reason to think, in other words, that this initial flash of freedom will not be short-lived. And there is certainly no justification for acting as if it will not.

We can already see the beginnings of this reconstruction. Already the architecture is being remade to reregulate what real-space architecture before made regulable. Already the Net is changing from free to controlled.

Some of these steps to reregulate are inevitable; some shift back is unavoidable. Before the change is complete, however, we must understand the freedoms the Net now provides and determine which freedoms we mean to preserve.

And not just preserve. The architecture of the Internet, as it is right now, is perhaps the most important model of free speech since the founding. This model has implications far beyond e-mail and web pages. Two hundred years after the framers ratified the Constitution, the Net has taught us what the First Amendment means. If we take this meaning seriously, then the First Amendment will require a fairly radical restructuring of the architectures of speech off the Net as well.

But all that is to get ahead of the story. In the balance of this chapter, I want to tell three stories—one about publication, one about access, and one about distribution. With each, I want to consider how "free speech" is regulated.

These stories do not all have the same constitutional significance. My aim in the first is to illustrate a relationship between architectures and institutions of free speech; the second identifies another latent ambiguity in our constitutional regime; and the third is a straightforward translation of the framing design. It is the third story that, if correct, would prove the most fundamental, though all three illustrate the relationship between values, architectures, and the choices they now present.

▪ ▪ ▪ The Regulators of Speech: Publication

Floyd Abrams is one of America's leading First Amendment lawyers. In 1971 he was a young partner at the law firm of Cahill, Gordon.[6] Late in the evening of Monday, June 14, he received a call from James Goodale, in-house counsel for the *New York Times*. Goodale asked Abrams, together with Alexander Bickel, a Yale Law School professor, to defend the *New York Times* in a lawsuit that was to be filed the very next day.

The *New York Times* had just refused the government's request that it cease all publication of what we now know as the "Pentagon Papers" and return the source documents to the Department of Defense.[7] These papers, mostly from the Pentagon's "History of U.S. Decision Making Process on Vietnam Policy," evaluated U.S. policy during the Vietnam War.[8] Their evaluation was extremely negative, and their conclusions were devastating. The papers made the government look extremely bad and made the war seem unwinnable.

The papers had been given to the *New York Times* by someone who did think the war was unwinnable; who had worked in the Pentagon and helped write the report; who at first did not believe the war was unwinnable but who over time had come to see the impossibility that the Vietnam War was.

This someone was Daniel Ellsberg. Ellsberg smuggled one of the fifteen copies of the papers from a safe at the RAND Corporation to an offsite photocopier. There, he and a colleague, Anthony Russo, photocopied the papers over a period of several weeks.[9] Ellsberg tried without success to make the papers public by having them read into the *Congressional Record*. He eventually contacted the *New York Times* reporter

Neil Sheehan in the hope that the *Times* would publish them. Ellsberg knew that this was a criminal act, but for him the war itself was a criminal act; his aim was to let the American people see just what kind of a crime it was.

For two and a half months the *Times* editors pored over the papers, working to verify their authenticity and accuracy. After an extensive review, the editors determined that they were authentic and resolved to publish the first of a ten-part series of excerpts and stories on Sunday, June 13, 1971.[10]

On Monday afternoon, one day after the first installment appeared, Attorney General John Mitchell sent a telegraph to the *New York Times* stating:

> I respectfully request that you publish no further information of this character and advise me that you have made arrangements for the return of these documents to the Department of Defense.[11]

When the *Times* failed to comply, the government filed papers to enjoin the paper from continuing to publish stories and excepts from the documents.[12]

The government's claims were simple: these papers contained government secrets; they were stolen from the possession of the government; to publish them would put many American soldiers at risk and embarrass the United States in the eyes of the world. This concern about embarrassment was more than mere vanity: embarrassment, the government argued, would weaken our bargaining position in the efforts to negotiate a peace. Because of the harm that would come from further publication, the Court should step in to stop it.

The argument was not unprecedented. Past courts had stopped the publication of life-threatening texts, especially in the context of war. As the Supreme Court said in *Near v Minnesota*, for example, "no one would question but that a government might prevent actual obstruction to its recruiting service or the publication of the sailing dates of transports or the number and location of troops."[13]

Yet the question was not easily resolved. Standing against precedent was an increasingly clear command: if the First Amendment meant anything, it meant that the government generally cannot exercise the power of prior restraint.[14] "Prior restraint" is when the government gets a court to stop publication of some material, rather than punish the publisher later for what was illegally published. Such a power is thought to present much greater risks to a system of free speech.[15] Attorney General Mitchell was asking the Court to exercise this power of prior restraint.

The Court struggled with the question, but resolved it quickly. It struggled because the costs seemed so high,[16] but when it resolved the question, it did so quite squarely against the government. In the Court's reading, the Constitution gave the *New York Times* the right to publish without the threat of prior restraint.

The Pentagon Papers is a First Amendment classic—a striking reminder of how powerful a constitution can be. But even classics get old. In a recent speech, Abrams asked an incredible question: Is the case really important anymore?

For the government to succeed in a claim that a printing should be stopped, it must show "irreparable harm"—harm so significant and irreversible that the Court must intervene to prevent it.[17] But the showing depends on the publication not occurring—if the Pentagon Papers had already been published by the *Chicago Tribune*, the government would have claimed no compelling interest to stop its publication in the *New York Times*. When the cat is already out of the bag, preventing further publication cannot prevent the cat from getting out of the bag.

This point is made clear in a case that came after *New York Times*—a case that could have been invented by a law professor. *The Progressive* was a left-wing magazine that in the late 1970s commissioned an article by Howard Morland about the workings of an H-bomb. *The Progressive* first submitted the manuscript to the Department of Energy, and the government in turn brought an injunction to block its publication. The government's claim was compelling: to give to the world the secrets of how to build a bomb would make it possible for any terrorist to annihilate any city. On March 26, 1979, Judge Robert Warren of the Western District of Wisconsin agreed and issued a temporary restraining order enjoining *The Progressive* from publishing the article.[18]

Unlike the Pentagon Papers case, this case stewed, no doubt in part because the district judge hearing the case understood the great risk this publication presented. The judge did stop the publication while he thought through the case. And for two and a half months he thought. The publishers went to the Court of Appeals, and to the Supreme Court, asking each to hurry the thinking along. No one did anything.

Until Chuck Hansen, a computer programmer, ran a "Design Your Own H-Bomb" contest and circulated an eighteen-page letter in which he detailed his understanding of how an H-Bomb works. On September 16, 1979, the *Press-Connection* of Madison, Wisconsin, published the letter. The next day the government moved to withdraw its case, conceding that it was now moot. The compelling interest of the government ended once the secret was out.[19]

Note what this sequence implies. There is a need for the constitutional protection that the Pentagon Papers case represents only because there is a real constraint on publishing. Publishing requires a publisher, and a publisher can be punished by the state. But if the essence or facts of the publication are published elsewhere first, then the need for *constitutional* protection disappears. Once the piece is published, there is no further *legal* justification for suppressing it.

So, Abrams asks, would the case be important today? Is the constitutional protection of the Pentagon Papers case still essential?

Surprisingly, Floyd Abrams suggests not.[20] Today there's a way to ensure that the government never has a compelling interest in asking a court to suppress publication. If the *New York Times* wanted to publish the Pentagon Papers today, it could ensure that the papers had been previously published simply by leaking them to a USENET newsgroup. More quickly than its own newspaper is distributed, the papers would then be published in millions of places across the world. The need for the constitutional protection would be erased, because the architecture of the system gives anyone the power to publish, quickly and anonymously.

The architecture of the Net, Abrams argues, eliminates the need for the constitutional protection; even better, the Net protects against prior restraint just as the Constitution did—by ensuring that strong controls on information can no longer be achieved. Abrams argues that the Net does what publication of the Pentagon Papers was designed to do—ensure that the truth does not remain hidden.

But there's a second side to this story.

On July 17, 1996, TWA Flight 800 fell from the sky ten miles off the southern coast of Center Moriches, New York. Two hundred and thirty people were killed. Immediately after the accident the United States launched the largest investigation of an airplane crash in the history of the National Transportation Safety Board (NTSB), spending $27 million to discover the cause of the crash, which eventually was determined to have been a mechanical failure.[21]

This was not, however, the view of the Internet. From the beginning stories circulated about missiles—people said they saw a streaking light shoot toward the plane just before it went down. There were also stories about missile tests conducted by the Navy seventy miles from the crash site.[22] And then there were reports of a cover-up by the U.S. government to hide its involvement in one of the worst civil air disasters in American history.

The government denied these reports, yet the more the government denied them, the more contrary "evidence" appeared on the Net.[23] There were repeated reports of sightings of missiles by witnesses on the ground. These reports, writers on the Net claimed, were being "suppressed" by the government. The witnesses were being silenced. And then, as a final straw in the story, there was a report purportedly by a government insider, claiming that indeed there was a conspiracy—because evidence suggested that friendly fire had shot down TWA 800.[24]

A former press secretary to President John F. Kennedy believed it. In a speech in France, Pierre Salinger announced that his government was hiding the facts of the case, and that he had the proof.

I remember this event well. I was talking to a colleague just after I heard Salinger's report. I recounted Salinger's report to this colleague, a leading constitutional scholar from one of the top American law schools. We both were at a loss about what to believe. There were cross-cutting intuitions about credibility. Salinger was no nut, but the story was certainly loony.

Salinger, it turns out, had been caught by the Net. He had been tricked by the flip side of the point that everyone can publish. In a world where everyone can publish, it is very hard to know what to believe. For publishers are also editors, and editors make decisions about what to publish—decisions that ordinarily are driven at least in part by the question, is it true? Statements cannot verify themselves. We cannot always tell from a sentence reporting a fact about the world, whether that sentence is true.[25] So in addition to our own experience and knowledge of the world, we must rely on structures of reputation that build credibility. When something is published, we associate the claim with the publisher. If the *New York Times* says that aliens have kidnapped the president, that is a different story from a story with the identical words published in the *National Enquirer*.

When a new technology comes along, however, we are likely to lose our bearings. This is nothing new. It is said that the word *phony* comes from the birth of the telephone—the phony was the con artist who used the phone to trick people who were familiar with face-to-face communication only. We should expect the same uncertainty in cyberspace, and expect that it too, at first, will shake expectations of credibility.

Abrams's argument then depends on a feature of the Net that we cannot take for granted. If there were credibility on the Net, the importance of the Pentagon Papers would indeed be diminished. But if speech on the Net lacks credibility, the protections of the Constitution again become important.

"Credibility," however, is not a quality that is legislated; nor is it coded. It comes from institutions of trust that help the reader separate reliable from unreliable sources. Flight 800 thus raises an important question: How can we reestablish credibility in this space so that it is not lost to the loons?[26]

Two solutions are possible. One, a top-down solution, would empower editors—people who select what should be published based on a host of considerations, including the truth of what is said. The other, bottom-up, would facilitate the construction of reputation—a measure of the significance of the speech that turns on who is actually uttering it. In real space, of course, the two go together—editing goes with publishing, and hence, because of the selections made by the editors at the *New York Times*, the reputation of the *New York Times* is different from the reputation of the *National Enquirer*. We might have thought that the *New York Times* sold newspapers. But cyberspace is teaching us that it sells editing services that happen to be delivered on paper.

In cyberspace, these two functions could be distinct. Editing could be separate from distribution, which means that there could be a greater competition among editors. And credibility would be one of the values that editing services would sell.

Traditionally such credibility has been created by an institution of some stability—the *New York Times*, for example—serving a credentialing function. Being hired as a reporter by the *New York Times* says something important about your status; the *Times* then has an interest in policing you—your misadventures would reflect negatively on the *Times*. The public gets the benefit of a clear structure of responsibility.

We could see just this kind of reintermediation—restoration of intermediaries—on the Net.[27] But it could happen in other ways too. Imagine a kind of rating service that, as with bonds or with medical malpractice insurance, rates the reputation of each reporter and source through some formula of its own determination. We could imagine any number of such agencies, each providing reporters with ratings that serve as their credential. The reporter's rating would become part of every story published on the Net. And the same with any source, anonymous or not, since any source could also receive a rating.

In this example, an architecture of trust would replace institutions of trust.[28] A reporter could gain credibility as a good and accurate reporter whether employed by the *New York Times* or not. Hence, reintermediation on the Net need not involve the re-creation of the relatively few trusted publishers in real space but instead could focus on the relocation of the credentialing service from the publishers to independent agencies.

The difference between these reregulations is a difference in the power of institutions. Without preferring one over the other, we may note the trade-off between an architecture and a market structure.

▮▮▮ The Regulators of Speech: Access

Pornography, in real space, is regulated extensively. Porn—not obscenity and not child porn, but what the Supreme Court calls sexually explicit speech that is "harmful to minors."[29] Obscenity and child porn are regulated too, but their regulation is different from that of porn. Obscenity and child porn are banned for all people in real space (United States); porn is banned only for kids.

We can understand porn's regulation by considering the four modalities of regulation. All four are directed to a common end: to keep porn away from kids while (sometimes) ensuring adults' access to it.

First, laws do this. Laws in many jurisdictions require that porn not be sold to kids.[30] Since at least 1968, when the Supreme Court decided *Ginsberg v New York*,[31] such regulation has been consistently upheld. States can require vendors of porn to sell it only to adults; they can also require vendors to check the ID of buyers.

But not only laws channel. Social norms do as well. Norms restrict the sale of porn generally—society for the most part sneers at consumers of porn, and this sneer undoubtedly inhibits its sale. Norms also support the policy of keeping porn away from kids. Porn dealers don't like to think of themselves as people who corrupt. Selling porn to kids is universally seen as corrupting, and this is an important constraint on dealers, as on anyone else.

The market too keeps porn away from kids. Porn in real space costs money. Kids, on average, do not have much money. Because sellers discriminate on the basis of who can pay, they thus help to discourage children from getting porn.

But the regulations of law, market, and norms all presuppose another regulation that makes the first three possible: the regulation of real-space architecture. In real space it is hard to hide that you are a child. A kid can don a mustache and climb onto stilts, but it would still be pretty hard for him to convince a salesperson that he's not a kid. Thus, because a kid cannot hide his age, and because porn is largely sold face to face, the architectures of real space make it relatively cheap for laws and norms to be effective.

This constellation of regulations in real space has the effect of controlling, to a reasonable degree, the distribution of porn to kids. It is not perfect—any child who really wants the stuff can get it—but regulation does not need to be perfect to be effective. It is enough that these regulations make porn generally unavailable—as they do in real space.

In cyberspace the regulation of porn is different. The first difference is the market. In real space porn costs money, but in cyberspace it need not—at least not much. If you want to distribute one million pictures of "the girl next door" in real space, it is not unreasonable to say that distribution will cost close to $1,000,000. In cyberspace distribution is practically free. So long as you have access to cyberspace and a scanner, you can scan a picture of "the girl next door" and then distribute the digital image across USENET to many more than one million people for just the cost of an Internet connection.

With this market for supply, much more porn can be produced for cyberspace than for real space. But there is also the market for demand. Porn in cyberspace can be retrieved—often and in many places—for free. Not from commercial porn sites, but from USENET servers, for example. Thus, the constraint of the market is absent in cyberspace.

More important than the market, however, is the difference in architectures. A crucial feature that makes regulation in real space possible is the difficulty of disguising who you are. In cyberspace there is no fact about your identity to disguise. You enter without an identity, and you identify only what you want to identify. Thus, a kid in cyberspace need not disclose that he is a kid. And therefore he need not suffer the discriminations applied to a child in real space. No one needs to know that Jon is Jonny; therefore no one needs to know the necessary preconditions for applying the restrictions of law, norms, and the market.

The result is what we all know: there are few limits on the distribution of porn to children in cyberspace. And this fact, in turn, gave birth to the "porn scare."[32]

Just about the time the Net was coming into the popular consciousness, a particularly seedy part of the Net came into view first. This was the extraordinary growth of sex available on the Net. This concern became widespread in the United States early in 1995.[33] Its source was an extraordinary rise in the number of ordinary users of the Net, and therefore a rise in use by kids and an even more extraordinary rise in the availability of what many call porn on the Net. An extremely controversial (and deeply flawed) study published in the *Georgetown University Law Review* reported that the Net was awash in porn.[34] *Time* ran a cover story about its availability.[35] Senators and congressmen were bombarded with demands to do something to regulate "cybersmut."

Congress responded in 1996 with the Communications Decency Act (CDA). A law of extraordinary stupidity, it practically impaled itself on the First Amendment. The law made it a felony to transmit "indecent" material on the Net to a minor, or to a place where a minor could observe it. But it gave speakers on the Net a defense—if they took good-faith, "reasonable, effective" steps to screen out children, then they could speak "indecently."[36]

There were at least three problems with the CDA, any one of which should have doomed it to well-deserved extinction.[37] The first was the scope of the speech it addressed: "indecency" is not a category of speech that Congress has the power to regulate (at least not outside the context of broadcasting.)[38] As I have already described, Congress *can* regulate speech that is "harmful to minors," or *Ginsberg* speech, but that is very different from speech called "indecent." Thus, the first strike against the statute was that it reached too far.

Strike two was vagueness.[39] The form of the allowable defenses was clear: so long as there was an architecture for screening out kids, the speech would be permitted. But the architectures that existed at the time for screening out children were relatively crude, and in some cases quite expensive. It was unclear whether, to satisfy the statute, they had to be extremely effective or just reasonably effective given the state of the technology. If the former, then the defenses were no defense at all, because an extremely effective block was extremely expensive; the cost of a reasonably effective block would not have been so high.

Strike three was the government's own doing. In arguing its case before the Supreme Court in 1997, the government did little either to narrow the scope of the speech being regulated or to expand the scope of the defenses. It stuck with the hopelessly vague, overbroad definition Congress had given it, and it displayed a poor understanding of how the technology might have provided a defense. As the Court considered the case, there seemed to be no way that an identification system could satisfy the statute without creating an extreme burden on Internet speakers.

But let's step back from the CDA for a moment and clarify just what is possible in a regulation of this kind. Since the case of *Ginsberg v New York*, it has been assumed that there is a class of speech that adults have a right to but children do not. States can regulate that class to ensure that such speech is channeled to the proper user.

Conceptually, then, before such a regulation could be applied, two questions must be answered:

1. Is this speech within the class of "regulable" speech?
2. Is this listener under a minimum age?

Clearly, the sender is in a better position to answer question one, and the receiver is in a better position to answer question two. Yet the CDA imposed the full burden of the regulation on the sender—he must determine both whether his speech is subject to regulation and whether the recipient is above the minimum age.

An alternative would be to place the burden on the receiver—or more precisely, on his parents. Parents know whether they have children who should be protected from porn; if they do, they arguably should take steps to block out speech they consider inappropriate for their children.

Both solutions—placing the burden on the recipient or on the sender—require a new architecture for the Net, not at the level of the TCP/IP protocol, but in the application space. Both require that changes be built into the most common suite of applications in a way that users can depend on.

What might these applications look like? Let's call the first a *zoning* solution. Speakers are zoned into a space from which children are excluded. The second is a *filtering* solution. Listeners are empowered to block speech they want to block. We could describe each as a version of the other—with zoning, people are filtered; with filtering, the listener zones speech. But let's keep the kinds distinct and consider what each would require.

Architectures That Zone Speech

Two kinds of zoning solutions are conceptually equivalent, but constitutionally distinct. One, that is, is constitutional; the other, not. Both solutions require a change in the architecture of the Net to facilitate the production of a certain kind of information. One solution requires a signal that the user is a kid (call this a "kids-ID"). The other requires a signal that the user is an adult (call this an "adult-ID").

The difference is crucial, but let's see first how each might work. With the kids-ID solution, we could imagine the government requiring browser manufacturers to modify their browsers to permit users to set up profiles. One option in that profile would be a check-off box where the user signals that he is a minor. If this check-off box is selected in a profile on a given machine, the other profiles on the machine would require a password. Many people could share a single machine, but if any of them were minors, the adult profiles would be secured with a password.

Take an example from a hypothetical family. Say a family of three shares a single computer. One member of that family is a minor. Using this modified browser, the adults would set up a profile for each member of the family. With the child's profile, the kids-ID box would be checked, and a password would be used to access that profile. Any member of the family using the system would select his or her own profile and browse according to the rules of that profile. (Netscape already provides something close to this. With Navigator Communicator 4.5, for example, you can set up profiles just as I have described, though they do not have a kids-ID option.)

Armed with such a browser, a kid-identified user would then transmit this fact to a web site when accessing the site. This scheme would require that the web site block *Ginsberg* speech to any self-identified minor.[40] The burden on the child (or more accurately, the burden on his parents) would be slight, and the burden on the web site would also be slight.

That is one kind of zoning solution. A second would require the opposite identification: rather than guaranteeing everyone access except those who identify themselves as children, this version would grant access to adult material only to those users who could certify that they were adults.

We have seen such a system already: an architecture of digital certificates. Users wanting to enter a regulable site would have their credentials checked automatically. Those holding the right certificate would be permitted to enter; those without one would be denied entry. Web sites would then bear the burden of verifying that certificates were authentic, and would also bear the burden of determining which elements, if any, of their speech were regulable. But they would bear this burden only when the site had *Ginsberg* speech.

This second zoning solution is the model of the first CDA and Congress's more recent (and constitutionally troubled) Child Online Protection Act (COPA).[41] The burden is placed on both the adult site and the adult who wants adult speech. He must secure an ID; the site must verify the ID.

These two ID systems both effect zoning, but at different costs. One burdens the parents of children slightly and web sites practically not at all; the other burdens adults significantly and web sites significantly as well.

This difference should be constitutionally significant. It should incline the Court against upholding a statute like COPA, while disposing it to uphold a statute that requires kid-IDs. If a zoning solution is selected, the Court should uphold the solution that imposes the least cost on free speech interests.

But both statutes are different from a filtering solution. Both zone the Net according to features of the users. A filtering solution zones the Net according to features of the speech. Would a zoning solution impose fewer costs on free speech interests than a filtering solution?

Architectures That Filter Speech

The filtering system is a bit more complex, though a ready model exists: the architecture of the World Wide Web Consortium's platform for Internet content selection (PICS).[42]

We have already seen a relative (actually, a child) of PICS in the chapter about privacy. P3P, like PICS, is a protocol for rating and filtering content on the Net. In the context of privacy, the content was assertions about privacy practices, and the regime was designed to help individuals negotiate those practices.

With online speech the idea is much the same. PICS divides the problem of filtering into two parts—labeling (rating content) and then filtering the content according to those labels. Software authors would compete to write software that could filter according to the ratings; content providers and rating organizations would compete to rate content. Users would then pick their filtering software and rating system. If you wanted the ratings of the Christian Right, for example, you could select its rating system; if I wanted the ratings of the Atheist Left, I could select that. By picking our raters, we would pick the content we wanted the software to filter.

This regime requires a few assumptions. First, software manufacturers would have to write the code necessary to filter material. (This has already been done—both Netscape and Microsoft have PICS-compliant filters within their browser software.) Second, rating organizations would actively have to rate the Net. This, of course, would be no simple task; organizations are only slowly taking up the challenge.[43] Third, organizations that rated the Net in a way that allowed for a simple translation from one rating system to another would have a competitive advantage over other raters. They could, for example, sell a rating system to the government of Taiwan and then easily develop a slightly different rating system for the "government" of IBM.

If all three assumptions held true, any number of ratings could be applied to the Net. As envisioned by its authors, PICS would be neutral among ratings and neutral among filters; the system would simply provide a language with which content on the Net could be rated, and with which decisions about how to use that rated material could be made from machine to machine.[44]

Neutrality sounds like a good thing. It sounds like an idea that policymakers should embrace. Your speech is not my speech; we are both free to speak and listen as we want. We should establish regimes that protect that freedom; PICS seems to be just such a regime.

But PICS contains more "neutrality" than we might like. PICS is not just *horizontally* neutral—allowing individuals to choose from a range of rating systems the one he or she wants; PICS is also *vertically* neutral—allowing the filter to be imposed at any level in the distributional chain. Most people who first endorsed the system imagined the PICS filter sitting on a user's computer, filtering according to the desires of that individual. But nothing in the design of PICS prevents organizations that provide access to the Net from filtering content as well. Filtering can occur at any level in the distributional chain—the user, the company through which the user gains access, the ISP, or even the jurisdiction within which the user lives. Nothing in the design of PICS requires that such filters announce themselves. Filtering in an architecture like PICS can be invisible, and indeed, in some of its implementations invisibility is part of its design.[45]

From a free speech perspective, how should we evaluate these two architectures? One regime—either the zoning regime of the CDA or the alternative kids-ID regime—requires those who have zonable speech to place that speech behind walls; the second regime permits listeners to adopt filters that block offending speech. The blockings of the first follow requirements in a law; the filterings of the second, while perhaps induced by law, follow from individual choice. One (zoning) looks like "censorship"; the other looks like "choice" (PICS). Thus, most people embrace the second while trashing the first.[46]

But from a free speech perspective, this is exactly backward. As a (perhaps) unintended consequence, the PICS regime not only enables nontransparent filtering but, by producing a market in filtering technology, engenders filters for much more than

Ginsberg speech. That, of course, was the complaint against the original CDA. But here the market, whose tastes are the tastes of the community, facilitates the filtering. Built into the filter are the norms of a community, which are broader than the narrow filter of *Ginsberg*. The filtering system can expand as broadly as the users want, or as far upstream as sources want.

The zoning solution is narrower. There would be no incentive for speakers to block out listeners; the incentive of a speaker is to have more, not fewer, listeners. The only requirements to filter out listeners would be those that may constitutionally be imposed—*Ginsberg* speech requirements. Since they would be imposed by the state, these requirements could be tested against the Constitution, and if the state were found to have reached too far, it could be checked.

The difference, then, is in the generalizability of the regimes. The filtering regime would establish an architecture that could be used to filter any kind of speech, and the desires for filtering then could be expected to reach beyond a constitutional minimum: the zoning regime would establish an architecture for blocking that would not have this more general purpose.

Which regime should we prefer?

Notice the values implicit in each regime. Both are general solutions to particular problems. The filtering regime does not limit itself to *Ginsberg* speech; it can be used to rate, and filter, any Internet content. And the zoning regime is not limited to facilitating zoning only for *Ginsberg* speech. The CDA zoning solution could be used to certify any number of attributes of the user—not only age but citizenship or credit-worthiness. The kids-ID zoning solution could be used to advance other child protective schemes. Both have applications far beyond the specifics of porn on the Net.

In principle at least. We should be asking, however, what the incentives are to extend the solution beyond the problem. In addition, what resistance is this extended solution likely to encounter?

Here we begin to see an important difference between the two regimes. When your access is blocked because of a certificate you are holding, you want to know why. When you are told you cannot enter a certain site, the claim to exclude is checked at least by the person being excluded. Sometimes the exclusion is justified, but when it is not, it can be challenged. Zoning, then, builds into itself a system for its own limitation. A site cannot block someone from the site without that individual knowing it.[47]

Filtering is different. If you cannot see the content, you cannot know what is being blocked. In principle at least, content could be filtered by a PICS filter somewhere upstream and you would not necessarily know this was happening. Nothing in the PICS design requires truth in blocking in the way that the zoning solution does. Thus, upstream filtering becomes easier, less transparent, and less costly with PICS.

This effect is even clearer if we take apart the components of the filtering process. Recall the two elements of filtering solutions—labeling content, and then blocking based on that labeling. We might well argue that the labeling is the more dangerous of the two elements. If content is labeled, then it is possible to monitor who gets what without even blocking access. That might well raise greater concerns than blocking, since blocking at least puts the user on notice.

These possibilities should trouble us only if we have reason to question the value of filtering generally, and upstream filtering in particular. I believe we do. But I must confess that my concern grows out of yet another latent ambiguity in our constitutional past.

There is an undeniable value in filtering. We all filter out much more than we process, and in general it is better if we can select our filters rather than have others select them for us. If I read the *New York Times* rather than the *Wall Street Journal,* I am selecting a filter according to my understanding of the values both newspapers bring to the process of filtering. Obviously, in any particular case, there cannot be a problem with this.

But there is also a value in confronting the unfiltered. We individually may want to avoid issues of poverty or of inequality, and so we might prefer to tune those facts out of our universe. But from the standpoint of society, it would be terrible if citizens could simply tune out problems that were not theirs. Those same citizens have to select leaders to manage these very problems.[48]

In real space we do not have to worry about this problem too much because filtering is usually imperfect. However much I'd like to ignore homelessness, I cannot go to my bank without confronting homeless people on the street; however much I'd like to ignore inequality, I cannot drive to the airport without passing through neighborhoods that remind me of how unequal a nation the United States is. All sorts of issues I'd rather not think about force themselves on me. They demand my attention in real space, regardless of my filtering choices.

This is not true for everyone. The very rich can cut themselves off from what they do not want to see. Think of the butler on a nineteenth-century English estate, answering the door and sending away those he thinks should not trouble his master. Those people lived perfectly filtered lives. And so do some today.

But on balance, most of us do not. We must confront the problems of others and think about problems that affect our society. This exposure makes us better citizens.[49] We can better deliberate and vote on issues that affect others if we have some sense of the problems they face.

What happens, then, if the imperfections of filtering disappear? What happens if everyone can, in effect, have a butler? Would such a world be consistent with the values of the First Amendment?

Some believe that it would not be. Cass Sunstein, for example, has argued quite forcefully that the framers embraced what he calls a "Madisonian" conception of the First Amendment.[50] This Madisonian conception rejects the notion that the mix of speech we see should solely be a function of individual choice. It insists, Sunstein claims, on ensuring that we are exposed to the range of issues we need to understand if we are to function as citizens. It therefore would reject any architecture that makes consumer choice trump. Choice is not a bad circumstance in the Madisonian scheme, but it is not the end of the matter. Ithiel de Sola Pool makes a very similar point:

> What will it mean if audiences are increasingly fractionated into small groups with special interests? What will it mean if the agenda of national fads and concerns is no longer effectively set by a few mass media to which everyone is exposed? Such a trend raises for society the reverse problems from those posed by mass conformism. The cohesion and effective functioning of a democratic society depends upon some sort of public agora in which everyone participates and where all deal with a common agenda of problems, however much they may argue over the solutions.[51]

On the other side are scholars such as Geoffrey Stone, who insists just as strongly that any such paternalistic ideal is nowhere found in the conception of free speech embraced by our framers.[52] The amendment, he says, is merely concerned with banning state control of private choice. Since enabling private choice is no problem under this regime, perfect filtering is likewise no problem.

This is another latent ambiguity, and as with others, I do not think we get far by appealing to Madison. To use Sunstein against Sunstein, the framers' First Amendment was an incompletely theorized agreement, and it is better simply to confess that it did not cover the case of perfect filtering.[53] The framers couldn't imagine a PICS-enabled world; they certainly didn't agree upon it. If we are to support one regime over another, we must do so by asserting the values we want to embrace rather than claiming they have already been embraced.

So what values should we choose? In my view, we should not opt for perfect filtering. We should not design for the most efficient system of censoring—or at least, we should not do this in a way that allows invisible upstream filtering. Nor should we opt for perfect filtering so long as the tendency worldwide is to overfilter speech. If there is speech the government has an interest in controlling, then let that control be obvious to the users. Only when regulation is transparent is a political response possible.

Thus, between the two, my vote is for the least transformative regime. A zoning regime that enables children to self-identify is less transformative than a filtering regime that in effect requires all speech to be labeled. A zoning regime is not only less transformative but less enabling (of other regulation)—it requires the smallest change to the existing architecture of the Net and does not easily generalize to a far more significant regulation.

I would opt for a zoning regime even if it required a law and the filtering solution required only private choice. If the state is pushing for a change in the mix of law and architecture, I do not care that it is pushing with law in one context and with norms in the other. From my perspective, the question is the result, not the means—does the regime produced by these changes protect free speech values?

Others are obsessed with this distinction between law and private action. They view regulation by the state as universally suspect and regulation by private actors as beyond the scope of constitutional review. And, to their credit, most constitutional law is on their side.

But as I've hinted before, and defend more below, I do not think we should get caught up in the lines that lawyers draw. Our question should be the values we want cyberspace to protect. The lawyers will figure out how.

The annoying skeptic who keeps noting my "inconsistencies" will like to pester me again at this point. In the last chapter, I embraced an architecture for privacy that is in essence the architecture of PICS. P3P, like PICS, would enable machine-to-machine negotiation about content. With P3P the content is rules about privacy practices, and with PICS it is rules about content. But how, the skeptic asks, can I oppose one yet favor the other?

The answer is the same as before: the values of speech are different from the values of privacy; the control we want to vest over speech is less than the control we want to vest over privacy. For the same reasons that we disable some of the control over intellectual property, we should disable some of the control over content. A little bit of messiness, or friction, is a value, not a cost.[54]

But are these values different just because I say they are? No. They are only different if *we* say they are different. In real space we treat them as different, and my only argument is that we choose what we want in cyberspace.

▪▪▪ The Regulators of Speech: Distribution

So far my arguments about architectures have been about architectures in cyberspace. In this final story, I blur the borders a bit. I want to use the architecture of cyberspace to show something important about the regulation of broadcasting.

The Federal Communications Commission regulates speech. If I wanted to broadcast a political speech on FM radio at a frequency of 98.6 MHz in Boston, the FCC would have me prosecuted.[55] To speak on 98.6 in Boston I need a license; I do not have such a license; to speak without a license is a crime. It is a crime despite the fact that the Constitution says, "Congress shall make no law . . . abridging the freedom of speech, or of the press." What gives?

The answer rests on a deeply held assumption at the core of our jurisprudence governing broadcasting technologies: only a fixed amount of spectrum is available for broadcasting, and the only way to facilitate broadcasting is to allocate slices of the spectrum to users, who are then solely entitled to use their allocated spectrum. Without allocation, there would be chaos, in which event there would be no broadcasting.

This view first came on the constitutional scene after Congress passed the Radio Act of 1927.[56] In 1926 Secretary of Commerce Herbert Hoover gave up the practice of controlling broadcasting after a number of circuit courts held that he did not have the power to do so. If he did not have the power, he said, then the invisible hand would have to govern. But Hoover was no friend of the invisible hand. He predicted what would happen if radio were left to the invisible hand (chaos), and some suggest that he helped bring about what he predicted. Stations would override other stations, he said; broadcasting would be a mess. When some confusion did arise, Hoover used this to justify new federal regulation.[57]

Congress then rode to the rescue by authorizing the FCC to regulate in a massively invasive way. Only the licensed could speak; what they said would be controlled by their license; they had to speak in the public interest; they had to share their resource with their opponents. In short, Congress said, broadcasting had to be regulated in the same way the Soviet Union regulated its economy.[58] We had no choice. As Justice Felix Frankfurter said in upholding the regime, it was compelled by the "nature" of broadcasting.[59]

From the beginning, however, there have been skeptics—not about the idea that spectrum must be regulated but about the means by which it is regulated. Was it necessary to have a central agency to allocate property? The common law, these skeptics argued, had done just fine.[60] Ronald Coase in 1959 proposed that if the spectrum were auctioned rather than licensed, it would be allocated to the highest value users.[61] Coase's idea caught on—fifty years later. In the United States the FCC has just begun to auction huge chunks of the broadcasting spectrum. Soon, much of the decision about who gets to say what will be made by private interests—but private interests backed by the force of the state.

Think for a second about the architecture implied by this development. If spectrum must be allocated, the argument goes, a governmental body should do the allocation. If this body licenses, then its right to do so must be extensive and powerful as it reviews the practices of licensees and allocates renewals accordingly. But even if the government simply auctions spectrum, it must still do extensive policing. Channels must be kept clear; interlopers must be punished. Under either regime—licensing or auctioning—both strong government and a great deal of private power are required. They are justified—indeed compelled—by the nature of broadcasting technology.

Many have noticed how different this architecture is from that of the press at the founding. The "press" in 1791 was not the *New York Times* or the *Wall Street Journal*. It did not comprise large organizations of private interests, with millions of readers associated with each organization. Rather, the press then was much like the Internet today. The cost of a printing press was low, the readership was slight, and anyone (within reason) could become a publisher—and in fact an extraordinary number did.[62] When the Constitution speaks of the rights of the "press," the architecture it has in mind is the architecture of the Internet.[63]

The market has erased this architecture in the print press; nature, we are told, has eliminated it in broadcasting. And so we are left with a world where the dominant architectures of free speech are fundamentally different from those the framers embraced.

In chapter 4, I said that architectures could differ both in the values they embrace and in the regulability of behavior within their space. But here we see a third way in which architectures differ. As the example of broadcasting shows, architectures differ in the justifications of regulation that they entail. Given an architecture of spectrum allocation, more regulation is justified, since someone must make choices about allocation.

So we have an architecture for broadcasting that is fundamentally different from the framers' design. It justifies a massive amount of state regulation over core areas of speech. Yet it is an architecture, we are told, that we are compelled to accept because nature gives us no other choice. Spectrum must be allocated if broadcasting is to occur.

But what if this assumption were no longer true?[64] Whatever the state of radio technology was in 1927, there's an emerging view that broadcasting today does not require spectrum allocation. There is a second architecture for broadcasting (which I will call "Spread Spectrum"—it has a few different names) that would not require any spectrum allocation at all.[65] If broadcasting were done through this technology, the extensive governmental regulation would no longer be justified.

How could this be? Your intuition about broadcasting is likely to that when two transmitters transmit on the same frequency, the signals "interfere" with each other in the sense that both are distorted. But in fact, the distortion we hear is caused by dumb receivers, not by conflicting signals. A dumb receiver needs a clear channel—or a clear difference between the channel it is receiving and everything else. If it does not receive a clear channel, then it does not know which signal to focus on. Thus, it sounds as if it were moving between the two, as if the transmissions were themselves mixed.

But a smart receiver could distinguish the transmissions. It could tell which it was to receive and ignore all others, without any coordination of the transmissions. The only requirement would be an agreement about the protocols for receivers. Receivers would wait until they received the proper packet, and only then would they open it.

This is the architecture of the Internet. Machines have addresses; they collect from the Net packets addressed to that machine.[66] No one allocates a particular channel to your machine; your machine shares the Net with every other machine on the Net. But the Net has a protocol about sharing this commons. Once this protocol is agreed on, no further regulation is required.

Broadcasting, many now argue, could be set up the same way. Broadcasts could be made using a spread spectrum design, and no one would have to allocate a particular bit of spectrum to a particular sender. Although this architecture in effect turns spectrum into a commons, there would be no tragedy of the commons since the technology of the receivers would regulate their use depending on global demand. Everyone could be a broadcaster.

So here we have an alternative architecture for broadcasting, one that does not require massive government regulation or state-supported oligopolies like NBC. It is an architecture that would facilitate far wider use of broadcast spectrum, and it would put those uses in competition with other ways of transmitting packets—copper and glass. All modes of transmission would compete with each other, and speakers would have the benefit of the most competitive mode.

Two architectures (spread spectrum and spectrum allocation), two structures of regulation (small and large), and two structures for industry (small and large broadcasters): Which, we might ask, is more consistent with the First Amendment's design?

Here, finally, we have an example of a translation that works. We have a choice between an architecture that is the functional equivalent of the architecture of the American framing and an architecture equivalent to the Soviet framing. One architecture distributes power and facilitates speech; the other concentrates power and raises the price of speech. Between these two choices, the American framers made a choice. The state was not to be in the business of licensing speakers either directly or indirectly. Yet that is just the business that spectrum allocation allows.

A faithful reading of the framers' Constitution, my colleague Yochai Benkler and I have argued,[67] would strike down the regime of spectrum allocation.[68] A faithful reading would reject an architecture that so strongly concentrates power. The model for speech that the framers embraced was the model of the Internet—distributed, noncentralized, fully free and diverse. Of course, we should choose whether we want a faithful reading—translation does not provide its own normative support. But if fidelity is our aim, this is its answer.

▮▮▮ Speech Lessons

What I described at the start of the book as modalities of constraint I have redescribed in this chapter as modalities of protection. While modalities of constraint can be used as swords against the individual (powers), modalities of protection can be used as shields (rights).

In principle we might think about how the four modalities protect speech, but I have focused here on architectures. Which architectures protect what speech? How does changing an architecture change the kind of speech being protected?

I have not tried to be comprehensive. But I have pushed for a view that addresses the relationship between architectures and speech globally and uses constitutional values to think not just about what is permitted, given a particular architecture, but also about which architectures are permitted. Our real-space constitution should inform the values of our cyberspace constitution. At the least, it should constrain the state in its efforts to architect cyberspace in ways that are inconsistent with those values.

ENDNOTES

1. Two excellent examples include Owen M. Fiss, *The Irony of Free Speech* (Cambridge, Mass.: Harvard University Press, 1996); and Cass R. Sunstein, *Democracy and the Problem of Free Speech* (New York: Free Press, 1993).
2. See 47 CFR § 73.658(e) (1998); see also Herbert J. Rotfeld et al., "Television Station Standards for Acceptable Advertising," *Journal of Consumer Affairs* 24 (1990): 392.
3. See Strafgesetzbuch (penal code) (SIGB) §§ 130–31, reprinted in *German Criminal Law*, vol. 1, edited by Gerold Harfst, translated by Otto A. Schmidt (Würzburg: Harfst Verlag, 1989), 75–76.
4. Built by industry but also especially by Cypherpunks—coders dedicated to building the tools for privacy for the Internet. As Eric Hughes writes in "A Cypherpunk's Manifesto" (in *Applied Cryptography*, 2d ed., by Bruce Schneier [New York: Wiley, 1996], 609): "We the Cypherpunks are dedicated to building anonymous systems. We are defending our privacy with cryptography, with anonymous mail forwarding systems, with digital signatures, and with electronic money. Cypherpunks write code. We know that someone has to write software to defend privacy, and since we can't get privacy unless we all do, we're going to write it. We publish our code so that our fellow Cypherpunks may practice and play with it. Our code is free for all to use, worldwide."
5. John Perry Barlow has put into circulation theme that, "in cyberspace, the First Amendment is a local ordinance"; "Leaving the Physical World," available at www.eff.org/pub/Publications/John_Perry_Barlow/leaving_the_physical_world.article (visited May 30, 1999).
6. See David Rudenstine, *The Day the Presses Stopped: A History of the Pentagon Papers Case* (Berkeley: University of California Press, 1996), 101, 139.

7. Ibid., 100.

8. See ibid., 2.

9. See ibid., 2, 42.

10. Ibid., 47–63.

11. Sanford J. Ungar, *The Papers and the Papers: An Account of the Legal and Political Battle over the Pentagon Papers* (New York: Columbia University Press, 1989), 120; cited in Rudenstine, *The Day the Presses Stopped*, 92.

12. See ibid., 105.

13. *Near v Minnesota*, 283 US 697, 716 (1931); cf. *United States v Noriega*, 917 F2d 1543 (11th Cir 1990) (affirming the prior restraint of audiotapes of the defendant's conversations with his attorney on the grounds that they might impede his right to a fair trial), cert. denied, 498 US 976 (1990) (Justice Thurgood Marshall dissenting).

14. See, for example, *Organization for a Better Austin v Keefe*, 402 US 415, 418–19 (1971); *Bantam Books, Inc., v Sullivan*, 372 US 58, 70 (1963); *Near v Minnesota*, 283 US 697, 713–14.

15. The standard arguments are summarized well by Kathleen M. Sullivan and Gerald Gunther: "(1) It is easier for an official to restrict speech 'by a simple stroke of the pen' than by the more cumbersome apparatus of subsequent punishment. . . . (2) Censors will have a professional bias in favor of censorship, and thus will systematically overvalue government interests and undervalue speech. (3) Censors operate more informally than judges and so afford less procedural safeguards to speakers. (4) Speech suppressed in advance never reaches the marketplace of ideas at all. (5) When speech is suppressed in advance, there is no empirical evidence from which to measure its alleged likely harms"; *First Amendment Law* (New York: Foundation Press, 1999), 339–40, citing Thomas Emerson, "The Doctrine of Prior Restraint," *Law and Contemporary Problems* 20 (1955): 648. Frederick Schauer offers a nice balance to this commonplace theory; see "Fear, Risk, and the First Amendment: Unraveling the 'Chilling Effect,'" *Boston University Law Review* 58 (1978): 685, 725–30.

16. In a particularly telling exchange, Justice Stewart asked Professor Bickel about a case in which disclosure "would result in the sentencing to death of a hundred young men whose only offense had been that they were nineteen years old and had low draft numbers. What should we do?" Bickel replied that his "inclinations of humanity overcome the somewhat more abstract devotion to the First Amendment in a case of that sort"; *May It Please the Court: The Most Significant Oral Arguments Made Before the Supreme Court Since 1955*, edited by Peter Irons and Stephanie Guitton (New York: Free Press, 1993), 173.

17. In a concurring opinion, Justice Potter Stewart wrote that the prior restraint at issue was invalid since he could not "say that disclosure of [the Pentagon Papers] will surely result in direct, immediate, and irreparable damage to our Nation or its people"; *New York Times Company v United States*, 403 US 713, 730 (1971) (per curiam). This standard has frequently been thought to reflect the position of the Court; see Laurence H. Tribe, *American Constitutional Law* (Meneola, N.Y.: Foundation Press, 1978), 731; Morton H. Halperin and Daniel N. Hoffman, *Top Secret: National Security and the Right to Know* (Washington, D.C.: New Republic Books, 1977), 147 n.22; see also *Alderman. v Philadelphia Housing Authority*, 496 F2d 164, 170 (3d Cir 1974), cert. denied, 419 US 844 (1974) (prior restraint must be supported by "compelling proof" that it is "essential to a vital government interest").

18. See *United States v Progressive Inc.*, 467 FSupp 990 (WDWis 1979); see also L. A. Powe Jr., "The H-Bomb Injunction," *University of Colorado Law Review* 61 (1990): 55, 56.

19. The *Milwaukee Sentinel* and *Fusion* magazine had published articles dealing with similar concepts; see A. DeVolpi et al., *Born Secret: The H-Bomb, The Progressive Case, and National Security* (New York: Pergamon Press, 1981), 102, 106; see also Howard Morland, *The Secret That Exploded* (New York: Random House, 1981), 223, 225–26.

20. See Floyd Abrams, "First Amendment Postcards from the Edge of Cyberspace," *St. John's Journal of Legal Commentary* 11 (1996): 693, 699.

21. NTSB Chairman Jim Hall announced later that investigations confirmed that a fuel tank explosion caused the crash; see "Statement of Jim Hall, Chairman, National Transportation Safety Board," July 16, 1998, available at www.ntsb.gov/pressrel/980716.htm (visited May 30, 1999).

22. See Robert E. Kessler, "TWA Probe: Submarines off Long Island/Sources: But No Link to Crash of Jetliner," *Newsday*, March 22, 1997, A8.

23. See, for example, James Sanders, *The Downing of TWA Flight 800* (New York: Kensington Publishing, 1997), 131–37; Accuracy in Media et al., "TWA 800—Missile Website Roadmap," available at www.angelfire.com/hi/TWA800/ (visited May 30, 1999); Mark K. Anderson, "Friendly Ire," available at www.valleyadvocate.com/articles/twa3.html (visited May 30, 1999); Ian W. Goddard, "TWA Flight 800 and Facts Pertaining to U.S. Navy Culpability," available at www.erols.com/lgoddard/twa-fact.htm (visited May 30, 1999).

24. See Sanders, *The Downing of TWA Flight 800*, 29–30, 75, 70–79, 171–73.

25. We can tell that it is false, of course, as in, "The cat was alive and not alive."

26. Andrew Shapiro has a powerful analysis of a particularly smart loon; see *The Control Revolution*, 133–41.

27. As Shapiro puts it, "What we need are trusted intermediaries: people to whom we entrust certain tasks because we recognize the value of their perspective, their expertise, their time, and their independence"; ibid., 188.

28. See Zucker, "Production of Trust," 63–65.

29. Obscenity is not constitutionally protected speech, and federal laws prohibit the transportation of obscene materials; see 18 USCA § 1462 (1984), amended by 18 USCA § 1462 (Supp 1999). In *Miller v California*, the Supreme Court described the test for obscenity as: "(a) whether 'the average person, applying contemporary community standards' would find that the work, taken as a whole, appeals to the prurient interest; (b) whether the work depicts or describes, in a patently offensive way, sexual conduct specifically defined by the applicable state law; and (c) whether the work, taken as a whole, lacks serious literary, artistic, political, or scientific value;" *Miller v California*, 413 US 15, 24 (1973) (5–4 decision), rehearing denied, 414 US 881 (1973). Porn, on the other hand, is protected by the First Amendment but may be regulated to promote the state's interest in protecting children from harmful materials so long as the regulation is the least restrictive means to further the articulated interest; see *Ginsberg v New York*, 390 US 629, 637–40 (1968). Child porn may be prohibited as obscene material even if it is not obscene under the *Miller* test, owing to the strong state interest in preventing the sexual exploitation of children; see *New York v Ferber*, 458 US 747, 764 (1982). Child porn is not constitutionally protected, and federal law prohibits the transportation of child porn; see 18 USCA § 2252 (1984), amended by 18 USCA § 2252 (Supp 1999).

30. Justice Sandra Day O'Connor listed more than forty states with such law in her concurrence in *Reno v ACLU*, 521 US 844, 887 n.2.

31. *Ginsberg v New York*, 390 US 629 (1968).

32. See Godwin, *CyberRights*, 206–59.

33. See Blake T. Bilstad, "Obscenity and Indecency in a Digital Age: The Legal and Political Implications of Cybersmut, Virtual Pornography, and the Communications Decency Act of 1996," *Santa Clara Computer and High Technology Law Journal* 13 (1997): 321, 336–37.

34. Marty Rimm, "Marketing Pornography on the Information Superhighway: A Survey of 917,410 Images, Descriptions, Short Stories, and Animations Downloaded 8.5 Million Times by Consumers in over 2,000 Cities in Forty Countries, Provinces, and Territories," *Georgetown University Law Journal* 83 (1995): 1849. Godwin provides the whole history of the Rimm article, describing the most significant problems and consequences of the "misleading" and "false" statements, and its eventual demise; *CyberRights*, 206–59; see also Jonathan Wallace and Mark Mangan, *Sex, Laws, and Cyberspace* (New York: M&T Books, 1996), ch. 6.

35. See Philip Elmer-Dewitt, "On a Screen Near You: Cyberporn—It's Popular, Pervasive, and Surprisingly Perverse, According to the First Survey of Online Erotica—And There's No Easy Way to Stamp It Out," *Time*, July 3, 1995.

36. 47 USCA § 223(e)(5)(A) (Supp 1999).

37. The law was extinguished (at least in part) at 521 US 844 (1997); see Eugene Volokh, "Freedom of Speech, Shielding Children, and Transcending Balancing," *Supreme Court Review* 1997 (1997): 141.

38. See *Federal Communications Commission v Pacifica Foundation* 438 US 726, 748–50 (1978) (plurality). Though *Pacifica* has been criticized strongly, see Steven H. Shiffrin, *The First Amendment, Democracy, and Romance* (Cambridge, Mass.: Harvard University Press, 1990), 80, as Jonathan Weinberg convincingly argues, *Pacifica* continues to have influence in the broadcasting context; "Cable TV, Indecency, and the Court," *Columbia-VLA Journal of Law and the Arts 21* (1997): 95.

39. See *Gentile v State Bar of Nevada*, 501 US 1030, 1048–51 (1991) (vague regulations of speech are void owing to the impermissible risk of chilling speech); *Dombrowski v Pfister*, 380 US 479, 494 (1965) (chilling speech).

40. For a more extensive discussion of this system, see Lawrence Lessig and Paul Resnick, "The Architectures of Mandated Access Controls," *Michigan Law Review* (forthcoming, 1999).

41. 47 USC § 230 (Supp 1999). Charles Nesson and David Marglin suggest that the constitutionality of the CDA—and by extension of COPA—will change over time: Even if it was not constitutional initially, technological change may render it constitutional later; see Charles Neason and David Marglin, "The Day the Internet Met the First Amendment: Time and the Communications Decency Act," *Harvard Journal of Law and Technology* 10 (1996): 113.

42. See World Wide Web Consortium, "Platform for Internet Content Selection (PICS)," available at www.w3.org/PICS/ (visited October 25, 1998).

43. See Diane Roberts, "On the Plurality of Ratings," *Cardozo Arts and Entertainment Law Journal* 15 (1997): 105, 113–15.

44. Paul Resnick, "PICS-Interest@w3.org, Moving On," January 20 1999, available at www//lists.w3.org/Archives/Public/pics-interest/1999Jan/0000.html (visited May 30, 1999); Paul Resnick, "Filtering Information on the Internet," *Scientific American* 106 (March 1997), also available at www.sciam.com/

0397issue/0397resnick.html (visited May 30, 1999); Paul Resnick, "PICS and Intellectual Freedom FAQ," available at www.w3.org/PICS/PICS-FAQ-980126.html (visited May 30, 1999); Paul Resnick and Jim Miller, "PICS: Internet Access Controls Without Censorship," *Communications of the ACM* 39 (1996): 87, also available at www.w3.org/PICS/iscwcv2.htm (visited May 30, 1999); Jim Miller, Paul Resnick, et al., "PICS 1.1 Rating Services and Rating Systems—and Their Machine-Readable Descriptions," October 31, 1996, available at www.w3.org/TR/REC-PICS-services) (visited May 30, 1999); Tim Krauskopf, Paul Resnick, et al., "PICS 1.1 Label Distribution—Label Syntax and Communication Protocols," October 31, 1996, available at www.w3.org/TR/REC-PICS-labels (visited May 30, 1999); Christopher Evans, Paul Resnick, et al., "W3C Recommendation: PICS Rules 1.1, REC-PICS, Rules-971229," December 29, 1997, available at www.w3.org/TR/REC-PICSRules (visited May 30, 1999).

45. See Jonathan Weinberg, "Rating the Net," *Hastings Communications and Entertainment Law Journal* 19 (1997): 453, 478 n.108.

46. See, for example, the Center for Democracy and Technology's endorsement of parental empowerment through rating systems and blocking software rather than government regulation in "Internet Family Empowerment White Paper," July 16, 1997, available at www.cdt.org/speech/empower.html (visited May 30, 1999); a similar point of view is found in Esther Dyson, "Release 1.0: Labels and Disclosure," December 1996, available at www.edventure.com/release1/1296body.html (visited May 30, 1999).

47. This claim, of course, is too strong. The site could block deceptively, making it seem as if the user were gaining access but actually not giving her access to what she believes she is gaining access to.

48. See Richard Thompson Ford ("The Boundaries of Race: Political Geography in Legal Analysis," *Harvard Law Review* 107 [1994]: 1841, 1844), who asserts that jurisdictional boundaries perpetuate racial segregation and inequality; Gerald E. Frug ("Universities and Cities," *Connecticut Law Review* 30 [1998]: 1199, 1200), explains how universities erect borders to divorce themselves from surrounding poverty and argues that universities should critique these borders; Lani Guinier ("More Democracy," *University of Chicago Legal Forum* 1995 [1995]: 1,3) advocates a cross-racial participatory democracy that demands a concern for, and a familiarity with, the views of others.

49. See *Regents of the University of California v Bakke*, 438 US 265, 312 (1978) (Justice Lewis F. Powell, quoting *Keyishian v Board of Regents*, 385 US 589, 603 [1967]: "The Nation's future depends upon leaders trained through wide exposure to that robust exchange of ideas which discovers truth 'out of a multitude of tongues, [rather] than through any kind of authoritative selection'").

50. See Fiss, *The Irony of Free Speech*, 3, 37–38; Sunstein, *Democracy and the Problem of Free Speech*, xvi-xx. Andrew Shapiro's powerful analysis of Sunstein's point is better tuned to the realities of the Net; see *The Control Revolution*, 107–12.

51. Ithiel de Sola Pool, *Technologies Without Boundaries: On Telecommunications in a Global Age*, edited by Eli M. Noam (Cambridge, Mass.: Harvard University Press, 1990), 15.

52. See Geoffrey R. Stone, "Imagining a Free Press," *Michigan Law Review* 90 (1992): 1246, 1264.

53. But see Thomas G. Krattenmaker and L. A. Powe Jr. ("Converging First Amendment Principles for Converging Communications Media," *Yale Law Journal* 104 [1995]: 1719, 1735), who argue that First Amendment principles urge that consumers, not the government, control the content they consume in the area of emerging media technologies; Sunstein ("The First Amendment in Cyberspace," *Yale Law Journal* 104 [1995]: 1757, 1765) contends that emerging media technologies produce new areas for applying old Madisonian First Amendment principles.

54. For an early and extraordinary work that struggles with the complexity of the question about which information you should be able to own, see Anne Wells Branscomb, *Who Owns Information?: From Privacy to Public Access* (New York: Basic Books, 1994). My conclusions are different from hers, but I agree with her insight that "ownership" cuts across different kinds of information in different ways. James Boyle advances a similar theme in *Shamans, Software, and Spleens*.

55. See 47 CFR § 73.277 (1998).

56. 47 USCA §§ 81–119 (1927) (repealed by the Communications Act of 1934).

57. See *Red Lion Broadcasting Company v Federal Communications Commission*, 395 US 367, 375–77 (1969); *National Broadcasting Company v United States*, 319 US 190, 212–13 (1943). Thomas Hazlett makes a powerful critique of Frankfurter's history of the emergence of any necessity for FOC regulation; see *Physical Scarcity*.

58. See *Turner Broadcasting System, Inc. v Federal Communications Commission*, 512 US 622, 637–38 (1997); see also Huber, *Law and Disorder in Cyberspace*.

59. See *National Broadcasting Company, Inc. v Columbia Broadcasting System*, 213.

60. See Huber, *Law and Disorder in Cyberspace*, 28–34. The dominant voice in this debate is Thomas W. Hazlett, who has argued strongly against the licensing regime for spectrum and in favor of a property

auction. His work on the history of the Radio Act is particularly good; see, for example, "Assigning Property Rights to Radio Spectrum Users: Why Did FCC License Auctions Take Sixty-seven Years?," *Journal of Law and Economics* 41 (1998): 529; "Oak Leaves and the Origins of the 1927 Radio Act: Comment," *Public Choice* 95 (1998): 277; "Physical Scarcity, Rent Seeking, and the First Amendment," *Columbia Law Review* 97 (1997): 905; "The Rationality of U.S. Regulation of the Broadcast Spectrum," *Journal of Law and Economics* 33 (1990): 133; Thomas W. Hazlett and David Sosa, "Was the Fairness Doctrine a 'Chilling Effect'?: Evidence from the Postderegulation Radio Market," *Journal of Legal Studies* 26 (1997): 279. For another historical account, see Morton I. Hamburg and Stuart N. Brotman, *Communications Law and Practice*, vol. 1 (New York: Law Journal Seminars–Press, 1995), 5–8. Ithiel de Sola Pool was an early advocate of a position close to Hazlett's; see *Technologies Without Boundaries*, 108–88.

61. See Ronald H. Coase, "The Federal Communications Commission," *Journal of Law and Economics* 2 (1959): 1.

62. See Patrick M. Garry, *Scrambling for Protection: The New Media and the First Amendment* (Pittsburgh: University of Pittsburgh, 1994), 97–106.

63. There is an important argument supporting a different treatment for the "press" under the First Amendment, though the Supreme Court has not yet developed this distinctive jurisprudence. Justice Potter Stewart sketched some of the potential in "Or of the Press" (*Hastings Law Journal* 26 [1975]: 631), and his argument takes on a new significance in the context of the Internet. For a persuasive account, see Garry, *Scrambling for Protection*, 107–21.

64. See Hazlett, *Physical Scarcity*, 911–12; Anna Couey, "The Birth of Spread Spectrum," available at www.sirius.be/lamarr.htm (visited May 30, 1999); Jack Glas, "The Principles of Spread Spectrum Communication," available at www.tas.et.tudelft.nl/~glas/ssc/techn/techniques.html (visited May 30, 1999). One important reason for the shortage of spectrum is its inefficient use; see de Sola Pool, "Technologies Without Boundaries," 42–45.

65. Yochai Benkler's article provides (for lawyers) the most extensive discussion of the technology; see "Overcoming Agoraphobia," 287. He describes the change in technology: "The technological shift derives from various techniques—such as spread spectrum and code division multiple access, time division multiple access, frequency hopping, and packet switching—for allowing multiple users to communicate at the same time using the same frequency range. Some of these technologies complement each other; some conflict with each other. What is crucial to understand about these technologies is that they challenge the underlying assumption of both licensing and privatization: that the only way to assure high quality wireless communications is to assign one person the right to transmit in a given frequency band" (324, footnote omitted). The appendix to his article then describes the related technologies, including spread spectrum (395), time division multiple access (TDMA) (397), and frequency hopping (399). For a discussion of code division multiple access and frequency division multiple access, see Ted Stevens, "Regulation and Licensing of Low-Earth-Orbit Satellites," *Santa Clara Computer and High Technology Law Journal* 10 (1994): 401.

66. Ethernet literally functions like this. Data on an Ethernet network are streamed into each machine on that network. Each machine sniffs the data and then pays attention to the data intended for it. This process creates an obvious security hole: "sniffers" can be put on "promiscuous mode" and read packets intended for other machines; see Loshin, *TCP/IP Clearly Explained*, 44–46.

67. See Yochai Benkler and Lawrence Lessig, "Net Gains," *New Republic*, December 14, 1998.

68. The founder of this argument must be Eli Noam; see "Spectrum Auctions: Yesterday's Heresy, Today's Orthodoxy, Tomorrow's Anachronism—Taking the Next Step to Open Spectrum Access," *Journal of Law and Economics* 41 (1998): 765. Benkler has spiced it up a bit (in my view, in critical ways) by adding to it the value of the commons. For an extraordinarily powerful push to a similar political (if not technological) end, see Eben Moglen, "The Invisible Barbecue," *Columbia Law Review* 97 (1997): 945. Moglen notes the lack of debate regarding the sociopolitical consequences of carving up telecommunication rights at the "Great Barbecue" and draws a parallel with the Gilded Age's allocation of benefits and privileges associated with the railroad industry.

Index

475

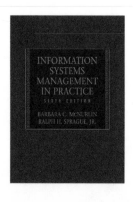